Constitutional Law

ANALYSIS AND CASES

Constitutional Law

ANALYSIS AND CASES

Ziyad Motala & Cyril Ramaphosa

OXFORD

OXFORD
UNIVERSITY PRESS

Great Clarendon Street, Oxford OX2 6DP

Oxford University Press is a department of the University of Oxford.
It furthers the University's objective of excellence in research, scholarship,
and education by publishing worldwide in

Oxford New York

Auckland Bangkok Buenos Aires Cape Town Chennai
Dar es Salaam Delhi Hong Kong Istanbul Karachi Kolkata
Kuala Lumpur Madrid Melbourne Mexico City Mumbai Nairobi
São Paulo Shanghai Singapore Taipei Tokyo Toronto

with an associated company in Berlin

Oxford is a registered trade mark of Oxford University Press
in the UK and certain other countries

Published in South Africa
by Oxford University Press Southern Africa, Cape Town

Constitutional Law
ISBN 0 19 571726 0

© Ziyad Motala and Cyril Ramaphosa 2002

The moral rights of the authors have been asserted
Database right Oxford University Press (maker)

First published 2002

Editors: Peggy Lipinski and Ken McGillivray
Designer: Christopher Davis
Indexer: Ina Lawson

Published by Oxford University Press Southern Africa
PO Box 12119, N1 City, 7463, Cape Town, South Africa

Set in 9pt on 11.5pt Galliard by Mckore Graphics, Cape Town
Imagesetting by Castle Graphics, Cape Town
Cover reproduction by The Image Bureau
Printed and bound by Clyson Printers, Maitland

Preface

This book is designed as a basic reference work on constitutional law. In many jurisdictions, constitutional law is viewed as coterminous with decisions of the highest court of the land. Consistent with this approach, and not as a slight to any other court, the text focuses primarily on precedent-setting decisions of the highest constitutional tribunal, the Constitutional Court of South Africa. It attempts to provide a summary of the Court's approach to constitutional questions as well as our analysis of its approach.

Many parts of the Constitution are open to different interpretations. Central to our approach is the belief that constitutional interpretation of open-ended phrases often involves a dynamic interplay between legal and political reality. No doubt the analysis and interpretation we prefer is influenced by our own normative and value judgements. However, we do attempt to provide a variety of scholarly critiques and an exposition of alternative constitutional positions, including a consideration of comparable foreign case law.

The Constitution calls upon the courts to take account of foreign case law in interpreting the Constitution. The presentation of foreign and comparative material provides alternative justifications and concepts of law, politics, and government and provides additional criteria for evaluating our Constitution and the decisions of the Constitutional Court.

In the main, our approach is to summarize the constitutional provisions, to give the interpretation of the Constitutional Court, to present major extracts of seminal Court decisions so that the reader can extract legal and policy principles from the Court's decisions; and to provide an analysis, a critique and, where relevant, a different perspective. We hope that our method and presentation of the material enables the reader to understand the approach of the Court as distinct from our analyses.

The treatment of the subject varies across different sections. There are parts where we simply summarize the Constitution or the approach of the Court. These parts are explanatory and to a large extent represent settled, or at least less controversial, constitutional principles. And there are other sections where we offer detailed analysis and critiques representing contested areas.

Constitutional law is a vast subject and it is impossible to do justice to the topic in a single treatise. Adopting a comparative approach makes the subject more extensive. This inevitably means that choices have to be made. For instance, we elected to omit the notes from the case extracts. Moreover, under the rights discourse, we decided to limit our discussion of right-to-fair-trial procedures and administrative action. One reason for this is that these areas are better covered in texts on criminal procedure and administrative law respectively. Another is that, in many jurisdictions, criminal procedure and administrative law are not addressed in a basic constitutional law class. We also decided, at the outset, to limit our discussion of statutes. Overall, then, we focus on those areas of the Constitution which we think invite greater controversy and litigation. Issues which we feel are peripheral to a basic understanding of the Constitution receive shorter treatment, even though they may have been the subject of a large amount of writing elsewhere.

Chapter 1 offers a basic overview of the Constitution and the constitution-making process. The remainder of the book is divided into a discussion of powers and rights. Chapters 2 to 6 discuss the powers aspects of the Constitution, namely which branch or level of government has the power to act. Chapters 7 to 14 deal with the rights provisions under the Constitution.

Central to the discussion in chapters 2 to 6 are: separation of powers between the judicial, legislative, and executive branches of government; and the distribution of powers between the national, provincial, and local levels of government. Chapters 2 to 4 deal with the role of the judiciary. The two major themes that permeate these chapters are the legitimacy of judicial review and the methodology the Constitutional Court employs in subjecting governmental and individual action to scrutiny. Chapter 2 deals with the process of constitutional adjudication and the methods of constitutional interpretation relied upon by the Court. Chapter 3 considers the tension between judicial review and democracy. This chapter also considers the jurisdiction of the Court and other courts to hear constitutional matters. Chapter 4 looks at possible political controls, and judicially imposed restraints (standards of justiciability) that the Court employs. Chapter 5 deals with the law-making powers of the national and provincial legislatures, and local government bodies. The critical enquiry is: which level of government has the power to exercise certain functions under the Constitution? Chapter 6 addresses executive power and the role of independent constitutional organs. Central to this enquiry is the doctrine of separation of powers and the definition of legislative, executive, administrative, and judicial powers.

Chapters 7 to 14 address the Bill of Rights. Chapter 7 provides an overview of pivotal provisions in the bill. Chapters 8 to 14 address the important fundamental rights (not addressed in chapter 7) which are more likely to invite litigation: equality and affirmative action in chapter 8; the right to property in chapter 9; horizontal versus vertical application of the Constitution in chapter 10; the right-to-fair-trial procedures and fair administrative action in chapter 11; freedom of speech, of assembly, and of religion in chapter 12; and socioeconomic rights in chapter 13. The final chapter deals with the derogation clause.

Regarding the citation of the Constitutional Court cases, although we provide both Juta and Butterworths citations to the cases, we elected to rely primarily on the official case citations as reported by the Court. Our decision was prompted by Butterworths withholding permission to reprint the case extracts in the absence of a royalty payment. Given that Constitutional Court decisions are of public record and freely available, we were not willing to make such payment. The text is current with regard to discussion of relevent Constitutional Court decisions decided before April 2001. The recent constitutional amendments adopted in November 2001 with respect to changes in the tenure of Constitutional Court judges are also not considered.

We are indebted to many people who read all or parts of the manuscript, and provided us with valuable comments. These include: Judges Zak Yacob, Evonne Mokgoro, Albie Sachs, and Siraj Desai. We also thank Nicholas Haysom and J Clay Smith, and Arthur Attwell of Oxford University Press. We wish to acknowledge the research, editorial, and computer assistance of Ama Bekoe, Shashana Crichton, Antonia Soares, Felicia Ayanbiola, David and Kirsten Butleritchie, and Irshad Motala. Special thanks are due to Luis Acosta and Antonia Soares for the many hours they spent working on different aspects of the manuscript. We are indebted to all the constitutional scholars who inspired us and whose ideas we have adopted, borrowed, or critiqued. Cyril Ramaphosa would like especially to thank Steyn Speed for inspiration provided during the drafting of the Constitution.

We also acknowledge permission from the following publishers and authors who provided consent to print or use excerpts from the following materials: Michael Asimov for his article 'Towards a South African Administrative Justice Act' in the *Michigan Journal for Race and International Justice*; Brice Dickson for his article 'Protecting Human Rights Through a Constitutional Court: The Case in South Africa' in the *Fordham Law Review*; Duke University Press for permission to quote from Donald P Kommers *The Constitutional Jurisprudence of the Federal Republic of Germany*; Kluwer Law International for permission to quote from *Human Rights and Judicial Review: A Comparative Perspective*; Juta & Co for permission to reprint South African case extracts, and Nomos Verlagsgesellschaft for permission to quote from P Kirchoff and DP Kommers *Germany and Its Basic Law. Past, Present and Future*, and *Hastings International Law and Comparative Law Review*; *Arizona International Law and Comparative Law Review*; *Albany Law Review*; *South African Law Journal*; *Comparative and International Law Journal of Southern Africa*, and the *South African Year Book of International Law* for permission to quote articles by Ziyad Motala.

Details of these publications are to be found in the bibliography.

ZIYAD MOTALA AND CYRIL RAMAPHOSA

Contents

3   The power of judicial review: the composition, election, and jurisdiction of the Constitutional Court

4   Control over the courts

5 Legislative power: national, provincial, and local

6   The executive

7   Fundamental rights

8 The right to equality

9 The right to own property

13   Social welfare rights

14   The limitations clause

Table of cases

FOREIGN CASES

Australia

Canada

Germany

India

Ireland

Japan

United Kingdom

United States of America

INTERNATIONAL AND REGIONAL TRIBUNALS

African Commission on Human and People's Rights

European Court of Human Rights and the European Commission on Human Rights

European Court of Justice

Inter-American Court and Inter-American Commission on Human Rights

International arbitration

International Court of Justice and Permanent Court

United Nations and International Human Rights Tribunals

Table of statutes

International covenants and treaties

Bibliography

Books

Agresto, John *The Supreme Court and Constitutional Democracy* New York: Cornell University Press 1984

American Law Institute *Restatement of the Law Third: Restatement of the Foreign Relations Law of the United States* St Paul: American Law Institute Publishers 1987

Amissah, Austin *The Contribution of the Courts to Governments: A West African View* Oxford: Oxford University Press 1981

Amoda, John M 'The Relationship of History, Thought and Action with Respect to the Nigerian Situation' in *Nigeria: Dilemma of Nationhood*, edited by Joseph Okpaku. New York: Third Press 1972

Andrews, William G 'Constitutionalism and Constitutions' in *Constitutions and Constitutionalism*, edited by William G Andrews. Princeton: Van Nostrand 1961

Awogu, F Olisa *Political Institutions and Thought in Africa: An Introduction* New York: Vantage Press 1975

Awolomo, Obafemi *Thoughts on the Nigerian Constitution* Ibadan: Oxford University Press 1966

Azikiwe, Nnamdi *Zik: A Selection from the Speeches of Nnamdi Azikiwe* Cambridge: Cambridge University Press 1961

Baker, H 'Reflections on the Economic Correlates of African Democracy' in *Democracy and Pluralism in Africa*, edited by Dov Ronen. Boulder: Lynne Rienner Publishers 1986

Bassiouni, Cherif M 'Characteristics of International Criminal Law Conventions' in *International Criminal Law*, edited by Cherif M Bassiouni. New York: Transnational Publishers 1986

— *Crimes Against Humanity in International Criminal Law* Dordrecht: M Nijhoff 1992

Beattie, John 'Checks on the Abuse of Political Power in some African States: A Preliminary Framework for Analysis' in *Comparative Political Systems: Studies in the Politics of Pre-Industrial Societies*, edited by Ronald Cohen and John Middleton. New York: Natural History Press 1967

Beatty, David M *Constitutional Law in Theory and Practice* Toronto: University of Toronto Press 1995

— 'The Last Generation: When Rights lose their Meaning' in *Human Rights and Judicial Review: A Comparative Perspective*, edited by David M Beatty. Dordrecht: M Nijhoff 1994

Bell, Derrick A, Jnr *Race, Racism and American Law* Boston: Little Brown, 2nd edition, 1980

Bell, J 'Three Models of the Judicial Function' in *Judges and the Judicial Power: Essays in Honour of Justice VR Krishna Iyer*, edited by Rajeev Dhavan, R Sudarshan, and Salman Khurshid. London: Sweet & Maxwell 1985

Benda, E 'The Position and Function of the *Bundesverfassungsgericht* (Federal Constitution Court) in a United Germany' in *Federalism-in-the-Making: Contemporary Canadian and German Constitutionalism, National and Transnational*, edited by Edward McWhinney, Jerald Zaslove, and Werner Wolf. Dordrecht: Kluwer Academic Publishers 1992

Bengoetxea, Joxerramon *The Legal Reasoning of the European Court of Justice: Towards a European Jurisprudence* Oxford: Clarendon 1993

Berg-Schlosser, Dirk *Tradition and Change in Kenya: A Comparative Analysis of Seven Major Ethnic Groups* Paderborn: F Schoningh 1984

Bhandara, MK *Basic Structure of the Indian Constitution: A Critical Consideration* New Delhi: Deep & Deep 1993

Bickel, Alexander *The Least Dangerous Branch: The Supreme Court at the Bar of Politics* Indianapolis: Bobbs-Merrill 1962

— *The Least Dangerous Branch: The Supreme Court at the Bar of Politics* New Haven: Yale University Press, 2nd edition, 1986

Bishin, William R, and Christopher D Stone *Law, Language, and Ethics: An Introduction to Law and Legal Method* New York: Foundation Press 1972

Bobbitt, Philip *Constitutional Fate: Theory of the Constitution* New York: Oxford University Press 1982

Bothe, Michael 'Final Report' in *Federalism and Decentralization: Constitutional Problems of Territorial Decentralization in Federal and Centralized States*, edited by Thomas Fleiner-Gerster and Silvan Hutter. Fribourg: Editions Universitaires 1987

Boulle, Laurence J *Constitutional Reform and the Apartheid State: Legitimacy, Consociationalism and Control in South Africa* New York: St Martin's Press 1984.

Brest, Paul *Processes of Constitutional Decision-making: Cases and Materials* Boston: Little Brown 1975

Brest, Paul, and Sanford Levinson *Processes of Constitutional Decision-making: Cases and Materials* Boston: Little Brown, 3rd edition, 1992

Brown, Brendan Francis *The Natural Law Reader* New York: Oceana Publications 1960

Busia, KA *Africa in Search of Democracy* London: Routledge and Kegan Paul 1967

Cappelletti, Mauro, and William Cohen *Comparative Constitutional Law: Cases and Materials* Indianapolis: Bobbs-Merrill 1979

Carter, Barry E, and Phillip R Trimble *International Law* Boston: Little Brown 1991

Cassese, Antonio *International Law in a Divided World* Oxford: Clarendon Press 1988

Chemerinsky, Erwin *Constitutional Law: Principles and Policies* New York: Aspen Law & Business 1997

Cockram, Gail-Maryse *Constitutional Law in the Republic of South Africa* Cape Town: Juta & Co 1975

Corder, Hugh *Judges at Work: The Role and Attitudes of the South African Appellate Judiciary, 1910–1950* Cape Town: Juta & Co 1984

Corwin, Edward Samuel *Court over Constitution: A Study of Judicial Review as an Instrument of Popular Government* New York: P Smith 1938

— 'The Passing of Dual Federalism' in *Essays in Constitutional Law*, edited by Robert G McCloskey. New York: Knopf 1957

Cowen, Denis V *The Foundations of Freedom, with Special Reference to South Africa* Cape Town: Oxford University Press 1961

Cranston, Maurice *What are Human Rights?* New York: Taplinger Publishing Co 1973

Dalberg-Larsen, Jurgen *The Welfare State and its Law* Berlin: Tesdorph 1987

Das, Kamleshwar 'United Nations Institutions and Procedures founded on Conventions on Human Rights and Fundamental Freedoms' in *The International Dimensions of Human Rights*, edited by Karel Vasak and Philip Alston. Westport: Greenwood Press 1982

Davis, Dennis, Halton Cheadle, and Nicolas Haysom *Fundamental Rights in the Constitution: Commentary and Cases: A Commentary on Chapter 3 on Fundamental Rights of the 1993 Constitution and Chapter 2 of the 1996 Constitution* Cape Town: Juta & Co 1997

Davidson, Basil *Which Way Africa? The Search for a New Society* Harmondsworth: Penguin, 3rd edition, 1971

De Silva, HL 'Pluralism and the Judiciary in Sri Lanka' in *The Role of the Judiciary in Plural Societies*, edited by Neelan Tiruchelvam and Radhika Coomaraswamy. London: F Pinter 1987

De Smith, Stanley A *The New Commonwealth and its Constitutions* London: Stevens 1964

De Waal, Johan, Iain Currie, and Gerhard Erasmus *The Bill of Rights Handbook* Cape Town: Juta & Co, 2nd edition, 1999

Duchacek, Ivo D *Comparative Federalism: The Territorial Dimensions of Politics* New York: Holt, Rinehart and Winston 1970

— *Power Maps: Comparative Politics of Constitutions* Santa Barbara: ABC-Clio 1973

Durham, Cole W 'General Assessment of the Basic Law: An American Overview' in *Germany and Its Basic Law, Past, Present and Future: A German-American Symposium*, edited by Paul Kirchhoff and Donald P Kommers. Baden-Baden: Nomos 1993

Elazar, Daniel J, and Ilan Greilsammer 'A Political Science Perspective' in *Integration Through Law: Europe and the American Federal Experience*, edited by Mauro Cappelletti, Monica Seccombe, and Joseph Weiler. Berlin: W de Gruyter 1986

Ely, John Hart *Democracy and Distrust: A Theory of Judicial Review* Cambridge: Harvard University Press 1980

Emerson, Thomas *The System of Freedom of Expression* New York: Random House 1970

Eze, Osita C *Human Rights in Africa: Some Selected Problems* Lagos: Nigerian Institute of International Affairs 1984

Folsom, Ralph H, and Michael W Gordon *International Business Transactions* St Paul: West Publishing Co, 3rd edition, 1995

Franck, Thomas M *Human Rights in Third World Perspective* London: Oceana 1982

Friedrich, Carl J *Constitutional Government and Democracy: Theory and Practice in Europe and America* Waltham: Blaisdell Publishing Co, 4th edition, 1968

Gerhardt, Michael J, and Thomas D Rowe Jnr *Constitutional Theory: Arguments and Perspectives* Charlottesville: Michie 1993

Gierke, Otto von *Natural Law and the Theory of Society, 1500–1800* Cambridge: Cambridge University Press 1958

Georges, Telford *Law and its Administration in a One-party State: Selected Speeches*, compiled and edited by RW James and FM Kassam. Nairobi: East African Literature Bureau 1973

Good, Robert C *Congo Crisis: The Role of the New States* (NP) 1962

Gordon, Michael W *The Cuban Nationalizations: The Demise of Foreign Private Property* New York: William S Hein 1976

Gotz, Volkmar 'Legislative and Executive Power under the Constitutional Requirements entailed in the Principle of the Rule of Law' in *New Challenges to the German Basic Law*, edited by Christian Starck. Baden-Baden: Nomos 1991

Greenstein, Fred I, and Nelson W Polsby (eds) *Handbook of Political Science* Reading: Addison-Wesley Publishing 1975

Greer, Patricia *Transforming Central Government: The Next Steps Initiative* Buckingham: Open University Press 1994

Grimm, Dieter 'Human Rights and Judicial Review in Germany' in *Human Rights and Judicial Review: A Comparative Perspective*, edited by David M Beatty. Dordrecht: M Nijhoff 1994

Gros Espiell, Hector *The Right to Self-determination: Implementation of United Nations Resolutions, Study* New York: United Nations 1980

Gunlicks, Arthur B 'Principles of American Federalism' in *Germany and its Basic Law, Past, Present and Future: A German-American Symposium*, edited by Paul Kirchoff and Donald P Kommers. Baden-Baden: Nomos 1993

Gwyn, William B *The Meaning of the Separation of Powers: An Analysis of the Doctrine from its Origin to the Adoption of the United States Constitution* New Orleans: Tulane University Press 1965

Hanf, Theodor, Heribert Weiland, Gerda Vierdag, and Mark Orkin *South Africa, the Prospects of Peaceful Change: An Empirical Enquiry into the Possibility of Democratic Conflict Regulation* London: R Collings 1981

Harlow, Carol 'Power from the People? Representation and Constitutional Theory' in *Law, Legitimacy and the Constitution: Essays Marking the Centenary of Dicey's Law of the Constitution*, edited by Patrick McAuslan and John F McEldowney. London: Sweet & Maxwell 1985

Harris, DJ *Cases and Materials on International Law* London: Sweet & Maxwell, 3rd edition, 1983

Hartley, Trevor C *The Foundations of European Community Law: An Introduction to the Constitutional and Administrative Law of the European Community* Oxford: Clarendon Press 1988

Hatch, John *Nigeria: The Seeds of Disaster* Chicago: Regnery Co 1970

Heady, Ferrell 'Bureaucracies' in *Encyclopedia of Government and Politics*, edited by Mary Hawkesworth and Maurice Kogan. London: Routledge 1992

Henkin, Louis, Richard C Pugh, Oscar Schachter, and Hans Smit *Cases on International Law* St Paul: West Publishing Co, 3rd edition, 1993

Hidayatullah, M *Constitutional Law of India* New Delhi: Bar Council of India Trust 1984

Hogg, Peter W *Constitutional Law of Canada* Scarborough: Carswell, 3rd edition, 1992

Holmes, Stephen 'Precommitment and the Paradox of Democracy' in *Constitutionalism and Democracy*, edited by

Jon Elster and Rune Slagstad. Cambridge: Cambridge University Press 1988

Hopkins, RF 'The influence of the Legislature on Development Strategy: The Case of Kenya and Tanzania' in *Legislatures in Development: Dynamics of Change in New and Old States*, edited by Joel Smith and Lloyd D Musolf. Durham: Duke University Press 1979

Horowitz, Morton *The Transformation of American Law, 1780–1860* New York: Oxford University Press 1992

Hosten, WJ, AB Edwards, Francis Bosman, and Joan Church (eds) *Introduction to South African Law and Legal Theory* Durban: Butterworths, 2nd edition, 1995

Humphrey, John P 'Political and Related Rights' in *Human Rights in International Law: Legal and Policy Issues*, edited by Theodor Meron. Oxford: Clarendon Press 1984

Hurst, Williard 'The Process of Constitutional Construction: The Role of History' in *Supreme Court and Supreme Law*, edited by Edmond Cahn. Bloomington: Indiana University Press 1954

International Commission of Jurists *First African Conference on the Rule of Law, Lagos, 1961: A Report on the Proceedings* Geneva: International Commission of Jurists 1961
— *Human Rights in a One-party State: International Seminar on Human Rights, Their Protection, and the Rule of Law in a One-party State* London: Search Press 1978

Jackson, John D *Justice in South Africa* London: Secker & Warberg 1980

Jackson, Vicki C, and Mark V Tushnet *Comparative Constitutional Law* New York: Foundation Press 1999

Jacobs, FG, and KL Karst 'The Federal Legal Order: The USA and Europe compared: A Juridical Perspective' in *Integration through Law: Europe and the American Federal Experience*, edited by Mauro Cappelletti, Monica Seacombe, and Joseph Weiler. Berlin, W de Gruyter 1986

Jaffe, Louis L *English and American Judges as Lawmakers* Oxford: Clarendon Press 1969

Jennings, Ivor *Law and the Constitution* London: University of London Press, 5th edition, 1977

Joseph, Francis, and Kenneth Karst 'A Juridical Perspective' in *Integration through Law: Europe and the American Federal Experience*, edited by Mauro Cappelletti, Monica Seccombe, and Joseph Weiler. Berlin: W de Gruyter 1986

Kaplan, William A *The Concepts and Methods of Constitutional Law* Durham: Carolina Academic Press 1982

Karpen, Ulrich 'Freedom of Expression' in *The Constitution of the Federal Republic of Germany: Essays on the Basic Rights and Principles of the Basic Law with a Translation of the Basic Law*, edited by Ulrich Karpen. Baden-Baden: Nomos 1988
— 'The Constitution in the Face of Economic and Social Progress' in *New Challenges to the German Basic Law*, edited by Christian Starck. Baden-Baden: Nomos 1991

Kartashkin, Vladimir 'Economic, Social and Cultural Rights' in *The International Dimensions of Human Rights*, edited by Karel Vasak and Phillip Alston. Westport: Greenwood Press 1982

Kateb, G 'Remarks on the Procedures of Constitutional Democracy' in *Constitutionalism: Nomos XX*, edited by J Roland Peacock and John W Chapman. New York: New York University Press 1979

Kaunda, Kenneth *A Humanist in Africa: Letters to Colin M Morris from Kenneth D Kaunda* London: Longmans 1966

Kavanagh, Dennis 'Politics of Great Britain' in *Modern Political Systems: Europe*, edited by Roy C Macridis. Englewood Cliffs: Prentice-Hall, 7th edition, 1990

Kelly, JM, Gerard Hogan, and Gerry Whyte *The Irish Constitution* Dublin: Butterworths, 3rd edition, 1994

Kelsen, Hans *What is Justice? Justice, Law and Politics in the Mirror of Science: Collected Essays* Berkeley: University of California Press 1960

King, Preston T *Federalism and Federation* Baltimore: Johns Hopkins University Press 1982

Klein, Eckart 'The Parliamentary Democracy' in *The Constitution of the Federal Republic of Germany: Essays on the Basic Rights and Principles of the Basic Law with a Translation of the Basic Law*, edited by Ulrich Karpen. Baden-Baden: Nomos 1988

Kommers, Donald P *The Constitutional Jurisprudence of the Federal Republic of Germany* Durham: Duke University Press 1989

Kunig, Philip 'The Principle of Social Justice' in *The Constitution of the Federal Republic of Germany: Essays on the Basic Rights and Principles of the Basic Law with a Translation of the Basic Law*, edited by Ulrich Karpen. Baden-Baden: Nomos 1988

Lane, PH *A Manual of Australian Constitutional Law* Sydney: Law Book Co 1995

Legasse, Asmarom 'Human Rights in African Political Culture' in *The Moral Imperatives of Human Rights: A World Survey*, edited by Kenneth W Thompson. Lanham: University Press of America 1980

Lillich, Richard B 'Civil Rights' in *Human Rights in International Law: Legal and Policy Issues*, edited by Theodor Meron. Oxford: Clarendon Press 1984

Locke, John 'An Essay Concerning the True Original Extent and the End of Civil Government' in *Social Contract, Essays by Locke, Hume, and Rousseau*, edited by Ernest Baker. Oxford: Oxford University Press 1971
— *Two Treatises on Government*, edited by Peter Laslett. New York: Cambridge University Press 1988

Lord Russell of Liverpool *The Tragedy of the Congo* London: (NP) 1962

Macklem, Patrick, RCB Risk, CJ Rogerson, KE Swinton, LE Weinrib, and JD Whyte *Constitutional Law of Canada* Toronto: Emond Montgomery Publications Limited 1994

Madison, James 'Federalist No 47' in Alexander Hamilton, James Madison, and John Jay *The Federalist Papers*, edited by Garry Wills. New York: Bantam 1982

Mallory, JR *The Structure of Canadian Government* Toronto: Gage, revised edition, 1984

Marashinge, L 'Traditional Conceptions of Human Rights in Africa' in *Human Rights and Development in Africa*, edited by Claude E Welch and Ronald I Meltzer. New York: State University of New York Press 1984

Markesinis, Basil S *Foreign Law Comparative Methodology: A Subject and a Thesis* Oxford: Hart 1997

Markowitz, Irving *Power and Class in Africa: An Introduction to Change and Conflict in African Politics* Englewood Cliffs: Prentice-Hall 1977

Marks, Stephen P 'Principles and Norms of Human Rights Applicable in Emergency Situations: Underdevelopment, Catastrophes and Armed Conflicts' in *The International*

Dimensions of Human Rights, edited by Karel Vasak and Philip Alston. Westport: Greenwood Press 1982

Marquard, Leo *The Peoples and Policies of South Africa* London: Oxford University Press 1969

Marsh, David S *The Welfare State* London: Longman 1970

Marshall, Geoffrey *Constitutional Theory* Oxford: Clarendon 1971

Martin, Francisco Forrest, Stephen J Schnably, Ronald C Slye, Richard Wilson, Richard Falk, Jonathan S Simon, and Edward Koren *International Human Rights Law and Practice: Cases, Treaties and Materials* Cambridge: Kluwer Law International 1997

May, Henry John *The South African Constitution* Westport: Greenwood Press, 3rd edition, 1970

Mbaye, Keba, and B Ndiaye 'The Organization of African Unity' in *The International Dimensions of Human Rights*, edited by Karel Vasak and Philip Alston. Westport: Greenwood Press 1982

McWhinney, Edward *Supreme Court and Judicial Law-making: Constitutional Tribunals and Constitutional Review* Dordrecht: M Nijhoff 1986

— 'Constitution-making in an Era of Transition' in *Federalism-in-the-Making: Contemporary Canadian and German Constitutionalism, National and Transnational*, edited by Edward McWhinney, Jerald Zaslove, and Werner Wolf. Dordrecht: M Nijhoff 1992

Meron, Theodor *Human Rights and Humanitarian Norms as Customary Law* Oxford: Clarendon 1989

Meron, Theodor (ed) *Human Rights in International Law: Legal and Policy Issues* Oxford: Clarendon 1984

Mojekwe, C 'International Human Rights: The African Perspective' in *International Human Rights: Contemporary Issues*, edited by Jack L Nelson and Vera M Green. Standfordville: Human Rights Publishing Group 1980

— 'Self-determination: The African Perspective' in *Self-determination: National, Regional and Global Dimensions*, edited by Yonah Alexander and Robert A Friedlander. Boulder: Westview Press 1980

Morin, Yvan-Jacques 'The Rule of Law and the *Rechtsstaat* Concept' in *Federalism-in-the-Making: Contemporary Canadian and German Constitutionalism, National and Transnational*, edited by Edward McWhinney, Jerald Zaslove, and Werner Wolf. Dordrecht: M Nijhoff 1992

Mueller, Susanne D *Government and Opposition in Kenya, 1966–1969* Boston: African Studies Center, Boston University 1983

Muller, Ingo *Hitler's Justice: The Courts of the Third Reich*, translated by Deborah Lucas Schneider. Cambridge: Harvard University Press 1989

Murphy, Walter F 'Excluding Political Parties: Problems for Democratic and Constitutional Theory' in *Germany and Its Basic Law, Past, Present and Future: A German-American Symposium*, edited by Paul Kirchoff and Donald P Kommers. Baden-Baden: Nomos 1993

Newman, Frank C and Karel Vasak 'Civil and Political Rights' in *The International Dimensions of Human Rights*, edited by Karel Vasak and Philip Alston. Westport: Greenwood Press 1982

Newman, Frank, and David Weissbrodt *International Human Rights: Law, Policy and Process* Cincinnati: Anderson Publishing, 2nd edition, 1996

Nkrumah, Kwame *Challenge of the Congo* New York: International Publishers 1967

Nowak, John E, and Ronald E Rotunda *Constitutional Law* St Paul: West, 5th edition, 1995

Nwabueze, BO *Constitutionalism in the Emergent States* London: C Hurst 1973

— *Presidentialism in Commonwealth Africa* London: C Hurst 1975

Nyerere, Julius K *Ujamaa – Essays on Socialism* Dar es Salaam: Oxford University Press 1968

Nziransanga, M 'Secession, Federalism and African Unity' in *Nigeria: Dilemma of Nationhood*, edited by Joseph Okpaku. New York: Third Press 1972

Odinga, Oajuma Oginga *Not Yet Uhuru: The Autobiography of Oginga Odinga* London: Heinemann 1967

Ogwurike, C *Concept of Law in English-speaking Africa* New York: NOK Publishers International 1979.

Orwin, C, and T Pangle 'The Philosophical Foundation of Human Rights' in *Human Rights in our Time: Essays in Memory of Victor Baras*, edited by Mark F Plattner. Boulder: Westview Press 1984

Partsch, Karl Joseph 'Fundamental Principles of Human Rights' in *The International Dimensions of Human Rights*, edited by Karel Vasak and Philip Alston. Westport: Greenwood Press 1982

Pennock, Roland J, and John W Chapman (eds) *Constitutionalism* New York: New York University Press 1979

Pollis, Admantia, and Peter Schwab (eds) *Human Rights: Cultural and Ideological Perspectives* New York: Praeger 1979

Potholm, Christian P *The Theory and Practice of African Politics* Englewood Cliffs: Prentice-Hall 1979

Pusey, Merlo J *Charles Evan Hughes* New York: McMillan 1951

Quaye, Christopher O *Liberation Struggles in International Law* Philadelphia: Temple University Press 1991

Railton, Peter 'Judicial Review, Elites and Liberal Democracy' in *Constitutionalism*, edited by J Roland Pennock and John W Chapman. New York: New York University Press 1979

Reddy, Jeewan BP 'The Jurisprudence of Human Rights' in *Human Rights and Judicial Review: A Comparative Perspective*, edited by David M Beatty. Dordrecht: M Nijhoff 1994

Rex, John 'The Plural Society: The South African Case' in *South Africa: Economic Growth and Political Change*, edited by A Leftwich. London: Allison & Busby 1971

Ridley, F, and J Blondel *Public Administration in France* London: Routledge, 2nd edition, 1969

Riker, William H *Federalism: Origin, Operation, Significance* Boston: Little Brown 1964

— 'Federalism' in *Handbook of Political Science, Volume 5: Government Institutions and Processes*, edited by Fred I Greenstein and Nelson W Polsby. Reading: Addison-Wesley 1982

Rivkin, Arnold *Nation-building in Africa: Problems and Prospects* New Brunswick: Rutgers University Press 1969

Rockefeller, Nelson A *The Future of Federalism* Cambridge: Harvard University Press 1962

Ross, George 'The Constitution and the Requirements of Democracy in Germany' in *New Challenges to the German*

Basic Law, edited by Christian Starck. Baden-Baden: Nomos 1991

Rossum, Ralph A, and Alan G Tarr *American Constitutional Law: Cases and Interpretation* New York: St Martin's Press, 3rd edition, 1991

Rothchild, Majimbo 'Schemes in Kenya and Uganda' in *Boston University Papers on Africa: Transition in African Politics*, edited by Jeffrey Butler and AA Castagno. New York: Praeger 1967

Schermers, Henry G, and Denis F Waelbroeck *Judicial Protection in the European Communities* Deventer: Kluwer Law and Taxation, 5th edition, 1992

Schmidt, Eberhard Abmann 'The Constitution and the Requirements of Local Autonomy' in *The Constitution of the Federal Republic of Germany: Essays on the Basic Rights and Principles of the Basic Law with a Translation of the Basic Law*, edited by Ulrich Karpen. Baden-Baden: Nomos 1988

Schroder, Meinhard 'Strengthening of Constitutional Law: Effort and Problems' in *The Constitution of the Federal Republic of Germany: Essays on the Basic Rights and Principles of the Basic Law with a Translation of the Basic Law*, edited by Ulrich Karpen. Baden-Baden: Nomos 1988

Schuppert, Gunnar Folke 'The Right to Property' in *The Constitution of the Federal Republic of Germany: Essays on the Basic Rights and Principles of the Basic Law with a Translation of the Basic Law*, edited by Ulrich Karpen. Baden-Baden: Nomos 1988

Schwarz, Frederick AO, Jnr *Nigeria: The Tribes, the Nation or the Race: The Politics of Independence* Cambridge: MIT Press 1965

Schwelb, Egon *Human Rights and the International Community: The Roots and Growth of the Universal Declaration of Human Rights* Chicago: Quadrangle Books 1964

Sonobe, Itsuo 'The System of Constitutional Review in Japan' in *Human Rights and Judicial Review: A Comparative Perspective*, edited by David M Beatty. Dordrecht: M Nijhoff 1994

Sontheimer, Kurt 'Principles of Human Dignity in the Federal Republic' in *Germany and its Basic Law, Past, Present and Future: A German-American Symposium*, edited by Paul Kirchhoff and Donald P Kommers. Baden-Baden: Nomos 1993

Starke, JG *Introduction to International Law* London: Butterworths, 10th edition, 1989

Steinberger, Helmut 'Political Representation in Germany' in *Germany and Its Basic Law, Past, Present and Future: A German-American Symposium*, edited by Paul Kirchhoff and Donald P Kommers. Baden-Baden: Nomos 1993

Stephen, Mark 'Principles and Norms of Human Rights Applicable in Emergency Situations: Underdevelopment, Catastrophes and Armed Conflicts' in *The International Dimensions of Human Rights*, edited by Karel Vasak and Philip Alston. Westport: Greenwood Press 1982

Stone, Geoffrey R, Louis M Seidman, Cass R Sunstein, and Mark V Tushnet *Constitutional Law* Boston: Little Brown, 3rd edition, 1996

Strayer, BL *The Canadian Constitution and the Courts* Toronto: Butterworths, 3rd edition, 1988

Strong, CF *Modern Political Constitutions: An Introduction to the Comparative Study of their History and Existing Forms* London: Sidgewick & Jackson, 6th edition, 1963

Sunstein, Cass R 'Constitutions and Democracies: An Epilogue' in *Constitutionalism and Democracy*, edited by Jon Elster and Rune Slagstad. Cambridge: Cambridge University Press 1988

Tabuwe, Aletum M *The One-party System and the Traditional African Institutions* Yaounde: A Tabuwe 1980

Tolley, Howard, Jnr *The UN Commission on Human Rights* Boulder: Westview Press 1987

Tribe, Laurence *American Constitutional Law* New York: Foundation Press, 2nd edition, 1988

Trubek, David M 'Economic, Social, and Cultural Rights in the Third World: Human Rights Law and Human Needs Programs' in *Human Rights in International Law: Legal and Policy Issues*, edited by Theodor Meron. Oxford: Clarendon 1984

Van Boven, Theodor C 'Distinguishing Criteria of Human Rights' in *The International Dimensions of Human Rights*, edited by Karel Vasak and Philip Alston. Westport: Greenwood Press 1982

Van den Berghe, Pierre L *South Africa: A Study in Conflict* Middletown: Wesleyan University Press 1965

Venter, F 'South African Constitutional Law in Flux' in *Change in South Africa*, edited by DJ van Vuuren, NE Wiehan, JA Lombard, and NJ Rhoodie. Durban: Butterworths 1983

Vile, MJC *Constitutionalism and the Separation of Powers* Oxford: Clarendon Press 1967

Wade, ECS, and AW Bradley *Constitutional and Administrative Law* London: Longman, 10th edition, 1985

Waltman, Jerald L, and Kenneth M Holland (eds) *The Political Role of Law: Courts in Modern Democracies* New York: St Martin's Press 1988

Watts, Ronald L *New Federations: Experiments in the Commonwealth* Oxford: Clarendon 1966

Welch, Claude E, Jnr 'Human Rights as a Problem in Contemporary Africa' in *Human Rights and Development in Africa*, edited by Claude E Welch Jnr and Ronald I Meltzer. Albany: State University of New York Press 1984

Wellington, Harry H *Interpreting the Constitution: The Supreme Court and the Process of Adjudication* New Haven: Yale University Press 1990

Wheare, KC *Federal Government* New York: Oxford University Press, 4th edition, 1964

— *Modern Constitutions* London: Oxford University Press, 2nd edition, 1966

Wraith, Ronald E *Corruption in Developing Countries* New York: Norton 1964

Wurtenberger, Thomas 'Equality' in *The Constitution of the Federal Republic of Germany: Essays on the Basic Rights and Principles of the Basic Law with a Translation of the Basic Law*, edited by Ulrich Karpen. Baden-Baden: Nomos 1988

Young, Crawford, and Thomas Turner *The Rise and Decline of the Zairian State* Madison: University of Wisconsin Press 1985

Journals

Asante, SKB 'Nation Building and Human Rights in Emergent African Nations' (1969) 2 *Cornell International Law Journal* 73

Asimov, Michael 'Towards a South African Administrative Justice Act' (1997) 3 *Michigan Journal of Race and Law* 1

Balkin, JM 'Deconstructive Practice and Legal Theory' (1987) 96 *Yale Law Journal* 743

Bandes, Susan 'The Negative Constitution: A Critique' (1990) 88 *Michigan Law Review* 2271

Barnett, Randy, 'The Relevance of the Framers Intent' (1996) 19 *Harvard Journal of Law and Public Policy* 403

Berger, Peter L 'Are Human Rights Universal?' (1997) September *Commentary* 60

Berger, Raoul 'The Activist Legacy of the New Deal Court' (1984) 59 *Washington Law Review* 62

Bilder, Richard B, and Mark A Weisburd 'Book Review and Note: Legal and Moral Constraints on Low-Intensity Conflict' Alberto R Coll, James C Ord, and Stephen A Rose (eds) (1995) 67 *US War College of International War Studies* 91) (1997) *American Journal of International Law* 205

Bouckaert, Peter N, 'Negotiated Revolution: South Africa's Transition to a Multiracial Democracy' (1997) 33 *Stanford Journal of International Law* 375

Budlender, Geoff 'A Common Citizenship' (1985) 1 *South African Journal of Human Rights* 210

Callahan, Maureen B 'Cultural Relativism and The Interpretation of Constitutional Texts' (1994) 30 *Willamette Law Review* 609

Cameron, Edwin, Harold Rudolph, and Dirk van Zyl Smit 'Judicial Appointments, Public Confidence, and the Court Structure: Proposals for a new Approach' (1980) *De Rebus* 430

Christenson, Gordon '*Jus Cogens*: Guarding Interests Fundamental to International Society' (1988) 28 *Virginia Journal of International Law* 585

Cox, Archibald 'Constitutional Adjudication and the Promotion of Human Rights' (1966) 80 *Harvard Law Review* 91

Currie, David P 'Positive and Negative Constitutional Rights' (1986) 53 *University of Chicago Law Review* 864

Cushman, B 'Rethinking the New Deal Court' (1994) 80 *Virginia Law Review* 201

Davis Dennis 'The Twist of Language and the Two Fagans: Please Sir may I have Some More Literalism!' (1996) 12 *South African Journal of Human Rights* 504

Davis Michael H 'The Law/Politics Distinction, the French *Conseil Constitutionnel*, and the United States Supreme Court' (1986) 34 *American Journal of Comparative Law* 45

Dawson, Frank G, and Burns H Weston 'Prompt Adequate and Effective Universal Standard of Compensation' (1962) 30 *Fordham Law Review* 727

Dickson, Brice 'Human Rights on the Eve of the Next Century: Aspects of Human Rights Implementation: Protecting Human Rights through a Constitutional Court: The Case of South Africa' (1997) 66 *Fordham Law Review* 531

Donders, Yvonne 'Commentary on the Maastricht Guidelines on Violations of Economic, Social and Cultural Rights' (1997) January–March *African Legal Aid Quarterly* 22

Fagan, Eduard 'The Longest Erratum Note in History' (1996) 12 *South African Journal of Human Rights* 89

— 'The Ordinary Meaning of Language – A Response to Professor Davis' (1997) 13 *South African Journal of Human Rights* 175

Finn, John E 'Federalism in Perpetuity: West German and United States Federalism in Comparative Perspective' (1989) 22 *New York University Journal of International Law and Politics* 1

Fish, Stanley 'Fish v Fiss' (1984) 36 *Stanford Law Review* 1325

Fiss, Owen 'Objectivity and Interpretation' (1982) 34 *Stanford Law Review* 739

— 'Comments on Conventionalism' (1985) 58 *Southern California Law Review* 177

Ford, Christopher A 'Challenges and Dilemmas of Racial and Ethnic Identity in American and Post-Apartheid South African Affirmative Action' (1996) 43 *University of California Los Angeles Law Review* 1953

Grey, Thomas C 'Do We Have an Unwritten Constitution?' (1975) 27 *Stanford Law Review* 703

— 'The Constitution as Scripture' (1984) 37 *Stanford Law Review* 1

Gunlicks, Arthur B 'Constitutional Law and the Protection of Subnational Governments in the United States and West Germany' (1988) 18 *Publius* 149

Hamalengwa, M 'The Political Economy of Human Rights in Africa: Historical and Contemporary Perspectives' (1983) 9 *Philosophy and Social Action* 25

Haysom, Nicolas 'Constitutionalism, Majoritarian Democracy and Socio-economic Rights' (1992) 8 *South African Journal of Human Rights* 451

Hegland, Kenny 'Goodbye to Deconstruction' (1985) 58 *Southern California Law Review* 1204

Hinden, Rita 'Africa and Democracy' (1962) *Encounter* 8

Howard, Dick AE 'The Indeterminacy of Constitutions' (1996) 31 *Wake Forest Law Review* 383

Hulsebosch, Daniel J 'Note, The New Deal Court: Emergence of a New Reason' (1990) 90 *Columbia Law Review* 1973

Humphrey, John P 'The International Bill of Rights: Scope and Implementation' (1976) 17 *William & Mary Law Review* 527

Hutchinson, Allen C, and Andrew Petter 'Private Rights, Public Wrongs: The Liberal Lie of the Charter' (1988) 38 *University of Toronto Law Journal* 278

Hutchinson, Allen C, and Patrick J Monahan 'The "Rights" Stuff: Roberto Unger and Beyond' (1984) 62 *Texas Law Review* 1477

Iglar, Richard F 'The Constitutional Crisis in Yugoslavia and the International Law of Self-determination: Slovenia and Croatia's Right to Secede' (1992) 15 *Boston College International and Comparative Law Review* 213

Ishihara, Brendon Troy 'Toward a More Perfect Union: The Role of Amending Formulae in the United States, Canadian, and German Constitutional Experiences' (1996) 2 *University of California at Davis Journal of International Law and Policy* 267

Kenn, Deborah 'One Dream, Another's Reality: Housing Justice in Sweden' (1996) 22 *Brooklyn Journal of International Law* 63

Kentridge, Sydney 'Telling the Truth about Law' (1982) 99 *South African Law Journal* 648

Kommers, Donald P 'German Constitutionalism: A Prolegomenon' (1991) 40 *Emory Law Journal* 837

Lapidoth, Ruth 'Freedom of Religion and of Conscience in Israel' (1998) 47 *Catholic University Law Review* 441

Ledda, Romano 'Social Classes and Political Struggle in Africa' (1967) August *International Socialist Journal* 568

Levinson, Sanford 'Law as Literature' (1982) 60 *Texas Law Review* 373

Lofchie, Michael F 'Representative Government, Bureaucracy, and Political Development: The African Case' (1976) 16 *African Administrative Studies* 133

MacDonald, R St J 'Derogations under Article 15 of the European Convention on Human Rights' (1997) 36 *Columbia Journal of Transnational Law* 225

MacKinnon, Catherine A 'Not a Moral Issue' (1984) 2 *Yale Law and Policy Review* 321

Magner, Ellis S 'Therapeutic Jurisprudence Forum: Therapeutic Jurisprudence: Its Potential for Australia' (1998) 67 *Revista Juridica de la Universidad de Puerto Rico* 121

Mazrui, Ali 'The Cultural Faith of African Legislatures: Rise, Decline and Prospects for Revival' (1979) 112 *Presence Africaine* 26

Miller, Arthur S 'On Politics, Democracy, and the First Amendment: A Commentary on First National Bank v Bellotti' (1981) 38 *Washington & Lee Law Review* 21

Minagawa, Takeshi '*Jus Cogens* in Public International Law' (1968) 6 *Hitotsubashi Journal of International Law and Politics* 16

Monaghan, Henry Paul 'The Supreme Court, 1974 Term-Forward: Constitutional Common Law' (1975) 89 *Harvard Law Review* 1

— '*Stare Decisis* and Constitutional Adjudication' (1988) 88 *Columbia Law Review* 723

Moore, Michael S 'The Semantics of Judging' (1981) 54 *Southern California Law Review* 151

Morton, RL 'Judicial Review in France: A Comparative Analysis' (1998) 36 *American Journal of Comparative Law* 89

Mosely, Emily 'Defining Religious Tolerance: German Policy toward the Church of Scientology' (1997) 30 *Vanderbilt Journal of Transnational Law* 1129

Motala, Ziyad 'Human Rights in Africa: A Cultural, Ideological and Legal Examination' (1989) 12 *Hastings International and Comparative Law Review* 373

— 'Independence of the Judiciary, Prospects and Limitations of Judicial Review in Terms of the United States Model in a New South African Order: Towards an Alternative Judicial Structure based on the Continental Models' (1991) 55 *Albany Law Review* 367

— 'Socio-economic Rights, Federalism and the Courts: Comparative Lessons for South Africa' (1995) 112 (1) *South Africa Law Journal* 61

— 'The Constitution is not Anything the Court wants It to be: The *Mhlungu* Decision and the Need for Disciplining Rules' (1998) 115 (1) *South African Law Journal* 141

— 'The Constitutional Court's Approach to International Law and Its Method of Interpretation in the *Amnesty* Decision: Intellectual Honesty or Political Expendiency (1996) 21 *South African Year Book of International Law* 29

— 'The Record of Federal Constitutions in Africa: Some Lessons for a Post-Apartheid South Africa' (1990) 7 *Arizona Journal of International and Comparative Law* 225

— 'The Promotion of National Unity and Reconciliation Act, the Constitution and International Law' (1995) XXVIII *Comparative and International Law Journal of Southern Africa* 338

— 'Towards an Appropriate Understanding of Separation of Powers, and Accountability of the Executive and Public Service under the New South African Order' (1995) 112 (3) *South African Law Journal* 503

— 'Under International Law, does the New Order in South Africa assume the Obligations and Responsibilities of the Apartheid Order: An Argument for Realism over Formalism' (1997) *South African Yearbook of International Law* 294

Motala, Ziyad, and David Butleritchie 'Self-defense in International Law, the United Nations, and the Bosnia Conflict' (1995) 57 *University of Pittsburgh Law Review* 1

Murchison, Brian C 'Interpretation and Independence: How Judges use the Avoidance Canon in Separation of Powers Cases' (1995) 30 *Georgia Law Review* 85

Mureinik, Etienne 'Beyond a Charter of Luxuries: Economic Rights in the Constitution' (1992) 8 *South African Journal of Human Rights* 464

Neuberger, Benyamin 'History and African Concepts of Nationhood' (1987) XIV (1) *Canadian Review of Studies in Nationalism* 161

Parker, Karen, and Lyn B Neylon '*Jus Cogens*: Compelling the Law of Human Rights' (1989) 12 *Hastings International and Comparative Law Review* 411

Rapczynski, Andrew 'From Sovereignty to Process: The Jurisprudence of Federalism after Garcia' (1985) 341 *Supreme Court Review* 341

Schachter, Oscar 'Editorial Comment, Compensation for Expiration' (1984) 78 *American Journal of International Law* 121

Schwartz, Herman 'Why Economic and Social Rights belong in the New Post-Communist Constitutions in Europe' (1992) Fall *East European Constitutional Review* 25

Spann, Girardeau 'Deconstructing the Legislative Veto' (1984) 68 *Minnesota Law Review* 473

Starck, Christian 'Europe's Fundamental Rights in their Newest Garb' (1982) 3 *Human Rights Law Journal* 103

Sunstein, Cass R 'Constitutionalism after the New Deal' (1987) 101 *Harvard Law Review* 421

Tarlton, Charles D 'Symmetry and Asymmetry as Elements of Federalism: A Theoretical Speculation' (1965) 27 *Journal of Politics* 861

Thayer, James Bradley 'The Origin and Scope of the American Doctrine of Constitutional Law' (1893) *Harvard Law Review* 129

Tushnet, Mark V 'Following the Rules laid down: A Critique of Interpretivism and Neutral Principles' (1983) 96 *Harvard Law Review* 781

Unger, Roberto Mungabeira 'The Critical Legal Studies Movement' (1983) 96 *Harvard Law Review* 561

Warren, Samuel D, and Louis D Brandeis 'The Right to Privacy' (1980) 4 *Harvard Law Review* 93

Weiler, Paul C 'The Supreme Court and the Law of Canadian Federalism' (1973) 23 *University of Toronto Law Journal* 307

Wortley, BA 'Political Crime in English Law and in International Law' (1971) 45 *British Yearbook of International Law* 228

Yacoob, Justice Zakeria Mohammed 'Salient Features of the Negotiating Process' (1999) 52 *Southern Methodist University Law Review* 1579

1

The making of the Constitution

Introduction

In July 1993, the South African government, represented by the National Party (NP), the African National Congress (ANC), and various other political organizations, agreed to hold South Africa's first non-racial election from 26 to 28 April 1994. In December 1993, the white-controlled South African parliament adopted the interim Constitution,[1] ending 300 years of white minority rule. This agreement on the Constitution is a story of leadership and prodding, of a coalition of leaders from different groups – once bitter enemies – now sitting together to discuss their differences. All parties had recognized the gravity of the situation they were facing, particularly the constant peril of violence. It is also a story of leadership on all sides, showing the pragmatism to compromise, to regulate the political conflict in the interests of all. A constitution was brokered that aimed to transcend the divisions of the past, to move away from apportioning blame or seeking revenge, and towards a society based on mutual respect, dignity, and freedom for all.[2]

In *Du Plessis and Others v De Klerk and Another*,[3] the Constitutional Court, *per* Kriegler J, observed:

... our constitution is unique in its origins, concepts, and aspirations. Nor am I a chauvinist when I describe the negotiations process which gave birth to that constitution as unique; so, too, the leap from minority rule to representative democracy founded on universal adult suffrage; the damascene about-turn from executive directed parliamentary supremacy to justiciable constitutionalism and a specialist constitutional court, the in gathering of discarded fragments of the country and the creation of new provinces; and the entrenchment of a true separation and devolution of powers. Nowhere in the world that I am aware of have enemies agreed on a transitional coalition and a controlled two-stage process of constitution-building.

South Africa's transition to democratic rule has been marked by a change in status from that of a pariah state to an example, to other divided societies, of a model democracy.[4] In this introductory chapter, we outline the process culminat-

---

[1] Constitution of the Republic of South Africa Act 200 of 1993 (interim Constitution).
[2] See the preamble to the interim Constitution.
[3] *Du Plessis and Others v De Klerk and Another* CCT 8/95 (15 May 1996), now cited as 1996 (3) SA 850 (CC); 1996 (5) BCLR 658 (CC).
[4] Protagonists in the conflict in Northern Ireland and Palestine have invoked the South African example of negotiation as a model to be emulated in their conflicts.

ing in the drafting of South Africa's final Constitution.[5] The constitution-making process can best be understood in terms of four stages. The first stage includes the constitutions of the apartheid era, beginning with the Union of South Africa in 1910[6] and ending with the tri-cameral Constitution of 1983.[7] The second stage covers the negotiations between the government and the liberation movements after the unbanning of the ANC, the Pan Africanist Congress (PAC), and other political movements in 1990. The third stage encompasses the talks within the Convention for a Democratic South Africa (Codesa) between 1992 and 1994, which culminated in the drafting of the interim Constitution. The fourth stage comprises the drafting and adoption of the final Constitution between 1994 and 1996 by the democratically elected Constitutional Assembly (CA).

Past constitutions

The first Constitution of South Africa was introduced at the formation of the Union of South Africa in 1909–1910 and took its inspiration from the British model. This was the framework of government for three quarters of the twentieth century.[8] The Republic of South Africa was proclaimed in 1961,[9] but this did not result in a change in the overall form of government.[10] Since the formation of the Union of South Africa, sovereignty of parliament has been a major constitutional principle.[11] Therefore, like Britain, South Africa has had an independent judiciary.

The judiciary, however, did not have the power to decide on the substance of legislation. At the formation of the Union of South Africa, the predominant view among the delegates was to allow the courts a testing right over legislation, which would amount to defeating the will of the people.[12] Supremacy of the legislature assumed the status of a predominant *Grundnorm*.[13] The Westminster form of government was finally abolished in 1984 with the introduction of the tri-cameral parliament.[14]

The *de facto* situation since the formation of the union was the separation of people on the basis of colour. With the advent of NP control in 1949, the dominant focus of the government became the institutionalization of separate development. In 1950, the Population Registration Act[15] was passed and required the registration of every citizen of the country as belonging to one of the defined population groups: 'White', 'Coloured', or 'Bantu'. Moreover, the 'Bantu' group was further subdivided into eight tribal units. After 1948, the exclusion of blacks from the central decision-making process took a new and somewhat sophisticated turn. The NP's political platform was the complete separation of the races in every sphere of life. This culminated in the creation of separate political institutions for 'Coloureds', 'Indians', and 'Bantu'. With respect to so-called coloureds and Indians, the Coloured Persons Representative Council (CPRC)[16] and the South African Indian Council[17] (SAIC) were formed as fora for these respective designated groups. Both the CPRC and SAIC failed to achieve any legitimacy because of their lack of real power and

---

[5] Constitution of the Republic of South Africa Act 108 of 1996 (final Consitution).

[6] South Africa Act 1909.

[7] Republic of South Africa Constitution Act 110 of 1983.

[8] South Africa Act 1909.

[9] Republic of South Africa Constitution Act 32 of 1961 (previously known as Provincial Government Act 32 of 1961).

[10] The proclamation of the Republic of South Africa merely entailed the severing of all links with the British Crown. Therefore, from the perspective of the white government, minimal changes were required in the form of government.

[11] Article 59 of the South Africa Act 1909.

[12] Denis V Cowen *The Foundations of Freedom with Special Reference to South Africa* Cape Town: Oxford University Press 1961, 139.

[13] F Venter 'South African Constitutional Law in Flux' in *Change in South Africa*, edited by DJ van Vuuren, NE Wiehan, JA Lombard, and NJ Rhoodie. Durban: Butterworths 1983, 3.

[14] Republic of South Africa Constitution Act 110 of 1983.

[15] Act 30 of 1950.

[16] Coloured Persons Representative Council Act 49 of 1964.

[17] South African Indian Council Act 31 of 1968.

their overall subordinate position relative to the government.[18]

With regard to the African majority, the primary forum for black political participation was supposed to be within the homelands. In the context of the policy of separate development, each African was identified in terms of one of the defined ethnic groups. Africans were supposed to exercise political rights as ethnic groups within the designated areas of their specific groups. The corollary was that Africans would no longer exercise political rights outside the specified areas that were areas of white rule. The National States Citizenship Act[19] specified that every black person in South Africa was a citizen of one of the homelands irrespective of where that person was born or resided throughout his or her life. Moreover, once a territory obtained so-called independence, all persons identified with that homeland were stripped of their South African nationality.[20] As a result, millions of Africans lost their nationality in what has been referred to as an exercise of denationalization.[21]

In 1983, a new constitution replaced the Westminster style of constitution. The new constitution established the tri-cameral parliament, which focused on a stronger executive president. The new dispensation provided for limited participation for the coloured and Indian groups in the central political process. In reality, the inclusion of these groups did not really alter the status quo of white supremacy, particularly NP dominance over South African politics.[22] Neither did it confer on the two groups significant decision-making powers. All it accomplished was to make coloured and Indian groups junior partners in the implementation of apartheid legislation. The constitutional machinery was designed in such a way that major decision-making power still resided in the hands of the white minority. The electoral college, responsible for electing the president, consisted of eighty-eight members, fifty of whom were from the white House of Assembly. In other words, the institutions were set up in such a way as to ensure that the choice of state president would be that of the dominant party in the white House of Assembly of the legislature.[23]

Factors that contributed to negotiations

Like preceding constitutions, the Constitution of 1983 experienced a legitimacy crisis. The introduction of the tri-cameral parliament served as a catalyst to move the underprivileged, dispossessed, and frustrated majority to greater resistance against the apartheid regime through strikes, boycotts, stay-aways, and other forms of resistance. The uprisings were met by massive repression by the state and a declaration of a state of emergency. After almost a decade of bitter and violent conflict, the protagonists entered into a process of negotiation. In *Certification of the Constitution of the Republic of South Africa*,[24] the Constitutional Court observed:

... remarkably and in the course of but a few years, the country's political leaders managed to avoid a cataclysm by negotiating a largely peaceful transition from the rigidly controlled minority regime to a wholly democratic constitutional dispensation. After a long history of 'deep conflict between a minority which reserved for itself all control over the political instruments of the state and a majority who sought to resist that domination', the overwhelming majority of South Africans across the

---

[18] Lawrence J Boulle *Constitutional Reform and the Apartheid State: Legitimacy, Consociationalism and Control in South Africa* New York: St Martin's Press 1984, 84. Both bodies were abolished with the introduction of the new Constitution setting up the tri-cameral parliament in 1984. See the discussion on the new Constitution below.

[19] Act 26 of 1970.

[20] Section 3 of the National States Citizenship Act 26 of 1970.

[21] Geoff Budlender 'A Common Citizenship' (1985) *South African Journal of Human Rights* 210.

[22] The exclusive power that the state president had in designating his or her own and general affairs allowed the dominant white group constituted in the NP to control the legislative agenda. See below.

[23] The members of the electoral college were chosen by the majority parties in each of the three houses of the legislature. The white legislature's share of members in the electoral college was greater than that of the other two houses combined.

[24] *In re: Certification of the Constitution of the Republic of South Africa* CCT 23/96 (6 September 1996), now cited as 1996 (10) BCLR 1253 (CC); 1996 (4) SA 744 (CC) (*First Certification* decision).

political divide realized that the country had to be rescued from imminent disaster by a negotiated commitment to a fundamentally new constitutional order premised upon open and democratic government and the universal enjoyment of fundamental human rights.

Thirty years of low-level military conflict between the NP government and the liberation movements (primarily the ANC) had resulted in stalemate. It did not appear that the liberation movements were in any position to defeat the apartheid regime militarily. Simultaneously, a multitude of global, regional, and domestic factors led the major protagonists, particularly the ANC and the NP government, to sitting down at the same table and discussing a negotiated settlement. At the international level, the sanctions and embargoes had taken a considerable toll on the economy. The Cold War was over, and the southern African region no longer held the same strategic position for the superpowers. At the regional level, the apartheid regime had sustained significant military losses in Angola, which contributed to the independence of Namibia. The protagonists of the conflicts in Angola and Mozambique were actively negotiating resolutions to their conflicts. Most significantly, the internal resistance against the regime, together with the strikes and boycotts, considerably undermined the economy. Large parts of the country had become ungovernable. Apartheid had simply become too costly to maintain. This confluence of factors finally led President FW de Klerk to announce, on 2 February 1990, the unbanning of the liberation movements, the release of high-level political prisoners, and a call for multi-party negotiations.

Negotiations towards a democratic constitution: the first phase

Before multi-party negotiations commenced, there were a series of meetings, referred to as *talks about talks*, between the ANC and the NP, to iron out the significant differences as to how negotiations would proceed, as well as the ground rules for the negotiations. The major protagonists had different perspectives on the nature of, and the objectives of, the negotiations. The NP did not approach the negotiations with a view to making a decisive break with the past. Instead, it sought to reform the existing system with a view to some form of inclusion, which would result in a decrease in international pressure and the halting of internal resistance. During the period of negotiations, the NP was determined to control all institutions of state. The ANC set the tone for a negotiated settlement with the Harare Declaration, a document adopted by the Organization of African Unity in 1989. The document articulated how the ANC envisaged the creation of a climate for negotiations and the process towards a negotiated settlement. The Harare Declaration emphasized the creation of a level playing field for all players, and the adoption of a constitution by an elected constituent assembly, the release of all political prisoners, the ending of the state of emergency, and the withdrawal of troops from the townships.

The NP and the Inkatha Freedom Party (IFP) initially favoured tri-lateral negotiations between the ANC, NP, and the IFP. The ANC argued that all political groupings with proven support be involved in the multi-party negotiations. All sides recognized that the nature of the process, coupled with the relative balance of forces between the parties, would determine the outcome of negotiations.

The initial meetings between the NP and the ANC culminated in the Groote Schuur Minute: the first agreement between the two organizations.[25] The government agreed to meet the demands outlined in the Harare Declaration within a short time frame. The ANC in turn agreed to help reduce the level of violence in the country. The Groote Schuur Minute was followed by the Pretoria Minute, in terms of which the ANC agreed to suspend the armed struggle while the government agreed to the release of political prisoners.[26]

---

[25] Signed on 2 May 1990.
[26] Signed on 7 August 1990.

Convention for a Democratic South Africa (Codesa)

The first formal meeting of all sides took place at the Convention for a Democratic South Africa (Codesa) on 20 December 1991. At this meeting, the major participants signed the Declaration of Intent in which they pledged to work towards the creation of a 'united, nonracial, and non-sexist state' and the creation of a 'multiracial democracy'. The declaration also bound all parties to abide by the decisions of Codesa which would itself draft the text of all legislation necessary to give effect to the negotiated agreements. Codesa established five working groups which were entrusted with the responsibility of hammering out the details of transition, including how to create a free political climate, details on the constitutional principles and the constitution-making body, the transitional government, the reincorporation of the home-lands, and the time frame for the transition period.[27]

At the second plenary session of Codesa in May 1992 (Codesa II), the major parties agreed that a democratically elected Constituent Assembly (CA) should write the new constitution. The parties agreed that the democratically elected CA would act as an interim parliament. Despite this agreement, the NP (supported by the IFP) insisted that decisions of the CA be made subject to minority veto. The NP also wanted the boundaries, powers, functions, and structures of regions, to be agreed to in the interim Constitution and to be immune to change by the CA. The NP further wanted decisions of the CA to be made by a seventy per cent majority, and a seventy-five per cent majority for decisions relating to the Bill of Rights. These demands by the NP led to an impasse that resulted in the ANC withdrawing from the negotiations. The ANC subsequently embarked on a campaign of mass action and nationwide strikes to push for an end to the violence and the creation of a CA. The political deadlock saw violence grow to even higher levels.

Parallel with the mass action, top-level ANC and NP officials secretly established informal talks to explore possible solutions to the impasse. These contacts focused on the major points of contention and culminated in the ANC–NP Summit of September 1992. Both parties signed a record of understanding which included agreement on a democratically elected CA with fixed time frames and adequate deadlock-breaking mechanisms; an interim government of national unity with the CA acting as an interim parliament; the phased release of political prisoners before November 1992; increased security and monitoring of measures at various hostels as a means of curbing the violence; the prohibition of the carrying of dangerous weapons in public; and the right of all political groups to engage in peaceful mass action.

The progress of the bilateral meetings opened the way for negotiations to resume. During the stalemate, the ANC had undertook a reassessment of its approach to negotiations, which culminated in the National Executive Committee (NEC) of the ANC adopting the Strategic Perspectives document in November 1992. The document reflected a realization that the country was in particularly severe crisis. To the NEC this meant that the following was required: establishment of a democratic constitution-making process; ending of the NPs monopoly on power; ensuring a continuing link between democracy and socioeconomic empowerment; and minimizing the threat to stability and the democratic process. The ANC document contained a number of clauses that became known as the *sunset clauses*. These clauses committed the ANC to an interim government of national unity and the contemplation of amnesty. For the ANC, the proposals in the document reflected a strategic concession that the ANC was prepared to make to achieve a resolution that would lead to a democratic South Africa.

By September 1993, with these concessions negotiated, a final agreement was reached on some of the key institutional mechanisms for managing the run-up to democratic elections, including the creation of the Independent Electoral Commission (IEC), the Independent Broadcasting Authority (IBA), and the Transitional Executive Constitution (TEC). On 18 November 1993, the multi-

---

[27] Peter N Bouckaert 'Negotiated Revolution: South Africa's Transition to a Multiracial Democracy' (1997) 33 *Stanford Journal of International Law*, edited by Thomas Fleiner-Gerster and Silvan Hutter. Fribourg: Editions Universitaires 1987, 390.

party forum, in a plenary session, adopted the interim Constitution, which would come into effect on 27 April 1994. The interim Constitution was to remain in effect until the final Constitution was drawn up by the democratically elected CA. The then existing parliament passed into law the resolutions of the multi-party forum.

The TEC was entrusted with the responsibility to monitor the run-up to South Africa's first election and to ensure a level playing field for all political parties. All twenty-one political parties that had negotiated the interim Constitution had representation on the TEC. During the run-up to the election, the TEC was empowered to order the government to take or refrain from certain courses of action that would contribute to a free and fair election. The TEC did not constitute an end to white minority rule because the cabinet under President FW de Klerk still remained in charge of day-to-day affairs. However, special sub-councils on matters such as defence, law and order, finance, and foreign affairs were created to supervise the work of the white cabinet until the election.

The compromise contained three pivotal aspects: an interim Constitution for a period of two years, during which time the final Constitution would be adopted by the democratically elected legislature; the final Constitution that was to conform to a set of agreed upon constitutional principles contained in Schedule 4 of the interim Constitution; and the certification of the final Constitution by the newly created Constitutional Court.

The idea of the interim Constitution was to allow for a democratic election and democratically elected representatives to draw up the final Constitution. Having an election before the drawing up of a constitution represented a victory for the ANC. Its members had consistently argued that the drawing up the final Constitution could only legitimately be done by democratically elected representatives. Under the principles contained in Schedule 4 of the interim Constitution, certain aspects of the final Constitution were already agreed upon, particularly the need for the protection of fundamental human rights. Other principles were mentioned on an abstract level, such as the requirement for separation of powers and the division of authority between the national, provincial, and local levels of government. The principles also contained conflicting norms, for example, individual liberties and the need for social and economic upliftment. These principles – some concrete, others abstract, and others apparently conflicting – helped the different political parties with their differing agendas (parties who could have contributed to greater strife and instability in the country), move the country towards a democratic and constitutional future.[28] In the *First Certification* decision, the Court observed:

Certification of the Constitution of the Republic of South Africa CCT 23/96 (6 September 1996), now cited as (10) BCLR 1253 (CC); 1996 (4) SA 744 (CC)
(*First Certification* decision)
(notes omitted)

[12] One of the deadlocks, a crucial one on which the negotiations all but foundered, related to the formulation of a new constitution for the country. All were agreed that such an instrument was necessary and would have to contain certain basic provisions. Those who negotiated this commitment were confronted, however, with two problems. The first arose from the fact that they were not elected to their positions in consequence of any free and verifiable elections and that it was therefore necessary to have this commitment articulated in a final constitution adopted by a credible body properly mandated to do so in consequence of free and fair elections based on universal adult suffrage. The second problem was the fear in some quarters that the constitution eventually favoured by such a body of elected representatives might not sufficiently address the anxieties and the insecurities of such constituencies and might therefore subvert the

---

28 Dick AE Howard 'The Indeterminacy of Constitutions' (1996) 31 *Wake Forest Law Review* 397.

objectives of a negotiated settlement. The government and other minority groups were prepared to relinquish power to the majority but were determined to have a hand in drawing the framework for the future governance of the country. The liberation movements on the opposition side were equally adamant that only democratically elected representatives of the people could legitimately engage in forging a constitution: neither they, and certainly not the government of the day, had any claim to the requisite mandate from the electorate.

[13] The impasse was resolved by a compromise which enabled both sides to attain their basic goals without sacrificing principle. What was no less important in the political climate of the time was that it enabled them to keep faith with their respective constituencies: those who feared engulfment by a black majority and those who were determined to eradicate apartheid once and for all. In essence the settlement was quite simple. Instead of an outright transmission of power from the old order to the new, there would be a programmed two-stage transition. An interim government, established and functioning under an interim Constitution agreed to by the negotiating parties, would govern the country on a coalition basis while a final Constitution was being drafted. A national legislature, elected (directly and indirectly) by universal adult suffrage, would double as the constitution-making body and would draft the new Constitution within a given time. But – and herein lies the key to the resolution of the deadlock – that text would have to comply with certain guidelines agreed upon in advance by the negotiating parties. What is more, an independent arbiter would have to ascertain and declare whether the new Constitution indeed complied with the guidelines before it could come into force.

Legal Context and Terminology

[14] The settlement was ultimately concluded by the negotiating parties in November 1993. Shortly thereafter and pursuant thereto the South African Parliament duly adopted the Interim Constitution. Although the formal date of commencement of the IC was 27 April 1994 (a date agreed upon in advance by the negotiating parties), its provisions relating to the election of the transitional national legislature came into operation earlier.

[15] The importance of the deadlock-breaking agreement is highlighted by the preamble to the IC, which, in its second paragraph, characterises the Constitutional Principles as 'a solemn pact' in the following terms:

AND WHEREAS in order to secure the achievement of this goal, elected representatives of all the people of South Africa should be mandated to adopt a new Constitution in accordance with a solemn pact recorded as Constitutional Principles.

It is also clear from the language that the Constitutional Principles constituted the formal record of the 'solemn pact'. They were contained in IC sch 4, which was incorporated by a reference under IC 71(1) *(a)*. Although they were numbered from I to IV and were often referred to as the 34 Constitutional Principles, they listed many more requirements than that. Henceforth they will be referred to collectively as the 'CPs' and individually as 'CP I' and so on. The wording and interpretation of the CPs will be discussed later; what is of importance at this stage is to note that they are acknowledged by the preamble to be foundational to the new constitution. As will be shown shortly, they were also crucial to the certification task with which the Court had been entrusted.

Key features of the compromise under the interim Constitution

Government of national unity

Under the interim Constitution, the new government installed after the elections was to be one of national unity, comprising all political parties which received over five per cent of the national vote. Decisions in the cabinet were to be taken by majority vote. Executive power vested in the president, who was elected by the National Assembly (NA). The interim Constitution made provision for every party that had a twenty per cent vote in the NA to designate a deputy president, or the party with the second highest vote to designate a deputy president.

The cabinet consisted of twenty-seven cabinet positions. All parties with at least twenty seats in the NA were given a right to obtain cabinet positions based on proportional representation. The president made the determination as to which portfolio would be given to which political party. The government of national unity was to serve a full five-year term.

Consensus on adoption of the final Constitution

The compromise provided that a sixty-six per cent majority was required in the legislature for the approval of the final Constitution. This super-majority was also a concession to minority parties. The ANC, however, achieved its goal of a deadlock-breaking mechanism. If the sixty-six per cent majority were not attained, then the final draft would have to be presented to the population in a referendum. In that case, it would be adopted if sixty per cent of the voters approved the new Constitution. If the Constitution were rejected in the referendum, an election for a new legislature would be conducted. This time around, there would not be a need for a sixty per cent majority in the legislature for the approval of the new Constitution.

Certification by the Constitutional Court

However, before the Constitution could take effect, or be put to the population in a referendum, the Constitutional Court needed to certify that the final Constitution incorporated the fundamental principles and guidelines contained in Schedule 4 of the interim Constitution. A new Constitutional Court was created to adjudicate over constitutional disputes and to enforce the Bill of Rights. The Constitutional Court also had an effective veto over the final Constitution.

The role of the judiciary is to protect adherence to the Constitution. The judiciary's function is to explain and to justify what the Constitution means, free from the hurly-burly of everyday politics encountered by the legislature and the executive. A continuous conflict exists between judicial review and democracy. The judiciary cannot play the role of a constituent body to dismiss or create the ground rules that the Constitution represents. However, as part of the certification function, the Constitutional Court was given a unique and, up to this time, unheard of duty, to evaluate and accordingly certify the new Constitution as consistent with the agreed constitutional principles. This was a one-off limited function that the Constitutional Court was given as part of the constitutional agreement ushering in the new order. The role given to the Constitutional Court enhanced the confidence of minority parties that the solemn pact agreed to under the interim Constitution and the ground rules required under Schedule 4 would be adhered to.

In the *First Certification* decision, the Court identified the basic structures and premises of the final Constitution, as required by the constitutional principles:

In order to answer the first question it is necessary to identify what are indeed the basic structures and premises of a new constitutional text contemplated by the CPs. It seems to us that fundamental to those structures and premises are the following:

(a) a constitutional democracy based on the supremacy of the Constitution protected by an independent judiciary;

(b) a democratic system of government founded on openness, accountability and equality, with universal adult suffrage and regular elections;

(c) a separation of powers between the legislature, executive and judiciary with appropriate checks and balances to ensure accountability, responsiveness and openness;

(d) the need for other appropriate checks on governmental power;

(e) enjoyment of all universally accepted fundamental rights, freedoms and civil liberties protected by justiciable provisions in the NT;

(f) one sovereign state structured at national, provincial and local levels, each of such levels being allocated appropriate and adequate powers to function effectively;

(g)   the recognition and protection of the status, institution and role of traditional leadership;

(h)   a legal system which ensures equality of all persons before the law, which includes laws, programmes or activities that have as their objective the amelioration of the conditions of the disadvantaged, including those disadvantaged on grounds of race, colour or creed;

(i)   representative government embracing multi-party democracy, a common voters' roll and, in general, proportional representation;

(j)   the protection of the NT against amendment save through special processes;

(k)   adequate provision for fiscal and financial allocations to the provincial and local levels of government from revenue collected nationally;

(l)   the right of employers and employees to engage in collective bargaining and the right of every person to fair labour practices;

(m)   a non-partisan public service broadly representative of the South African community, serving all the members, and

(n)   the security forces required to perform their functions in the national interest and prohibited from furthering or prejudicing party political interests.

Proportional representation

With respect to the interim legislature, there was a two-chamber legislature comprising of a 400-member popularly elected NA and a senate consisting of ninety members. The 400 seats in the NA were filled in the following manner: first, 200 seats were filled through election from a regional list with a fixed number being allocated to each region. The remaining 200 seats were filled from a national list compiled by the various political parties. Each party received an allocation of seats from both the national list and the regional list based on proportional representation. The senate was composed of ten senators from each of the nine provinces. The senators were nominated by the various political parties in their respective provincial and state legislatures. These nominations were also based on proportional representation.

Regional power and the creation of additional provinces

The interim Constitution created nine defined provinces and conferred powers on the provinces and local governments. The new provinces replaced the four provinces and the ten homelands or 'bantustans'. The creation of provinces and regional autonomy was a compromise to the NP and IFP which both favoured the exercise of regional power.

Compromise to cultural sensitivities

A few days before the elections, various constitutional amendments were made which provided for the possibility of a *Volkstaat* and for a possible role for the Zulu king.[29] These concessions were couched as possibilities and not certainties. It is likely that a definite concession to provide a *Volkstaat* would have been intolerable to the ANC and its supporters. The concession of a possibility of such autonomy catered to the sensitivities of the Freedom Front (FF) and the IFP and made it possible for the Afrikaner right wing and the IFP to enter the elections.

The final Constitution

The process of creating the final Constitution began after the 27 April 1994 election. The task ahead was, in many ways, easier because this time, the CA had a clearer sense of what was expected from it. The CA also knew the parameters within which it was supposed to operate and the mechanisms for reaching finality, and it had a clear time frame within which the final Constitution was to be completed. Moreover, there were fewer uncertainties in the process because embodied in the ground rules were deadlock-breaking mechanisms. The level of violence had decreased since the election. The relative peace and order allowed the constitution-makers to concentrate on the content of the Constitution and its long-term implications for democracy, without having to

---

[29] Section 235 of the interim Constitution (Constitution of the Republic of South Africa Act 200 of 1993).

continually be concerned as to whether the country would explode into violence and terror.

The process for drawing up the final Constitution was far more inclusive than that for the interim Constitution. The CAs public participation programme reached out to millions of South Africans across the country through the media and community fora. Hundreds of workshops and meetings were held throughout the country. The CA printed copies of literature that were widely distributed to the public, who were requested to comment on the proposals. By the end of the process, the CA had received over two million submissions from members of the public. The staff of the CA did their best to process each submission and feed them to the relevant Theme Committees. Not every submission had an impact on the final product, nor did every submission influence the positions taken by the various parties. However, the submissions highlighted some of the key concerns shared by all South Africans, and allowed ordinary people to engage directly in the process of shaping the Constitution.

Inside the CA, each of the Theme Committees examined in detail its assigned area of the Constitution. In coming to consensus on the issues, the Theme Committees examined international practice and consulted local and international experts and stakeholders. As the negotiations unfolded, differences such as the distribution of power between the national government and the provinces and the protection of minority rights again came to the fore. As was the case with the interim Constitution, the process was accompanied by drama, deadlocks, and walkouts. Two months before the May 1996 deadline, the ANC and the NP negotiators were meeting to resolve their differences over issues such as language, the national anthem, the death penalty, the lockout, and the seat of parliament. There was divergence on the questions of single-medium instruction in schools, property rights, and employers' rights to lockouts, all representing different concepts of equality and property rights. As was the

case with the interim Constitution, a deal was eventually struck, with the ANC, NP, Democratic Party (DP), and PAC voting in favour of the final Constitution.[30]

Theme Committees[31]

In order to effectively deal with the wide variety of issues to be covered in the new Constitution, and to ensure the involvement of as many members of the CA as possible, Theme Committees were set up to work on different aspects of the Constitution. Each Theme Committee consisted of thirty members who were nominated by their political parties according to a system of proportional representation. The members of each Theme Committee elected three chairpersons. Together with a core group of seven to eight members of the Constitutional Committee, the chairpersons were responsible for managing and coordinating the work of the Theme Committees.

The Theme Committees were given the tasks of receiving and processing the views of political parties and the broader community, and compiling reports for discussion by the Constitutional Committee. A Technical Committee of four advisers was appointed for each Theme Committee to give technical advice and assist in compiling reports and some Theme Committees were assigned additional technical advisers because of the broad scope of their work.

The Theme Committees started work in September 1994. Their first major task was to draw up work programmes to ensure that work was completed timeously. These programmes were finalized by the Constitutional Committee in December 1994. A target date of 30 June 1995 was set for the Theme Committees to complete their assignments.

By 13 February 1995 – a mere six weeks after the annual December recess – the first Theme Committee reports were received. As planned, the

---

30 The CA adopted the final Constitution on 8 May 1996.
31 For a list of all the Theme Committees and their respective tasks, see the CA internet site.

Theme Committees completed most of their work by the end of June. The final reports from the Theme Committees were presented to the CA in September 1995. Theme Committee reports to the CA were accompanied by draft constitutional text after revised drafting procedures were agreed to by the CA.[32]

The certification process: a basic understanding of the Constitution

The Constitution did not provide any guidance with respect to how the Constitutional Court should evaluate whether the final Constitution passed muster. The Constitutional Court called for both oral and written representations from the CA, political parties, and any other person or body who objected to the certification of the Constitution.[33] The objections had to be submitted in writing, the specific grounds for the objections had to be stated, and the objectors to the text had to be identified.[34]

The Court went about the certification process by asking two questions. The first was: were the basic structures and premises of the text in compliance with what was required by the constitutional principles? If the answer to the first question was positive, then the second question was: did the details of the text comply with the constitutional principles?[35] In performing the certification function, the Court sought to avoid a rigid and technical interpretation of the constitutional principles.[36] Instead, it favoured a purposive and teleological approach to give expression to what the Court characterized as a new sovereign and democratic constitutional order in which all citizens are able to enjoy and exercise fundamental rights and freedoms.[37] In terms of the Court's approach, the constitutional principles were read 'holistically with an integrated approach'.[38] Also, if a provision in a constitutional principle had more than one meaning, the Court would give deference to the CAs choice, providing that meaning was permissible.[39] The Court, in the *First Certification* decision, failed to certify the Constitution because a number of provisions did not comply with the constitutional principles.[40]

The CA went back to the drawing board and reformulated the provisions the Court determined were non-conforming. The revised text was referred back to the Court and the final Constitution was certified on 4 December 1996.[41] The final Constitution provides for a constitution which is the supreme law of the land, and provides for protection of basic rights; a constitutional duty to advance socioeconomic rights; separation of powers; distribution of power between national, provincial, and local government, and an independent judiciary. The essence of the final Constitution[42] was summed up by the Court in the *Second Certification* decision.

---

[32] This discussion is adapted and reprinted with permission from the CAs internet site.

[33] *First Certification* decision para 22.

[34] *Supra*.

[35] *Supra* para 44.

[36] *Supra* para 36.

[37] *Supra* para 34.

[38] *Supra* para 37.

[39] Supra para 42.

[40] The provisions that failed to comply with the constitutional principles are summarized in the order of the Constitutional Court in the *First Certification* decision para 482.

[41] *Certification of the Amended Text of the Constitution of the Republic of South Africa, 1996* CCT 37/95 (4 December 1996), now cited as 1997 (2) SA 97 (CC); 1997 (1) BCLR 1 (CC) (*Second Certification* decision).

[42] Constitution of the Republic of South Africa Act 108 of 1996 (final Constitution).

**Certification of the Amended Text
of the Constitution of the Republic of
South Africa, 1996
CCT 37/95 (4 December 1996), now
cited as 1997 (2) SA 97 (CC);
1997 (1) BCLR 1 (CC).**
(*Second Certification* decision)
(notes omitted)

[25] The AT [Amended Text] is based on founding values which include human dignity, the achievement of equality, the recognition and advancement of human rights and freedoms, the supremacy of the Constitution and the rule of law. It makes provision for a multi-party system of democratic government, with provision for three levels of government, to ensure account-ability, responsiveness and openness. This provides a protective framework for civil society, which is enhanced by institutional structures such as the Public Protector, the Human Rights Commission, the Commission for the Promotion and Protection of Rights of Cultural, Religious and Linguistic Communities, and the Commission for Gender Equality, and ultimately by AT ch 2 which contains a justiciable Bill of Rights. The Bill of Rights is described as a 'cornerstone of democracy', and the state is required to respect, protect, promote and fulfil these rights, which are enforceable by an independent judiciary.

[26] AT ch 2 protects a range of individual rights of association including freedom of association, freedom to form and participate in the activities of political parties, and freedom to form and join a trade union or employers' organisation and participate in its activities. Freedom of association is conferred upon everyone. In addition AT 30 separately pro-tects the right of all people to use the language and to participate in the cultural life of their choice. AT 8(4) extends the protection of the Bill of Rights to juristic persons, 'to the extent required by the nature of the rights and the nature of that juristic person'. AT 38 permits all these rights to be enforced by an association acting in the interest of its members, and a person acting in the interest of a group or class of persons. The clear protection of rights of association coupled with the generous standing provisions protect the rights of collective self-determination stipulated by the CP [Constitu-tional Principle] for those communities not expressly protected by AT 31.

2

Interpretation of the Constitution

Constitutional interpretation

Historically, former South African constitutions took inspiration from the British Westminster model. The most important principle was the doctrine of parliamentary or legislative supremacy. This principle held that no court of law could set aside an act of the legislature, even if the court found the legislation morally repugnant. The traditional view, inherited from the British tradition, was that judges, as unelected officials, should not be responsible for shaping the law in terms of morality or their own concepts of what is right.[1] Chief Justice Stein, former Chief Justice of South Africa, stated that the task of the courts in interpreting a statute was to ascertain the intention of parliament.[2] The new constitutional order marks a fundamental change in the *Grundnorm* of the South African legal order; a departure from parliamentary supremacy towards the supremacy of the Constitution (subject to judicial review). Section 2 of the final Constitution[3] proclaims:

> **Supremacy of Constitution**
> 2 This Constitution is the supreme law of the Republic; law or conduct inconsistent with it is invalid, and the obligations imposed by it must be fulfilled.

The Constitution now makes the Constitutional Court the final arbiter over the Constitution.[4]

Against this background of thrusting the judiciary into the centre of constitutional adjudication, we are reminded of the statement made by former Chief Justice of the United Sates, Charles Evans Hughes, '[W]e are under a Constitution but the Constitution is what the judges say it is, and the judiciary is the safeguard of our liberty and of our property under the Constitution.'[5] This is an erroneous and dangerous position if accepted on its face. The Chief Justice is saying that a constitution is without meaning until the judges pour meaning into its provisions. Many of the provisions of the constitutions in South Africa, the

---

[1] J Bell 'Three Models of the Judicial Function' in *Judges and the Judicial Power: Essays in Honour of Justice VR Krishna Iyer*, edited by Rajeev Dhavan, R Sudarshan, and Salman Khurshid. London: Sweet & Maxwell 1985, 58–9.

[2] Chief Justice Steyn as quoted in Hugh Corder *Judges at Work: The Role and Attitudes of the South African Appellate Judiciary, 1910–1950* Cape Town: Juta & Co 1984, 12.

[3] Constitution of the Republic of South Africa Act 108 of 1996.

[4] Section 167(5) proclaims 'The Constitutional Court makes the final decision whether an Act of Parliament, a provincial Act or conduct of the President is Constitutional'.

[5] Merlo J Pusey *Charles Evan Hughes* New York: McMillan 1951, 204.

United States, and elsewhere have settled meanings, and we do not have to go to the justices to interpret them. The position of Kentridge AJ in *Zuma*, the first rendered judgment by the Constitutional Court, is the better approach. Here Kentridge AJ stated: 'I am well aware of the fallacy of supposing that general language must have a single "objective" meaning. Nor is it easy to avoid the influence of one's personal intellectual and moral preconcepts. But it cannot be too strongly stressed that the Constitution does not mean whatever we might wish it to mean'.[6] Kentridge AJ goes on to remark that 'if the language used by the lawgiver is ignored in favour of a general resort to "values" the result is not interpretation but divination'.[7]

There is, however, an important element to Chief Justice Hughes' statement that Kentridge AJ recognized in *Zuma*: there are many provisions in the Constitution that are not self-defining, and have been, or will be in time, the objects of judicial interpretation. The Constitutional Court has recognized that there are provisions in the Constitution that do not lend themselves to precise measurement, and often call for a 'value judgement in an area where personal opinions are prone to differ, a value judgement that can easily become entangled with or be influenced by one's own moral attitude and feelings'.[8] For example, s 9 of the Constitution while providing for equality before the law for every person, also provides for affirmative action. Under the new constitutional scheme, the Constitutional Court has the competence to determine the correct balance between affirmative action and equality. Section 25 of the Constitution provides for a right to acquire and hold rights in property: stating that property can only be expropriated for public purposes,[9] and when there is an expropriation of private property, there has to be just and equitable compensation taking into account all relevant factors. The factors to determine compensation include: the use to which the property is being put; the history of its acquisition; the market value of the property; the extent of state investment and subsidy in the acquisition and improvement of the property; and the purpose of the expropriation.[10] Chapter 2 of the Constitution, containing the Bill of Rights, has a host of other provisions including freedom of expression, association, and political rights to name a few, which are also couched in open-ended terms. Chapter 3 of the Constitution refers to cooperative government[11] and the distribution of national and provincial powers, many provisions of which are also couched in open-ended terms and require interpretation.[12] The Constitutional Court as the final arbiter over the Constitution has the power to determine what vague provisions mean.

Where do the judges look to interpret the Constitution? There are two divergent approaches: one approach views constitutional interpretation as a wholly discretionary exercise that treats the entire text as capable of many meanings. Under this view, the judge is free to invent whatever meaning he or she thinks is appropriate.[13] We agree with Kentridge AJ that judges are not free to interpret the Constitution in terms of their own value preferences. The test for constitutionality must be found in the Constitution itself.[14] In the words of Alexander Bickel, it is wrong:

---

[6] *S v Zuma and Others* CCT 5/94 (5 April 1995) para 17, now cited as 1995 (2) SA 642 (CC); 1995 (4) BCLR 401 (SA). See also Chaskalson P in *Mistry v Interim National Medical and Dental Council of South Africa and Others* CCT 13/97 (29 May 1998) para 3, now cited as 1998 (4) SA 1127 (CC); 1998 (7) BCLR 880 (CC).

[7] *Zuma* para 18.

[8] Didcott J, in *S v Makwanyane and Another* CCT 3/94 (6 June 1995) para 177, now cited as 1995 (3) SA 391 (CC); 1995 (6) BCLR 665 (CC).

[9] Section 25(2) of the Constitution.

[10] Section 25(3).

[11] Sections 40 and 41.

[12] eg s 146 of the Constitution speaks about conflicts between national and provincial legislation and sets out certain conditions (such as the maintenance of national security and the maintenance of economic unity), when national override can be used in cases of open-ended provisions.

[13] Stanley Fish, 'Fish v Fiss' (1984) 36 *Stanford Law Review* 1325.

[14] *S v Mhlungu and Others* CCT 25/94 (8 June 1995) para 78, now cited as 1995 (3) SA 867 (CC); 1995 (7) BCLR 793 (CC).

to conclude that behind all judicial dialectic there is personal preference and personal power and nothing else. In any event, there is a reality, if it be true, on which we cannot allow the edifice of judicial review to be based, for if that is all judges do, then their authority over us is totally intolerable and totally irreconcilable with the theory and practice of political democracy.[15]

The second polar approach is to view all constitutional interpretation as wholly mechanical, namely that the meaning of the Constitution is embedded in the text.[16] This theory, as an absolute method of interpretation, is also not satisfactory. Under the Bill of Rights, for example, the Constitution does not define either equality or freedom of speech. In the distribution of powers, the Constitution does not define the maintenance of national security or the maintenance of economic unity, both of which are conditions that would make national legislation supersede provincial legislation. Interpretation of provisions like these cannot be effected in a mechanical fashion. Constitutional interpretation is neither fixed nor wholly discretionary, but as characterized by Owen Fiss, it often involves a 'dynamic interaction between reader and text' from which meaning is derived.[17]

Disciplining rules within the interpretive community

To explain the concept of constraints in the law, Fiss introduces two additional concepts. The first concept is the notion of disciplining rules or theories of interpretation, which limit the interpreter and represent the standards by which the validity of the interpretation is judged.[18] The second concept is the notion of an 'interpretive community, which recognizes these rules as authoritative'.[19]

In trying to find answers to what a constitution means, judges and scholars of constitutional law have developed different approaches (theories or constitutional principles) to constitutional interpretation. These approaches seek to both justify judicial review and to ensure that decisions are not rendered in terms of the subjective preferences of judges. They attempt to provide the judiciary with overarching principles, as opposed to the judges' own ideas of correctness, to be employed in the interpretation of a constitution. The judges are constrained by these principles and theories that seek to limit the value determinations they make in constitutional cases.[20] At the heart of the debate over constitutional theory is an attempt to ensure that judicial review is performed in a principled manner using reasoned standards. Any judgment must be reached on analysis and reasons that transcend the immediate result achieved in the case before the court.[21] Fiss describes the importance of these rules as not simply the standards or principles of individual judges, but standards that are part of the legal institution itself.[22] As Fiss proclaims, these rules are recognized as authoritative in the interpretive community of professionals of which judges are a part.[23] Judges are part of this interpretive community not because they share the same values, but by virtue of a commitment to uphold the rule of law.[24] If judges deny the authority of the interpretive community, they relinquish their authority to speak on what constitutes the law.[25]

---

[15] Alexander Bickel *The Least Dangerous Branch: The Supreme Court at the Bar of Politics* Indianapolis: Bobbs-Merrill 1962, 80.

[16] One of the leading constitutional writers who best encapsulates this approach is John Hart Ely in *Democracy and Distrust: A Theory of Judicial Review* Cambridge: Harvard University Press 1980.

[17] Owen Fiss 'Objectivity and Interpretation' (1982) 34 *Stanford Law Review* 739.

[18] Op cit 744.

[19] Ibid.

[20] See Harry H Wellington *Interpreting the Constitution: The Supreme Court and the Process of Adjudication* New Haven: Yale University Press 1990, 30.

[21] Op cit 43.

[22] Fiss 745.

[23] Owen Fiss 'Conventionalism' (1985) 58 *Southern California Law Review* 183.

[24] Fiss 'Objectivity and Interpretation' 745.

[25] Op cit 747.

This is not to suggest that constitutional interpretation is a smooth, harmonious process. It also does not mean that there is only one constitutional theory. The judges of the Constitutional Court sometimes disagree over the appropriate method of interpretation. The disciplining rules are methods widely accepted in the interpretive community even though they might not be accepted by everyone in that community. There is a potential contingency in the temporal sense as to what is acceptable.[26] The authority of a disciplining rule is legitimized if it is widely accepted and similarly eroded where there is pervasive disagreement.[27] For example, historically in South Africa, courts did not consider parliamentary debates and explanatory memoranda providing reasons for a bill as an aid in interpretation. The Constitutional Court recognized the relevance of such material in interpreting the Constitution for the first time in *Makwanyane*[28] and again in *Ferreira v Levin NO and Others; Vryenhoek and Others v Powell NO and Others*.[29] Original intent or legislative history is now also a legitimate method of interpreting the Constitution.

The fact that judges disagree on which method of interpretation to adopt does not undermine the disciplining rules. For example, in interpreting a contentious provision some may prefer to look at the intent of the legislature, whereas others may prefer to look at the overall purpose and object of the Constitution. The interpretation that other judges give can be found through a path using other disciplining rules including the text, precedent, and fundamental rights protections developed by the interpretive community.[30] Each represents a theory to constrain the interpreter.

Differences of this nature do not erode the legitimacy of disciplining rules, but instead pose issues of application.[31] Different judges and scholars come to be associated with particular methods of interpretation. They employ different methods of interpretation depending on the provision of the constitution at issue.[32] It is fair to say that no sane judge or jurist can rely on one approach only in addressing all constitutional issues.[33] In *Makwanyane*, for example, Mahomed J commented on the judicial role in interpreting the Constitution as follows:[34]

What the Constitutional Court is required to do in order to resolve an issue, is to examine the relevant provisions of the Constitution, their text and their context; the interplay between the different provisions; legal precedent relevant to the resolution of the problem both in South Africa and abroad; the domestic common law and public international law impacting on its possible solution; factual and historical considerations bearing on the problem; the significance and meaning of the language used in the relevant provisions; the content and the sweep of the ethos expressed in the structure of the Constitution; the balance to be struck between different and sometimes potentially conflicting considerations reflected in its text; and by a judicious interpretation and assessment of all *these* factors to determine what the Constitution permits and what it prohibits.

The application of a principle has to be consistent, however. If the application of any particular principle is tempered because there is a need for a compromise, then the concept of disciplining rules breaks down.[35] For example, in *Azanian People's Organisation and Others v The President of*

---

[26] Sanford Levinson 'Law as Literature' (1982) 60 *Texas Law Review* 373, 384.

[27] Fiss 748.

[28] *Makwanyane* paras 15–17.

[29] *Ferreira v Levin NO and Others; Vryenhoek and Others v Powell NO and Others* CCT 5/95 (6 December 1995) para 46, now cited as 1996 (1) BCLR 1 (CC); 1996 (1) SA 984 (CC).

[30] Bickel 50.

[31] Stanley Fish '*Fish v Fiss*' (1984) 36 *Stanford Law Review* 747.

[32] See Sachs J in *Coetzee v Government of the Republic of South Africa and Others; Matiso v The Commanding Officier, Port Elizabeth Prisons and Others* CCT 19/94 (22 September 1995) para 46, now cited as 1995 (4) SA 631 (CC); 1995 (10) BCLR 1382 (CC).

[33] Philip Bobbitt *Constitutional Fate: Theory of the Constitution* New York: Oxford University Press 1982, 124. Bobbitt likens the process of interpretation to a carpenter using different tools 'and often many tools in a single project.'

[34] *Makwanyane* para 266.

[35] Bickel 58.

the Republic of South Africa,[36] the Constitutional Court was faced with the question of what the position of international law is under the interim Constitution. Mahomed DP adopted an inconsistent position in stating that the word 'shall' in the epilogue mandates that some form of amnesty be provided.[37] However, when it came to s 35(1) of the interim Constitution, which stated the court 'shall, where applicable, have regard to public international law on the protection of human rights entrenched in this Chapter ...', the word 'shall' was given a discretionary meaning.[38]

The number of theories of interpretation to be created by a judge is not infinite. Stanley Fish describes the process of interpretation differently from Fiss and considers the judge's conduct as a learned endeavour acquired through the judge's operation in the legal enterprise.[39] The judge understands what rule to apply because he or she is deeply embedded in the context in which the rule is given meaning. In other words, the judge is not free to conjure up his or her own meanings, but applies a set of meanings which he or she acquired through his or her operation in the legal system.[40] For Fiss, it is the interpretive community that provides the different disciplining rules to understand a constitution, whereas for Fish it is the enterprise within which judges are situated that provides the different meanings of a constitution.[41] Regardless of whether one subscribes to the view that an *a priori* category of disciplining rules exists, as Fiss suggests, or that the conduct of interpretation is acquired in practice following Fish, or if one wants to be eclectic and say that there are disciplining rules whose application is better understood in practice, both Fish and Fiss

correctly note that the number of different methods of interpretation to be conjured up by a judge is not infinite.[42]

Constitutional interpretation: interpretivist versus non-interpretivist

There are a multitude of different methods of interpretation. The different methods come under two broad categories, namely interpretivist and non-interpretivist.[43] The interpretivist method, also referred to as formalist or strict constructionist, relies on the four corners of a constitution to provide meaning.[44] This method considers a limited set of materials, namely the text itself and the history (or original intent). This approach is formalistic and technical, and views as illegitimate any method of interpretation that relies on sources other than the text of a constitution and historical documents that show evidence of the framers' intent. The only time one can resort to extrinsic sources, under the interpretive paradigm, is to consider historical material to ascertain the original intent of the framers.[45]

A non-interpretivist does not confine constitutional interpretation solely to the text or history of the document itself. Instead, this method draws on extrinsic sources and values. For example, theorists from this school draw on moral philosophy, human rights, and other theoretical frameworks concerning what is socially desirable in ascertaining the meaning of a constitution.[46] This approach is sometimes characterized as the 'living Constitu-

---

[36] *Azanian People's Organisation (Azapo) and Others v The President of the Republic of South Africa* CCT 17/96 (25 July 1996), now cited as 1996 (4) SA 671 (CC); 1996 (8) BCLR 1015 (CC) (*Azapo* decision).

[37] *Azapo* decision para 14.

[38] *Supra* para 27.

[39] See Fish 1328–33.

[40] Op cit 1332–3.

[41] Op cit 1336.

[42] Ibid.

[43] Maureen B Callahan 'Cultural Relativism and The Interpretation of Constitutional Texts' (1994) 30 *Willamette Law Review* 621.

[44] Thomas Grey 'Do we have an Unwritten Constitution?' (1975) 27 *Stanford. Law Review* 703, 706.

[45] Grey 1.

[46] Callahan 621–2.

tion' approach, and calls on the judiciary to give content and expression to a constitution, based on the realities of the time.[47]

The interpretivist versus non-interpretivist debate reflects deep differences concerning whether the exercise of the court's authority is in terms of actual legal canons, or whether the court can also base its judgment on what it considers desirable social policy.[48] The interpretivist or formalist approach, based on text and history, operates in the main on the assumption that a judge can deduce a single correct answer in most cases.[49] These answers are supposedly arrived at in an impersonal, restrained, and apolitical method.[50] An example would be *Makwanyane*, where Mahomed J stated that there is a difference between the political role performed by the legislature and the legal role performed by the courts.[51]

Non-interpretivists theories commonly criticize the idea that there is a Cartesian distinction between law and politics that can be maintained in constitutional adjudication.[52] Under this view, constitutional integration, despite Mahomed Js distinction between the political and the judicial roles,[53] often involves a profound interplay between legal and political factors. For example, how far affirmative action programmes can be taken cannot be determined on legal factors alone.

Central to this debate is the distinction between judicial activism and judicial self-restraint. Those favouring judicial self-restraint give greater deference to the legislature, which is the democratically-elected organ of government. Advocates of judicial activism assert that the judiciary was designed to be an intermediary between the people and government in order to keep the government within the limits assigned to them in the Constitution.[54] They argue that the judiciary is responsible for articulating what is socially good, and is ultimately the arbiter of social morality.[55] These two different approaches to interpretation have their strengths and weaknesses.

Methods of interpretation

Textualism

In interpreting a constitution, the starting point preferred by most jurists is the text of the constitution itself. In terms of this approach, if the words of the text are clear on their face, the interpretation should be based on the text itself. This approach was defined by Justice Owen Roberts in *United States v Butler*:[56]

There should be no understanding as to the function of this court in such a case. It is sometimes said that the court assumes a power to overrule or control the action of the people's representatives. This is a misconception. The Constitution is the supreme law of the land ordained and established by the people. All legislation must conform to the principles it lays down. When an act of Congress is appropriately challenged in the courts as not conforming to the Constitutional mandate the judicial branch of the government has only one duty – to lay the article of the Constitution which is invoked beside the statute which is challenged and to decide whether the latter squares with the former. All the court does, or can do, is to announce its considered judgment upon the question. The only power it has, if such it may be called, is the power of judgment. This court neither approves nor condemns any legislative policy. Its delicate and difficult office is to ascertain and declare whether the legislation is in accordance with, or in contravention of, the provisions of the Constitution; and, having done that, its duty ends.

---

[47] See Grey 709.

[48] Michael J Gerhardt and Thomas D Rowe Jnr *Constitutional Theory: Arguments and Perspectives* Charlottesville: Michie 1993, 3.

[49] Michael S Moore 'The Semantics of Judging' (1981) 54 *Southern California Law Review* 151, 157.

[50] Roberto Mungabeira Unger 'The Critical Legal Studies Movement' (1983) 96 *Harvard Law Review* 564–5.

[51] *Makwanyane* para 266.

[52] *Supra* para 563.

[53] *Supra* para 266.

[54] Ralph A Rossum and Alan G Tarr *American Constitutional Law: Cases and Interpretation* New York: St Martin's Press, 3rd edition, 1991, 56.

[55] Op cit 57.

[56] *United States v Butler* 297 US 1, 62–63 (1936).

Most textualists operate on the assumption that there is only one answer to be ascertained from the text. It is important to note, though, that the textual method need not always result in a literal interpretation of the text. Some textualists, like John Hart Ely, seek meaning not in the isolated examination of individual words themselves, but instead look at the overall structure of a constitution.[57] The textualists consider the interplay between concepts and structures for guidance if the individual words themselves are not clear.[58] Although this approach might avoid a strict literal interpretation, the approach still operates within the text of the constitution and proceeds from the premise that constitutional interpretation and valid inferences are drawn directly from the text of the constitution.[59]

In South Africa, the textual approach finds its clearest expression in Kentridge AJ's dissenting opinion in *Mhlungu*.[60] In *Mhlungu*, the accused was charged with murder and other crimes for which indictments were served on 11 March 1994. At the trial, the state relied on a confession that the accused had made to a magistrate. The state also relied on the presumptions contained in s 217(1)(b) of the Criminal Procedure Act[61] that the confession was made voluntarily. In its very first decision in *Zuma*, the Constitutional Court, in a decision written by Kentridge AJ, had ruled that the reverse onus presumption in s 217(1)(b) was unconstitutional.[62] The specific issue before the court in *Mhlungu* was whether the accused enjoyed the right to fair-trial protections provided in the interim Constitution, where the trial of the accused began before the commencement of the interim Constitution on 27 April 1994. The answer to this question depended upon the

interpretation of s 241(8) of the interim Constitution which stated that:

> [A]ll proceedings which immediately before the commencement of this Constitution were pending before the court of law, including any tribunal or reviewing authority established by or under law, exercising jurisdiction in accordance with the law in force shall be dealt with as if this Constitution had not been passed.

Mahomed J, in a plurality opinion, in which Langa, Madala, Mokgoro, and O'Regan JJ concurred, surveyed the different approaches to s 241(8) that the various provincial divisions had adopted. He stated that a literal reading of the text would deny the accused the protections provided in the interim Constitution because the proceedings began before the commencement of the Constitution.[63] Such an interpretation, he stated, would result in unjust and perhaps absurd results since an accused, who was indicted before 27 April 1994, would enjoy less protection than an accused who was tried after 27 April 1994.[64] This interpretation, he felt, was irrational and would deny the equal protection of the laws to different accused individuals.[65] Moreover, it was inconsistent with the guarantee of human rights (including the guarantee of a right to a fair trial) to be accorded to all people.[66]

Section 241(8), according to the plurality decision, should be interpreted to provide the most benefit in the widest possible way.[67] Section 241(8), according to their preferred interpretation, was meant to extend the authority and jurisdiction of the courts in matters that were pending before

---

[57] See generally Ely – a leading constitutional writer who best encapsulates this approach.
[58] Levinson 379.
[59] See Callahan 623.
[60] *Mhlungu* para 32.
[61] Act 51 of 1977.
[62] *Zuma* para 39.
[63] *Mhlungu* para 2.
[64] *Supra* paras 4–5.
[65] *Supra* para 8.
[66] *Supra*.
[67] *Supra* para 9.

27 April 1994, and not to deny an accused the protections guaranteed in the Constitution.[68] The plurality supported this interpretation by stating that the phrase 'shall be dealt with' as used in s 241(8) is a colloquial phrase that has different meanings. One of its meanings is to 'proceed with' or 'take action' and not necessarily 'continued and concluded'. For the plurality, the use of the phrase 'dealt with' in s 241(8), if interpreted in the first way, is more consistent with preserving the authority of the courts from the previous order, as opposed to denying the fair-trial protections to an accused whose trial began before the Constitution took effect.[69] The plurality felt that a literal interpretation would have radical consequences by denying to a large group of people the equal protection of fundamental human rights.[70] The plurality also felt that its interpretation was more consistent with the fundamental objectives of the Constitution.[71]

In his separate concurring opinion, Kriegler J also interpreted s 241(8) as preserving the authority of the courts.[72] Kriegler J went further, and stated that the Bill of Rights 'recognizes for every person a comprehensive set of rights and freedoms enforceable in a court of law ... which imperiously makes the chapter [Chapter 3 of the Constitution containing the Bill of Rights] binding on "all legislative and executive organs of state" and applicable to all law in force'.[73]

Sachs J, in his separate concurring opinion, went further than Mahomed and Kriegler JJ and stated that the rights enshrined in the Bill of Rights 'are deeply entrenched, not only in relation to Parliament, but in respect of the rest of the Constitution'.[74] He stated further that the

strength of the Bill or Rights 'and the intensity of the values they promote are central to the whole constitutional scheme, and fundamental to our role as defenders of the constitution'.[75] Sachs J observed that when the courts are in a position to interpret some sections of the Constitution, they must contemporaneously consider the provisions of the Bill of Rights.[76] He conceded that there are words in the Constitution that are very clear, though he declined to spell out the terms he was referring to.[77] His preferred approach was that words in the Constitution should not be considered on their own, or in terms of a plain-meaning approach, but in relation to protections of fundamental rights.[78] He further stated that '[o]nly the most compelling language would justify a departure from such a clear responsibility'.[79] According to his interpretation, every provision in the Constitution has to be evaluated against the protection of fundamental rights entrenched in the Bill of Rights.

Underlying the approach of the majority of justices, the plurality, and the individual concurring opinions of Kriegler and Sachs JJ, was the idea that s 241(8) should be interpreted purposively, that is, in relation to the fundamental rights protections contained in the Bill of Rights. Kentridge AJ, writing for the dissent (in which Chaskalson P, Ackermann, and Didcott JJ concurred), stated that s 241(8) not only preserved the jurisdiction of the courts from the previous order, but also required that cases which commenced before the introduction of the interim Constitution should be disposed of as if the Constitution had not been passed.[80] The dissent was emphatic that there was no ambiguity in the

---

[68] *Supra* para 23.
[69] *Supra* para 26.
[70] *Supra* para 33.
[71] *Supra* para 45.
[72] *Supra* para 95.
[73] *Supra* para 90.
[74] *Supra* para 110.
[75] *Supra*.
[76] *Supra* para 107.
[77] *Supra* para 108.
[78] *Supra*.
[79] *Supra* para 110.
[80] *Supra* paras 70 and 71.

wording of s 241(8) by stating explicitly that the words contained in s 241(8) 'echo wordings used for 100 years by legislators wishing to make it clear that new statutes did not affect pending proceedings'.[81] Moreover, the dissent maintained that the words 'dealt with' were not of uncertain meaning but related to acting, disposing of, and handling in 'the conduct of pending proceedings in the period after the Constitution has come into force'.[82] The dissent refers to two previous decisions where the Appellate Division used the word 'dealt with' as synonymous with 'continued' and 'concluded', which contradicts the interpretation of the plurality opinion. The dissent, while recognizing the legitimacy of the purposive approach to interpretation, felt that there are limits to interpreting the Constitution generously. One of those limits is the notion that the clear words in the Constitution itself should be dispositive. Kentridge AJ also refers to his decision in *Zuma*, where the unanimous Court accepted that it must pay respect to the language used in the Constitution.[83]

The dissent conceded that a literal interpretation may bring about harsh results. However, the dissent felt that the Court simply cannot override the Constitution itself.[84] Any possible harsh effects should be corrected by the legislative and executive branches of government, which are also bound to respect and enforce the Constitution. As far as the Court is concerned, the dissent maintained, s 241(8) is very clear, and there was no justification to depart from the clear, express language of the Constitution. Moreover, there was no justification for 'doing violence to the language of the Constitution in order to remedy what may seem a hard case.'[85]

Was *Mhlungu* an easy case, as Kentridge AJ asserted in the dissent, or was it a 'hard case' as Mahomed J concluded in the plurality opinion? How does one decide whether one is confronted with a hard or easy case? 'Hard cases' can arise from vague or unambiguous terms. A word is ambiguous if it is capable of two or more different meanings.[86] For example, if we glance at the equality provision of s 9 of the Constitution which states that, '[E]veryone is equal before the law', the phrase 'equal before the law' is not clear. As we have asserted, there are many phrases in constitutions that are expected to govern a broad range of problems. These phrases are not meant to be static. Instead, it is intended that certain phrases should be able to grow, to prevent certain evils, and not be restricted to the meaning of a certain era.[87] Constitutional interpretation as it pertains to broad phrases in the Constitution (such as equality, liberty, and free speech, to name a few) invites such broad interpretation. In such a situation, it is difficult to find an answer to the problem based on a simple reading of the Constitution. Instead of relying solely on the text, judges can employ different interpretive tools recognized in the interpretive community. Kentridge AJ, however, correctly noted that s 241(8) of the interim Constitution did not present a vague or ambiguous phrase capable of conflicting interpretations.[88]

The plurality's interpretation of s 241(8) turns on the interpretation of the words 'dealt with', which it held to be subject to different meanings. The words 'dealt with' in s 241(8) are not as elusive as the plurality makes them out to be. The plurality correctly notes that dictionaries define 'to deal with' as "to treat a topic',[89] 'to struggle', 'to

---

[81] *Supra* para 75.

[82] *Supra* para 77.

[83] *Supra* para 78.

[84] *Supra* para 85.

[85] *Supra* para 84.

[86] Paul Brest and Sanford Levinson *Processes of Constitutional Decision-making: Cases and Materials* Boston: Little Brown, 3rd edition, 1992, 37.

[87] Ely 12–3.

[88] *Mhlungu* para 75. See also Eduard Fagan 'The Ordinary Meaning of Language – A Response to Professor Davis' (1997) 13 *South African Journal of Human Rights* 175. Fagan who, while conceding that s 241(8) may be poorly drafted, asserts that the section still lends itself to only one meaning – the one the dissent adopted.

[89] *New Webster's Comprehensive Dictionary of the English Language* 1991 edition.

contend', or 'to take action,[90] or 'to behave in a specified way towards'.[91] However, none of these interpretations supports the limited meaning that they give to the terms as relating only to preserving the territorial jurisdiction of the courts. Also, as the dissent noted, the Appellate Division previously used the term 'dealt with' as synonymous with 'continued' or 'concluded'.[92] Simply put, the term 'dealt with' in s 241(8) cannot be interpreted as simply preserving the territorial jurisdiction of the courts. If any of the above meanings were substituted for the words 'dealt with' in s 241(8) in terms of the plain meaning approach, the courts would have had to dispose of the issue as though the provisions of the interim Constitution did not apply to the case at hand.

The second circumstance where we encounter a hard case is when a case may seem linguistically easy but the result is inconsistent with the purpose of the rule.[93] In such a case, there is a tension between the ordinary meaning of the word and the reason for using the word.[94] The problem in this instance arises due to clumsy drafting where the purpose enunciated conflicts with the wording of the law. For example, the s 1 of the XIII Amendment of the United States Constitution provides: '[N]either slavery nor involuntary servitude, except as punishment for crime whereof the party shall have been duly convicted, shall exist within the United States' The object of the XIII Amendment (which together with the XIV and XV Amendments comprise the Civil Rights Amendments) was to abolish slavery. These amendments were drawn up after the American Civil War to accord the former slaves the full protection of the law. Yet a literal reading of the section could mean that slavery is a competent punishment for a crime. Section 248(8) in *Mhlungu* does not present a

constitutional provision which conflicts with the purpose of the section.[95]

The third, and sometimes the most controversial way, a case is made 'hard' is when the judge finds the meaning of a provision in a constitution clear, but feels that the clause should not be interpreted on its own, but instead should be balanced against other provisions in the constitution. One can think of many examples where this might legitimately arise in the Constitution. For example, although everyone has the right to freedom of expression, this right has to be balanced against the outlawing of hate speech.[96] While everyone is entitled to equal protection and benefit of the law, this equality has to be balanced against the need to assist historically disadvantaged persons.[97] Similarly, while everyone is entitled to fundamental rights protected in the Bill of Rights, there are circumstances in which legislation can encroach on fundamental rights.[98] In the above examples the Constitution itself requires the courts to balance the different parts of the text. The courts are required to balance different interests and seek some proportion in harmonizing these different interests.

The problem in constitutional interpretation is that competing texts can almost always be found, and when the judge resorts to these other provisions the text in question does not really count in the decision.[99] In *Mhlungu*, Mahomed J in his plurality opinion, and Kriegler and Sachs JJ in their concurring opinions, stated that s 248(8) had to be interpreted against the human rights protections contained in Chapter 3 of the interim Constitution. The position of Mahomed, Kriegler and Sachs JJ is problematic, though. To the extent that there will always be competing texts, and no rule to tell us which one to give priority to,

---

[90] *Webster's Third International Dictionary of the English Language* 1993 unabridged edition.

[91] *Rogets's II: The New Thesaurus* by the editors of the *American Heritage Dictionary* 1988 expanded edition.

[92] *Mhlungu* para 76.

[93] Gerhard & Rowe 46.

[94] Ibid.

[95] See Eduard Fagan 'The Longest Erratum Note in History' (1996) 12 *South African Journal of Human Rights* 89.

[96] Section 16(2) of the Constitution.

[97] Section 9.

[98] Section 36(1).

[99] Bobbitt 60.

following the approach of the majority in *Mhlungu* leaves us bereft of any textual argument.[100] While constitutional interpretation sometimes calls for balancing different parts of a constitution (as the above examples demonstrate), s 241(8) was not such an example. Where the text is very clear in spelling out what the Constitution requires, the judge has no discretion to invoke another section of the Constitution to cut back the scope of the text in question. The majority's approach in *Mhlungu* made an easy case hard. The question is 'Why did the majority do this'? This leads us to the fourth example of a hard case.

Despite the existence of only one rule that could be applied in a straightforward fashion, and the fact that the application of that rule would be consistent with its purpose, the majority in *Mhlungu* took an approach that is an unfortunate example of judges making a case hard when the application of the literal approach is morally hard for them to swallow.[101] Ultimately, the plurality in *Mhlungu* disregarded the strict, literal approach because such an application of the section would, in their opinion, lead to 'some very unjust, perhaps even absurd, consequences'.[102] Therefore, the majority of the judges preferred to interpret s 241(8) as preserving the authority of courts dealing with pending matters to continue to discharge their functions, as opposed to the literal interpretation, which would have deprived an accused who had been indicted before the commencement of the interim Constitution, of the protections provided in the interim Constitution.

The approach of the majority in *Mhlungu* is particularly problematic. It undermines the very idea of the rule of law that is so central to constitutional jurisprudence.[103] Judges should not, when faced with a text that is clear on its face, project their own preferences or values, or create fringe meanings. Instead, they must uphold what a constitution requires.[104] Professor Dennis Davis adopts a contrary approach and rejects the employment of ordinary language in interpreting any provision of the Constitution.[105] He asserts that the interpretation of the text is dependent on political struggle and political experience that he claims 'introduce[s] new and different contexts, themes and meaning[s] into the work'.[106] Such arguments are not novel in legal interpretation. For example, the critical legal studies movement presents a nihilistic assumption of the Constitution as always capable of infinite interpretations, and maintains that the role of the judge is to choose one interpretation from the many available.[107] The text is a maze of many dimensions and there is no exclusive or original meaning in the text.[108] There are no constraints on interpretive meaning such as, for example, plain literary meaning.[109]

This school of thought does not accept that there are easy cases.[110] To name just two examples, s 88(2) which states that '[N]o person may hold office as President for more than two terms', and s 103 which lists the provinces of South Africa, are clear on their face and not capable of more than one interpretation. These phrases (along with many other such examples) present easy cases, and do not require the wisdom

---

[100] Op cit 61.

[101] Gerhard & Rowe 46.

[102] *Mhlungu* para 4.

[103] In *Mphahlele v First National Bank of South Africa Ltd* CCT 23/98 (1 March 1999) para 12, now cited as 1999 (3) BCLR 253 (CC); 1999 (2) SA 667 (CC), Goldstone J observed that the rule of law requires judges to not act arbitrarily.

[104] Gerhardt & Rowe 67. See Fagan 'Erratum Note' 80–1.

[105] Dennis Davis 'The Twist of Language and the Two Fagans: Please Sir may I have Some More Literalism!' (1996) 12 *South African Journal of Human Rights* 504, 508.

[106] Ibid.

[107] Levinson 373. See also Allen C Hutchinson and Patrick J Monahan 'The "Rights" Stuff: Roberto Unger and Beyond' (1984) 62 *Texas Law Review*, 1504. This approach is also referred to as 'deconstruction'. For an overview of the history of this movement, see JM Balkin 'Deconstructive Practice and Legal Theory' (1987) 96 *Yale Law Journal* 743.

[108] Hutchinson & Monahan 1504.

[109] Unger 565.

[110] For this distinction between easy and hard cases, see William R Bishin and Christopher D Stone *Law, Language and Ethics: An Introduction to Law and Legal Method* Mineola: Foundation Press 1972, 246.

of judges to give their meaning to them before we understand what they mean. When the Constitution states '[N]o person may hold office as President for more than two terms', the fact that there is a fierce political struggle among several candidates to succeed a popular president whose second term has expired, cannot permit an interpretation that would allow the president to seek a third term. Contrary to what Davis asserts, no political struggle or historical experience could give meaning to s 88(2) which would allow a president to stand for office for a third term. To say that political struggle and historical experience do permit a president to seek a third term represents a nihilistic assumption of the Constitution, which ignores the text of the Constitution as binding on the judges.

The majority approach in *Mhlungu* represents an example of legal nihilism. A judge that takes this sort of interpretive freedom is unable to ground his or her claim of obedience on virtue; the authoritativeness proceeds from institutional power alone.[111] Fiss uses the work of Hart and Kelsen to argue that in this instance, the individual has an ethical claim of obedience to obey a judicial interpretation not because of its intellectual correctness, but because the judge is part of an authority structure that is good to preserve. Compliance with the judge's opinion 'derives from institutional virtue, rather than institutional power'.[112] Acceptance of the judicial interpretation because of the belief in the institutional virtue of judicial interpretation will not diminish the perception of the fundamental or egregious error.[113]

It does not bode well for the legitimacy of judicial review if members of the judiciary give their own meaning to clauses in the Constitution regardless of how clear the text is. Admittedly, it might prove difficult at times to draw a line between texts that are clear and those that are not. *Mhlungu*, however, clearly did not present a hard case. It could have been disposed of relatively easily. The interpretation that the majority provided, as Kentridge AJ warned against in *Zuma*, is divination. The decision replaces principled decision-making with the subjective preferences of the judges.[114] It bolsters cynicism, and fuels the perception that the rule of law is a fiction and that no case is determined by legal doctrine.[115] The majority approach gives credence to the view that legal discourse is simply judges doing what their political and moral views. command.[116] The approach has unpalatable ramifications in eroding the meaning of the Constitution, and reducing it to an instrument of judicial fancy. It also gives credence to the position of those in the critical legal studies movement who assert that the judge who has been given power to serve the goals of society invariably utilizes this power to serve his or her own goals.[117] If a constitutional provision leads to unjust results, as Kentridge AJ observed, it is the lawmakers who ultimately must change it. Indeed, the lawmakers in the final Constitution did cater to the situation that the majority in *Mhlungu* was concerned about, by providing that 'all proceedings which were pending before a court when the new Constitution took effect, must be disposed of as if the new Constitution had not been enacted, unless the interests of justice requires otherwise'.[118]

Intent of the framers

This approach is premised on the idea that the interpretation of ambiguous terms must proceed from what the drafters of the document intended.[119] It has received its clearest expression

---

[111] Fiss 'Objectivity and Interpretation' 757.

[112] Op cit 756.

[113] Op cit 757.

[114] Kenny Hegland 'Goodbye to Deconstruction' (1985) 58 *Southern California Law Review* 1204. See also Fagan 'Erratum Note', 84.

[115] Girardeau Spann 'Deconstructing the Legislative Veto' (1984) 68 *Minnesota Law Review* 473 (1984). See also Unger 565.

[116] This is the position of Mark V Tushnet in 'Following the Rules laid down: A Critique of Interpretivism and Neutral Principles' (1983) 96 *Harvard Law Review* 781, 819.

[117] Hegland 1204.

[118] Section 17 of the Constitution, Schedule 6: Transitional Arrangements

[119] See Williard Hurst 'The Process of Constitutional Construction: The Role of History' in *Supreme Court and Supreme Law*, edited by Edmond Cahn. Bloomingdale: Indiana University Press 1954, 57.

by Chaskalson P in *Makwanyane*. This case involved the constitutionality of the death penalty. The Constitution did not explicitly outlaw the death penalty – neither did it permit it. The question was whether the death penalty violated various clauses in the Constitution, including the right to life and the right not to be subjected to cruel, inhuman, and degrading treatment. In his opinion, Chaskalson P refers to the intent of the framers and other background evidence to support the position that the drafters of the Constitution wanted the courts to decide whether the death penalty was consistent with the fundamental rights protections and other values the Constitution seeks to promote.[120] This approach was also employed by Ackerman J in *Ferreira*, where he refers to the Report of the Technical Committee to interpret the term 'liberty'.

S v Makwanyane and Another
CCT 3/94 (6 June 1995), 1995 (3) SA 391 (CC), now cited as 1995 (6) BCLR 665 (CC); 1994 (3) SA 868 (A).
(notes omitted)
CHASKALSON P

[16] In countries in which the Constitution is similarly the supreme law, it is not unusual for the Courts to have regard to the circumstances existing at the time the Constitution was adopted, including the debates and writings which formed part of the process. The United States Supreme Court pays attention to such matters, and its judgments frequently contain reviews of the legislative history of the provision in question, including references to debates, and statements made, at the time the provision was adopted. The German Constitutional Court also has regard to such evidence. The Canadian Supreme Court has held such evidence to be admissible, and has referred to the historical background including the pre-confederation debates for the purpose of interpreting provisions of the Canadian Constitution, although it attaches less weight to such information than the United States Supreme Court does. It also has regard to ministerial statements in parliament in regard to the purpose of particular legislation. In India, whilst speeches of individual members of parliament or the conventions are apparently not ordinarily admissible, the reports of drafting committees can, according to Seervai, 'be a helpful extrinsic aid to construction'. Seervai cites Kania CJ in *AK Gopalan v The State* for the proposition that whilst not taking '. . . into consideration the individual opinions of Members of Parliament or Convention to construe the meaning of a particular clause, when a question is raised whether a certain phrase or expression was up for consideration at all or not, a reference to debates may be permitted'. The European Court of Human Rights and the United Nations Committee on Human Rights all allow their deliberations to be informed by *travaux preparatoires*.

[17] Our Constitution was the product of negotiations conducted at the multi-party negotiating process. The final draft adopted by the forum of the multi-party negotiating process was, with few changes adopted by Parliament. The multi-party negotiating process was advised by technical committees, and the reports of these committees on the drafts are the equivalent of the *travaux preparatoires*, relied upon by the international tribunals. Such background material can provide a context for the interpretation of the Constitution and, where it serves that purpose, I can see no reason why such evidence should be excluded. The precise nature of the evidence, and the purpose for which it may be tendered, will determine the weight to be given to it.

[18] It has been said in respect of the Canadian Constitution that:

. . . the Charter is not the product of a few individual public servants, however distinguished, but of a multiplicity of individuals who played major roles in the negotiating, drafting and adoption of the Charter.

---

[120] *Supra* para 25.

How can one say with any confidence that within this enormous multiplicity of actors ... the comments of a few federal civil servants can in any way be determinative.

Our Constitution is also the product of a multiplicity of persons, some of whom took part in the negotiations, and others who as members of parliament enacted the final draft. The same caution is called for in respect to the comments of individual actors in the process, no matter how prominent a role they might have played.

[19] Background evidence may, however, be useful to show why particular provisions were or were not included in the Constitution. It is neither necessary nor desirable at this stage in the development of our constitutional law to express any opinion on whether it might also be relevant for other purposes, nor to attempt to lay down general principles governing the admissibility of such evidence. It is sufficient to say that where the background material is clear, is not in dispute, and is relevant to showing why particular provisions were or were not included in the Constitution, it can be taken into account by a court in interpreting the Constitution. These conditions are satisfied in the present case.

[20] Capital punishment was the subject of debate before and during the constitution-making process, and it is clear that the failure to deal specifically in the Constitution with this issue was not accidental.

[22] In August 1991, the South African Law Commission in its interim report on group and human Rights described the imposition of the death penalty as 'highly controversial'. A working paper of the Commission which preceded the interim report had proposed that the right to life be recognized in a bill of rights, subject to the proviso that the discretionary imposition of the sentence of death be allowed for the most serious crimes. As a result of the comments it received, the law commission decided to change the draft and to adopt a 'Solomonic solution' under which a constitutional court would be required to decide whether a right to life expressed in unqualified terms could be circumscribed by a limitations clause contained in a bill of rights. 'This proposed solution' it said 'naturally imposes an onerous task on the Constitutional Court. But it is a task which this Court will in future have to carry out in respect of many other laws and executive and administrative acts. The Court must not shrink from this task, otherwise we shall be back to parliamentary sovereignty.'

Resorting to legislative history is undoubtedly a valid method of interpretation. However, as Chaskalson P observed, legislative history poses problems because it can be difficult to determine what the framers intended. This is so even where there is a homogeneous body of people drafting the Constitution (such as, for example, was the case with the founding fathers in the United States). At a fundamental level, we can ask exactly who are the framers? Are we going to pay attention to what the drafters said, or what the members of the CA who voted for the provisions understood the provisions to mean?[121] Many decisions are made based on compromise, and it is often difficult to agree upon what all the delegates intended when they approved a particular provision. This approach might be very difficult to apply, for example, with respect to things such as the distribution of power between the national parliament and the provinces. The power provisions are largely based on compromise between the principle actors, namely the NP, and the ANC. Moreover, they have different concepts of what the various provisions were meant to represent. The ANC favoured a more centralized state, whereas the NP and its allies favoured a decentralized model. It might prove difficult to rely on the intent of the framers in arriving at a result of what the appropriate distribution of power is, or what the appropriate balance between equality and affirmative action is. Similarly, there would be differences with respect to what the socioeconomic clauses meant.

---

121 Randy Barnett 'The Relevance of the Framers Intent' (1996) 19 *Harvard Journal of Law and Public Policy* 403–4.

Invocation of original intent in the *Makwanyane*,[122] and *Du Plessis*,[123] cases raises the question whether a court can really infer intent from the silence of the lawmaker? It also raises a troubling issue; namely the avoidance of difficult questions by the democratically elected body, as they did with the death penalty issue. Instead of facing the issue of the death penalty head-on, the delegates at Codesa, and later the CA, decided not to face the hard question. Instead, the question was left for the Court to decide. It seems a similar debate surrounded the applicability of the Bill of Rights to private action. Rather then face the issue directly, the framers in the interim Constitution did not mention whether the Bill of Rights applies (or does not apply) to private action. In *Du Plessis*, Mahomed J read the silence in the Constitution as an indication that the framers did not intend the Bill of Rights to apply to private action.[124] The final Constitution mentions explicitly, in s 8(1), that the Bill of Rights applies to both natural and juristic persons. On issues of such profound consequence, the court should not have to infer legislative intent from silence. These are hard choices that the legislature should make, as opposed to passing the buck on to the courts; thus hiding behind the decision of the court as in the death penalty case.

A more fundamental objection to the use of legislative history is why succeeding generations should be bound to the will of a previous generation. Let us imagine s 12(1)(e) of the Constitution which speaks about freedom from cruel, inhuman, and degrading punishment. If this phrase is fixed in terms of the framers' idea, it limits the protection of the clause to a fixed concept of a specific era. It might be that the framers did not even think about the situation at hand at all. A rigid adherence to original intent precludes adaptation of the Constitution to changed circumstances.[125]

Precedent

Precedent, namely relying on previous decisions of the court, is an important method of interpretation in the common-law system. Relying on precedent provides stability, coherence, efficiency, and predictability to the Constitution. The Constitutional Court relied on precedent in the *Certification of the Amended Text of the Constitution of the Republic of South Africa*.[126] Here, the Constitutional Court was requested to revisit its approach to the certification of the Constitution in the *First Certification* decision. In a unanimous decision, the Court stated that it might have erred in its previous analysis in certifying various parts of the new Constitution.[127] The Court held that it should not vacillate and that there is a 'sound jurisprudential basis for the policy that a court should adhere to its previous decisions unless they are shown to be clearly wrong'.[128] Apart from stability and continuity, following precedent instills a belief in the rule of law. More specifically, precedent instills a belief that like other organs of government, the Court is bound by the law.[129]

In many constitutions, over a period of time, certain constitutional norms achieve particular importance and become so entrenched that they are no longer open to question. If the principle is reviewed and approved many times, it becomes a doctrine of the Constitution.[130] The difficulty with precedent is that constitutional law often involves great social and political issues, which cannot be resolved on the basis of the past. Relying on precedent gives you a good idea of where you

---

[122] *Per* Chaskalson P, *Makwanyane* paras 16–19.

[123] *Per* Mahomed DP, in *Du Plessis and Others v De Klerk and Another* CCT 8/95 (15 May 1996) para 76, now cited as 1996 (3) SA 850 (CC); 1996 (5) BCLR 658 (CC).

[124] *Supra*.

[125] Tushnet 781.

[126] *Certification of the Amended Text of the Constitution of the Republic of South Africa, 1996* CCT 37/95 (4 December 1996), now cited as 1997 (2) SA 97 (CC); 1997 (1) BCLR 1 (CC) (*Second Certification* decision).

[127] *Supra* para 8.

[128] *Supra*.

[129] See Henry Paul Monaghan '*Stare Decisis* and Constitutional Adjudication' (1988) 88 *Columbia Law Review* 723, 728–9.

[130] See Bickel 131.

came from but not where you should be heading.[131] The Constitution, as a broad outline of government, seeks to achieve certain political and social goals that might be difficult to achieve if decided in terms of what previous Courts have held.[132] Blind adherence to precedent often perpetuates wrong decisions; as was the case when the United States Supreme Court upheld the separate but equal doctrine for over fifty years.

Living Constitution as an open-ended experiential approach

This approach to Constitutional interpretation operates on the premise that the Constitution must be moulded to reflect present day realities and the sum total of the national experience.[133] This method sometimes conceives the Constitution more as a political document. The approach was summed up by Brandeis J, when he wrote that a Constitution 'is not a strait-jacket. It is a living organism. As such it is capable of growth-expansion and of adaptation to new conditions. Growth implies changes, political, economic and social. Growth which is significant manifests itself rather in intellectual and moral concepts than in material things. Because our Constitution possesses the capacity of adaptation, it has endured as the fundamental law of an ever-developing people.'[134]

The living Constitution approach was first employed by the United States Supreme Court in *McCulloch v Maryland*, where Chief Justice Marshall declared that a constitution is not meant to contain an accurate detail of all its powers nor the means by which they may be carried into execution.[135] The Constitution only contains the great outlines of government. To spell out all details in the Constitution 'would partake of the prolixity of a legal code' which could scarcely be embraced.[136] According to this interpretation, the Constitution should be adapted to confront crisis based on the reality of the times. There are two ways in which a constitution can be viewed as a living document. The first is in terms of its structure, and the second is in terms of the rights it confers on individuals.[137]

The Constitution as a living structure

The courts can interpret the Constitution as a living document in terms of the structural argument. Here courts are less concerned about particular provisions, in terms of how they impact on individuals, but more in terms of who has the competence under the Constitution to adopt particular decisions. In other words, structural arguments relate to the power aspects of the Constitution: namely which branch or level of government has the requisite authority.

In the United States, for example, disputes have arisen in the separation of powers context where the Court is faced with the question of whether it is strictly limited to the distribution of power as laid out in the text of the Constitution, or whether they can adopt a functionalist approach to allow some reallocation of power between the legislative and executive branch of government based on the exigencies of a modern twentieth-century state. There is a line of cases where the majority of justices have insisted that there are executive functions which cannot be encroached upon by the legislative branch.[138] Similarly, they have stated that there are legislative functions, which cannot be encroached upon by the executive branch of government.[139] In these lines of cases, the decisions were premised on a formalistic assumption: namely that the text and intention of

---

[131] Rossum & Tarr 4.

[132] Ibid.

[133] See eg Paul Brest *Processes of Constitutional Decision-making: Cases and Materials Boston:* Little, Brown 1975, 1329. For a criticism of this approach, see Raoul Berger 'The Activist: Legacy of The New Deal Court' (1984) 59 *Washington Law Review* 751, 783–8.

[134] See Bickel 107.

[135] *McCulloch v Maryland,* 17 US 316, 332 (1819).

[136] *Supra.*

[137] In the US, the SC has on occasions embraced this approach to give content to basic individual rights. See Callahan 624.

[138] *Myers v United States* 272 US 52 (1962); *Buckely v Valeo* 424 US 1, 135–37 (1976); *INS v Chadha* 462 US 919, 958 (1983); *Metropolitan Washington Airports Authority v Citizens for the Abatement of Aircraft Noise* 501 US 252 (1991).

[139] *NIRA Panama Refining Co v Ryan* 293 US 388 (1935); ALA *Schechter Poultry Corp v United States* 295 US 495 (1935).

the framers were dispositive, and that new political and social realities are not relevant to Constitutional adjudication.[140] There is another line of cases that suggests the allocation of power between the different branches of government should not be approached in such a mechanical fashion.[141]

Morrison v Olson best represents the functionalist approach to Constitutional interpretation. In *Morrison*, a challenge was brought to the independent council provisions of the Ethics in Government Act, which provided for the appointment of an independent council to investigate – and, if appropriate – prosecute high-ranking executive officials for violations of federal criminal law. The United States Constitution provides that the president is the Chief Executive Officer and is responsible for executing the laws of the United States. The power to prosecute relates to the enforcement powers, which are a quintessential executive function. The statute in question took away the president's ability to control prosecutorial powers in an important group of cases. The Supreme Court, in a departure from the formalist approach, stated that it was not going to adhere to rigid categories of legislative or quasi-legislative powers.[142] Instead, the Court approached the statute in terms of whether the restrictions impeded the president in the exercise of his executive power. The statute in question was designed to investigate high-ranking executive officials. The majority of justices felt that they should look at the factual situation in this case, which offered a compelling reason to limit the presidential power.[143] Limiting the president's power would not impede the executive functions, if the president did not have the same degree of control over cases that investigated the conduct of executive officials.

The functional approach was adopted by the Constitutional Court in *Transvaal Agricultural*

Union.[144] At issue here was whether s 122(1)(b) of the interim Constitution required the Commission on Restitution of Land Rights to personally deal with all mediation of land disputes. Parliament had adopted a statute that authorized the Chief Land Claims Commissioner to appoint mediators or other persons to assist in settling land disputes. The applicants contended that under s 122(1)(b) of the interim Constitution, the Commission on Restitution of Land Rights was required to conduct all mediation on land disputes personally. The Court noted that the acceptance of the applicants' arguments would result in inordinate delays, since the commission would be required to deal personally with all two million potential claims lodged. A formalist would have argued that the Constitution, in setting up the Commission on Restitution of Land Rights and giving it certain powers, required that only this body could carry out the functions for which it was set up. The unanimous court, *per* P Chaskalson, declared that the Constitution should not be interpreted with 'the austerity of tabulated legalism'.[145]

The difficulty with this living approach is that it creates a large degree of discretion and uncertainty as to the allocation of power in the Constitution.[146] Whereas the formalist approach is predictable, the living approach allows the Court to cure defects such as those that arose in *Transvaal Agricultural Union*.

The purposive approach

The purposive method proceeds on the basis that a provision in the Constitution must be interpreted in a way that is consistent with the overall purpose and objectives of the Constitution itself.[147] It was first referred to by Kentridge AJ in *Zuma* (the first decision of the Court), where Kentridge AJ refers to the use of this approach by the Canadian

[140] See Cass R Sunstein 'Constitutionalism after the New Deal' (1987) 101 *Harvard Law Review* 421, 493.
[141] *Morrison v Olson* 487 US 654 (1988); *Mistretta v United States* 488 US 361 (1989).
[142] *Morrison*, 487 US at 658.
[143] *Supra* at 711.
[144] *Transvaal Agricultural Union v The Minister of Land Affairs and the Commission on Restitution of Land Rights* CCT 21/96 (18 November 1996), now cited as 1996 (12) BCLR 1573 (CC); 1997 (2) SA 621 (CC) paras 42–43.
[145] *Supra* para 44.
[146] Sunstein 496.
[147] See Kriegler J (dissenting), in *Du Plessis* para 123.

Supreme Court.[148] The purposive approach was quoted by Chaskalson P in *Makwanyane*, where the president stated that the Court's interpretation, while paying regard to the language that is used, 'is "generous" and "purposive" and gives expression to the underlying values of the Constitution'.[149] Inherent in the purposive method is the notion expounded upon by the German Constitutional Court in the *Southweste State 1* case, where that Court observed that the Basic Law represents a logical unity, and that no clause or provision must be interpreted on its own.[150] Every clause or provision must be seen in relation to every other clauses, as well as the Constitution as a whole.[151]

The Constitutional Court has stated that while it will pay due regard to the language of the Constitution, it needs to be generous and purposive and give expression to the underlying values of the Constitution.[152] This necessitates the development of overarching principles by the Court, which are meant to give direction to the interpretation of the Constitution. Some of the principles that have been suggested are the promotion of human rights, justice, and equality.[153]

There are two different strands to the use of the purposive approach.[154] The first (and more narrow) position maintains, whenever there is an ambiguity in the interpretation of any provision in the Constitution, the Court must favour an interpretation that is consistent with human rights protections (as contained in the Bill of Rights). Under this approach, a resort to human rights values only arises when the text of the Constitution is unclear.[155]

For example, in *Du Plessis* the Court was faced with the question of whether the Bill of Rights, under the interim Constitution, applied horizontally as a restraint on private action. Mahomed DP in his concurring opinion referred to the text of s 7(1) of the interim Constitution, which stated that '[T]his Chapter shall bind all legislative and executive organs of state at all levels of government.' The text indicated that the Bill of Rights under the interim Constitution only applied to the legislative and executive organs.[156] If the chapter was to apply to private actions as well, the Constitution would have provided so in clear terms. Where the text in question was clear, there was no need to draw any other inference from other provisions in the Constitution.[157]

The wider purposive approach is that all constitutional interpretation must be performed against the recognition of the overall purpose of the Constitution, particularly the protection of fundamental human rights.[158] In *Du Plessis* Kriegler J, in his dissenting opinion, stated that the better approach was to interpret the Constitution 'purposively and as a whole, bearing in mind its manifest objectives'.[159] In ascertaining whether the Bill of Rights was to apply to private action, Kriegler J argued that the Court must look at the entire Constitution and the values and purposes the Constitution seeks to achieve. Therefore, even though the Bill of Rights in the interim Constitution did not explicitly cover private action, Kriegler J would have read it to cover private action. His reading of the overall purpose of the Constitution

---

[148] *Zuma* para 15.

[149] *Makwanyane* para 9.

[150] *Southweste State 1* case (1951) 14 BVerfGE. Donald P Kommers *The Constitutional Jurisprudence of the Federal Republic of Germany* Durham: Duke University Press 1989, 76.

[151] Ibid.

[152] *Makwanyane* para 9.

[153] Dennis Davis, et al *Fundamental Rights in the Constitution: Commentary and Cases: A Commentary on Chapter 3 on Fundamental Rights of the 1993 Constitution and Chapter 2 of the 1996 Constitution* Cape Town: Juta & Co 1997, 19–20.

[154] The different approaches are best reflected in the plurality opinion of Mahomed J, and the concurring opinions of Kriegler J and Sachs J in *Mhlungu*, which three opinions adopt the wider purposive approach. The dissenting opinion of Kentridge AJ in *Mhlungu* represents the narrower approach.

[155] As reflected in the dissenting opinion of Kentridge AJ in *Mhlungu*. This was the approach of Mahomed DP in his concurring opinion in *Du Plessis* para 76.

[156] *Du Plessis* para 76.

[157] *Supra.*

[158] As reflected in the plurality opinion of Mahomed J, and the separate concurring opinions of Kriegler J and Sachs J in *Mhlungu*.

[159] *Du Plessis* para 123.

Du Plessis and Others v De Klerk and Others
CCT 8/95 (15 May 196), now cited
as 1996 (5) BCLR 658 (CC); 1995 (1)
SA 40 (T).
(notes omitted)
KRIEGLER and DIDCOTT JJ (dissenting):

[125] I make no apology for starting the exercise by examining the document with which we are concerned, the Constitution. Nor do I think one errs in commencing the exercise with an open mind, one untrammeled by subjective perceptions of evils of the past which the Constitution was intended to combat. The way I read the Preamble and the Postscript, the framers unequivocally proclaimed much more sweeping aims than those identified by the judge *a quo*, and apparently accepted by some of my colleagues. Our past is not merely one of repressive use of state power. It is one of persistent, institutionalized subjugation and exploitation of a voiceless and largely defence-less majority by a determined and privileged minority. The 'untold suffering and injustice' of which the Postscript speaks do not refer only to the previous forty years, nor only to Bantu education, group areas, security and the similar legislative tools used by the previous govern-ment. The Postscript mentions 'a divided society characterised by strife [and] conflict'. That is not a reference to governmental action only, or even primarily. The 'reconciliation and reconstruc-tion' mentioned in the last paragraph relate not so much, if at all, to the oppressed and the oppressive government, but to reconciliation of whites and blacks, to reconstruction of a skewed society. Likewise, when the Preamble speaks of 'citizenship in a sovereign democratic constitu-tional state' the emphasis immediately falls on racial equality.

[126] The Constitution bracketed by that Preamble and that Postscript is unabashedly egalitarian and libertarian.

The past was pervaded by inequality, author-itarianism and repression. The aspiration of the future is based on what is 'justifiable in an open and democratic society based on freedom and equality'.

This is underscored by the very presence of the Chapter 3 rights. It is re-emphasized by the unusual length and detail of the catalogue of rights and freedoms listed, as also by the broad sweep of much of its language. Nor is it coincidental that the very first right enunciated is that of equality before, and equal protection of, the law. It is equally significant that such right is coupled with a most detailed, if not vehement, proscription of discrimination. Viewed in context, textually and historically, the fundamental rights and freedoms have a poignancy and depth of meaning not echoed in any other national constitution I have seen.

[127] It is therefore no spirit of isolationism which leads me to say that our Constitution is unique in its origins, concepts and aspirations. Nor am I a chauvinist when I describe the negotiation process which gave birth to that Constitution as unique; so, too, the leap from minority rule to representative democracy founded on universal adult suffrage; the Damas-cene about-turn from executive directed parlia-mentary supremacy to justiciable constitution-alism and a specialist constitutional court, the ingathering of discarded fragments of the country and the creation of new provinces; and the entrenchment of a true separation and devolution of powers. Nowhere in the world that I am aware of have enemies agreed on a transitional coalition and a controlled two-stage process of constitution building. Therefore, although it is always instructive to see how other countries have arranged their constitu-tional affairs, I do not start there. And when I do conduct comparative study, I do so with great caution. The survey is conducted from the point of vantage afforded by the South African Constitution, constructed on unique founda-tions, built according to a unique design and intended for unique purposes.

was to transcend the subjugation, suffering, and injustice of the past, even in the private realm.

The purposive approach also underlies the separate opinions of the majority in *Mhlungu*. Sachs J observed in *Mhlungu* that when the courts are in a position to interpret some section of the Constitution contemporaneously, they must consider the provisions in the Bill of Rights.[160] Sachs J observed that the rights 'enshrined in Chapter 3 ... are deeply entrenched, not only in relation to Parliament, but in respect of the rest of the Constitution'.[161] The learned judge further states that 'the strength of Chapter 3 right[s] and the intensity of the values they promote are central to the whole Constitutional scheme, and fundamental to our role as defenders of the Constitution'.[162] Kriegler J observed that the Bill of Rights 'recognizes for every person a comprehensive set of rights and freedoms enforceable in a court of law which imperiously makes the chapter binding on "all legislative and executive organs of state" and applicable to all law in force ...'.[163]

The purposive method of interpretation is generous in fulfilling the full benefits of human rights protections, even though a provision on its face appears to limit such a right.[164] In *Mhlungu*, Mahomed J stated that 'the Court must avoid a literal interpretation which has radical constitutional consequences, and which denies to a substantial group of people [the fundamental rights guaranteed in the Bill of Rights]'.[165] Similarly, Mahomed DP has stated that a provision in the Constitution often has to be interpreted not on its own, but in relation to other clauses in the Constitution.[166] The Bill of Rights 'seeks not to invade but to expand rights'.[167] Mahomed DP goes on to state that the Chapter containing the Bill of Rights 'imperiously makes the Chapter binding on all legislative and executive organs of state, and applicable to all law in force during the operation of this Constitution'.[168] Earlier in this chapter we argued that the broader purposive approach could make the text bereft of any meaning. When faced with the interpretation of a particular provision, it is not difficult to find competing texts or another competing value, and no rule which tells us to which one gives priority.

The purposive method, however, using human rights as a yardstick to measure whether a statute passes the Constitutional muster, can proceed from both an interpretivist or a non-interpretivist perspective. For example, an interpretivist could interpret human rights protections in the Constitution based on textualism and original intent, which is what Mahomed DP did in *Du Plessis*. Using original intent and the text, an interpretivist could still measure the constitutionality of legislation against human rights protections; except that their terms of reference would be limited. It is more usual to associate this method with a non-interpretivist approach, because often the Court has to go outside the Constitution to give expression to what fundamental human rights entail, which was the approach of Kriegler J in *Du Plessis*.

Protection of vulnerable groups: representation–reinforcement

Not only is the role of the judiciary to protect fundamental rights, this approach is also associated with the view that the role of the judiciary is to protect groups that are particularly vulnerable to the tyranny that may accompany majoritarian impulses. This approach was relied upon by Mokgoro J in *Larbi-Odam and Others v MEC for Education (North West Province) and Another*.[169] The notion that courts have to protect

---

[160] *Mhlungu* para 133.
[161] *Supra* para 110.
[162] *Supra*.
[163] *Supra* para 89.
[164] *Supra* para 8.
[165] *Supra*.
[166] *Supra* para 46.
[167] *Supra* para 38.
[168] *Supra*.
[169] *Larbi-Odam and Others v MEC for Education (North West Province) and Another* CCT 2/97 (26 November 1997) paras 27–28, now cited as 1997 (12) BCLR 1655 (CC); 1998 (1) SA 745 (CC).

certain groups that are not able to fully participate in the political process is also referred to as the representation–reinforcement theory.[170]

In *Larbi-Odam*, the Court was presented with a challenge to a regulation issued by the North West Province, which regulation precluded the appointment of aliens as permanent teachers.[171] The executive of the North West Province argued that the regulation was negotiated between the relevant education officials and employee organizations. The Court stated that despite the majority consensus that accompanied the adoption of the regulations, the effect of the regulations was to unfairly discriminate against a vulnerable group, whose interests the Court had to protect.

The living Constitution and problems of interpretation with respect to socio-economic rights

A problem with the living Constitution approach arises when the judiciary makes policy choices which could have profound social, economic, and political implications.[172] The critical question is when should the Court intervene to substitute their opinion for a decision that parliament has made on a social or economic matter? The democratically elected legislature should be given the greatest degree of latitude to mould the Constitution, and to enact socioeconomic legislation. The judiciary is not the best institution to mould the Constitution to social, economic, and political realities.[173]

Larbi-Odam and Others v MEC for Education (North West Province) and Another CCT 2/97 (26 November 1997), now cited as 1997 (12) BCLR 1655 (CC); 1998 (1) SA 745 (CC)
(notes omitted)
MOKGORO J (unanimous decision)

[27] A precondition to the applicability of section 33(1) is that the limitation of a right occur 'by law of general application'. I hold that precondition to be met in this case. Regulation 2(2) is subordinate legislation which applies generally to all educators in South Africa. The respondents' main argument on justification is the interest of a government in providing employment to its own nationals. They also argued that the regulation was negotiated and agreed upon in the Education Labour Relations Council, which included employee organizations, including non-citizen teachers. Finally, the respondents stated that due to the potential temporary nature of the residence of a foreigner who can return to his or her country of origin at any time, it is against the public interest to

appoint a non-citizen in a permanent capacity as an educator. I shall consider these arguments in turn.

[28] The respondents' second and third arguments can be dealt with summarily. Although it may be that in certain circumstances the fact that a provision is the product of collective bargaining will be of significance for section 33(1), I cannot accept that it is relevant in this case. Where the purpose and effect of an agreed provision is to discriminate unfairly against a minority, its origin in negotiated agreement will not in itself provide grounds for justification. Resolution by majority is the basis of all legislation in a democracy, yet it too is subject to constitutional challenge where it discriminates unfairly against vulnerable groups. The respondents' third argument, that the ability of foreign citizens to return to their country of origin reduces their commitment to South Africa, also lacks merit. This argument applies with equal force to the many thousands of South Africans who hold dual nationality. The regulations do not, however, impose any bar on their eligibility for permanent employment.

---

[170] See Geoffrey R Stone, et al *Constitutional Law* Boston: Little Brown, 3rd edition, 1996, 70–1.
[171] *Larbi-Odam* paras 1–2.
[172] Ely 12–14.
[173] *United States v Carolene Products* 304 US 144 (1938).

When a court overturns the legislature's policy choices and substitutes them with the court's preferences, it undermines the democratic process and the policy-making power of the representative organ of government.[174]

The Constitutional Court visited this issue in *Ferreira*.[175] The Court was faced with the question of whether s 11(1) of the interim Constitution, which provided for freedom and security of the person, also contained an implied liberty protection. Ackermann J adopted the position that the section protects liberty interests, and that an individual under the section has a right not to have obstacles placed before him or her with respect to possible choices and activities.[176] Interpreted in this way, all legislative policy judgments would be subject to the strictest scrutiny. Chaskalson P in his concurring opinion, recognized the danger of this interpretation, which would give individual freedom such a wide application. The President of the Court stated (notes omitted):

If freedom were to be given the wide meaning suggested by Ackerman J all regulatory laws, which are a feature of any modern society, would have to be justified as being necessary. In my view this is not what is contemplated by the provisions of section 11(1), nor is it a conclusion to which we need to be driven. It would require courts to sit in judgment on what are essentially political decisions, and in doing so to require the legislature to justify such decisions as being necessary. This is not something that is required either by the words or the context of the section. If the intention had been to vest the control of freedom in that sense in the courts, I would have expected this to have been clearly stated and not left to be inferred from an extensive interpretation of the section.[177]

Another problem with the living Constitution approach arises when there is a need to reconcile a conflict between individual rights protection with social, political, and economic policies that are in the interest of the majority. The question is when, if at all, the legislature's policy choices should be overturned in favor of individual rights? How should the limitations clause be interpreted when these kinds of conflicts are presented? The Constitution is the product of compromise, and reflects different – and sometimes conflicting – philosophies, visions, and ideals. The legislature's choices with respect to visions and ideals need particular respect on socioeconomic questions. In the words of James Bradley Thayer, 'the Constitution often admits of different interpretations; that there is often a range of choices; when there is a range of choices, the legislature is the appropriate body to determine what is the appropriate choice'.[178] The Court should not overturn the legislature's choices unless the decision is so wrong that it is not open to any rational debate.[179] There will be occasions when individual rights have to be balanced against the collective welfare.[180] For the Court to substitute their positions for the policy choices made by the legislature, is the equivalent of the Court engaging in politics; which is an inappropriate exercise of its power. In South Africa, it is likely that the judiciary is going to be presented with an activist legislature concerned with the legacies of the apartheid system. The Constitution offers broad outlines and a wide range of legislative discretion and choices.[181] The Court should not act as a super legislature substituting its policies for those of the legislature.[182] Chaskalson P recognized in *Ferreira* that a welfare state requires regulation and redistribution

---

[174] *Williamson v Lee Optical Company* 348 US 483 (1955). *Lawrence and Others v The State and Another* CCT 38/96; CCT 39/96; 40/96 (6 October 1997) para 36, now cited as 1997 (10) BLLR 1348 (CC); 1997 (4) SA 1176 (CC).

[175] *Ferreira NO v Levin and Others; Vryenheok and others v Powell NO and Others.*

[176] *Supra* para 54.

[177] *Supra* para 174.

[178] James Bradley Thayer 'The Origin and Scope of the American Doctrine of Constitutional Law' (1893) *Harvard Law Review* 7.

[179] Ibid.

[180] This is discussed in chapter 8 under equality and in chapter 9 under the right to property.

[181] Brian C Murchison 'Interpretation and Independence: How Judges use the Avoidance Canon in Separation of Powers Cases' (1995) 30 *Georgia Law Review* 85, 103.

[182] This theme is explored in greater detail in chapter 8.

in the public interest. If individual freedom is given a broad meaning, in terms of the judges' concept, this impedes social policies.[183]

Lessons can be drawn from the New Deal crisis in the United States in the 1930s and before, where the Supreme Court consistently struck down elementary economic regulations of every sort on the grounds that they violated the principles of federalism (or interfered with freedom of contract), and amounted to the denial of liberty and property without due process of law. The right to form trade unions, minimum wage laws, and regulations stipulating maximum working hours were set aside.[184] The judiciary interpreted vague provisions in the Constitution in a way that protected minority interests at the expence of the majority. The Court's position on state rights was favoured by the conservative wing and wealthy class in society because the outlawing of labour laws, antitrust laws, and federal income-tax laws protected big business.[185] With massive unemployment and widespread lack of food and shelter during the Depression, there was a feeling of frustration on the part of ordinary people, and a restlessness for an overhaul of the existing economic and social system.[186] The crisis over the New Deal era led to one of the greatest constitutional crises in the United States, as President Roosevelt threatened to stack the Court with new judges to counteract the obstruction of the sitting judges. The constitutional crisis was averted when the majority of justices of the Supreme Court reversed course.

There are troublesome constitutional issues that judges are incapable of addressing, and which can only be addressed by a responsible legislature.[187] For these issues, the legislature must be recognized as having the power and duty to interpret the Constitution.[188] Monaghan advocates a theory of interpretation whereby the legislature would have the upper hand with respect to decisions in a particular sphere of activity.[189] Such deference is particularly required with respect to social and economic policy choices. Similarly, the appropriate distribution of power between the provinces and the central government is a determination that is better made in the political arena than by the judiciary.[190] The judiciary does not have the same fact-finding capacity, knowledge and experience of public affairs as the legislature, nor are they accountable to any electorate.[191] Chaskalson P recognized the importance of deference to the legislature on economic and social policies in *Ferreira* where he declared:

Whether or not there should be regulation and redistribution is essentially a political question which falls within the domain of the legislature and not the Court. It is not for the courts to approve or disapprove of such policies. What the courts must ensure is that the implementation of any political decision to undertake such policies conforms with the Constitution. It should not, however, require the legislature to show that they are necessary if the Constitution does not specifically require that this be done.[192]

Background values used to interpret the Constitution

When faced with vague, open-ended provisions, where does the Court look to ascertain what values underlie an open and democratic society based on human dignity, equality, and freedom? In inter-

---

[183] *Ferreira* para 180.

[184] *Lochner v New York* 198 US 45 (1905); *United States v EC Knights* 156 US 1 (1895); *NLRB v Jones & Laughlin Steel Corp* 301 US 1 (1937); *ALA Schechter Poultry Corp v United States* 295 US 495 (1935).

[185] Derrick A Bell Jnr *Race, Racism and American Law* Boston: Little Brown, 2nd edition 1980, 36–7.

[186] DJ Hulsebosch 'Note, The New Deal Court Emergence of a New Reason' (1990) 90 *Columubia Law Review* 1973, 1977.

[187] Laurence Tribe *American Constitutional Law* Moneola: Foundation Press, 2nd edition, 1988, 39.

[188] Ibid.

[189] Henry Paul Monaghan 'The Supreme Court, 1974 Term-Forward: Constitutional Common Law' (1975) 89 *Harvard Law Review* 1.

[190] See Ziyad Motala 'Socio-Economic Rights, Federalism and the Courts: Comparative Lessons for South Africa' (1995) 112 *South African Law Journal* 63, 78–86. This is discussed further in chapter 5.

[191] See Peter W Hogg *Constitutional Law of Canada* Scarborough: Carswell, 3rd edition 1992, 121–2.

[192] *Ferreira* para 180.

preting the Bill of Rights, s 39(1)(b) requires the Court to consider international law. Section 8(3) of the Constitution requires the Court to apply and develop the common law. The justices have also stated that the Court needs to take account of indigenous values in giving expression to the Bill of Rights.[193]

Influence of international and foreign law

Section 39 of the Constitution provides:

> **39 (1)**
> When interpreting the Bill of Rights, a court, tribunal or forum—
> (a) must promote the values that underlie an open and democratic society based on human dignity, equality and freedom;
> (b) must consider international law; and
> (c) may consider foreign case law.

The provisions in s 39(1) resemble s 35(1) of the interim Constitution which required the Court to 'have regard to public international law applicable to the protection of the rights entrenched ... and may have regard to comparable foreign case law'. In *Makwanyane*, pertaining to the applicability of the death penalty, Chaskalson P observed that s 35(1) of the interim Constitution enables the court to look at both binding and non-binding international law.[194] Chaskalson P further observed that international agreements and customary international law provide a framework to evaluate and understand Chapter 3.[195] Chaskalson stated that the work of other tribunals,

such as the United Nations Committee on Human Rights, the Inter-American Commission on Human Rights, the Inter-American Court of Human Rights, and in appropriate instances, the specialized agencies, may provide guidance as to the correct interpretation of the provisions of Chapter 3.[196] Judge Mokgoro was even more emphatic when he stated that s 35(1) required 'courts to proceed to public international law and foreign case law for guidance in Constitutional interpretation, thereby promoting the ideal and internationally accepted values in the cultivation of a human rights jurisprudence for South Africa'.[197] Judge Mokgoro further emphasizes that the 'Constitution [sic] makes it particularly imperative for courts to develop the entrenched fundamental rights in terms of a cohesive set of values, ideal to an open and democratic society'.[198]

Similarly, Sachs J observed in *Coetzee*[199] that in interpreting whether a limitation is justifiable in an open and democratic society based on freedom and equality, 'we need to locate ourselves in the mainstream of international democratic practice'.[200] The learned judge makes reference to practices from which there can be no derogation such as slavery and torture.[201]

Use of international law in the *Azapo* decision

In *Azanian Peoples Organisation (Azapo) and Others v The President of the Republic of South Africa*,[202] the applicants challenged the validity of certain provisions of the Promotion of National Unity and Reconciliation Act (Amnesty Act).[203] Section 20(7) of the Amnesty Act precludes any criminal or civil actions against any individual who confesses to any wrongdoing related to political

---

[193] See eg Mokgoro J, in *Du Plessis* paras 172–175.
[194] *Makwanyane* para 35.
[195] *Supra*.
[196] *Supra*.
[197] *Supra* para 304.
[198] *Supra* para 302.
[199] *Coetzee* para 51.
[200] *Supra*.
[201] *Supra* para 52.
[202] *Azanian Peoples Organisation (Azapo) and Others v The President of the Republic of South Africa* CCT 17/96 (25 July 1996), now cited as 1996 (4) SA 671 (CC); 1996 (8) BCLR 1015 (CC).
[203] Act 30 of 1995 (Amnesty Act).

acts of the past. The applicants argued that under principles of international law, it was unconstitutional for the Amnesty Committee to grant amnesty for crimes such as murder and torture. They further argued that the amnesty provisions violate s 22 of the interim Constitution, which provided that 'every person shall have the right to have justiciable disputes settled by a court of law or, where appropriate, another independent or impartial forum'.[204] They also argued that under international law, the state was obliged to prosecute those who were responsible for gross human rights violations.[205] Mahomed DP ruled that international law has relevance to the interpretation of the Constitution, but is not part of the law of South Africa until, and unless, it is incorporated into domestic law by legislative enactment.[206] The interim Constitution of South Africa provided that a court of law 'shall where applicable, have regard to public international law applicable to the protection of the rights entrenched' in Chapter 3 of the Constitution.[207] Mahomed DP interpreted the words 'have regard' to mean something that the Court may consider and which parliament could override through ordinary legislation.[208] The Constitution in the section under 'Transitional Arrangements', further provided that all international agreements shall be binding on the republic unless provided otherwise by an Act of Parliament.[209] Under the transitional arrangements section, there was a clawback clause in s 231(1) that allowed parliament to change treaty obligations and customary international-law rules with respect to international agreements, Mahomed DP stated that the same clawback clause that applied to s 231(1) also applied to s 35(1), now contained in s 39(1), which deals with public international law as it pertains to the protection of fundamental rights. Mahomed DP also interpreted the provisions of s 35(1), which

says that courts 'shall, where applicable, have regard to public international law', as providing discretion whether regarding public international law should be considered.[210]

Contrary to the Constitutional Court's finding in the *Azapo* decision, under s 35(1) of the interim Constitution, and now under s 39(1) of the Constitution, the courts of South Africa are required to consider principles of public international law in their interpretation of statutes that affect fundamental rights.[211] Under the transitional arrangements section in the interim Constitution, there was a clawback clause that allowed parliament to change treaty obligations and customary international-law rules with respect to international agreements, but the same clawback clause was not present in s 35(1) with respect to public international law, as it pertains to the protection of fundamental rights. Section 35(1) of the interim Constitution provided discretion with respect to the Court's considering foreign case law by providing '[i]n interpreting the provisions of this Chapter a court of law ... may have regard to comparable foreign case law'. The final Constitution also provides the same discretion with respect to foreign case law in s 39(1)*(c)*. However, the obligation to consider international law is not discretionary under s 39(1)*(b)*.

The Court's position on the role of international law in the Constitution is a departure from its earlier decisions.[212] The Court's opinion in *Makwanyane* is an affirmation of the 'monistic' view of international law, which considers international law and national law as one integrated legal system. In contradistinction, the Court's position in *Azapo* – a unanimous decision with a separate concurring opinion by Didcott J – reflects the competing theory of international law, called 'dualism', which states that national law and domestic law are two distinct legal systems. This

---

[204] *Azapo* para 8.
[205] *Supra* para 25.
[206] *Supra* para 26.
[207] Article 35(1) of the interim Constitution.
[208] *Azapo* para 27.
[209] Section 231(1) of the interim Constitution.
[210] *Azapo* para 27.
[211] See Mokgoro J in *Makwanyane* para 304.
[212] eg the various opinions in *Makwanyane* and *Mhlungu*.

anachronistic position goes against what some of the judges have said in the past, as well as mitigates against the fundamental development in international law since the Second World War, that domestic law cannot override the protection of fundamental human rights.[213] It is now a general proposition of international law that states cannot invoke their domestic law as a justification for not adhering to international norms.[214] States no longer have an unrestricted freedom to legislate, and have to act in terms of international law principles. Particular respect has to be paid to *jus cogens* which, in international law, signifies the highest form of international law from which there can be no derogation.

A peremptory norm of international law 'is a norm accepted . . . by the international community of States as a whole as a norm from which no derogation is permitted'.[215] Such a norm transcends all positive expressions of law.[216] In effect, peremptory norms lie at the foundation of the international community itself. This means that some principles are so fundamental to the very functioning of the state system that their existence is presupposed and cannot be overridden by positive law. Therefore, even without the incorporation of international-law norms into the Constitution of South Africa, the South African State absolutely cannot act legislate in a way that contravenes *jus cogens* principles. This means that under modern international law a state still has sovereignty, but this sovereignty is limited by certain norms of international law.[217] The Court erroneously adopted the position, in *Azapo*, that international human rights protections are not part of the South African Constitution unless they are adopted by the legislature. In the *Azapo* decision, the Court should have interpreted s 35(1) of the interim Constitution as Mokgoro J did in *Makwanyane*, as an obligation that requires 'courts to proceed to public international law and foreign case law for guidance in constitutional interpretation, thereby promoting the ideal and internationally accepted values in the cultivation of a human rights jurisprudence for South Africa'.[218]

If the Constitutional Court located itself in the mainstream of democratic international practice, it would have seen that from the time of the Nuremberg Tribunal, international law has imposed duties on states to prosecute for serious human rights violations and attaches liabilities upon both individuals and states.[219] The Nuremberg principles are codified in a wide range of international instruments. Underlying these instruments is an assumption that each state will enforce the provisions of the treaty within its domestic criminal law, and will cooperate in the prosecution and punishment of individuals engaged in international crime.[220] The duty to prosecute is a peremptory norm of international law.[221] The state is bound to search and prosecute, and the state cannot waive or forgive an incident — doing so it violates international law, and this violation on the part of the state does not bind the victim.[222] A war crime is not a 'common' criminal offence, nor is it a political offence, and a person alleged to be involved in war crimes cannot receive

---

[213] Theodor Meron *Human Rights and Humanitarian Norms as Customary Law* Oxford: Clarendon 1989, 190–1.

[214] Polish Nationals in Danzig (1931) PCIJ Ser A/B 44. See also Antonio Cassese *International Law in a Divided World* Oxford: Clarendon Press 1988, 15.

[215] Article 53 of the Vienna Convention on the Law of Treaties, UN Doc A/Conf 39/27 (1969), entered into force 23 May 1980, 1155 UNTS 331, 344.

[216] 216 Barry E Carter and Phillip R Trimble *International Law* Boston: Little Brown 1991, 98.

[217] JG Starke *Introduction to International Law* London: Butterworths 1989, 75.

[218] *Makwanyane* para 304.

[219] *Nuremberg* judgment (1946) 41 AJIL 172, 221.

[220] Cherif M Bassiouni 'Characteristics of International Criminal Law Conventions' in *International Criminal Law*, edited by Cherif M Bassiouni. New York: Transnational Publishers 1986.

[221] Karen Parker and Lyn B Neylon '*Jus Cogens*: Compelling the Law of Human Rights' (1989) 12 *Hastings International and Comparative Law Review* 455.

[222] Ziyad Motala 'The Promotion of National Unity and Reconciliation Act, the Constitution and International Law' (1995) XXVIII *Comparative and International Law Journal of Southern Africa* 338, 350.

amnesty by claiming that the crime was of a political nature.[223]

The principles enunciated by the Nuremberg Tribunal have been codified in various conventions, most notably the four Geneva Conventions of 1949 which are regarded as instruments with binding force on the international community.[224] The apartheid regime ratified the four Geneva Conventions of 1949. The Geneva Conventions were updated in 1977 with two subsequent protocols.[225] Mahomed DP remarks that these conventions have no force because there was no instrument of ratification deposited with the Swiss Federal Council.[226] This position is most surprising. Mahomed DP failed to investigate the status of these conventions in terms of customary international law or, more importantly, principles of *jus cogens*. These conventions either codified obligatory norms at the time they were adopted, or over the years have come to reflect peremptory norms of international law from which no state can derogate. The main purpose of these conventions is to further the protection of the fundamental rights of individuals, and therefore, in view of the Court's previous decisions should have come under the purview of the Bill of Rights.

Reliance on the common law

The requirement to resort to common law

The Constitution in ss 8(3)(a) and (b) calls on the courts:

> in order to give effect to a right in the Bill, must apply, or if necessary develop, the common law to the extent that legislation does not give effect to that right; and may develop rules of common law to limit the right, provided that the limitation is in accordance with section 36(1).

In any legal system, jurists (academics, practising lawyers, judges, and other legal officers) develop a legal culture and doctrine through socialization which is reinforced in law schools.[227] Legal doctrine seeks to be a science of law to 'order, clarify, and structure the law'.[228] Jurists in South Africa go through a law socialization process against a background of Roman-Dutch law and the British common law. Under apartheid, some jurists placed greater emphasis on Roman-Dutch law principles as the foundation of South African law. With the demise of apartheid, it would not be surprising to find less emphasis placed on Roman-Dutch law and greater emphasis on the common law as the final Constitution does. Jurists in South Africa are socialized in both Roman-Dutch law and the common law, and in the words of Bengoetxea, have assumed 'this ideal of law as a system, adopting the internal point of view'.[229] The common law and Roman-Dutch law provide the ontological and epistemological tools for legal theory. The legal theory in turn explains the legal order, the normative values that underlay the order, and the sources of law that the judiciary rely upon to justify their decisions. It is not surprising that even before the adoption of s 8(3) of the final

---

[223] BA Wortley 'Political Crime in English Law and in International Law' (1971) 45 *British Yearbook of International Law* 228–9.

[224] Geneva Conventions of 1949, (1950) 75 UNTS at 75, 85, 135, 287 (1950), done at Geneva on 12 August 1949 and, entered into force on 21 October 1950 (First, Second, Third, or Fourth Geneva Convention of 1949). For an excellent overview of the evolution of war crimes, crimes against humanity and crimes against peace as a *jus cogens* norm, see the comprehensive work of Cherif M Bassiouni *Crimes Against Humanity in International Law* Dordrecht: M Nijhoff 1992.

[225] Protocol Additional to the Geneva Conventions of 12 August 1949, and Relating to the Protection of Victims of International Armed Conflicts (1977) 16 ILM 1391, adopted 8 June 1977 and entered into force 7 December 1978, (Geneva Convention Protocol I); Protocol Additional to the Geneva Conventions of 12 August 1949, and Relating to the Protection of Victims of Non-International Armed Conflicts, (1977) 16 ILM 1442, adopted 8 June 1977 and entered into force 7 December 1978, (Geneva Convention Protocol II).

[226] *Azapo* decision para 30.

[227] Joxerramon Bengoetxea *The Legal Reasoning of the European Court of Justice: Towards a European Jurisprudence* Oxford: Clarendon 1993, 57.

[228] Ibid.

[229] Ibid.

Constitution, the Constitutional Court in interpreting the interim Constitution frequently resorted to legal theory based on the common law to justify their decisions. For example, in its very first decision, the Constitutional Court, *per* Kentridge AJ, relied extensively on the common law in evaluating the constitutionality of the reverse onus in s 217(1)*(b)*(ii) of the Criminal Procedure Act.[230] In giving expression to the right to remain silent under s 25 of the interim Constitution, the Court unanimously resorted to the common-law presumptions that the right to remain silent is a basic principle of an open and democratic society.[231] Based on these presumptions, it concluded that the reverse onus presumption of the Criminal Procedure Act as applied in this case was not consistent with the promotion of an open and democratic society.

Section 8(3)*(a)* requires a court to develop rules of common law to give effect to a right in the Bill of Rights where there is no legislation. Section 8(3)*(b)* allows a court to develop rules of the common law to limit the right, provided that the limitation is in accordance with s 36(1). Under s 36(1), a right in the Bill of Rights may only be limited in terms of a general law that 'is reasonable and justifiable in an open and democratic society based on human dignity, equality and freedom, taking into account' a number of relevant factors included in the limitations clause.

Arguably, the tenor of s 8(3) is to require the courts to mould and infuse the common law with progressive human rights thinking. In *Amod v Multilateral Motor Vehicle Accident Fund*,[232] the Supreme Court of Appeal, *per* Mohamed CJ, held that the respondent was liable to pay compensation to the plaintiff, who was married under Islamic law and had lost her husband in a motor-vehicle accident. The common law previously did not recognize a marriage contracted under Islamic law because the marriage was potentially polygamous. The Court, *per* Mohamed CJ, held that an interpretation of the common law which recognizes a duty of support 'flowing from a marriage solemnized and recognized by one faith or philosophy to the exclusion of others' was untenable.[233] The Chief Justice cited Farlam J in *Ryland v Edros*[234] for the proposition that it is wrong for one group to impose its values on another. The constitutional mandate is to make one common law inclusive as possible. The recognition of the common law under the Constitution does not entail the acceptance of a separate system of law. Instead, it entails a recognition of a common-law frame of reference which has to be shaped by the Constitution.[235] In *Pharmaceuticals Manufacturers Association*, the Constitutional Court, *per* Chaskalson P, held that the common law no longer controls the exercise of public power. Instead, the exercise of public power flows from the Constitution, 'and the common law, in so far as it has any application, must be developed consistently with its end subject to constitutional control'.[236] The framers recognized certain limitations in the common law. For example, if the values under the common law as understood for many years were to control the interpretation of many sections in the Constitution, would the Constitution serve as a viable framework for achieving socioeconomic transformation? Whether calling on the common law in its present form to evaluate, for example, the nature and importance of the right in an open and democratic society would allow an interpretation of socioeconomic rights which is responsive to the needs of the majority? Are the common-law assumptions as to what is reasonable and justifiable in an open and democratic society necessarily

---

[230] *Zuma* para 1.

[231] *Supra* paras 29–33.

[232] *Amod v Multilateral Motor Vehicle Accident Fund* 444/98 (29 September 1999) now cited as 1999 (4) SA 1319 (SCA); 1999 [4] All SA 421 (A).

[233] *Supra* para 20.

[234] 1997 (2) SA 690 (C) at 707E–H.

[235] *Pharmaceutical Manufacturers Association of SA, In re the ex parte Application of the President of the RSA and Others* CCT 31/99 (25 February 2000) para 44, now cited as 2000 (3) BLLR 241 (CC); 2000 (2) SA 674 (CC).

[236] *Supra* para 45.

in the interests of the underprivileged majority? The short answer is, probably, no.

The common law and problems with socioeconomic rights

In weighing the different – and sometimes conflicting – ideals, philosophies, and visions the Constitution espouses, the Constitutional Court must look critically at the myth of the common law (particularly with respect to socioeconomic rights), which in the Anglo-American tradition has been regarded as immemorial by judges.[237] Sachs J recognized the limitations of the common law in *Mhlungu*, when he remarked that 'a question mark has to be placed over the usefulness of common-law presumptions in interpreting the Constitution'.[238] The common law is neither natural nor pre-political, but embodies a particular social theory that serves some interest at the expense of others.[239] It might not be conducive to social change for the common good of society.[240] It often serves as a mechanism to prevent the distribution of property and wealth with little protection for the poor, elderly, or unemployed.[241] The common-law rules derive from a particular strain of liberal theory which places the individual at the top of the social order.[242] The judiciary will have to grow, and look beyond the values derived from the common law and the British tradition.[243] The majority of the justices recognized the need to move beyond the common law in *Du Plessis*, where the Court was faced with the question of whether the Bill of Rights was merely a restraint against state action, or whether it applied horizontally, to cover private action as well.[244] Although the majority found that the Bill of Rights under the interim Constitution did not apply to private action, Kentridge AJ stated that the values which are embodied in the Bill of Rights will permeate the common law in all respects, including private litigation.[245]

In interpreting the socioeconomic provisions, and conducting the balancing that s 36 of the Constitution requires, there should be no deference to the common law in a way that freezes the economic status quo. Moreover, law in the new South African order should not be seen as only protecting the individual, but should instead be seen as a tool to empower the underprivileged and dispossessed. Mahomed DP states this very concisely in *Du Plessis*, when he says in *dicta*. that there can be no interpretation of the common law by private persons seeking perpetuation of unfair privilege.[246] He warns there would be a need to re-examine contracts and public policy of the past.[247] It is the duty of the Constitutional Court to ensure that all courts infuse the common law with the proper spirit of the Bill of Rights.[248]

This once again raises important questions on judicial discretion and when judges should intervene to substitute their decisions for those of the legislature. As previously stated, the Constitution is the product of compromise, and reflects different, sometimes conflicting philosophies, visions, and ideals. Against the background of the divergent tendencies and approaches to Constitutional interpretation, the Constitutional Court should first take into account the social consequences of a choice that favours the individual against the community. The Court should exercise

---

[237] Trevor C Hartley *The Foundations of European Community Law: An Introduction to the Constitutional and Administrative Law of the European Community* Oxford: Clarendon Press 1988, 129.

[238] *Mhlungu* para 115.

[239] Sunstein 423.

[240] Morton Horowitz *The Transformation of American Law, 1780–1860* New York: Oxford University Press 1992, 1.

[241] Ibid.

[242] This view of the common law finds expression in Ackerman J's minority opinion in *Ferreira* para 39.

[243] We see this growth beyond the individualistic perspective in the opinions of Chaskalson P in *Ferreira* para 180 and in the approach of Mokgoro J in *Makwanyane* para 308.

[244] *Du Plessis* para 124.

[245] *Supra* para 60. See also Ackermann J (concurring opinion) para 110, where he states that the common law has to prove flexible and adapt to the requirements of the Bill of Rights

[246] *Supra* para 86.

[247] *Supra.*

[248] *Supra* para 87.

its choice in the social setting of South Africa's reality as South African society emerges from the apartheid era. Patrick Monaghan, writing on the Canadian Charter (Bill of Rights), offers the view that the charter does not provide some independent theory of justice or fairness. Instead, the charter represents a broadening of the values of democracy and public debate.[249] The function of judicial review is to protect the political process, rather then ensuring some particular result. This does not mean that individuals are obliterated. Instead, it means that individuals do not exist on their own, but are part of a larger community.[250] The assumption is that individuals can be enhanced if the community is enhanced.

Another way of approaching the issue is to argue that the Court has to use a contextual and systemic interpretation whereby the Constitutional Court seeks to achieve legitimacy in light of what is in the best interest of the survival of the new order.[251] The Constitutional Court, in *Makwanyane*, described its duty to protect the rights of the marginalized, the social outcasts, and the weakest members of society without playing to public opinion.[252] There is a school of thought that judicial review must in some way link itself to public consensus,[253] because judicial review cuts against the grain of representative democracy.[254] This is not to advocate the electoral theory: namely the notion that the Court should follow the election returns and adopt the position of the majority party for which the electorate voted.[255] Nor is it 'founded on what may be uninformed or

indeed prejudiced public opinion'[256] which Mokgoro J warns against in *Makwanyane*. However, as the President of the Court noted in *Makwanyane*, the Court has a duty to protect the weakest members of society. In the social and economic realm it should defer to the legislature, where the legislature's goal is to advance the interests of the weakest members of society. The reality is that South Africa, with its legacy of apartheid, is a very polarized society with haves and have-nots divided over access to resources. Apartheid rule over the black population represented the deliberate and systematic impoverishment of the majority by the minority. As far as the majority black population is concerned, they have fought for a better order and have an expectation that the end of apartheid will result in material changes to their socioeconomic conditions. Ultimately, the success of the new order is dependent upon whether it is responsive to the needs of the impoverished majority.

The European Court of Justice has, from time to time, also considered the possible economic and social repercussions of its decisions.[257] It is appropriate for the South African Constitutional Court to consider the principle of legitimate expectations, or what Hartley refers to as 'protection of legitimate confidence'.[258] This principle of legitimate expectations is used as a principle of interpretation by the European Court of Justice. Arguably, s 8(3) requires courts in South Africa to be conscious of their environment, and to adopt a method of interpretation (and use of background factors) guided by the 'unique'

---

[249] See P Macklem, et al *Constitutional Law of Canada* Toronto: Emond Montgomery Publishers 1994, 139.

[250] Ibid.

[251] For an analysis of the use of this approach by the ECJ, see Bengoetxea 98. In *Bongani Dlamini v The State* CCT 21/98 (3 June 1999), now cited as 1999 (7) BCLR 771 (CC); 1999 (4) SA 623 (CC), the Constitutional Court, *per* Kriegler J, para 55 and 67, accepted the view that the constitutionality of the restrictive bail provisions as provided in terms of ss 60(4)*(c)*, 8*(a)* and s 60(11)*(a)* of the Criminal Procedure Act 51 of 1997 (as amended by the Criminal Procedure Second Amendment Act 75 of 1995 and the Criminal Procedure Second Amendment Act 85 of 1997) should be viewed against the backdrop of violent crime which is deeply affecting the fabric of SA society.

[252] *Makwanyane, per* Chaskalson P, para 88, and Langa J, para 230.

[253] In *Dlamini* para 55, the Constitutional Court accepted the view that they should take the public opinion into account in considering whether restrictive bail conditions can be sustained under the limitations clause. See Tribe 63.

[254] Tribe 62.

[255] See divergent views of this approach as applied to the USSC at the time of the New Deal crisis in B Cushman 'Rethinking the New Deal Court' (1994) 80 *Virginia Law Review* 201, 228.

[256] *Makwanyane* para 306.

[257] See *Foglia v Novello* 244/80 (1981) ECHR 3045. For a discussion of this approach adopted in the EEC, see Bengoetxea 57.

[258] Hartley 142.

social and political environment within which they operate. For example, in the European Community, the European Court of Justice has been the most important institution in the promotion of European integration.[259] The European Court of Justice has adopted an activist stance where the object is to compensate society for social consequences in instances when the legislature has failed to act.[260] In South Africa, the legislature will most likely be the focal institution to provide social legislation, and the Constitutional Court should defer to the legislature to allow for compensation for the social consequences of apartheid. The common law and its assumptions of rugged individualism should not serve as the background 'conscience' for judges to invalidate affirmative social action or redistribution choices enacted by the legislature. The provision in the Constitution which permits the Court to consider foreign law should move the Court to look beyond the common law, to other traditions including the welfare constitutions in European countries, African constitutions, and traditional African society, to fill in the gaps in the Constitution.

Traditional African society

Historically, the creation of laws in South Africa

has not been performed in an impartial manner based on the consent of the majority. The assumptions of South African law, in the main, operate in terms of Western principles derived from Roman, Dutch, and English traditions. The indigenous majority had little input into the shaping of legal principles. Historically, there was very little recognition of indigenous or customary law. The Constitution, apart from recognizing the common law, recognizes customary law.[261] In the development of customary law, the Constitution requires that the spirit, purport, and objects of the Bill of Rights must be promoted.[262]

Historically, the concept of rights in the legal system operated in individualistic terms, while the concept of rights in the traditional African setting was in terms of the group or unit.[263] In traditional African society, the institution of private property, which is central to the concept of private rights in the present South African order, was non-existent.[264] In traditional societies, the right to life extended beyond how it is conceived in the present South African legal system to include an obligation by the society to provide subsistence to the needy members of the community.[265] The lack of recognition for indigenous values was recognized by Mokgoro J in the death penalty case.

S v Makwanyane and Another
CCT 3/94 (6 June 1995) (3) SA 391 (CC),
now cited as 1995 (6) BCLR 665 (CC);
1994 (3) SA 868 (A).
(notes omitted)

MOKGORO J:

[300] I give this brief concurring opinion to highlight what I regard as important: namely

that, when our courts promote the underlying values of an open and democratic society ... when considering the constitutionality of laws, they should recognise that indigenous South African values are not always irrelevant nor unrelated to this task. In my view, these values are embodied in the Constitution and they impact directly on the death penalty as a form of punishment.

---

[259] FG Jacobs and KL Karst 'The Federal Legal Order: The USA and Europe Compared: A Juridical Perspective' in *Integration Through Law* edited by Mauro Cappelletti, et al. Berlin: W de Gruyter 1986, 169–238.

[260] Bengoetxea 102.

[261] Section 39(3) of the Constitution.

[262] Section 39(2).

[263] For a discussion of the different concept of rights, see Ziyad Motala 'Human Rights in Africa: A Cultural, Ideological and Legal Examination' (1989) 12 *Hastings International and Comparative Law Review* 373–410.

[264] Op cit 382–3.

[265] RT Nhlapo 'Limitations on Human Rights: The Cultural Argument', unpublished paper presented at the Seminar and Human Rights and Law in Development at Gaberone, Botswana (24–28 May 1982).

Mokgoro J goes on to proclaim that the Constitution acknowledges . . .

[304] [T]he paucity of home-grown judicial precedent upholding human rights, which is not surprising considering the repressive nature of the past legal order. It requires courts to proceed to public international law and foreign case law for guidance in Constitutional interpretation, thereby promoting the ideal and internationally accepted values in the cultivation of a human rights jurisprudence for South Africa. However, I am of the view that our own (ideal) indigenous value systems are a premise from which we need to proceed and are not wholly unrelated to our goal of a society based on freedom and equality. She states further that there is a [306] need to develop an all-inclusive South African jurisprudence.

She goes on to proclaim that [307] 'although South Africans have a history of deep divisions characterised by strife and conflict, one shared value and ideal that runs like a golden thread across cultural lines, is the value of *ubuntu* – a notion now coming to be generally articulated in this country. It is well accepted that the transitional Constitution is a culmination of a negotiated political settlement. It is a bridge between history of gross violation of human rights and humanitarian principles, and a future of reconstruction and reconciliation'.

[308] Generally, *ubuntu* translates as *humaneness*. In its most fundamental sense, it translates as *personhood* and *morality*. Metaphorically, it expresses itself in *umuntu ngumuntu ngabantu*, describing the significance of group solidarity on survival issues so central to the survival of communities. While it envelops the key values of group solidarity, compassion, respect, human dignity, conformity to basic norms and collective unity, in its fundamental sense it denotes humanity and morality. Its spirit emphasises respect for human dignity, marking a shift from confrontation to conciliation. In South Africa *ubuntu* has become a notion with particular resonance in the building of a democracy. It is part of our 'rainbow' heritage, though it might have operated and still operates differently in diverse community settings.

Sachs J in his concurring opinion expressed similar sentiments. He stated:

[361] To begin with, I wish firmly to express my agreement with the need to take account of the traditions, beliefs and values of all sectors of South African society when developing our jurisprudence.

[365] Above all, however, it means giving long overdue recognition to African law and legal thinking as a source of legal ideas, values and practice. We cannot, unfortunately extend the equality principle backwards in time to remove the humiliations and indignities suffered by past generations, but we can restore dignity to ideas and values that have long been suppressed or marginalized.

[371] It is a distressing fact that our law reports and legal textbooks contain few references to African sources as part of the general law of the country. That is no reason for this court to continue to ignore the legal institutions and values of a very large part of the population, moreover, of that section that suffered the most violations of fundamental rights under previous legal regimes, and that perhaps has the most to hope for from the new constitutional order.

[373] The evolution of core values in all sections of the community . . . requires this court not only to have regard to public international law, and foreign case law, but also to all the dimensions of the evolution of South African law . . . . This would require reference not only to what in legal discourse is referred to as 'our common law' but also to traditional African jurisprudence.

African contributions to human rights jurisprudence[266]

It is sometimes assumed that traditional society and values have no contribution to 'modern' human rights. This position is wrong, and ignores the presence of many human rights values in traditional African society.

All societies, traditional or modern, manifest some notions of human rights, but the way these rights are conceptualized varies across different cultural settings.[267] Traditional African societies had a system of law comparable to any legal system, with one major point of difference. In traditional societies – in most instances – the law existed outside the framework of a state as we know it in a modern sense.[268] Obedience to the law was maintained through custom and religion, and there were established patterns of sanction. Old African societies had a high level of organization, and political, economic, and social control was maintained.[269]

Unfortunately, some Western scholars view customary law – or the traditional patterns of maintaining social control – in disparaging terms because of the influence of religion, custom, or magic.[270] To adopt the above approach is to commit a fundamental error by failing to see the reality and working of this form of law, as opposed to where the law was derived from.[271] Even natural-law principles of human rights (which form the basis of Western concepts of human rights), contain 'inherent rights' derived from a supreme being, and carry religious overtones.[272]

Most African societies had a sense of justice, and were remarkably democratic insofar as the way all members of the group participated in the decision-making process.[273] The rights to life and security were essential components, as were the elaborate mechanisms and procedures for decision-making.[274] An important feature of the African concept of human rights was the group or community aspect: the group was seen as more important than the individual.[275] Moreover, it was humanist in orientation.[276]

In the community, decisions were taken for the benefit of the overall group and were achieved by overall consensus.[277] The core of African society was egalitarian in character, and all economic benefits achieved were shared by the group.[278] This is not to say there were no discrepancies between different members of the group in a

---

[266] This section is largely adapted, with permission, from, Ziyad Motala 'Human Rights in Africa: A Cultural, Ideological and Legal Examination' (1989) 12 *Hastings International and Comparative Law Review* 373–410 (notes have been renumbered).

[267] See Raoul Berger 'Are Human Rights Universal?' (1997) September *Commentary* 62.

[268] Osite C Eze *Human Rights in Africa: Some Selected Problems* Lagos: Nigerian Institute of International Affairs 1984, 10.

[269] Ibid.

[270] C Mojekwe 'Self-determination: The African Perspective' in *Self-determination: National, Regional and Global Dimensions*, edited by Yonah. Alexander and Robert A Friedlander. Boulder: Westview Press 1980, 223.

[271] Christian P Potholm *The Theory and Practice of African Politics* Englewood Cliffs: Prentice-Hall 1979, 25.

[272] F Olisa Awogu *Political Institutions and Thought in Africa: An Introduction* New York: Vantage Press 1975, 47.

[273] John Beattie 'Checks on the Abuse of Political Power in Some African States: A Preliminary Framework for Analysis' in *Comparative Political Systems: Studies in the Politics of Pre-industrial Societies*, edited by Ronald Cohen and John Middleton. New York: Natural History Press 1967, 361–73. Beattie selects four traditional African societies in different parts of the continent and identifies various social institutions which have the effect of restraining the abuse of political power. The conformity to these norms are built into the political institutions and acts to circumscribe the actions of the ruler from departing from established norms, eg making it a requirement that a leader first act on the advice of his council or else he may be fined or deposed. In some societies where the leader departed from established norms, subjects could refuse customary economic services, revolt or have the chief deposed.

[274] I Asante 'Nation Building and Human Rights in Emergent African Nations' (1969) 2 *Cornell International Law Journal* 73.

[275] Keba Mbaye and B Ndiaye 'The Organization of African Unity' in *The International Dimensions of Human Rights*, edited by Karel Vasak and Philip Alston. Westport: Greenwood Press 1982, 588.

[276] Kenneth Kaunda *A Humanist in Africa: Letters to Collin M Morris from Kenneth D Kaunda* London: Longmans 1966, 24–5.

[277] Oajuma Oginga Odinga *Not Yet Uhuru: The Autobiography of Oginga Odinga* London: Heinemann 1967, 12.

[278] Awogu 83.

society. Overall, there were mechanisms to ensure that individuals did not deviate much from the norm so as to overpower the other members of society.[279] President Kaunda of Zambia describes the practice of African humanism stating:

The tribal community was a mutual society. It was organised to satisfy the basic human needs of all its members ... individualism was discouraged .... Human need was the supreme criterion of behavior ... social harmony was a vital necessity .... Chief and tribal elders ... adjudicated between conflicting parties ... and took whatever action was necessary to strengthen the fabric of social life.[280]

Pollis and Schwab, when referring to human rights in indigenous society and the position today, state:

... individuals still perceive themselves in terms of their group identity .... The concept of an autonomous individual possessed of inherent, inalienable rights has been meaningless .... Regardless of the particular traditional cultural patterns and the specific social relations, the individual has been perceived as an integral part of a group within which he or she has a defined role or status ... and if the concept of rights has any relevance, it is derived from relations with others.[281]

Hence, in traditional societies the individual was not viewed as standing apart or alienated from the society. The individual enjoyed a great number of rights, but had duties as well.[282] These rights and duties, however, were enjoyed through or within the society of which the individual was a part.[283] Within the framework of the group, the individual enjoyed freedom of expression, freedom of religion, freedom of movement, freedom of association, the right to work, and the right to education.[284]

Colonial rule curtailed much of the traditional freedoms and African practices in the name of improvement and the betterment of the African condition.[285] However, the classical Western concepts of human rights were not allowed to be assimilated into the African life style.[286] Instead, colonial rule, as a practice, applied standards different from classical liberal traditions to the indigenous African population.[287]

In terms of tradition, it was considered a fundamental right to be part of the extended family.[288] A person who failed to conform to the norms of the society lost his or her status, and no longer enjoyed the protection of the social unit.[289] Freedom of thought, speech, and beliefs were considered a common communal right.[290] It was, however, subject to one qualification; namely the 'principle of respect'. Marashinge states that this respect involved both a respect for oneself and for others.[291] The individual members of society recognized and respected the position and rights of other members The degree of respect varied according to age, ability, and sex.[292] This respect towards others did not constitute merely the morals of the society, but as Marashinge states,

---

[279] Asmaron Legasse 'Human Rights in African Political Culture' in *The Moral Imperatives of Human Rights: A World Survey*, edited by Kenneth W Thompson. Lanham: University Press of America 1980, 125.

[280] Kaunda 24–5.

[281] See Admantia Pollis and Peter Schwab (eds) *Human Rights Cultural and Ideological Perspectives* New York: Praeger 1979, 16.

[282] Awogu 82.

[283] Ibid.

[284] Mbaye & Ndiaye 589–91.

[285] KA Busia *Africa in Search of Democracy* London: Routledge and Keagan 1967, 49.

[286] Asante 100.

[287] Ibid.

[288] L Marashinge 'Traditional Conceptions of Human Rights in Africa' in *Human Rights and Development in Africa*, edited by Claude E Welch Jnr and Ronald I Meltzer. Albany: State University of New York Press 1984, 16.

[289] Ibid.

[290] Op cit 37.

[291] Ibid.

[292] Julius K Nyerere *Ujamaa – Essays on Socialism* Dar es Salaam: Oxford University Press 1968, 107.

was very much a part of the normative structure of the legal system,[293] and determined the extent to which freedom of speech could be expressed.[294] The limitations imposed on freedom of speech were more to preserve the common fabric of the society.[295] It is arguable that this is similar to the limitations imposed in modern-day society. The enjoyment of wealth and property also occurred within the collective framework. For the most part, the wealth of African societies was distributed evenly, and security was provided for all members of the society.[296]

All members in society had to work for their living. Idleness was an almost non-existent feature, and to be classified as a loiterer carried a social stigma.[297] The elder of the society was a custodian of the wealth.[298] It was not as though everyone worked for the elder, because the elder did not personally possess the wealth but only held it as custodian due to his position.[299] Hence, there was deference to old age as the elders had served the society in their youth. The elder's prestige and power was not enhanced by the wealth he held for the community. If the elder in any way abused his position or squandered the wealth he could be removed, which demonstrates the democratic nature of the system.[300]

Traditional African society did not permit a situation of a leisured class of landowners, since land was viewed as the property of the community.[301] Article 17 of the Universal Declaration states that everyone has the right to own property and this goes against traditional African concepts.[302] In African societies the individual had the right to use the land so as to feed himself and his family, but the right did not extend beyond this.[303] Moreover, there did not exist the phenomenon of land existing as a commodity that was marketable.[304]

In its approach to human beings, African humanism viewed man as a totality.[305] The idea of concentrating on one or some aspects of man at the neglect of other aspects is to upset the traditional balance of viewing man in this way.[306] Clearly, the approach of looking at human rights in terms of economic goals, or only in terms of political or civil rights, is not in keeping with African traditions.

African humanism has a contribution to make in the area of humanitarian law. Fasil Nahum emphasizes the extent of African humanism in war and stresses that African wars never embodied the concept of all-out total destruction.[307] The sense of humanity is illustrated in the unwritten rules by which wars were fought. For example, a war started in the morning and ended at sundown, and further ceased in the ploughing and harvesting season.[308] Moreover, only men were involved in war, and cruelty to enemy casualties was not permitted.[309]

In looking at the future for the protection of human rights, with particular respect to those

---

[293] The point made is that although the law existed outside the framework of the state it still worked effectively albeit in the form of custom to regulate the actions of its members. See Eze 10.

[294] Marashinge 37.

[295] Ibid.

[296] Awogu 82.

[297] Nyerere 5.

[298] Ibid.

[299] Ibid.

[300] Beattie 361.

[301] Schwab & Pollis 8.

[302] The article states that everyone has the right to own property individually as well as collectively.

[303] Nyerere 7.

[304] Ibid.

[305] See generally, Fasil Nahum 'African Contributions to Human Rights', unpublished paper presented at the Seminar on Law and Human Rights in Development at Gaberone, Botswana (24–28 May 1982).

[306] See generally Nahum.

[307] Nahum 220.

[308] Ibid.

[309] Ibid.

aspects considered fundamental, a rethinking of current approaches is called for in light of the philosophic differences outlined. Although such major differences do exist, there are common features which all societies share. There is, therefore, a compelling need to first disentangle some fundamental current notions of human rights from particular ideologies, and conceptualize them in terms of a common denominator.[310]

Traditional African society showed a great respect for human dignity, conceptualized in what is today referred to as African humanism.[311] No traditional African society, like any present ideological system, permitted torture, killings, and detention of its members.[312] The widespread torture, killings, and other abuses in Africa (or for that matter practised anywhere else in the world), would be objectionable in terms of Africa's own traditional standards of human rights. The major difficulties arise when human rights theories are framed in a form that requires African countries to accept replicas of Western governments and notions of individualism and natural law.[313] Moreover, a broader flexibility is called for in accepting African concepts, which may depart from Western thinking, as valid expressions of human rights.

There is a need to explore beyond the conventional values and institutions for other possibilities that can be implemented in Africa for the protection of human rights. These values must be examined within the social traditions and priorities of African societies[314] While praising traditional values, and criticizing the institutions that African countries adopted in the post-colonial era, this discussion is not meant to elevate traditional structures (for reasons which will become apparent) as a model framework to be emulated in present-day African society. The traditional systems of law, and the values underlying them, are mechanisms intrinsic to each society. While colonial rule succeeded in destroying African political institutions, it was unsuccessful in destroying African traditional political values and ideas.[315] Therefore, the attainment of human rights (such as the right to life, right against torture, freedom of movement, and right to participate in the political decision-making) will be enhanced by promoting the concepts of human rights located in the particular society's customs and laws. The form of human rights here, should derive from a set of values common to members of a particular society which are essential in maintaining the fabric of that society.[316] The discarding of colonial constitutions by African leaders would not mean much to the people when the newly instituted Constitution itself does not represent values and traditions common to the people of that society.[317]

Concepts such as individual ownership of land should no longer be perceived as a universal right.[318] In a society where there is a perception that land belongs to all the people, it would be legitimate for the land to be developed for the benefit of all the people.[319] Moreover, where traditional patterns do not permit a situation where only the moneyed are able to develop the land, it is legitimate to promote equality according to standards acceptable to the peoples' way of life.[320] Hence, the concept of equality has to be

---

[310] Raoul Berger 'The Activist Legacy of the New Deal Court' (1984) 59 *Washington Law Review* 62.

[311] Kaunda 24–5.

[312] See generally Marashinge 16.

[313] See C Mojekwe 'International Human Rights: The African Perspective' in *International Human Rights: Contemporary Issues*, edited by Jack L Nelson and Vera M Green. Standfordville: Human Rights Publishing Group 1980, 85–95.

[314] Marashinge 32.

[315] Ali Mazrui 'The Cultural Faith of African Legislatures: Rise, Decline and Prospects for Revival' (1979) 112 *Presence Africaine* 26.

[316] Marashinge 32.

[317] Thomas M Franck *Human Rights in Third World Perspective* London: Oceana 1982, xvi.

[318] See C Orwin and T Pangle 'The Philosophical Foundation of Human Rights' in *Human Rights in Our Time: Essays in Memory of Victor Barnes*, edited by Mark F Plattner. Boulder: Westview Press 1984, 6. The authors emphasize that the right to accumulate private property is at the heart of the original notion of human rights. Private property is viewed as an institution allowing the expression of every man's labour.

[319] Odinga 13.

[320] Ibid.

analysed beyond conventional Western thinking and the individual's equality does not necessarily have to be promoted apart from the rest of society. Nahum, in describing African society, states that: '[T]o the ancient question, am I my brothers keeper, the answer is an emphatic "yes", and so is your brother your keeper! In traditional African society every value is shared both good and bad'.[321]

It follows then, that the promotion of human rights could include the promotion of cooperativeness and working together for the benefit of the community. Nyerere, when discussing Tanzanian society, called for a revision of the educational system to inculcate in the younger generation the skills and values needed and cherished in their own society.[322] The colonial education system was designed to serve colonial interests and – not surprisingly – reflected values for this purpose.[323] Moreover, equality is further perceived in reorganizing society so that the stronger members of society, intellectually and physically put their strength for the benefit of all.[324]

In a modern setting, one can argue that the state has replaced the tribe or clan. Issues that were previously looked at in terms of the tribe or clan now become national issues, and it would not be inconsistent for past group identities to be replaced by the state.[325] Moreover, in considering Africa's economic plight, the state in Africa cannot be viewed in negative terms, but instead needs to be a positive institution through which economic and developmental goals can be achieved.[326]

The notion of democracy has to be considered in a much broader and flexible manner to allow for methods of participation in the decision-making process beyond the casting of periodic votes. This calls for a recognition that the manner and form of participation can vary across different societies.[327] Democracy in the traditional African setting entailed participation in the social and economic institutions of the society that extended beyond the electing of a head of state or local representative.[328] This was in accordance with African humanism and its emphasis on human needs in the fullest sense.[329]

The foregoing discussion is not meant to elevate traditional institutions as a model framework to be emulated. It merely highlights the concept of human rights, particularly the notion of democracy, in terms of traditional values.[330] The institutions that exist to implement democracy and human rights can vary across different societies in different ages. The problem a jurist faces in Africa is that of determining the kind of jurisprudence and institutional arrangements that are appropriate for African society.[331] This would depend on the values of the community, the history of the society, and the lessons learned from the introduction of different institutional arrangements in Africa.[332] In the context of second millennium Africa, the nation-state as it was geographically defined by the colonial powers is a

---

[321] Nahum.

[322] Nyerere 52.

[323] Ibid.

[324] Ibid.

[325] Schwab & Pollis 11–12; see also Nyerere 85.

[326] The point is repeatedly made that economic deterioration is a major factor for military interventions in African states. See H Baker 'Reflections on the Economic Correlates of African Democracy' in *Democracy and Pluralism in Africa*, edited by Dov Ronen. Boulder: Lynne Rienner Publishers 1986, 53, 59.

[327] Rita Hinden 'Africa and Democracy' (1962) 8 *Encounter* 7–8.

[328] Nyerere 171.

[329] International Commission of Jurists *Human Rights in a One-party State: International Seminar on Human Rights, their Protection, and the Rule of Law in a One-party State* London: Search Press 1978, 26.

[330] Hinden 8–9.

[331] C Ogwurike *Concept of Law in English-speaking Africa* New York: NOK Publishers International 1979, 7.

[332] Ibid.

reality that Africa has accepted.[333] Traditional African institutions revolved primarily around the family, clan, or lineage which constituted the basic unit of organization. With the reality of the nation-state, feelings of allegiance have to be transferred to the new entity: the state. Traditional institutions would, in many instances, be incompatible with such a transformation.[334] In this respect, traditional practices – to the extent that they interfere with the nation-building process – should be halted. Discrimination against any group retards the nation-building process.[335]

In *Makwanyane*, Sachs J correctly observed:

We do not automatically invoke each and every aspect of traditional law as a source of values, just as we do not rely on all features of the common law. Thus, we reject the once powerful common-law traditions associated with patriarchy and the subordination of servants to masters, which are inconsistent with freedom and equality, and we uphold and develop those many aspects of the common law which feed into and enrich the fundamental rights enshrined in the Constitution. I am sure that there are many aspects and values of traditional African law, which will also have to be discarded or developed in order to ensure compatibility with the principles of the new constitutional order.

---

[333] African leaders, though they all emphasize the arbitrary nature of their borders, have since independence, done nothing to redraw their boundaries. See RB Neuberger 'Concepts of Nationhood' in *The Thought of Selected African Leaders* (1980) 211–14 (on microfilm at University of Ann Arbor, Michigan).

[334] Romano Ledda 'Social Classes and Political Struggle in Africa' (1967) August *International Socialist Journal* 568–70.

[335] The process of nation-building has been defined as a process of bringing people together. See Awogu 47.

3

The power of judicial review: the composition, election, and jurisdiction of the Constitutional Court

Introduction

One of the great tensions in democratic theory arises from the principle that the elected representatives of the people should exercise sovereign authority, as opposed to the competing principle of constitutionalism and limited government. The Constitution assigns the ultimate power to interpret the Constitution to the judiciary: namely the Constitutional Court. This power includes the power to declare an act of the legislature, the executive, or the provinces, to be unconstitutional. First, this chapter looks at the justification for judicial review. Secondly, it considers the jurisdiction of the Constitutional Court and the powers of the Court over constitutional matters. Thirdly, the chapter concerns itself with the process of, and circumstances for, engaging the Constitutional Court. Fourthly, it considers the problem of constitutional review by courts other than the Constitutional Court. Fifthly, the concept of 'independence of the judiciary', under the doctrine of separation of powers is explored. Finally, the chapter considers the different enforcement mechanisms available to the Constitutional Court.

Judicial review and democracy

Judges in interpreting open-ended provisions of the Constitution are engaged in lawmaking which – strictly speaking – flies against a popular strain in Western political theory, of law being made by the elected representatives of the people.[1] This leads to a crucial question, is the judicial lawmaking exercise legitimate? On what basis can an unelected and unaccountable judiciary exercise the discretionary lawmaking power? The judiciary in many societies is not always reflective of the wider society, hence should judges be able to impose their views on the rest of society?[2] The judiciary in South Africa are far from representative of the population. The overwhelming majority of judges are white (mostly Afrikaner) males. A non-representative judiciary can misconstrue what is in the public's interest. At a time where there is a need for great social and economic change, the judiciary has the potential to serve as an obstructionist force. This was particularly evident in the United States, in the New Deal era, when the justices of the Supreme Court continually frustrated the urgent economic reforms initiated in

---

[1] The type of lawmaking that the judiciary is engaged in is not identical to that of the legislature. Some categorize it as secondary lawmaking or interstitial lawmaking. For a view on the different models of the role of the judge see J Bell 'Three Models of the Judicial Function' in *Judges and the Judicial Power: Essays in Honour of Justice VR Krishna Iyer*, edited by Rajeev Dhavan, et al. London: Sweet & Maxwell 1985, 55–75.

[2] See Peter W Hogg *Constitutional Law of Canada* Scarborough: Carswell, 3rd edition, 1992, 121.

the inter-war era following the Great Depression.[3] Similarly, in France after the election of the socialist government, the *Conseil Constitutionnel* (the French equivalent of the Constitutional Court) initially thwarted the social and economic policies of the Mitterrand government.[4] The other two branches of government are accountable for their actions, and have to present themselves for periodic re-election.

Clearly rights such as the right to life, liberty, and freedom against torture are very important rights. However, the judiciary is not always in the best position to balance individual rights against group rights, such as social, economic, and cultural rights. It is arguably inconsistent with democracy that an unelected body can frustrate the wishes of a popularly elected legislature on matters of economic and social affairs.[5] In the United States, prior to the New Deal, judicial review extended beyond mere protection of 'fundamental' rights, toward the determination of economic and social policies.[6] Criticizing the Court's early positions, Justice Felix Frankfurter summed up the situation best by stating that 'democracy does not need an oligarchic and irresponsible body for its preserva-

tion'. According to Justice Frankfurter, history has shown that the judiciary can misconceive what is in the public's good. For Justice Frankfurter, the best protector of democracy is the people and their vigilance over their representatives.[7] The conservative posture of the United States Supreme Court at the turn of the century is an example of the court misconceiving the public good.[8] Many of the provisions which the Court struck down are today accepted as norms in society.[9] It was during this era that there were clamours to recall members of the judiciary or have their decisions recalled.[10] Even today some argue that the judiciary in many societies is the guardian of the privileges of the rich, which is their own social position.[11] Judicial review could amount to an elite group protecting the vested interest of the status quo. Such a scenario is not compatible with democracy, as it entails an unelected minority being able to frustrate the wishes of the majority. In South Africa, since the democratic elections in 1994, there have been several decisions rendered by lower court judges (many appointed under the old order), which in effect protect the privileges and actions of the status quo.[12]

---

[3] Edward McWhinney *Supreme Court and Judicial Lawmaking: Constitutional Tribunals and Constitutional Review* Dordrecht: M Nijhoff 1986, 275–6. See *United States v Butler* 297 US 1 (1936) and *ALA Schechter Poultry Corp v United States* 295 US 495 (1935)(SC decisions).

[4] RL Morton 'Judicial Review in France: A Comparative Analysis' (1988) 36 *American Journal of Comparative Law* 94.

[5] See Jerald L Waltman and Kenneth M Holland (eds) *The Political Role of Law Courts in Modern Democracies* New York: Martin Press 1988, 1.

[6] The USSC determines the scope of abortion and education. See *Roe v Wade* 410 US 113 (1973); *Brown v Board of Education* 349 US 753 (1954).

[7] *Supra* at 557. Frankfurter accepts that the courts have the power to rule on the validity of legislation but he asserts the courts have to keep the implications of that right in mind. Frankfurter rightly asserts that the courts have to leave policy judgments to the legislative body which is chosen by the people.

[8] Cass R Sunstein 'Constitutions and Democracies: An Epilogue' in *Constitutionalism and Democracy*, edited by Jon Elster and Rune Slagstad. Cambridge: Cambridge University Press 1988, 343.

[9] eg formation of trade unions, minimum wage, and other economic regulations pertaining to safety at the workplace. See previous discussion of conservative judiciary at the time of the New Deal.

[10] Louis L Jaffe *English and American Judges as Lawmakers* Oxford: Clarendon Press 1969, 87.

[11] See the criticisms of the SC justices by Arthur S Miller 'On Politics, Democracy, and the First Amendment: A Commentary on First National Bank v Bellotti' (1981) 38 *Washington & Lee Law Review* 25, 38–40. In the above decision the SC invalidated a Massachusetts statute that prohibited banks and corporations from spending money to influence the vote on a referendum. The SC position was that a corporation was a constitutional person and, therefore, was entitled to protection of First Amendment freedom of speech. Miller points out that the above decision serves the interests of the dominant economic interests as it ignores the enormous disparities in wealth between corporations and natural persons which will affect the outcome of the referendum. See Miller 36. See Hogg 121–2. Michael H Davis 'The Law/Politics Distinction, the French *Conseil Constitutionnel* and the United States Supreme Court' (1986) 34 *American Journal of Comparative Law* 47–8.

[12] *Grove Primary School v Minister of Education and Others* 1997 (4) SA 982 (C); *South African Rugby Union and Others v President of the RSA and Others* 1998 (10) BCLR 1256 (T). See *Walker v Stadsraad van Pretoria* 1997 (3) BCLR 416 (T), where the provincial division

There are various justifications for judicial review. Some scholars assert that democracy does not entail majority rule alone; as it is only one element of democracy.[13] For instance, George Kateb asserts that the majority has 'no right to abridge or defeat the rights of individuals'.[14] Some liberal theorists are prepared to concede that the judiciary is an elitist body and judicial review is inconsistent with democracy.[15] However, while democracy may be promoted in the short term by abolishing judicial review, in the long-term basic rights and freedoms would be eroded.[16] Seen in a different light, constitutionalism aims to limit the scope of government action even though the majority may decide on the particular course of action. In terms of 'pure' democratic theory there is a tension between constitutionalism and 'pure' democracy. Constitutionalism aims to tie the community's hands in regard to certain decisions.[17] In *Larbi-Odam v The Member of the Executive Council For Education*,[18] Mokgoro J stated that the role of the judiciary is to protect groups that are particularly vulnerable to the tyranny that may accompany majoritarian decisions.[19]

In chapter 2, the theory of representation-reinforcement was considered and the notion that the courts have to protect certain groups that are not able to fully participate in the political process.[20] A variation of this argument posits judicial review as particularly important to reconcile ethnic and other cleavages in a plural society. The plural notion has been applied extensively by social scientists and academics to describe South African society.[21] South Africa is described as 'a house divided among itself'.[22] Its history is characterized as one of strife between various groups, with conflict between various tribes, and between black and white.[23] It is a society seen as having a multitude of different groups with extreme cultural heterogeneity influenced from three continents.[24] Judges enjoy a unique status in having a secure tenure: their detached position away from the hurly-burly of political pressures, together with their legal training (to consider matters on principle rather than expediency), make them better equipped to deal with strife.[25] It is the function of the legislature to attend to social and

---

upheld a challenge by white residents that different bases for assessment for water and electricity in white and black areas constituted a violation of the equality clause. The decision was reversed on appeal to the Constitutional Court in *City Council of Pretoria v Walker* CCT 8/97 (17 February 1998) now cited as 1998 (3) BCLR 257 (CC); 1998 (2) SA 363 (CC).

13 BO Nwabueze *Constitutionalism in the Emergent States* London: C Hurst 1973, 230–1. See also Peter Railton 'Judicial Review, Elites and Liberal Democracy' in *Constitutionalism*, edited by J Roland Pennock and John W Chapman. New York: New York University Press 1979, 156. The other and more important element is the protection of individual and minority rights, which cannot be infringed upon even by the majority.

14 G Kateb 'Remarks on the Procedures of Constitutional Democracy' in *Constitutionalism: Nomos XX*, edited by J Roland Pennock and John W Chapman. New York: New York University Press 1979, 148.

15 Ziyad Motala 'Independence of the Judiciary, Prospects and Limitations of Judicial Review in Terms of the United States Model in a New South African Order: Towards an Alternative Judicial Structure' (1991) 55 *Albany Law Review* 392.

16 Railton 158.

17 Stephen Holmes 'Precommitment and the Paradox of Democracy' in *Constitutionalism and Democracy*, edited by John Elster and Rune Slagstad. Cambridge: Cambridge University Press 1979.

18 *Larbi-Odam and Others v MEC for Education (North West Province) and Another* CCT 2/97 (26 November 1997), now cited as 1997 (12) BCLR 1655 (CC); 1998 (1) SA 745 (CC).

19 *Supra* paras 27–28.

20 See Geoffrey R Stone, et al *Constitutional Law* Boston: Little Brown, 3rd edition, 1996, 70–1.

21 Theodor Hanf, et al *South Africa, the Prospects for Peaceful Change: An Empirical Enquiry into the Possibility of Democratic Conflict Regulation* London: R Collings 1981, 3; John Rex 'The Plural Society: The South African Case' in *South Africa: Economic Growth and Political Change*, edited by A Leftwich. London: Allison & Busby 1971, 40.

22 Leo Marquard *The Peoples and Policies of South Africa* London: Oxford University Press 1969, 28.

23 Ibid.

24 Pierre L van den Berghe *South Africa: A Study in Conflict* Miiddletown: Wesleyan University Press 1965, 38.

25 HL de Silva 'Pluralism and the Judiciary in Sri Lanka' in *The Role of the Judiciary in Plural Societies*, edited by Neelan Tirucheluam and Radhika Coomaraswamy. London: F Pinter 1987, 81.

welfare functions. However, in fulfilling its functions the legislature is seen as being subject to various influences of lobby and pressure groups.[26] The judiciary, which is detached from politics, is the best protector of individual and minority rights.[27] In *Makwanyane*, Mahomed J observed:

The difference between a political election made by a legislative organ and decisions reached by a judicial organ, like the Constitutional Court, is crucial. The legislative organ exercises a political discretion, taking into account the *political preferences* of the electorate which votes political decision-makers into office. Public opinion therefore legitimately plays a significant, sometimes even decisive, role in the resolution of a public issue such as the death penalty. The judicial process is entirely different. What the Constitutional Court is required to do in order to resolve an issue, is to examine the relevant provisions of the Constitution, their text and their context; the interplay between the different provisions; legal precedent relevant to the resolution of the problem both in South Africa and abroad; the domestic common law and public international law impacting on its possible solution; factual and historical considerations bearing on the problem; the significance and meaning of the language used in the relevant provisions; the content and the sweep of the ethos expressed in the structure of the Constitution; the balance to be struck between different and sometimes potentially conflicting considerations reflected in its text; and by a judicious interpretation and assessment of all these factors to determine what the *Constitution* permits and what it prohibits.

While there are examples of the judiciary misconstruing what is in the public's good, it has been shown that an unfettered executive or legislature in many societies (as in apartheid South Africa), can run roughshod over fundamental rights and liberties. The African continent is rife with torture, brutality, and other abuses of fundamental rights. Undoubtedly, judicial review and an independent judiciary[28] enhance the protection of important individual rights, such as freedom of person, speech, assembly, and conscience, and the right against torture and arbitrary detention. If we say that the Constitution represents the will of the people and stands for limited government, then when the judiciary declares an act of the legislature unconstitutional, it is representing the wishes of the people.[29] This is a legitimate exercise to prevent tyranny. With respect to policy choices, we have argued in chapter 2 that there are certain substantive principles that the Court should observe when exercising judicial review in order to prevent the type of above-mentioned problems. One of those principles is that the Court should limit its intervention with respect to socio-economic legislation.

The problem that the framers of the Constitution faced was whether the judges – largely unrepresentative of the population – appointed by the apartheid order, could be trusted as custodians of the new constitutional order, given their record of being largely an instrument of the apartheid state.[30] On the one hand, one had a judiciary in South Africa which was tainted by the previous order and had the potential of being an obstructionist element in a new order. On the other hand, in those societies where there was no independent judiciary, there was a tendency for gross violations of fundamental rights.[31] In order to harmonize judicial review with the democratic ideals of the new order, the framers borrowed important features from the European model of judicial review of the Constitution.

---

[26] Jaffe.

[27] Op cit 34–5. See also John Agresto *The Supreme Court and Constitutional Democracy* New York: Cornell University Press 1984, 142.

[28] Independence in this context is used to denote a judiciary free of political manipulation by the government or any other state agency.

[29] Alexander Bickel *The Least Dangerous Branch: The Supreme Court at the Bar of Politics* New Haven: Yale University Press, 2nd edition, 1986, 16–17.

[30] Motala 383–6.

[31] See the events surrounding the dismissal of judges of the SC of Ghana by President Nkrumah and the subsequent actions by the executive, as reported in KA Busia *Africa in Search of Democracy* London: Routledge and Keagan 1967.

The specialized Constitutional Court

The Constitutional Court as a specialized tribunal

In terms of the British and United States systems, judicial review is exercised by the ordinary courts of the land. The courts under the above two systems are courts of general jurisdiction with authority to rule on all disputes, whether the disputes relate to the private or public realm. The judges in most instances have security of tenure.[32] Prior to the new constitutional order, the courts in South Africa operated like the Anglo-American model and exercised general jurisdiction.

In the period after the Second World War, many European countries introduced novel court structures – departing fundamentally from the Anglo-American model – entrusted with specific jurisdiction. The most notable development was the creation of a special constitutional court to adjudicate on constitutional disputes and to prevent government tyranny.[33] This has given rise to the classification of centralized versus non-centralized, or decentralized judicial review.[34] Under the centralized system, judicial review of a constitution is exercised by a single, or special, judicial organ. Under the decentralized system, judicial review is exercised by all the judicial organs in the legal system.[35]

The most important difference in the European constitutional tribunals is that they are specialized courts whose jurisdiction is limited to constitutional issues. There are other courts that exist separately from the specialized constitutional tribunals. The other courts fulfil all the other functions which courts fulfil in any system, except to decide disputes which involve constitutional issues. Members of the ordinary courts – as opposed to the constitutional courts – enjoy security of tenure, much like their counterparts in the Anglo-American model.

The South African Constitution has borrowed from the European model except that the ordinary courts are not completely deprived of authority to adjudicate over the Constitution.[36] The ordinary courts are deprived of jurisdiction to hear a number of constitutional disputes, which are reserved exclusively for the Constitutional Court. For example, under s 167(4), only the Constitutional Court may:

(a) decide disputes between organs of state in the national or provincial sphere concerning the constitutional status, powers or functions of any of those organs of state;

(b) decide on the constitutionality of any parliamentary or provincial Bill, but may do so only in the circumstances anticipated in section 79 or 121;

(c) decide applications envisaged in section 80 or 122;

(d) decide on the constitutionality of any amendment to the Constitution;

(e) decide that Parliament or the President has failed to fulfil a constitutional obligation; or

(f) certify a provincial constitution in terms of section 144.

Significantly, s 167(5) states that an order by any other court declaring that an Act of Parliament or a provincial act is invalid, or that the conduct of the president is unconstitutional, has to be first confirmed by the Constitutional Court before that order has any force. Section 167(5) provides:

(5) The Constitutional Court makes the final decision whether an Act of Parliament, a provincial Act or

---

[32] This means the judge, providing he or she is able, once appointed will continue to sit on the bench until he or she chooses to retire unless there is a mandatory retirement age as in the Anglo-American systems.

[33] Cole W Durham 'General Assessment of the Basic Law: An American Overview' in *Germany and its Basic Law, Past, Present and Future: A German-American Symposium*, edited by Paul Kirchoff and Donald P Kommers Baden-Baden: Nomos 1989, 43. Several European countries have these centralized constitutional Courts; namely: Germany, Italy, Belgium and France.

[34] For this classification, see Mauro Cappelletti and William Cohen *Comparative Constitutional Law: Cases and Materials* Indianapolis: Bobbs-Merrill 1979, 73–5.

[35] Cappelletti & Cohen 73.

[36] The term ordinary court refers to all the other courts apart from the Constitutional Court referred to under s 166 of the Constitution.

> conduct of the President is constitutional, and must confirm any order of invalidity made by the Supreme Court of Appeal, a High Court, or a court of similar status, before that order has any force.

The Constitution essentially limits the power of the ordinary courts to, unilaterally, declare an Act of Parliament or an act of the president unconstitutional. This is further affirmed in s 172(2), which provides:

> (2) (a) The Supreme Court of Appeal, a High Court or a court of similar status may make an order concerning the constitutional validity of an Act of Parliament, a provincial Act or any conduct of the President, but an order of constitutional invalidity has no force unless it is confirmed by the Constitutional Court.
> (b) A court which makes an order of constitutional invalidity may grant a temporary interdict or other temporary relief to a party, or may adjourn the proceedings, pending a decision of the Constitutional Court on the validity of that Act or conduct.

A magistrates' court has jurisdiction to apply the Constitution as determined by an Act of Parliament.[37] However, unlike the High Court, a magistrates' court does not have the authority to decide on the constitutionality of any legislation or any conduct of the president.[38]

Selection of judges

An important difference between the specialized tribunals and the Anglo-American model is the recognition of the political nature of judicial review – particularly as it pertains to constitutional issues.[39] There is an explicit recognition of the interplay between law and politics in the realm of constitutional interpretation. This recognition of the political functions is most vividly reflected in the method of election and limited tenure of members of the Constitutional Court, which is a departure from the tenure of ordinary judges. The assumptions underlying the specialized Constitutional Court structures (in European countries) recognize the political nature of the judicial function. For example, judges in the German Federal Constitutional Court are selected by the two houses of the legislature, with each house choosing half the judges of the Constitutional Court.[40] The lower house, the *Bundestag*, selects an electoral college of twelve members. The twelve-member electoral college represents the political parties in proportion to their strength in the lower house.[41] The upper house, the *Bundesrat*, selects its half of the members of the Constitutional Court by a two-thirds vote. The actual appointment is made by the Federal President.[42]

In Germany, invariably the members of the Constitutional Court consist of members of all the major political parties.[43] This marks a recognition that many functions considered judicial are in fact political activity. The judges, once appointed, are independent and free from political pressures. The South African Constitution provides for more representative judicial appointments in the future, not only for Constitutional Court judges, but also for judges of the lower courts. Under the German system (like most European systems), the selection of members of the Constitutional Court is entrusted to the political parties in the legislature. The South African Constitution has created a Judicial Service Commission (JSC) and has entrusted this body with the responsibility of proposing judicial nominees to the president. Section 178 of the Constitution describes the JSC as follows:

---

37 Section 170 of the Constitution.
38 Section 170.
39 Contrary to what Mahomed DP stated in *Makwanyane* para 266
40 Article 94(1) of the German Basic Law.
41 Waltman & Holland 93.
42 Ibid.
43 Cappeletti & Cohen 77.

178(1) There is a Judicial Service Commission consisting of—

(a) the Chief Justice, who presides at meetings of the Commission;

(b) the President of the Constitutional Court;

(c) one Judge President designated by the Judges President;

(d) the Cabinet member responsible for the administration of justice, or an alternate designated by that Cabinet member;

(e) two practising advocates nominated from within the advocates' profession to represent the profession as a whole, and appointed by the President;

(f) two practising attorneys nominated from within the attorneys' profession to represent the profession as a whole, and appointed by the President;

(g) one teacher of law designated by teachers of law at South African universities;

(h) six persons designated by the National Assembly from among its members, at least three of whom must be members of opposition parties represented in the Assembly;

(i) four permanent delegates to the National Council of Provinces designated together by the Council with a supporting vote of at least six provinces;

(j) four persons designated by the President as head of the national executive, after consulting the leaders of all the parties in the National Assembly; and

(k) when considering matters specifically relating to a provincial or local division of the High Court, the Judge President of that division and the Premier, or an alternate designated by the Premier, of the province concerned.

(2) If the number of persons nominated from within the advocates' or attorneys' profession in terms of subsection (1)*(e)* or *(f)* equals the number of vacancies to be filled, the President must appoint them. If the number of persons nominated exceeds the number of vacancies to be filled, the President, after consulting the relevant profession, must appoint sufficient of the nominees to fill the vacancies, taking into account the need to ensure that those appointed represent the profession as a whole.

(3) Members of the Commission designated by the National Council of Provinces serve until they are replaced together, or until any vacancy occurs in their number. Other members who were designated or nominated to the Commission serve until they are replaced by those who designated or nominated them.

(4) The Judicial Service Commission has the powers and functions assigned to it in the Constitution and national legislation.

(5) The Judicial Service Commission may advise the national government on any matter relating to the judiciary or the administration of justice, but when it considers any matter except the appointment of a judge, it must sit without the members designated in terms of subsection (1)*(h)* and *(i)*.

(6) The Judicial Service Commission may determine its own procedure, but decisions of the Commission must be supported by a majority of its members.

The JSC reflects an expansion of the number of legal interests responsible for the selection of judges to include the Chief Justice, the President of the Constitutional Court, the Minister of Justice, four members of the legal profession (two representing the attorneys' profession and two representing the advocates' profession), an academic designated by law teachers, six persons from the National Assembly (NA) – at least three of whom must represent opposition parties – four members from the National Council of Provinces, and four persons designated by the president after consulting the leaders of all political parties in the NA. These different interests have a chance of influencing the social, political, and economic course of the country in their selection of members of the judiciary.

The second striking difference between the specialized tribunals and the Anglo-American model is the tendency of the European systems to limit the tenure of judges to the Constitutional Court. The judicial tenure of members of the German Constitutional Court is limited to a single term of twelve years. This curtails the spectre of a judiciary appointed to the bench giving judgments based on their own values, for periods long after their appointment. This also allows the elected representatives a measure of political control over the actions of the judiciary in that there is periodic renewal of the bench. The South African Constitution replicates the German model by providing a single non-renewable term of twelve years.[44] The judicial tenure with respect to all other judges is left intact. Under s 176(2) of the Constitution, this limitation of a single non-renewable term does not apply to other judges.[45]

Once elected, the members of the Constitutional Court are free from political pressures since they have a fixed security of tenure. This means that while in office, there is little incentive for a Constitutional Court judge to be swayed by politicians because there is no threat that the judge can be removed from office and no prospect that the judge is going to have to face re-election. On the bench the judge can act fearlessly without pressure or domination from the executive or any other branch of the government. This is not the same thing as saying the judges are apolitical, because their political views are canvassed by the JSC before any nomination is made to the president. At the same time, with the periodic renewal of the Court's membership, there is no spectre of a judiciary appointed for a life term, imposing opinions that belong to a previous era. A Constitutional Court representative of the broader South Africa is more likely to take into account different interests and more likely to enjoy greater legitimacy. Moreover, a Constitutional Court whose membership can be renewed at periodic intervals, is more likely to be sensitive to the realities of South African society.

Access to the Constitutional Court

Introduction

The Constitutional Court receives numerous applications for review. The Court can only decide cases that it is empowered to hear under the Constitution. The Constitutional Court's jurisdiction is limited to constitutional disputes.[46] In this role, it acts as the ultimate guardian and arbiter over the Constitution.[47] Its decisions on constitutional matters are final and binding on all other courts and institutions. Once the jurisdictional requirement is fulfilled, the Constitutional Court has broad discretion in selecting which cases it will adjudicate upon. In this section, we review the pivotal constitutional and statutory provisions on jurisdiction, as well as the approach the Constitutional Court has adopted in the selection of cases.

Exclusive jurisdiction

The Constitutional Court has original and exclusive jurisdiction over a range of matters for which it functions as a trial court. Under the final Constitution, matters of exclusive jurisdiction include the authority to decide: the constitutionality of an Act of Parliament on the request of one-third of the members of the NA;[48] disputes over a provincial statute on the request of twenty per cent of the members of the provincial legislature;[49] certain disputes between organs of state;[50] the constitutionality of constitutional amendments;[51] whether parliament or the president has failed to fulfil a constitutional obligation;[52] and to certify a provincial constitution.[53] Most of the above proceedings will only arise in an abstract context

---

[44] Section 176(1) of the Constitution provides that a Constitutional Court judge is appointed for a non-renewable term of twelve years, but must retire at the age of seventy.

[45] Under s 176(2). Other judges hold office until they are discharged from active service in terms of an Act of Parliament.

[46] Section 167(3)(b) of the Constitution.

[47] Section 167(3)(a).

[48] Section 80.

[49] Section 122.

[50] Section 167(4)(a).

[51] Section 167(4)(d).

[52] Section 167(4)(e).

[53] Section 167(4)(f).

because they are unlikely to arise during the course of normal litigation.[54] The procedures for referring matters pertaining to the Court's exclusive jurisdiction are spelled out in ss 13–16 of the Constitutional Court Rules.[55]

Under the interim Constitution, the Constitutional Court had exclusive power to determine whether an Act of Parliament was unconstitutional. The final Constitution permits the High Court or Supreme Court of Appeal (SCA) to make such determinations. However, under s 167(5), any order that an Act of Parliament, a provincial act, or conduct of the president is unconstitutional, must be confirmed by the Constitutional Court before the order has any force. The High Court has the power to grant a temporary interdict, pending a decision by the Constitutional Court on the validity of the Act or conduct.[56] In 1997, parliament passed the Constitutional Court Complementary Amendment Act.[57] The amendment to the Act provides rules with respect to the process whereby a referral is made to the Constitutional Court for confirmation after the High Court has made a ruling of invalidity pertaining to an Act of Parliament, a provincial act or the conduct of the president.[58]

Review over matters pertaining to the common law

There is no need for a referral to the Constitutional Court under the interim and final Constitution where a lower court makes a determination of constitutional invalidity relating to the common law.[59] In *Gardener v Whitaker*,[60] Kentridge AJ, referring to the Court's earlier decision in *Du Plessis and Others v De Klerk and Another*,[61] stated '. . . the development and application of the common law and customary law is the task of the Supreme Court, including the Appellate Division . . . . [I]t is not within the powers of this Court to choose between competing versions of the common law, all of which may be consistent with the Constitution.'[62] Where the Supreme Court of Appeals fails to develop the common law in terms of its obligations under the Constitution, the Constitutional Court would intervene to ensure obedience to the Constitution.[63] In *Du Plessis*, the Court, *per* Kentridge AJ and Mahomed J, stated that the Constitutional Court had an oversight function to ensure that the interpretation and development of the common-law accords with the spirit and purport and objects of the Bill of Rights.[64]

Whether something relates to the interpretation of the common law sometimes involves a value judgement.[65] To the extent that the Constitutional Court adopts the approach that the interpretation pertains to the application of the common law, it might be that in given situations the Court's approach could constitute an avoidance technique. In *De Freitas and Another v The Society of Advocates of Natal and Another*,[66] application was made to the Constitutional Court against an order of the Natal High Court for two

---

[54] It might be possible disputes involving organs of state under s 167(4)*(a)* might arise in litigation.

[55] Government Notice R757, *Regulation Gazette* 6199 of 29 May 1998 (Constitutional Court Rules).

[56] Section 172(2)*(b)* of the Constitution.

[57] Act 79 of 1997.

[58] Section 8.

[59] *National Coalition for Gay and Lesbian Equality and Another v Minister of Justice and Others* CCT 11/98 (9 October 1998) para 3, now cited as 1998 (12) BCLR 1517 (CC); 1999 (1) SA 6 (CC) (*National Coalition for Gay and Lesbian Equality 1*).

[60] *Gardener v Whitaker* CCT 26/94 (15 May 1996) para 16, now cited as 1996 (6) BCLR 775 (CC); 1996 (4) SA 337 (CC).

[61] *Du Plessis* para 64.

[62] *Gardener* para 16.

[63] *Boesak v The State* CCT 25/00 (1 December 2000) para 15, now cited as 2001 (1) BCLR 36 (CC); 2001 (1) SA 912 (CC).

[64] *Du Plessis* paras 63 and 87.

[65] *Mistry v Interim National Medical and Dental Council of South Africa and Others* CCT 13/97 (29 May 1998) para 2, now cited as 1998 (7) BCLR 880 (CC); 1998 (4) SA 1127 (CC).

[66] *De Freitas and Another v Society of Advocates of Natal (Natal Law Society Intervening)* CCT 2/98 (15 September 1998), now cited as 1998 (11) BCLR 1345 (CC).

rulings. First, suspending the first applicant from practice as an advocate for a period of six months, as a consequence of a finding by the High Court that the first applicant was guilty of unprofessional conduct in that he accepted work directly from members of the public without the intervention of an attorney. Secondly, dismissing the second applicant's counter application in the High Court, in which the second applicant sought an order finding that advocates, who are not members of the respondent, are not bound by the referral rule and are therefore entitled to accept work directly from the public. There were two issues before the Court: namely, the constitutionality of s 7(2) of the Admission of Advocates Act[67] which entitles respondent to initiate proceedings of a disciplinary nature against any advocate; and whether the referral rule, that prohibits advocates from accepting work directly from the public, is an unconstitutional infringement of an advocate's right to practise his or her trade. The applicants wanted direct access before the Constitutional Court. The Court held that the first issue relating to who has a right to intervene in proceedings before a court was a matter under the common law. Therefore, the application for leave to appeal on this question had to fail.[68] With respect to the challenge to the referral rule, the Court held that the challenge concerned an issue, which related to both the common law and the Constitution, and the appeal should first proceed to the SCA.[69] The difficulty with the Constitutional Court's approach to the second issue is that one can find justifications for many unjust practices based on established patterns of conduct outside the legislation. Where the Court is faced with a challenge that a piece of legislation violates a fundamental right under the Constitution, as was the case in *De Freitas*, the Court should render a judgment on that legislation. Arguably, the effect of the Right of

Appearance in the Courts Act,[70] was to distinguish between different categories of legal practitioners The Court should have independently reviewed the validity of the statute. The mere fact that the rules embodied in the statute reflect long-standing customs and practices, which can come under the rubric of the common law, should not prevent the Court from ruling on the validity of the statute. The Constitutional Court, when confronted with a racial discrimination statute, would not require that the validity of the statute should first be approached by the SCA, since racial discrimination was countenanced by earlier courts and was part of the practices and morés of society. The Court's approach in *De Freitas* reflects an unfortunate avoidance technique, which allows the Court to pass on rendering a decision.

Rules for engaging the Constitutional Court: criteria for case selection

For matters outside its exclusive jurisdiction, the Constitutional Court exercises both original and appellate jurisdiction.[71] The Court controls access to it 'by granting "leave" only in cases where it is in the interests of justice to do so'.[72] The Constitutional Court hears the majority of these cases on appeal from the High Courts or the SCA, in which instance it acts as an appellate tribunal.

The interim Constitution contained detailed provisions on the requirements for reference to the Constitutional Court.[73] These requirements will continue to apply to proceedings pending before the application of the final Constitution. Sections 102(1) and (2) provide the conditions for referrals of those cases to the Constitutional Court on a constitutional issue that may be decisive for the case, and which falls within the exclusive jurisdiction of the Constitutional Court, providing the

---

[67] Act 74 of 1964.
[68] *De Freitas, per* Langa DP, para 9–10.
[69] *Supra* para 23.
[70] Act 62 of 1995.
[71] *Pennington & Summerley v The State* CCT 14/97(18 September 1997) para 11, 1997 (4) SA 1076 (CC); 1997 (10) BCLR 1413 (CC).
[72] *Supra. Boesak* para 12.
[73] Sections 102 and 103 of the interim Constitution.

referral was in the interest of justice. It was envisaged that the procedures for engaging the Constitutional Court would be further amplified in the Rules of the Court. Section 100(1) of the interim Constitution gave the President of the Constitutional Court, acting in consultation with the Chief Justice, the power to create rules for bringing matters before the Constitutional Court. Section 100(2) provided that rules may be adopted with respect to direct access to the Court, where it was in the interest of justice to do so, on any matter over which the Constitutional Court had jurisdiction. The rules were promulgated in January 1995.[74] The Court Rules provided greater details as to how to engage the Constitutional Court. Rule 18 of the Court Rules provided the requirements that needed to be met to appeal a decision from the SCA to the Constitutional Court. Rules pertaining to direct access are contained in Rule 17 of the 1995 Court Rules.

The final Constitution does not contain the same procedures for referral to the Constitutional Court. Instead, it appears the framers wanted the procedures to be worked out through legislation, court-created rules, and through procedures developed by the Constitutional Court through its inherent powers. These appear in three provisions in the Constitution, namely: s 167(6), s 171, and s 173. Section 167(6) provides that national legislation or the rules of the Constitutional Court must allow a person, when it is in the interest of justice and with the leave of the Constitutional Court, to bring a matter directly to the Constitutional Court,[75] or to appeal directly to the Constitutional Court from any other court. Section 171 provides that all courts function in

terms of national legislation, and their rules and procedures must be provided for in terms of national legislation. Finally, s 173 provides that the Constitutional Court, the SCA and the High Courts have the inherent power to protect and regulate their own processes and to develop the common law, taking into account the interests of justice.

Unlike the interim Constitution, under the final Constitution, the Court does not have the power to adopt its own rules in the absence of an enabling statute. In 1995, parliament passed the Constitutional Court Complementary Amendment Act.[76] The 1997 Act provides rules with respect to the process whereby a referral is made to the Constitutional Court for confirmation, where the High Court has made a ruling of invalidity pertaining to an Act of Parliament, a provincial act, or the conduct of the president.[77] The Act further provides enabling legislation which confers power on the President of the Constitutional Court, in consultation with the Chief Justice, to make rules for the Constitutional Court. These rules were created in May 1998.[78] The Constitutional Court has preferred that parliament adopt appropriate legislation on procedure for engaging the Constitutional Court.[79] In a number of cases before the legislation was passed, the Court fashioned its own procedure for bringing appeals to the Court pursuant to the inherent powers conferred by s 173, allowing the Constitutional Court to regulate its own process.[80] Prior to the passing of enabling legislation authorizing the Court to draw up its rules as envisaged under s 171, the Constitutional Court required applicants to seek leave to appeal to the Constitutional Court.[81]

---

[74] *Regulation Gazette* 5450 of 6 January 1995.

[75] Section 167(6)*(a)*.

[76] Act 79 of 1997.

[77] Section 8.

[78] Government Notice R757, *Regulation Gazette* 6199 of 29 May 1998 (Constitutional Court Rules).

[79] *Pennington* para 22.

[80] *Supra; Parbhoo and Others v Getz NO and Another* CCT 16/97 (18 September 1997) para 4–5, now cited as 1997 (10) BCLR 1337 (CC); 1997 (4) SA 1095 (CC).

[81] *Pennington* paras 22, 26.

Pennington & Summerley v The State
CCT 14/97 (18 September 1997), now
cited as 1997 (10) BCLR 1413 (CC);
1997 (4) SA 1076 (CC).
(notes omitted)
CHASKALSON P.:

[10] On a proper construction of the 1996 Constitution there can be no doubt that this Court has appellate jurisdiction, including jurisdiction to hear appeals from decisions of the Supreme Court of Appeal on constitutional matters. Section 167(3)(a) of the 1996 Constitution provides that the Constitutional Court 'is the highest court in all constitutional matters'.

Section 168(3) provides that the Supreme Court of Appeal 'may decide appeals in any matter. It is the highest court of appeal except in constitutional matters . . .'.

The 'highest' court of appeal in respect of constitutional matters is therefore the Constitutional Court. This is made explicit by section 167(6) of the 1996 Constitution which provides:

National legislation or the rules of the Constitutional Court must allow a person, when it is in the interests of justice and with leave of the Constitutional Court:
(a) to bring a matter directly to the Constitutional Court; or
(b) to appeal directly to the Constitutional Court from any other court.

The words 'any other court' would include the Supreme Court of Appeal.

[11] Section 167(6) makes clear that the Constitutional Court is to have both original and appellate jurisdiction, and the power to control access to it by granting 'leave' only in cases where it is in the interests of justice to do so. In other words, litigants will not ordinarily have the right to insist upon a matter being heard by the Constitutional Court. What has to be decided in the present matter is whether in the period between the coming into force of the 1996 Constitution and the enactment of the legislation or rules required by section 167(6), the Court can hear appeals from the Supreme Court

of Appeal, and if so, whether it can regulate the procedure to be followed in such appeals.

[20] At common law a court has no jurisdiction to hear an appeal against a decision of another court. It can only do so if that authority is conferred on it by the statute under which it is constituted, and then it must function in terms of that statute. This Court was established under the interim Constitution, and its authority as a court was recognised and reaffirmed by the 1996 Constitution. The question is whether on a proper construction of the Constitution it has the power in the circumstances of the present case to regulate its procedure so as to require the appellants to secure its leave to the noting and prosecuting of their appeals to it.

The Court's power to regulate its own procedure

[21] In terms of the interim Constitution the Court was given jurisdiction to deal with constitutional issues referred to it by a provincial or local division of the Supreme Court, or the Appellate Division, and appellate jurisdiction to hear appeals from decisions of provincial or local divisions on constitutional issues. It also had an original jurisdiction to deal with matters by way of direct access, and with the constitutionality of bills before Parliament or a provincial legislature. As the Appellate Division then had no jurisdiction in respect of constitutional matters, neither the interim Constitution nor the rules of Court made provision for appeals from its decisions to this Court.

[22] A person who wishes to approach this Court to uphold or protect his or her constitutional rights should not be prevented from doing so solely because the legislation or rules contemplated by sections 167(6) and 171 have not been passed. Section 173 of the 1996 Constitution gives this Court an 'inherent power' to 'protect' and 'regulate' its process. It is a power which has to be exercised with caution. It is not necessary to decide whether it is subject to the same constraints as the 'inherent reservoir of power to regulate its procedures in the interests of the proper administration of

justice' which vested in the Appellate Division prior to the passing of the 1996 Constitution. Even if it is subject to such constraints, the present situation, in which there is a vacuum because the legislation and rules contemplated by the Constitution have not been passed, is an extraordinary one in which it would be appropriate to exercise the power.

[23] The power is to 'protect and regulate' the process of this Court taking into account 'the interests of justice'. When this power is exercised it should be done in a way which accords with the requirements of the Constitution and as far as possible with the procedure ordinarily followed by this Court in similar cases. Section 167(6) of the 1996 Constitution indicates the procedure that is contemplated by the Constitution. It is to

... allow a person, when it is in the interests of justice and with leave of the Constitutional Court ... to appeal directly to the Constitutional Court from any other court.

[25] Section 167(6) of the 1996 Constitution is the only provision of the Constitution which addresses the procedure to be followed in engaging the Constitutional Court. It prescribes that legislation must be enacted to allow appeals to be brought to this Court from decisions of another court when it is in the 'interests of justice' to do so

and 'with leave of the Constitutional Court'.

[26] The appellants purport to note their appeal in terms of section 167. Leave of this Court is a requirement prescribed by section 167(6). Section 173 of the Constitution allows this Court to 'protect and regulate [its] own process'. 'Leave to appeal' is also a requirement needed to 'protect' the process of this Court against abuse by appeals which have no merit, and it is in the 'interests of justice' that this requirement be imposed, for if appeals without merit were allowed against decisions of the Supreme Court of Appeal, justice would be delayed.

[27] I would therefore hold that in regulating its process to fill the vacuum caused by the absence of the necessary legislation and rules, this Court should adopt the procedure contemplated by section 167(6) of the Constitution and require leave of this Court to be obtained for the noting of appeals to it against decisions of the Supreme Court of Appeal on constitutional matters – a procedure that is consistent with the rules regulating appeals from the High Court to this Court. This procedure requires a consideration of the merits of the appeal and is an exercise of the appellate jurisdiction vested in the Court. It will be necessary to lay down the details of the procedure to be followed in such matters and this will be done in the order that is made later in this judgment.

The 1998 Constitutional Court Rules provide detailed requirements for engaging the Court, covering among other important matters: the application procedure;[82] urgent applications;[83] argument;[84] referral of a bill under the Court's exclusive jurisdiction including referrals by the president or premier of a province;[85] applications under the Court's exclusive jurisdiction under s 80(1) and s 122(1);[86] confirmation of an order of constitutional invalidity;[87] certification of a provincial Constitution;[88] direct access in the interest of justice;[89] appeals from courts other than the SCA;[90] procedure on appeal;[91] and appeal against a decision of the SCA.[92]

---

[82] Section 10 of the Constitutional Court Rules.
[83] Section 11.
[84] Section 12.
[85] Section 13.
[86] Section 14.
[87] Section 15.
[88] Section 16.
[89] Section 17.
[90] Section 18.
[91] Section 19.
[92] Section 20.

Apart from matters within its exclusive jurisdiction, the Constitutional Court has great discretion over which cases it will hear. Under Constitutional Court Rule 17, which deals with direct access, applicants require the leave of the Constitutional Court. Similarly, under rule 18, an applicant needs the leave of the Court from which he or she is appealing an adverse decision,[93] or the leave of the Constitutional Court.[94] Both s 17 and s 18 contain substantive and procedural prerequisites. Under ss 17 and 18 of the rules, an applicant has to provide grounds which satisfy the Court that it is in the interests of justice for direct access to be granted.[95] Under s 18, which deals with appeals from courts other than the SCA, in addition to the requirement that 'it is in the interest of justice', the relevant rules require:

S 18(2): A litigant who is aggrieved by the decision of a court and who wishes to appeal against it directly to the Court shall, within 15 days of the order against which the appeal is sought to be brought and after giving notice to the other party or parties concerned, apply to the court which gave the decision to certify that it is in the interests of justice for the matter to be brought directly to the Constitutional Court and that there is reason to believe that the Court may give leave to the appellant to note an appeal against the decision on such matter.

S 18(6) (6)/a/: If it appears to the court hearing the application made in terms of subrule (2) that–
(i) the constitutional matter is one of substance on which a ruling by the Court is desirable; and
(ii) the evidence in the proceedings is sufficient to enable the Court to deal with and dispose of the matter without having to refer the case back to the court concerned for further evidence; and

(iii) there is a reasonable prospect that the Court will reverse or materially alter the judgment if permission to bring the appeal is given, such court shall certify on the application that in its opinion, the requirements of subparagraphs (i), (ii) and (iii) have been satisfied or, failing which, which of such requirements have been satisfied and which have not been so satisfied.
(b) The certificate shall also indicate whether, in the opinion of the court concerned, it is in the interests of justice for the appeal to be brought directly to the Constitutional Court.

Sections 17 and 18 of the 1998 Constitutional Court Rules mirror the provisions of ss 17 and 18 of the 1995 Constitutional Court Rules. Therefore, the Court's approach to appeals under the interim Constitution would also be applicable to appeals under the final Constitution. The Court summarized the salient features of rule 18 under the 1995 rules, in *Mistry v The Interim National Medical and Dental Council of South Africa.*[96]

The Constitutional Court has become increasingly selective (under both the interim and final Constitutions), in deciding which cases it will hear, and under what circumstances it will grant direct access to the Court. Central to the Constitutional Court's approach is an insistence that, first, lower courts having jurisdiction to hear the issue not refer the issue to the Constitutional Court without the prior rendering of a decision.[97] Secondly, disputes of fact should be resolved at the level of the trial Court.[98] Thirdly, direct access to the Constitutional Court should be reserved for exceptional situations.[99]

[93] Section 18(2).
[94] Section 18(7).
[95] Sections 17(2)/a/ and 18(2).
[96] See *Mistry v Interim National Medical and Dental Council of South Africa and Others*, paras 5 and 7.
[97] *S v Vermaas, S v Du Plessis* CCT 1/94; CCT 2/94 (8 June 1995) para 7, now cited as 1995(7) BCLR 851 (CC); 1995 (3) SA 292 (CC).
[98] *Hekpoort Environmental Preservation Society and Another v Minister of Land Affairs and Others* CCT 21/97 (8 October 1997) para 10, now cited as 1997 (11) BCLR 1537 (CC); 1998 (1) SA 349 (CC).
[99] *Bruce and Another v Fleecytex Johannesburg CC and Others* CCT 1/98 (24 March 1998) para 8, now cited as 1998 (4) BCLR 415 (CC); 1998 (2) SA 1143 (CC).

Mistry v The Interim National Medical and Dental Council of South Africa and Others CCT 13/97 (29 May 1998) 1997 (7) BCLR 880 (CC); 1998 (4) SA 1127 (CC) (notes omitted)

CHASKALSON P.

[5] Rule 18*(e)* of the Constitutional Court Rules provides as follows:

If it appears to the judge or judges of the division of the [High Court] concerned, hearing the application [for a certificate], that–
  (i) the constitutional issue is one of substance on which a ruling by the Court is desirable; and
  (ii) the evidence in the proceedings is sufficient to enable the Court to deal with and dispose of the matter without having to refer the case back to the division concerned for further evidence; and
  (iii) there is a reasonable prospect that the Court will reverse or materially alter the decision given ... if permission to bring the appeal is given, such judge or judges ... shall certify on the application that in his or her or their opinion, the requirements of subparagraphs (i), (ii) and (iii) have been satisfied or, failing which, the judge or judges shall certify which of such requirements have been satisfied, and which have not been satisfied.

[6] A party wishing to appeal against a decision of the High Court applies formally to that court for a certificate in terms of Rule 18. Considerations relevant to deciding whether a certificate should be positive or negative are in many respects similar to those which should influence a court in deciding whether or not to grant leave to appeal to the Supreme Court of Appeal. In both instances the High Court is required to consider whether or not there are reasonable prospects of success and whether the issues raised are of sufficient substance to be dealt with by such court. It is appropriate, therefore, that an application for a certificate in terms of Rule 18 should be dealt with in the same manner as a conventional application for leave to appeal. In both instances a judgment on the application is required.

[7] The purpose of the certificate is to assist this Court in the decision that it has to make as to whether or not leave to appeal should be granted. Where the relevant constitutional issues have been fully traversed in the judgment in respect of which the certificate is given, there may be no need for a detailed judgment on the certificate. But where the application for a certificate raises issues which have not been fully canvassed in the judgment, or where the reasoning in the judgment is subjected to challenge which calls for comment, the judgment on the certificate may have to be more comprehensive. Ultimately what is necessary is that the judge or judges in the High Court to whom the application is made, should, as McLaren J did in the present matter, consider the issues identified in Rule 18*(e)* and give reasons for the findings made.

Under the interim Constitution, there were various provisions under which the Constitutional Court could hear a matter directly. The interim Constitution, in s 102(8), permitted any division of the SCA, having disposed of a matter, to refer the matter to the Constitutional Court if the Supreme Court felt that the issues raised were of such public importance that a ruling should be given on it. Section 103(4) permitted the referral to the Constitutional Court of matters within the exclusive jurisdiction of the Constitutional Court, if the provincial or local division felt that a decision regarding the validity of the law or provision was material to the adjudication of the matter, that there was a reasonable prospect that the relevant law or provision would be held to be invalid, and that it was in the interests of justice to do so. Moreover, under s 100(2) of the interim Constitution, the Court could create its own rules for direct access in the interests of justice.

In interpreting the various provisions to engage the Constitutional Court, the Court has insisted that the matter filter through the ordinary court system and only reach the Constitutional Court after other courts have pronounced on the dispute. In its very first decision, the Constitutional Court, *per* Kentridge AJ, held that where the Constitution confers jurisdiction on other courts, the jurisdiction was not optional and had to be exercised.[100] A judge had to make his or her own decision on a constitutional issue within his or her jurisdiction before the matter can be referred to the Constitutional Court.[101] The necessity for this approach was stressed in *Bernstein and Others v Bester and Others*[102] where Ackerman J observed:

[2] ... While provincial and local divisions might initially have been hesitant to grapple with the implications and application of the new Constitution and might have preferred to refer constitutional issues to this Court, it must be stressed that, for the proper development of our law under the Constitution, it is essential that these courts and indeed all other courts empowered to do so, play their full role in developing our post-constitutional law. It would greatly assist the task of the provincial and local divisions of the Supreme Court, and in so doing ultimately the task of this Court, if counsel were called upon to justify rigorously why it was contended that the particular provision of the Constitution relied upon renders the law or provision in question invalid and why it is necessary or advisable to refer the issue in question to the Constitutional Court at that particular juncture. This would lead to narrower and more closely focused referrals and enable the provincial and local divisions to furnish more comprehensive reasons for any particular referral which would in turn assist the task of this Court and the development of our constitutional jurisprudence. Such an approach would also decrease the risk of wrong referrals and avoid the unsatisfactory expedient in such cases of having to try to invoke, at the last moment, in a forced manner and in unsatisfactory circumstances, the direct access procedure provided for in Constitutional Court Rule 17.

Similarly, in interpreting the procedures for recourse to the Constitutional Court under the final Constitution, the Court observed in *Bruce and Another v Fleecytex Johannesburg CC and Others*, that '[i]f as a matter of course, constitutional matters could be brought directly to it, we could be called upon to deal with disputed facts on which evidence might be necessary, to decide constitutional issues which are not decisive of the litigation and which might prove to be purely academic, and to hear cases without the benefit of the views of other courts having constitutional jurisdiction'.[103] The Court further noted that it is '... not ordinarily in the interest of justice for a court to sit as a court of first and last instance, in which matters are decided without there being any possibility of appealing against the decision given'.[104]

In its earlier decisions in cases such as *Zuma*,[105] *Mhlungu*,[106] and *Mbatha*,[107] the Constitutional Court considered the substantive issues presented in these cases even though the questions considered were not within its exclusive jurisdiction. The Court, in essence, overlooked what were otherwise faulty references. In other cases such as *S v Vermaas* and *S v Du Plessis*, the Court refused to countenance a faulty referral.[108] In the United States, Chief Justice Earl Warren once remarked that the selection process in determining which cases it will decide 'cannot be captured in any rule or guidelines that would be meaningful'.[109] Similarly, the interpretation of the substantive requirements for referral to the Constitutional Court are sometimes elusive. The Court's approach on access is sometimes contradictory and

---

[100] *S v Zuma and Others* CCT 5/94 (5 April 1995) para 10, now cited as 1995 (2) SA 642 (CC); 1995 (4) BCLR 401 (SA).

[101] *Supra.*

[102] *Bernstein and Others v Bester and Others NNO* CCT 23/95 (27 March 1996) para 2, now cited as 1996 (4) BCLR 449 (CC); 1996 (2) SA 751 (CC).

[103] *Bruce* para 7.

[104] *Supra* para 8.

[105] *Zuma* paras 9, 11.

[106] *Mhlungu* paras 55–56, 59.

[107] *Mbatha* paras 28, 29.

[108] *Vermaas* para 13.

[109] Quoted in Ralph A Rossum and Alan G Tarr *American Constitutional Law: Cases and Interpretation* New York: St Martin's Press, 3rd edition, 1991, 26.

confusing.[110] Even though a case may incorrectly be referred to the Constitutional Court, the Court may still grant direct access if it feels that it is in the interest of justice for it to decide the matter.[111] In *Dladla*, the Court, despite procedural flaws in the referral, proceeded to examine the constitutionality of the bail provisions under the Criminal Procedure Act.[112] The Court felt it was in the interest of justice that uncertainty surrounding the constitutionality of the bail provisions, which affected the rights of thousands of people be put to rest.[113] As the Court recognized, the phrase 'interest of justice' is an imprecise term and ultimately marks a value judgement.[114]

Arguably, the inconsistent approach in the early days can be attributed to the 'novelty' of the new Constitution. As a rule, a referral to the Constitutional Court cannot be undertaken simply on the presentation of a constitutional dispute. Where a referral is made, under s 102(1) of the interim Constitution, on a matter within the exclusive jurisdiction of the Constitutional Court, the Court has insisted that the two requirements of s 102(1) must be satisfied. First, the issue referred must be decisive for the case and, secondly, it must be in the interest of justice to refer the issue to the Constitutional Court.[115]

The Court has interpreted 'decisive for the case' to mean that the ruling 'may have a crucial bearing on the eventual outcome of the case as a whole, or any significant aspect of the way in which its remaining parts ought to be handled'.[116] Where there are multiple issues presented and the provincial division refers one issue to the Constitutional Court, it cannot be said that issue is decisive for the case, since the case may be decided on the other issues.[117]

The Constitutional Court has suggested a number of factors that are important in considering whether it is in the interest of justice for the Court to hear an issue. A recurring theme in the Court's approach as to whether it is in the interest of justice, is the requirement that there must be a reasonable prospect that the Court will uphold the challenge.[118] Commenting on the reasonable prospect that the relevant law or provision will be held to be invalid, Kentridge AJ observed in *Mhlungu*.[119]

It is convenient at this point to say something about the practice of referrals to this Court under section 102(1) of the Constitution. The fact that an issue within the exclusive jurisdiction of this court arises in a Provincial or Local Division does not necessitate an immediate referral to this Court. Even if the issue appears to be a substantial one, the court hearing the case is required to refer it only

(i) if the issue is one which may be decisive for the case; and

(ii) if it considers it to be in the interest of justice to do so.

In section 103(4) of the Constitution, which deals with the referral to this Court of matters originating in inferior courts, the referring Provincial or Local Division must in addition be of the opinion 'that there is a reasonable prospect that the relevant law or provision will be held to be invalid'. In *S v W and Others* 1994 (2) BCLR 135 (C), 147G; *S v Williams and Five Similar Cases* 1994 (4) SA 126 (C), 139F, Farlam J said that although that was not an express requirement of section 102(1) it was implicit therein. I respectfully agree. See also *Matiso and Others v*

---

[110] Brice Dickson 'Human Rights on the Eve of the Next Century: Aspects of Human Rights Implementation: Protecting Human Rights through a Constitutional Court: The Case of South Africa' (1997) 66 *Fordham Law Review* 531.

[111] *Vusi Dladla and Others v The State* CCT 22/98 (3 June 1999) para 34, now cited as 1999 (7) BCLR 771 (CC); 1999 (4) SA 623 (CC).

[112] Act 51 of 1977, as amended.

[113] *Dladla* para 35.

[114] *Supra* para 46.

[115] *Brink v Kitshoff NO* CCT 15/95 (15 May 1996) para 8, now cited as 1996 (6) BCLR 752 (CC); 1996 (4) SA 197 (CC). *S v Bequinot* CCT 24/95 (18 November 1996) para 7, now cited as 1997 (2) SA 887 (CC); 1996 (12) BCLR 1588 (CC). *Dlamini* para 35.

[116] *Luitingh v Minister of Defence* CCT 29/95 (4 April 1996) para 9, now cited as 1996 (4) BCLR 581 (CC); 1996 (2) SA 909 (CC). *Brink* para 10.

[117] *Luitingh* para 9.

[118] *Brink* para 9; *Mhlungu* para 59; *Tsotetsi v Mutual and Federal Insurance Co Ltd* CCT 16/95 (12 September 1996) para 4, now cited as 1996 (11) BCLR 1439 (CC); 1997 (1) SA 585 (CC). *Pennington & Summerley* para 27; *Bruce* para 6; *Boesak* para 12.

[119] *Mhlungu* para 59.

The Commanding Officer, Port Elizabeth Prison and Others 1994 (3) BCLR 80 (SE), 89G – 90D; *Matiso and Others v The Commanding Officer, Port Elizabeth Prison and Another* 1994 (4) SA 592 (SE), 599G – 600E. The reasonable prospect of success is, of course, to be understood as a *sine qua non* of a referral, not as in itself a sufficient ground. It is not always in the interest of justice to make a reference as soon as the relevant issue has been raised. Where the case is not likely to be of long duration it may be in the interests of justice to hear all the evidence or as much of it as possible before considering a referral. Interrupting and delaying a trial, and above all a criminal trial, is in itself undesirable, especially if it means that witnesses have to be brought back after a break of several months. Moreover, once the evidence in the case is heard it may turn out that the constitutional issue is not after all decisive. I would lay it down as a general principle that where it is possible to decide any case, civil or criminal, without reaching a constitutional issue, that is the course which should be followed. One may conceive of cases where an immediate reference under section 102(1) would be in the interests of justice – for example, a criminal trial likely to last many months, where a declaration by this Court of the invalidity of a statute would put an end to the whole prosecution. But those cases would be exceptional. One may compare the practice of the Supreme Court with regard to reviews of criminal trials It is only in very special circumstances that it would entertain a review before verdict. See Hiemstra, *Suid-Afrikaanse Strafproses* (5de uitgawe), 764. In any event, the convenience of a rapid resort to this Court would not relieve the trial judge from making his own decision on a constitutional issue within his jurisdiction.

The 'interest of justice' also means there must be compelling reasons to deal with the Constitutional issue.[120] Moreover, it is not ordinarily in the 'interest of justice' for a matter to be heard piecemeal, and the constitutional issue should, as far as possible, be avoided.[121] The requirements of 'interest of justice' and 'reasonable prospect that

the Court will reverse the decision' are contained as two separate standards in Constitutional Court Rule 18, which provides the criteria and procedure for appeals from courts other than the Supreme Court of Appeal under the final Constitution. Under Rule 18, an aggrieved litigant who wants to appeal to the Constitutional Court is required to obtain a certificate from the court, which rendered the decision, that it is in the interests of justice for the matter to be heard by the Constitutional Court.[122] The certificate should also state whether, in the opinion of the judge, there is a reasonable prospect that the Court will reverse or materially alter the judgment if permission to bring the appeal is given,[123] and whether the constitutional matter is one of substance.[124] The Court Rules now require that the matter be one of substance. There is great latitude in the determination of whether the matter is one of substance. In the United States, the Supreme Court has considered the intrinsic importance of the issues raised in the case in determining which cases it will review.[125] In exercising its power of review, the United States Supreme Court is less concerned with individual cases of miscarriage of justice, and tends instead to concern itself with questions the resolution of which could have an impact far beyond the facts and parties involved.[126] It is to be seen how the Constitutional Court determines whether a matter 'is one of substance'.

Section 101(2) of the interim Constitution dealing with matters within the exclusive jurisdiction of the Constitutional Court required that the issue must be decisive for the case. Constitutional Court Rule 18 does not deal with matters within the exclusive jurisdiction of the Constitutional Court. In light of the litany of judgments in which the Court has stated that they should not deal with a constitutional question unless it is necessary, (even on matters on which the Constitutional Court has exclusive jurisdiction under the interim

---

[120] *Zantsi v The Council of State, Ciskei and Others* CCT 24/94 (22 September 1995) para 4, now cited as 1995 (4) SA 615 (CC); 1995 (10) BCLR 1424 (CC).

[121] *Mhlungu* para 59; *Brink* para 9.

[122] Constitutional Court Rules, 18(2) and 18(6)*(b)*.

[123] Section 18(6)(iii).

[124] Sections 18(6)(i) and (iii).

[125] Rossum & Tarr 27.

[126] Ibid.

Constitution), the Constitutional Court is likely to insist that the requirement that the issue being referred be decisive for the case, is an implicit requirement.

Appeals through the Supreme Court of Appeal (SCA)

Consistent with its approach that a matter must filter its way through the ordinary court system, the Constitutional Court would not ordinarily grant access to a litigant directly from the provincial division without hearing the views of the SCA.[127] Under the interim Constitution, the Appellate Division did not have the power to adjudicate over constitutional issues. If one applied the interim Constitution strictly, the SCA would not have jurisdiction over disputes pending under the interim Constitution. In *Fedsure Life Assurance Ltd. and Others v Greater Johannesburg Transitional Metropolitan Council and Others,*[128] the Constitutional Court held that it was in the interest of justice for the SCA to exercise jurisdiction, conferred in terms of Chapter 8 of the final Constitution, which is to say over constitutional issues arising under the interim Constitution.[129] This means that appeals should proceed first from the High Courts to the SCA and only reach the Constitutional Court as a last resort. It is only in exceptional situations, where the Constitutional Court accepts that it is in the interest of justice, that the Constitutional Court will hear an appeal directly from a provincial division.[130]

In *Member of the Executive Council For Development Planning and Local Government in the Provincial Government of Gauteng v The Democratic Party and Others,*[131] the Constitutional Court was asked to hear a matter on appeal from the provincial division of the High Court without an appeal to the SCA. The issue pertained to the voting procedure for the adoption of the budget under local government structures. A ruling by the Constitutional Court would have consequences for other local authorities in terms of how they adopted their budgets. In their application for leave to appeal, the applicants argued that litigation would be protracted by requiring the matter to pass through the SCA.[132] An appeal to the Constitutional Court would also reduce costs and avoid delays.[133] The Constitutional Court held that the interest of justice would depend on the facts of each case.[134] A direct appeal to the Constitutional Court would deny the Court of the advantage of having the views of the SCA. Where there are both constitutional issues and other issues on appeal, the Court would be reluctant to grant access without hearing the views of the SCA. However, where the appeal was concerned only with the interpretation of constitutional provisions, a direct appeal from the High Court to the Constitutional Court would save time and costs.[135] Moreover, the Court held a ruling in this case would involve issues of local government that had to be resolved as a matter of urgency.[136]

However, where a matter involves a mixed issue involving both constitutional law and the common law, the Constitutional Court is very reluctant to grant access without the matter first being heard by the SCA.[137] In *De Freitas and Another v The Society*

[127] *Member of the Executive Council for Development Planning and Local Government, Gauteng v The Democratic Party and Others* CCT 33/97 (29 May 1998), now cited as 1998 (7) BCLR 855 (CC); 1998 (4) SA 1157 (CC).
[128] *Fedsure Life Assurance Ltd and Others v Greater Johannesburg Transitional Metropolitan Council and Others* CCT 7/98 (14 October 1998), now cited as 1998 (12) BCLR 1458 (CC); 1999 (1) SA 374 (CC).
[129] *Supra* para 113.
[130] 126 *Supra.*
[131] *Member of the Executive Council of Gauteng para 29.*
[132] *Supra.*
[133] *Supra.*
[134] *Supra* para 32.
[135] *Supra* para 30.
[136] *Supra* para 33.
[137] *Amod v Multilateral Motor Vehicle Accidents Fund* CCT 4/98 (27 August 1998) para 33, now cited as 1998 (10) BCLR 1207 (CC); 1998 (4) SA 753 (CC).

of Advocates of Natal and Another,[138] the Court refused to grant access to the applicant without first hearing the views of the SCA. The applicant challenged the referral rule under which practising advocates were prevented from accepting work directly from the public. The applicants argued that it was in the interest of justice for the Constitutional Court to hear this matter directly, because the issues affected the livelihood of over 300 advocates.[139] The applicants further argued that the matter had far-reaching implications, in terms of litigation costs, for the general public. Finally, the applicants argued that their own litigation costs would increase if they had to proceed to the SCA.[140] The Constitutional Court held that the challenge to the referral rule related to an issue under the common law and the Constitution.[141] Seeing that it was a matter of mixed law, the appeal first had to proceed to the SCA.[142]

The Constitutional Court will not entertain an appeal to a decision of the SCA on the grounds that it was wrong on the facts.[143] In *Boesak*, the Constitutional Court held that disagreement with the SCAs interpretation of the facts whether evidence was sufficient to justify a finding of guilt beyond reasonable doubt, did not in itself present a constitutional issue.[144]

Hearing of oral evidence

The Constitutional Court has expressed reservations as to whether it is best suited to hear oral evidence and resolve disputes of fact.[145] It is only where 'the circumstances are so exceptional and the public interest, or the ends of justice or good government, are of such overriding importance, that the Court might be disposed to grant direct access under rule 17…'.[146] Similarly, under the interim Constitution, the trial court was required to hear evidence and make factual findings before it made a referral to the Constitutional Court.[147] The duty of the trial court to hear evidence before an appeal could be made from a provincial division is found both in the 1995 Constitutional Court Rules,[148] and the current 1998 Constitutional Court Rules.[149]

Criteria for direct access

There are circumstances where the Constitutional Court will expedite consideration of cases. Direct access will only be granted in exceptional circumstances.[150] Under the 1995 Constitutional Court Rules, the Constitutional Court would allow direct access where the matter was of urgency or public importance, and where the use of ordinary procedures would prejudice the public interest or prejudice the ends of justice and good government.[151] Uncertainty in the law will not on its own constitute a ground for direct access.[152] The applicant must show the public importance of resolving the uncertainty.[153] In *S v Mbatha* and *S v Prinsloo*, the Constitutional Court was faced with the constitutionality of reverse onus presumptions

---

[138] CCT 2/98 (15 September 1998), now cited as 1998 (11) BCLR 1345 (CC).

[139] *Supra* para 19.

[140] *Supra*.

[141] *Supra* para 23.

[142] *Supra*.

[143] *Boesak* para 15.

[144] *Supra*.

[145] *Hekpoort* para 10; *Brink* para 11.

[146] *Hekpoort* paras 10, 11.

[147] Sections 102(1) and 102(3) of the interim Constitution.

[148] 1995 Constitutional Court Rules, s 18*(e)*(ii).

[149] Section 18(6)(ii).

[150] *Moseneke and Others v The Minister of the High Court* CCT 51/00 (6 December 2000) para 19, now cited as 2001 (2) BCLR 103 (CC); 2001 (2) SA 18 (CC).

[151] 1995 Constitutional Court Rules, s 17(1). *S v Vermaas; S v Du Plessis* para 7.

[152] *Christian Education of South Africa v The Minister of Justice* CCT 13/98 (14 October 1998) paras 10–11, now cited as 1998 (12) BCLR 1449 (CC); 1999 (2) SA 83 (CC).

[153] *Transvaal Agricultural Union v The Minister of Land Affairs and the Commission on Restitution of Land Rights* CCT 21/96 (18 November 1996) para 18, now cited as 1996 (12) BCLR 1573 (CC); 1997 (2) SA 621 (CC).

under which a multitude of accused were imprisoned.[154] The Court held that clarity with regard to the presumption was of public importance because there were many trials either pending or proceeding, in which the presumption might be invoked, which made the granting of direct access under the interim Constitution appropriate.[155] In *Tsoetsi v Mutual and Federal Insurance Company Ltd.*, the Court summarized the approach to direct access by stating that:

In several cases, this court has confirmed that it has a discretion to allow direct access and that it will not allow direct access to it in the absence of exceptional circumstances (See *S v Zuma and Others* 1995 (2) SA 642 (CC); 1995 (4) BCLR 401 (CC) at paragraph 11; *Executive Council of the Western Cape Legislature and Others v President of the Republic of South Africa and Others* 1995 (4) SA 877 (CC); 1995 (10) BCLR 1289 (CC) at paragraphs 15 – 17; *Ferreira v Levin NO and Others; Vryenhoek and Others v Powell NO and Others* 1996 (1) SA 984 (CC); 1996 (1) BCLR 1 (CC) at paragraph 10; *S v Mbatha; S v Prinsloo* 1996 (2) SA 464 (CC); 1996 (3) BCLR 293 (CC) at paragraph 29; *Luitingh v Minister of Defence* at paragraph 15; *Besserglik v Minister of Trade, Industry and Tourism and Others* 1996 (6) BCLR 745 (CC) at paragraph 6; *Brink v Kitshoff NO* at paragraph 18.)

[12] The court has been willing to exercise its discretion to permit direct access in several cases: where it was satisfied that there was a pressing need for a particular issue to be determined in order to avoid substantial dislocation in the criminal justice process (*S v Zuma* at paragraph 11); or to prevent significant delays and disruption in the procedures relating to the liquidation of companies (*Ferreira v Levin NO and Others; Vryenhoek and Others v Powell NO and Others* at paragraph 10); where a litigant had no other avenue for relief available (*Besserglik v Minister of Trade, Industry and Tourism and Others* at paragraph 6); where there was a compelling national interest in the determination of an issue in the light of a pending election (*Executive Council of the Western Cape Legislature and Others v President of the Republic of South Africa and Others* at paragraphs 15 – 17) and where parties consented to direct access and there was a real prospect that the order made by the court will in fact be decisive for the case (*Brink v Kitshoff NO* at paragraph 18). The grant of direct access remains a discretionary power of the court which will be exercised in exceptional circumstances only and in the light of the facts of each particular application.

Even though the new Constitutional Court Rules do not mention urgency and public importance, the Constitutional Court has invoked the need for urgency and public importance in order to achieve direct access under the final Constitution.[156] The current Constitutional Court Rules require an applicant, who seeks direct access, to lodge an application with the registrar setting out: the grounds on which it is claimed that it is in the interests of justice that an order for direct access be granted;[157] the nature of the relief sought and the grounds upon which such relief is based;[158] whether the matter can be dealt with by the Court without the hearing of oral evidence;[159] and if the matter cannot be heard without oral evidence, how such evidence can be adduced and how conflicts of fact can be resolved.[160] Direct access will be permitted in 'exceptional circumstances only'.[161]

---

[154] *S v Mbatha, S v Prinsloo* CCT 19/95 (9 February 1996), now cited as 1996 (2) SA 464 (CC); 1996 (3) BCLR 293 (CC).

[155] *Supra* para 30.

[156] *Christian Education South Africa* para 11.

[157] Constitutional Court Rules, s 17(2)*(a)*.

[158] Section 17(2)*(b)*.

[159] Section 17(2)*(c)*.

[160] Section 17(2)*(d)*.

[161] *Bruce* para 4.

Bruce and Another v Fleecytex
Johannesburg CC and Others
CCT 1/98 (24 March 1998), now
cited as 1998 (4) BCLR 415 (CC);
1998 (2) SA 1143 (CC)
(notes omitted)
CHASKALSON P:

[1] This is an application for direct access brought in terms of Rule 17 of the Constitutional Court Rules in a matter in which the applicant seeks an order declaring that the provisions of section 150(3) of the Insolvency Act are unconstitutional.

[5] In terms of the 1996 Constitution the President, Premiers, Members of Parliament and Members of Provincial Legislatures are entitled to bring certain matters directly to this Court. There are also certain matters in respect of which this Court has exclusive jurisdiction. But subject to these exceptions the 1996 Constitution recognises that there should not ordinarily be an unqualified right to approach this Court directly.

[6] This applies to both the Court's appellate jurisdiction and its original jurisdiction to hear matters as a court of first instance. In dealing with applications for leave to appeal against a decision of the Supreme Court of Appeal this Court has held that the prospects of success are of fundamental importance. Such an appeal is the only remedy left to the applicant and if there are reasonable prospects that the appeal will succeed there are compelling reasons for granting the leave that is necessary. As yet no decision has been given on the circumstances in which it would be appropriate to note an appeal directly to this Court from a court other than the Supreme Court of Appeal. In such matters, however, the relevant consideration may well be different for the aggrieved litigant has other remedies which can be pursued before approaching this Court for its decision on the matter.

[7] Whilst the prospects of success are clearly relevant to applications for direct access to this Court, there are other considerations which are at least of equal importance. This Court is the highest court on all constitutional matters If, as a

matter of course, constitutional matters could be brought directly to it, we could be called upon to deal with disputed facts on which evidence might be necessary, to decide constitutional issues which are not decisive of the litigation and which might prove to be purely academic, and to hear cases without the benefit of the views of other courts having constitutional jurisdiction. These factors have been referred to in decisions given by this Court on applications for direct access under the interim Constitution, and are clearly relevant to the granting of direct access under the 1996 Constitution.

[8] It is, moreover, not ordinarily in the interests of justice for a court to sit as a court of first and last instance, in which matters are decide without there being any possibility of appealing against the decision given. Experience shows that decisions are more likely to be correct if more than one court has been required to consider the issues raised. In such circumstances the losing party has an opportunity of challenging the reasoning on which the first judgment is based, and of reconsidering and refining arguments previously raised in the light of such judgment.

[9] Under the 1996 Constitution, High Courts as well as the Supreme Court of Appeal have constitutional jurisdiction including the jurisdiction to make an order concerning the validity of the provisions of an Act of Parliament. Although an order made by such Courts declaring an Act of Parliament to be invalid has no force unless confirmed by this Court, the court making the order may grant a temporary interdict or other temporary relief pending the decision of this Court. The procedure contemplated by the 1996 Constitution is that such orders of constitutional invalidity will be referred to this Court for confirmation, and that appropriate procedures in such cases will be provided for by national legislation . . .. Bearing in mind the jurisdiction of the High Courts and the Supreme Court of Appeal, and the matters referred to in paragraphs 7 and 8 of this judgment, compelling reasons are required to justify a different procedure and to persuade this Court that it should exercise its discretion to grant direct access and sit as a court of first instance.

[10] The background to the present application is as follows. The first applicant (Bruce) is the sole member of a close corporation (Baby Angel) which was placed in liquidation on 4 December 1997 by an order of the Witwatersrand High Court. On the same day an application for leave to appeal against the liquidation order was noted. A liquidator appointed pursuant to the winding up order sought to proceed with the winding up of Baby Angel but Bruce objected to this. She contended that in terms of Rule 49(11) of the Uniform Rules of Court the winding up order had been suspended by the noting of the application for leave to appeal, and that as sole member of Baby Angel she was still entitled to control its affairs. On 23 January 1998 Bruce brought an urgent application in the High Court in the name of Baby Angel for an interdict restraining the liquidator from proceeding with the winding up.

[11] The liquidator opposed the application contending that section 150(3) of the Insolvency Act is applicable to the winding up of close corporations, and that the provisions of the winding up order were accordingly not suspended by the noting of the application for leave to appeal. The liquidator's contention was upheld by Wunsch J and the application for an interdict was dismissed with costs.

[12] On 29 January 1998 Bruce applied urgently to this Court for an order declaring that section 150(3) of the Insolvency Act is invalid in that it

... deprives individuals, companies and Close Corporations who appeal against sequestration or liquidation orders of the right of access to the Court in terms of Rule 49(11) which is part of section 20 of Act 59 of 1959 and which gives an individual and/or a company and/or a Close Corporation the right of access to the Court pending an Appeal against a Sequestration Order or a Liquidation Order, in conflict with [section] 34 of the [1996] Constitution.

In the alternative an order of invalidity was sought on the grounds that the section '... deprives an individual and/or a company and/or a Close Corporation of the right to exercise its trade or profession freely pending an Appeal ...' against a sequestration or liquidation order.

[13] Apart from a reference to the importance to her of a decision on the constitutionality of the section, the only ground advanced by Bruce in support of her contention that the case was one in which direct access should be permitted was that the delay caused by following the ordinary court procedures would prejudice her. She stated in her application:

[I]f I had to wait for some Higher Court, including the Appeal Court, to decide whether Wunsch J [sic] was right or wrong in applying section 150(3), which he was bound to apply as it stands as part of an Act of Parliament, then the whole purpose of the appeal will be defeated ....

[14] If the constitutionality of the section had been raised before him, Wunsch J would not have been bound to apply section 150(3) of the Insolvency Act. He would have been entitled in terms of section 172(2) of the 1996 Constitution to consider that question, and if he was of the opinion that the section was inconsistent with the 1996 Constitution, to declare it to be invalid, and to grant the applicant interim relief pending a decision by this Court in the confirmation proceedings. I express no opinion on whether there is any substance in the applicant's contention that the section is invalid and nothing in this judgment should be construed as indicating support for such a proposition. What is important as far as this judgment is concerned is that the High Court has jurisdiction to consider the constitutionality of Acts of Parliament and to deal with the matters raised by the applicant in her application for direct access.

[15] The constitutionality of section 150(3) of the Insolvency Act was apparently not raised in the hearing before Wunsch J. The application for direct access contains no explanation for this omission, nor does it say why it was considered necessary to approach this Court directly instead of applying to the High Court for the relief that is claimed in the notice of motion. The application seems to have been launched on the incorrect

assumption that this Court is the only court with jurisdiction to deal with the matter.

[16] A direction was given by the President of the Court calling upon the applicant to make written submissions as to why direct access should be granted, having regard in particular to the provisions of section 172(2) of the 1996 Constitution and the decisions of this Court, *inter alia*, in *Transvaal Agricultural Union* and *Besserglik v Minister of Trade, Industry and Tourism and Others (Minister of Justice Intervening)*.

[17] In *Transvaal Agricultural Union* it was said that:

... jurisprudential policy dictates, that this Court should ordinarily not deal with matters as both a Court of first instance and as one of last resort.

And in *Besserglik* it was held that in applications for direct access one of the relevant considerations will be:

... whether an applicant can show that he or she has exhausted all other remedies or procedures that may have been available.

[18] In the written argument submitted pursuant to the direction, counsel contended that the relief sought could not be secured through the use of ordinary procedures, and that the matter was of such urgency and of such public importance that direct access should be granted. He also contended that a failure to follow the correct procedures was not necessarily fatal to an application for direct access, and sought to rely on the decision of this Court in *Besserglik* for that proposition.

[19] It was pointed out in *Transvaal Agricultural Union* that the mere fact that the validity of a provision of an Act of Parliament is in issue does not in itself justify an application for direct access. There must in addition be sufficient urgency or public importance, and proof of prejudice to the public interest or the ends of justice and good government, to justify such a procedure. There is no greater importance in securing a definitive ruling on the constitutionality of section 150(3) of the Insolvency Act than would ordinarily exist in securing a ruling on the constitutionality of provisions of other Acts of Parliament, and there is no substance in the contention that the matter is of such public importance that direct access should be allowed. The relief claimed in the present case is within the jurisdiction of the High Court. If Bruce had followed the normal procedures she could have pursued her claim in that court, and if successful, she could have secured effective relief there. There was no need for her to launch an urgent application in this Court for that purpose.

[22] Kentridge AJ made it clear in his judgment in *S v Zuma and Others* that applications for direct access are to be entertained only in exceptional circumstances and not merely to avoid the consequences of incorrect procedures that have been followed. If, notwithstanding the pending appeal, Bruce is entitled to raise the constitutionality of section 150(3) of the Insolvency Act in separate proceedings, she can initiate such proceedings in the High Court; but if she is not entitled to do so, she cannot avoid the consequences of her earlier omission by applying to this Court for relief.

[23] I am satisfied that grounds for direct access have not been established and that this is not a proper case for the granting of such relief. The application for direct access is accordingly dismissed.

Mechanics of case selection

The mechanics of case selection are relatively simple. Once an application for leave to appeal is lodged with the Constitutional Court, the President of the Court refers the application to all members of the Court. The judges decide in conference whether or not to grant the leave to appeal.[162] At least eight judges are present at the conference.[163] Leave to appeal would be refused if a majority of the justices took the view that there

---

[162] *Member of the Executive Council Government of Gauteng* para 15.
[163] *Pennington* para 51.

were no reasonable prospects of success.[164] Applications for direct access,[165] or applications for leave to appeal[166] are usually dealt with summarily without oral or written argument. However, the president may give further directions to the parties for further submissions as to whether to grant direct access.[167] In appeals from courts other than the SCA which are of an urgent nature, and when the Court is not in term, the President of the Court may grant, but not refuse, leave to appeal.[168] The President of the Court may vest this power (or for that matter any other power or authority under the Court Rules) in any other judge or judges whom the president designated for that purpose.[169]

Constitutional review by the ordinary courts and transformation[170]

The creation of the new Constitutional Court allowed for the selection of judges who would be more likely to be sensitive to the realities of the new order. Unfortunately, the final Constitution permits the ordinary courts to pronounce on constitutional questions. South Africa would possibly have done better to have adopted the European approach and divested ordinary courts of the ability to rule on constitutional questions, at least until the majority of the judiciary was made more legitimate. Most of the judges on the bench

were appointed by the heads of state of the apartheid order.[171] The apartheid governments mostly appointed judges who were sympathetic to its racial policies.[172] Political factors were given greater priority than merit, with better qualified persons being passed over and preference being given to pro-government Afrikaners, and relatively unknown candidates favouring government's views.[173] Sydney Kentridge asserts that most lawyers knew about these appointments but refrained from discussing them because to do so would have impaired the dignity and reputation of the Supreme Court.[174] There is an erroneous assumption that a lawyer's training and experience at the bar will produce an independent frame of mind and a quest for justice.[175] This is not to say there were no judges who were opposed to the philosophies of the government. However, the majority of appointees to the bench were pro-apartheid and arguably continue to hold political views and attitudes of the previous era. To presume that a judge, on assuming the position on the bench, will become liberated and espouse different values and behave differently from his or her previous disposition, is to re-echo the assumption that the judiciary is a majestic institution. Members of the judiciary come to the bench with their individual political assumptions and social values, which colour their view of issues. In exercising his or her discretionary powers, each judge's choice is influenced by his or her background and personality.[176]

---

[164] *Supra.*

[165] Constitutional Court Rules, s 17(5).

[166] Section 18(9)*(b)*.

[167] Section 17(4)(4)*(a)*.

[168] See generally Constitutional Court Rules.

[169] Section 1(2).

[170] Part of this discussion is adapted, with permission, from Ziyad Motala 'Independence of the Judiciary, Prospects and Limitations of Judicial Review in Terms of the United States Model in a New South African Order: Towards an Alternative Judicial Structure' (1991) 55 *Albany Law Review* 367.

[171] In terms of s 10 of the previous Supreme Court Act 59 of 1959.

[172] A number of eminent jurists have alluded to the government appointing judges in terms of political preferences both during and in the pre-NP rule era. Sydney Kentridge 'Telling the Truth about Law' (1982) 99 *South African Law Journal* 652.

[173] John D Jackson *Justice in South Africa* London: Secker & Warberg 1980, 24–5.

[174] Ibid.

[175] Edwin Cameron, Harold Rudolph, and Dirk van Zyl Smit 'Judicial Appointments' (1980) *De Rebus* 430.

[176] This is not to posit that there will be at all times will be a harmony of political and social values between the judge and the executive responsible for appointing the particular member of the judiciary. Eg Chief Justice Warren of the USSC was appointed by a conservative Republican President Eisenhower and proved to be a great social engineer. It was during Warren's era on the bench that

It would have been better if the new order had the option of legitimizing the judiciary by re-staffing the entire court system. This would also have prevented the likelihood of a rearguard action being mounted by backward-looking judges. For example, in the period immediately following the Second World War, the German judges appointed by the defunct Nazi party posed a potentially grave problem of pronouncing judgments that 'be-longed' to the disgraced order.[177] The Allied forces resorted to closing down all the German courts and dismissing all judges and prosecutors. Initially, they contemplated keeping the courts closed for a period of ten years. During this period they hoped to re-educate a whole new generation of judges.[178] They encouraged retired judges (who sat on the bench before the Nazi era), to return to the bench. However, the drastic action of dismissing all the Nazi-era judges would have caused a rupture in the entire judicial system. Subsequently, the Allied powers allowed the former judges back after conducting individual background checks into their roles in the Third Reich courts.[179] If such a course of action were followed in South Africa, it would have necessi-tated an investigation and profile of each and every judge sitting on the bench – a very difficult undertaking.[180] Such a course of action was not available in South Africa, and would have caused a rupture of the entire judicial system, as discovered in the German situation.

A variation on the above course of action would have been to allow the judges appointed by the previous order to sit on the bench at the discretion of the new government. This was the course of action was followed in some African countries, particularly Tanzania, at independence.[181] In terms of the arrangement, the expatriate judges served on a temporary basis and their services could be terminated after having been given six months notice.[182] The arrangement is undesirable because it gives the government of the day the power to dismiss judges with whom the govern-ment feels uncomfortable. It is not possible, in these circumstances, for the judges to fulfil their duty fearlessly, because there is always a danger that their services will be terminated. Therefore, the creation of the new Constitutional Court was necessary to provide legitimacy for judicial review.

In light of the reality of facing reactionary judges in the lower courts, it would have been preferable for the ordinary courts not to have been afforded the opportunity of ruling on constitu-tional questions, even though the decisions can ultimately be overturned on appeal to the Constitutional Court. In a litany of decisions, such as the *South African Rugby Union*[183] case in which the president was dragged into court to justify his use of his constitutional powers; the *City Council of Pretoria* case pertaining to different assessments for electricity and water in white and black areas;[184] the matter involving affirmative action in the Justice Department,[185] and the *Western Province Education*[186] case involving criteria for hiring teachers, the lower court judges identified with the ideology and, arguably, the orientation of the old order. Legal purists could argue that legal rules and not ideology should be

---

most of the historic decisions striking down racial segregation such as *Brown v Board of Education* were delivered. Overall, however, it is impossible to ignore the history, socialization, training, and background of the judiciary.

[177] Ingo Muller *Hitler's Justice: The Courts of the Third Reich*, translated by Deborah Lucas Schneider. Cambridge: Harvard University Press 1989, 196. See the judgment of Hans Karl Filbinger where the judge after the war sentenced a soldier to six months imprisonment because the soldier refused to obey his commander who ordered the soldier to wear the swastika and other Nazi symbols on his uniform, 196.

[178] Muller 204.

[179] Ibid.

[180] As the Germans had discovered it was difficult to interview and profile each of the judges.

[181] Telford Georges *Law and its Administration in a One-party State: Selected Speeches of Telford Georges*, compiled by RW James and FM Kassam. Nairobi: East African Literature Bureau 1973, 25.

[182] Ibid.

[183] *South African Rugby Union and Others v President of the RSA and Others* 1998 (10) BCLR 1256 (T).

[184] *Walker v Stadsraad van Pretoria* 1997 (3) BCLR 416 (T).

[185] *Public Servants Association of South Africa v Minister of Justice* 1997 (5) BCLR 577 (T).

[186] *Grove Primary School v Minister of Education and Others* 1997 (4) SA 982 (C).

the guiding force in the decisions of judges.[187] From a legal point of view, it is conceivable that both the decision of the lower court and the Constitutional Court could be supported in cases such as *City Council of Pretoria*[188] and the *Rugby Union* cases.[189] The cases, however, highlight the problems associated with decisions made by a judiciary from an old order in matters involving a profound interplay between legal and political factors. In the *SARFU 2* decision, the Constitutional Court ruled that the lower court had erred in requiring the president to testify, before an open court, in order to justify the president's appointment of a commission of enquiry into the affairs of the *South African Rugby Football Union*. The Court held that the lower court judge, De Villiers J, had on a litany of issues, misconstrued the facts and the law.[190] The *SARFU 2* decision portrays a disturbing picture, and it is almost as if the lower court judge and the Constitutional Court judges were reading from two different scripts and emerged with two opposite understandings of the facts.

While politically South Africa has moved beyond apartheid rule, the majority of lower court judges have not necessarily 'decolonized'. South Africa is in need of severe social, economic, and racial transformation. The challenges in several cases pertained to government action directed towards the necessary transformation. The lower court judges at times do not show sufficient understanding of the nature of many of these actions directed towards transformation and integration.

In a society in need of transformation and integration, a central and decisive judicial organ which has legitimacy and the vision to provide uniform standards is necessary. When we look at the European Union (EU), which consists of fifteen member states, the treaties of the EU as amended – as in art 41 of the ECSC Treaty –[191] gave the European Court of Justice the 'sole jurisdiction to give preliminary rulings on the validity of acts of the High Authority and the Council where such validity is in issue in proceedings before a national court or tribunal'. Similarly, under art 177 (*c*) of the EEC Treaty, and under art 150 of the Euratom Treaty,[192] the highest courts in the various jurisdictions are called upon to refer a matter of EU law to the European Court of Justice for a ruling, where a decision on EU law is necessary to enable the Court to give a judgment. The three treaties collectively represent the Constitution of the EU.[193] According to some scholars, the EU is evolving into a new federal entity.[194] The provisions in the treaties which require reference to the European Court of Justice are designed to assist integration and harmonization of law in the EU, by preventing different courts from providing divergent interpretations on important aspects of EU law.[195] The preliminary ruling by the European Court of Justice helps the courts in member countries to apply EU law, and effectively give EU law its full effect.[196] In other words, there is a recognition that courts used old habits and customs that may not be best suited to the process of integration and harmonization which the political leaders seek to accomplish.

---

[187] See the views quoted by BO Nwabueze *Presidentialism in Commonwealth Africa* London: C Hurst 1975.

[188] Which was overturned on appeal to the Constitutional Court in the *City of Pretoria v Walker* CCT 8/97 (17 February 1998), now cited as 1998 (2) SA 363 (CC); 1998 (3) BCLR 257 (CC).

[189] *South African Rugby Football Union* case, which was overturned by the Constitutional Court in *The President of the Republic of South Africa and Others v South African Rugby Football Union and Others* CCT 16/98 (2 December 1998), now cited as 1999 (2) SA 14 (CC); 1999 (2) BCLR 175 (CC) (*SARFU 2*).

[190] *SARFU 2*, paras 28, 36, 193, 196–197, 234, 249.

[191] Signed in May 1952 and came into effect in July 1952.

[192] The EEC and Euratom were signed in terms of the Treaty of Rome in March 1957, and both came into effect in January 1958.

[193] Daniel J Elazar and Ilan Greilsammer 'A Political Science Perspective' in *Integration through Law: Europe and the American Federal Experience*, edited by Mauro Cappelletti, et al. Berlin: W de Gruyter 1986, 93.

[194] Francis Joseph and Kenneth Karst 'A Juridical Perspective' in *Integration through Law: Europe and the American Federal Experience*, 170–2.

[195] Henry G Schemers and Denis F Waelbroeck *Judicial Protection in the European Communities* Deventer: Kluwer Law and Taxation, 5th edition, 1992, 393.

[196] Op cit 394.

At end of the Third Reich, Germany experienced similar problems from conservative judges, who were appointed under Hitler and who failed to come to grips with what the past represented.[197] In Germany, the old-guard judges were less able to act as an obstructionist element in seminal cases such as the *Civil Servant Loyalty* case, and the *Gestapo* case, where the Constitutional Court upheld the termination of benefits to former Nazi officials.[198] The Constitutional Court decisions were criticized by the civil courts who fortunately were not in the constitutional position to provide relief to the former Nazi officials.[199]

The creation in South Africa of the new Constitutional Court was a logical choice. In hindsight, the framers made a critical mistake in allowing the lower courts the power to continue exercising review over the Constitution. Perhaps the new Constitutional Court should have been granted exclusive power over the Constitution for a few years. During this critical period, they could have fleshed out and clarified what the Constitution represents. Once the Constitutional Court has rendered a decision, which interprets the Constitution, it would then be appropriate for the lower courts to apply the law in terms of the standards enunciated by the Constitutional Court.

The approach we are suggesting is based on the practice in the EU pursuant to art 177. Under art 177, the courts of member states are required to refer certain matters to the European Court of Justice for a decision on EU law. The European Court of Justice has, however, held that where the European Court has previously rendered a decision on a matter, and a materially identical matter comes up, there is no need to refer the subsequent matter to the European Court.[200] In other words, where the provision is so clear that there is no 'reasonable doubt as to the manner in which the question raised is to be resolved', only then should there be no reference to the constitutional court.[201] In contrast the Constitutional Court in South Africa has been very reluctant to sit as a court of first instance.[202] There are other alternatives available to prevent any overload, such as the creation of screening communities to filter out frivolous complaints and the setting up of different chambers within the Court.[203] The current situation – which allows recourse to lower courts where the mindset of many judges is still rooted in the old order – wastes time, energy, and resources. It also slows down transformation and nation-building. It would have been preferable to allow the lower court to make a finding of facts but leave the interpretation of the Constitution to the Constitutional Court.

Politics and the appointment of judges

Independence of the judiciary and political appointments of judges

The Constitution provides that the courts are independent and subject only to the Constitution.[204] There are at least nine members on the JSC who are appointed by the legislature and the president. In addition, the Chief Justice and the President of the Constitutional Court are also appointed by the president. One of the conclusions of the African Conference on the Rule of Law held in Nigeria in 1961 was that ways and means should

---

[197] Kurt Sontheimer 'Principles of Human Dignity in the Federal Republic' in *Germany and its Basic Law Past, Present and Future: A German-American Symposium*, edited by Paul Kirchoff and Donald P Kommers Baden-Baden: Nomos 1993, 217.

[198] Donald P Kommers *The Constitutional Jurisprudence of the Federal Republic of West Germany* Durham: Duke University Press 1989, 263 (*Civil Servant Loyalty* case (1975) 39 BVerfGe 334; *Gestapo* case (1957) 6 BVerfGe 132).

[199] Ibid.

[200] *De Costa v Nederlandse Belastingadministratie* (1963) 31 ECR 8010.

[201] *CILFIT Srl v Ministro Della Sanita* 1982 ECR 3415, CCH Common Mkt Rep December, 8875.

[202] *Bruce*, para 8; *Transvaal Agricultural Union v Minister of Land Affairs and the Commission on Restitution of Land Rights* CCT 21/96 (18 November 1996) para 17, now cited as 1997 (2) SA 621 (CC); 1996 (12) BCLR 157 3 (CC); *Besserglik v Minister of Trade, Industry and Tourism and Others* CCT 34/95 (14 May 1996) para 18, now cited as 1996 (6) BCLR 745 (CC); 1996 (4) SA 331 (CC).

[203] As is found in Germany. See Kommers 21–2.

[204] Section 165(2) of the Constitution.

be found to ensure an absolute independence of the judiciary, and to ensure control of the judiciary, by the legal profession.[205] Several constitutions of African states drafted at independence incorporated extraordinary measures to create a non-political appointing process and non-involvement in politics by the judiciary.[206] They attempted to do this by creating JSCs made up of lawyers not involved in politics.[207] The JSCs were entrusted with the responsibility of judicial appointments.[208] This marked a departure from the Anglo-American model where judicial appointments are essentially an executive decision, and sometimes performed in recognition of the judge's political services and social views.

The extraordinary attempts to isolate the judicial appointments from the other political branches is impractical and short-sighted. It ignores the reality that many judicial decisions entail political judgements. In the exercise of this political judgement, the political outlook of the judge is extremely important, particularly to a new nation on the threshold of major social and economic changes. If the judiciary is entrusted with interpretive powers that may have critical political implications, it is crucial that the political views of the judges are taken into account.

The dominant involvement of the other two branches of government in the selection of judges does not undermine the independence of the judiciary. The involvement of the other two branches in the selection of judges is part of the system of checks and balances which accompany separation of powers.[209] In the *First Certification* decision, the Constitutional Court emphasized that legislative and executive appointment of judges do not undermine the independence of the judiciary. The test for independence of the judiciary is whether the judiciary enforces the law impartially and independently of the legislature and the executive.[210]

In re: Certification of the Constitution of the Republic of South Africa
CCT 23/96 (6 September 1996), now cited as (10) BCLR 1253 (CC);
1996 (4) SA 744 (CC)
(notes omitted)
Unanimous decision

[121] It was contended that Parliament and the executive are over-represented on the JSC and that the President, who appoints the Minister of Justice, the Chief Justice, the President of the Constitutional Court and four members of the JSC, and who selects the Constitutional Court judges from the JSC list or lists, has been given too dominant a role in the appointment of judges. The President also has the power in terms of NT 178(2) to select a profession's nominees if there is disagreement within a profession as to who its nominees should be. The President is required to do this after consulting the profession concerned and is also required to consult the JSC before appointing the Chief Justice, and the JSC and the leaders of parties represented in the NA before appointing the President of the Constitutional Court.

[122] CP VI makes provision for a separation of powers between the legislature, executive and judiciary and CP VII requires the judiciary to be 'appropriately qualified, independent and impar-

---

[205] International Commission of Jurists *First African Conference of the Rule of Law, Lagos 1961: A Report on the Proceedings* Geneva: International Commission of Jurists 1961.

[206] Austin Amissah *The Contribution of the Courts to Governments: A West African View* Oxford: Oxford University Press 1981, 98.

[207] Op cit 105–6. Various rules and qualification criteria were imposed pertaining to previous office and eligibility to serve on the bench.

[208] The countries included Kenya, Zambia, Lesotho, Swaziland, Gambia, and Ghana. See Amissah 102. There were variations in the composition of the JSC with members being appointed by the professional societies as well as the Ministry of Justice or a combination of both.

[209] *In re: Certification of the Constitution of The Republic of South Africa* CCT 23/96 (6 September 1996) para 123, now cited as 1996 (10) BCLR 1253 (CC); 1996 (4) SA 744 (CC).

[210] *Supra* para 124.

tial'. NT 174(1) requires that a person appointed to judicial office be 'appropriately qualified' and a 'fit and proper person' for such office. These are objective criteria subject to constitutional control by the courts, and meet the requirements of CP VII in that regard. The CPs do not, however, require a JSC to be established and contain no provision dealing specifically with the appointment of judges.

[123] The requirement of CP VI that there be a separation of powers between the legislature, executive and judiciary is dealt with elsewhere in this judgment. An essential part of the separation of powers is that there be an independent judiciary. The mere fact, however, that the executive makes or participates in the appointment of judges is not inconsistent with the doctrine of separation of powers or with the judicial independence required by CP VII. In many countries in which there is an independent judiciary and a separation of powers, judicial appointments are made either by the executive or by Parliament or by both. What is crucial to the separation of powers and the independence of the judiciary is that the judiciary should enforce the law impartially and that it should function independently of the legislature and the executive. NT 165 is directed to this end. It vests the judicial authority in the courts and protects the courts against any interference with that authority. Constitutionally, therefore, all judges are independent.

[124] Appointment of judges by the executive or a combination of the executive and Parliament would not be inconsistent with the CPs. The JSC contains significant representation from the judiciary, the legal professions and political parties of the opposition. It participates in the appointment of the Chief Justice, the President of the Constitutional Court and the Constitutional Court judges, and it selects the judges of all other courts. As an institution it provides a broadly based selection panel for appointments to the judiciary and provides a check and balance to the power of the executive to make such appointments. In the absence of any obligation to establish such a body, the fact that it could have been constituted differently, with greater representation being given to the legal profession and the judiciary, is irrelevant. Its composition was a political choice which has been made by the CA within the framework of the CPs. We cannot interfere with that decision, and in the circumstances the objection to NT 178 must be rejected.

Judicial review as independent from other branches of government: no ouster of the Court's jurisdiction

Under the previous constitutional order, parliament frequently adopted statutes which ousted the jurisdiction of the courts from ruling on the validity of executive actions. In some constitutions, even though there is a bill of rights the jurisdiction of the High Court may be curtailed. For example, the United States Constitution provides – in art III s 2 – that the Supreme Court shall exercise appellate jurisdiction with 'such Exceptions, and under such Regulations, as the Congress shall make'. The United States Congress has exercised its authority to withdraw the Courts appellate jurisdiction on politically sensitive issues. For example, after the Civil War, the Congress of the United States adopted a statute that revoked the jurisdiction of the Supreme Court to hear petitions of *habeas corpus* under a previous 1867 Act. In *Ex parte McCardle*, the Supreme Court agreed that such a radical exercise of power, which in effect curtailed the Court's appellate jurisdiction, lay within the power of congress.[211]

Would such an ouster of the Court's jurisdiction pass constitutional muster in South Africa? In addressing this question there are two interrelated issues that need to be addressed. First, what is the judicial role under South Africa's constitutional scheme of separation of powers? Secondly, under the Constitution, who is the final protector of

---

[211] *Ex parte McCardle* 74 US 506 (1868).

individual rights? On the first question, s 165 of the Constitution establishes the independence of the judiciary. Section 165(3) affirms that no person or organ of state may interfere with the functioning of the courts. On the second question, the Constitution provides that everyone has the right to have all legal disputes decided before a court or another independent and impartial tribunal or forum.[212] The Constitution further affirms that everyone has the right to approach a competent court alleging that a right in the Bill of Rights has been infringed or threatened.[213] Arguably, judicial review is made an absolute postulate of the Constitution, both in terms of separation of powers, and as an instrument to secure fundamental liberties. Even actions taken under extraordinary times, such as a declaration of a state of emergency,[214] and other actions taken pursuant to a state of emergency,[215] are subject to judicial review.

In its *First Certification* decision, the Constitutional Court rejected the proposed new text of the Constitution which tried to maintain the provisions of the Labour Relations Act,[216] and the Promotion of National Unity and Reconciliation Act,[217] without constitutional review. Although the decision was rendered in the context of certification of the new Constitution, s 165(2) by providing that the 'courts are independent and subject only to the Constitution and the law', and s 165(3) which states, '[N]o person or organ of state may interfere with the functioning of the courts', should preclude any ouster of the Court's jurisdiction.

In *Azapo*,[218] the Constitutional Court visited the question of the ouster of the Court's jurisdiction, and addressed the denial to an individual of the right to have justiciable disputes settled by a court. The dispute in *Azapo* arose out of the adoption of the Promotion of National Unity and Reconciliation Act.[219] The epilogue contained in the last clause of the interim Constitution as a post-end bill[220] stated 'that the adoption of this Constitution provides a foundation for South Africans to transcend the divisions and strife of the past'. It further proclaimed that there is a need for reconciliation, understanding, and reparation, but not for vengeance and retaliation. In pursuit of such reconciliation and reconstruction, the epilogue required that 'amnesty shall be granted in respect of acts, omissions and offences associated with political objectives and committed in the course of the conflicts of the past'.[221] It went on to provide that parliament 'shall adopt a law providing for the mechanisms, criteria and procedures, including tribunals, if any through which such amnesty shall be dealt with at any time after the law has been passed'.[222] Pursuant to the above mandate, parliament passed the Promotion of National Unity and Reconciliation Act to grant amnesty to persons who had committed political acts in the past, and who make a full disclosure of their past deeds.

The Amnesty Act provides that the Amnesty Committee shall grant amnesty to all persons who comply with the provisions of the Act: that 'they have committed a political offence during the prescribed period, and have made a full disclosure'.[223] 'A person who has been granted amnesty in respect of any act, omission or offence shall henceforth enjoy full immunity from all criminal and civil actions'.[224] In *Azapo*, the applicants

---

[212] Article 34 of the Constitution.

[213] Article 38.

[214] Section 37(3).

[215] Such as eg detention or derogation from fundamental rights under ss 37(5), 37(6), and 37(7).

[216] *First Certification* decision para 149.

[217] *Supra* para 150.

[218] *Azanian Peoples Organization (Azapo) and Others v President of the Republic of South Africa* CCT 17/96 (25 July 1996), now cited as 1996 (8) BCLR 1015 (CC); 1996 (4) SA 671 (CC).

[219] Act 30 of 1995 (Amnesty Act).

[220] Constitution of the Republic of South Africa Act 200 of 1993 (interim Consitution).

[221] The post-amble of the interim Constitution.

[222] The post-amble.

[223] Section 21 of the Amnesty Act.

[224] Section s 21(7).

challenged the Constitutionality of s 20(7) of the Amnesty Act by arguing that it is unconstitutional for the Amnesty Committee to grant amnesty for crimes such as murder and torture. The applicants further argued that the amnesty provisions violate s 22 of the interim Constitution which provides that 'every person shall have the right to have justiciable disputes settled by a court of law or, where appropriate, another independent or impartial forum'.[225] The applicants in oral argument also asserted that s 20(7) of the Amnesty Act was unconstitutional in all respects because the Constitution did not authorize the granting of such civil or criminal amnesty.[226] The Court ruled that s 20(7) of the Amnesty Act impacts upon fundamental rights,[227] but does not violate the Constitution because the Constitution itself in the epilogue authorized such a violation.[228]

This finding of the Court is open to serious question. Like the final Constitution, the interim Constitution provided that the judicial authority of the country is vested in the courts.[229] The interim Constitution was more explicit than the final Constitution in providing that the Constitutional Court shall be the final arbiter over all matters relating to the Constitution, including any alleged violation – or threatened violation – of any fundamental right entrenched in Chapter 3 of the Constitution.[230] It also provided that '[No] person and no organ of state shall interfere with judicial officers in the performance of their function.'[231] Any person whose rights (as entrenched in the Bill of Rights) were violated, had a right to apply to a competent court of law, or other independent and impartial forum for appropriate relief.[232] While the post-end bill provided that

parliament shall provide for procedures and tribunals, if any, through which amnesty shall be granted, this provision had to be read in relation to the other provisions of the Constitution; particularly the power of judicial review, and the right of individuals to seek enforcement of their rights before the courts. The post-end bill did not authorize the ouster of the courts' traditional function of adjudicating over disputes. Such function is guaranteed in other parts of the Constitution as a fundamental principle of the Constitution.

A cardinal principle of constitutionalism is separation of powers. The legislature makes law, the executive executes the law, and as the interim Constitution and the final Constitution provide, the judiciary adjudicates over disputes with respect to the law. The Promotion of National Unity and Reconciliation Act took away the competence of the court in a particular category of disputes (very much like ouster clauses under the apartheid regime), and placed the adjudicative function in a number of executive appointees. In the interests of efficiency and prevention of tyranny, the separation of powers doctrine, as a cardinal principle of constitutionalism, requires that the three branches of government fulfil their respective functions within their domain. The adjudicative function and interpretation of statutes is a quintessential judicial function. The Court should have found that it is untenable and unconstitutional for executive appointees (as provided for in the Promotion of National Unity and Reconciliation Act), who clearly were not part of the judicial branch of government, to carry out what is essentially an adjudicative function.[233] It is the function of a

---

[225] *Azapo* para 8.

[226] *Supra* para 15.

[227] *Supra* para 9.

[228] *Supra* paras 10 and 14.

[229] Article 96(1) of the interim Constitution.

[230] Section 98(1)*(a)*.

[231] Section 96(3).

[232] Article 22.

[233] Under separation of powers, it is the judicial branch of government that interprets a statute, and decides the rights of specific persons under a statute as laid out in criteria prescribed by the legislature. For a very compelling presentation of this argument, see Justice Powell's concurring opinion in the *Chadha* decision where Justice Powell ruled that reviewing the law in an individual setting is a judicial function upon which other branches of government cannot encroach. *INS v Chadha* 462 US 919, 952–954 (1983).

competent court to determine the essential facts and apply the relevant law in justiciable disputes between parties.

The Irish Supreme Court has stated that under modern constitutions the administration of justice is confined exclusively to the judges and courts.[234] Where the legislature attempted to conclusively remove such determinations from the courts, the Irish Supreme Court ruled it is an invalid infringement of the judicial power.[235] Similarly, the German Constitutional Court has ruled that access to the courts cannot be substituted with recourse to review by auxiliary bodies appointed by parliament.[236] In the absence of any constitutional change that deprives the courts of their jurisdiction, the Constitutional Court in South Africa should have protected the overarching principle of judicial review. Through ordinary legislation such as the Promotion of National Unity and Reconciliation Act, there can be no ouster of the courts' jurisdiction, nor exercise of the adjudicative process by an ad hoc body, which is an extension of the executive.

In his concurring opinion in *Azapo*, Didcott J stated that the Committee on Amnesty and the Committee on Reparation and Rehabilitation are independent and impartial.[237] This finding is not consistent with international human rights interpretations. A temporary commission appointed by the executive branch of government, as the Promotion of National Unity And Reconciliation Act provided for, without the trappings and independence of a 'true' court, cannot be deemed to be an independent and impartial forum. The ordinary meaning of 'independent' is separation of other organs of government in terms of the doctrine of separation of powers.[238] Such impartiality and independence cannot be achieved

through ad hoc or special tribunals. It is required that the tribunal be 'competent'. A competent tribunal means that the jurisdiction of the court must have been previously established by law.[239] The Court's decision in *Azapo*, validating the diminution of the Court's authority and denial of access to the Court, is understood narrowly as flowing from the post-amble of the interim Constitution, and as only applying to crimes under the apartheid era. In *Bernstein and Others v Bester NO and Others*,[240] the Court, *per* Ackermann J, warned against allowing the legislature from turning themselves into courts.[241]

Enforcement Mechanisms

The Court's discretionary power

The Constitution, in various sections, speaks to the issue of remedies: s 2 provides that 'this Constitution is the supreme law' and that any 'law or conduct inconsistent with it is invalid, and the obligations imposed by it must be fulfilled'. Under s 38 of the Bill of Rights, any person covered in the section 'has a right to approach a competent court, alleging that a right in the Bill of Rights has been infringed or threatened, and the court may grant appropriate relief, including a declaration of rights'. The Court has several enforcement mechanisms available, including declaring that a statute or conduct is invalid.[242] Section 172(1)(a) requires a declaration of invalidity only to the extent that the law or conduct is inconsistent with the Constitution. Moreover, s 172(1)(b) permits the granting of any order that is just and equitable, including limiting the retrospective effect of the order,[243] and suspending the declaration of

---

[234] JM Kelly, et al *The Irish Constitution* Dublin: Butterworths 1994, 370, 386.

[235] Op cit 386.

[236] Kommers 140.

[237] *Azapo* para 53.

[238] Richard B Lillich 'Civil Rights' in *Human Rights in International Law: Legal and Policy Issues*, edited by Theodor Meron. Oxford: Clarendon Press 1984, 141.

[239] Ibid.

[240] *Bernstein and Others v Bester and Others NO* CCT 23/95 (27 March 1996), now cited as 1996 (4) BCLR 449 (CC); 1996 (2) SA 751 (CC).

[241] *Supra* para 105.

[242] Section 172(1) of the Constitution.

[243] Section 172(1) *(b)*(i).

invalidity for any period and on any conditions to allow the authorities to correct the defect.[244]

The Court has considerable discretion in the way it frames its orders. For example, it could make an order that would be prospective, or it could make an order of invalidity with respect to all cases which have not yet been finalized.[245] Under the interim Constitution, the nature of the Court's order would depend on considerations such as 'justice and good government'.[246] Also, under the interim Constitution if an order of retrospective application would cause great uncertainty and dislocation in the administration of justice, the Court would limit the application of its order.[247] For example, if retrospective application of the law would result in the rehearing of a large number of trials, this might not be in the interest of good government.[248] Under the final Constitution, the Court would still consider the interest of good government in determining what is a just and equitable order.[249] However, under the final Constitution the interest of good government, although it might be the most decisive factor, is only one of many possible factors to consider.[250] Where a person has been wronged, as a general rule, the Court will try to place the aggrieved person in the same position the person would have been if the wrong was not committed.[251] In *Hoffmann*, the appellant was unfairly discriminated against by being denied employment with South African Airways (SAA) because of his HIV status. The Court ordered SAA to employ the appellant as a cabin steward with immediate effect.[252] There are situations where a court may rule in the plaintiff's favour, but in the interest of justice and good government, still not grant the plaintiff any consequential relief.[253] In *East Zulu Motors*, the Constitutional Court found that the local government had violated the applicant's constitutional rights by not providing the applicant the right to appeal against the local government's decision to permit rezoning of certain land. In the meanwhile, development had already taken place on the rezoned property. The Constitutional Court upheld the lower court decision that the failure to provide an appeal, although it may have been unconstitutional, should not be made effective immediately.[254] The Court, *per* Madala J, in refusing leave to appeal, held that there was no prospect that the Court would make an order on appeal which would be of benefit to the applicant.[255] This was an instance where the interest of good government required the Court to deny consequential relief.

There are times when the Court interprets the 'interests of good government' as requiring no special treatment for a particular litigant. In *Steyn v The State*, applicant succeeded in getting the Constitutional Court to validate s 309 *(b)* and *(c)* of the Criminal Procedure Act. The said provisions of the Act required the permission of the magistrate or of Judge President of of the division of the High Court having jurisdiction, before a convicted person could lodge an appeal against a decision of a magistrate. Despite their legal success, the Court felt that there was no reason why applicants should be singled out for relief whilst others on the same position would not obtain the same relief.[256]

A person who suffers an infringement of a right

---

[244] Section 172(1)*(b)*(ii).

[245] O'Regan J in *Scagell* para 36.

[246] *S v Mbatha, S v Prinsloo* para 30.

[247] *Zuma* para 43.

[248] *Supra*.

[249] Ackermann J in *National Coalition for Gay and Lesbian Equality* para 94.

[250] *Supra. First National Bank of South Africa Limited v Land and Agriculture Bank of South Africa* CCT 15/00 (9 June 2000) para 18.

[251] *Hoffmann v South African Airways* CCT 17/00 (28 September 2000) para 50, now cited as 2000 (10) BCLR 1211 (CC); 2001 (1) SA 1 (CC).

[252] *Supra* paras 50 and 61.

[253] *Steyn v The State* CCT 19/00 (29 November 2000) para 52, now cited as 2001 (2) BCLR 118 (CC); 2001 (2) SA 1 (CC); *East Zulu Motors* para 9.

[254] *East Zulu Motors (Pty) Ltd v Empangeni/Ngwlezane Transitional Local Council and Others* CCT 44/96 (4 December 1997) paras 8–9, now cited as 1998 (2) SA 61 (CC); 1998 (2) BCLR 1 (CC).

[255] *Supra* para 10.

[256] *Steyn v The State* CCT 14/97 (29 November 2000) para 52, now cited as 2001 (1) BCLR 52 (CC); 2001 (1) SA 1146 (CC).

under the Bill of Rights is entitled to 'appropriate relief'. What appropriate relief is would depend on the particulars of each case.[257] In *Fose*, Ackerman J stated that:

appropriate relief will in essence be relief that is required to protect and enforce the Constitution. Depending on the circumstances of each particular case the relief may be a declaration of rights, an interdict, a *mandamus* or such other relief as may be required to ensure that the rights enshrined in the Constitution are protected and enforced. If it is necessary to do so, the courts may even have to fashion new remedies to secure the protection and enforcement of these all-important rights.[258]

A declaration of invalidity is the most far-reaching remedy. In addition to invalidations, granting an interdict, and a declaration of rights, additional remedies recognized by the Constitutional Court include reading down, severance, temporary invalidations, *mandamus*, and damages – all of which limit the extent to which a law may be declared unconstitutional.

Reading down: presumption of constitutionality

Where a constitutional provision is open to different interpretations, there is an interpretive technique whereby the Court will read the statute in a way which makes it compatible with the Constitution.[259] The Court will not engage in reading down where the language of the statute is clear.[260] To do so would mean the Court is rewriting the statute.[261]

In *Mistry*, the Constitutional Court declared s 28(1) of the Medicines and Related Substances Control Act[262] to be in violation of the right to privacy. Section 28(1) permitted an inspector to enter upon any premises, place, vehicle, vessel, or aircraft where there are reasonable grounds to believe that any medicine or schedule substance is contained therein.[263] An inspector also had powers to inspect items,[264] and to seize any item as evidence of contravention of the provisions of the Act.[265] The Court held that the search provisions were overbroad in permitting entry and inspection of any premises, including private residences.[266] Respondents asked the Court to preserve the constitutionality of the statute by reading it down by interpreting s 28(1) to only allow searches 'for the proper enforcement of this Act'.[267] The Court held that where the terms of the statute are clear on its face, as in this case, the Court could not provide a reading down, which in effect would mean rewriting the statute.[268]

On the other hand, where the law is unclear in terms of its meaning, the Court feels obliged to interpret the statute in a way that is consistent with the Constitution (as opposed to striking down the provision as unconstitutional). When the Court makes such a ruling, it is in effect telling the state what are the permissible applications of the statute.[269]

In *Bernstein and Others v Bester and Others*,[270] the Constitutional Court was presented with a

[257] *City Council of Pretoria v Walker* para 95.

[258] *Fose* para 19.

[259] *S v Bhulwana; S v Gwadiso* CCT 12/95 (29 November 1995) para 28, now cited as 1995 (12) BCLR 1579 (CC); 1996 (1) SA 388 (CC). Hogg likens this approach to a method of interpretation tied to the notion of judicial restraint. See Hogg 859.

[260] *Bhulwana* para 21. *Mistry* para 32.

[261] *Bhulwana* para 29.

[262] Act 101 of 1965.

[263] Section 28(1)*(a)*.

[264] Section 28(1)*(b)*.

[265] Sections 28(1)*(c)* and *(d)*.

[266] *Mistry* para 23.

[267] *Supra* para 31.

[268] *Supra* para 32. See also Mokgoro J in *Case and Another v Minister of Safety and Security and Others; Curtis v Minister of Safety and Security and Others* CCT 20/95; CCT 21/95 (9 May 1996) para 78, now cited as 1996 (3) SA 617 (CC); 1996 (5) BCLR 609 (CC).

[269] Patrick Mackelem, et al *Constitutional Law of Canada* Toronto: Edmond Montgomery Publishers 1994, 264.

[270] CCT 23/95 (27 March 1996), now cited as 1996 (4) BCLR 449 (CC); 1996 (2) SA 751 (CC).

challenge to ss 417 and 418 of the Companies Act.[271] Under these sections, the Master of the Court could summon and question directors and officers of a company in connection with the winding up of that company. The applicants argued that the section violated their right to privacy and their right to be free from self-incrimination, both protected under the interim Constitution. The Court, *per* Ackerman J, held there was nothing in ss 417 and 418 of the Act which compelled a witness to answer any incriminating question.[272] Instead, the section obliged a witness who was summoned to appear before a hearing. The Court interpreted the sections in the statute by distinguishing between an obligation to attend a hearing, as opposed to an obligation to answer any question put to the witness. The Court in effect construed ss 417 and 418 in a way which recognized the applicant's constitutional rights to privacy and not to incriminate themselves.

By ruling that any person summoned was not compelled to answer a question that would incriminate them, the Court in effect limited the possible application of the sections.

Reading in

Where a statute is under inclusive in terms of the category of persons it covers, the Court could adopt the technique of reading in. Rather than declaring the statute, or parts of the statute, invalid, by reading in, the Court extends the coverage to include protected persons who should not have been omitted from the statute.[273] In *National Coalition for Gay and Lesbian Equality*, the Court was faced with a challenge to s 25(5) of the Aliens Control Act,[274] which provided preferential treatment to a foreign national applying for an immigrant permit who is 'the spouse of a person permanently and lawfully resident in the Republic'. The section did not accord the same treatment to a foreign national who was similarly placed in all other respects except that they were in a same-sex relationship with a permanent resident in the republic.[275] The Court cured the omission in s 25(5) of the Act by reading in after the word 'spouse' the following additional words: 'or partner, in a permanent same-sex life partnership'.[276] The Court will only resort to this remedy when it is able to read in words with sufficient precision and when reading in does not intrude on budgetary decisions.[277]

> *National Coalition for Gay and Lesbian Equality and Others v Minister of Home Affairs and Others*
> **CCT 10/99 (2 December 1999), now cited as 2000 (2) SA 1 (CC); 2000 (1) BCLR 39 (CC)**
> (notes omitted)
>
> [15]...The attack on the constitutional validity of section 25(5) concentrated on the fact that it enables preferential treatment to be given to a foreign national applying for an immigration permit who is 'the spouse ... of a person permanently and lawfully resident in the Republic', but not to a foreign national who, though similarly placed in all other respects, is in a same-sex life partnership with a person permanently and lawfully resident in the Republic.
>
> [75] In deciding to read words into a statute, a court should also bear in mind that it will not be appropriate to read words in, unless in so

---

[271] Act 61 of 1973, as amended.

[272] *Bernstein* para 60.

[273] *National Coalition for Gay and Lesbian Equality and Others v Minister of Home Affairs and Others* CCT 10/99 (2 December 1999) para 64, now cited as 2000 (1) BCLR 39 (CC); 2000 (2) SA 1 (CC) (*National Coalition for Gay and Lesbian Equality 2*).

[274] Act 96 of 1991.

[275] *National Coalition for Gay and Lesbian Equality 2* para 15.

[276] *Supra* para 86.

[277] *Supra* para 75.

doing a court can define with sufficient precision how the statute ought to be extended in order to comply with the Constitution. Moreover, when reading in (as when severing) a court should endeavour to be as faithful as possible to the legislative scheme within the constraints of the Constitution. Even where the remedy of reading in is otherwise justified, it ought not to be granted where it would result in an unsupportable budgetary intrusion. In determining the scope of the budgetary intrusion, it will be necessary to consider the relative size of the group which the reading in would add to the group already enjoying the benefits. Where reading in would, by expanding the group of persons protected, sustain a policy of long standing or one that is constitutionally encouraged, it should be preferred to one removing the protection completely.

[97] Section 25(5) of the Aliens Control Act 96 of 1991, by omitting to confer on persons, who are partners in permanent same-sex life partnerships, the benefits it extends to spouses, unfairly discriminates, on the grounds of their sexual orientation and marital status, against partners in such same-sex partnerships who are permanently and lawfully resident in the Republic. Such unfair discrimination limits the equality rights of such partners guaranteed to them by section 9 of the Constitution and their right to dignity under section 10. This limitation is not reasonable or justifiable in an open and democratic society based on human dignity, equality and freedom and accordingly does not satisfy the requirements of section 36(1) of the Constitution. This omission in section 25(5) of the Act is therefore inconsistent with the Constitution. It would not be an appropriate remedy to declare the whole of section 25(5) invalid. Instead, it would be appropriate to read in, after the word 'spouse' in the section, the words 'or partner, in a permanent same-sex life partnership'. The reading in of these words comes into effect from the making of the order in this judgment.

Severance

Where the court is faced with a statute which is unconstitutional, and it is possible to separate the good from the bad, the Court will invalidate the bad part and give effect to the part which is constitutional.[278] In other words, the Court will limit the invalidation of the statute to the parts which are unconstitutional, while preserving those parts which are constitutional. Severance will only be performed when the bad parts can be 'cleanly' deleted without interfering with the good.[279] Commenting on the doctrine of severance, the Constitutional Court in *Prinsloo v Van der Linde and Another*,[280] observed that their task is not to find the one 'correct' interpretation of a statutory provision, but given more than one reasonably possible construction, to prefer one which is consistent with the interim Constitution: '. . . [A]mbiguity must be resolved by favouring the construction which keeps the provision constitutionally alive, provided the construction is reasonable.'[281] Where it is not possible to delete the bad parts from the good, or where severance will result in the statute having a meaning different from what the legislature envisaged, the Court would be reluctant to engage in severance.[282]

In *Coetzee v The Government; Matiso v The Commanding Officer, Port Elizabeth Prison and Others*,[283] the Court ruled that s 65A to 65M of the Magistrates' Courts Act,[284] which permitted

---

[278] *Case* para 70.

[279] *Scagell and Others v Attorney-General of the Western Cape and Others* CCT 42/95 (12 September 1996) para 20, now cited as 1996 (11) BCLR 1446 (CC); 1997 (2) SA 368 (CC); *Case* para 70. *Chief Direko Lesapo* para 31.

[280] *Prinsloo v Van der Linde and Another* CCT 4/96 (18 April 1997), now cited as 1997 (6) BCLR 759 (CC); 1997 (3) SA 1012 (CC).

[281] *Supra* para 13.

[282] *Case*, per Mokgoro J, paras 72–73.

[283] *Coetzee v Government of South Africa and Others; Matiso v The Commanding Officer, Port Elizabeth Prison and Others* CCT 19/94, 22/94 (22 September 1995), now cited as 1995 (10) BCLR 1382 (CC); 1995 (4) SA 631 (CC).

[284] Act 32 of 1944, as amended.

the imprisonment of judgment debtors who were unable to make payment because of a lack of financial resources, was unconstitutional.[285] The Court further considered whether the sections could be severed so as to distinguish between those debtors who fail to pay because of lack of means, as opposed to other debtors who refuse to pay for other reasons. There were parts of the statute that related to the categories of debtors that could not be severed. It was not possible to sever the parts relating to imprisonment.[286] The Court, *per* Kriegler J, set out the approach to severance by stating:

[15] This conclusion obliges one to consider the question of severability. Indeed, there are two questions to be answered with regard to the possible severance of the provisions of the law not consistent with the Constitution. First, can one excise the provisions which render the option of imprisonment unconstitutional because they do not distinguish between those who can pay but will not from those who cannot pay? If not, can the provisions which provide for imprisonment itself be severed from the rest of the system for enforcement of judgment debts?

[16] Although severability in the context of constitutional law may often require special treatment, in the present case the trite test can properly be applied: if the good is not dependent on the bad and can be separated from it, one gives effect to the good that remains after the separation if it still gives effect to the main objective of the statute. The test has two parts: first, is it possible to sever the invalid provisions and second, if so, is what remains giving effect to the purpose of the legislative scheme?

[17] In the present instance, it is not possible to excise only those provisions of sections 65A to 65M of the Magistrates' Courts Act which fail to distinguish between the two categories of debtors. In order to do so this Court would have to engage in the details of law making, a constitutional activity given to the legislatures It is, however, possible to sever the provisions which make up

the option of imprisonment. The question then is whether in severing such provisions, the object of the statute will nevertheless remain to be carried out. The answer to this question clearly is yes. The object of sections 65A to 65M of the Magistrates' Courts Act is to provide a system to assist in the collection of judgment debts. Removing one of the options available under the system does not render the system that remains contrary to the purpose of the legislative scheme. Accordingly, the infringing provisions can be severed and the balance of the system can usefully remain in force.

Central to the Court's approach is the idea that severance should not be resorted to where the good part is so bound up with the bad that the good cannot survive on its own.[287] Also, the Court should not engage in severance so as to end up rewriting the statute.[288] In *Case*,[289] Mokgoro J observed:

[72] On the other hand, if we apply a blue pencil to each and every noun form and transitive verb that presents overbreadth problems, we effectively write a new provision that bears only accidental resemblance to that enacted by Parliament. If, as appears to be the case, the scheme behind the statute was to impose a comprehensive scheme of censorship to give effect to a particular moral, cultural and political world-view, it hardly does justice to the 'main object' thereof for this Court to pare it down to prohibit only that discrete set of sexually-oriented expressions that this Court believes may constitutionally be restricted.

[73] For this Court to attempt that textual surgery would entail it departing fundamentally from its assigned role under our Constitution. It is trite but true that our role is to review, rather than to re-draft, legislation. This Court has already had occasion to caution against judicial arrogation of an essentially legislative function in the guise of severance. In *Coetzee v Government of the Republic of South Africa; Matiso v Commanding Officer, Port Elizabeth Prison*, Kriegler, J, noted that

---

285 *Coetzee* paras 10 and 14.
286 *Supra* para 17.
287 *Scagell* para 20. Hogg 391.
288 *Fraser v Children's Court, Pretoria North and Others* CCT 31/96 (5 February 1997) paras 46–49, now cited as 1997 (2) BCLR 153 (CC); 1997 (2) SA 261 (CC).
289 *Case, per* Mokgoro J, paras 72–73.

'In order to [excise only offending provisions] ... this Court would have to engage in the details of law-making, a constitutional activity given to the legislatures'.

Temporary invalidations

There are situations where the Court may declare a law invalid, but suspend the declaration of invalidity for a period of time in order to allow the lawmakers to correct the invalidity.[290] The Court resorts to this option when immediate invalidations would create a legal vacuum resulting in greater detriment to the Constitution.[291] The need for this power was described by the Constitutional Court in *Executive Council of Western Cape Legislature and Others v The President of the Republic of South Africa and Others*,[292] where Chaskalson P stated when the new Constitution came into effect there were many statutes inconsistent with the Constitution. If all of the inconsistent statutes were to be immediately struck down, and all action taken under them were declared to be invalid, there would be a legislative vacuum and chaotic conditions.[293] Therefore, there is a need for the Court to exercise its powers so as to 'avoid or control the consequences of a declaration of invalidity ... where the result of invalidating everything ... is disproportional to the harm which would result from giving the legislation temporary validity'.[294] Special regard will be given to laws enacted before the coming into force of the Constitution.[295]

Generally, a successful litigant should obtain the relief requested. Therefore, a party that wishes an unconstitutional provision to be granted temporary validity is required to place information before the Court justifying why the Court should grant such an order.[296] In *S v Bhulwana; S v Gwadiso*,[297] the Constitutional Court, *per* O'Regan J, held '[it] is only where the interest of good government outweigh the interest of the individual litigants that the court will not grant the relief to successful litigants'.[298]

In *S v Ntuli*, the Constitutional Court invalidated s 309(4)(a) of the Criminal Procedure Act. This section required that any person in prison pursuant to a conviction in a magistrates' court would not be able to proceed with an appeal in person, without a lawyer, unless a judge of the provincial division certifies that there are reasonable grounds for the appeal. Didcott J, for a unanimous Court, declared that the certificate procedure violated the right to appeal and the right to equality under the interim Constitution. However, the Court suspended its declaration of invalidity for almost a year and a half during which period parliament was given an opportunity to remedy the defect.[299] The Court suspended the invalidity because of a concern that absent the laying out of a new procedure, there would be a great increase in the number of appeals which the provincial courts might not be able to handle. Parliament did not effect the changes to the law within the year-and-a-half grace period. Shortly before the deadline, the Minister of Justice applied to the Court for an additional extension of time to correct the defect.[300] The Court, *per* Chaskalson P, found that parliament had failed to take the necessary steps required under the Constitution; nor did they place information before the Court

---

[290] *Fraser* para 50.
[291] Ibid; *S v Ntuli* CCT 17/95 (8 December 1995) para 46, now cited as 1996 (1) BCLR 141 (CC); 1996 (1) 1207 (CC); *Steyn v The State*.
[292] *Executive Council of Western Cape Legislature and Others v President of the Republic of South Africa and Others* CCT 27/95 (22 September 1995), now cited as 1995 (10) BCLR 1289 (CC); 1995 (4) SA 877 (CC).
[293] *Supra* para 107.
[294] *Supra.*
[295] *Supra* para 108.
[296] *Mistry* para 37.
[297] *S v Bhulwana; S v Gwadiso* CCT 12/95; CCT 11/95 (29 November 1995), now cited as 1995 (12) BCLR 1579 (CC); 1996 (1) SA 388 (CC).
[298] *Supra* para 32.
[299] *Ntuli* para 30.
[300] *The Minister of Justice v Ntuli* CCT 15/97 [17/95] (5 June 1997), now cited as 1997 (3) SA 772 (CC); 1997 (6) BCLR 677 (CC).

justifying why the order of invalidity should be further suspended.[301] The Court, therefore, refused to grant the state further time to implement the changes.[302]

In *Executive Council of Western Cape Legislature and Others v The President of the Republic of South Africa and Others*,[303] the Constitutional Court unanimously declared s 16A of the Local Government Transition Act,[304] which conferred powers on the president to effect amendments by proclamation, to be unconstitutional.[305] The attempt by parliament to give the president the power to adopt legislative changes by executive decree was found to be an unconstitutional delegation of power.[306] The Court majority further found that certain proclamations issued by the president, pursuant to the powers conferred under s 16A of the Act, were unconstitutional.[307] An immediate declaration of invalidity would necessitate the invalidation of various proclamations under s 16A of the Act. This, the Court found, would have resulted in the invalidations of many structures and arrangements, which would have made the pending local elections, which were due to take place in six weeks, impossible to undertake, unless parliament was able to reconvene and adopt new legislation.[308] In view of the national importance of local elections, and the need to establish democratic local government, an immediate order of invalidity would frustrate such endeavours and not be in the interest of good government.[309] The Court, therefore, allowed the defect to continue for a temporary period of just under five weeks. During

this period parliament would be afforded an opportunity to correct the defect before the elections were held.[310] In other words, parliament was given an opportunity to validate the proclamations, made by the president through its ordinary legislative power.

The Court may also make the suspension of the order of invalidity subject to the executive abiding by a specific interpretation of the law during the suspension period. In *Moseneke*, the Constitutional Court invalidated s 23(7)(a) of the Black Administration Act[311] and reg 3(1)[312] in terms of which provisions a local magistrate was required to deal with the estate of an African person who died intestate. For all other races, the estate is administered by the Master of the High Court. The Court held that the entire statute constituted unfair discrimination and an impairment of human dignity.[313] The Court suspended its order of invalidity and allowed the provisions on administrations of African estates to stay in place for a period of two years so as to allow parliament to come up with an alternate scheme. The suspension of the order of invalidity was made in order to prevent dislocation and injustice.[314] At the same time, the Court did not want African people to continue suffering the indignity of racist treatment. Therefore, the Court ordered that the term 'shall' in reg 3 must be read for the period of suspension as 'may'.[315] This interpretation would allow an African the choice of either having the state administered by the Master of the Supreme Court or in terms of the Black Administration Act.

Where there are no compelling considerations

---

[301] *Supra* para 41.

[302] *Supra* para 39.

[303] *Executive Council of Western Cape Legislature.*

[304] Act 209 of 1993.

[305] *Executive Council of Western Cape* para 101.

[306] *Supra* para 64.

[307] *Supra.*

[308] *Supra* para 109.

[309] *Supra* paras 109–110.

[310] *Supra* para 124.

[311] Act 38 of 1927.

[312] Promulgated in terms of s 23(10) of the Act.

[313] *Moseneke* para 22.

[314] *Supra* paras 25 and 27.

[315] *Supra* para 27.

such as 'justice and good government', the Courts would not grant a temporary declaration of invalidity.[316] In *S v Mbatha; S v Prinsloo*, the state asked the Court to suspend its order declaring that the reverse onus presumption in s 32 of the Arms and Ammunition Act 75 of 1969 was unconstitutional. The Court held that a prolonging of the presumption would prolong the risks to accused persons who might be convicted despite the existence of reasonable doubt.[317] There were no compelling considerations of 'justice and good government' that justified the continuing of unconstitutional actions.[318] A continuation of the action would have grave consequences for potentially innocent persons.[319]

Mandamus

Where there is a violation of a right in the Bill of Rights, a complainant can apply to a court for a *mandamus* to vindicate the breach of the right.[320] In *City Council of Pretoria*, the Court found that the city council had discriminated against white residents by taking selective enforcement measures to collect for electricity and water use.[321] The Court held that although there was a breach of a right, the respondent was not entitled to take measures on his own, such as the withholding of payments to the city council. Instead, the respondent should have applied to a court 'for a declaration of rights or a *mandamus* in order to vindicate the breach. By means of such an order the council could have been compelled to take appropriate steps as soon as possible to eliminate

the unfair discrimination and to report back to the court in question.'[322]

Damages

In various jurisdictions, under appropriate circumstances, a successful litigant can be awarded damages for violation of their constitutional rights.[323] In *Fose v Minister of Safety and Security*, the plaintiff sued the Minister of Safety and Security for damages arising from a series of alleged assaults committed by the police.[324] The plaintiff sought constitutional damages for the alleged assaults, which he claimed was a violation of various rights under the interim Constitution (including the guarantees of human dignity, freedom and security of the person, privacy, and the right against unlawful detention).[325] The Witwatersrand Provincial Division rejected a claim for damages as a remedy for a constitutional wrong. The Constitutional Court, *per* Ackerman J, (concurred by Chaskalson P, Mahomed DP, Langa J, Madala J, and Sachs J), held that in appropriate circumstances, damages can be given to vindicate a constitutional wrong.[326] The purpose of the award would be 'to compensate persons who have suffered loss as a result of the breach of a statutory right if, on a proper construction of the statute in question, it was the legislature's intention that such damages should be payable ...'.[327] On the facts of this case, Ackerman J held that under the common law, the plaintiff was entitled to sufficient damages to vindicate his constitutional rights. Therefore,

---

[316] *S v Mbatha; S v Prinsloo* para 30. *Coetzee* para 18. *Mistry* para 37.

[317] *Supra* para 30.

[318] *Supra.*

[319] *Supra.*

[320] *City Council of Pretoria v Walker* para 95; *Fose* para 19.

[321] *Supra* paras 87 and 91.

[322] *Supra* para 95.

[323] In the US, see s 1983 of the Civil Rights Act. *Fose v Minister of Safety and Security* CCT 14/96 (5 June 1997) para 60, now cited as 1997 (3) SA 786 (CC); 1997 (7) BCLR 851 (CC).

[324] *Fose* para 11.

[325] *Supra* para 12.

[326] *Supra* para 60.

[327] *Supra.*

there was no need for an additional award of constitutional damages.[328] The majority of the justices refused to award punitive damages. They felt that punitive damages would not serve as a deterrent and would be a drain on scarce resources which need to be used for many important purposes. The majority felt that there is no justification for such damages, particularly where the victims are compensated for the injuries committed against them.[329] Didcott J, in his concurring opinion, stated that he would apply the same policies to large and wealthy corporations against whom punitive damages may be awarded.[330] Kriegler J, on the other hand, felt that punitive damages should not be foreclosed and could be awarded even against the state in appropriate circumstances.[331]

Since the decision in *Fose*, parliament has passed the Promotion of Equality and Prevention of Unfair Discrimination Act.[332] The Act provides that the Equality Court could order payment of damages 'in respect of any proven financial loss, including future loss, or in respect of impairment of dignity, pain and suffering or emotional and psychological suffering, as a result of the unfair discrimination, hate speech or harassment in question'.[333] Arguably, the said Act, in terms of the majority approach in *Fose*, signifies a legislative intent to award constitutional damages.

---

[328] *Supra* para 67.
[329] *Supra* para 72.
[330] *Supra* para 87.
[331] *Supra* paras 93, 102–103.
[332] Act 4 of 2000.
[333] Section 21(2)*(d)*.

4

Control over the courts

Introduction

In this chapter we look at the external and internal controls exercised over and by the judiciary. First, in discussing external control, we look at political methods to curtail unpopular decisions; constitutional amendment, and the power of removal. Secondly, we look at self-imposed restraints employed by the judiciary, which limit the circumstances under which courts will adjudicate constitutional issues.

Political control over the courts

Constitutional amendment

If the Constitutional Court renders a decision with which the majority disagrees, the legislature has the option of adopting a constitutional amendment. Special and extraordinary machinery are required for constitutional amendment, as contained in s 74:

> 74 (1) Section 1 and this subsection may be amended by a Bill passed by—
>   (a) the National Assembly, with a supporting vote of at least 75 per cent of its members; and

> (b) the National Council of Provinces with a supporting vote of at least six provinces.
> (2) Chapter 2 may be amended by a Bill passed by—
>   (a) the National Assembly, with a supporting vote of at least two thirds of its members; and
>   (b) the National Council of Provinces supported by a vote of at least six provinces.
> (3) Any other provision of the Constitution may be amended by a Bill passes—
>   (a) by the National Assembly, with a supporting vote of at least two thirds of its members; and
>   (b) also by the National Council of Provinces, with a supporting vote of at least six provinces, if the amendment—
>   (i) relates to a matter that affects the Council;
>   (ii) alters provincial boundaries, powers, functions or institutions; or
>   (iii) amends a provision that deals specifically with a provincial matter.
> (4) A Bill amending the Constitution may not include provisions other than constitutional amendments and matters connected with the amendments.
> (5) At least 30 days before a Bill amending the Constitution is introduced in terms of section

74 (2) the person or committee intending to introduce the Bill must—

(a) publish in the national *Government Gazette*, and in accordance with the rules and orders of the National Assembly, particulars of the proposed amendment for public comment;

(b) submit, in accordance with the rules and orders of the Assembly, those particulars to the provincial legislature for their views; and

(c) submit in accordance with the rules and orders of the National Council of Provinces, those particulars to the Council for a public debate, if the proposed amendment is not an amendment that is required to be passed by the Council.

The process for amending the Constitution is both rigid and different from ordinary legislation. An amendment to s 1 of the Constitution (which entrenches human dignity and equality, non-racialism, and non-sexism, supremacy of the Constitution and the rule of law, and the right to vote under universal suffrage in a multi-party and open democratic system), requires a minimum of seventy-five per cent support in the National Assembly and the support of six of the nine provinces in the National Council of Provinces. To amend the Bill of Rights, the Constitution requires a majority of at least two thirds in the NA and at least the supporting votes of six provinces in the National Council of Provinces. For all other constitutional amendments, the Constitution requires at least a two-thirds majority in the NA and the support of at least six provinces (if the amendment relates to a matter which affects the National Council of Provinces, alters provincial boundaries, or relates to a provision that deals specifically with a provincial matter).

The Constitution is a special document that sets out the outlines of government, and the important values of society. It should not be subject to the whims of transient majorities. This is not the same as saying that there can be no amendment at all. However, all laws, especially the Constitution, must be adaptable to changing social, political, and economic realities. If the Constitution cannot be changed to meet new realities, it is likely to experience a legitimacy crisis. However, changes should not come about through transient changes implemented by a simple majority in the country. If there is to be change to this basic document, there should be widespread consensus about the change. Therefore, it is not unusual to find modern constitutions subject to a rigid amendment procedure.

Some jurists argue that there are certain constitutional values that are not capable of change, and that it is the function of the judiciary to ensure the protection of these values. In two cases – *Premier of KwaZulu-Natal and Others v The President the Republic of South Africa and Others*,[1] and *Executive Council of the Western Cape Legislature and Others v President of the Republic of South Africa and Others*[2] – at least two of the justices expressed the idea that there are certain constitutional features which are absolute. In the *Premier of KwaZulu-Natal* case, Mahomed DP alluded to a constitutional amendment that has the 'effect of destroying or abrogating the very essentials upon which the Constitutional Principles are premised'; such a situation which he said, did not arise in that case.[3] Similarly Sachs J, in *Executive Council of the Western Cape*, stated that there are certain 'fundamental features of parliamentary democracy which are not spelled out in the Constitution, but which are inherent in its very nature, design and purpose'.[4] Judge Sachs goes on to state that 'there are certain features of the constitutional order so fundamental that even if parliament followed the necessary amendment procedures, it could not change them'.[5] Ma-

---

[1] *Premier of KwaZulu-Natal and Others v President of the Republic of South Africa and Others* CCT 36/95 (29 November 1995), now cited as 1995 (12) BCLR 1361 (CC); 1996 (1) SA 769 (CC).

[2] *Executive Council of the Western Cape Legislature and Others v President of the Republic of South Africa and Others* CCT 27/95 (22 September 1995) para 204, now cited as 1995 (10) BCLR 1289 (CC); 1995 (4) SA 877 (CC).

[3] *Premier of KwaZulu-Natal* para 12.

[4] *Executive Council of the Western Cape* para 204.

[5] *Supra.*

homed DP, in *Premier of KwaZulu-Natal*, echoed the same sentiments by stating that 'a purported amendment to the Constitution, following the formal procedures prescribed by the Constitution, but radically and fundamentally restructuring and re-organizing the fundamental premises of the Constitution, might not qualify as an "amendment" at all'.[6] Mahomed DP refers to the decision of the Indian Supreme Court, in the case of *Raj Narain*, where that Court concluded that a constitutional amendment could not be employed 'to the extent of destroying the basic features and structure of the Constitution'.[7] Given the facts, Mahomed DP felt it unnecessary to pursue the line of authorities dealing with unconstitutional constitutional amendment in the *Premier of KwaZulu-Natal* case.

There is a concept in Indian jurisprudence called the basic structure doctrine, which posits the idea that there are certain, 'permanent, immutable, sacrosanct and basic features' that can never be interfered with, even through an amending process by the legislature.[8] According to this concept, there are two parts to the Indian Constitution; the basic and the circumstantial. The first remains constant whereas the latter can be subject to change.[9] The Indian Supreme Court has, over the years, added features to the basic structure to include the power of judicial review, free and fair elections, *habeas corpus*, freedom of assembly, and a host of other activities.[10] The Court has reserved the power to determine the basic features of the Constitution.[11] In the case of Germany, German Basic Law expressly declares that certain rights pertaining to democracy and federalism cannot be deleted.[12] The German Constitutional Court, in interpreting this provision, has expressed this idea

of an unconstitutional constitutional amendment, declaring that it reserves the right to invalidate even a constitutional amendment if the amendment conflicts with a higher norm that is basic to the German Basic Law.[13] Similarly, the Constitution of Italy, in art 112, provides that the republican form of state can never be modified.[14]

The South African Constitution does not explicitly contain references to any norm or structural features not subject to constitutional amendment. If the Court reserves the right to strike down a constitutional amendment adopted in terms of ordinary democratic practice because the amendment conflicts with the Court's preferences, this does not bode well for democracy. Abraham Lincoln, in his first inaugural address as President of the United States, remarked that 'if the policy of the Government upon vital questions affecting the whole people is to be irrevocably fixed by decisions of the Supreme Court, the instant they are made in ordinary litigation between parties in personal actions, the people will have ceased to be their own rulers, having to that extent practically resigned their Government into the hands of that eminent tribunal'.[15] There is always a conflict between judicial review and democracy. The approach that the judiciary can decide ultimately on the propriety of constitutional norms undermines democracy, and elevates the anti-majoritarian reality of judicial review to an unacceptable level.

The danger in Mahomed DPs and Sachs Js approach is that they fail to indicate from where they would draw these values or higher norms. Under what standards do the justices reserve the power to strike down a constitutional amendment? The highest courts in some jurisdictions have espoused the idea that natural law imposes

---

[6] *Premier of KwaZulu-Natal* para 64.

[7] *Supra*.

[8] MK Bhandara *Basic Structure of The Indian Constitution: A Critical Reconsideration* New Delhi: Deep & Deep 1993, 341–2.

[9] Op cit 6–7.

[10] Op cit 9–11.

[11] Op cit 10.

[12] Article 79 of the German Basic Law.

[13] Donald P Kommers *Constitutional Jurisprudence of the Federal Republic of Germany* Durham: Duke University Press 1989, 76.

[14] Brandon Troy Ishihara 'Toward a more Perfect Union: The Role of Amending Formulae in the United States, Canadian, and German Constitutional Experiences' (1996) 2 *University of California at Davis Journal of International Law and Policy* 268.

[15] Quoted in Harry H Wellington *Interpreting the Constitution: The Supreme Court and the Process of Adjudication* New Haven: Yale University Press 1990, 133.

limitations on the legislature, in both ordinary lawmaking and in the area of constitutional amendment.[16] However, scholars constantly disagree about natural law.[17] Since natural law does not offer a consistent theory, it is difficult to apply this doctrine and any invocation of natural law ultimately is a preference of the judge. Does this mean that there are no absolute principles which are not subject to any derogation at all? For example, what happens if the legislature, with the requisite majority, reintroduces apartheid, or slavery, or condones torture? There are absolute principles in international law from which there can be no derogation.[18] Unfortunately, in *Premier of KwaZulu-Natal*, Mahomed DP failed to identify exactly where these principles would be derived. If the Court is saying that it places itself in the mainstream of international democratic practice, and accordingly would strike down a law permitting slavery or apartheid, it is on stronger ground, because it seeks to uphold a peremptory and higher norm of international law, from which there can be no derogation – even via a constitutional amendment.

It is now a general proposition of international law that states cannot invoke their domestic law as a justification for not adhering to international norms.[19] States no longer have an unrestricted freedom to legislate, and have to act in terms of international-law principles Particular respect has to be paid to *jus cogens* which, in international law, signifies the highest form of international law from which there can be no derogation. A peremptory norm of international law 'is a norm accepted by the international community of States as a whole, as a norm from which no derogation is permitted'.[20] *Jus cogens* has been described as embodying a notion 'that is foundational, guarding the most fundamental and highly-valued interests of international society'.[21] Such a norm transcends all positive expressions of law.[22] In effect, peremptory norms lie at the foundation of the international community itself; meaning some principles are so fundamental to the very functioning of the state system that their existence is presupposed and cannot be overridden by positive law. Once a norm reaches the status of *jus cogens*, all states are bound to refrain from any actions which are prohibited by the peremptory norm. Thus, any action on the part of the state which infringes on a peremptory norm is null and void.[23] As in the case with any norm of international law, in order to determine whether particular conduct violates a principal of *jus cogens*, one needs to look at the sources of international law as laid out specifically in the most authoritative source; namely the statute of the International Court of Justice.[24] As the Constitutional Court recognized in *Makwanyane*, art 38(1) of the Statute of the International Court of Justice provides that the Court shall apply the following sources: international conventions, customs, general principles of law, and judicial decisions and teachings of the publicists as subsidiary means.[25] A law that

---

[16] See eg the Irish cases of *The State v Donoghue* [1976] IR 325 and *Murphy v PMPA Insurance* [1978] ILRM 25. In the US see Justice Chase's opinion in *Calder v Bull* 3 US (3 Dall) 386 (1798). See JM Kelly, et al *The Irish Constitution* Dublin: Butterworths, 3rd edition, 1994, 677.

[17] Hans Kelsen *What is Justice? Justice, Law and Politics in the Mirror of Science: Collected Essays* Berkeley: University of California Press 1960, 259. See also Kelly 677, 683.

[18] Ziyad Motala and David Butleritchie 'Self-defense in International Law, the United Nations, and the Bosnia Conflict' (1995) 57 *University of Pittsburg Law Review* 1, 14.

[19] Polish Nationals in Danzig (1931) PCIJ Ser A/B 44. See also Antonio Cassese *International Law in a Divided World* Oxford: Clarendon 1988, 15.

[20] Article 53 of the Vienna Convention on the Law of Treaties, UN Doc A/Conf 39/27 (1969), entered into force on 23 May 23 1980, 1155 UNTS 331, 344.

[21] Gordon Christenson '*Jus Cogens*: Guarding Interests Fundamental to International Society' (1988) 28 *Virginia Journal of International Law* 585, 587.

[22] Barry E Carter and Phillip R Trimble *International Law* Boston: Little Brown 1991, 98.

[23] Takeshi Minagawa '*Jus Cogens* in Public International Law' (1968) 6 *Hitotsubashi Journal of International Law and Politics* 16, 25.

[24] Statute of the International Court of Justice, 59 Stat 1055, TS 993 3 Bevans 1179.

[25] *S v Makwanyane and Another* CCT 3/94 (6 June 1995): 1995 (3) SA 391 (CC) para 36, now cited as 1995 (6) BCLR 665 (CC); 1994 (3) SA 868 (A).

authorizes torture, apartheid, arbitrary deprivation of life, slavery, and war crimes, to name a few, violates principles of *jus cogens*. It is appropriate for the Court to strike down legislation which violates peremptory norms of international law. The Constitutional Court was presented with this issue in the *Azapo* case, dealing with the validity of the amnesty provision in the Promotion of National Unity and Reconciliation Act. As we have argued in chapter 2, it was required of the Court to invalidate those provisions of the Amnesty Act which violated peremptory norms of international law, such as the granting of amnesty for crimes against humanity. Unfortunately, in *Azapo*, the Court failed to fully canvass international law for guidance on the duty of the state when gross violations of human rights had been alleged. The Constitutional Court failed to consider the significant international law authority affirming the responsibilities of a state where international law imposes a peremptory duty to prosecute for war crimes and crimes against humanity.[26] As opposed to the approach of Mahomed DP in *Premier of KwaZulu-Natal* (where he fails to tell us from where he would draw his values to strike down a constitutional amendment), this approach argues that the South African state absolutely cannot act or legislate in a way which contravenes *jus cogens* principles.

The examples that arise in many of the decisions rendered by the Indian Supreme Court, the republican provision in the Italian Constitution, the federalism provision in the German Constitution, and the Irish case where natural law were evoked, mostly relate to principles where *jus cogens* norms were not violated. For example, a constitutional amendment which deprives the Constitutional Court of review may upset the state structure doctrine, and separation of powers, but is not a violation of a peremptory norm of international law. However, the Amnesty Act in *Azapo* did not present a constitutional amendment. It presented an ordinary statute which ousted the jurisdiction of all review, and violated other principles of *jus cogens*.

When faced with a constitutional amendment, even though it may radically alter the structure of the state, and providing it is not a violation of *jus cogens*, there is a competing argument that sanctions should lie in public opinion and not in the judicial process.[27] Criticizing the Indian Supreme Court's approach, Bhandari states that 'the Court's restriction on the legislature's amending power flows from the total lack of faith or trust in democracy or in Parliament'.[28] The judiciary is there to protect adherence to the Constitution. The judiciary's function is to explain and justify what the Constitution means, free from the hurly-burly of everyday politics which the legislature and executive encounter. There is always a conflict between judicial review and democracy. Judicial review over legislative and executive conduct is the price we pay for the long-term protection of liberty. This function of judicial review should not be confused with a claim of power on the part of the judiciary to prevent changes in the Constitution itself. The judiciary cannot play the role of a constituent body to dismiss or create the ground rules, which the Constitution represents. As part of the certification function, the Constitutional Court was given a unique – and previously unheard of – function: to evaluate, and accordingly to certify, the new Constitution as consistent with the agreed constitutional principles. This was a one-time limited function that the Constitutional Court was given, as part of the constitutional agreement that ushered in the new order, at a particular period in South African constitutional history. The ground rules are not easy to change. If the ground rules are changed through the rigid process of amendment, and if there is a problem with the new ground rules, the accountability of, and check on, the legislature should come through the political process. The rules and structures that the Constitution create have to emanate from the people and not from the judiciary. The decision of the Constitutional Court in the *First Certification* decision supports the position that the Bill of Rights is entrenched but not unamendable:

---

[26] For a partial listing of these cites see Ziyad Motala 'Promotion of National Unity and Reconciliation Act, the Constitution and International Law' (1995) 28 *Comparative International Law Journal of Southern Africa* 338.

[27] Bhandara 62.

[28] Op cit 88.

In re: Certification of the Constitution of the Republic of South Africa, 1996
CCT 23/96 (6 September 1996), now cited as 1996 (10) BCLR 1253 (CC); 1996 (4) SA 744 (CC)
(notes omitted)
Unanimous Decision

Entrenchment of the Bill of Rights
[157] CP II requires that 'all universally accepted rights, freedoms and civil liberties … shall be provided for and protected by entrenched and justiciable provisions in the Constitution'.

The complaint is that the provisions of the Bill of Rights contained in NT ch 2 do not enjoy the protection and entrenchment required by CP II. In particular there is nothing in the NT which elevates the level of protection of the Bill of Rights above that afforded the general provisions of the NT.

[158] In defence of the NT it was argued that the relevant provisions enjoy the requisite protection and entrenchment and that CP II is satisfied once those rights, freedoms and civil liberties are placed beyond the reach of ordinary legislative procedures and majorities, as has been done in the NT.

[159] We do not agree that CP II requires no more than that the NT should ensure that the rights are included in a constitution the provisions of which enjoy more protection than ordinary legislation. We regard the notion of entrenchment 'in the Constitution' as requiring a more stringent protection than that which is accorded to the ordinary provisions of the NT. The objection of non-compliance with CP II in this respect therefore succeeds. In using the word 'entrenched', the drafters of CP II required that the provisions of the Bill of Rights, given their vital nature and purpose, be safeguarded by special amendment procedures against easy abridgement. A two-thirds majority of one House does not provide the bulwark envisaged by CP II. That CP does not require that the Bill of Rights should be immune from amendment or practically unamendable. What it requires is some 'entrenching' mechanism, such as the involvement of both Houses of Parliament or a greater majority in the NA or other reinforcement, which gives the Bill of Rights greater protection than the ordinary provisions of the NT. What that mechanism should be is for the CA and not for us to decide.

Removal of judges

The Constitution provides:

Section 177
(1) A judge may be removed from office only if—
   (a) the Judicial Service Commission finds that the judge suffers from an incapacity, is grossly incompetent or is guilty of gross misconduct; and
   (b) the National Assembly calls for that judge to be removed, by a resolution adopted with a supporting vote of at least two thirds of its members.
(2) The President must remove a judge from office upon adoption of a resolution calling for that judge to be removed.
(3) The President, on the advice of the Judicial Service Commission, may suspend a judge who is the subject of a procedure in terms of subsection (1).

The procedure for removal of judges is not easy. First, s 177(1) requires a finding from the Judicial Service Commission (JSC) that a judge suffers from incapacity, is grossly incompetent, or is guilty of gross misconduct. Secondly, the NA must vote, by at least a two-thirds majority, calling for the judge's removal, in which case the president is obliged to remove the judge from office. The crucial question is whether a finding by the JSC and an affirmative two-thirds vote in the NA to remove a judge (based on gross incompetence or gross misconduct), is subject to judicial review? This raises the question whether the terms, grossly incompetent or guilty of gross misconduct, are subject to judicial standards.

Article III of the United States Constitution, s 1, provides that judges 'shall hold their Offices during good behaviour'. Further, the United States Constitution – in art II, s 4 – provides that judges may be removed from office for impeachment, conviction of treason, bribery, or other high crimes or misdemeanours. Finally, in art I, ss 2 and 3, the United States Constitution, provides that the House of Representatives shall have the sole power of impeachment and the senate shall have the sole power to try all impeachments. Former President Ford, when he was a member of the House of Representatives, argued that the grounds for impeachment were 'whatever a majority of the House of Representatives considers them to be at a given moment in history'.[29] Under this interpretation, it is not necessary that someone be impeached for misconduct that is a crime. During impeachment proceedings against President Nixon, the staff of the House of Representatives Judiciary Committee concluded that impeachment could be based 'upon conduct seriously incompatible with either the constitutional form and principles of our government or the proper performance of constitutional duties of the presidential office'.[30] The House of Representatives Judiciary Committee subsequently voted articles of impeachment based in part on non-criminal conduct.[31]

Under this interpretation, incapacity, grossly incompetent or gross misconduct, for purposes of interpreting s 177 of the South African Constitution in the context of removal proceedings, would mean whatever a majority in the JSC and two-thirds of the NA think it is. Interpreting gross misconduct, for example, is not the same as guilt in a criminal setting. When the JSC votes to remove someone from office, and the NA affirms this decision with the requisite two-thirds majority, this means that the JSC and the relevant political branch feel that the judge is engaged in conduct which is inappropriate to the office, and that the judge should be removed from such office. This removal does not carry any criminal sanction. If criminal wrongdoing is involved, this will have to be determined in a separate trial before a competent court.

Is it necessary for there to be a criminal conviction before the gross misconduct standard is applied?[32] In *Hastings*, Alcee Hastings – a judge in the District Court of Florida – was charged with taking bribes, but was acquitted by a jury. Subsequent to his acquittal, the House of Representatives voted articles of impeachment and the senate confirmed the impeachment. Hastings questioned the constitutionality of the impeachment proceedings against him on several grounds, namely that an impeachment action could only be performed on affirmation of guilt in the criminal sense. The district court for the District of Columbia held that a federal judge could not be impeached unless the judge was brought up on real charges and had a full trial before the Senate of the United States.[33] The district court further stated that impeachment proceedings are not political proceedings, but are judicial proceedings.[34] The approach of the district court was repudiated by the United States Supreme Court in *Nixon v United States*.[35] The Court held that the word 'try' in the Constitution is not the same as try in the criminal context. Nixon, a district court judge, was convicted of making a false statement and was subsequently removed from office by impeachment. He then sought judicial review of the impeachment proceedings against him. The majority of the justices approached the issue in terms of the political question doctrine. When applying the political question doctrine, the United States Supreme Court must ask a number of questions:

---

[29] Quoted in Geoffrey R Stone, et al *Constitutional Law Boston: Little Brown*, 3rd edition, 1996, 80.

[30] 'Report of the Staff of the Impeachment Enquiry' quoted in Paul Brest and Sanford Levinson *Process of Constitutional Decision-Making* Boston: Little Brown, 3rd edition, 1992, 1476.

[31] Brest & Levinson 1476–7.

[32] *Alcee Hastings v United States* 802 F Supp 490 (DC 1992).

[33] *Supra* at 505.

[34] *Supra* at 497. Judges could not be removed for political reasons because to do so would be the 'antithesis of creating and sustaining an independent judiciary'. *Supra* at 494. The Court goes on to proclaim that '[impeachment was never intended to be an ominous weapon that the legislature could hold over the head of the judiciary and invoke at will without limitation or reason'. *Supra* at 494–495. The Court therefore reserved a right to exercise judicial review over any impeachment proceeding to review whether the impeachment was appropriate.

[35] *Nixon v United States* 506 US 224 (1993).

whether there is a textually demonstrable commitment to leave the issue to a coordinate political department; whether a decision by the Court would cause embarrassment to the government abroad; whether there are judicially discoverable and manageable standards for resolving the problem?[36] The nature of the impeachment proceeding is to remove a person from judicial office, and does not involve any criminal proceedings, which come in a separate trial, before a competent court.[37] More importantly, Chief Justice Rehnquist correctly observed that removal of judges through impeachment is the only avenue to check against abuse by the judiciary, and further maintained it is illogical to allow the judiciary to review themselves.[38] Justices White, Blackman, and Souter concurred that the removal here was a non-justiciable political question. However, they left open the possibility of reviewing the impeachment if the senate abused its discretion – they felt this was not present in this case.[39]

Chief Justice Rehnquist's approach denies the judiciary any power to review the removal of judges. Justices White, Blackman and Souter state that it is difficult to judge removals wisely. The common theme which runs through the opinions is that the standards for removal are better left to be determined by the other constitutional organs. The Court's decision is premised largely on prudential reasons. The Court recognizes that removal of judges is an extraordinary action. However, as Rehnquist correctly observed, this does not mean that politicians would routinely remove judges who render unpopular decisions.[40] As in the United States, the South African Constitution has checks and balances, namely a vote of the JSC and a two-thirds majority of the NA.

Self-imposed judicial restraints in constitutional adjudication

Introduction

To maintain the legitimacy of judicial review, courts in many jurisdictions have developed a set of justiciability rules which Alexander Bickel calls 'passive virtues'.[41] These rules limit the circumstances under which the courts will adjudicate constitutional disputes. If a dispute does not satisfy these justiciability rules, the court will stay its hand and let the matter be resolved by the other branches of government. These devices serve as vehicles for judicial self-restraint, thereby reducing the opportunity for friction between the judiciary on the one hand, and the legislative and executive branches on the other hand. These restraints, though constitutionally based, are really self-defined by the Court. They mark a recognition by the Court that prudence requires it to use substantial discretion when exercising subject-matter jurisdiction.[42] These policies contribute to the legitimacy of the Court. In the words of John Roche, '[J]udicial self-restraint and judicial power seem to be the opposite sides of the same coin: it has been by judicious application of the former that the latter has been maintained. A tradition suggests that the Court's power has been maintained by a wise refusal to employ it in unequal combat'.[43] This set of rules marks an institutional psychology of the Court's view of its role of judicial review.[44] The court-imposed restraints include the requirements of a case and controversy, standing, ripeness, mootness, and avoidance of the dispute, if the matter can be resolved without looking at the constitutional issue.

---

36 *Supra* at 239.
37 Chief Justice Rehnquist uses both a textualist and original intent method of interpretation and concludes that the senate has the sole power to try impeachments. *Supra* at 229.
38 *Supra* at 235.
39 *Supra* at 239.
40 *Supra* at 235–246.
41 Alexander Bickel *The Least Dangerous Branch: The Supreme Court at the Bar of Politics* New Haven: Yale University Press, 2nd edition, 1986, 111.
42 Lawrence Tribe *American Constitutional Law* Mineola: Foundation Press, 2nd edition, 1998, 68.
43 John P Roche 'Judicial Self-restraint' (1955) 49 *American Political Science Review* 722.
44 Tribe 68.

Case and controversy

The courts will generally not render an abstract opinion on the constitutionality of state or private action.[45] There are few situations where the Constitution allows the rendering of an abstract opinion. For example, under s 80, a third of the members of the NA may apply to the Constitutional Court to review the constitutionality of an Act of Parliament:

> 80 (1) Members of the National Assembly may apply to the Constitutional Court for an order declaring that all or part of an Act of Parliament is unconstitutional.
> (2) An application—
> (a) must be supported by at least one third of the members of the Assembly; and
> (b) must be made within 30 days of the date on which the President assented to and signed the Act.
> (3) The Constitutional Court may order that all or part of an Act that is the subject of an application in terms of subsection (1) has no force until the Court has decided the application if—
> (a) the interests of justice require this; and
> [(b) the application has a reasonable prospect of success].

A similar provision is contained in s 122 allowing members of the provincial legislature the option of applying to the Constitutional Court for an abstract decision on the constitutionality of provincial legislation:

> 122 (1) Members of a provincial legislature may apply to the Constitutional Court for an order declaring that all or part of a provincial Act is unconstitutional.

> (2) An application—
> (a) must be supported by at least 20 per cent of the members of the legislature; and
> (b) must be made within 30 days of the date on which the Premier assented to and signed the Act.
> (3) The Constitutional Court may order that all or part of an Act that is the subject of an application in terms of subsection (1) has no force until the Court has decided the application if—
> (a) the interests of justice require this; and
> (b) the application has a reasonable prospect of success.

The Constitution also allows the president the option of requesting an abstract review from the Constitutional Court before he or she assents to a bill.[46] A similar option is given to the premier of the provinces.[47] Before the president petitions the Constitutional Court to consider the constitutionality of a bill, the president must first refer the bill, with his or her reservations, back to parliament for reconsideration.[48]

In *Ferreira*, Ackerman J stated that the Constitutional Court cannot entertain abstract questions except under ss 98(2)*(d)* and 101(3)*(e)* of the interim Constitution,[49] these sections are analogous to ss 80 and 122 of the Constitution. Outside the above situation, the Court will not generally entertain abstract questions. Questions before the Court have to arise in the context of a real dispute, as opposed to a hypothetical, feigned, or collusive suit. The case and controversy requirement is part of the common-law tradition that requires the issues to be addressed in a concrete adversarial context. This context is to prevent speculative suppositions of facts that are unknown.

---

[45] *Zantsi v The Council of State, Ciskei, and Others* CCT 24/94 (22 September 1995) para 7, now cited as 1995 (4) SA 615 (CC); 1995 (10) BCLR 1424 (CC).

[46] Section 79(4) of the Constitution. The first time the Court was called to exercise review under this section was in *Ex parte the President of the Republic of South Africa: In re: Constitutionality of the Liquor Bill* CCT 12/99 (11 November 1999) para 19, now cited as 2000 (1) SA 732 (CC); 2000 (1) BCLR 1 (CC).

[47] Section 121(2)*(b)* of the Constitution.

[48] *In re: Constitutionality of the Liquor Bill* para 19.

[49] *Ferreira v Levin NO and Others; Vryenhoek and Others v Powell NO and Others* CCT 5/95 (6 December 1995) para 35, now cited as 1996 (1) SA 984 (CC); 1996 (1) BCLR 1 (CC).

Zantsi v The Council of State, Ciskei and Others
CCT 24/94 (22 September 1995), now
cited as 1995 (4) SA 615 (CC);
1995 (10) BCLR 1424 (CC)
(note omitted)

Authors' note: Zantsi *involved an interpretation of*
s 102(8) of the interim Constitution dealing with
referrals to the Constitutional Court, from the former
Supreme Courts, on a constitutional matter on which
the Supreme Court has already rendered an opinion.

CHASKALSON P [unanimous decision]

[2] In the United States of America, and as long
ago as 1885, Matthews, J said:

[N]ever ... anticipate a question of constitutional law in
advance of the necessity of deciding it; ... never ...
formulate a rule of constitutional law broader than is
required by the precise facts to which it is to be applied.

This rule, though not absolute, has ordinarily
been followed by courts in the United States of
America since then. Although the United States
jurisprudence is influenced by the 'case' and
'Controversy' requirement of Article III of the
US Constitution, the rule stated by Matthews, J
is a salutary rule which has been followed in
other countries.

[3] It is also consistent with the requirements
of section 102 of our Constitution and the
decision of this Court in *S v Mhlungu and Others*
where Kentridge AJ said:

I would lay it down as a general principle that where it
is possible to decide any case, civil or criminal, without
reaching a constitutional issue, that is the course which
should be followed.

[4] The same principle ... require appeals from a
provincial or local division of the Supreme Court
to be dealt with first by the Appellate Division
and, where possible, to be disposed of by that
Court without the constitutional issue having to
be addressed. It is only where it is necessary for
the purpose of disposing of the appeal, or where
it is in the interest of justice to do so, that the
constitutional issue should be dealt with first by
this Court. It will only be *necessary* for this to be

done where the appeal cannot be disposed of
without the constitutional issue being decided;
and it will only be in the *interest of justice* for a
constitutional issue to be decided first, where
there are compelling reasons that this should be
done.

[5] This rule allows the law to develop
incrementally. In view of the far reaching
implications attaching to constitutional decisions, it is a rule which should ordinarily be
adhered to by this and all other South African
courts before whom constitutional issues are
raised. It is within this context that the
provisions of section 102(8) should be viewed
and interpreted.

[6] Section 102(8) of the Constitution
applies only to cases which have been disposed
of. A referral of the moot issue in such
circumstances is the exception, and it follows
that the section should be invoked only in
exceptional circumstances. In other words, there
must be a compelling public interest that
requires the reference to be made.

[7] It is not ordinarily desirable for a court to
give rulings in the abstract on issues which are
not the subject of controversy and are only of
academic interest, and section 102(8) should
not be invoked in order to refer to this court an
issue which was not relevant to the case which
had to be decided. In the present case, it is not
clear from the judgments of the Ciskei Provincial Division whether the issue concerning the
jurisdiction of provincial and local divisions of
the Supreme Court generally, as distinct from
the jurisdiction of the Ciskei Provincial Division,
was in fact raised during the proceedings, or
whether it was raised only in the judgments. But
even if the issue was raised during the proceedings, it was not, as appears from the judgment of
Trengove AJ, relevant to the case which had to
be decided. Section 102(8) should therefore not
have been invoked.

[8] The issue has, however, become one of
public importance as a result of the judgments
given by the Ciskei Supreme Court. The
judgments held that provincial and local divisions of the Supreme Court have jurisdiction to
enquire into the validity of Acts of Parliament

passed prior to the 27th April 1994. For the reasons given by Trengove AJ this is not correct, and to avoid the uncertainty that might otherwise result from such judgments, it has been necessary

for this Court to deal with that issue. This Court is not, however, obliged to, and will not ordinarily decide issues, which are not correctly referred to it under Section 102(8).

There are, however, exceptional situations where the Court would consider issues that are hypothetical. In *Du Plessis v De Klerk*,[50] the Court was faced with the question of whether the Bill of Rights, under the interim Constitution, had horizontal application. The dispute between two parties arose before April 1994, which meant that the provisions did not apply to the dispute at hand. The Court, however, proceeded to determine the issue of horizontality because it felt that the matter was of public importance, especially given the conflicting approaches adopted by the various lower courts.[51]

Standing

Closely tied to the requirement of a case and controversy is the requirement of standing, or *locus standi* as it is more commonly known in South Africa.[52] The concern is whether the party bringing an action has a sufficient stake in the outcome of the case, and not whether there is any merit to the legal argument of wrongdoing on the part of the defendant. Therefore, it is not sufficient for the party to show that the defendant's action is invalid. The plaintiff has to show that he or she has sustained (or is in immediate danger of sustaining) some immediate injury as a result of the action.[53] The Constitution adopts different standards on standing depending on whether the plaintiff's case is based on a mere claim of wrongdoing on the

part of the defendant, versus a claim of wrongdoing which affects rights protected in the Bill of Rights. In the former instance the standards are more rigid; in the latter instance the standards for standing are more flexible.

Standing based on claim of mere wrongdoing

First, the party bringing an action must have a direct interest in the outcome of the case. Chaskalson P, writing for a six-judge majority affirmed the requirement of standing, in the absence of which the Court would not adjudicate over an issue.[54] The Court majority stated emphatically that it would not adjudicate over hypothetical or academic disputes.[55] Applicants, therefore, need to show direct harm or a threat of harm against them. The Court's reference to s 7 of the Constitution refers to s 7 of the interim Constitution. The provisions on standing are now contained in s 38 of the final Constitution.

In the United States, the courts insist that the injury must be 'distinct and palpable' and not 'abstract' or 'conjectural' or 'hypothetical'.[56] Moreover, the injury must be traceable to the challenged action, and relief from the injury must be 'likely to follow from a favorable decision'.[57] In *Allen v Wright*, the respondents who were black parents, brought a claim for injunctive and declaratory relief to require the Internal Revenue Service (IRS) to deny tax-exempt status to all

---

[50] *Du Plessis and Others v De Klerk and Others* CCT 8/95 (15 May 1996), now cited as 1996 (5) BCLR 658 (CC); 1995 (3) SA 850 (CC).

[51] *Supra* para 30.

[52] *Locus standi*: the capacity of parties to participate in legal proceedings. If a person is found not to have the requisite capacity to sue, that person may not be a party to any civil action. To establish *locus standi*, a person needs to show enough facts to substantiate an interest to institute the proceedings. WJ Hosten, AB Edwards, Francis Bosman, and Joan Church (eds) *Introduction to South African Law and Legal Theory* Durban: Butterworths, 2nd edition, 1995, 1145–6.

[53] *Frothingham v Mellon* 262 US 447, 488 (1923).

[54] See *Ferreira v Levin and Others* paras 164–165.

[55] *Supra*.

[56] *Allen v Wright* 468 US 737, 751 (1984).

[57] *Supra*.

private schools that discriminated on the basis of race. The respondents' children had not applied to any of the alleged racially discriminatory schools. The respondents' claim of injury was based on an assertion that the government was violating IRS regulations that denied giving tax-exempt status to private schools that had racially discriminatory practices.[58] The defendants argued that the government's failure to carry out the statutory requirement amounted to federal support of segregated schools, and perpetuated racially segregated schools. The Court held that respondents' claim of injury was twofold: first, to have the government not violate the law; and secondly, a claim of stigmatic injury when the government discriminates on the basis of race.[59] The Court majority held that defendants did not have standing simply based on the government's

violation of the law.[60] The Court does not have jurisdiction to simply order the government not to violate the law when the defendants themselves did not suffer injury.[61] With respect to the defendants' claim of injury, the Court held that the injury must not be an abstract or stigmatic injury. The defendants themselves must be racially discriminated against. To hold otherwise would mean that a black person in Hawaii could challenge a racially discriminatory action in Maine (over six thousand miles away) that does not affect him or her. Similarly, in *Valley Forge Christian College v Americans United for Separation of Church and State*, the United States Supreme Court stated that claimants cannot 'roam the country in search of governmental wrongdoing and to reveal their discoveries in federal court'.[62]

Ferreira v Levin NO and Others; Vryenhoek and Others v Powell NO and Others
CCT 5/95 (6 December 1995), now cited as 1996 (1) SA 984 (CC); 1996 (1) BCLR 1 (CC)
(notes omitted)
CHASKALSON P [concurred by MAHOMED DP, DIDCOTT, LANGA, MADALA JJ and TRENGOVE AJ]

[162] In the present case the Applicants allege that section 417(2)(b) is inconsistent with section 25(3) of the Constitution. This is a matter which this Court has jurisdiction to enquire into, and it can do so in the present case if the Applicants have standing to seek such an order from it. Ordinarily a person whose rights are directly affected by an invalid law in a manner adverse to such person, has standing to challenge the validity of that law in the courts. There can be no question that the Applicants have such an interest in the present case. Their right to refuse to answer questions that incriminate them is in issue and they seek to vindicate that right by challenging the only

obstacle to their assertion of it. It was argued, however, that this does not apply to the present Applicants because section 7(4) of the Constitution limits constitutional challenges to persons whose constitutional rights have been impaired or threatened. And, so the argument went, this could occur only if they are charged with a criminal offence and the evidence given by them at the enquiry is tendered against them at the criminal trial.

[163] If there is a conflict between section 25(3) of the Constitution and section 417(2)(b) which, viewed objectively, renders section 417(2)(b) invalid to the extent of that inconsistency, it seems to me to be highly technical to say that a witness called to a section 417(2)(b) enquiry lacks standing to challenge the constitutionality of the section. A witness who genuinely fears prosecution if he or she is called upon to give incriminating answers cannot be said to lack an interest in the decision on the constitutionality of the section. To deny the witness the right to challenge the constitutionality of the section in

---

[58] *Supra* at 737.
[59] *Supra* at 754.
[60] *Supra* at 759.
[61] *Supra* at 759–760.
[62] *Valley Forge Christian College v Americans United for Separation of Church and State* 454 US 464, 766 (1982).

such circumstances is in effect to say to the witness: the only obstacle to your right to refuse to answer incriminating questions is an unconstitutional provision, but you cannot ask this Court to declare the provision unconstitutional because you have not yet been charged. What if the witness refuses to answer and is threatened with imprisonment? Surely the witness would then be entitled to challenge the constitutionality of the section on which the prosecution is based. The fact that the witness might be entitled to turn to section 11(1) of the Constitution to found a constitutional challenge is not in my view an adequate answer to that dilemma. The right to challenge the constitutionality of a statute which affects you directly cannot be made dependent on the finding of some other constitutional right on which to base the challenge. What if there is no such right?

[164] The objection to constitutional challenges brought by persons who have only a hypothetical or academic interest in the outcome of the litigation is referred to in *Zantsi v Council of State, Ciskei and Others*. The principal reasons for this objection are that in an adversarial system decisions are best made when there is a genuine dispute in which each party has an interest to protect. There is moreover the need to conserve scarce judicial resources and to apply them to real and not hypothetical disputes. The United States courts also have regard to 'the proper role of the Courts in a democratic society' which is to settle concrete disputes, and to the need to prevent courts from being drawn into unnecessary conflict with coordinate branches of government. These objections do not apply to the present case. The Applicants have a real and not a hypothetical interest in the decision. The decision will not be academic; on the contrary it is a decision which will have an effect on all section 417 enquiries and there is a pressing public interest that the decision be given as soon as possible. All the requirements ordinarily set by a court for the exercise of its jurisdiction to issue a declaration of rights are therefore present. The question is whether different considerations apply in constitutional cases.

[165] Whilst it is important that this Court should not be required to deal with abstract or hypothetical issues, and should devote its scarce resources to issues that are properly before it, I can see no good reason for adopting a narrow approach to the issue of standing in constitutional cases. On the contrary, it is my view that we should rather adopt a broad approach to standing. This would be consistent with the mandate given to this Court to uphold the Constitution and would serve to ensure that constitutional rights enjoy the full measure of the protection to which they are entitled. Such an approach would also be consistent in my view with the provisions of section 7(4) of the Constitution on which counsel for the Respondents based his argument. I will deal later with the terms of this section and the purpose that it serves.

[166] The Canadian courts accept that persons have a standing to challenge unconstitutional law if they are liable to conviction for an offence under the law even though the unconstitutional effects are not directed against [them] per se. It is sufficient for the accused to show that he or she is directly affected by the unconstitutional legislation. If this is shown '... it matters not whether he is the victim'.

[167] I do not read section 7(4) as denying the Applicants this right. The section deals with the situation where '... an infringement of or threat to any right entrenched in this Chapter is alleged ...'. It therefore applies specifically to the jurisdiction vested in the courts by section 98(2)(a) and 101(3)(a) of the Constitution to deal with 'any alleged violation or threatened violation of any fundamental right entrenched in Chapter 3'. But section 98(2) vests a general jurisdiction in this Court to interpret, protect and enforce the provisions of the Constitution. Section 7(4) in dealing with the section 98(2)(a) jurisdiction provides that where an infringement or threat to the infringement of a constitutional right is alleged, any of the persons referred to in section 7(4)(b) will have standing to bring the matter to 'a competent court of law'. The category of persons empowered to do so is broader than the category of persons who have hitherto been allowed standing in cases

where it is alleged that a right has been infringed or threatened, and to that extent the section demonstrates a broad and not a narrow approach to standing.

[168] Once it is accepted, as Ackermann J has, that the issue of constitutionality has to be tested objectively and not subjectively, there is no valid reason for denying persons in the position of the Applicants standing to secure a ruling on the validity of a law that directly affects their interests. Even if section 7(4) were to be read extensively as applying by inference to all the subsections of section 98(2), I would not see it as an obstacle to the Applicants' case. In that event it would have to be read as meaning 'where an infringement of or threat to any right entrenched in this Chapter [or any dispute over the constitutionality of any executive or administrative act or conduct or threatened administrative act or conduct of any organ of the state, or any enquiry into the constitutionality of any law, including an Act of Parliament, irrespective of whether such law was passed or made before or after the commencement of this Constitution ...] is alleged' the persons referred to in paragraph (b) shall have standing. There would be no need on this extensive interpretation of the section to construe section 7(4)(b)(i) as meaning that the person acting in his or her own interest must be a person whose constitutional right has been infringed or threatened. This is not what the section says. What the section requires is that the person concerned should make the challenge in his or her own interest. It is for this Court to decide what is a sufficient interest in such circumstances. In my view, on the facts of the present case, the Applicants have a sufficient interest to seek such a ruling. If that is so they can rely on the argument that viewed objectively section 417(2)(b) is inconsistent with the Constitution because it infringes the right to a fair trial guaranteed by section 25(3).

Ferreira establishes clearly that the plaintiff does not have to sustain injury.[63] The standing requirement is satisfied when there is a reasonable apprehension of injury. Here the plaintiff, if forced to testify, could have faced the prospect that the testimony could be used against him or her in subsequent criminal proceedings. The application of the statute posed a threat the right of the plaintiff against self-incrimination.

The requirement of injury or threat to injury precludes adjudication of a case based on possible harm to a hypothetical plaintiff.[64] To rule otherwise would open up the judicial process to 'cranks and busybodies'.[65] The fact that an individual is a taxpayer is not sufficient to confer standing to prevent government wrongdoing.[66]

There are some jurisdictions – such as Canada and India[67] – which adopt a lenient attitude to standing. In the Canadian case of *Finlay*,[68] the plaintiff sought a ruling that the federal government's payments to the Province of Manitoba was illegal because Manitoba was not complying with the requirements of cost-sharing called for by the statute.[69] A ruling in the plaintiff's favour would not have redressed the plaintiff's real grievance which was entitlement to income support – a matter governed by provincial legislation. The challenge to the federal legislation amounted to the plaintiff wanting the government to stop engaging in wrongful conduct. There was an absence of any injury, or threat of injury, to the plaintiff, which could be traced to the defendant's conduct. A ruling by the court that the Government of Canada was not complying with the statute would not have any effect on the plaintiff's income. Despite the absence of injury, the

---

[63] *Ferreira* para 167.
[64] *Supra* para 164. See also the Irish case of *Cahill v Sutton* [1980] IR 269. See also Kelly 439.
[65] Ibid.
[66] *Frothingham v Mellon* 486–489.
[67] *Wadhwa v State of India* AIR (1987) SC 579.
[68] *Finlay v Minister of Finance of Canada* [1986] 2 RCS 342. See also the Indian case of *Wadhwa v State of India*.
[69] *Finlay* at 611.

Supreme Court of Canada ruled that the plaintiff had standing because the issue presented a question of law relating to the legality of government action.[70]

The Canadian courts – when extending standing to a party who has no special interest in the case – usually require the party to establish, first, that the action raises a serious legal issue, secondly, that the plaintiff has a genuine interest in having the issue resolved, and thirdly, that there is no other reasonable or effective manner to bring the matter before the court.[71] In our opinion, the liberal practice with respect to standing in Canada should not be followed in South Africa. The Canadian approach arguably amounts to judicial overreaching. To ask an open question such as whether there is any other way of bringing the matter before the court lays the standing doctrine open to the potential for manipulation. It also opens the court to criticism that it is pursuing extraneous ends or pursuing its views on the merits.[72] The standing requirement serves several goals. First, it is a prudential tool of self-restraint on an unelected and unaccountable judiciary. Secondly, it prevents bystanders or intermediaries from litigating the rights of others. Thirdly, it prevents the opening of the floodgates of litigation. Fourthly, by insisting on the standing requirement, the court assures the concrete adverseness which is more likely to ensure that the issues are presented in a sharpened form, thus avoiding the rendering of advisory opinions.[73] Fifthly, and arguably most important, is that the standing requirement is related to the doctrine of separation of powers – that the judicial role should be limited to concrete disputes involving real contending parties. The reluctance of both the Irish and United States Supreme Courts to adjudicate over a matter in the absence of the standing requirement is premised largely on separation of powers arguments, namely that it is undesirable that political opposition when it loses in the legislature (without incurring any legal harm) subsequently attempts to win the political battle in the courts.[74] Instead of allowing busy-bodies to bring challenges to laws which might affect the interest of other parties, ways should be found to extend legal assistance to individuals to vindicate their own rights.

Standing based on a claim of violation of the Bill of Rights

The Constitution provides very broad standing where there is a violation of fundamental rights Section 38 of the Constitution provides:

> Anyone listed in this section has the right to approach a competent court, alleging that a right in the Bill of Rights has been infringed or threatened, and the court may grant appropriate relief, including a declaration of rights. The persons who may approach a court are:
> (a) anyone acting in their own interest;
> (b) anyone acting on behalf of another person who cannot act in their own name;
> (c) anyone acting as a member of, or in the interest of, a group or class of persons;
> (d) anyone acting in the public interest; and
> (e) an association acting in the interest of its members.

Whereas the traditional rule in a court case is that only the party that is affected by the defendant's conduct has any right to bring an action, the framers of the Constitution provided that harm or threat of harm to the plaintiff is not required to raise a constitutional question where there is a violation of the Bill of Rights. The most far-reaching provision is s 38(d), which allows standing to anyone acting in the public interest. This broad approach to standing, where fundamental human rights are involved, is consistent with developments in the field of international human rights. In international law, if an individual is harmed by a second state, only the state of which

---

[70] *Supra* at 613.

[71] *Supra* at 625. See also Peter W Hogg *Constitutional Law of Canada* Scarborough: Carswell, 3rd edition, 1992, 1269.

[72] Tribe makes the point that in applying the standing doctrine, courts are often criticized in this way. Arguably, by extending standing in terms of such an open question exacerbates criticism of the court pursuing unacknowledged and impermissible ends. Tribe 110.

[73] *Flast v Cohen* 392 US 83, 99 (1968).

[74] Kelly 439. For the argument that court's insistence on standing is based on separation of powers principles in the US, see *Allen v Wright* 468 US at 752.

the individual is a national can bring an action on behalf of the aggrieved individual.[75] To rule otherwise would open the floodgates of legal claims by third states on behalf of nationals from other states.[76] However, where there is a violation of an obligation *erga omnes* (a duty owed to the international community, such as respect for fundamental human rights), and there is consent to the jurisdiction of the International Court of Justice, any state party has standing to bring an action before the Court.[77]

Ultimately the scope of s 38 *(d)* would depend on the Court's interpretation of 'the public interest'. The Canadian Supreme Court began its relaxed interpretation of standing in areas pertaining to human rights.[78] It later extended standing to individuals not harmed by governmental conduct, and outside the human rights area, to defend against wrongful government action.[79] Under the South African Constitution, the wide-standing requirement is limited to protection of fundamental human rights contained in the Bill of Rights. However, at least one judge of the Constitutional Court, namely O'Regan J in *Ferreira*, has endorsed the wide Canadian view of standing in interpreting s 7(4) of the interim Constitution (which provisions are identical in substance to s 39(1) of the Constitution.[80]

Ferreira v Levin NO and Others; Vryenhoek and Others v Powell NO and Others
CCT 5/95 (6 December 1995), now cited as 1996 (1) SA 984 (CC); 1996 (1) BCLR 1 (CC)
(notes omitted)
O'REGAN J (dissenting)

[224] The applicants allege that section 417(2)*(b)* constitutes a breach of the rights of accused persons, in that it permits the admission of evidence in a criminal trial which has been compelled from those accused persons in a section 417 enquiry. The difficulty the applicants face is that they have not yet been charged, nor is there any allegation on the record to suggest that they consider that there is a threat that a prosecution may be launched against them, after they have given evidence at the section 417 enquiry, in which that evidence will be used against them.

[225] Section 7(4) of the Constitution provides that:

(a) When an infringement of or threat to any right entrenched in this Chapter is alleged, any person referred to in paragraph (b) shall be entitled to apply to a competent court of law for appropriate relief, which may include a declaration of rights

(b) The relief referred to in paragraph (a) may be sought by—

  (i) a person acting in his or her own interest;

  (ii) an association acting in the interest of its members;

  (iii) a person acting on behalf of another person who is not in a position to seek such relief in his or her own name;

---

[75] JG Starke *Introduction to International Law* London: Butterworths, 10th edition, 1989, 315.

[76] Ibid.

[77] Case concerning *The Barcelona Traction Light and Power Company Limited* (*Belgium v Spain*), Second Phase International Court of Justice, (1970) 1970 ICJ 3. However, to bring the matter before the ICJ, there has to be consent to jurisdiction of the Court by all parties, either under art 35(2) of the Statute of the Court, or by treaty.

[78] eg *Thorson v Attorney-General of Canada* (1975) 1 SCR 138 (pertaining to language rights); *Nova Scotia Board of Censors v McNeil* (1976) 2 SCR 265 (pertaining to film censorship); *Minister of Justice Canada v Borowski* (1981) 2 SCR 575 (dealing with the right to abortion).

[79] *Finlay* at 613.

[80] *Ferreira* para 73. See also *Executive Council of the Province of the Western Cape v The Minister for Provincial Affairs and Constitutional Development and Another* CCT 15/99 (15 October 1999) para 10, now cited as 2000 (1) SA 661 (CC); 1999 (12) BCLR 1360 (CC), where Ngcobo J in dicta stated that any person could raise the constitutionality of various provisions of the Local Government: Municipal Structures Act 117 of 1998 before the High Court.

(iv) a person acting as a member of or in the interest of a group or class of persons; or

(v) a person acting in the public interest.

[226] Ackermann J (at para 38) finds that persons acting in their own interest (as contemplated by section 7(4)(b)(i)) may only seek relief from the court where their rights, and not the rights of others, are infringed. I respectfully disagree with this approach. It seems clear to me from the text of section 7(4) that a person may have an interest in the infringement or threatened infringement of the right of another which would afford such a person the standing to seek constitutional relief. In addition, such an interpretation fits best contextually with the overall approach adopted in section 7(4).

[227] There are many circumstances where it may be alleged that an individual has an interest in the infringement or threatened infringement of the right of another. Several such cases have come before the Canadian courts. In *R v Big M Drug Mart Ltd* [1985] 13 CRR 64, a corporation was charged in terms of a statute which prohibited trading on Sundays. The corporation did not have a right to religious freedom, but nevertheless it was permitted to raise the constitutionality of the statute which was held to be in breach of the Charter. A similar issue arose in *Morgentaler, Smoling and Scott v R* [1988] 31 CRR 1 in which male doctors, prosecuted under anti-abortion provisions, successfully challenged the constitutionality of the legislation in terms of which they were prosecuted. In both of these cases, the prosecution was based on a provision which itself directly infringed the rights of people other than the accused. The Canadian jurisprudence on standing is not directly comparable to ours, however, for their constitutional provisions governing standing are different, but the fact that situations of this nature arise is instructive of the need for a broad approach to standing.

[228] In this case, however, although the challenge is section 417(2)(b) in its entirety, the constitutional objection lies in the condition that evidence given under compulsion in an enquiry, whether incriminating or not, may be used in a subsequent prosecution. There is no allegation on the record of any actual or threatened prosecution in which such evidence is to be led.

[229] There can be little doubt that section 7(4) provides for a generous and expanded approach to standing in the constitutional context. The categories of persons who are granted standing to seek relief are far broader than our common law has ever permitted. (See, for a discussion, Erasmus *Superior Court Practice* (1994) A2-17 to A2-33.) In this respect, I agree with Chaskalson P (at paras 165–166). This expanded approach to standing is quite appropriate for constitutional litigation. Existing common-law rules of standing have often developed in the context of private litigation. As a general rule, private litigation is concerned with the determination of a dispute between two individuals, in which relief will be specific and, often, retrospective, in that it applies to a set of past events. Such litigation will generally not directly affect people who are not parties to the litigation. In such cases, the plaintiff is both the victim of the harm and the beneficiary of the relief. In litigation of a public character, however, that nexus is rarely so intimate. The relief sought is generally forward-looking and general in its application, so that it may directly affect a wide range of people. In addition, the harm alleged may often be quite diffuse or amorphous. Of course, these categories are ideal types: no bright line can be drawn between private litigation and litigation of a public or constitutional nature. Not all non-constitutional litigation is private in nature. Nor can it be said that all constitutional challenges involve litigation of a purely public character: a challenge to a particular administrative act or decision may be of a private rather than a public character. But it is clear that in litigation of a public character, different considerations may be appropriate to determine who should have standing to launch litigation. In recognition of this, section 7(4) casts a wider net for standing than has traditionally been cast by the common law.

[230] Section 7(4) is a recognition too of the particular role played by the courts in a

constitutional democracy. As the arm of government which is entrusted primarily with the interpretation and enforcement of constitutional rights, it carries a particular democratic responsibility to ensure that those rights are honoured in our society. This role requires that access to the courts in constitutional matters should not be precluded by rules of standing developed in a different constitutional environment in which a different model of adjudication predominated. In particular, it is important that it is not only those with vested interests who should be afforded standing in constitutional challenges, where remedies may have a wide impact.

[231] However, standing remains a factual question. In each case, applicants must demonstrate that they have the necessary interest in an infringement or threatened infringement of a right. The facts necessary to establish standing should appear from the record before the court. As I have said, there is no evidence on the record in this case which would meet the requirements of section 7(4)(b)(i). The applicants have alleged neither a threat of a prosecution in which compelled evidence may be led against them, nor an interest in the infringement or threatened infringement of the rights of other persons. This situation, may have arisen because the case was referred by Van Schalkwyk J in terms of section 102(1); it did not arise originally as an application for direct access. Accordingly, there are no affidavits before the court in support of a direct access application. The only document on the record in this court was the decision of Van Schalkwyk J.

[233] In the special circumstances of this case, it appears to me that the applicants may rely upon section 7(4)(b)(v), as applicants acting in the public interest. The possibility that applicants may be granted standing on the grounds that they are acting in the public interest is a new departure in our law. Even the old *actiones populares* of Roman Law afforded a right to act in the public interest only in narrowly circumscribed causes of action. Section 7(4)(b)(v) is the provision in which the expansion of the ordinary rules of standing is

most obvious and it needs to be interpreted in the light of the special role that the courts now play in our constitutional democracy.

[234] This court will be circumspect in affording applicants standing by way of section 7(4)(b)(v) and will require an applicant to show that he or she is genuinely acting in the public interest. Factors relevant to determining whether a person is genuinely acting in the public interest will include considerations such as: whether there is another reasonable and effective manner in which the challenge can be brought; the nature of the relief sought, and the extent to which it is of general and prospective application; and the range of persons or groups who may be directly or indirectly affected by any order made by the court and the opportunity that those persons or groups have had to present evidence and argument to the court. These factors will need to be considered in the light of the facts and circumstances of each case.

[235] Although in this case too, section 7(4)(a) requires applicants to allege an infringement of or threat to a right contained in Chapter 3, applicants under section 7(4)(b)(v) need not point to an infringement of or threat to the right of a particular person. They need to allege that, objectively speaking, the challenged rule or conduct is in breach of a right enshrined in Chapter 3. This flows from the notion of acting in the public interest. The public will ordinarily have an interest in the infringement of rights generally, not particularly.

[236] In this case, it is clear from the referral that the applicants consider that section 417(2)(b) is, objectively speaking, in breach of chapter 3. Although the challenge could be brought by other persons, a considerable delay may result if this court were to wait for such a challenge. It is also clear that the challenge is to the constitutionality of a provision contained in an Act of Parliament and that the relief sought is a declaration of invalidity. It is relief which falls exclusively within the jurisdiction of this court and it is of a general, not particular, nature. In addition, adequate notice of the constitutional challenge has been given and a wide range of different individuals and organisations have

lodged memoranda and *amicus curiae* briefs in the matter. At the hearing also, the matter of the constitutionality of section 417 was thoroughly argued. There can be little doubt that those directly interested in the constitutionality of section 417 have had an opportunity to place their views before the court.

[237] In these special circumstances, it seems to me that the applicants have established standing to act in the public interest to challenge the constitutionality of section 417(2)*(b)*. It is also clear that the exceptional circumstances necessary to warrant a grant of direct access exist. Accordingly, I agree with Ackermann J that the applicants should be granted direct access in respect of the first issue referred to this court by the Transvaal Provincial Division of the Supreme Court. In my view, however, the application for direct access on the other issues referred to this court should fail. None of these issues fall within the exclusive jurisdiction of this court. They are best dealt with by the Supreme Court, as they arise in litigation before it.

O'Regan's approach is flawed for several reasons: first, she fails to identify the limited area for an expansive standing in the Constitution; secondly, she fails to identify where she obtains the standards for standing, and thirdly, she provides standards but fails to show us how she applied these to the case at hand.

O' Regan J adopts a very broad interpretation of the public interest. This approach contrasts with the text which provides broad standing based on public interest only to vindicate the protection of fundamental rights. The text does not support the broad approach, which the Canadian Supreme Court has adopted and which the majority rightly resisted. She also states that the court will be 'circumspect in affording applicants standing' and will require the applicant to show that he or she is 'genuinely acting in the public interest'.[81] She provides a three-part test to determine whether a person is acting in the public interest, namely, first, whether there is another reasonable and effective manner in which the challenge can be brought; secondly, whether the nature of the relief sought and the extent to which it is of general and prospective application, and thirdly, whether the range of persons or groups who may be directly or indirectly affected by an order made by the court and the opportunity that those persons or groups have had to present evidence and argument to the court. O'Regan J fails to mention from where she derives this three-part test. She concludes that the applicants did not sustain direct injury and that there was no threat of injury. O'Regan J also fails to individually apply each part of her test to the case at hand. Instead, she grants standing based on the possibility of considerable delay if the court were to wait for a challenge by other persons affected by the statute.

We see the opinion as an alarming manipulation of the standing doctrine. It opens the court to criticism of what Professor Tribe cautions against; namely unprincipled decision-making, pursuing extraneous ends, or pursuing its views on the merits.[82]

---

[81] *Ferreira* para 234.

[82] Tribe makes the point that in applying the standing doctrine, courts are often criticized in this way. See Tribe 110.

S v Lawrence; S v Negal; S v Solberg
**CCT 38/96; 39/96; 40/96 (6 October
1997), now cited as 1997 (10)
BCLR 1348 (CC); 1997 (4)
SA 1176 (CC).**
(notes omitted)

*Authors' note: The Court was faced with a challenge to
the Liquor Act 27 of 1989, which Act prohibited some
vendors from selling certain kinds of alcoholic beverages
on Sundays, and certain Christian holidays. The
appellants challenged the Act on various grounds
including freedom of religion. They argued that the
Act, by forcing them not to sell alcohol on Christian days
of worship, violated their freedom of religion. There was
no evidence on the appellants religious belief, and there
was no evidence that their freedom of religion was
harmed. However, since the challenge was based on a
purported violation of the Bill of Rights, the appellants
had standing to challenge the constitutionality of the
Act.*

O'REGAN J

[113] There is no evidence on the record to establish the
appellant's religious beliefs. There can be no doubt
however that she has a direct interest in the
constitutionality of the provisions under scrutiny. If
they are held to be unconstitutional on the grounds she
has raised, then her conviction may be set aside. If they
are found not to be inconsistent with the interim
Constitution on those grounds, then the conviction will
stand. This interest is clearly sufficient to found her
challenge to the provisions.

SACHS J

[140] To complicate the matter further, the
challenge based on section 14 came not from
believers whose faith was being threatened, but
from grocers whose profits were being limited.
The applicants were, of course, quite entitled to
raise the issue of the constitutionality, in terms
of section 14, of a law which placed restrictions
on their commercial activities. Yet, the result
was an air of artificiality in relation to this aspect
of the case, and a lack of evidence, from the side
both of the applicants and of the state, on the
question of the purpose and impact of closed
days. If ever there was a case which required
close contextual rather than purely abstract
analysis, it was this one, and if ever a cupboard
was bare of concrete contextual information it
was the one in the present matter.

[154] As I have said, although the section 14
issue of principle is real, the way it came to us
was artificial. The objective was to abolish a
commercial restraint, not to secure a religious
freedom. Thus, the matter before us arises out of
a prosecution of an employee of a grocery chain
store whose actual complaint was that she was
compelled by the state not to sell liquor on a
Sunday. She did not allege that she was obliged
by her religion not to sell liquor on a day other
than Sunday as well, and, as a result of her belief,
subjected by the state to an invidious choice
between following her religion or pursuing her
trade. Nevertheless, it was not a precondition for
her bringing of the case that she establish that
her own rights of religion, belief or opinion were
trespassed upon. It was sufficient for her to
complain that her rights were infringed as a
result of her being prosecuted in terms of a
statutory provision which, objectively speaking,
was invalid because it violated section 14.

Ripeness

Another court-created barrier to adjudication is
ripeness. Ripeness means that a matter which is
premature should not be decided until all the
factors necessary for a decision have developed.[83]
In *Ferreira*, Kriegler J defined ripeness as serving
'the useful purpose of highlighting that the
business of a court is generally retrospective; it
deals with situations or problems that have already
ripened or crystallized, and not with prospective or
hypothetical [problems]'.[84] A decision that a
matter is not ripe entails a judgment that the
matter is not yet fit for judicial decision.[85] For
example, assume that we have a statute which if

---

[83] Ralph A Rossum and Alan G Tarr *American Constitutional Law: Cases and Interpretation* New York: St Martin's Press, 3rd edition, 1991, 53.

[84] *Ferreira* para 199.

[85] *Abbott Laboratories v Gardner* 387 US 136 (1967).

implemented may target a group of individuals. The fact that the statute if implemented may affect individuals is not sufficient for the court to adjudicate the issue. It may be that the government may not target the individuals at all. It is only when the statute is implemented, or when it definitely will be implemented, and might cause harm to the plaintiff, does it present a ripe issue for adjudication.[86] In the absence of a well-developed and sufficiently real dispute, the Court will not be able to render a principled decision. Any decision rendered while the relationship between the parties is still in a state of flux will hinge on speculation about how the parties may behave.[87]

Transvaal Agricultural Union v The Minister of Land Affairs and the Commission of Restitution of Land Rights
CCT 21/95 (18 November 1996), now cited as 1996 (12) BCLR 1573 (CC); 1997 (2) SA 621 (CC).
(notes omitted)

Authors' note: Applicants representing the interests of various farmers brought an action to have various sections of the Restitution of Land Rights Act 22 of 1994 set aside. Applicants argued that the Act violated their constitutional rights as landowners, and that the statute denied them a right of hearing. The unanimous court, per Chaskalson P, ruled that the latter claim depended on how the Commission on Restitution of Land Rights interpreted its mandate.[88] The court ruled that there was a need for all the factors that are necessary for the resolution of a dispute to develop, before the court considers the matter.

CHASKALSON P [unanimous court]

Introduction
[1] The Transvaal Agricultural Union is a body established to represent the interests of its members who are farmers. It has applied directly to this Court for an order declaring that sections 6(1)(c), 9(1)(b), 11(1), 11(6)(b), 11(7), 11(8), and 13(2)(b) of the Restitution of Land Rights Act 22 of 1994, and rules 13 and 14 of the rules regarding the procedure of the Commission on Restitution of Land Rights, promulgated in terms of section 16(1) of that Act, are inconsistent with the Constitution, and accordingly invalid. The provisions are material to the interests of members of the applicant, and it was not disputed that it has standing . . . to bring this application.

[5] The Restitution of Land Rights Act was enacted pursuant to the provisions of sections 121 to 123 of the Constitution. The provisions of these sections that are relevant to the present dispute are as follows:

121 Claims – (1) An Act of Parliament shall provide for matters relating to the restitution of land rights, as envisaged in this section and in sections 122 and 123.

(2) A person or a community shall be entitled to claim restitution of a right in land from the state if–

(a) such person or community was dispossessed of such right at any time after a date to be fixed by the Act referred to in subsection (1); and

(b) such dispossession was effected under or for the purpose of furthering the object of a law which would have been inconsistent with the prohibition of racial discrimination contained in section 8(2), had that section been in operation at the time of such dispossession.

(5) No claim under this section shall be lodged before the passing of the Act contemplated in subsection (1).

(6) Any claims under subsection (2) shall be subject to such conditions, limitations and exclusions as may be prescribed by such Act, and shall not be justiciable by a court

---

[86] See *Laird v Tatum* 408 US 1, 57 (1972).
[87] Rosum & Tarr 53.
[88] *Transvaal Agricultural Union* paras 25–26.

of law unless the claim has been dealt with in terms of section 122 by the Commission established by that section.

122 Commission.–

(1) The Act contemplated in section 121(1) shall establish a Commission on Restitution of Land Rights, which shall be competent to –

(a) investigate the merits of any claims;

(b) mediate and settle disputes arising from such claims;

(c) draw up reports on unsettled claims for submission as evidence to a court of law and to present any other relevant evidence to the court; and

(d) exercise and perform any such other powers and functions as may be provided for in the said Act.

(2) The procedures to be followed for dealing with claims in terms of this section shall be as prescribed by or under the said Act.

[6] The Restitution of Land Rights Act established the Commission to deal with matters referred to in section 122 of the Constitution, and a special court, the Land Claims Court, with the powers contemplated by section 123 of the Constitution. It is not necessary for the purposes of this judgment to set out the details of these powers.

[7] The principal function of the Commission is to process claims for restitution, by investigating the claims lodged with it, and where possible, securing settlement of claims through negotiations or mediation. Where this does not prove to be possible, the Commission is required to refer the claim to the Land Claims Court which is empowered to resolve it.

[8] The applicant does not dispute the validity of the legislation as such, or the need to make provision for the restitution of land rights. Its objection is confined to certain provisions of the legislation dealing with the

Commission, which it contends are inconsistent with the object, spirit and provisions of the Constitution.

The Challenge to Sections 11(1), 11(6)(b), 11(7), 11(8) and Rules 13 and 14

[9] The applicant objects in the first instance to certain provisions of section 11 of the Act. It contends that these provisions are inconsistent with the administrative justice provisions of section 24 of the Constitution, and in particular, with section 24(b) which vests in every person the right to procedurally fair administrative action where any of his or her rights or legitimate expectations is affected or threatened.

[12] A decision to publish a notice of the claim in the *Gazette* has certain consequences. Sections 11(7)(b) and (c) provide that no claimant who was resident on the land in question at the date of commencement of the Act may be evicted from the land, and no improvement on the land may be removed or destroyed, without the written authority of the Chief Land Claims Commissioner. Section 11(8) empowers a regional land claims commissioner who has reason to believe that any improvement on the land is likely to be removed, damaged or destroyed or that any person resident on such land may be adversely affected as a result of the publication of such notice to authorise officials or delegates of the Commission to enter upon the land to draw up an inventory of assets on the land, a list of persons employed or resident thereon, and to report on the agricultural condition of the land and of any excavations, mining or prospecting thereon. Rules 13 and 14 deal with the terms of the section 11(1) notice and the compilation of the inventory.

[24] The main objection, and the one primarily relied upon by the applicant as the basis for its contention that landowners have been prejudiced by the legislation, is that no provision is made in the statute for regional land claims commissioners to hear owners before issuing a section 11(1) notice.

[25] The mere fact that the legislation does not specifically make provision for such a hearing does not mean that there is indeed no such right. It is well established that:

... when a statute empowers a public official or body to give a decision prejudicially affecting an individual in his liberty or property or existing rights, the latter has a right to be heard before the decision is taken (or in some instances thereafter — see [*Cabinet for the Territory of South West Africa v Chikane and Another* 1989 (1) SA 349 (A)] at 379G), unless the statute expressly or by implication indicates the contrary.

[26] The question whether such right has been excluded by the Act in the present case depends, therefore, upon the proper interpretation of the statute. That, in the first instance, is a task for and within the jurisdiction of the Supreme Court. Counsel for the applicant contended, however, that the Act clearly excludes a right to a hearing, and that it was not necessary in the circumstances to approach the Supreme Court for such a ruling. He pointed out that rule 13(2) requires the section 11(1) notice to be given to all possible interested parties, including the registered landowner and contended that this implies that notice will not have been given to the owner earlier. The question whether a right to a hearing has been excluded depends, however, on an interpretation of the Act; if required by the Act, it cannot be excluded by the rules.

[27] The Act contemplates that regional land claims commissioners will scrutinise claims lodged with them to satisfy themselves that claims comply with the formal requirements of the Act, and are not frivolous or vexatious. If a claim is considered to be frivolous or vexatious, it can be dismissed summarily. If a claim meets the formal requirements of the Act, and is not considered by the regional land claims commissioner to be frivolous or vexatious, it will be accepted and the process laid down by the Act must then be followed.

[28] The registration of the claim in the deeds registry, which is required by section 11(6)(*b*) of the Act, does not in itself detract from the rights of the landowner or other persons interested in the property. The owner remains free to alienate or deal with the property and other interested parties are free to assert their rights. Registration is no more than notice to the world at large that the land in question is subject to a claim under the Act, information which the landowner would in any event have been obliged to disclose to any potential buyer or mortgagor.

[29] Section 11(7) of the Act which precludes evictions of claimants who are residing on the land, or interference with improvements upon the land, and section 11(8) which authorises entry upon land for the purposes of drawing up an inventory do detract from the rights of a landowner, and possibly of other interested parties as well. The Chief Land Claims Commissioner is, however, vested with the power to allow evictions and interference with improvements, and decisions of the Commissioner in that regard are subject to review by the Land Claims Court. Such decisions will have to be taken with due regard to rights which the landowner may have under the Constitution, and any justifiable limitation imposed upon such rights by the Act.

[30] In deciding whether the constitutional requirement that there be procedurally fair administrative action requires notice to be given by regional land claims commissioners to the landowners before issuing a section 11(1) notice, or whether their interests are sufficiently protected by notice given to them after such claims have been accepted, various matters would have to be considered by the Court. Without attempting to lay down what will be involved in such an enquiry, it seems clear that a Court would have to weigh up the interests of the claimants against those of the landowners, and consideration would have to be given to issues such as the temporary nature of the impediment; the purpose served by the status quo provision of section 11(7); whether there is a need for expedition in securing that purpose once a claim has been lodged; the harm done to landowners by the impediments placed upon them by sections 11(7) and (8); the vulnerability of the claimants and the harm that might be suffered by them if the status quo is not preserved; and the fact that there is an unrestricted right to approach a different official, the Chief Land Claims Commissioner, for authority to evict a claimant or interfere with improvements on the land. It might also be necessary to

consider whether the Act reasonably requires claims to be processed expeditiously.

[31] These are all matters on which the Supreme Court can and should give a decision, and which ought to be canvassed in the Supreme Court in the light of any evidence placed before it, before any approach is made to this Court for relief. A constitutional issue will arise only if the Supreme Court were to hold that on a proper construction of the Act, it requires claims to be dealt with in a manner inconsistent with procedurally fair administrative action. It is premature to approach this Court for a decision, before that issue has been determined.

Mootness

Closely related to the case and controversy requirement is the requirement of mootness. Where there is a succession of developments that bring about a change in the circumstances resulting in the plaintiff no longer having a stake in the outcome of the case, the courts in many jurisdictions will not adjudicate the matter because they consider the matter moot.[89] In other words, the plaintiff had a real dispute when the proceedings began, but subsequent developments caused the case or controversy to disappear. In contrast to the case and controversy requirement, which is considered at the time the proceedings first reach the Court, mootness relates to the plaintiff's stake in the outcome of the case after the commencement of proceedings A case can become moot by various circumstances including the death of a party, or the repeal of the offending law.[90] In other words, the case or controversy requirement has to exist not only at the beginning of the plaintiff's complaint but throughout the court's review. In the absence of this requirement, the plaintiff will not have standing.[91]

The mootness doctrine is not fully developed in South African constitutional jurisprudence and is unlikely to mirror the American approach because even if the issue becomes moot, the Court may still need to consider some aspect of the merits for purposes of determining costs. This was born out in *JT Publishing*:

> *JT Publishing (Pty) Ltd and Another v Minister of Safety and Security and Others* CCT 14/95 (21 November 1996), now cited as 1997 (3) SA 514 (CC); 1996 (12) BCLR 1599 (CC) (notes omitted)
>
> Authors' note: Here the applicants wanted an order from the Court declaring the Publication Act, the Indecent or Obscene Photographic Matter Act, or certain parts of both Acts, constitutionally invalid. The state opposed the application before the Supreme Court. By the time the matter came on appeal to the Constitutional Court, the two Acts in question were repealed by parliament. This made a rendering of a declaration by the Constitutional Court moot. Didcott J (for a unanimous Court) reiterated the need for a case or controversy. Nevertheless, the question of costs still had to be determined. While parliament had changed the law in question, the plaintiffs were still entitled to the legal costs they incurred before the law was changed.
>
> DIDCOTT J [unanimous opinion]
>
> [15] The reversal of the decision reached in the Court below brings duly before us the claim for a declaratory order which the applicants wish us to grant on the constitutional issues presented by them. That does not necessarily mean, however, that we are now bound to resolve those issues. Whether we should say anything at all about them must be settled first. I interpose that enquiry because a declaratory order is a discretionary remedy, in the sense that the claim lodged by an interested party for such an order

---

[89] *Janse van Rensburg and Another v Minister of Trade and Industry and Another* CCT 13/99 (29 September 2000) para 9. In the US, see *De Funis v Odegaard* 416 US 312 (1974). In Canada, see *R v Mercure* [1988] 1 SCR 234.

[90] Hogg 1275.

[91] *United States Parole Commission v Geraghty* 445 US 388, 397 (1980).

does not in itself oblige the Court handling the matter to respond to the question which it poses, even when that looks like being capable of a ready answer. A corollary is the judicial policy governing the discretion thus vested in the Courts, a well established and uniformly observed policy which directs them not to exercise it in favour of deciding points that are merely abstract, academic or hypothetical ones. I see no reason why this new Court of ours should not adhere in turn to a rule that sounds so sensible. Its provenance lies in the intrinsic character and object of the remedy, after all, rather than some jurisdictional concept peculiar to the work of the Supreme Court or otherwise foreign to that performed here. Perhaps, what is more, a declaratory order on an issue quite unsuitable for one does not even amount to appropriate relief, the type which section 7(4)(*a*) empowers us to grant. The description may well encompass not only the form of the relief but also the setting for it. We do not need to consider that suggestion, however, once our adoption of the rule appears to be wise in any event. We should no doubt regard it, like most general rules, as one that is subject in special circumstances to exceptions, in our field those necessitated now and then by factors which are fundamental to a proper constitutional adjudication. But, for reasons that will emerge in a moment, nothing warrants a departure from the policy this time. A further word or two had better be said on the topic before I leave it. Section 98 (5) admittedly enjoins us to declare that a law is invalid once we have found it to be inconsistent with the Constitution. But the requirement does not mean that we are compelled to determine the anterior issue of inconsistency when, owing to its wholly abstract, academic or hypothetical nature should it have such in a given case, our going into it can produce no concrete or tangible result, indeed none whatsoever beyond the bare declaration.

[16] The current state of affairs differs significantly from the situation that existed at the time when Daniels J heard the application for a referral. No staunch effort was made before us to defend the parts of the Publications Act that had come under fire, and by the time when the argument ended it seemed to have become common cause that, in some important respects at least, the statute could not survive constitutional scrutiny. The only question then remaining in dispute on those features of it was whether their consequent invalidation should ensue immediately or be suspended for a limited period in order to afford Parliament the opportunity of repairing the defects in them. The occasion for that opportunity which was thought to have arisen has disappeared, however, since we reserved our judgment in the case. For Parliament has now achieved the purpose that the suspension was meant to serve by passing in the meantime the Films and Publications Act (65 of 1996), which repeals entirely both the Publications Act and the Indecent or Obscene Photographic Matter Act, replacing the pair with a substantially different scheme. The new statute was enacted very recently, and it has not yet been brought into operation. But that will no doubt happen soon, in all probability sooner than the time when the suggested suspension would have expired. The old statutes, which are already obsolete, will both then terminate. Neither of the applicants, nor for that matter anyone else, stands to gain the slightest advantage today from an order dealing with their moribund and futureless provisions. No wrong which we can still right was done to either applicant on the strength of them. Nor is anything that should be stopped likely to occur under their rapidly waning authority.

[17] In all those circumstances there can hardly be a clearer instance of issues that are wholly academic, of issues exciting no interest but an historical one, than those on which our ruling is wanted have now become. The repeal of the Publications Act has disposed altogether of the question pertaining to that. And any aspect of the one about the Indecent or Obscene Photographic Matter Act which our previous decision on it did not answer finally has been foreclosed by its repeal in turn. I therefore conclude that we should decline at this stage to grant a declaratory order on either topic.

[18] The costs of the litigation in its

consecutive phases remain to be considered. Once the view is taken that the application for a referral ought to have succeeded in the Court below, it must follow that the applicants should not have been saddled with the entire costs of those proceedings. They were liable for the ones that would have been incurred had their application encountered no resistance, since they could not have avoided going to Court for the referral in any event. But those occasioned by the opposition which eventuated should be made payable, now that it has failed, by the second and third respondents. The applicants had to come here on appeal in order to obtain that reversal of the adverse order for costs. So they deserve, I believe, to be awarded the costs of both the appeal and the application for leave to appeal.

Although the Constitutional Court in *JT Publishing* considered mootness as a technical barrier to adjudication, like the United States courts, it is unlikely that the barrier will be absolute. The United States courts, as evidenced in *Roe v Wade*, will adjudicate over matters that are moot, yet 'capable of repetition yet evading review'.[92] *Roe* involved a challenge to a Texas law restricting abortion. The case was initiated in 1970 and decided by the Supreme Court in 1973 when the plaintiff was no longer pregnant. The Supreme Court felt it necessary to decide the case because pregnancy could occur in the future, and because a holding of mootness would mean that pregnancy litigation would never go beyond the trial stage.[93] The Constitutional Court would also decide an issue which has become academic because of its public importance. In *Du Plessis v De Klerk*,[94] the Court addressed the question of whether the Bill of Rights under the interim Constitution had horizontal application. The dispute in question arose before April 1994, which meant that the provisions did not apply to the dispute at hand. Despite the academic nature of the inquiry, the Court considered the horizontality issue because it was of public importance and because it kept coming up before the lower courts.[95]

Avoiding constitutional adjudication

There is an established principle of self-restraint that a court should not pass on a constitutional question if there is some other ground on which the case may be disposed.[96] If a case can be decided on either constitutional grounds or some other ground, the Court should only decide the issue on the non-constitutional ground. The constitutional issue should only be looked at as a last resort.[97]

---

[92] *Roe v Wade* 410 US 113, 113 (1973).

[93] *Supra* at 128.

[94] See *Du Plessis and Others v De Klerk and Another* CCT 8/05 (15 May 1996), now cited as 1996 (3) SA 850 (CC); 1996 (5) BCLR 658 (CC).

[95] *Supra* para 30.

[96] *S v Vermaas; S v Du Plessis* CCT 1/94 CCT 2/94 (8 June 1995) para 13, now cited as 1995 (3) SA 292 (CC); 1995 (7) BCLR 851 (CC), quoting Kentridge AJ from *S v Mhlungu* CCT 25/94 (8 June 1995), now cited as 1995 (7) BCLR 793 (CC); 1995 (3) SA 867 (CC). *Gardener v Whitaker* CCT 26/94 (15 May 1996) para 14, now cited as 1996 (6) BCLR 775 (CC); 1996 (4) SA 337 (CC). In the US see *Ashwander v Tennessee Authority* 297 US 288, 341 (1936).

[97] *Per* Chaskalson P in *Zantsi* para 2. See also Langa J's opinion in *S v Mbatha; S v Le Roux and Others* CCT 19/95; CCT 35/95 (9 February 1996) para 28, now cited as *S v Mbatha; S v Prinsloo* 1996 (3) BCLR 293 (CC); 1996 (2) SA 464 (CC). This approach is followed in other jurisdictions as well. In the US, see eg *Ashwander v Tennessee Authority* 297 US 288, 341 (1936). For a discussion of Irish cases, see Kelly 449.

S v Bequinot
CCT 24/95 (18 November 1996), now cited as 1997 (2) SA 887 (CC); 1996 (12) BCLR 1588 (CC)
(notes omitted)

Authors' note: The Court was presented with the constitutionality of a reverse onus presumption in the General Law Amendment Act. The accused was convicted under this Act for knowingly receiving stolen goods. The unanimous Constitutional Court refused to consider the constitutionality of the Act without first knowing whether the trial court would have convicted the accused despite the reverse onus presumption in the statute, either in terms of the common law or some other statutory basis. The Constitutional Court ruled that the court below did not establish that the constitutional question was crucial for the resolution of the case. Therefore, the referral of the matter to the Constitutional Court was not a competent referral.

KRIEGLER J [unanimous opinion]:

[2] The appellant was one of eight accused charged in the Regional Court on fourteen counts, including robbery of 7 000 pounds sterling in traveler's cheques. The appellant received all but two of the cheques at his pawnbroker's shop shortly after the robbery. The trial court, holding that the appellant could not be linked to the robbery, focused on his admitted receipt of the stolen cheques. That, so it reasoned, brought into play the provisions of section 37 of the General Law Amendment Act 62 of 1955, a conviction of which is a competent verdict on a charge of robbery. The regional magistrate did not consider a verdict of knowingly receiving stolen property, likewise a competent verdict. He analysed section 37 in the light of the applicable authorities and concluded that its effect was that the appellant had to establish on a balance of probabilities that, at the time he received the cheques, he reasonably believed that the person who gave them to him was legally entitled to do so. The regional magistrate rejected the evidence proffered by the appellant in exculpation of such receipt and found that he could not possibly have believed that the cheques being offered to him had been obtained honestly:

[He] had no reasonable belief that the person who handed cheques over was the owner or was authorized by the owner thereof. There is no doubt about that.

It is more than arguable that such finding was tantamount to concluding that the appellant had received the cheques knowing them to have been stolen. The magistrate did not reason along such lines, however, but found that the prosecution had proved all the elements of section 37 on which it bore the onus and that the appellant had not established the genuineness or reasonableness of his alleged belief. The appellant's conviction of a contravention of that section followed. The sentence was a fine of R4 000 plus a wholly suspended period of imprisonment. An appeal against the conviction only was noted to the Witwatersrand Local Division of the Supreme Court (the WLD).

[3] Counsel for the appellant lodged heads of argument in the WLD challenging the trial court's findings on a variety of grounds.

[4] When the appeal was called in the WLD the learned judge presiding, of his own volition, raised the question whether the constitutional validity of section 37 ought not there and then to be referred to this Court for its decision. After a brief debate with counsel, who had not been forewarned of the constitutional question and could understandably make little meaningful contribution, the learned judges made an order, the transcript of which reads:

... [O]n the question as to whether Section 37 of the General Law Amendment Act No 62 of 1955 is in conflict with Section 3 *(c)* [sic] of the Constitution Act No 200 of 1993. The terms of reference are to be settled by counsel and an order will be made in due course.

The formal order of court supplements the transcription by commencing with the words [t]hat this matter be referred to the Constitutional Court and the section of the Constitution targeted is said to be 23(3)*(c)*. Neither section is of course relevant, the provision intended being section 25(3)*(c)* of the Constitution.

[5] It took some considerable time for

counsel to 'settle' the 'terms of reference' and for the learned judges to consider them …. Be that as it may, the document signed by the learned judges reads as follows:

1 The Appellant was convicted of the offence of contravening Section 37 of the General Law Amendment Act, 62 or 1955.

2 As a result of the reverse onus contained in the aforementioned provision, it was necessary for the Appellant to prove on a balance of probabilities that he had reasonable cause for believing at the time of the acquisition or receipt that the goods were the property of the person from whom he received them or that such person had been duly authorised by the owner thereof to deal with or to dispose of them.

3 Section 25(3)(c) of Act 200 of 1993 provides that:
Every accused person shall have the right to a fair trial … which shall include the right to be presumed innocent and to remain silent during plea proceedings or trial and not to testify during trial.

4 The ruling required from the Court is whether Section 37 of the General Law Amendment Act, No 62 of 1955, is in conflict with Section 25(3)(c) of Act 200 of 1993.

5 It is in the interests of justice that the matter be referred so that the apparent conflict between the Constitution and Section 37 of the General Law Amendment Act, 62 of 1995 may be resolved.

6 The issue of the constitutionality of Section 37 of the General Law Amendment Act, 62 of 1955 is decisive for the determination of this case.

[7] Indeed, in the very first reported judgment of this Court, in *Zuma*, Kentridge AJ mentioned, and in the associated case of *Mhlungu*, Kentridge AJ discussed the procedure under section 102(1) of the Constitution. Thereafter the Court considered and explained not only the statutory requirements of that subsection and associated provisions of the Constitution, but identified additional questions of judicial policy that come into play when referral of a constitutional issue is being considered by a provincial or local division. Thus:

[T]he power and duty to refer only arises when …

(a) there is an issue in the matter before the Court in question which may be decisive for the case;

(b) such issue falls within the exclusive jurisdiction of the Constitutional Court; and

(c) the Court in question considers it to be in the interests of justice to refer such issue to the Constitutional Court.

….

These conditions are conjunctive and all have to be fulfilled before the Court has the power to refer an issue to the Constitutional Court in terms of section 102(1).

[T]he subsection requires the Provincial or Local Division of the Supreme Court to be of the opinion that there is a reasonable prospect that the relevant law or provision will be held to be invalid.

[T]he judge or judges referring to the Constitutional Court the issue of the constitutionality of an Act of Parliament are obliged to furnish written reasons why it is considered that:

(a) there is a reasonable prospect that the Act of Parliament in question will be held to be invalid; and

(b) the interest of justice requires this issue to be referred at this particular stage.

It is only where it is necessary for the purpose of disposing of the appeal, or where it is in the interest of justice to do so, that the constitutional issue should be dealt with first by this Court. It will only be necessary for this to be done where the appeal cannot be disposed of without the constitutional issue being decided; and it will only be in the interest of justice for a constitutional issue to be decided first, where there are compelling reasons that this should be done.

This rule allows the law to develop incrementally. In view of the far-reaching implications attaching to constitutional decisions, it is a rule which should ordinarily be adhered to by this and all other South African Courts before whom constitutional issues are raised.

[C]onstitutional issues within the exclusive jurisdiction of the Constitutional Court will be raised formally in proceedings before the Supreme Court or other courts, and will only be referred to the Constitutional Court for its decision in circumstances where it would be appropriate to do so. It is in the first instance the responsibility of the Supreme Court to decide whether or not the circumstances are appropriate.

[I]t is not ordinarily in the interest of justice for cases to be heard piecemeal, and ... as a general rule if it is possible to decide a case without deciding a constitutional issue this should be done.

[8] The circumstances of the present case demonstrate the advisability of adhering to those principles. The record of the trial proceedings exceeds 300 pages; there were eight accused charged on fourteen counts and a number of state witnesses who testified to four distinct facets of the case. The trial court's judgment on the merits runs to over 40 pages and not only analyses the evidence in detail, but also deals with the legal issues raised by the provisions of section 37 of Act 62 of 1955 read with section 260 (f) of Act 51 of 1977. The judgment contains fairly extensive factual and legal reasoning, the crucial elements of which were canvassed in the heads of argument filed by the parties in the WLD. But, because of the course adopted in the latter court, none of those issues was debated there and no views thereon were formulated – or at least expressed – by the learned judges a quo. Nor was any view expressed on the severability of the reverse onus provision from the remainder of section 37 and whether there was any prospect of the appeal being upheld if such provision were to be severed.

[9] In the result this Court is in the dark as to whether the learned judges endorsed the trial court's rejection of the appellant's evidence as false beyond reasonable doubt. Nor do we know if they considered whether, upon an endorsement of the trial court s credibility finding and its analysis of the probabilities, a conviction under section 37 was not warranted without applying the reverse onus. This was a crucial issue to resolve before a referral was warranted. It depended upon forming a view as to whether there was any reasonable prospect that the Constitutional Court, if it held the reverse onus provision to be unconstitutional, would find that such provision was not severable from the remainder of section 37. If there was no such prospect, a conviction under section 37, after severance, might well be justified, if the trial court s credibility finding and its analysis of the probabilities were accepted. Without deciding these issues it was not possible for the court a quo to determine whether the constitutionality of the reverse onus provision had any relevance at all to the conviction in question. A further possibility to which the court a quo did not advert is whether there was scope for substituting on appeal a conviction of the common law crime of receiving stolen property knowing it to have been stolen, a verdict unaffected by the statutory reversal of onus giving rise to the constitutional issue referred to this Court. There is yet another possibility not addressed by the court a quo. That is that the trial court should have found that the appellant had indeed discharged the onus cast on him by section 37.

[10] Obviously any of those conclusions would preclude a positive finding as to the first requirement for a referral under ... the Constitution, namely, that resolution of the constitutional question may be decisive for the case. As Didcott J pointed out in *Luitingh*, that requirement entails a finding that the constitutional ruling may have a crucial bearing on the eventual outcome of the case as a whole or on any significant aspect of the way in which its remaining parts ought to be handled. The prospects of successfully upsetting the trial court's factual findings on appeal constituted an essential factor in evaluating the potential materiality of the incidence of the onus. Yet

there is no indication on the record that the court *a quo* applied its mind to that factor and it is clear that the parties were afforded little if any opportunity to be heard on the point.

[11] There is, moreover, no indication that the desirability of interrupting the ordinary course of the criminal justice system was considered. ... [T]he Constitution, as this Court has pointed out, obliges a provincial or local division of the Supreme Court to consider under the rubric of interests of justice not only the whether but also the when of a referral. In a case such as this, where the appeal court's evaluation of the trial court s findings of fact may well dispose of the matter, there is no warrant for a referral at the outset. In the event of the incidence of the onus eventually proving decisive, and the constitutional validity of the provisions of section 37 of Act 62 of 1955 affecting the onus becoming crucial, a referral would be both necessary and timely. At this stage it is neither. Consequently the statement of the court *a quo* as to the interest of justice cannot be supported. On the contrary, the interest of justice is not served by the interruption of a criminal appeal for the determination of a constitutional question which is not – and may well never become – necessary for the decision of the case.

[12] There are sound policy reasons why constitutional questions should not be antici-

pated. The judgment of Chaskalson P in *Zantsi's* case, which all the members of this Court endorsed, was dedicated to a discussion and explanation of those reasons. The instant case illustrates the wisdom of adhering to the policy of deciding cases on constitutional grounds only if and when it is necessary to do so. The receipt of stolen goods is a vital link in the chain of gainful disposal of the spoils of criminality. It is, of course, also a powerful incentive to such criminality and statutory devices aimed at facilitating the successful apprehension and prosecution of receivers of stolen property, such as section 37 clearly is, cannot lightly be invalidated. Serious consideration will still have to be given whether such a provision, which is found to offend some or other provision of the Bill of Rights, is not saved either under section 33(1) of the Constitution or by severing the reverse onus provision from the rest of the section.

[13] A referral at the appropriate juncture, where the constitutional issue is vital to the determination of the case and has been thoroughly canvassed in one or more other courts, serves to define the constitutional issues and focus the development of our constitutional jurisprudence. But a case such as this, where the parties did not raise the issue themselves and the constitutional point may well prove peripheral, is inappropriate for grappling with the difficult legal and policy issues involved in invalidating a long-standing weapon in society's war against crime.

Political question

Courts in various jurisdictions have adopted the position that cases which it considers to fall under the rubric of the political question doctrine are non-justiciable.[98] Matters identified as a political question can be best resolved through the political process. In the United States, courts apply the political question doctrine when: first, the Constitution shows a textually demonstrable commitment to leave the

decision to a coordinate branch of government; secondly, there is a lack of judicial standards for resolving the issue; thirdly, there is a need for the nation to act with one voice with respect to the matter at hand, and finally when a decision by the court would cause grave embarrassment to the government abroad.[99]

In *Luther v Borden*, the plaintiff brought an action for trespass against a government official.[100] The invasion of the plaintiff's home occurred at the

---

[98] In the US, see *Luther v Borden* 48 US (7 Howard) 1 (1849). In Germany, see *Pershing 2* and *Cruise Missile 1* case (1983) 66 BVerfGE 39 translated in Kommers 166–8. The Canadian Supreme Court, however, does not recognize the political question doctrine. See Hogg 805.

[99] *Baker v Carr* 369 US 186, 222–26 (1962).

[100] See *Luther v Borden* 48 US (7 Howard) 1 (1849).

time there was a conflict as to which was the legitimate government of Rhode Island. The plaintiff's action would have succeeded if the court ruled that the government of Rhode Island at the time was illegitimate. However, the executive branch of the United States had made a choice with respect to which was the legitimate government of Rhode Island. The court ruled that a decision by the court that the government of Rhode Island was illegitimate would have caused an embarrassment to the executive branch of government, which had recognized one of the factions as the government of Rhode Island.[101] A decision by the Court that the government of Rhode Island was illegitimate would also have resulted in the invalidation of all actions taken by the government, including tax collections, enacted laws and salaries paid. Rather than render an opinion as to whether the government of Rhode Island was a legitimate government, the Court adopted the position that the choice of which was the proper government of Rhode Island was, a political question and better left to the determination of the other coequal branches of government.[102] The Court also stated it did not have the same fact finding capacity as the legislature to make the determination as to which was the legitimate government.[103]

The political question doctrine is based on both prudential and functional arguments. The prudential argument is that the court should not render a judgment on the merits if rendering a judgment would compromise an important principle or erode the court's legitimacy.[104] The functional argument, also part of separation of powers, recognizes the difficulty of the judiciary rendering certain decisions, because the judiciary does not have all the relevant information, and there is a need for uniformity of action. In achieving uniformity, the court needs to take into consideration decisions of other branches of government, in determining whether or not to decide the issue.[105]

It remains to be seen whether the Constitutional Court would accept the political question doctrine. There are situations where the political question doctrine should arguably apply in the South African context. For example, with respect to a majority vote of no confidence, and subsequent removal of the president or the cabinet, it is clearly not appropriate for the court to render a decision on the conditions for the validity of such an action. There are no judicial standards for determining what is appropriate for purposes of determining lack of confidence. Similarly, for prudential reasons, a court should not subject to judicial enquiry, a finding by the JSC to remove a judge supported by the two-thirds vote of the NA.[106] A decision to remove a judge affected under s 177, is the only check against the judiciary. The validity of such removals should be judged as a political question. In *Nixon v United States*,[107] the United States Supreme Court ruled that impeachment is the only method for removal of federal judges under the United States Constitution, and that the senate has broad discretion in terms of the political question doctrine in exercising the power of impeachment.[108] A political question does not mean that the judiciary abdicates its responsibility of judicial review. What it means, is that prudence and functionalism require the court, at times, to defer to the judgment of the coordinate branches of government.

Another candidate for the political question doctrine is the internal arrangements, proceedings and procedures of parliament, which is entrusted to the NA[109] and the National Council of Provinces.[110] In *De Lille and Another v Speaker of the National Assembly*,[111] The Cape High

---

[101] *Supra* at 40–44.
[102] *Supra* at 51.
[103] *Supra* at 53.
[104] Tribe 96.
[105] Ibid.
[106] Section 117 of the Constitution.
[107] *Nixon v United States* 506 US 224, 243 (1993).
[108] *Supra* at 244.
[109] *Section 57(1) of the* Constitution.
[110] *Section* 70(1).
[111] *De Lille and Another v Speaker of the National Assembly* 1998 (3) SA 430 (C).

Court, *per Nhlope J*, invalidated the fifteen-day suspension order imposed against PAC Member of Parliament, Patricia de Lille for violating the parliamentary rules on speech. Ms de Lille alleged in parliament that certain ANC members worked as spies for the apartheid government. The Constitution s 557(1)(a) supports a finding that parliament is to be given a wide latitude to conduct its affairs, including the disciplining of its members. The Court held that the house appointed ad hoc committee was stacked with ANC members Moreover, the Court found that the majority in the committee had acted in bad faith because they had formulated a conclusion before the hearings had commenced.[112] The Constitution does not authorize parliament to act *mala fides*.[113] The Court further held that Ms de Lille's freedom of speech was also violated by the suspension.[114] Parliament's decision and conduct are subject to the Constitution and Bill of Rights as the Court correctly observed.[115] However, freedom of speech, as indeed many other rights in the Bill of Rights, have a different application in different settings.[116] The Court unfortunately failed to recognize that under separation of powers,

parliament should be accorded greater deference in the conduct of its affairs and the disciplining of its members if a member acts in a disruptive manner. The real issue in *De Lille* was whether the applicant had acted in a way which was obstructive or disruptive of parliamentary proceedings. On appeal to the Supreme Court of Appeal, Mahomed CJ held that the statement made by De Lille did not obstruct or disrupt the proceedings of parliament. Therefore, the suspension of Ms De Lille was invalid.[117]

Foreign affairs is also recognized as a political question because there are few, if any, judicial standards to apply in this area. Foreign affairs is an area where the country needs to speak with one voice. The other branches of government are better equipped to make decisions in this area. Even though the German Constitution – like the South African Constitution – requires the Court to decide all matters rightly placed before it, the German Constitutional Court in the *Pershing 2* case ruled that foreign affairs is an area where it lacks manageable judicial standards and should be treated as a political question better left to be decided by the other branches of government.[118]

Pershing 2 and *Cruise Missile 1* case (1983) 66 BVerfGe 39[119]

Authors' note: In 1983 several persons filed constitutional complaints against the Federal Republic's forthcoming deployment of weapons equipped with nuclear warheads on West German territory. This deployment was to be undertaken in accordance with a decision of the foreign and defence ministers of member states of the North Atlantic Treaty Organization (NATO). On 22 November 1983, the Bundestag passed a resolution supporting the federal government's decision. The Gravamen of the complaint was that the missiles would endanger the life and health of the complainants in

violation of art 2 (2). Article 2 (2) provides that the right to life and personal inviolability may only be encroached upon pursuant to a law. The legislature s failure to support deployment in the form of a statute, they argued, violated this provision.

Judgment of the Second Senate ...

A. II.5 ... The complainants base their constitutional complaints on the following arguments: The quality of the new weapons and their deployment on European territory near the Soviet Union change the political-strategic constellation of chances and risks in

---

[112] *Supra para 443–44.*

[113] *Supra para 445.*

[114] *Supra para 449.*

[115] *Supra.*

[116] *S v Lawrence* para 167.

[117] *The Speaker of the National Assembly v De Lille MP and Another* 297/98 para 29.

[118] *Pershing 2* and *Cruise Missile 1* case quoted in Kommers 167.

[119] Kommers *Constitutional Jurisprudence of The Federal Republic of Germany* 164–8. Reprinted with permission.

favor of the United States of America. There are several possible Soviet reaction to this, each of which brings with it the risk of a destructive strike by the Soviet Union against Pershing 2 and Cruise missile sites. Deploying these weapons, therefore, endangers the lives of the population of the Federal Republic. In addition, the Soviet Union has announced the installation of a computer-controlled responsive-strike system which may give rise to the use of nuclear weapons even in the case of limited military operations by the member states of NATO. [The possibility] also cannot be precluded that an atomic attack may be brought about by a technical failure in this system. Deploying Pershing 2 and Cruise missiles in therefore incompatible with the state's duty to protect life pursuant to Article 2 (2) [I] of the Basic Law. The Constitution s decision to provide for a national defense does not authorize the impending destruction of the entire or significant portions of the population of the Federal Republic. It is true that the competent government authorities have the basic responsibility to decide how to fulfill their duty to protect life arising under Article 2 (2) [I] of the Basic Law. However, [they] cannot justify the instillation of new weapons as a measure to protect life. [The deployment of new weapons] is also an inappropriate defensive measure because it neither averts a Soviet attack with SS-2 missiles nor permits a first strike aimed at disarmament. The new weapons have no defensive value for the Federal Republic because the Federal Republic has no control over their use. If the federal government believes it must modernize its weapons, it can choose the less dangerous alternative of deploying new weapons at sea.

[Complaints argue that (I) the Basic Law permits defensive weapons only, (2) the Pershing and Cruise missiles are not necessary for the defense of the Federal Republic, (3) the missiles are more dangerous than alternative means of defence (eg, sea-based missiles), (4) American control of the weapons violates German sovereignty, and (5) deployment violates the Federal Republic s duties under international law.]

C ... The constitutional complaints are inadmissible.

1 To the Extent that the complainants can be interpreted as assailing the conduct of non-German state power in connection with the deployment of Pershing 2 and Cruise missiles, their constitutional complaint is inadmissible. It is true that the protected sphere of human rights, including the basic rights and freedoms recognized in the Basic Law, applies against every form of sovereign power. But Article 93 (I)[4a] of the Basic Law and section 90 of the FCCA grant the constitutional complaint as a legal remedy only against German state action subject to the Basic Law.

2 To the extent that they attack conduct attributable to German sovereign power, it follows neither from the complainants allegations nor from other circumstances that German state action caused the asserted threat and therefore would fall within the realm of protected basic rights claimed to have been injured by an act of the German state ....

Even accepting the complainant s premise that deploying Pershing 2 and Cruise missiles increases the danger of a Soviet nuclear attack against targets in the Federal Republic, and therefore the risk to legal rights protected by Article 2(2) of the Basic Law, it is still questionable whether the asserted violation of complainants' life and limb by German sovereign power rises to the level of an injury. In those cases where the Federal Constitutional Court has issued an opinion on the degree of intervention necessary to endanger basic rights, [it was possible] to make certain, not entirely indefinite statements about the probability that the asserted dangers would actually occur. In those cases the essential sources of risk were susceptible to investigation by scientific methods, even if such methods were naturally conditioned upon and limited by the state and type of knowledge at the time. In the [resent case, on the contrary, no suitable, reliable process exists by which the [judge] might ascertain the increased degree of danger to complaints life and limb. For, in dealing with the ultimate source of this danger, we are dealing with the decisions of a foreign sovereign state in the context of the general world political situation and changing political and military relations Under the prevailing circumstances, [we cannot make] judicially verifiable findings concerning such decisions in advance. Morever, the possible violation of basic rights asserted in this case does not fall within the protective purview of these rights because [basic rights] are aimed at German state action; this, however, is the action which complainants have attacked.

(b) ... Because [we] lack legally manageable criteria, the Federal constitutional Court cannot determine whether or not the German state action challenged by complainants had any influence on decisions of the Soviet Union which may or may not trigger the military measures (a preventative responsive nuclear strike) complainants fear. The federal organs responsible for the foreign and defence policy of the Federal Republic must make such evaluations. Within the intended goals of the Basic Law, especially as they have been expressed in the present context in Article 1(2) and Article 24(2), and within the scope of what is permissible under international law, the constitutional authority of these organs for foreign defence policy includes the authority to defend the Federal Republic effectively. It is within their political decision-making power and responsibility to decide what measures promise success. To the extent that unpredictable areas of risk remain, as will often

be the case, the political body constitutionally responsible for the decision must include these [considerations] in their deliberations and assume political responsibility. It is not the function of the Federal Constitutional Court to substitute its opinion for the opinions and deliberations of the competent political branch of the federation over and above standard legal handicaps in this area. This applies equally for the question of how the state should fulfil its affirmative legal duty to protect the basic rights in the sphere of foreign policy and defence matters *vis-à-vis* foreign states In the light of the fact that the dangerous situation which complainants presume to exist depends significantly on the political decision of a foreign sovereign state in the context of the global political situation, the Federal Constitutional Court has no legally manageable criteria for judging whether the German state action being challenged is the decisive [factor] in the creation of this situation or whether it is at least contributory and therefore casual. It is quite possible that the danger of a Soviet nuclear attack, as the complainants fear it, already existed before the federal government agreed to station or before the deployment itself, or will come into being independent of the deployment. Nor do we have legally manageable standards to judge whether one may correctly say, based on empirical knowledge, that the creation of the danger of a Soviet nuclear attack represents a change of existing circumstances legally connected to the conduct that complainants censure ....

D This decision is issued unanimously as to the result, with one vote dissenting as to the grounds of judgment.

5

Legislative power: national, provincial, and local

Introduction

Since the formation of the Union of South Africa, and until April 1994, sovereignty of parliament was the central principle underpinning the Constitution.[1] Under the new Constitution, parliament can only legislate if there is express or implied authority. Section 43 *(a)* provides that the legislative authority of the national government is vested in parliament. Section 44(1)(ii) provides that parliament has the power to pass legislation with respect to any matter within its competence. In addition, parliament's ability to legislate is limited by the Bill of Rights which provides in s 8(1): 'The Bill of Rights applies to all law, and binds the legislature, the executive, the judiciary and all organs of state'.

Therefore, in evaluating the constitutionality of any Act of Parliament, there are two questions to be asked. First, does parliament have the competence to legislate? This question is one of power, namely which branch or level of government has the competence to take action. The second question is an issue of rights, and asks whether there are any other constitutional provisions that have been violated, such as a provision in the Bill of Rights.[2]

In looking at the distribution of power, this chapter will consider several questions. First, the nature of the South African state, which involves looking at the federal unitary dichotomy; secondly, the virtues and pitfalls of classical federalism; thirdly, the scope of national power and provincial power; fourthly, different concepts of federalism and the nature of the distribution of power under the Constitution; fifthly, the exercise of provincial power and the limits imposed by the provincial power on the exercise of national power; sixthly, exercise of power by local government, and finally, we look at other bases for the exercise of national power such as the treaty-making power.

Different forms of state

Federal–unitary dichotomy

The two primary forms of state organizations are the unitary and federal arrangements. The basic principle of a unitary state is that it displays 'one supreme, ultimate and unified center of authority'.[3] The federal arrangement is associated with a more delegated form of authority with greater

---

[1] Article 59 of the South Africa Act 1909.
[2] This is the focus of chapters 7 to 14.
[3] Preston T King *Federalism and Federation* Baltimore: Johns Hopkins University Press 1982, 133.

territorial divisions. Broadly speaking, the unitary form of state is associated with a stronger form of central government with few territorial divisions. Greater emphasis is placed on unity and central control of activities. It is a system aimed at achieving greater homogeneity in a country, be it in the realm of economic or legal affairs. A unitary state is more amenable to central control of economic and cultural affairs. However, this does not mean that there is no delegation of power in a unitary system. Regardless of the nature of the decisions or the way they are reached, almost all states will find it necessary to delegate power in the interest of efficiency.[4] An important distinction has to be drawn between local government under a unitary arrangement and the powers of the units in a federal arrangement. In the former instance, the powers of central government are not fettered by the local governments who essentially owe their existence to the central government. Just as the local governments are created by the central government, the powers and existence of the local government can be terminated by the central government. No smaller part of the state can impose any restriction on the central government.[5] While power may be delegated to lower levels, such as the different territories, this is not carried out because of any ideal, but more to achieve efficiency.[6]

A federal system is essentially a constitutional arrangement that allows for territorial diversity in the organizational structure of the state. It is a situation where there is a national government and a territorial government both ruling over the same territory, with the latter government having the predominant prerogative over some defined inter-est.[7] Under a federal constitution, the various local units exercise authority in respect to certain affairs which power, under the classical federal models, invariably cannot be infringed upon by the central government. In the words of Wheare, 'the general and regional governments are each, within a sphere, co-ordinate and independent'.[8] An individual is, in a sense, subject to the laws of two authorities: a central authority and a regional authority.[9] By giving the local units power, a federal constitution allows the units to act as a brake on the ability of the central government to act in regard to certain matters.[10] A federal constitution operates according to anti-majoritarian principles in that it calls for bargains and compromises between the various units and the central government in governmental and state problems. In this sense, federalism can rightly be associated with a weaker form of central government.

The evolution of power distribution: from unitary to federal

With respect to the form of state, the South Africa Act of 1909 introduced a variation from the British unitary form of state by providing for the continuation of four separate provinces. The provinces were able to elect members of the Upper House, or senate. Moreover, they were given certain powers in respect to taxation, education, health, and various local works.[11] The previous form of state was not federal as its constitution did not confer on the provinces any separate powers upon which the central government could not encroach.[12] All the powers exercised by the provinces were at the discretion

4   Ivo D Duchacek *Power Maps: Comparative Politics of Constitutions* Santa Barbara: ABC-Clio 1973, 93.
5   CF Strong *Modern Political Constitutions: An Introduction to the Comparative Study of their History and Existing Forms* London: Sidgewick & Jackson, 6th edition, 1963, 64.
6   Ivo D Duchacek *Comparative Federalism: The Territorial Dimensions of Politics* New York: Rinehart and Winston 1970, 3.
7   PH Lane *A Manual of Australian Constitutional Law* Sydney: Law Book Co 1995, 3. William H Riker 'Federalism' in *Handbook of Political Science: Government Institutions and Processes*, edited by Fred I Greenstein and Nelson W Polsby. Reading: Addison-Wesley 1982, 101.
8   KC Wheare *Federal Government* New York: Oxford University Press, 4th edition, 1964, 10.
9   Peter W Hogg *Constitutional Law of Canada* Scarborough: Carswell, 3rd edition, 1992, 98.
10 Carl J Friedrich *Constitutional Government and Democracy: Theory and Practice in Europe and America* Waltham: Blaisdell Publishing Co, 4th edition, 1968, 226–7.
11 Section 85 of the South Africa Act of 1909.
12 For a contrary view, see Henry John May *The South African Constitution* Westport: Greenwood, 3rd edition, 1970, 191.

of the central legislature and the latter could abridge and remove the power of the provinces.[13] For political and legal purposes, the country was regarded as a single unit for decision-making.

At the Convention for a Democratic South Africa (Codesa) talks, the various political parties decided that the Constitution should distribute power between the central government and the provinces. Although there was no mention of the word federalism in the interim Constitution, the interim Constitution and the terms of reference for the final Constitution (contained in Schedule 4) required power to be distributed along national and provincial lines. For example, art XVIII and XIX of Schedule 4 addressed the powers, boundaries, and functions of the national government and provincial government which had to be protected in the final Constitution. Article XIV addressed the functions of national and provincial governments were to include exclusive and concurrent powers. Not only did the interim Constitution require distribution of power along national and provincial lines, but it also required power to be given to local governments. For example, s 174 required that parliament or the provincial legislature would not encroach upon the powers, functions and structures of a local government so 'as to compromise the fundamental status, purpose and character of local government'. The final Constitution proclaims that government power is based on national, provincial, and local government power.[14]

The Constitution apportions power to the national legislature, provincial legislature, and local government. There are matters of 'exclusive' provincial power and local power,[15] as well as matters of concurrent power which the provinces and local government share with the national government.[16] All the remaining legislative power (not given or shared with provincial or local government) belongs to the national legislature. The Constitution provides criteria in terms of which national power will predominate over provincial or local power on matters of concurrent power.[17] The Constitution also provides criteria under which national power will supercede provincial or local power on matters which are listed as exclusive to the provinces or local government.[18]

Reasons for the selection of one or other form of state

The task of advancing reasons for the selection of one or the other form of state is contentious Some theorists assert that there are 'objective' or 'rational' reasons for the adoption of a unitary or federal constitution.[19] A unitary form of state is more conducive to central planning and is better suited to a society faced with major dislocation, famine, and economic crisis.[20] Moreover, a unitary state is less costly than a federal state because there is no duplication of government at different levels.[21] Because there is no duplication, it is more likely that a unitary system be administratively and economically efficient.[22]

The advantages or 'objective reasons' put forward for a federal state are more contentious. In the first instance, in terms of liberal political theory, federalism is sometimes associated with freedom and liberty.[23] Federalism, according to

---

[13] For a discussion of the difference between the provincial system and federalism, see Gail-Maryse Cockram *Constitutional Law in the Republic of South Africa* Cape Town: Juta & Co 1975, 61.

[14] Section 40(1) of the Constitution.

[15] Defined in Schedule 5 of the Constitution.

[16] Defined in Schedule 4 of the Constitution.

[17] Section 146(3).

[18] Section 44(2).

[19] Michael Bothe 'Final Report' in *Federalism and Decentralization: Constitutional Problems of Territorial Decentralization in Federal and Centralized States*, edited by Thomas Fleiner-Gerstner and Silvan Hutter. Fribourg: Editions Universitaires 1987, 412.

[20] KC Wheare *Modern Constitutions* London: Oxford University Press, 2nd edition, 1966, 11.

[21] Majimbo Rothchild 'Schemes in Kenya and Uganda' in *Boston University Papers on Africa: Transition in African Politics*, edited by Jeffrey Butler and AA Castagno. New York: Praeger 1967, 298–9.

[22] Friedrich 227.

[23] Nelson A Rockefeller *The Future of Federalism* Cambridge: Harvard University Press 1962, 4.

the Madisonian concept of democracy, minimizes tyranny by dispersing power among different governmental authorities.[24] Dispersal of government power is posited as the best framework for individual freedom to flourish.[25] While it may be inefficient, the trade-off is seen in the greater freedom it allows.[26] In the twentieth century, one could criticize the notion of a limited national government and argue the contrary; namely, that uniform national action is vital in many spheres. The better way to protect against tyranny is to entrench individual rights and make the protection of the rights subject to judicial review.[27]

In contra-distinction to the previous position which viewed federalism as possibly inefficient, under the second view, federalism is offered as the most efficient framework for a country with a large land area. By having a decentralized government close to the people, it is more likely that the people's concerns and needs will be taken into account.[28] Moreover, the government would be better able to offer solutions suited to local conditions.[29]

A third argument for federalism is that it allows for social and economic experimentation which cannot always occur in a unitary state.[30] Provinces can serve as laboratories for experimentation and if the result proves successful, these can be duplicated in the rest of the country. If it is not successful, the entire country does not suffer as a result of the bad choice.[31]

The fourth contention, and arguably the most controversial, is the notion that a federal form of state is most appropriate for a plural or heterogeneous society characterized by cultural, linguistic, national, or religious diversities.[32] A federal arrangement in many African countries, including Nigeria,[33] Kenya,[34] Uganda,[35] and Congo,[36] was seen as a mechanism that allowed each of the diverse elements in the population a measure of autonomy in respect to matters which were considered of local concern.[37]

Self-determination

Section 1 of the Constitution proclaims South Africa as 'one sovereign, democratic state'. The interim Constitution spoke about the self-determination of groups.[38] The Constitution in s 235 speaks about self-determination and the possibility, by national legislation, for recognition of communities sharing a common cultural and linguistic heritage. The term 'self-determination' is generally understood as the right of the people to be free from foreign domination.[39] More recently, self-determination has come to mean, under certain circumstances, the right of a part of an existing state to cede and form a new state.[40] In s 235 the

---

[24] Patrick Macklem, et al *Canadian Constitutional Law*, Vol 1. Toronto: Edmond Montgomery Publishers 1994, 176.

[25] Op cit 68–9.

[26] Friedrich 227. See last part of chapter 5, where it is argued that the federal state offers a better opportunity for protection of individual rights and the protection of values of liberal society.

[27] Erwin Chemerinsky *Constitutional Law: Principles and Policies* New York: Aspen Law & Business 1997, 224.

[28] Andrew Rapczynski 'From Sovereignty to Process: The Jurisprudence of Federalism after Garcia' (1985) *Supreme Court Review* 391.

[29] Geoffrey Stone, et al *Constitutional Law* Boston: Little Brown, 3rd edition, 1996, 150.

[30] See Justice Brandeis dissenting opinion in *New State Ice Co v Liebman* 285 US 262, 311 (1932).

[31] Hogg 107–8.

[32] Obafemi Awolomo *Thoughts on the Nigerian Constitution* Ibadan: Oxford University Press 1966, 29.

[33] Nnamdi Azikiwe *Zik: A Selection from the Speeches of Nnamdi Azikiwe* Cambridge: Cambridge University Press 1961, 120–1 (delivered to the NCNC delegation to the United Kingdom conference for the revision of the MacPherson Constitution at Lagos on 29 August 1953).

[34] Rothchild 293. See BO Nwabueze *Presidentialism in Commonwealth Africa* London: C Hurst 1975, 139.

[35] Rothchild 293.

[36] Kwame Nkrumah *Challenge of the Congo* New York: International Publishers 1967, 67; Robert C Good *Congo Crisis: The Role of the New States* (NP) 1962, 5.

[37] Arnold Rivkin *Nation-building in Africa: Problems And Prospects* Brunswick: Rutgers University Press 1969, 100.

[38] The interim Constitution in Constitutional Principle XII in Schedule 4.

[39] See Ziyad Motala 'Under International Law, does the New Order in South Africa assume the Obligations and Responsibilities of the Apartheid Order: An Argument for Realism over Formalism' (1997) *South African Yearbook of International Law* 294.

[40] For a discussion of the historical evolution of the right to self-determination starting from the restrictive view of self-determination

Constitution provides that the South African people as a whole have a right to self-determination. This section also states that national legislation can recognize the right of self-determination of 'any community sharing a common cultural and language heritage'. The Province of KwaZulu-Natal argued in the *Certification of the Amended Text of the Constitution* that the new Constitution did not adequately promote the right to self-determination of all communities, as required in the interim Constitution in constitutional principle XII. The Constitutional Court stated emphatically that self-determination as used in the Constitution does not embody any notion of separation or political independence.[41] Self-determination as used in the Constitution protects associational rights and institutions providing for democratic governance.[42] Similarly, the African Commission on Human and Peoples Rights recently held that self-determination did not provide a right on the part of Katanga to separate from the rest of the former Zaire.[43]

Certification of the Amended Text of the Constitution of the Republic of South Africa, 1996
CCT 37/96 (4 December 1996), now cited as 1997 (1) BCLR 1 (CC); 1997 (2) SA 97 (CC).
(notes omitted).

Civil Society
[22] CP XII requires that:

Collective rights of self-determination in forming, joining and maintaining organs of civil society, including linguistic, cultural and religious associations, shall, on the basis of non-discrimination and free association, be recognised and protected.

[23] Counsel for KZN contended that this CP has not been complied with. He referred to AT 31, which protects the right of persons belonging to cultural, religious or linguistic communities to form, join and maintain cultural, religious and linguistic associations and other organs of civil society, but does not extend its protection to other communities. His argument was that the wording of this clause does not comply with the requirements of CP XII.
[24]CP XII does not indicate how the

collective rights of self-determination are to be recognised and protected. That was a matter for the CA to decide. Having regard to the CPs as a whole, the '[c]ollective rights of self-determination' mentioned in CP XII are associational individual rights, namely, those rights which cannot be fully or properly exercised by individuals otherwise than in association with others of like disposition. The concept 'self-determination' is circumscribed both by what is stated to be the object of self-determination, namely, 'forming, joining and maintaining organs of civil society' as well as by CP I which requires the state for which the Constitution has to provide, to be 'one sovereign state'. In this context 'self-determination' does not embody any notion of political independence or separateness. It clearly relates to what may be done by way of the autonomous exercise of these associational individual rights, in the civil society of one sovereign state. The objects of the AT 31 rights do not differ from the objects of the CP XII rights of self-determination; both sets of objects comprise various activities in relation to organs of civil society, 'organs of civil society' being specifically mentioned in AT 31(1)(b). One ostensible difference is the fact that the subjects of the CP XII rights are unspecified and

---

(meaning only the right to be free from colonial rule), to an expanded meaning (allowing for fragmentation of existing states), see Richard F Iglar 'The Constitutional Crisis in Yugoslavia and the International Law of Self-determination: Slovenia and Croatia's Right to Secede' (1992) 15 *Boston College International and Comparative Law Review* 213.
[41] *Certification of Amended Text* CCT 37/95 (4 December 1996) para 24, now cited as 1997 (2) SA 97 (CC); 1997 (1) BCLR 1 (CC).
[42] *Supra.*
[43] *Katangese People's Congress v Zaire*, African Commission on Human and People's Rights Communication 75/92 Eighth Annual Activity Report of the African Commission on Human and People's Rights 1994–1995 ACHPR /RPT/8th / Rev 1, Annex VI at 9.

therefore unrestricted, whereas AT 31 confers them on persons belonging to the three specified communities. It was this perceived difference that gave rise to the objection.

[25] The AT is based on founding values which include human dignity, the achievement of equality, the recognition and advancement of human rights and freedoms, the supremacy of the Constitution and the rule of law. It makes provision for a multi-party system of democratic government, with provision for three levels of government, to ensure accountability, responsiveness and openness. This provides a protective framework for civil society, which is enhanced by institutional structures such as the Public Protector, the Human Rights Commission, the Commission for the Promotion and Protection of Rights of Cultural, Religious and Linguistic Communities, and the Commission for Gender Equality, and ultimately by AT ch 2 which contains a justiciable Bill of Rights. The Bill of Rights is described as a 'cornerstone of democracy', and the state is required to respect, protect, promote and fulfil these

rights, which are enforceable by an independent judiciary.

[26] AT ch 2 protects a range of individual rights of association including freedom of association, freedom to form and participate in the activities of political parties, and freedom to form and join a trade union or employers' organisation and participate in its activities. Freedom of association is conferred upon everyone. In addition AT 30 separately protects the right of all people to use the language and to participate in the cultural life of their choice. AT 8(4) extends the protection of the Bill of Rights to juristic persons, 'to the extent required by the nature of the rights and the nature of that juristic person'. AT 38 permits all these rights to be enforced by an association acting in the interest of its members, and a person acting in the interest of a group or class of persons. The clear protection of rights of association coupled with the generous standing provisions protect the rights of collective self-determination stipulated by the CP for those communities not expressly protected by AT 31.

Composition of the national legislature

Introduction

National legislative power is vested in parliament, which consists of the National Assembly (NA) and the National Council of Provinces (NCOP). The NA consists of representatives who are elected by the population directly, whereas the NCOP consists of representatives of the provincial governments.

National Assembly

The composition of the NA is governed by s 46 of the Constitution, which requires that the NA be elected under universal adult franchise in terms of proportional representation. The NA consists of a

minimum of 350 members and a maximum of 400 members. The number of members must be determined by an Act of Parliament and they are elected for a term of five years.

National Council of Provinces (NCOP)

The composition of the NCOP is governed by s 60 of the Constitution. Under s 60(1), the NCOP is 'composed of a single delegation' consisting of ten members from each province. The ten delegates are made up of the premier of the province (or a member of the provincial legislature designated by the premier),[44] three special delegates,[45] and six permanent delegates.[46] The number of delegates from each party to the NCOP is determined by a proportional representation formula contained in Schedule 3, Part B of the Constitution.

---

[44] Section 60(2)(a)(II) of the Constitution.

[45] Supra.

[46] Supra 60(2)(b).

Powers of the national legislature

National legislative authority

Section 44 of the Constitution provides in part as follows:

> 44 (1) The national legislative authority as vested in Parliament—
> (a) confers on the National Assembly the power:
> (i) to amend the Constitution;
> (ii) to pass legislation with regard to any matter, including a matter within a functional area listed in Schedule 4, but excluding, subject to subsection (2), a matter within a functional area listed in Schedule 5;

Parliament has the power 'to pass legislation with regard to any matter' except a matter subject to the powers of the provinces under Schedule 5.[47] Therefore, the power of parliament in South Africa is residual whereas the power of the provinces is enumerated. This means parliament has the power to pass legislation on any matter not assigned to the provinces. This contrasts with the power of the national legislature in the United States and Australia. The power of the legislature in these instances is one of enumerated powers, whereas the power of the states is one of residual power.[48]

The distribution of power between the parliament and the provinces[49] takes three forms: first, the exclusive power of the national legislature, which is the residual power covering all activities, not covered in Schedule 4 and Schedule 5; secondly, the concurrent power of parliament and the provinces to regulate activities which are covered in Schedule 4, and thirdly, the power of the provinces to regulate matters under Schedule 5 subject only to the override provisions.

> *In re: Certification of the Constitution of the Republic of South Africa, 1996*
> **CCT 23/96 (6 September 1996), now cited as 1996 (10) BCLR 11253 (CC); 1996 (4) SA 744 (CC)**
> (notes omitted)

[309] CP XVIII.2 clearly requires a comparison between the powers of the provinces in the IC and those provided for in the NT. Before making that comparison it is necessary to understand the scheme according to which power is distributed between the national and provincial levels of government under the IC. At the national level Parliament has the power to make laws for the Republic. This is a general plenary legislative competence and is not confined to specific functional areas. At the provincial level, a provincial legislature has a limited competence to make laws for its province with regard to those matters which fall within the functional areas of IC sch 6. Provincial legislatures also have the power to adopt a constitution for the province and enjoy certain financial and fiscal powers specified in the IC. None of the IC sch 6 powers is exclusive to the provinces. Parliament is also competent to make laws in regard to IC sch 6 matters, and the IC regulates the manner in which conflicts between IC sch 6 laws enacted by Parliament and IC sch 6 laws enacted by a provincial legislature are to be resolved.

[310] The distribution of power between the national and provincial levels of government under the NT is substantially similar. At the national level Parliament has the power to pass legislation with regard to any matter other than a matter within the functional areas of exclusive provincial legislative competence set out in NT sch 5. In respect of such matters Parliament has only a limited power to intervene by passing legislation when it is necessary to do so for the purposes set out in NT 44(2)(a)-(e). Provincial legislatures have the exclusive powers referred to in NT sch 5, which are subject to intervention by

---

47 Unless they can provide a justification under s 44(2).
48 See the Tenth Amendment to the US Constitution. See also the Constitution of Australia, s 107. See Lane 8–9.
49 Which was described in the *First Certification* decision CCT 23/96 para 309–310.

Parliament in the special circumstances set out in NT 44(2), and powers set out in NT sch 4 which are exercisable concurrently with Parliament. The resolution of conflict between national legislation and provincial legislation in respect of NT sch 4 matters is regulated by the provisions of NT 146 to 150. A provincial legislature also has the power to adopt a constitution for the province and enjoys the fiscal and financial powers set out in NT ch 13.

Exclusive national power

The provinces cannot legislate on any matter unless there is an express grant of authority to the provinces. In the *Certification of the Constitution of KwaZulu-Natal*,[50] the provincial constitution attempted to regulate the status of the province by providing that the province was a self-governing territory. It also provided for the establishment of a provincial constitutional court, and the regulation of fundamental rights. The Constitutional Court refused to certify the KwaZulu-Natal constitution because the provincial constitution attempted to regulate matters which were of exclusive national concern under the interim Constitution.[51] Similarly, the Constitutional Court has held that when the president has assigned administrative powers to the province, a provincial legislature cannot regulate such matters which require national treatment, such as the registration of land titles.[52]

In re: Certification of the Constitution of the Province of Kwa-Zulu-Natal, 1996 CCT 15/96 (6 September 1996), now cited as 1996 (4) SA 1098 (CC); 1996 (11) BCLR 1419 (CC)
(notes omitted)

[1] In terms of section 160(1) of the Constitution of the Republic of South Africa, Act 200 of 1993 (the 'interim Constitution') a provincial legislature is entitled to pass a constitution for its province by a resolution of a majority of at least two-thirds of all its members. Before such a constitution can have the force of law, this Court must certify, under section 160(4) of the interim Constitution, that none of its provisions is inconsistent with any provision of the interim Constitution, including the Constitutional Principles set out in Schedule 4.

[14] In a number of provisions, the provincial Constitution purports to usurp powers and functions of Parliament and the national Government. This process begins in Chapter 1

dealing with 'Fundamental Principles'. The majority of these principles are those that one would expect to find and would be appropriate in a national constitution. Clause 1(1), for example, provides that:

The Province of KwaZulu Natal is a self-governing Province within the Republic of South Africa.

That purports to be an operative provision of the provincial Constitution and not a record of a fact or an aspiration. It is clearly beyond the capacity of a provincial legislature to pass constitutional provisions concerning the status of a province within the Republic. After all, the provinces are the recipients and not the source of power. In *The National Education Policy Bill* case Chaskalson P, writing for the Court and after emphasising the distinction between the history, structure and language of the United States Constitution which brought several sovereign states together in a federation and that of our interim Constitution, explained the powers of

---

[50] *In re: Certification of the Constitution of the Province of KwaZulu-Natal, 1996* CCT 15/96 (6 September 1996), now cited as 1996 (4) SA 1098 (CC); 1996 (11) BCLR 1419 (CC).
[51] *Supra.*
[52] *Certification of KwaZulu-Natal; DVB Behuising (Pty) Ltd v North West Provincial Government and Another* CCT 22/99 (2 March 2000) para 64, now cited as 2000 (4) BCLR 347 (CC). Under s 238 of the final Constitution, the president is able to delegate administrative power to the provincial executive.

the provinces under the interim Constitution as follows –

Unlike their counterparts in the United States of America, the provinces in South Africa are not sovereign states. They were created by the Constitution and have only those powers that are specifically conferred on them under the Constitution.

There is no provision in the interim Constitution which empowers a province to regulate its own status.

[16] Clause 1(5) of Chapter 1 purports to arrange the relationship between the province and the national Government. Clause 1(6) purports to confer autonomous powers in respect of local government. Clause 1(8) states that the provincial Constitution sets out the basis of the interaction between the province and the rest of the Republic. The provincial Constitution is replete with other examples of this attempted usurpation of power.

[19] The powers of a provincial legislature to enact a bill of rights are limited in different ways In the first place the legislature cannot provide for the provincial bill of rights to operate in respect of matters which fall outside its legislative or executive powers. Bills of rights, with the exception of provisions which may not always be regarded as capable of direct enforcement (such as, for example, certain of the types of provisions which have come to be known as 'directive principles of state policy') are conventionally enforced by courts of law striking down or invalidating, for example, legislation and administrative action even when such power of review is not expressly granted in the constitution or bill of rights concerned.

[20] Chapter 8 of the provincial Constitution purports to make provision for a provincial constitutional court and clause 1(4)(b) thereof empowers the provincial constitutional court to declare 'a law of the Province' unconstitutional. But a provincial bill of rights or other constitutional provision could not authorise the striking down of a law with regard to a matter in respect whereof the province had no legislative power in terms of section 126(1) of the interim Constitu-

tion, because such provision would be in conflict with such section and accordingly in breach of the inconsistency provision of section 160(3). The KZN Legislature appears to have been aware of this source of conflict, for in Chapter 14 clause 2(8) it purports to limit the enforcement of the 'human rights recognised and protected in this Constitution' (obviously a reference to the Chapter 3 rights which are described as 'Fundamental Rights, Freedoms and Duties' in the chapter heading) to the 'sphere of competence and to the powers and functions of the Province' with a similar limitation on the power of judicial review referred to above. Whether this purported limitation has in truth and in fact been successful will be dealt with later.

[27] The way is now clear to consider whether any provision in the bill of rights (Chapter 3) of the provincial Constitution is inconsistent with the interim Constitution or the Constitutional Principles because it purports to usurp powers or functions of Parliament. The contents of a right to a fair trial are, for instance, referred to in some detail in clause 19(3). Similarly, in clause 21, labour relations are dealt with in some detail. In clause 31 one finds detailed provisions for states of emergency and their suspension. These are all examples of areas falling patently outside the domain of competence of provincial legislatures. Another attempt to usurp national power is the provision in Chapter 3 clause 30(3) where, amongst others, it is asserted that the entrenchment of the rights in terms of the provincial Constitution shall not be construed as –

denying the existence of any other rights or freedoms recognised or conferred by the Constitution of the Republic of South Africa ... to the extent that they are not inconsistent with this Constitution.

This bears all the hallmarks of a hierarchical inversion. The provincial Constitution is presented as the supreme law recognising what is or is not valid in the national Constitution. It has no power to do so.

[32] In clause 1(2) of Chapter 5, exclusive

135

legislative powers are conferred upon the KZN Legislature. In clause 1(4) executive authority is 'conferred' upon the province in certain circumstances. It is unnecessary even to consider whether this conflicts with any corresponding powers of the national Legislature or executive in the interim Constitution for the simple reason that a province has no authority at all to 'confer' any legislative or executive authority, of whatsoever nature, on itself. All such power emanates exclusively from the interim Constitution.

[33] A related and equally serious attempted usurpation of power is the provision made in Chapter 8 for the establishment of a constitutional court for KZN and in clause 2(7) of Chapter 14 for the functions of such court to be performed by the provincial division of the Supreme Court pending its establishment. Chapter 8 clause 1(3) purports to confer on such constitutional court exclusive power to decide on the constitutional nature of a dispute and clause 1(4) exclusive jurisdiction to decide disputes in constitutional matters between organs and powers 'established or recognised in terms of this Constitution' and to 'declare a law of the Province unconstitutional'. The interim Constitution nowhere confers any power on a province to establish courts of law, whatever their jurisdiction may be. Chapter 7 of the interim Constitution establishes and makes comprehensive provision for court structures. It is also made explicitly clear by sections 101(3)(c), (d) and (e) respectively that it is the provincial or local division of the Supreme Court as established by the interim Constitution which has jurisdiction to enquire into the constitutionality of 'any law applicable within its area of jurisdiction, other than an Act of Parliament'; jurisdiction in relation to disputes of a constitutional nature between local governments or between a local government and a provincial government; and jurisdiction in respect of the determination of questions whether any matter falls within its jurisdiction. The KZN Legislature simply does not have the power it purports to exercise in Chapter 8 of the provincial Constitution.

[34] Clause 2(1) of Chapter 5 proclaims that '[t]his Constitution recognises' the exclusive legislative and executive authority of the 'national Government' over certain matters and clause 2(2) similarly purports to recognise the 'competence' of the 'national Parliament' in certain respects. These assertions of recognition purport to be the constitutional acts of a sovereign state. They are inconsistent with the interim Constitution because KZN is not a sovereign state and it simply has no power or authority to grant constitutional 'recognition' to what the national Government may or may not do.

[48] We are unable to and therefore decline to certify that the text of the Constitution of the Province of KwaZulu-Natal, 1996 adopted on 15 March 1996 by the KwaZulu-Natal Legislature is not inconsistent with the provisions of the Constitution of the Republic of South Africa, Act 200 of 1993 and the Constitutional Principles which constitute Schedule 4 to the said Constitution.

Concurrent powers under Schedule 4

The Constitution, while vesting national legislative power in parliament, confers certain concurrent powers to the provinces under Schedule 4, and certain administrative powers which are spelled out in Part B of Schedule 4:

Functional Areas of Concurrent National and Provincial Legislative Competence
Part A
Administration of indigenous forests
Agriculture

Airports other than international and national airports
Animal control and diseases
Casinos, racing, gambling and wagering, excluding lotteries and sports pools
Consumer protection
Cultural matters
Disaster management
Education at all levels, excluding tertiary education
Environment
Health services
Housing
Indigenous law and customary law subject to Chapter 12 of the Constitution

Industrial promotion

Language policy and the regulation of official languages to the extent that the provisions of section 6 of the Constitution expressly confer upon the provincial legislature legislative competence

Media services directly controlled or provided by the provincial government, subject to section 192

Nature conservation, excluding national parks, national botanical gardens and marine resources

Police to the extent that the provisions of Chapter 11 of the Constitution confer upon the provincial legislature legislative competence

Pollution control

Population development

Property transfer fees

Provincial public enterprises in respect of the functional areas in this Schedule and Schedule 5.

Public transport

Public works only in respect of the needs of provincial government departments in the discharge of their responsibilities to administer functions specifically assigned to them in terms of the Constitution or any other law

Regional planning and development

Road traffic regulation

Soil conservation

Tourism

Trade

Traditional leadership subject to Chapter 12 of the Constitution

Urban and rural development

Vehicle licencing

Welfare services

Part B
The following local government matters to the extent set out in section 155(6)*(a)* and (7):

Air pollution

Building regulations

Child care facilities

Electricity and gas reticulation

Firefighting services

Local tourism

Municipal airports

Municipal planning

Municipal health services

Municipal public transport

Municipal public works only in respect of the needs of municipalities in the discharge of their responsibilities to administer functions specifically assigned to them under this Constitution or any other law

Pontoons, ferries, jetties, piers and harbours excluding the regulation of international and national shipping and matters related thereto

Stormwater management systems in built-up areas

Trading regulations

Water and sanitation services limited to portable water supply systems and domestic waste-water and sewage disposal systems

Exclusive provincial and local government powers under Schedule 5

The Constitution also confers certain exclusive powers to the provinces spelled out in Part A of Schedule 5, and certain administrative powers which are spelled out in Part B of Schedule 5:

Functional Areas of Exclusive Provincial Legislative Competence

Part A

Abattoirs

Ambulance services

Archives other than national archives

Libraries other than national libraries

Liquor licences

Museums other than national museums

Provincial planning

Provincial cultural matters

Provincial recreation and amenities

Provincial sport

Provincial roads and traffic

Veterinary services excluding regulation of the profession

Part B
The following local government matters to the extent set out for provinces in section 155(6)*(a)* and (7):

Beaches and amusement facilities

Billboards and the display of advertisements in public places

Cemeteries, funeral parlours and crematoria Cleansing Control of public nuisances Control of undertakings that sell liquor to the public Facilities for the accommodation, care and burial of animals Fencing and fences Licensing of dogs Licensing and control of undertakings that sell food to the public Local amenities Local sport facilities Markets Municipal abattoirs Municipal parks and recreation Municipal roads Noise pollution Pounds Public places Refuse removal, refuse dumps and solid waste disposal	Street trading Street lighting Traffic and parking

The provincial legislature under s 142 of the Constitution has exclusive power to adopt a provincial constitution, provided that at least two-thirds of its members vote in favour of the bill. Section 143(1) provides that a provincial constitution cannot be inconsistent with the national Constitution. Section 143(2)(b) states that a provincial constitution cannot confer on the province any power or function outside the provincial competence, in terms of Schedule 4 or Schedule 5, or in terms of any other sections of the Constitution. For example, a provincial constitution cannot regulate the jurisdiction of the Constitutional Court.[53] Similarly, a provincial constitution cannot alter the nature of the electoral system.[54]

Certification of the Constitution of the Western Cape, 1997
CCT 6/97 (2 September 1997), now cited as 1997 (4) SA 795 (CC); 1997 (9) BCLR 1167 (CC)
(notes omitted).

[4] The constitution-making powers of provinces are contained in NC chap 6, which establishes the provinces, defines their territories and generally describes their organs, powers and functions. The chapter has five interrelated provisions relating to provincial constitution making. The first is NC 104(1)(a) which confers the power to adopt a constitution on a provincial legislature; the second is NC 142, which demands a two-thirds majority of its members for the exercise of that power. Then follows NC 143, which prescribes the permissible contents of provincial constitutions and reads as follows:

(1) A provincial constitution, or constitutional amendment, must not be inconsistent with this Constitution, but may provide for –
  (a) provincial legislative or executive structures and procedures that differ from those provided for in this Chapter; or
  (b) the institution, role, authority and status of a traditional monarch, where applicable.
(2) Provisions included in a provincial constitution or constitutional amendment in terms of paragraph (a) or (b) of subsection (1) –
  (a) must comply with the values in section 1 and with Chapter 3 and
  (b) may not confer on the province any power or function that falls
    (i) outside the area of provincial competence in terms of Schedules 4 and 5; or
    (ii) outside the powers and functions conferred on the province by other sections of the Constitution.

---

[53] *Certification of the Constitution of Western Cape, 1997* CCT 6/97 (2 September 1997) para 25, now cited as 1997 (4) SA 795 (CC); 1997 (9) BCLR 1167 (CC).
[54] *Supra* para 46.

That provision is followed by NC 144, requiring certification by this Court as an essential criterion for validity; and lastly, NC 145 providing for the signing, publication and safekeeping of a provincial constitution once it has been certified.

[8] The constitution-making powers of provinces provided for in NC 104(1)(*a*) are to be viewed in the broader context of the other provisions of the NC relating to provincial powers. Quite clearly, although a constitution-making power is a significant power, it is not a power to constitute a province with powers, functions or attributes in conflict with the overall constitutional framework established by the NC. The provinces remain creatures of the NC and cannot, through their provincial constitution-making power, alter their character or their relationship with the other levels of government. Nevertheless the power is a significant one, enabling a province to regulate its governance in its own fashion, subject to the provisions of NC 143 ....

[11] Although a provincial constitution may accordingly provide for legislative and executive *structures* and *procedures* which are different from those prescribed by the NC, such provisions must nevertheless comply with the values in NC 1 and NC chap 3 and *may not confer powers or functions* on the province in question beyond those conferred on them by the NC. The scope of permitted difference is therefore clearly and strictly limited to such structures and procedures. It is impermissible for a provincial constitution, under the guise of making provision for such legislative or executive structures or procedures, to grant the province powers or functions going beyond those conferred by the NC ....

[15] It is clear from these provisions in chapter 6 that it is not necessary for any province to enact a constitution ....

Repetition of Provisions in the NC

[21] The ANC objected to the repetition in the WCC of provisions of the NC which relate to matters falling outside the competence of the provincial legislature. As these provisions re-peated in the provincial constitution are identical to those in the national constitution, there obviously can be no textual inconsistency between them. But the question still arises whether the provincial legislature has the power even to repeat such provisions in its own constitution. In this regard it is necessary to recall what was said in the *KZN* case.

[T]here are two principal ways in which provisions in a provincial bill of rights could be inconsistent with the interim Constitution. Firstly, where the provision relates to a matter falling outside the power of the province, the inconsistency in this instance being in respect of s 126 of the interim Constitution. Secondly, where the provision, although relating to a matter within the province's power, is inconsistent with a provision in chap 3 of the interim Constitution. It needs to be emphasised that in the first case an inconsistency can occur even if the provincial bill of rights were to repeat *verbatim* a corresponding provision in chap 3 of the interim Constitution.

[22] What appeared in the KZN constitutional text was the repetition of matters which had nothing to do with provincial powers or competence. Those matters were contained principally in the bill of rights of the KZN constitutional text. Examples are the provisions which provided for the right to a fair trial and for states of emergency. In those instances this Court held that the 'consistency clauses' did not justify that repetition. Such repetition was not germane to the provincial constitution-making process.

[23] By contrast, in the WCC all of the provisions of the NC that are repeated relate to matters which directly affect governance within the province, that is, the provincial legislature and the members of the provincial executive or legislature. Thus, as examples, one finds the repetition of NC 106, which sets out the qualifications for membership of provincial legislatures, in WCC 15(1), (2) and (3), which set out the qualifications for membership of the Western Cape provincial parliament; of NC 108 in WCC 17 (the duration of the provincial legislature and related matters); and of NC 109

in WCC 18 (dissolution of the provincial legislature before the expiry of its term). It would indeed have been difficult for the WCC to be coherent and comprehensible without the repetition of those NC provisions which form the matrix for the related provisions of the WCC. We can find no fault with such provisions.

[24] In particular the ANC objected to WCC 32(1) on the ground that it purports to confer a competence on members of the Western Cape legislature to apply to the Constitutional Court for a declaration that a provincial Act is unconstitutional, thereby affecting the jurisdiction of this Court which is beyond the competence of a provincial legislature. We do not agree.

[25] Certainly a provincial legislature does not have the power to expand or contract the scope of jurisdiction of the Constitutional Court. In particular it has no power to regulate access to this Court. But WCC 32(1) does not purport to confer such power on the Western Cape legislature by virtue of the WCC itself. Rather, the challenged clause merely mirrors NC 122(1), the source of the power to regulate access by provincial legislators to the Constitutional Court. It is not an attempt at usurpation of power such as disqualified the KZN constitutional text.

[27] It should be noted that where provisions of the NC are repeated in the WCC, any future amendment of the NC provision in respect of a matter falling outside the competence of the provincial parliament under NC 104(1) or NC 143 would to that extent render the repeated provision in the WCC unconstitutional and of no effect. This conclusion follows from the provisions of the NC and, indeed, is recorded in WCC 3(2) which states:

The legislative and executive powers and functions of the Western Cape recorded in this Constitution emanate exclusively from the national Constitution.

[43] ... The provisions of the WCC differ from the provisions contained in the NC in two respects. First, WCC 14(d) stipulates that the electoral system be 'based predominantly on the representation of geographic multi-member constituencies'. This is in conflict with the list provided for in NC sch 6, item 11 read with IC sch 2 items 10-14. Secondly, WCC 14(a) provides that provincial legislation must prescribe an electoral system for the province in contrast to NC 105(1)(a) which provides that national legislation must prescribe the electoral system.

[44] Counsel for the Speaker acknowledged that these differences between the respective provisions of the NC and the WCC constituted inconsistencies within the meaning of NC 143(1), but argued that they fell within the scope of permissible deviation allowed by NC 143(1)(a). In particular, it was argued, the provision for a different form of proportional representation (a number of geographic multi-member constituencies as opposed to a single list system) and the provision that the electoral system is to be prescribed by the provincial and not the national legislature, were 'legislative structures' as contemplated by NC 143(1)(a).

[45] ... The choice made in the NC is straightforward: NC sch 6, read with IC sch 2, stipulates a list system of proportional representation for both national and provincial elections and seat allocation mechanisms designed to promote optimal proportionality. WCC 14(d) seeks to establish a different form of proportional representation for its legislature based on a division of the province into geographic multi-member constituencies.

[46] Therefore, whereas the NC requires the province to be regarded as a single multi-member constituency, that is, an outright list system of proportional representation with a specific seat allocation method, the WCC envisages a system which is inconsistent with that prescribed by the NC.

[48] It is true that an electoral system determines the selection or identification of representatives to function in the one or more elected elements constituting a legislature. It is also true that different electoral systems have a direct bearing on such selection or identification of legislators elected to the various elements constituting a legislature. But this has no effect at all on the constituent elements of the legislative structure. Their nature and number

remain exactly the same. There are other factors, such as the level of a threshold for party participation in the allocation of seats, which also affect the number of representatives of the various political parties who are elected to the constituent elements of a legislature. But no such factor can have any effect on the nature or number of such constituent elements. When NC 143(1)*(a)* permits a provincial constitution to provide for a provincial legislative structure different from that provided for in NC chap 6, it permits no more than a difference regarding the nature and number of the elements constituting the legislative structure. An electoral system not only does not constitute one of these elements but also has no effect on the nature or the number of such elements. It is accordingly not encompassed within the permissive provisions of NC 143(1)*(a)*.

[49] ... Applying this test, it is clear that an electoral system is not an aspect or part of a legislative structure. It is equally clear that an electoral system is not an aspect or part of a legislative procedure or an executive structure or procedure. We therefore conclude that WCC 14*(a)* and *(d)*, WCC 15(4), WCC sch 3, items 4(3) and 9(3) are inconsistent with the provisions of the NC and are not saved by NC 143(1)*(a)*.

[52] Under NC 110(1), the first sitting of a provincial legislature after an election must take place at a time and on a date determined by a judge designated by the President of the Constitutional Court. WCC 19(3) provides that the first sitting of the provincial parliament is to take place at a time and on a date determined by the Judge President of the High Court of the Western Cape or a judge designated by him or her.

[53] Under NC 111(2), a judge designated by the President of the Constitutional Court must preside over the election of a Speaker of a provincial legislature. WCC 20(2) provides that the Judge President of the High Court of the Western Cape, or a judge designated by the Judge President, must preside over the election of a Speaker. Under NC 128(2), a judge designated by the President of the Constitu-

tional Court must preside over the election of a provincial premier. WCC 38(2) provides that the Judge President of the High Court in the Western Cape or a judge designated by him or her is to preside at such election of the premier of the Western Cape.

[55] According to WCC 39 the premier must assume office by swearing or affirming faithfulness to the Republic and the Western Cape and obedience to the NC and the WCC in accordance with WCC sch 1. WCC 41(3) makes similar provision in respect of an acting premier. So, too, WCC 45 in respect of provincial ministers and WCC 16 in respect of members of the provincial parliament. In WCC sch 1 provision is made for a premier, acting premier, provincial ministers and members of the provincial parliament to swear or affirm before the Judge President of the High Court of the Western Cape or a judge designated by him or her.

[56] These provisions of the NC are clearly inconsistent with the corresponding provisions of the WCC. Counsel for the Speaker argued that the inconsistency concerns legislative or executive procedure and is thus sanctioned by NC 143(1). There is, however, an antecedent question, and that is whether a provincial legislature, in exercising its constitution-making power, has jurisdiction to remove from the President of the Constitutional Court a duty imposed on him or her by the NC and to impose that duty on a Judge President. Neither the President of the Constitutional Court nor Judges President are functionaries of any province. Members of the judiciary are independent and subject only to the Constitution and the law. A province does not have the power to impose duties on a Judge President, or to relieve the President of the Constitutional Court of duties imposed on him or her by the NC. It follows that, on this ground, these provisions of the WCC cannot be certified as being in compliance with NC 143. It is unnecessary, therefore, to consider whether the administration of an oath is a 'legislative' or 'executive' procedure within the meaning of NC 143(1).

WCC 70 : Provincial Cultural Council

[73] WCC 70 provides that

Provincial legislation must provide for the establishment and reasonable funding, within the Province's available resources, of a cultural council or councils for a community or communities in the Western Cape, sharing a common cultural and language heritage.

It was contended by the ANC that the provision was inconsistent with NC 185 and that provincial legislation emanating from it would fall foul of NC 146. According to the ANC, NC 185 contemplates the establishment of a single national commission whose powers will be regulated by national legislation. This, it was claimed, precluded the establishment of cultural councils at provincial level through provincial legislation.

[74] The relevant NC provisions are as follows:

Commission for the Promotion and Protection of the Rights of Cultural, Religious and Linguistic Communities

Functions of Commission

185 (1) The primary objects of the Commission for the Promotion and Protection of the Rights of Cultural, Religious and Linguistic Communities are—

(a) ....

(b) ....

(c) to recommend the establishment or recognition, in accordance with national legislation, of a cultural or other council or councils for a community or communities in South Africa.

[75] That a province is competent to pass legislation on cultural matters is clear. There is a concurrent national and provincial legislative competence in terms of NC sch 4 and an exclusive provincial legislative competence in terms of NC sch 5. The establishment, through provincial legislation of a provincial council, is therefore not inconsistent with the provision sanctioning the establishment of a national council.

[76] There is likewise no merit in the objection based on NC 146, a provision which deals with conflicts between national and provincial legislation. NC 146 clearly contemplates the concurrent existence of both national and provincial legislation on a matter falling within an NC sch 4 functional area and provides a procedure to resolve the conflict between the two pieces of legislation. On the other hand, the enquiry in certification proceedings relates to inconsistency between provisions of the national and provincial constitutions.

WCC Chapter 10: Directive Principles of Provincial Policy

[77] WCC chap 10, headed 'Directive Principles of Provincial Policy', was objected to by the ANC on the ground that uncertainty and confusion would flow from the fact that the directive principles are contained in a peremptory clause that declares that the Western Cape government must adopt and implement policies aimed at achieving fifteen specified goals, while the next clause provides that such principles are not legally enforceable but simply guide the Western Cape government in making and applying laws. We do not agree with this objection. WCC chap 10 contains only two clauses, WCC 81 and 82, and it is obvious that they are meant to be read together. When so read, WCC chap 10 is neither contradictory nor designed to create uncertainty or confusion. WCC 82 does nothing more than clearly describe the legal status of the guiding principles of provincial policy found in WCC 81. They are stated to be mere guiding principles relating to and not the source of enforceable legal obligations which have to be within the competence of the provincial parliament as set out in NC schs 4 and 5. Similar non-justiciable directive principles of state policy are found in the constitutions of India, Ireland and Namibia.

[78] It is worth considering that in the *KZN* case we stated that '[t]here can in principle be no objection to a province embodying a bill of rights in its constitution', provided that it did not purport to intrude on the field covered by the Bill of Rights contained in the NC. On similar and even stronger grounds, there can in principle be

no objection to non-justiciable directive principles of provincial policy being contained in a provincial constitution. If a bill of rights, a direct constraint on the legislative and executive organs of state, is permissible if it is consistent with the NC, then surely the limited constraint provided by non-enforceable directive principles fall within the competence of the drafters of the WCC.

Apart from the matters covered in Part B of Schedule 4 and Schedule 5, s 156(4) of the Constitution requires the national and provincial governments to assign a matter to a municipality, by agreement, the administration of matters in Part A of Schedule 4 and Part A of Schedule 5, if the matter relates to local government and it can be more effectively administered locally, and the municipality has the capacity to administer it. A municipality may make bye-laws to fulfil its functions. However, the power of local government under part B of Schedules 4 and 5 is merely executive and administrative.[55]

Interpretation of the override provisions

Introduction

If there is a conflict between national and provincial legislation on a Schedule 4 matter, ss 146(2) and (3) spell out how conflicts should be resolved. The sections provide:

> **Conflicts between national and provincial legislation**
>
> 146(1) This section applies to a conflict between national legislation and provincial legislation falling within a functional area listed in Schedule 4.
>
> (2) National legislation that applies uniformly with regard to the country as a whole prevails over provincial legislation if any of the following conditions is met:
>
> (a) The national legislation deals with a matter that cannot be regulated effectively by legislation enacted by the respective provinces individually.
>
> (b) The national legislation deals with a matter that, to be dealt with effectively, requires

> uniformity across the nation, and the national legislation provides that uniformity by establishing—
>
> (i) norms and standards;
> (ii) frameworks; or
> (iii) national policies
>
> (c) The national legislation is necessary for—
>
> (i) the maintenance of national security;
> (ii) the maintenance of economic unity;
> (iii) the protection of the common market in respect of the mobility of goods, services, capital and labour;
> (iv) the promotion of economic activities across provincial boundaries;
> (v) the promotion of equal opportunity or equal access to government services; or
> (vi) the protection of the environment.
>
> (3) National legislation prevails over provincial legislation if the national legislation is aimed at preventing unreasonable action by a province that—
>
> (a) is prejudicial to the economic, health or security interests of another province or the country as a whole; or
>
> (b) impedes the implementation of national economic policy.

With respect to Schedule 5 matters, the national government can, under s 44(2), intervene and pass national legislation when it is necessary:

> (a) to maintain national security;
> (b) to maintain economic unity;
> (c) to maintain essential national standards;
> (d) to establish minimum standards required for the rendering of services; or
> (e) to prevent unreasonable action taken by a province which is prejudicial to the interests of another province or to the country as a whole.

---

[55] Section 156(1) of the Constitution.

How should the Court approach the override provisions? If the Constitutional Court adopts a strict provincial rights approach to interpreting s 146(2) and s 146(3) (Schedule 4 override provisions), or s 44(2) (Schedule 5 override provisions), it might be very difficult for the national government to act on matters such as agriculture, education, housing, public transport, trade, and urban development to name only a few.[56] The Constitutional Court could read the criteria in the Schedule 4 and Schedule 5 override provisions as requiring a strong threshold for national intervention. The Court's interpretation of the override provisions, and its deference (or lack thereof) to parliament for the exercise of national power, will ultimately determine the nature of the distribution of power under the Constitution.

There are two broad and divergent approaches available to the Constitutional Court with respect to the distribution of power between the national legislature and the provinces. The first approach would be to look at the distribution of power in a formal way, as requiring a strict demarcation of power between the national government and the provinces. Only the most extreme circumstances would permit national prerogatives to supersede provincial interests. In Canada, the Canadian Supreme Court interprets the Canadian Constitution as strictly demarcating the power of the federal government and the provinces.[57] In the United States, right up to the New Deal era the Supreme Court operated on the notion of 'dual federalism', and interpreted the Constitution as placing a limit on the federal government's ability to regulate matters which were considered to be of concern to the states.[58]

The second approach is to look at federalism disputes as political issues that have to be largely resolved through the political process, within the democratically elected legislature. Under this approach, the preference is for all spheres of government to work out the distribution of power through the political process, rather than through the courts. This is the method of interpretation adhered to by the German Constitutional Court and the United States Supreme Court up to the mid-1980s. This approach recognizes that disputes concerning the allocation of power between the central government and the provinces is not a purely legal determination. Therefore, appropriate deference is given to compromises reached through the political process.

The static model of federalism: classical federalism in Canada

Canada represents the first federal system erected by the British Empire. The British North America Act of 1861 (BNA Act),[59] which is now the Canadian Constitution, apportions power between the provinces and the national government in ss 91 and 92. Section 91(2) provides that the federal government has the power to make laws with respect to '[T]he regulation of trade and commerce'.[60] Section 92(13) of the Canadian Constitution provides that the provinces shall have authority over property and civil rights. The commerce power under the Canadian Constitution is more expansive than the United States Commerce Clause, which provides that Congress has the power to 'regulate commerce with foreign nations, and among the several states'.[61] The framers of the BNA Act wanted a strong national government, contrary to United States position at that time. The framers, therefore, stated in the Constitution that the provinces would only have enumerated powers to make laws, whereas the rest of the legislative power would belong to the federal government.[62] Section 91 of the Canadian Constitution grants parliament the power to make

---

[56] The two override provisions together will be referred to as the override provisions

[57] *Labatt v Attorney-General of Canada* [1980] 1 SCR 914 (Supreme Court of Canada).

[58] *Hammer v Dagenhart* 247 US 251 (1918); *ALA Schechter Poultry Corp v United States* 295 US 495 (1935).

[59] Now referred to as the Constitution Act of 1867 (Canada Constitution).

[60] Section 91(2) of the Canada Constitution.

[61] Article 1, s 8(1) of the US Constitution.

[62] Hogg 108–9.

laws for the Peace, Order and Good Government (POGG) of Canada. The POGG power was intended to provide the federal legislature with a general grant of power.[63]

The framers of the BNA Act intended to empower the central government to act on behalf of the entire nation with respect to economic policy. At the time, there was no fear of an omnipotent legislature.[64] The Canadian Constitution's POGG power, was (according to many scholars) meant to be a residual catch-all clause of the Constitution, designed to allow national legislation on matters that were not explicitly assigned to the provinces.[65] As a matter of fact, the preamble of the Canadian Constitution states that its purpose is to create a union 'with a Constitution similar in principle to that of the United Kingdom'. This means the framers intended to have the principle of legislative supremacy.[66] The Canadians, however, failed to see the potential of the Court interpreting the Constitution in a different way.[67] Until 1949, judicial review was performed by the Judicial Committee of the Privy Council in England, which was considered to be an impartial body, with the ability to enforce the Constitution in a disinterested manner.[68] The Privy Council approached the BNA Act's distribution of power between the central government and the provinces in a rigid and literal manner by attempting to provide compartments for federal and provincial powers.[69] For example, if the central government regulated the federal power over trade and commerce, such legislation would likely have implications for provincial power over property rights. The highest court in Canada has attempted to do the impossible, namely eliminate overlapping, and make the powers of the federal government and the provinces exclusive.[70] The Court has employed an approach to federalism, which requires the federal government (when adopting trade and commerce legislation), not to encroach upon provincial powers. The Court requires parliament, when acting under s 91 (particularly in terms of the POGG power), not to encroach upon the power of the provinces.[71] The Supreme Court has interpreted the POGG power not as a general grant of power to the central legislature, but as a grant of power in the case of an emergency which threatens the life of Canada.[72] For example, the Court has struck down labour legislation enacted by the national legislature providing for maximum working hours and minimum wages, because it sees relations between employers and employees as a civil rights matter, which is subject to provincial legislation.[73] The Court struck down many economic and social legislation at the time of the 1930s Great Depression, which by most accounts was a period of national emergency.[74] After the abolition of appeals to the Privy Council,[75] the Supreme Court broadened its interpretation of emergency to include economic measures to cure rampant inflation.[76] It is only in exceptional situations that the Court would permit parliament to use the

---

[63] Op cit 278.

[64] BL Strayer *The Canadian Constitution and the Courts* Toronto: Butterworths, 3rd edition, 1988, 4.

[65] David M Beatty *Constitutional Law in Theory and Practice* Toronto: University of Toronto Press 1995, 32.

[66] JR Mallory *The Structure of Canadian Government* Toronto: Gagem, revised edition, 1984, 39.

[67] Martha Field notes that the departure in Canada from the original understanding has been accomplished primarily by judicial interpretation by the Canadian SC. Martha Field, quoted in Vicki C Jackson and Mark V Tushnet *Comparative Constitutional Law* New York: Foundation Press 1999, 794.

[68] Op cit 334–5.

[69] Op cit 346.

[70] Hogg 522.

[71] *Attorney-General for Ontario v Attorney-General for Canada* [1896] AC 348.

[72] Mallory 454.

[73] *A-AG Can v A-G Alta* (Insurance) [1916] 1 AC at 412; A-G Can v A-G Ont [1937] AC 355.

[74] The Court felt the Great Depression was not of an emergency nature. *Reference re Natural Products Marketing Act* [1936] AC 193.

[75] This was done in 1949.

[76] Reference re Inflation Act [1976] 68 DLR (3d) at 458.

POGG powers to override provincial powers.[77] Despite the development of doctrines such as the 'double aspect rule', 'pith and substance', and the 'ancillary rule' the broad approach of federalism elevated the provinces to an equal status with the federal government and provided a limited interpretation of federal powers, that has been maintained in Canada up to this day.[78]

McWhinney characterizes the Canadian interpretation of federalism as judgments of 'a strongly decentralized, centrifugal orientation'.[79] Through its interpretation of federalism, the Court sided with forces opposed to national social and economic protection and against the interest of the poorer sector of society. By getting the Court to rule that labour issues, civil rights, and property rights belonged exclusively to the provinces, private interests were able to protect themselves from national legislation.[80] Mallory makes the point that although the Court gave the provinces jurisdiction over many of these matters, the provinces at various times did not have the resources to meet needs such as unemployment benefits, social security, and economic direction. There was a need for an energized central government which the Court said was excluded from acting on behalf of the entire country.[81] Despite the POGG power, the Canadian judiciary has approached federalism in a very static way, which regards the provinces as a buffer against the central government. For example, the Canadian Court's interpretation of emergency is highly restrictive and not something that can be readily resorted to for national solutions.[82]

The Canadian interpretation of the distribution of power represents the classical and static model of federalism. If the Constitutional Court in South Africa adopts this approach, they could conceivably adopt criteria for the interpretation of, for example, necessary economic unity or national standards under the override provisions that are very demanding and difficult to meet. This could have adverse consequences for transformation as illustrated below.

Classical federalism in African states: an overview [83]

Most African states at independence were plural societies. They consisted of various linguistic, cultural or religious groups. The question is whether the classical federal model offers a viable framework to deal with sub-nationalism, socio-economic change, and nation-building. Critics of the federal model argue that it does not operate neutrally, but instead works in favour of certain societal interests.[84] The federal model often operates in a way which leads to conflict between those elements representing the status quo and those elements advocating change.[85] By dividing authority between various units and entrenching the rights of those units, a minority can frustrate the will of the majority. Federalism may thus operate to protect the interests of the minority at the expense of the majority. Riker asserts that the federal model in the United States has historically allowed a privileged class in the South to tyrannize African Americans.[86] The plea for the rights of states has worked to guarantee the privilege of the majority in the South over African Americans, first

---

[77] In *R v Crown Zellerbach Canada Ltd* [1988] 1 SCR 401 (SC of Canada), the Court (in a four-to-three vote) validated federal legislation to control marine pollution in terms of the POGG powers.

[78] Beaty 44–6. Hogg 111, who suggests that it is unlikely that there will be a wholesale rejection of this judicial interpretation.

[79] Edward McWhinney 'Constitution-making in an Era of Transition' in *Federalism-in-the-making: Contemporary Canadian and German Constitutionalism, National and Transnational*, edited by Edward McWhinney, et al. Dordrecht: M Nijhoff 1992, 21.

[80] Mallory 342.

[81] Op cit 343–5.

[82] Beatty 35.

[83] The following is adapted with permission from: Ziyad Motala 'The Record of Federal Constitutions in Africa: Some Lessons for a Post-Apartheid South Africa' (1990) 7 *Arizona Journal of International And Comparative Law* 235–42 (note numbers changed).

[84] Bothe 414.

[85] Ibid.

[86] William H Riker *Federalism: Origin, Operation, Significance* Boston: Little Brown 1964, 140, 142.

as slaves and later as an underprivileged sector of the population.[87] The equation of federalism and freedom is rejected because a majority at the national level can have their wishes blocked by a minority at the regional level.[88] Despite these criticisms the federal system in the United States has survived for over two hundred years. There are, however, differences in the conditions under which the federal system was introduced in many African countries. The overall desirability of a classical federal system must be examined in light of the social and political conditions present in African societies. The potential for success of a classical federal government must also be gauged by analysing the factors which contribute to the success of a federal system.[89]

Proponents of federalism assert that it is the most suitable model for societies characterized by major cleavages in the population. The United States represents the longest surviving federal system. The United States is one of the most diverse countries in the world, made up of a myriad of ethnic and national groups. The federal model in the United States is essentially a symmetrical model, in that the units do not in any way coincide with cleavages in the population. There are no major differences in the religious, linguistic, or ethnic composition of the states which lead to friction. The federal model in the United States was not designed to protect the integrity of a culturally distinctive group as in some African countries, Canada and other countries using asymmetric models of federalism. This distinction undercuts the notion that a federal model is most successful in a society made up of different ethnic, national, or religious groups. The

relationship between federalism and nationalism is very complex.[90] Some societies have been able to overcome their obstacles by dividing into various units, whereas in other circumstances, it has had the opposite effect. In the United States the federal system has worked well in a symmetrical society, where 'each particular section, state or region partakes of a character general and common to the whole'.[91] If follows then, that there is no simple relationship between federalism and pluralism.[92]

In several African states classical federalism has been espoused and implemented as though it act as a panacea for diversity. Unlike the United States, federal states in African countries did not operate in a symmetrical manner. It is important to understand the strengths and pitfalls of classical federal states.[93] In many African nations, the federal model has not resulted in the freedom and compromises identified with federal institutions, but has instead resulted in greater instability, and even chaos, in some states.[94] Introduction of the classical federal model in many African states has led to a mobilization of ethnic minorities. The notion that minority communities should have special representation has resulted in divided loyalties and has thwarted the development of national consciousness.[95] In Nigeria, the federal system gave institutional expression to tribalized politics and froze the situation as it was at the time of the departure of the colonial power.[96] The regions created under federal plans were each identified with a major ethnic community.[97] Each region saw itself as a distinct political entity. Political parties identified with certain regions and with particular ethnic groups. The political parties invariably sought support from their

---

[87] Op cit 152.

[88] Op cit 142.

[89] Charles D Tarlton 'Symmetry and Asymmetry as Elements of Federalism: A Theoretical Speculation' (1965) 27 *Journal of Politics* 861.

[90] Friedrich 227.

[91] Tarlton 861.

[92] Friedrich 872.

[93] Tarlton 874.

[94] See Lord Russell of Liverpool *The Tragedy of the Congo* London: 1962, 2. See also FAO Schwarz Jnr *Nigeria: The Tribes, The Nation or the Race: The Politics of Independence* Cambridge: MIT Press 1965, 194.

[95] Stanley A de Smith *The New Commonwealth and its Constitutions* London: Stevens 1964, 117.

[96] John M Amoda 'The Relationship of History, Thought and Action with Respect to the Nigerian Situation' in *Nigeria: Dilemma of Nationhood*, edited by Joseph Okpaku. New York: Third Press 1972, 37.

[97] John Hatch *Nigeria: The Seeds of Disaster* Chicago: Regnery Co 1970, 257.

regional and ethnic bases.[98] It becomes difficult to achieve a national party representing common national interests. Nigeria exemplifies the adverse affects that a preoccupation with regional or ethnic self-interests can have on the development of a sense of common identity. The parochialism of political parties in Nigeria has severely strained unifying mechanisms essential for nation-building.[99]

In Uganda, the federal system was marked by tribal loyalties which severely compromised nation-building. The region of Buganda was given a privileged position under the Constitution with respect to a host of matters.[100] The leader of Buganda was identified with the traditional kingdom and claimed the loyalty of the Buganda people over that of the Ugandan state.[101] Again, the federal state permitted a situation of divided loyalties. The federal structure gave institutional expression to a competition for loyalty between the region and the centre: this posed a threat of dismembering the Ugandan state.[102] The abolition of the federal state was considered necessary if Uganda was to remain as a single country.[103]

Similarly, the first Republic of the Congo provided for a fragmentation of provincial autonomy. The post-independence period was characterized by violent tribal riots flowing from widespread communal insecurities created by ethnic rivalries.[104]

These examples illustrate that communal representation within a federal system has had a poor track record in Africa. It tends to exacerbate communal differences and communal prejudices.[105] This institutionalized parochialism resulted in great political ruptures in the Congo, Uganda, and Nigeria. In many instances there was

unrelenting competition between the centre and the region for the loyalty of the people. This was evident in Nigeria during the Biafran crisis, when the Eastern region attempted to secede from the federal state. A similar phenomenon occurred in the Congo with the attempted secession of Katanga. The central governments in all three instances could not effectuate national policies without meeting the resistance of regional or ethnic political groups. This has resulted in a political system consistently fragmented by parochial loyalties. The ability of the central government to act decisively on issues of national concern was crippled by local self-interest. Weak central governments subject to the political restraints of the regions under the classical federal systems have not been able to implement and carry out national policies in education, housing, agriculture, and other important areas. It has also resulted in the entrenchment of tribalism and the squandering of resources, something the struggling nations could ill afford.[106] A country with scarce resources cannot afford the dual system of local and central governments which consumes a great deal of resources. For example, under the Independence Constitution in Nigeria, economic and social planning was duplicated four times with the central and local governments carrying out their programmes in parallel.[107] Similarly, duplication of government functions in Uganda and Kenya imposed a high administrative cost on the state.[108]

African states came into existence at a time when the attitudes toward the proper role of government had changed.[109] During the twentieth century, unlike the seventeenth and eighteenth centuries, it has been generally accepted that government must play an active role in economic

[98] Ibid.

[99] Schwarz 194.

[100] M Nziramsanga 'Secession, Federalism and African Unity' in *Nigeria: Dilemma of Nationhood*, edited by Joseph Okpaku. New York: Third Press 1972, 231.

[101] Nwabueze 147.

[102] Op cit 146, 149.

[103] Op cit 148.

[104] Crawford Young and Thomas Turner *The Rise and Decline of the Zairean State* Madison: University of Wisconsin Press 1985, 42.

[105] De Smith 118.

[106] Aletum M Tabuwe *The One-party System and the Traditional African Institutions* Yaounde: A Tabuwe 1980, 19.

[107] Ronald L Watts *New Federations: Experiments in the Commonwealth* Oxford Clarendon 1966, 128.

[108] Rothchild 298–9.

[109] Schwarz 195.

and social development.[110] Constitutionalizing widespread regional autonomy and limiting the power of the central government has resulted in even greater economic and social disparities.

Non-classical federalism: independence, cooperative government, and compromise

As the foregoing discussion illustrates, classical federalism operates in terms of legalisms and rigid legal categories. There is a competing concept of federalism that espouses political flexibility, co-operation, negotiation, compromise and less reliance on legalisms, and legal analyses. From the override provision, the distribution of power under the South African Constitution was not meant to be in terms of rigid categories. The Constitution arguably marks a departure from classical federalism and stresses instead two interrelated principles namely, 'cooperative government'[111] (much akin to the German example), and 'political federalism'. Cooperative government, among other things, requires all organs of government to work together in exercising the proper allocation of power. In terms of the doctrine of political federalism, if one (or more) provinces attempted to prevent the exercise of national power on a Schedule 4 or Schedule 5 matter, the Constitutional Court could give great deference to the political process. In other words, under this doctrine, the Court would be reluctant to spell out a strict demarcation of power between the national legislature and the provinces, but instead would prefer that the distribution of power be resolved through compromise and negotiation through the political process. The Constitution expressly provides for cooperative government and states:

40 (1) In the Republic, government is constituted as national, provincial and local spheres of government, which are distinctive, interdependent and interrelated.

(2) All spheres of government must observe and adhere to the principles in this Chapter and must conduct their activities within the parameters that the Chapter provides.

Principles of cooperative government and inter-governmental relations

41 (1) All spheres of government and all organs of state within each sphere must—
 (a) preserve the peace, national unity and the indivisibility of the Republic;
 (b) secure the well-being of the people of the Republic;
 (c) provide effective, transparent, accountable and coherent government for the Republic as a whole;
 (d) be loyal to the Constitution, the Republic and its people;
 (e) respect the constitutional status, institutions, powers and functions of government in the other spheres;
 (f) not assume any power or function except those conferred on them in terms of the Constitution;
 (g) exercise their powers and perform their functions in a manner that does not encroach on the geographical, functional or institutional integrity of government in another sphere; and
 (h) co-operate with one another in mutual trust and good faith by—
  (i) fostering friendly relations;
  (ii) assisting and supporting one another;
  (iii) informing one another of, and consulting one another on, matters of common interest;
  (iv) co-ordinating their actions and legislation with one another;
  (v) adhering to agreed procedures; and
  (vi) avoiding legal proceedings against one another.
(2) An Act of Parliament must —
 (a) establish or provide for structures and institutions to promote and facilitate inter-governmental relations; and

---

[110] Ibid.
[111] Chapter 3 of the Constitution.

(b) provide for appropriate mechanisms and procedures to facilitate settlement of intergovernmental disputes.

(3) An organ of state involved in an intergovernmental dispute must make every reasonable effort to settle the dispute by means of mechanisms and procedures provided for that purpose, and must exhaust all other remedies before it approaches a court to resolve the dispute.

(4) If a court is not satisfied that the requirements of subsection (3) have been met, it may refer a dispute back to the organs of state involved.

Chapter 3 of the Constitution stresses two main themes: first, that the division of power between different levels of government needs to be respected, and secondly, that this division of power is not exclusive but has to be exercised in a cooperative manner. The division of power is described as constituted in national, provincial, and local spheres, 'which are distinctive, interdependent and interrelated'.[112] This leads to the question what is the meaning of 'distinctive', 'interdependent', and 'interrelated'?

Meaning of distinctive nature of government

What do we understand by the phrase 'government is distinctive'? In the *Premier of the Province of Western Cape*, the Constitutional Court observed that '[d]istinctiveness lies in the provision made for elected governments at national, provincial, and local levels'.[113] It requires that all spheres of government respect the constitutional status,

institutions, powers, and functions of government in other spheres.[114] It requires that all spheres of government must exercise only the power conferred upon them by the Constitution.[115] It further requires that the institutional integrity and functions of government in all spheres be respected.[116] This principle was best described in *Fedsure*, where the Court stated: 'It seems central to the conception of our constitutional order that the legislative and executive in every sphere are constrained by the principle that they may exercise no power and perform no function beyond that conferred by law'.[117]

What this means, first and foremost, is that the provinces or any other sphere of government cannot legislate on matters which are within parliament's exclusive competence. This could change if parliament delegated power to the provinces.[118] In the absence of any delegated authority, the provinces absolutely cannot, for example, legislate on matters such as defence, foreign affairs, or post offices. An attempt on the part of a province to legislate on, for example, arms reductions would be inconsistent with cooperative behaviour and the obligation not to assume 'any power or function except those conferred on them in the Constitution'. Apart from preventing any attempt on the part of the provinces to legislate directly, there should be limits on other spheres of government taking independent action, that would pressurize parliament to adopt the 'will of the province' in a matter which is within the exclusive power of the national legislature.[119] For example, the NP-majority government in the Western Cape provincial legislature has threatened to hold a referendum on the death

---

[112] Section 40(1).

[113] *Premier of the Province of the Western Cape v The President of South Africa and Another* CCT 26/98 (29 March 1999) para 50, now cited as 1999 (4) BCLR 382 (CC); 1999 (3) SA 657 (CC).

[114] Section 41(1)*(e)* of the Consitution.

[115] Section 41(1)*(f)*.

[116] Section 41(1)*(g)*.

[117] *Fedsure Life Assurance Ltd and Others v The Greater Johannesburg Transitional Metropolitan Council and Others* CCT 7/98 (14 October 1998) para 58, now cited as 1998 (12) BCLR 1458 (CC); 1999 (1) SA 374 (CC).

[118] Under s 44(2), parliament can assign its legislative powers (except the power to amend the Constitution) to a legislative body in another sphere of government.

[119] See eg the *Atomic Weapons Referenda I* case translated in Donald P Kommers *The Constitutional Jurisprudence of the Federal Republic of Germany* Durham: Duke University Press 1989, 87–8, where the German Constitutional Court ruled one state cannot hold a referendum to ascertain the will of the population on a matter that is within the exclusive domain of the national government.

penalty. The death penalty violates various provisions in the Bill of Rights.[120] The propriety of introducing the death penalty is a matter exclusively within the domain of the national parliament.[121] Action by the provincial parliament on a matter of exclusive national concern should be ruled unconstitutional. In *Certification of the Constitution of the Western Cape*, the Constitutional Court observed:

[8] The constitution-making powers of provinces provided for in NC 104(1)*(a)* are to be viewed in the broader context of the other provisions of the NC relating to provincial powers. Quite clearly, although a constitution-making power is a significant power, it is not a power to constitute a province with powers, functions or attributes in conflict with the overall constitutional framework established by the NC. The provinces remain creatures of the NC and cannot, through their provincial constitution-making power, alter their character or their relationship with the other levels of government. Nevertheless the power is a significant one, enabling a province to regulate its governance in its own fashion, subject to the provisions of NC 143.

The distinctive nature of government also means respect for the integrity and functions of provincial and local government. In the *Premier of the Western Cape*, the Constitutional Court held that s 53(3)(3)*(b)* of the Public Service Laws Amendment Act,[122] which attempted to vest the power of implementation of provincial laws with the national minister was unconstitutional.[123] The section infringed on the executive power of the provinces to administer their own laws.[124]

Similarly, where the Constitution grants exclusive power to the provinces, the national government cannot interfere with provincial power. The Constitutional Court has held that the national government cannot dictate to the provinces on the different types of municipalities to be established in the provinces because this decision under s 155(5) of the Constitution is reserved for the provinces.[125]

Meaning of interdependent and interrelated

Just as it stresses the power of different levels of government, the Constitution also stresses the need for all spheres of government to cooperate with one another[126] by assisting and supporting one another,[127] and informing and consulting one another on matters of common interest,[128] and (interestingly) calls on all spheres of government to avoid legal proceedings against one another.[129] The Constitution requires national legislation to create a framework to facilitate intergovernmental relations,[130] and to provide for mechanisms and procedures to settle intergovernmental disputes.[131] The interdependence and interrelatedness relates to activities which are integral to the preservation of South Africa as a single sovereign democratic state. In *Premier of the Western Cape*,[132] the Court held that the national legislature could, under s 197(1) of the Constitution, compel the provincial Directors-General to carry out certain functions over the objections of Western Cape that the provinces should be able to appoint their own functionaries to attend to these functions.[133] The Court further held that the

---

[120] As held in *Makwanyane*.

[121] Which will have to be effected via a constitutional amendment.

[122] Act 86 of 1998.

[123] *Premier of the Western Cape* para 86.

[124] *Supra*.

[125] *Executive Council of the Province of the Western Cape* para 47. See also *Premier of the Western Cape* para 80, where the Court held that the national minister cannot dictate to the provinces as to how to administer provincial laws.

[126] Section 41(1)*(h)* of the Constitution.

[127] Section 41(1)*(e)*(ii).

[128] Section 41(1)*(e)*(iii).

[129] Section 41(1)*(e)*(vi).

[130] Section 41(2)*(a)*.

[131] Section 41(2)*(b)*.

[132] *Premier of the Western Cape* para 50.

[133] *Supra* para 68.

provisions under the Public Service Act,[134] which required the premier of a province, if he or she wanted to establish or abolish provincial departments, to make a request to the president, was not unconstitutional. The requirement that the president and the premier of the province achieve consensus on restructuring of the public service is consistent with cooperative government, and does not constitute an invasion of the executive power of the provinces, or of the functional or institutional integrity of the provincial governments.[135]

In Germany, the German Constitutional Court has provided the expression cooperative federalism and federal comity. The German Basic Law, provides that the federal government can exercise authority only on those matters expressly conferred on it,[136] which might lead to the conclusion that Germany has a federal system which attempts to strictly demarcate the powers of the national government and the states (*Länders*). However, the predominant view of German federalism is one of comity and cooperation, which obliges the federal government and the *Länders* to work together in their relations with each other.[137] There is nothing in the German Basic Law (unlike the South African Constitution) which mentions the principle of cooperation between the states and the central government. Comity is a principle that the German Constitutional Court has arrived at through dynamic interpretation. As McWhinney observed, the German Constitutional Court in interpreting the distribution of power in the Basic Law was able to break from the classical British imperial thinking of federalism.[138]

The German approach is also instructive in interpreting the requirement of all spheres *assisting and supporting one another*. For example, art 109 of the German Basic Law states that the federation and the states are 'independent of each other with regard to their respective budgets'.[139] The federal government in Germany consistently enacts equalization statutes which require richer states to transfer tax resources to poorer states. In the *Finance Equalization* case, the equalization measures were challenged by the rich states as violating the principles of federalism.[140] The German Constitutional Court ruled that the states have rights as well as duties and where the stronger states are concerned, they have a duty to assist the financially poorer states.[141] Arguably, s 41(1) of the Constitution requires similar cooperation and assistance, as opposed to a static concept of federalism, with the provinces and national government in perpetual conflict with each other.

The corollary is that the national legislature must not encroach upon the exercise of provincial power, particularly Schedule 5 matters, unless there is a constitutional basis to support parliament's intervention.[142] Over time, judgments have to be made with respect to the levels of cooperation, consultation, and as to which levels are best placed to exercise power with respect to various functions, particularly specific functional areas under Schedule 4 and Schedule 5. This leads to the question: what are the standards for national intervention for Schedule 4 and Schedule 5 matters, and what degree of deference should the Constitutional Court give to the national political institutions to make this determination, which leads to the notion of political federalism?

Standard of deference: political federalism

The Constitution in South Africa is being introduced in an era where the national government is expected to act for the benefit of the entire country. Therefore, rather then using imperial and

---

[134] Act 86 of 1998, ss 7, 5*(a)* and *(b)*.

[135] *Premier of the Western Cape* para 83.

[136] Article 70(1) of the German Basic Law.

[137] Kommers 70.

[138] McWhinney 6, 27.

[139] Article 109 of the German Basic Law.

[140] The *Finance Equalization* case (1952) 1 BVerfGE 117, quoted in Kommers 100.

[141] Kommers 100.

[142] *Ex parte the President of the Republic of South Africa; In re: Constitutionality of the Liquor Bill* CCT 12/99 (11 November 1999) para 21, now cited as 2000 (1) SA 732 (CC); 2000 (1) BCLR 1 (CC).

archaic concepts of federalism, all spheres of government are called upon in s 41 to apply themselves in a cooperative manner through the political process and work out the best distribution of power. But what happens if there is a stalemate in the political institutions resulting in disagreement between parliament and the provinces on, for example, appropriate policy with respect to housing, or education, both of which are Schedule 4 matters? This brings us to the question of how the courts are going to interpret the override provisions. While there is merit in the devolution of power to the provinces and local areas, the interests of citizens, to borrow a phrase from Simeon, 'in terms of economic and social goals – as consumers, workers, businessmen, homeowners' are more important to the entire country 'than their interests as members of territorially defined communities'.[143] It is hoped that the Constitutional Court will be influenced by the notion of political federalism in interpreting the override provisions. The concept of political federalism is embodied in the approaches of the United States Supreme Court in *Garcia v San Antonio Metro. Transit Authority*,[144] and that of the German Constitutional Court in a series of cases.[145] Under this approach, power disputes on matters of concurrent power should in the main be resolved through the political process. Arguably, the South African Constitution more so than the United States and German Constitutions, emphasises that disputes with respect to the appropriate distribution of power should be resolved through the political process.[146]

The evolution of political federalism is best reflected in the federalism decisions of the United States Supreme Court after 1937. The Tenth Amendment of the United States Constitution provides that '[T]he powers not delegated to the United States by the Constitution, nor prohibited by it to the states, are reserved to the States respectively, or to the people'. Prior to the New Deal crisis of the 1930s, the United States Supreme Court consistently held that the Tenth Amendment prohibited the federal government from exercising functions which belonged to the states. The Court in the period before the New Deal adopted a very formalistic approach to federalism and in a number of cases held that the federal government could not regulate manufacturing, local labour conditions, maximum working hours, or minimum wages.[147] (This early approach was akin to the Canadian approach to federalism.) The Court operated in terms of the notion of dual federalism and traditional functions that belonged to the federal government and the states. Under this concept, there were certain powers that belonged exclusively to the federal government, and there were certain powers that belonged exclusively to the states. In exercising its national power, the national government could not usurp the power of the states.[148] The federal government was a government of enumerated powers. The Tenth Amendment reserved all the remaining powers, not enumerated to the federal government, to the states. The parameters of federal and national power were timeless and immutable.[149]

While Schedule 4 provides for dual power, and Schedule 4 and 5 provide override provisions, the Constitutional Court could interpret the override

---

[143] R Simeon, quoted in Macklem 174.

[144] *Garcia v San Antonio Metro Transit Authority* 469 US 528, 105 SCt 1005, 83 L Ed2d 1016 (1985).

[145] The *First Television* case (1961) 12 BVerfGE 205 (Federal Constitutional Court of Germany) translated in Jackson & Tushnet 827–31. JE Finn 'Federalism in Perpetuity: West German and United States Federalism in Comparative Perspective' (1989) 22 *New York University Journal of International Law and Politics* 30.

[146] eg section 41(2)*(a)* requires parliament to adopt legislation to facilitate intergovernmental relations. Section 41(2)*(b)* further requires legislation to provide for mechanisms and procedures to settle intergovernmental relations. Very significantly, under s 41(3) all organs of government are required to settle disputes through the political process and only approach the Court for a remedy as a last resort. *Premier of the Western Cape* para 54.

[147] *Hammer v Dagenhart* 247 US 251 (1918); *United States v EC Knight* 156 US 1 (1895); *ALA Schechter Poultry Corp v United States* 295 US 495 (1935).

[148] For a comprehensive discussion of the notion of dual federalism, see Edward Samuel Corwin 'The Passing of Dual Federalism' in *Essays in Constitutional Law*, edited by Robert G McCloskey. New York: Knof 1957.

[149] Edward Samuel Corwin *Court over Constitution: A Study of Judicial Review as an Instrument of Popular Government* New York: P Smith 1938, 13.

provision in a rigid fashion almost akin to dual federalism. With this approach to dual federalism, the United States Supreme Court prevented the national government from regulating a range of activities such as manufacturing, labour, and mining, which the Court considered to be traditionally under the regulation of the states. The Supreme Court became the protector of property interests. Elementary economic regulations of every sort were held unconstitutional on the grounds that they violated the principles of federalism, or interfered with freedom of contract and amounted to the taking of liberty and property without due process of law. The right to form trade unions, to set minimum wages, and stipulate maximum working hours were set aside.[150] The judiciary interpreted the distribution of power in a way that protected state and minority interests at the expense of the majority. The Court's position on state rights was favoured by the conservative wing and the wealthy classes in society, because the outlawing of labour laws, anti-trust laws, and federal income tax laws protected big business.[151] With the massive unemployment and widespread lack of food and shelter, there was a feeling of frustration on the part of ordinary people, and a restlessness for an overhaul of the existing economic and social system.[152] The crisis over the New Deal era led to one of the greatest constitutional crises. President Roosevelt threatened to stack the Court with new judges to counteract the obstruction of the sitting judges. A major constitutional crisis was averted when the majority of the nine justices on the Supreme Court reversed course in what has now come to be characterized as *a switch in time saved nine*.

Starting in 1937,[153] the United States Supreme Court in a matter of a few years, transformed its position on federalism and state rights culminating in *Garcia v San Antonio Metropolitan Transit Authority*,[154] where the majority stated that they could not adhere to the 'traditional government functions test'. This test, the Court said was too rigid a standard and was unworkable because it prevented the Court from adapting to historical changes in functions of the state.[155] What we see in cases after the New Deal era, particularly in the period between 1937 and 1992, is a break from formalism[156] and *a priori* categories of state and national government functions.[157] Since 1937, the United States Supreme Court has never invalidated national legislation on private sector economic activity on the grounds that the activity belonged to the states.

Recently, the majority in the United States Supreme Court has retreated somewhat in resurrecting the Tenth Amendment as a limitation on the exercise of national power.[158] In *New York v United States*, the state government challenged a provision in the Low-Level Radioactive Waste Policy Amendment Act, which required the states to take title to nuclear waste after 1996, if the state did not provide facilities for the disposition of nuclear waste. The effect of the statute was to make the states agents of the national government. The federal government argued that the statute was drawn up with the consent of the states, including the state of New York, through a process of cooperation.[159] The response of the majority was that federalism was for the protection of individual liberties and not for the states.[160] Therefore, the principles of federalism cannot be

---

[150] *Lochner v New York* 198 US 45 (1905).

[151] Derrick A Bell Jnr *Race, Racism and American Law* Boston: Little Brown 1980, 36–7.

[152] DJ Hulsebosch 'The New Deal Court Emergence of a New Reason' (1990) 90 *Columbia Law Review* 1973.

[153] Starting with *National Labor Relations Board v Jones & Laughlin Steel Corporation* 301 US 1 (1937).

[154] 469 US 528 (1985).

[155] *Supra.*

[156] There was one aberration in the Court's approach in *National League of Cities v Usery* 426 US 833 (1976), where the Court upheld a federalism based limitation on the federal government, preventing it from regulating the operations of state governments. The approach in *Usery* was overruled in *Garcia*.

[157] *Garcia v San Antonio Metro Transit Authority* 469 US 528, 548 (1985).

[158] *New York v United States* 505 US 144 (1992); *United States v Lopez* 115 SCt 1624 (1995). *United States v Morrison* 120 SCt 1578 (2000).

[159] *New York v United States* 505 US at 180–181.

[160] *Supra.*

given away by the states. The Supreme Court ruled that the federal government could not compel the states to act as agents for the federal government.[161]

The South African Constitution reflects a different concept with respect to the relationship between the national government and the provinces. Indeed, parliament can pass legislation which requires the provincial government to act in furtherance of national policies.[162] In *In re: The National Education Policy Bill No 83 of 1995*,[163]

the Constitutional Court rejected the approach to federalism that the United States Supreme Court adopted in *New York v United States*. The crucial issue was whether parliament could force the provincial political head of education to participate in cooperative structures, and to prepare a plan as to how national standards on education could be implemented. The Constitutional Court ruled that parliament could require the provincial Head of Education to cooperate in the preparation of national education standards.[164]

In re: Dispute Concerning the Constitutionality of Certain Provisions of the National Education Policy Bill No 83 of 1995
CCT 46/95 (3 April 1996), now cited 1996 (3) SA 289 (CC); 1996 (4) BCLR 518 (CC)
(notes omitted)

[22] It was pointed out in *Executive Council of the Western Cape Legislature and Others v President of the Republic of South Africa and Others* that the powers of Parliament depend ultimately upon 'the language of the Constitution, construed in the light of [our] own history'. Our history is different to the history of the United States of America, and the language of our Constitution differs materially from the language of the United States Constitution. The history and structure of the United States Constitution are discussed in the judgment of O'Connor J in the *New York* case. The Constitution addressed a situation in which several sovereign states were brought together in a federation. The constitutional scheme agreed upon was that each state would surrender part of its sovereignty to the federal government and retain that part which had not been surrendered. This is reflected in the language of the Constitution. Congress has only those powers

specifically vested in it by the Constitution. All other power is vested in the states Congress can make laws which encroach upon state sovereignty through the supremacy clause, commerce clause, the spending power and the power to make all laws which may be necessary and proper for the implementation of its powers, but cannot otherwise interfere with the rights vested in the states under the Tenth Amendment.

[23] Unlike their counterparts in the United States of America, the provinces in South Africa are not sovereign states. They were created by the Constitution and have only those powers that are specifically conferred on them under the Constitution. Their legislative power is confined to schedule 6 matters and even then it is a power that is exercised concurrently with Parliament. Decisions of the courts of the United States dealing with state rights are not a safe guide as to how our courts should address problems that may arise in relation to the rights of provinces under our Constitution. And this is so whether the issue arises under the provisions of section 126 or any other provision of the Constitution.

[33] It was suggested in argument that the cooperation of a provincial political head of education who wishes to ignore a request made for the submission of a remedial plan, could be secured through a *mandamus*, or through a

---

[161] *Supra.*

[162] *Premier of the Western Cape* para 52.

[163] *In re: The National Education Policy Bill No 83 of 1995* CCT 46/95 (3 April 1996).

[164] *The National Education Policy Bill* para 34. See also *Premier of the Western Cape* para 71, where the Constitutional Court affirmed the power of parliament, under s 197(2) of the Constitution, to direct certain public servants in the provincial administration to exercise certain management, administrative and training functions in their departments.

threat to withhold financial support for the province's education system, or through some other coercive action. It is by no means clear that a political obligation such as that contemplated by clause 8(6) could be made the subject of a *mandamus*, particularly if the province is not willing to implement the plan; nor is it clear that the offering or withholding of financial incentives (if otherwise lawful) would be open to objection. If the financial incentives or other action taken to persuade the provinces to agree to national policy are not legitimate they can be challenged under the Constitution or under the well established principle that a power given for a specific purpose may not be misused in order to secure an ulterior purpose; if they are legitimate, then they are not open to objection. These are not, however, issues that need trouble us in this case. It can be assumed that provincial administrations will act in accordance with a law which is consistent with the Constitution. If a law requires a provincial administration to act in a particular manner and that requirement is not constitutional, the law cannot be saved from constitutional challenge simply because there may be inadequate forensic mechanisms under the Constitution for its enforcement. It is therefore necessary to confront and answer the question: can an Act of Parliament require a provincial political head of education to cause a plan to be prepared as to how national standards can best be implemented in the province?

[34] Where two legislatures have concurrent powers to make laws in respect of the same functional areas, the only reasonable way in which these powers can be implemented is through cooperation. And this applies as much to policy as to any other matter. It cannot therefore be said to be contrary to the Constitution for Parliament to enact legislation that is premised on the assumption that the necessary cooperation will be offered, and which requires a provincial administration to participate in cooperative structures and to provide information or formulate plans that are reasonably required by the Minister and are relevant to finding the best solution to an impasse that has arisen.

[36] ... Provinces are free to develop and implement their own education policies If they do so in a way that conflicts with national education policy, and that conflict is in respect of matters falling within the purview of section 126(3)(a) to (e) of the Constitution, the provinces concerned may possibly be required by the Minister to amend their policies. But, in the absence of agreement or legislation lawfully enacted by Parliament that requires them to do so, they have no obligation to comply with any demand that might be made by the Minister, the

---

Not only are the provinces obligated to fulfil national legislation under s 100 of the Constitution, but where the provinces cannot or do not fulfil their constitutional or statutory obligations, the national executive can intervene to ensure that the legal obligations are fulfilled. The Constitution provides:

National supervision of provincial administration

100(1) When a province cannot or does not fulfil an executive obligation in terms of legislation or the Constitution, the national executive may intervene by taking any appropriate steps to ensure fulfilment of that obligation, including—

(a) issuing a directive to the provincial executive, describing the extent of the failure to fulfil its obligations and stating any steps required to meet its obligations; and

(b) assuming responsibility for the relevant obligation in that province to the extent necessary to—

(i) maintain essential national standards or meet established minimum standards for the rendering of a service;

(ii) maintain economic unity;

(iii) maintain national security; or

(iv) prevent that province from taking unreasonable action that is prejudicial to the interests of another province or to the country as a whole.

(2) If the national executive intervenes in a province in terms of subsection (1)(b)—

(a) notice of the intervention must be tabled in the National Council of Provinces within 14 days of its first sitting after the intervention began;

(b) the intervention must end unless it is approved by the Council within 30 days of its first sitting after the intervention began; and

(c) the Council must review the intervention regularly and make any appropriate recommendations to the national executive.

(3) National legislation may regulate the process established by this section.

The Constitutional Court interpreted the scope of s 100 in the *First Certification* decision, and again in the *Second Certification* decision.

In re: Certification of the Constitution of the Republic of South Africa, 1996
CCT 23/96 (6 September 1996), now cited as 1996 (10) BCLR 1253 (CC); 1996 (4) SA 744 (CC)
(notes omitted)

[263] NT 100 creates an exception to the general principle that the implementation of provincial legislation in a province is an exclusive provincial executive power. It provides that when a province cannot or does not fulfil an executive obligation the national executive may take appropriate steps to ensure fulfilment of that obligation.

[264] The right to intervene is subject to the provisions of NT 41(1)(e), (f) and (g), which require all levels of government to:

(e) respect the constitutional status, institutions, powers and functions of government in the other spheres;

(f) not assume any power or function except those conferred on them in terms of the Constitution; [and]

(g) exercise their powers and functions in a manner that does not encroach on the geographical, functional or institutional integrity of government in another sphere.

It is also subject to the requirements of NT

100(2), which are that such intervention be approved by the NCOP.

[265] The action of the national executive contemplated by NT 100 is either to put the province on terms to carry out its obligations (and presumably to intervene if it then fails to do so) or to assume responsibility for such functions itself to the extent that it is necessary to do so for any of the purposes set out in NT 100(1)(b). These are the same purposes referred to in NT 44(2) and intervention for such purposes is also authorised and required by CP XXI.2.

[266] NT 100 serves the limited purpose of enabling the national government to take appropriate executive action in circumstances where this is required because a provincial government is unable or unwilling to do so itself. This is consistent not only with CP XXI.2 but also with CP XX, which requires the allocation of powers to be made on a basis that is conducive to effective public administration. Any attempt by the national government to intervene at an executive level for other purposes would be inconsistent with the NT and justiciable. NT 100 does not diminish the right of provinces to carry out the functions vested in them under the NT; it makes provision for a situation in which they are unable or unwilling to do so. This cannot be said to constitute an encroachment upon their legitimate autonomy.

The Constitution, therefore, envisages that the national legislature can pass laws that the provincial government must adhere to, and if the provinces fail to adhere to the national laws, the national executive can intervene.

The Court further amplified on the scope of s 100 in the *Second Certification* decision as follows:

Certification of the Amended Text of the Constitution of the Republic of South Africa 1996
CCT 37/96 (4 December 1996), now cited as 1997 (1) BCLR 1 (CC); 1997 (2) SA 97(CC)
(notes omitted)

[123] 'Appropriate steps' within the meaning of AT 100(1) will not ordinarily include the assumption of a provincial obligation by the national executive. That is clear from the language of AT 100(1), which gives an extended meaning to 'appropriate steps' to permit such action in the circumstances referred to in AT 100(1)(b). The extended meaning is confined, however, to the intervention dealt with in AT 100(1)(b).

[124] The reference to 'appropriate steps' in AT 100(1) must be construed in the context of the Constitution as a whole and the provision that it makes for the distribution of power between different levels of government. If regard is had to the CPs and the constitutional scheme embodied in the AT, it would not be appropriate for the national executive to attempt to intervene in provincial affairs in a manner other than that authorised by the Constitution or by legislation enacted in accordance with the Constitution. 'Appropriate steps' would thus include action such as a resort to the procedures established under AT 41(2) for the promotion of intergovernmental relations and the settlement of intergovernmental disputes and the exercise of the treasury control powers under AT 216. It would not, however, include resort to means that would be inconsistent with AT ch 3, and in particular, with the obligation under AT 41(1)(g) to exercise its powers in a manner that 'does not encroach on the geographical, functional or institutional integrity' of provincial governments.

[125] On this construction of the clause, AT 100 means–
(a) when an obligation is not performed by a province the national executive can intervene through taking appropriate steps;
(b) 'appropriate steps' must be construed to mean steps that are appropriate in the context of the Constitution; and
(c) where it is necessary to intervene for the purposes referred to in AT 100(1)(b) 'appropriate steps' has an extended meaning, and permits the assumption of responsibility by the national executive for an obligation of the provincial executive, to the extent that it is necessary to do so for such purposes.

The role of the National Council of Provinces (NCOP) in political federalism

Political federalism operates from the premise that all provinces have appropriate representation in the political process. It is through the political process that the appropriate distribution of power between the national government and the provinces must be determined. For example, the majority in *Garcia* stated that the United States Supreme Court cannot indulge in the exercise of drawing up the boundaries of state and national power.[165] The Court held that issues of federalism are fundamentally political decisions and, therefore, cannot be determined by the judiciary in a legal manner. The Court would defer to the legislature to determine what is local and what is national in nature. If the states wanted any protection, they were represented in the political process and must, therefore, look to the political process for protection.[166]

---

[165] *Garcia*, 469 US at 548.
[166] *Supra* at 551–554.

Under the Court's interpretation in *Garcia*, it is the legislative branch of the national government which is primarily responsible for erecting the distribution of power between the states and the national government. Finn refers to this as 'political federalism'.[167] The political nature of this federalism makes it unsuitable for judicial protection.[168] The South African Constitution best represents political federalism; not just as a construct but also from an institutional perspective. The institutional framework for political federalism is best represented in the composition of the NCOP:

> **National Council of Provinces**
> Composition of National Council
> 60 (1) The National Council of Provinces is composed of a single delegation from each province consisting of ten delegates.
> (2) The ten delegates are—
>   (a) four special delegates consisting of-
>   (i) the Premier of the province or, if the Premier is
>   (ii) not available, any member of the provincial legislature designated by the Premier either generally or for any specific business before the National Council of Provinces; and
>   (iii) three other special delegates; and
>   (b) six permanent delegates appointed in terms of section 61(2).
> (3) The Premier of a province, or if the Premier is not available, a member of the province's delegation designated by the Premier, heads the delegation.

Herbert Wechsler, in a seminal article, argues that judicial enforcement of federalism in America is unnecessary because the interests of states under the United States Constitution are represented in the political process.[169] In South Africa, the institutions created[170] are designed to channel all organs of state in the direction of political federalism, and achieving consensus on the distribution of power through the political process. The NCOP is a key institution in achieving political federalism. The composition of the NCOP ensures direct provincial representation in the principal lawmaking body. Provincial governments chose the members to sit on the NCOP to represent the interests of the provinces in the national legislature. The delegates to the NCOP act as one unit, which is led by the head of the provincial delegation.[171] In effect, members of the NCOP are subject to the instructions of their provincial legislature.[172] The unique composition of the NCOP allows for three 'roving' delegates who are selected based on the legislative issue. In other words, the provinces send their 'expert' politicians to parliament as representatives of the province. The provinces also send representatives who might have special expertise in the specific area in which legislation might be contemplated. Not only is the NCOP representative of provinces, it is also meant to represent the views of local government. Section 163(*b*)(ii) of the Constitution requires that an Act of Parliament determine procedures whereby local government may designate representatives to participate in the NCOP.

All bills emanating from the NA have to be referred to the NCOP, whose views must be considered by the NA. However, if the bill does not affect the provinces, the NA can pass the bill again without incorporating the views of the NCOP.[173] If the bill affects the provinces, and the NCOP rejects the bill (against the wishes of the NA), the bill (in terms of s 75(1)) has to be

---

[167] See Finn 34.

[168] Ibid.

[169] Herbert Wechsler 'The Political Safeguards of Federalism: The Role of the States in the Composition and Selection of the National Government' (1954) 54 *Columbia Law Review* 543.

[170] Under Chapter 3 and under Chapter 4.

[171] Section 65(1)*(a)* of the Constitution.

[172] Section 65(2) requires an Act of Parliament must provide a uniform procedure 'in terms of which provincial legislatures confer authority on their deletions to cast votes on their behalf'.

[173] Section 75(1)*(c)*(i).

referred to a Mediation Committee. If the bill is initiated in the NCOP and is rejected by the NA, the bill pursuant to s 75(2), also has to be referred to a Mediation Committee. The Mediation Committee consists of an equal number of members (nine) from the NA and the NCOP (one from each province). Where the bill is initiated by the NA, and where the Mediation Committee is unable to achieve consensus, or if one of the houses rejects the bill as suggested by the Mediation Committee, the NA can pass its original version of the bill with supporting votes of at least two thirds of its members.[174]

What are matters that could affect the provinces and could trigger intervention of the Mediation Committee under s 75(1) or s 75(2)? Under s 76(3), apart from matters under Schedule 4, the following matters are also considered to affect the provinces: s 65(2) (procedure for conferring authority on delegates to NCOP); s 163 (dealing with organized local government); s 182 (functions of Public Protector); ss 195(3) and (4) (legislation pertaining to the values and principles governing public administration, and the appointment of public administrators on policy grounds); s 196 (Public Service Commission), and s 197 (the public service). Under s 76(4) (a) and (b) the following are also deemed to affect the provinces: matters under Schedule 5 which parliament seeks to regulate under s 44(2); s 220(3)(bills dealing with the functions of the Financial And Fiscal Commission), and Chapter 13 (bills which affect the financial interests of the provincial government).

The NCOP is a key institution under cooperative federalism in representing the interests of the provinces. However, the NCOP cannot defeat the national will[175] as represented by the NA. While the NCOP has the right to consider all bills, in the final analysis, it can only delay the adoption of bills. Providing for Schedule 4 and 5 matters, the NA can muster the two-thirds majority required to override a negative vote of the NCOP.

In the Federal Republic of Germany, the role the *Bundesrat* performs under the Basic Law of Germany in protecting the interests of the *Länders* is basically similar to the role that the NCOP performs for the provinces. There will inevitably be many debates in South Africa as to whether legislation in some way involves a matter listed in ss 76(3), or (4) of the Constitution, and therefore affects the provinces. Just as in the German example,[176] it is objectively justiciable whether a particular bill involves a matter which affects the provinces.

Justiciability of the override provisions

Towards a non-legalistic interpretation

Judicial review is important to ensure, for example, that the government follows the procedures laid out in the Constitution, or for that matter does not trample on fundamental liberties. It is, however, controversial to say that the override standards are equally justiciable in an objective manner. In the *Certification of the Amended Text*, the Constitutional Court suggested that the override provisions, such as whether national legislation is necessary for the maintenance of national security, economic unity, or protection of the common market are objectively justiciable.[177]

---

[174] For an overview of the procedure and the role of the NCOP, under ss 75(1) and 75(2), see *Ex parte The President of the Republic of South Africa, In re: Constitutionality of the Liquor Bill* CCT 12/99 (11 November 1999) para 25, now cited as 2000 (1) SA 732 (CC); 2000 (1) BCLR 1 (CC)..

[175] With the exception of constitutional amendments covered by s 74(1)(b).

[176] See eg the *Pension Insurance* amendment case (1975) 37 BVerfGE 363 translated in Kommers 109–10.

[177] *Certification of the Amended Text* para 159.

In re: Certification of the Amended Text of the Constitution of the Republic of South Africa, 1996
CCT 37/95 (4 December 1996), now cited as 1997 (2) SA 97 (CC); 1997 (1) BCLR 1 (CC)
(notes omitted)

[155] The effect of AT 146(4) is to remove the presumption in favour of national legislation which was contained in NT 146(4). The issue as to whether or not the particular national legislation dealt with a matter which was necessary for the maintenance of national security or economic unity or the protection of the common market or any of the others factors listed in NT 146(2)*(c)* is now objectively justiciable in a court without any presumption in favour of such national legislation. If it is not established that the legislation is necessary for any of the purposes identified by AT 146(2)*(c)*, the national government will not be entitled to rely on AT 146(2)*(c)* in order to ensure that such national legislation prevails over any conflicting provincial legislation dealing with the matter in that, such national legislation, which has been approved by the NCOP, will not create any presumption in favour of the national legislation. All that the court is enjoined to do is to have 'due regard to the approval or rejection of the legislation' by the NCOP. The obligation to pay 'due regard' means simply that the court has a duty to give to the approval or rejection of the legislation by the NCOP the consideration which it deserves in the circumstances. This is a consideration which the court might in any event have been entitled to take into account without an express provision to that effect.

[159] Although we accept that there may have been some increase in the range of national legislation which may now take precedence over provincial legislation, we are not of the view that this is a substantial increase. In terms of AT 146(2)*(b)*, a framework or national policy can only take precedence over provincial legislation if it is a framework or national policy which 'deals with a matter that, to be dealt with effectively, requires uniformity across the nation' and it provides that uniformity. This is effectively the same criterion as applies in terms of IC 126(3)*(b)*. The criterion of uniformity is a significant limitation of the range of national policies and frameworks which may override provincial legislation. One of the definitions of 'uniform' given in the *Concise Oxford Dictionary* is 'conforming to the same standard, rules or pattern'. The achievement of uniformity in the context of AT 146(2)*(b)* therefore requires the establishment of standards, rules or patterns of conduct which can be applied nationally. As we have stated above, this is an objectively justiciable criterion. Under the IC, an override for the purpose of uniformity is permitted where legislation contained 'norms or standards'. Neither of these words is capable of precise definition. The *Concise Oxford Dictionary* defines 'standard' as 'an object or quality or measure serving as a basis or example or principle to which others conform or should conform or by which the accuracy or quality of others is judged'. 'Norm' is defined as a 'standard or pattern or type'. Given the ill-defined import of the words 'norms and standards', and the governing criterion of uniformity, it is likely that even under the IC, framework legislation and national policies which sought to establish uniformity by establishing standards, rules or patterns of conduct would have been held to fall within the scope of 'norms and standards'.

Although the override provisions are justiciable, there are no clear standards available for the Constitutional Court to enforce distribution of power limits on parliament, *vis-à-vis* the provinces or local governments. The Court's understanding of words such as 'uniform' and 'standards' in the *Second Certification* decision reflected an over reliance on narrow and legalistic definitions. It is arguable that the Court's approach to the override provisions as it pertains to a Schedule 4 matter should be more deferential to compromises reached through the political process. On the other hand, Schedule 5 matters reflect a set of activities (such as abattoirs, ambulance services, provincial roads, and traffic, to name a few) which parliament realistically has little reason to regulate at a national level.[178] Where parliament seeks to regulate a Schedule 5 matter, the Court should be less deferential and should require parliament to justify its intrusion, arguably, in terms of a stricter threshold. In *Premier of the Western Cape*, the Constitutional Court, *per* Chaskalson P, held that the national legislature is more powerful than the provincial legislatures, having the legislative competence in respect of any matter including the matters in Schedule 4.[179] However, the Court emphasized that parliament's competence to legislate in respect of matters in Schedule 5 'is limited to making laws that are necessary for one of the purposes referred to in section 44(2)'.[180] In *Constitutionality of the Liquor Bill*, the Constitutional Court held that parliament could not regulate the granting of a liquor licence (a Schedule 5 matter) in the absence of a showing that the regulation was necessary to achieve the objectives outlined in s 44(2).[181] The Court held that the national government's attaching importance to 'consistency of approval' did not amount to necessity.[182] However, the Court held that parliament could regulate cross-holdings of ownership between producers, distributors, and retailers as part of its power to regulate trade, production, and racial equality, which was a concurrent power under Schedule 4 and subject to an override under s 44(3).[183] Similarly, the Court held that the establishment of uniform conditions under a national registration for liquor manufacturers and distribution was directed at activity of an extra-provincial or international market.[184] The national government's interest in maintaining economic unity entitles it to override the provincial interests by providing a single set of rules for production and distribution of liquor.[185] The oneness of the South African economy means that provinces should not create separate regulations which impede the flow of goods across provincial boundaries.[186] Perhaps, the Court did not sustain the part of the legislation which attempted to regulate retail liquor licences because the state did not attempt to show that the regulation was related to the exercise of power concerning a matter listed in Schedule 4, as contained in s 44(3).[187] Section 44(3) provides that '[l]egislation with regard to a matter that is reasonably necessary for, or incidental to, the effective exercise of power concerning any matter listed in Schedule 4 is, for all purposes, legislation with regard to a matter listed in Schedule 4'. The Court in *Constitutionality of the Liquor Bill* passed on the opportunity to define 'reasonably necessary for, or incidental to'.

In interpreting the override provisions, it would be a grave error for the Court to adopt a narrow and legalistic definition of national power in interpreting words and phrases such as 'reasonably necessary or incidental to', 'necessary', 'national security', 'economic unity', or 'minimum standards', as the United States Supreme Court did in interpreting the scope of national power under the Commerce Clause prior to the New Deal. The Court is not better placed to second-guess the legislature on issues of national security, economic unity, or protection of the common market. As the United States Supreme Court majority said in *Garcia*, there has to be greater deference to the national legislature.[188] As Justice Breyer stated in his dissent in *Lopez*, in determining whether a local activity will have an impact on the national economy, the court is required to judge the connection 'not directly, but

[178] *In re: Constitutionality of the Liquor Bill* para 49.
[179] CCT 26/98 para 52.
[180] *Supra* para 52.
[181] *In re: Constitutionality of the Liquor Bill, supra* para 79–80.
[182] *Supra* para 80.
[183] *Supra* para 70.
[184] *Supra* para 72.
[185] *Supra* para 75.
[186] *Supra.*
[187] *Supra* para 81.
[188] *Garcia v San Antonio Metro Transit Authority* 469 US 547 (1985).

at one remove'.[189] Courts must give the legislature a 'degree of leeway in determining the existence of a significant factual connection between the regulated activity and interstate commerce'.[190] Justice Breyer goes on to affirm that such a determination 'requires an empirical judgment of a kind that a legislature is more likely than a court to make with accuracy'.[191] In the United States, the standard that the courts traditionally employ is the 'rational basis' test. When the courts utilize this test, the question that they ask is not whether national intervention is sufficiently connected with the criteria for intervention, but rather whether the legislature has a rational basis for making the conclusion. When the courts employ the rational basis test, the courts largely presume the existence of the facts on which the legislature has made the choice, and defer to the legislature on questions of degree and proportion.[192] Commenting on the Canadian situation, Hogg makes the observation, 'that the judge's lack of democratic accountability, coupled with the limitations inherent in the adversarial judicial process, dictates that the appropriate posture for the courts in disputes over the distribution of power is one of restraint: the legislative decision should be overridden only where its invalidity is clear'.[193] Hogg goes on to remark that '[t]here should be, in other words, a presumption of constitutionality. In this way a proper respect is paid to the legislators, and the danger of covert (albeit unconscious) imposition of judicial policy preferences is minimized'.[194] It seems that the framers of the South African Constitution foresaw that situations might arise where the Constitutional Court will not be able to resolve disputes over allocation of power. In such a situation, the Constitution provides in s 148 that 'national legislation prevails over the provincial legislation or provincial constitution'.

Federal models of state have been introduced in a number of African countries at the time of independence.[195] All the federal models introduced in African countries contained provisions which attempted to divide the power between the regions and the centre in the classical mould. Inevitably, they led to the immobilization of the central government which was unable to act in vital areas such as housing, education, land tenure, and infrastructure.[196] If the distribution of power under the Constitution is interpreted in the same classical mould or what McWhinney characterizes as the British imperial system[197] in South Africa, this would lead to the kind of constitutional ruptures which have taken place in other parts of the African continent.

The United States Supreme Court's position on federalism after the New Deal approached social and economic problems in national terms. Federalism is not necessarily viewed in terms of state and national power which has to be defined in an *a priori* fashion. In the context of a modern state, it is the national government which should resolve social and economic conflicts. The Constitutional Court in South Africa should not look at the terms and phrases in the override provisions in terms of the static conception of the Canadian judges trained in the British tradition. Instead it should look at the demarcation of power as a political judgement. All nine provinces have direct representation in the legislature. Questions of federalism in the final analysis pertain to the distribution and execution of political power, and not the interpretation and application of legal rules.[198]

---

[189] *United States v Lopez* 115 SCt 1624, 1658 (1995).

[190] *Supra.*

[191] *Supra.*

[192] See Archibald Cox 'Constitutional Adjudication and the Promotion of Human Rights' (1966) 80 *Harvard Law Review* 91, 107.

[193] Hogg 122.

[194] Op cit 123.

[195] Such as in Nigeria, Kenya, Uganda and the Congo. See Awolomo 29; Rothchild 293; Nwabueze 139; Nkrumah 67.

[196] For a comprehensive overview of the failure of federal models in African states, see Ziyad Motala 'The Record of Federal Constitutions in Africa: Some Lessons for a Post-Apartheid South Africa' (1990) 7 *Arizona Journal of International and Comparative Law* 225.

[197] McWhinney 6.

[198] Finn 11.

Meaning of 'necessary'

What interpretation will the Constitutional Court give to the term 'necessary', contained in s 146 (c) and in s 44 (2) of the Constitution? In *R v Magana*,[199] the Supreme Court was faced with an interpretation of the word 'necessary' as used in a road traffic ordinance. The ordinance gave the administrator the power to do any act or thing 'so far as necessary' to bring the law into operation.

The administrator promulgated regulations to bring the road traffic ordinance into effect. The question before the Court was whether the making of the regulations was necessary for bringing the ordinance into operation. The Court, *per* Trollip J, proceeded on the basis that the regulation was necessary.[200] The Court further held that it 'ought generally to be presumed that the condition precedent was fulfilled',[201] unless the contrary is proved.[202] In interpreting the word 'necessary', Justice Trollip held that necessary does not mean absolute necessity, or indispensability. All that it means is 'reasonably necessary'.[203] In other words, the term 'necessary' must not be given a restrictive meaning. Instead, it should be liberally interpreted.[204]

The interpretation of necessary in the context of the distribution of power should not be confused with the interpretation of necessary under the limitations clause of the interim Constitution. Where the lawmaker acts in a way which transgresses on fundamental liberties, and argues that the action was necessary, the threshold for proving necessity must be greater, by virtue of the interests involved, namely fundamental liberties. In *Coetzee*,[205] Justice Sachs surveyed the different meanings attached to the word 'necessary'. Sometimes, the word is interpreted liberally, and other times it is understood as more rigid.[206] Where fundamental human rights are implicated, necessary is usually understood in a more strict sense as pressing or urgent, and would require a high degree of justification.[207] Necessary when used in the context of the distribution of power cannot be subjected to such a rigid definition. Instead, the approach in *Magana*, and that of the United States Supreme Court's decision in *McCulloch v Maryland*,[208] is the appropriate approach. Both these cases stand for the proposition that necessary does not mean absolute necessity or indispensability.

In *McCulloch*, the State of Maryland claimed that the United States government did not have the power to incorporate a bank because the Constitution did not confer this power on the federal government. The legitimacy of the federal government action depended in part on the proper interpretation of the necessary and proper clause of the Constitution. The necessary and proper clause gives congress the power to make all laws which are necessary and proper for carrying out all the foregoing powers vested by the Constitution. The State of Maryland argued that the word 'necessary' required that the government action, in order to be legitimate, had to be something the federal government absolutely could not do without. The Court disagreed and instead said that the word 'necessary' as used in the Constitution, did not mean indispensable, but instead meant something that was useful and convenient.[209]

Just as the Court will have to interpret 'necessary', the Court will also have to interpret what is national security, economic unity, essential national standards, or action on the part of one province where it is prejudicial to the interests of

---

[199] *R v Magana* 1961 (2) SA 654 (T).

[200] *Supra* para 656.

[201] *Supra*.

[202] *Supra* para 657.

[203] *Supra* para 658.

[204] *Supra* para 656.

[205] *Coetzee v The Government of the Republic of South Africa and Others; Matiso v The Commanding Officer, Port Elizabeth Prisons and Others* CCT 19/94, 22/94 (22 September 1995), now cited as 1995 (10) BCLR 1382 (CC); 1995 (4) SA 631 (CC).

[206] *Coetzee* para 57.

[207] *Supra* paras 58, 60.

[208] *McCulloch v Maryland* 17 US 316 (1819).

[209] *Supra* at 316, 418.

another province. The Court's approach to these questions will determine the nature of the distribution of power and what concept of federalism it follows. If the Constitutional Court adopts the idea of political federalism, it would refrain from a narrow, legalistic, or technical interpretation in favour of a standard based on flexibility and compromise achieved through the political process.

Conflict between legislation adopted at different levels of government

National and provincial legislation regulating the same matter

If the national legislature and a provincial legislature legislate on a Schedule 4 or Schedule 5 matter, a situation might arise where a choice has to be made as to which legislation takes precedence. The fact that both the provinces and

the national government regulate a particular activity does not always mean that a choice has to be made between which to apply. In *In re: The National Educational Policy Bill*, the Constitutional Court in interpreting ss 126(3) and 126(4) of the interim Constitution override provisions, for concurrent national and provincial authority, ruled that where an Act of Parliament and a provincial law regulate the same activity, they 'should be construed as being consistent with each other'.[210] The interim Constitution override provisions mirror the override provisions in ss 146(2) and s 146(3) of the final Constitution.

If the two pieces of legislation are incompatible and providing national intervention is legitimate in terms of the override provisions, the national legislation will prevail over the provincial legislation. If the national legislation override requirements are not fulfilled, the provincial legislation will prevail.[211] This is not the same as saying the national legislation will invalidate provincial legislation. It merely keeps the provincial legislation in abeyance so long as the national legislation remains in force.[212]

In re: Dispute Concerning The Constitutionality of Certain Provisions of the National Education Policy Bill No 83 of 1995
CCT 46/95 (3 April 1996), now
cited 1996 (3) SA 289 (CC);
1996 (4) BCLR 518 (CC)
(notes omitted).

[15] Section 126(5) of the Constitution requires that if it is possible to do so an Act of Parliament and a provincial law should be construed as being consistent with each other. If, or to the extent that, this cannot be done, then the provisions of sections 126(3) and (4) determine which of the conflicting provisions is to prevail. The solution provided is as follows: To the extent that the criteria specified in subsections (a) to (e) of section 126(3) are met the

provisions of an Act of Parliament that is of general application will prevail; if, or to the extent that, such criteria are not met, the provisions of the provincial law will prevail.

[16] The legislative competences of the provinces and Parliament to make laws in respect of schedule 6 matters do not depend upon section 126(3). Section 126(3) comes into operation only if it is necessary to have resort to it in order to resolve a conflict. If the conflict is resolved in favour of either the provincial or the national law the other is not invalidated; it is subordinated and to the extent of the conflict rendered inoperative. There is an important difference in this regard between laws that are inconsistent with each other and laws that are inconsistent with the Constitution. Section 4 provides that a law inconsistent with the Constitution is 'of no force and effect an

---

[210] *In re: National Education Policy Bill* para 15. This approach is also adhered to in the US and Canada. *Pacific Gas & Electric v State Energy Resources Conservation Commission* 461 US 190 (1983). Beatty 46–7.
[211] See *Certification of the Constitution of the Province of KwaZulu-Natal* para 9.
[212] *Supra* para 19.

its terms of section 98(5) such a law has to be declared by this court to be invalid to the extent of the inconsistency'. Section 126(3), which deals with laws that are consistent with the Constitution but inconsistent with each other, does not stipulate that either law will be invalid as a result of the inconsistency; only that the provisions of one of the laws shall prevail over the other.

[17] Hogg, discusses the difference between inconsistency and invalidity in Chapter 16. He concludes that:

Once it has been determined that a federal law is inconsistent with a provincial law, the doctrine of federal paramountcy stipulates that the provincial law must yield to the federal law. The most usual and most accurate way of describing the effect on the provincial law is to say that it is rendered inoperative to the extent of the inconsistency. Notice that the paramountcy doctrine applies only to the extent of the inconsistency. The doctrine will not affect the operation of those parts of the provincial law which are not inconsistent with the federal law, unless of course the inconsistent parts are inseparably linked with the consistent parts. There is also a temporal limitation on the paramountcy doctrine. It will affect the operation of the provincial law only so long as the inconsistent federal law is in force. If the federal law is repealed, the provincial law will automatically 'revive' (come back into operation) without any reenactment by the provincial Legislature.

[18] A similar conclusion has been reached by the High Court of Australia in respect of conflicts between state laws and laws of the Commonwealth Parliament. Section 109 of the Australian Constitution provides that a state law that is inconsistent with a Commonwealth law shall to the extent of such inconsistency be 'invalid'. The High Court has held that section 109 does not nullify the inconsistent provisions of the state law; it simply renders them 'inoperative and ineffective' as if they had been suspended. They would revive and be of full force and effect if the Commonwealth law were to be repealed, or amended in a manner that removed the inconsistency.

[19] This reflects in my view the way in which our Constitution requires inconsistencies that cannot be resolved by the application of the provisions of section 126(5) to be dealt with. Neither Parliament nor a provincial legislature has the competence to invalidate laws of the other passed in accordance with the Constitution; nor does the Constitution lay down that a consequence of inconsistency will be the invalidity of one of the laws. It follows that a law that is subordinated by virtue of the application of section 126(3) is not nullified; it remains in force and has to be implemented to the extent that it is not inconsistent with the law that prevails. If the inconsistency falls away the law would then have to be implemented in all respects.

Stating the rule may be easier then applying it in real situations. Both parliament and the provinces may regulate a matter and the regulation may not, on its face, be incompatible. For example, parliament may provide particular standards for education, and a particular province may provide a different standard. Under Schedule 4 both parliament and the provinces have the authority to regulate education. The province's reasons for adopting a separate standard may be different from the reason parliament adopted its standards. Parliament, in adopting educational standards, may have intended to provide uniform rules in order to achieve certain goals. In adopting the standards, parliament also intended to occupy the field completely with respect to appropriate education standards. Where the national legislation is clear on its face in stating national standards are important, it will be easier for the Court to infer that national policy must prevail. If national legislation does not contain any reference to the need for national standards, the Court will have to go behind the legislation and look at, for example, parliamentary debates to ascertain the intent behind the national legislation. It cannot be said that the goals of national and provincial law are the same if the provincial law interferes with the methods by which the national legislation was designed to reach that goal.[213] The Court will, therefore, have to ascertain whether provincial legislation is consistent with national goals and objectives.[214]

Incompatibility between local government law and national or provincial legislation

While a national law cannot preempt a provincial law (and vice versa), this is not the case with regard to municipal law. Under s 156(3) of the Constitution, a bye-law that conflicts with national or provincial legislation is invalid.

Local power

A unique feature of the Constitution is the constitutional status of local governments,[215] that, like the national and provincial governments are

recognized as a separate sphere of government.[216] Chapter 7 of the Constitution deals with local governments. Section 151(1) states that local governments consist of municipalities which must be established throughout the entire country. Under s 151(2), the executive and legislative authority of a municipality is vested in the municipal council. Under s 151(3), the local affairs of a community should be governed by the municipality, subject to national and provincial legislation as laid out in the Constitution. The national and provincial government under s 151(4) must not compromise or impede a municipality in the exercise of its powers and functions. In the *First Certification* decision, the Constitutional Court summarized the different categories of municipalities, the role of parliament in establishing criteria for the different types of municipalities, and the scope of power of municipalities.

Certification of the Amended Text
(notes omitted)

[76] The CA amended NT 155, dealing with the establishment of municipalities, NT 160 dealing with the internal procedures of municipalities, and NT 229 dealing with municipal fiscal powers. It contended that these amendments adequately address the problem identified in the *CJ*.

[77] The effect of these amendments is to specify three different categories of municipalities that can be established. In substance these are (a) self-standing municipalities, (b) municipalities that form part of a comprehensive coordinating structure, and (c) municipalities that perform coordinating functions. In the terminology of existing legislation the third category would include structures such as regional and metropo-

litan councils. It has been made clear that it is a national function to establish the criteria for determining which category of municipality should be established in a particular area and how powers and functions are to be divided between municipalities with shared powers. National legislation must also define the types of municipality that may be established within each category but it is for the provincial legislature to determine which types should be established in its province. The internal procedures for the functioning of municipalities have been defined more precisely than was the case in the NT, but national legislation must still provide the criteria for determining the size of a municipal council, the types of committees it may have and the size of committees that are established.

[78] The AT sets out the categories of LG

---

[213] *International Paper Co v Ouellette* 479 US 481, 494 (1987).

[214] See *Gade v National Solid Waste Management Association* 505 US 88, 91(1992).

[215] Constitutional recognition of local government is also found in art 28 s 2 of the German Basic Law, which gives municipalities and counties powers of self-administration.

[216] Section 40(1) of the Constitution. See the Constitutional Court's discussion of the status of local government under the interim Constitution in *Fedsure Life Assurance Ltd and Others v Greater Johannesburg Transitional Metropolitan Council and Others* CCT 7/98 (14 October 1995) paras 35–36, now cited as 1998 (12) BCLR 1458 (CC); 1999 (1) SA 374 (CC). As in the interim Constitution, the final Constitution imposed an obligation to establish local government, para 36. See also *Executive Council of the Province of Western Cape v The Minister for Provincial Affairs and Constitutional Development and Another* CCT 15/99 (15 October 1999) paras 12–15, now cited as 2000 (1) SA 661 (CC); 1999 (12) BCLR 1360 (CC).

that can be established, and a scheme for LG within which LG structures are to function. The scheme is one which involves the establishment of municipalities for the whole of the territory of the Republic. A municipality will have legislative and executive powers in respect of the local government matters listed in part B of AT sch 4 and part B of AT sch 5, and any other matter assigned to it by national or provincial legislation. These powers will be vested in its Council. The legislative power is to be exercised by the making of by-laws, a power which must be exercised by the Council itself and may not be delegated by it to any person. A framework for an electoral system according to which members of the Council are to be elected is set out in AT 157, and the manner in which decisions are to be taken and by-laws passed is prescribed by AT 160. A framework for the demarcation of municipal boundaries and wards is provided. AT ch 13 establishes a framework for the fiscal powers and functions of municipalities, revenue allocation to municipalities, the preparation of budgets, treasury control, and the procurement of goods and services. The objects of LG are defined in AT 152, and municipalities are required to observe and adhere to the principles of cooperative government set out in AT ch 3.

A main objective of local government, spelled out in ss 152(1) and 152(4), is to promote democracy and participation in local affairs. Under the principles of cooperative government, the national and provincial governments are required to 'support and strengthen the capacity of municipalities to manage their own affairs', and 'to exercise their powers and to perform their functions'.[217]

Under s 156 (1), a municipality has executive and administrative authority over matters listed in Part B of Schedule 4 and Part B of Schedule 5. The national and provincial governments are required to assign functions to local government under s 156(4) which provides:

The national government and provincial governments must assign to a municipality, by agreement and subject to any conditions, the administration of any matter listed in Part A of Schedule 4 or Part A of Schedule 5 which necessarily relates to local government, if—

(a) that matter would most effectively be administered locally; and

(b) the municipality has the capacity to administer it.

(5) A municipality has the right to exercise any power concerning a matter reasonably necessary for, or incidental to, the effective performance of its functions.

Under s 160(1), a municipal council has certain powers to make decisions concerning its internal procedures, including election of its office bearers and employment of personnel.

The constitutionalizing of the status of local government is akin to what one finds under the Basic Law of Germany, which in art 28 provides that local governments 'must be guaranteed the right to regulate on their own responsibility all the affairs of the local community within the limits set by law'. The German Constitutional Court has said that local government functions include what the Court considers core functions such as 'territorial integrity, and autonomy in organisation, personnel, finance, local rule-making, and at least in part, land-use planning'.[218]

The Constitution, in s 155(2), says that national legislation must provide for the different categories of municipalities. Section 155(3) states that national legislation must establish the criteria for determining the categories of municipalities. Parliament has passed several pieces of legislation to establish different types of municipalities, the criteria for municipalities, appropriate division of functions and powers between categories of municipalities, and the internal systems, structures and office-bearers of municipalities.[219] While local governments have territorial integrity, as in

---

[217] Section 154(1) of the Constitution.

[218] Arthur B Gunlicks 'Constitutional Law and the Protection of Sub-national Governments in the United States and West Germany' (1998) 18 *Publius* 149.

[219] The seminal legislation is Local Government: Municipal Structures Act 117 of 1998. Other legislation include: Local Government: Municipal Demarcation Act 27 of 1998; Disestablishment of the Local Government Affairs Council Act 59 of 1999; Repeal of Local Government Laws Act 42 of 1997.

Germany, they can be consolidated or have their borders changed. As in Germany, the guarantee of local government is an institutional guarantee, and not one that protects the status of individual local governments.[220]

Local government is designed to promote autonomy on matters which intimately affect a locality such as street lights, and building permits. As the Constitutional Court, *per* Ngcobo J, observed in *Executive Council of the Province of the Western Cape*, the Constitution 'protects the role of local government, and places certain constraints upon the powers of Parliament to interfere with local government decisions. It is neither necessary nor desirable to attempt to define these constraints in any detail. It is sufficient to say that the constraints exist, and if an Act of Parliament is inconsistent with such constraints it would to that extent be invalid'.[221] As Schmidt-Ambann notes, in Germany, the reality is that some tasks cannot be assigned in such a clear-cut fashion, because the function might consist of a mixture of local and national concerns.[222] As with the distribution of power between the national government and the provinces, there will likely be disputes as to the proper distribution of power between the national government and local government, and provincial government and local government. As in the situation of disputes between the national government and provinces, it is debatable whether these disputes are amenable to legal resolution or better resolved through the political process. It is arguable that the judiciary is not better placed to resolve a dispute as to whether a matter in Part A of Schedule 4, or Part A of Schedule 5, can be best administered locally, nationally, or provincially, or whether the municipality has the capacity to administer it.[223] The dispute is likely to centre on the proper interpretation of s 156(4), whether a matter necessarily relates to local government, and can be best administered locally, or whether the municipality has the capacity to administer it. Commenting on such disputes in Germany, Kommers concludes that in Germany even though the German Constitutional Court speaks about core functions, it is difficult to spell out what are the core functions of local government, which he argues are best resolved through the political process.[224] At the level of reality, the approach the Germans follow on local government is akin to the United States Supreme Court's approach to political federalism.[225] The German Constitutional Court sanctions the transfer of competences to the detriment of municipalities if the transfer facilitates better execution of functions.[226] Intrusions have been permitted despite a belief that local authority in an area was paramount, such as land-use control.[227] However, on matters where parliament does not have concurrent authority with local government or the provinces, parliament cannot intervene to supercede local or provincial power. For example, where the Constitution provides that 'provincial legislation must determine the different types of municipalities to be established in the province',[228] parliament cannot

---

[220] Gunlicks 150.

[221] *Executive Council of the Province of the Western Cape v The Minister for Provincial Affairs and Constitutional Development and Another* CCT 15/99; *Executive Council of KwaZulu-Natal v The President of the Republic of South Africa and Another* CCT 18/99 (15 October 1999) para 29, now cited as 2000 (1) SA 661 (CC); 1999 (12) BCLR 1360 (CC).

[222] Eberhard Abman Schmidt 'The Constitution and the Requirements of Local Autonomy; in *The Constitution of the Federal Republic of Germany: Essays on the Basic Rights and Principles of the Basic Law with a translation of the Basic Law*, edited by Ulrich Karpen. Baden-Baden: Nomos 1988, 173.

[223] As s 156(4) requires

[224] Kommers 118–19.

[225] Gunlicks 142.

[226] Meinhard Schroder 'Strengthening of Constitutional Law: Effort and Problems' in *The Constitution of the Federal Republic of Germany: Essays on the Basic Rights and Principles of the Basic Law with a translation of the Basic Law*, edited by Ulrich Karpen. Baden-Baden: Nomos 1988, 35.

[227] Arthur B Gunlicks 'Principles of American Federalism' in *Germany and its Basic Law, Past, Present and Future*, edited by Paul Kirchoff and Donald P Kommers. Baden-Baden: Nomos 1989, 109.

[228] Section 155(5) of the Constitution.

intervene in a way which encroaches on the provinces prerogatives.[229] In *Executive Council of the Province of the Western Cape*, the Constitutional Court, *per* Ngcobo J, held that the Constitution confers executive power on the provinces to establish municipalities within the framework of national legislation.[230] Once national legislation is adopted, the national government cannot prescribe to the provinces guidelines which the provinces must take into account in determining the types of municipalities to be established in the provinces.[231]

Other sources of national power

Introduction

We have dealt with the residual power of parliament under the Constitution. There are a number of other provisions in the Constitution which confer specific powers on parliament, such as the power to enforce and promote the rights in the Bill of Rights,[233] the power to enter into treaties,[234] and the power to declare a state of emergency.[235] The next section will address the scope of parliament's power under these provisions. Does parliament have broader powers under these provisions, or is parliament's authority subject to the same limitations as in the override provisions?

The Constitutional Jurisprudence of the Federal Republic of Germany[232]

Authors' note: The Core Functions (Kernbereich) of Local Government. When the Constitutional Court speaks of the essence of communal autonomy, it is referring to certain 'core functions' (Kernbereich) of local government that must be protected against federal or state encroachment. Not all local affairs, however, fall within the definition of a core function. The transfer of certain powers to the national government, the expansion of cooperative federalism, and the consequent reduction in the number of policy areas deemed exclusively municipal complicate any effort to distinguish between local and non-local affairs. On the other hand, the court's historical approach to determining the essence of local government 'could also be used to protect newly acquired local functions'. German commentators are unable to agree on any complete list of functions protected by the Kernbereich theory – 'some reject the theory of core functions altogether', but they, like the court, do include local rule-making, internal governmental organization, and certain aspects of land-use planning as well as personnel and finance administration.

The *Kernbereich* theory reminds us of the federalism controversy in the United States triggered by *National League of Cities v Usery* (1976). Usery held that the commerce clause did not permit Congress to impair the states' 'ability to function effectively in a federal system' or to displace their 'integral governmental functions'. In 1985, however, the Supreme Court overruled Usery, claiming contrary to the approach of the Federal Constitutional Court, that any '[r]eliance on history as an organizing principle [for determining the "core functions" of state governments', thus rendering them immune to federal regulation] results in linedrawing of the most arbitrary sort'. But as Gunlicks noted, 'it is much easier for the German Court to take a position in favor of local governments, since Article 28(2) of the Basic Law grants local governments explicit protection, while there is sharp disagreement whether the Tenth Amendment is relevant to protecting American local governments from federal incursions'.

---

[229] *Executive Council of the Province of the Western Cape* paras 30 and 57.
[230] *Supra* para 72.
[231] *Supra* paras 78–79.
[232] Kommers 118–19.
[233] Section 7(2) of the Constitution.
[234] Section 231.
[235] Section 37.

Power to protect and fulfil the rights contained in the Bill of Rights

Under s 8(1), the Constitution provides that the Bill of Rights applies to all organs of state and spheres of government. Section 7(2) provides, '[T]he state must respect, protect, promote and fulfil the rights in the Bill of Rights'. Nowhere in the Constitution is the word 'state' defined. Is the term state a reference to the responsibility of the national, provincial, or municipal government – or all three? If it is all three, does the national government have primary responsibility or is the responsibility equal among all centres of authority? For example, housing is a matter of concurrent jurisdiction contained in Schedule 4. Section 26(1) requires the state to take legislative measures to progressively realize this right. Similarly, s 9(4) requires national legislation to prevent or prohibit unfair discrimination.[236] If parliament adopts legislation in furtherance of this requirement, is the legislation subject to scrutiny in terms of the override provisions contained in s 146? The obligation to promote and fulfil the rights in the Bill of Rights provides an independent source of national power arguably not subject to the override provisions. The Court's scrutiny of parliamentary action taken pursuant to the power granted under s 7(2) or other provisions in the Bill of Rights should be constrained only by the limitations clause of s 36. The limitation of fundamental rights is considered in a separate chapter.[237] Suffice it to say that it is trite that legislation which erodes the enjoyment of fundamental rights, and which cannot surmount the test in the limitations clause, is going to be ruled invalid.

Where parliament acts to further human rights contained in Chapter 2 of the Constitution, provincial or municipal rights should not be used as a limitation on the exercise of national power. In the discussion of federalism in the United States and Canada we saw that historically the Court sided with the states (or provinces), by ruling that fundamental human rights issues such as labour, civil rights, and property rights were matters of state or provincial rights. The Courts, in effect, sided with the private interests that wanted protection from national legislation which threatened to enlarge the scope of protection of these rights.[238] Very significantly, the provinces in Canada and the states in the United States often did not have the resources to meet needs such as unemployment benefits, social security, and economic direction.[239] While the Bill of Rights is binding on all organs and spheres of government, arguably primary responsibility for promoting, protecting and fulfilling the rights has to fall with the national government (particularly parliament). The courts have to accord appropriate deference to parliament if it acts in the furtherance of fundamental human rights. For example, returning to the hypothetical, a province may adopt housing legislation which affords greater subsidies to the middle class as opposed to the wealthy and the poorer sectors of the population. The effect of the provincial action is to deny the majority of provincial residents access to funds for housing. Parliament has the power under s 7(2) to adopt standards to advance housing rights, or to take action to prevent the occurrence of acts that transgress on fundamental rights. The power to take action 'to respect, protect, promote and fulfil the rights in the Bill of Rights' allows parliament to act proactively, without first requiring a finding by the Court that the provincial action is unconstitutional. This applies even more forcefully with respect to the power under s 9(4), which requires parliament to adopt legislation to prevent or prohibit unfair discrimination.

The power under s 9(4) is arguably akin to the power under s 5 of the XIV Amendment to the United States Constitution, which provides that '[T]he Congress shall have power to enforce, by appropriate legislation, the provisions of this article'. Section 9(4) or s 7(2) of the South African Constitution, much like s 5 of the XIV Amendment, enlarges the scope of national power.

---

[236] Pursuant to this mandate, parliament adopted the Promotion of Equality and Prevention of Unfair Discrimination Act 4 of 2000.

[237] The full implication of the limitations clause is discussed in chapter 14.

[238] Mallory 342.

[239] Ibid.

In *Katzenbach v Morgan*,[240] the United States Supreme Court was asked to rule on the validity of s 4*(e)* of the Voting Rights Act of 1965 that congress adopted which prohibited the administration of literacy testing as a precondition to exercising the right to vote. The effect of the legislation was to invalidate New York's English literacy test; this had disenfranchised several thousand native Puerto Ricans. The State of New York argued that congress could only act under s 5 if the Court found that its literacy requirement was unconstitutional.[241] The Supreme Court ruled that s 5 of the XIV Amendment enlarged the power of congress, and allowed congress to adopt appropriate legislation to enforce prohibitions.[242] The Court was not going to look into each piece of legislation enacted by the states to see whether the legislation was inconsistent with the Constitution in order to approve congressional action. If the Court accepted New York's argument, this would have meant that any and all legislation to enforce the equality prevision of the XIV Amendment, would be subject to judicial approval before it could take effect. The scope of s 7(2) of the Constitution is also to allow parliament to decide, over the provinces, whether particular legislation is appropriate to advance the rights contained in the Bill of Rights. Providing parliament has a rational basis for this belief, the courts should defer to parliament.

Treaty power

Under Chapter 14 of the Constitution, parliament is given treaty powers. Under s 231(2), parliament is given the power by resolution of both the NA and the NCOP to bind the republic to an international treaty. Under s 231(3), the executive is given power to enter into executive agreements of a technical or administrative nature, which are also binding on the republic. Under s 231(4), any international agreement becomes law when it is enacted by national legislation. Parliament can approve international agreements as self-executing (that is, it can be invoked as domestic law), unless it is inconsistent with the Constitution or an Act of Parliament.

Once again, the question arises whether this legislative power, particularly under s 231(4), enlarges the scope of national power, or whether it is subject to power limitations? Section 231(2) does not contain the same fetters; it simply proclaims that an international agreement binds the republic by virtue of a resolution adopted by both houses of parliament. Can this mean that an international agreement is binding on the republic in terms of s 231(2), but it cannot be enforced before the domestic courts of the republic if it conflicts with the Constitution? The difference between treaties entered into under s 231(2) and s 231(4) is not spelled out. Arguably, s 231(2) was meant to cover political treaties and treaties of friendship.[243] If this *is* the case, one would need to make a determination of the nature of the treaty in order to conclude whether it is binding. While s 231(2) says an international agreement is binding upon adoption of a resolution of both houses of parliament, it does not say who has standing to bring an action to enforce a resolution adopted pursuant to s 231(2). Assuming that s 231(2) is meant to cover political treaties,[244] surely it could not have been envisaged that an individual or a foreign sovereign would be able to bring the government of South Africa before a domestic court in order to enforce a political treaty.[245] A treaty which is to be binding in the domestic context has to be adopted in terms of s 231(4).

Section 231, particularly s 231(4), creates an additional source of national power. Does this source enlarge the scope of parliament's power, or is the power subject to the federalism and other distributions of power limitations in the Constitution? Section 231(4) affirms that a treaty provision

---

[240] *Katzenbach v Morgan* 384 US 641 (1966).

[241] *Supra* at 648.

[242] *Supra* at 650–651.

[243] The German Basic Law does make a distinction between political treaties and other treaties. See Kommers 162–3.

[244] The difference between political and non-political treaties is discussed below.

[245] See the Irish case of *Hutchinson v Minister of Justice* [1993] ILRM 602.

cannot be inconsistent with the Constitution, which some might argue could include the federalism limitations. It is logical that parliament cannot change the Constitution by virtue of its treaty power. For example, parliament cannot change its composition by virtue of an international agreement duly approved by a resolution of both houses. In *Reid v Covert*, the United States Supreme Court, *per* Justice Black, stated that no agreement with a foreign power can confer on the legislature or any other branch of government powers which go against the Constitution.[246] Also where a treaty provision attempts to limit a fundamental right contained in the Bill of Rights, the Court should come out in favour of upholding the protection of fundamental human rights.[247] However, regarding the distribution of power over which the Constitution is open ended, s 231(4) should be interpreted as enlarging the scope of parliament's power. For example, assume parliament approves by resolution a multilateral international agreement on the environment. Assume that a province has also adopted legislation on environmental control – a Schedule 4 matter – which conflicts with the international agreement. Assume the provincial legislation is more rationally related to the needs of the province, and ultimately related to environmental control in the republic. However, parliament, in adopting the resolution approving the international agreement, did so in the context of international comity, and an emerging consensus on what ought to be appropriate conduct in environmental control. Arguably, the constitutionality of the international agreement should not be subject to scrutiny in terms of the override provisions For example, in Australia the Australian High Court has ruled that national intervention, even though it affects interests of the states when adopted pursuant to a treaty, is legitimate.[248] The Court in that case considered the treaty power as an additional source of legislative power.

Similarly, the United States Supreme Court has ruled that the treaty power under the United States Constitution is an additional source of congressional power. In *Missouri v Holland*,[249] the Court was faced with a challenge to a bird treaty which was entered into with Britain. The treaty prohibited the killing, capturing, or selling of certain species of birds. Missouri argued that the activity being regulated was a matter of state concern. A few years earlier, the district court had ruled that a similar statute adopted as ordinary legislation, was invalid because it conflicted with the state power under the Tenth Amendment to the United States Constitution.[250] In evaluating the constitutionality of the subsequent treaty, the United States Supreme Court ruled that treaties 'must be ascertained in a different way' and enlarged the scope of federal power. However, the German Constitutional Court has adopted a contrary position that the powers of the *Länders* cannot be undermined through a treaty.[251] In the *Concordat* case, the Court ruled that a treaty concluded by the federal government with the Vatican binding the *Länder* to support Catholic schools violated the power of the *Länder* under the Basic Law arts 7 and 141.[252]

---

[246] *Reid v Covert* 354 US 1 (1957).

[247] *Sonderup v Tondelli and Another* CCT 53/00 (4 December 2000) para 27, now cited as 2001 (2) BCLR 152 (CC); 2001 (1) SA 1171 (CC). Many countries, including Ireland, Germany and Italy have faced the situation where their domestic courts have had to make a choice between a treaty provision and protection of fundamental human rights. The tendency has been to uphold the fundamental human rights over other treaty obligations. For an overview of how courts in Ireland, Germany and Italy have dealt with this dilemma, see JM Kelly et al *The Irish Constitution* Dublin: Butterworths, 3rd edition 1994, 287–8.

[248] This is the approach of the Australian High Court. The Australian position is that the foreign affairs power is an additional source of power enabling the national government to regulate the matter even though the matter is considered a state concern. Eg even though aviation between the states was a state matter, the High Court in *R v Burgess; Ex parte Henry* (1936) 55 CLR 608, upheld federal intervention to regulate intrastate aviation where the federal statute was adopted pursuant to a treaty. See also *Commonwealth v Tasmania* (1983) 158 CLR 1, where the High Court ruled that the federal government statute which prevented the State of Tasmania from constructing a dam (ordinarily a state matter) was valid because the statute was adopted pursuant to a treaty.

[249] *Missouri v Holland* 252 US 416 (1920).

[250] *Supra* at 432.

[251] The *Concordat* case (1959) 6 BVerfGE 309 quoted in Jackson & Tushnet 832.

[252] Ibid.

Political versus non-political treaties

The Constitution makes provisions for three types of treaties. First, international agreements which are approved by ordinary resolution of parliament. Secondly, treaties of an executive nature involving technical and administrative matters, and thirdly, treaties which are required to be passed through the ordinary legislative process. The first type are referred to as political treaties. A political treaty relates to an agreement which does not require any change to the domestic law in order for it to be implemented. For example treaties of friendship, mutual cooperation, and diplomatic relations could all conceivably be implemented by executive action. On the other hand, a treaty on double taxation and environmental control would require a change in domestic law which could only be accomplished by legislative authority. In this instance, there might be a need for appropriation of funds which also could not be implemented by either ordinary resolution of parliament or by executive action. The different mechanisms for political treaties and other treaties is probably a legacy of the British constitutional tradition, under which a treaty would not be given effect in the domestic sphere unless it had been adopted into law by the legislature.[253] In terms of s 233, the courts, when interpreting legislation, are called upon to prefer a reasonable interpretation that is consistent with international law. However, where domestic law contains something contrary to the treaty, and where the treaty has been approved by resolution but not adopted by the legislature, there is an anomaly where South Africa would, under international law, be obligated to follow a particular conduct, but under its domestic law would be obligated to behave differently. In the United States, on the other hand, where there is a conflict between a treaty and a federal statute, the one that is passed last will be deemed to be the law. In *Azapo*, Mahomed DP adopted the position that international law is only binding on South Africa if adopted by the legislature.[254]

Emergency powers

The Constitution in s 37 contains detailed provisions as to the conditions which have to be fulfilled, and the procedure which needs to be followed for the declaration of a state of emergency. Whenever emergency powers are used, the only limitations on parliament's power are those contained in s 37. This means that federalism arguments cannot be used to invalidate the national exercise of power in an emergency. The emergency power is an additional source of power enabling parliament to take extraordinary measures when the life of the nation is threatened. Emergency powers raise special problems (which will be addressed fully under fundamental rights),[255] because a declaration of a state of emergency often involves the suspension of fundamental liberties.

---

[253] See Hogg 286. The Constitution of Ireland also requires legislative approval before a treaty becomes part of domestic law. See Kelly 296–7.

[254] *Azanian Peoples Organisation (Azapo) and Others v The President of the Republic of South Africa* CCT 17/96 (25 July 1996) para 27, now cited as 1996 (4) SA 671 (CC); 1996 (8) BCLR 1015 (CC).

[255] See chapter 7.

6

The executive

Introduction

The two core principles of constitutionalism include the limitation on the exercise of arbitrary power on the part of the government, and the guarantee of individual and civil liberties enforceable by the courts.[1] An important mechanism to prevent government tyranny is through the principle of separation of powers. This principle seeks to distribute power among the three agencies of government the legislative, executive, and judicial branches. The Constitution achieves these core principles of constitutionalism by distributing government power among the three agencies, as well as limiting the power to within certain prescribed boundaries.

In this chapter, we explore the meaning of separation of powers. First, in the case of executive power, we consider a number of questions, including the meaning and scope of executive power under the Constitution. Secondly, we look at the method of election of the president and the cabinet. Thirdly, we consider the concept of separation of powers, particularly the relationship between parliament and the executive. Fourthly, we look at the Office of the Attorney-General and

the prosecutorial function, in relation to executive power, and separation of powers. Fifthly, we consider administrative power, particularly the role of the civil service. Political control over the agenda of transformation, and the protection of jobs for civil servants engaged in executive tasks are two ends in conflict. On the other hand, there is also a need for certain administrative functions to be performed in a non-partisan manner and without executive interference. This chapter suggests that the question of job security for public servants should be approached in terms of a functional classification whether the function of the public servant is in the area of an executive or administrative activity. Finally, we look at the role of the various independent agencies created under the Constitution, such as the Human Rights Commission, the Auditor-General, the Public Service Commission, and the Reserve Bank. Agencies of government, independent of the executive or legislative branches of government, do not fit comfortably within the tripartite system of government. We look at what limits, if any, there are on the ability of parliament to delegate lawmaking power to the executive, or to independent agencies. If parliament is able to delegate

---

[1] BO Nwabueze *Constitutionalism in the Emergent States* London: C Hurst 1973, 1, 10; KC Wheare *Modern Constitutions* London: Oxford University Press, 2nd edition, 1966, 137; Denis V Cowen *The Foundations of Freedom, with Special Reference to South Africa* Cape Town: Oxford Univeristy Press 1961, 197.

lawmaking power to independent agencies, what does this do to the concept of separation of powers?

This chapter offers a theory of separation of powers that suggests constitutionalism and separation of powers should not mean the tying of the hands of the executive so as to prevent the executive from fulfilling its function of executing the law. The executive branch of government is responsible for implementing the laws of the country, and ought to be in a position to control those functionaries responsible for executing the law. For example, the duties of the Office of the Attorney-General are a quintessential executive function in that they involve the enforcement and execution of the law, and should come under the executive branch of government. However, to the extent that the public service activity in question is administrative or mechanical in nature, the Constitution allows these public servants to be insulated from executive control through appropriate legislation. The Constitution also requires the creation of independent constitutional organs to fulfil certain tasks free of political interference.

Constitutionalism and the three levels of government.

Constitutionalism stands for limited government, and seeks to introduce certain substantive and institutional limits to restrict the scope of governmental power. First, constitutionalism means accountable government, the holding of free elections, the existence of pluralism in political organizations (multi-party political systems), and legal guarantees for civil liberties protected by an independent judiciary.[2] The Constitution provides for democratic multi-party elections, as well as legal guarantees for civil and political rights. Under constitutionalism, the judiciary is the main agency for exercising control over the government and protecting fundamental civil and political rights.[3] The Constitution of South Africa is consistent with the principles of constitutionalism by making the judiciary the custodians of the Constitution.[4]

Secondly, constitutionalism operates on the premise that there are certain demonstrable relationships between institutional forms and the attainment of certain values.[5] The issue is presented as an ongoing contradiction between the government and the people. Power is in the hands of the government and this power has to be brought under control. One way of achieving this control is to limit the scope and extent of government power. The Constitution is consistent with the principles of constitutionalism in limiting governmental power and preventing transgression beyond certain rights. For example, the Constitution provides that it shall be the supreme law of the land, and any act (whether performed by the legislative, executive, or judicial organs of government) that is inconsistent with it shall be without legal effect.[6] Moreover, under constitutionalism, the procedure the government is to follow in exercising its powers is spelt out.[7] The Constitution provides very detailed rules with respect to how legislative and executive powers are exercised. Furthermore, the Constitution provides for separation of powers as important additional method of control of government under constitutionalism.

The doctrine of separation of powers can be traced back to the writings of the French philosopher Montesquieu and the American statesman Madison, who both argued that the best way to control governmental power is to divide it among the various branches of government: the legislative, executive, and judicial

---

2   Stanley A de Smith *The New Commonwealth and its Constitutions* London: Stevens 1964, 106.
3   Fred I Greenstein and Nelson W Polsby (eds) *Handbook of Political Science* Reading: Addison-Wesley Publishing 1975, 36.
4   Section 165(1) of the Constitution.
5   MJC Vile *Constitutionalism and the Separation of Powers* Oxford: Clarendon Press 1967, 8.
6   Section 2 of the Constitution.
7   William G Andrews 'Constitutionalism and Constitutions' in *Constitutions and Constitutionalism*, edited by William G Andrews. Princeton: Van Nostrand 1961, 13.

branches.[8] Some writers link the doctrine to the notion of checks and balances, while others view it as an institutional arrangement of limiting government.[9]

The notion of checks and balances seeks to make the separation of power effective by balancing the power of one agency against that of the other. The United States operates in terms of a more strict concept of separation of powers in that the members of the executive branch are separate from the legislature. In this instance, the separation operates at both the institutional level and in the composition of the personnel.[10] Nevertheless, there is a system of checks and balances in terms of which one agency can intervene in the activities of the other agency. For example, although the United States Congress has the power to pass all laws, the president has the ability to veto all legislation. Similarly, although the president is the Chief Executive Officer responsible for executing the law, his or her executive appointees are subject to confirmation by the United States Senate. However, once the president's appointees are confirmed, the president has complete control over officers engaged in activities of an executive nature. Similarly, the legislature can override a presidential veto and ultimately have the final say over particular legislation.

Separation of powers in South Africa operates in terms of the 'weaker' parliamentary theory, more akin to the Australian model.[11] Section 6(1) requires that the president be elected from the legislature, namely the National Assembly (NA). According to s 86(3), once elected the president ceases to be a member of the NA. Although no longer part of the legislature, under the parliamentary model, the president in terms of s 92(2) is ultimately accountable to the legislature. Section 91(3)(a) requires that the president choose the deputy president from the NA. The president is also required by s 91(3)(b) to choose the ministers from the NA. Under the weaker version of separation of powers, there is no separation of personnel in that the cabinet members originate from the legislature, and continue to serve in the legislature while serving in the cabinet. However, in terms of s 91(3)(c), the president may choose no more then two ministers from outside the NA. The deputy president and the ministers serve at the will of the president. The president assigns the powers and functions of cabinet ministers.

While executive authority is vested in the president, under the weaker version of separation of powers, not only is the president responsible to the NA, but under s 92(2) the 'cabinet are accountable collectively and individually to parliament for the exercise of their powers and the performance of their functions'. Members of the cabinet are required 'to provide parliament with full and regular reports concerning matters under their control'. Section 92(2) of the Constitution provides for both individual and collective responsibility of cabinet members. Collective responsibility means that the cabinet is responsible as a group for all decisions made by the executive. All members of the cabinet (including those that may have opposed the decision within the cabinet) will defend an individual cabinet minister subjected to criticism in the legislature. The cabinet is bound to secrecy with regard to executive discussions.[12] Collective responsibility can impact on whether the NA has confidence in the executive. Under

---

8 Carol Harlow 'Power from the People? Representation and Constitutional Theory' in *Law, Legitimacy and the Constitution: Essays marking the Centenary of Dicey's Law of the Constitution*, edited by Patrick McAuslan and John F McEldowney. London: Sweet & Maxwell 1985, 67; James Madison 'Federalist No 47' in Alexander Hamilton, et al *The Federalist Papers*, edited by Garry Wills. New York: Bantam 1982.

9 For a discussion of the theory of separation of powers, see William B Gwyn *The Meaning of the Separation of Powers: An Analysis of the Doctrine from its Origin to the Adoption of the United States Constitution* New Orleans: Tulane University Press 1965, especially chapter 1.

10 To some extent the arguments over the different meanings to the doctrine of separation of powers revolves around the debate between a preference for the US presidential system or the British parliamentary Westminster system of government. For a discussion of the different meanings to the separation of powers, *see* Geoffrey Marshall *Constitutional Theory* Oxford: Clarendon 1971, 97–100.

11 *South African Association of Personal Injury Lawyers v Heath and Others* CCT 27/00 (28 November 2000) para 23, now cited as 2001 (1) BCLR 52 (CC); 2001 (1) SA 1146 (CC).

12 ECS Wade and AW Bradley *Constitutional and Administrative Law* London: Longman, 10th edition, 1985.

s 102(1), the NA can pass a vote of no confidence in the cabinet. If the majority of members of the NA pass a vote of no confidence in the cabinet, the president has to reconstitute the cabinet. Under s 102(2), the majority of members in the NA can also pass a no-confidence vote which would require the president and the entire cabinet to resign.

In re: *Certification of the Constitution of The Republic of South Africa*
CCT 23/96 (6 September 1996), now cited as 1996 (10) BCLR 1253 (CC); 1996 4 SA 744 (CC)
(*The First Certification* decision)
(notes omitted)

Unanimous Decision

[107] The objector does not suggest that there has not been an adequate separation of the judicial power from the legislative and executive power, or that there has not been an adequate separation of the functions between the legislature, the executive and the judiciary. His complaint is that members of the Cabinet continue to be members of the legislature and, by virtue of their positions, are able to exercise a powerful influence over the decisions of the legislature. He contends that this is inconsistent with the separation of powers and cites as examples to be followed the United States of America, France, Germany and the Netherlands.

[108] There is, however, no universal model of separation of powers, and in democratic systems of government in which checks and balances result in the imposition of restraints by one branch of government upon another, there is no separation that is absolute. This is apparent from the objector's own examples. While in the USA, France and the Netherlands members of the executive may not continue to be members of the legislature, this is not a requirement of the German system of separation of powers. Moreover, because of the different systems of checks and balances that exist in these countries, the relationship between the different branches of government and the power or influence that one branch of government has over the other, differs from one country to another.

[109] The principle of separation of powers, on the one hand, recognizes the functional independence of branches of government. On the other hand, the principle of checks and balances focuses on the desirability of ensuring that the constitutional order, as a totality, prevents the branches of government from usurping power from one another. In this sense it anticipates the necessary or unavoidable intrusion of one branch on the terrain of another. No constitutional scheme can reflect a complete separation of powers: the scheme is always one of partial separation. In Justice Frankfurter's words, '[t]he areas are partly interacting, not wholly disjointed'.

[110] NT 43 vests the legislative authority of government in the national sphere in Parliament and in the provincial sphere in the provincial legislatures NT 85 and 125 vest the executive power of the Republic in the President and the executive power of the provinces in the Premiers, respectively. NT 165 vests the judicial authority of the Republic in the courts. This constitutional separation of powers has important consequences for the way in which and the institutions by which power can be exercised.

[111] As the separation of powers doctrine is not a fixed or rigid constitutional doctrine, it is given expression in many different forms and made subject to checks and balances of many kinds. It can thus not be said that a failure in the NT to separate completely the functionaries of the executive and legislature is destructive of the doctrine. Indeed, the overlap provides a singularly important check and balance on the exercise of executive power. It makes the executive more directly answerable to the elected legislature. This is emphasized by the provisions of NT 92(2), which indicate that members of the Cabinet are 'accountable collectively and individually to Parliament for the performance of their functions'. In terms of NT 92(3)(*b*), Cabinet members are compelled to provide Parliament with full and regular reports concerning matters under their control. And finally, the legislature has the power to

remove the President and indirectly the Cabinet (which is presidentially appointed) under NT 89.

[112] Within the broad requirement of separation of powers and appropriate checks and balances, the CA was afforded a large degree of latitude in shaping the independence and interdependence of government branches. The model adopted reflects the historical circumstances of our constitutional development. We find in the NT checks and balances that evidence a concern for both the over-concentration of power and the requirement of an energetic and effective, yet answerable, executive. A strict separation of powers has not always been maintained; but there is nothing to suggest that the CPs imposed upon the CA an obligation to adopt a particular form of strict separation, such as that found in the United States of America, France or the Netherlands.

[113] What CP VI requires is that there be a separation of powers between the legislature, executive and judiciary. It does not prescribe what form that separation should take. We have previously said that the CPs must not be interpreted with technical rigidity. The language of CP VI is sufficiently wide to cover the type of separation required by the NT, and the objection that CP VI has not been complied with must accordingly be rejected.

The one outstanding thread common to the both interpretations of the separation of powers is the belief in the separation and independence of the judiciary from the executive and legislative branches of government.[13] The Constitution enshrines the role of the judiciary as the bulwark to protect the fundamental values of the Constitution.

Giving content to executive power

A parliamentary system provides for checks and balances in terms of which one branch of government has power to interfere and check the actions of another. Section 85(1) of the Constitution proclaims that 'the executive authority of the Republic is vested in the President'. The Constitution further proclaims that the president together with the cabinet exercises executive authority by implementing legislation subject to the Constitution or an Act of Parliament.[14] The question is, how far can an Act of Parliament limit or control the exercise of executive power? Can an Act of Parliament limit the president in the choice of executive officers? Can an Act of Parliament provide for the direct supervision of the way the executive fulfills its functions? Can parliament intervene in implementing legislation?

Answers to these questions depend on what concept of separation of powers the Constitution represents. Under a parliamentary executive, parliament can hold the executive accountable. Even though there is a blurring of lines between the executive and the legislature under the parliamentary executive, arguably there are core functions that belong to each branch of government, which should not be encroached upon by the other. The core function of the executive is the execution of the law. The legislature cannot take it upon itself to execute the law. Similarly, the executive cannot encroach upon the core functions of the legislature, or the judiciary, even though there may be some overlap between the functions of the different branches. For example, the executive branch of government appoints judges from a list given by the Judicial Service Commission (JSC). Judicial appointments are not completely insulated from the political process as the president's power to appoint judges allows for an executive choice as to who serves on the bench. Just as parliament cannot take upon itself the power to execute the law, neither parliament nor the executive can perform the adjudicative function belonging to the judiciary. Also, the Constitution gives the president some check in the legislative sphere by referring a bill back to the NA

---

[13] Marshall 103. Independence of the judiciary is discussed in chapter 4.

for reconsideration of the bill's constitutionality.[15] The president can also refer a bill to the Constitutional Court for a decision on the bill's constitutionality.[16] If the Constitutional Court decides the bill is constitutional, the president must sign it.[17]

This check and balance is not the same as usurpation of the role of the other branch. A coherent concept of separation of powers requires that the legislature fulfil the traditional function of lawmaking, and the executive fulfil the traditional function of executing and administering the law. Courts in many jurisdictions have struggled to arrive at an appropriate concept of legislative, executive, administrative and quasi-judicial functions.[18] Some jurisdictions view the distinction between legislative, executive and administrative powers largely in terms of whether the activity pertains to lawmaking, law enforcement, or merely the administration of the law without discretion.[19] Lawmaking involves the creation of rules. Under the United States concept, if the activity involves enforcement powers, then it is executive in nature. The South African Constitutional Court, on the other hand, has interpreted 'executive power' as the discretionary power which the president and executive have under the Constitution, such as the power to appoint a commission of enquiry.[20] The Constitutional Court considers implementation of legislation through the executive as administrative power.[21] However, even in the interpretation of legislation, there may be a discretionary element which can make it difficult to decide whether the exercise of power by the executive is 'executive' or 'administrative' in nature. For example, a statute may give the president the power to interpret facts and take appropriate action based on the president's interpretation of the facts.[22] The Constitutional Court has recognized this difficulty and noted the following in *SARFU 2* (notes omitted):

[143] Determining whether an action should be characterised as the implementation of legislation or the formulation of policy may be difficult. It will, as we have said above, depend primarily upon the nature of the power. A series of considerations may be relevant to deciding on which side of the line a particular action falls. The source of the power, though not necessarily decisive, is a relevant factor. So too is the nature of the power, its subject matter, whether it involves the exercise of a public duty, and how closely it is related on the one hand to policy matters, which are not administrative, and on the other to the implementation of legislation, which is. While the subject matter of a power is not relevant to determine whether constitutional review is appropriate, it is relevant to determine whether the exercise of the power constitutes administrative action for the purposes of section 33. Difficult boundaries may have to be drawn in deciding what should and what should not be characterised as administrative action for the purposes of section 33. These will need to be drawn carefully in the light of the provisions of the Constitution and the overall constitutional purpose of an efficient, equitable and ethical public administration. This can best be done on a case-by-case basis.

The legislature should neither execute the law itself, nor be the supervising or executing the officers (beyond the president and cabinet) selected by the president and cabinet to execute

---

[14] Section 85(2) of the Constitution.

[15] Section 84(2)*(b)*.

[16] Section 84(2)*(c)*.

[17] Section 79(5). *Ex parte The President of the Republic of South Africa, In re: Constitutionality of the Liquor Bill* CCT 12/99 (11 November 1999) para 18, now cited as 2000 (1) SA 732 (CC); 2000 (1) BCLR 1 (CC).

[18] *Fedsure Life Assurance Ltd and Others v Greater Johannesburg Transitional Metropolitan Council* CCT 7/98 (14 October 1998) paras 26–46, now cited as 1998 (12) BCLR 1458 (CC); 1999(1) SA 374(CC).

[19] *Buckley v Valeo* 424 US 1, 121–124 (1976).

[20] *The President of the Republic of South Africa and Others v South African Rugby Football Union and Others* CCT 16/98 (2 December 1998) para 147, now cited as 1999 (2) SA 14 (CC); 1999 (2) BCLR 175 (CC)(*SARFU 2*).

[21] *Supra* para 142. *Permanent Secretary of the Department of Education Eastern Cape and Another v Ed-U College (PE) Inc* CCT 26/00 (29 November 2000) para 18, now cited as 2001 (2) BCLR 118 (CC); 2001 (2) SA 1 (CC).

[22] See discussion below on power to prosecute.

the law. In *Bowsher v Synar*,[23] the United States Supreme Court ruled that the United States Constitution does not provide for the legislature to directly supervise or remove individual officers charged with the execution of the law. The Court ruled that it is inappropriate for the United States Congress to directly supervise or remove officers charged with the execution of the law. The Court ruled that 'congressional participation in the removal of executive officers is unconstitutional'.[24] To permit the legislature to supervise and remove an individual who is responsible for the execution of the law, would mean that the legislature has control over the execution of the law.[25] The issue in *Bowsher* was whether congress could assign to the Comptroller-General historically is regarded as an agent of the legislature the power to make executive decisions pertaining to budget cuts. The Court discussed the differences between an executive, legislative, or administrative act. The essence of an executive act is the exercise of judgement concerning facts and the interpretation of law in relation to the facts. This judgement must be made by the executive.[26] An administrative act is ministerial and mechanical in character and need not be made by the executive.[27]

Separation of powers is important to prevent tyranny, and the concentration of power in one agency. The check and balance of one agency against that of the other is an important facet in the control and exercise of power. This function of check and balance is not the same as one agency usurping the role of the other. The Constitution envisages that the NA should hold the president and cabinet accountable for their actions, and the actions of subordinate officers appointed by the executive. The NA can pass a vote of no confidence against the executive but it cannot, with the exception of the president, choose and dismiss individual ministers. If there is any criminal wrongdoing, the particular official should be held legally accountable. Under separation of powers principles, the Court should make the determination as to whether there was any criminal wrongdoing.

While the South African Constitution, like those of other parliamentary systems (unlike that of the United States), speaks about individual responsibility of cabinet members to parliament, this responsibility is a political responsibility. It does not speak about the legislature passing a vote of no confidence in individual cabinet members. It also does not mean that parliament can replace executive decisions with decisions of its own.[28] Unlike the strict separation of powers, the Constitution creates an important political check on the cabinet, meaning the cabinet in its entirety, through the motion of no confidence.[29] Outside passing legislation, or the motion of no confidence, parliament should not be able to overrule the executive on how to fulfil the executive function. Just as the legislature cannot supervise the executive, the courts cannot give judgment on the validity of a properly[30] passed vote of no confidence in the cabinet or president. More importantly, a judicial officer cannot exercise executive or prosecutorial functions.[31]

In *South African Association of Personal Injury Lawyers*, the Constitutional Court was faced with a challenge to s 3(1) of the Special Investigating and Special Tribunals Act[32] and two proclamations[33] made by the president pursuant to the Act. Section 3(1) of the Act provides that the president must appoint a judge or an acting judge of the High

---

[23] *Bowsher v Synar* 478 US 714 (1986).

[24] *Supra* at 725.

[25] *Supra* at 726.

[26] *Supra* at 732.

[27] *Supra*.

[28] Helmut Steinberger 'Political Representation in Germany' in *Germany and its Basic Law, Past, Present and Future: A German-American Symposium*, edited by Paul Kirchoff and Donald P Kommers Baden-Baden: Nomos 1993, 153.

[29] Section 102(1) of the Constitution.

[30] The word 'properly' is used to mean correct procedure.

[31] *South African Association of Personal Injury Lawyers* paras 45–46.

[32] Act 74 of 1996.

[33] Proclamation R24 of 1997, *GG* 17854 RG 5884 and Proclamation R31 of 1999, *GG* 19882 RG 6469, 26 March 1999.

Court as head of the Special Investigating Unit (SIU). The SIU was created to investigate and aid in the prosecution of serious malpractice or mal-administration of state institutions, assets and public money. The judge appointed in terms of the Act performs executive functions including the appointment of staff, police functions, and prose-cutorial functions. The exercise of these functions is inconsistent with the role of the judiciary.[34] While it is permissible for judges to head commissions of enquiry and sanction search warrants,[35] it is incompatible under separation of powers for a judge to act as litigator on behalf of the state.[36]

The president and discretionary powers

The president and cabinet have a large degree of discretion in the exercise of executive power. Section 84 of the Constitution gives the president various powers. These include the power to refer bills back to the NA;[37] to refer a bill to the Constitutional Court for a decision on the bill's constitutionality;[38] to summon parliament to an extraordinary sitting;[39] to appoint commissions of inquiry;[40] to receive and recognize foreign diplomatic and consular representatives;[41] to appoint diplomatic officials;[42] to grant a par-don;[43] and to confer honours.[44] Under s 91(2), the president appoints the deputy president and the ministers. Under s 97(a), the president may

transfer, by proclamation, the administration of any function to another cabinet member. Under s 174, even though the president is required to provide reasons for rejecting nominees presented by the JSC, he or she has the final say on the appointment of judges. In the exercise of executive power, the president is always constrained by the principle of legality.[45] This means the president must exercise executive power in good faith and not misconstrue his or her power.[46] However, the exercise of the discretion is not easily amenable to judicial review. It is only in rare circumstances such as fraud, bad faith, or error that a court will intervene to invalidate an exercise of discretionary power.[47]

Where the discretionary power is properly exercised, the conduct of the executive branch should not, in terms of separation of powers, be subject to scrutiny by the judiciary. On 19 March 1997, the South African Rugby Football Union (SARFU) challenged the decision of, the then President Mandela to appoint a commission of inquiry into the affairs of SARFU. The president's decision was based on a recommendation from his Minister of Sport. SARFU argued that the president merely rubber-stamped a decision made by the Minister of Sport. The Transvaal Provincial Division, *per* De Villiers J, upheld the challenge.[48] The president's appearance before the Court was the first occasion that a South African Head of State had been subpoenaed and made to account for an executive decision before a court. The president's appearance before the lower court set

---

[34] *South African Association of Personal Lawyers* paras 17 and 38.

[35] *Supra* para 34.

[36] *Supra* para 45.

[37] Section 84(2)*(b)* of the Constitution.

[38] Section 84(2)*(c)*.

[39] Section 84(2)*(d)*.

[40] Section 84(2)*(f)*.

[41] Section 84(2)*(h)*.

[42] Section 84(2)*(i)*.

[43] Section 84(2)*(j)*.

[44] Section 84(2)*(k)*.

[45] *Fedsure Life Assurance Ltd* paras 56–59. *Hugo* paras 12–13. *SARFU 2* para 121.

[46] *SARFU 2* para 121.

[47] *President of the Republic of South Africa and Another v Hugo* CCT 11/96 (18 April 1997) paras 12–13, now cited as 1997 (4) SA 1 (CC); 1997 (6) BCLR 708 (CC); *SARFU 2* para 121; *In re: Pharmaceutical Manufacturers Association of SA: The ex parte Application of the President of the RSA and Others* CCT 31/99 (25 February 2000) paras 83 and 85.

[48] *South African Rugby Union and Others v President of the RSA and Others* 1998 (10) BCLR 1256 (T).

the unfortunate precedent of subjecting the presidential discretionary power to judicial review. On appeal, the Constitutional Court held that the lower court had erred in requiring the president to give evidence.[49] The doctrine of separation of powers requires a court to protect the status, dignity, and efficiency of the Office of the Presidency.[50] The president should not as a rule be called upon to justify, in open court, the performance of his or her official duties.[51]

In *Marbury v Madison*,[52] the first decision which affirmed the justification for judicial review in the United States, the United States Supreme Court was faced with the question of whether the Court could issue a writ of *mandamus* to a member of the president's cabinet, ordering the executive official to perform a duty. In addressing this question, Chief Justice Marshall draws an important line between law and politics, and further states that there are some matters entirely political in nature left entirely to the discretion of the executive.[53] With regard to such matters, the executive is only politically accountable.[54] For example, Marshall CJ says that when an executive official, such as a minister, is assisting the president in making a political decision, the acts of the official are not subject to judicial review.[55] However, where the law imposes specific duties

on executive officials, the officer is not an agent of the president but an officer of the law.

The South African Constitution gives the president the power to appoint a commission of inquiry.[56] This appointment is a judicial act, not a political one, to assist the political branches to ascertain facts.[57] To the extent that the president decides to exercise this discretionary power, this falls within the president's purview even if he or she does so pursuant to a recommendation of one of his or her officials. This is not to say that every discretionary power is not amenable to judicial review. If the president appoints a commission of inquiry to achieve illegal objectives such as smearing political opponents, or because of a bribe, the exercise of power could be subject to review.[58] In the absence of any illegality, separation of powers requires the court to stay its hand and defer to the executive branch of government, providing the power is exercised in terms of criteria laid out in the Constitution.[59] The exercise of this power is a discretionary power, and more aptly comes under the political question doctrine.[60] Similarly, the internal deliberations of the government, such as cabinet discussions, and the preparation of cabinet and departmental decisions, should also be subject to a special privilege.[61]

Marbury v Madison
5 US (1 Cranch) 137 (1803)
(notes omitted).

It follows, then, that the question, whether the legality of an act of the head of a department be

examinable in a court of justice or not, must always depend on the nature of that act. If some acts be examinable, and others not, there must be some rule of law to guide the court in the exercise of its jurisdiction. In some instances, there may be difficulty in applying the rule to

---

[49] *President of the RSA and Others v South African Rugby Football Union and Others* CCT 16/98 (2 December 1998), now cited as 1999 (2) SA 14 (CC); 1999 (2) BCLR 175 (CC)(*SARFU 2*).

[50] *Supra* para 36.

[51] *Supra* para 85.

[52] *Marbury v Madison* 5 US (1 Cranch) 137 (1803).

[53] *Supra* at 166.

[54] *Supra*.

[55] *Supra* at 166.

[56] Section 84 (2)*(e)* of the Constitution.

[57] *SARFU 2* paras 146–147.

[58] *Hugo* para 29.

[59] *Supra*.

[60] *SARFU 2* para 146. The political question doctrine is discussed more fully in chapter 5.

[61] Steinberger *154*.

particular cases; but there cannot, it is believed, be much difficulty in laying down the rule.

By the constitution of the United States, the president is invested with certain important political powers, in the exercise of which he is to use his own discretion, and is accountable only to his country in his political character, and to his own conscience. To aid him in the performance of these duties, he is authorized to appoint certain officers, who act by his authority and in conformity with his orders. In such cases, their acts are his acts; and whatever opinion may be entertained of the manner in which executive discretion may be used, still there exists, and can exist, no power to control that discretion. The subjects are political. They respect the nation, not individual rights, and being entrusted to the executive, the decision of the executive is conclusive. The application of this remark will be perceived by adverting to the act of congress for establishing the department of foreign affairs. This officer, as his duties were prescribed by that act, is to conform precisely to the will of the president: he is the mere organ by whom that will is communicated. The acts of such an officer, as an officer, can never be examinable by the courts. But when the legislature proceeds to impose on that officer other duties; when he is directed peremptorily to perform certain acts; when the rights of individuals are dependent on the performance of those acts; he is so far the officer of the law; is amenable to the laws for his conduct; and cannot at his discretion sport away the vested rights of others.

The conclusion from this reasoning is, that where the heads of departments are the political or confidential agents of the executive, merely to execute the will of the president, or rather to act in cases in which the executive possesses a constitutional or legal discretion, nothing can be more perfectly clear than that their acts are only politically examinable. But where a specific duty is assigned by law, and individual rights depend upon the performance of that duty, it seems equally clear that the individual who considers himself injured has a right to resort to the laws of his country for a remedy.

1. With respect to the officer to whom it would be directed. The intimate political relation, subsisting between the president of the United States and the heads of departments, necessarily renders any legal investigation of the acts of one of those high officers peculiarly irksome, as well as delicate; and excites some hesitation with respect to the propriety of entering into such investigation. Impressions are often received without much reflection or examination; and it is not wonderful that in such a case as this, the assertion, by an individual, of his legal claims in a court of justice, to which claims it is the duty of that court to attend, should at first view be considered by some, as an attempt to intrude into the cabinet, and to intermeddle with the prerogatives of the executive.

It is scarcely necessary for the court to disclaim all pretensions to such a jurisdiction. An extravagance, so absurd and excessive, could not have been entertained for a moment. The province of the court is, solely, to decide on the rights of individuals, not to inquire how the executive, or executive officers, perform duties in which they have a discretion. Questions, in their nature political, or which are, by the constitution and laws, submitted to the executive, can never be made in this court.

In *The President v Hugo*,[62] the Constitutional Court discussed the scope of executive powers (specifically in relation to the discretion of the president to grant pardons), under the interim Constitution. The scope of executive power, and the power of the president to grant pardons under the interim Constitution, is the same as that contained in the final Constitution. In *Hugo*, the president granted a rescission of prison sentences to certain categories of female prisoners, specifically mothers in prison with minor children under the age of twelve years. The respondent was a

---

[62] *President of the Republic of South Africa and Another v Hugo* CCT 11/96.

father with minor children under twelve years old. He argued that the act of the president discriminated against him and violated the equality provisions of the Constitution. The specific question before the Court was whether the powers of the president to grant pardons, where it is performed in terms of the criteria laid out in the Constitution, is subject to fetters, specifically the equality provisions in the Bill of Rights. The Court stated that in the exercise of his or her executive powers, the president under the interim and final Constitution is always subject to the Constitution.[63] In the exercise of the executive power, it is possible that the equality provisions in the Bill of Rights may be contravened. The Court referred to English authorities for the proposition

that whether the Court will be able to determine if the exercise of executive power is subject to judicial review will depend on the subject-matter.[64] Under this reasoning, there are a range of policy choices for which the judiciary is ill-equipped to perform judicial review. Under the South African Constitution, this does not mean that the Court does not have the power to exercise judicial review, but it could mean that for certain matters judicial review may not provide an effective remedy.[65] However, where there is blatant discrimination and abuse in the exercise of prerogative power such as, for example, granting pardons based on race, gender, or religion, the exercise of the prerogative power may be reviewed.[66]

President of the Republic of South African and Another v Hugo CCT 11/96 (18 April 1997), now cited as 1997 (6) BCLR 708 (CC), 1997 (4) SA 1 (CC)
(notes omitted)
GOLDSTONE, J

(30855) The foregoing discussion indicates that there has been a distinct movement in modern constitutional states, (and, I include, for this purpose, England) in favour of recognising at least some power of review of what are or were prerogative powers of the head of state.

(30856) The approach of the English courts whereby the jurisdiction of the courts to review the exercise of prerogative powers depends upon the subject-matter of the power is one that is not open to us. The interim Constitution obliges us to test impugned action by any organ of state against the discipline of the interim Constitution and, in particular, the Bill of Rights. That is a fundamental incidence of the constitutional state which is envisaged in the Preamble to the interim Constitution, namely:

... a new order in which all South Africans will be entitled to a common South African citizenship in a sovereign and democratic constitutional state in which there is equality between men and women and people of all races so that all citizens shall be able to enjoy and exercise their fundamental rights and freedoms; ....

In my view, it would be contrary to that promise if the exercise of presidential power is above the interim Constitution and is not subject to the discipline of the Bill of Rights. However, it may well be that, because of the nature of a section 82(1) power or the manner in which is it is exercised, the provisions of the interim Constitution, and, in particular, the Bill of Rights, provide no ground for an effective review of a presidential exercise of such a power. The result, in a particular case, may be the same as that in England, but the manner in which that result is reached in terms of the interim Constitution is a different one. On the English approach the courts, in certain cases, depending on the subject-matter of the prerogative power exercised, would be deprived of jurisdiction. Under the interim Constitution the jurisdiction would

---

63 *Supra* paras 12–13.
64 *Supra* para 18.
65 *Supra* para 14.
66 *Supra* paras 18–19.

be there in all cases in which the presidential powers under section 82(1) are exercised.

(30857) The way is now open to consider the review in the instant case, that is the exercise by the President of his power of pardon and reprieve of prisoners under section 82(1)(k) of the interim Constitution. I would emphasize that we are not required to consider the question of the reviewability of other powers which may be exercised by the President under section 82(1). In cases where the President pardons or reprieves a single prisoner it is difficult, (save in an unlikely situation where a course of conduct gives rise to an inference of unconstitutional conduct), to conceive of a case where a constitutional attack could be mounted against such an exercise of the presidential power. Even the provisions of section 8 of the interim Constitution – the equality clause – would have only limited application. No prisoner has the right to be pardoned, to be reprieved or to have a sentence remitted. The interim Constitution places such matters within the power of the President. This does not mean that if a president were to abuse this power vested in him or her under section 82(1)(k) a court would be powerless, for it is implicit in the interim Constitution that the President will exercise that power in good faith. If, for instance, a president were to abuse his or her powers by acting in bad faith I can see no reason why a court should not intervene to correct such action and to declare it to be unconstitutional. For example, a decision to grant a pardon in consideration for a bribe, could no doubt be set aside by a court. So, too, if a president were to misconstrue his or her powers I can see no objection to a court correcting such an error, though it could not exercise the

discretion itself. This is what happened in *R v Home Secretary, ex p Bentley* but even then the court declined to issue a *mandamus* or a declaration. It simply invited the Home Secretary to consider the case again in the light of the decision that he had misconstrued his powers. As it was put by Wilson J in *Operation Dismantle Inc v The Queen*:

[T]he courts should not be too eager to relinquish their judicial review function simply because they are called upon to exercise it in relation to weighty matters of state. Equally, however, it is important to realize that judicial review is not the same thing as substitution of the court's opinion on the merits for the opinion of the person or body to whom a discretionary decision-making power has been committed. The first step is to determine who as a constitutional matter has the decision-making power; the second is to determine the scope (if any) of judicial review of the exercise of that power.

In that case, the Canadian Supreme Court had been requested to review and set aside a decision by the Government to allow the testing of United States cruise missiles in Canada. Wilson J concluded that:

[I]f we are to look at the Constitution for the answer to the question whether it is appropriate for the courts to 'second guess' the executive on matters of defence, we would conclude that it is not appropriate. However, if what we are being asked to do is to decide whether any particular act of the executive violates the rights of the citizens, then it is not only appropriate that we answer the question; it is our obligation under the Charter to do so.

In *Hugo*, there was blatant discrimination against male prisoners. The Court majority on reviewing the facts found that the exercise of the power in this case was not capricious even though it may have discriminated against fathers. The Court majority, while stating that the exercise of prerogative powers is subject to the Constitution, did not subject the executive action to constitu-

tional scrutiny in the same way that it would have subjected to scrutiny such a discriminatory measure, if adopted by another organ of government. The majority says so in so many words by stating that 'if the President decides to approach the issue of pardon or reprieve not in individual cases, but by reference to a category of offender, then it may be well nigh impossible to do so other than by the "blunt-axe" method. In the legislative or administrative context other methods would usually be available and over or under inclusive classifications would be less likely to be held fair'.[67]

This raises serious questions as to whether the majority seriously subjected the president's actions to judicial review. If the president's exercise of prerogative powers transgresses on a fundamental right in the Bill of Rights, and if the Court says that the exercise of the president's power is subject to judicial review to ensure that it was exercised in terms of the Constitution, particularly the Bill of Rights, then the majority ought to have applied the limitations test as Mokgoro J required in her concurring opinion,[68] and Kriegler J required in his dissenting opinion.[69] Instead, the majority stated that they preferred to express no view in this regard.[70] Instead, they create a difference depending on the source of the discrimination. They then stated that whether the impact was unfair to the group discriminated against depended on 'the nature of the power in terms of which the discrimination was effected and, also at the nature of the interests which have been affected by the discrimination'.[71]

Arguably, what the majority is saying is that when the president exercises prerogative power, it is almost impossible to subject that power to judicial review. It is only in the most extreme circumstances, and where there is manifestly outrageous conduct (such as the pardon being granted with bribery as a factor), would the court intervene. Even though the Constitution obliges the Court to 'test impugned action by any organ of state' against the Constitution and Bill of Rights, the majority acknowledges that the subject matter may not provide an effective remedy because of the nature of the discretionary power.[72] For example,

let us assume that the president stipulates that the Minister of Defence should always be male. The president has discretion in choosing the cabinet. Arguably, it is not possible for a court to guarantee a change in the policy even though such discriminatory policy is in flagrant disregard of the Constitution.

In another example, if the president says 'I will only have two women (one of whom will be a Zulu) members of the Constitutional Court', again assuming that we can objectively prove that the next best candidate is not a woman, or is a non-Zulu, it is unlikely that the Court can provide effective review of the president's actions.[73] There are a host of other measures including the president's discretion in foreign affairs, granting honours, and appointing commissions of enquiry, that do not easily lend themselves to judicial review.[74] Where the Court adjudicates over the prerogative power, as it did in *Hugo*, it cannot apply the Bill of Rights to prerogative powers in the same way it applies the limitations clause to violations of fundamental human rights. For example, the Constitutional Court in *SARFU 2* held that the president's appointment of a commission of enquiry was not readily subject to judicial review.[75] When the president decides to appoint a commission of enquiry, this act is related to the exercise of executive power, namely, to gather information and advice.[76] The respondents' argument that they were entitled to administrative review, before the commission of enquiry was appointed, showed a misunderstanding of the nature of executive power. Providing the president's actions conform to all the legality requirements under the Constitution, the Court will not second-guess the president in the exercise of executive power.[77]

---

[67] *Supra* para 48.
[68] *Supra* paras 95–6, 105.
[69] *Supra* para 86.
[70] *Supra* para 50.
[71] *Supra* para 43.
[72] *Supra* para 28.
[73] Even though s 174 (4)*(b)* of the Consitution says he or she must present reasons for rejection of candidates presented by the JSC.
[74] *SARFU 2* para 146.
[75] *Supra.*
[76] *Supra* para 147.
[77] *Supra* para 148.

To prove a violation of the legality principle may be difficult in the context of discretionary executive power.[78] In *Mayor of Philadelphia v Educational Equity League*,[79] the applicant challenged the mayor's appointments to an Educational Nominating Panel, arguing that discrimination against blacks was present in violation of the equal protection clause of the United States Constitution. The United States Supreme Court, *per* Powell J, characterized the mayor's power to appoint officials as 'discretionary'.[80] The Court was reluctant to perform judicial oversight over discretionary acts.[81] Part of the problem is the difficulty of showing bad faith and an abuse of authority by the executive. It would require exceptional situations with evidence such as fraud, bribery or gross error for the Court to intervene to invalidate executive conduct. For example, in *Pharmaceutical Manufacturers Association*, the president made an application to the Court, requesting the Court to set aside the president's decision to bring an Act of Parliament dealing with pharmaceuticals into force.[82] Before the Pharmaceutical Act could take effect, a regulatory base and essential regulations to govern medicines had to be put into place.[83] The president, in error, purported to bring the Pharmaceutical Act into operation without the essential regulatory base. The effect of the president's error was that a host of dangerous substances would be unregulated. While the president had discretion as to when to bring the Act into operation, this discretion had to be exercised after the necessary steps, namely the creation of the regulatory base, had been established.[84] The Constitutional Court invalidated the president's action and held that the president had made an error which resulted in an irrational act.[85] Rationality is a minimum threshold for the exercise of all public power.[86] The Court pointed out that its determination of rationality was not based on its value preferences. However, its decision in this case was supported by the president and other executive officials having themselves approached the Court to set aside the president's decision.[87]

Enforcement versus discretionary power

Where the law imposes a duty on the executive to act in a certain way, the president has a duty to act in terms of the letter of the law. Suppose, for example, parliament passes an appropriations law that appropriates R1 billion to finance the construction of roads and railways. The president and the cabinet are opposed to the appropriation, and therefore the president decides not to spend the money even though it is available. The president arguably does not have the constitutional authority to 'swallow-up' the law by refusing to enforce it. In *Kendell*,[88] the United States Supreme Court ruled that where the legislature directed the executive to spend funds in a particular way, the executive did not have the authority to change the law by impounding the funds.[89] Where the executive fails to follow the requirements, it would be appropriate for the Court to issue an order directing the executive to act in terms of the appropriations law.

What happens if the costs decrease and the executive can complete the construction of the roads

---

[78] *Pharmaceutical Manufacturers Association* para 90.
[79] *Mayor of Philadelphia v Educational Equity League* 415 US 605 (1974).
[80] *Supra* at 614.
[81] *Supra* at 615.
[82] The Act was promulgated on 18 December 1998. The president issued a proclamation R49 on 30 April 1999, purporting to bring the Act into force.
[83] *Pharmaceutical Manufacturers Association* para 5.
[84] *Supra* paras 58 and 76.
[85] *Supra* paras 68 and 89.
[86] *Supra* para 90.
[87] *Supra.*
[88] *Kendell v United States ex rel Stokes* 37 US (12 Pet) 524 (1838).
[89] *Kendell* at 611.

and railways for R750 million? Here, the executive has neither intention to impound the funds, nor to frustrate the project, but merely wants to spend the money effectively. As part of the executive power, the president and cabinet have discretion as to how the funds are spent. However, in terms of separation of powers, the rescission of budget authority must be validated by the legislature.[90]

Where a statute gives the executive the power to interpret facts and take action based on its interpretation of the facts, the Court should be circumspect in allowing another branch of government to intervene to compel executive action in a particular way. Previously, the Attorney-General Act of 1992 removed the power of the executive branch of government over all prosecutions by providing for security of tenure for the Attorney-General (A-G).[91] During the period before and after the introduction of the final Constitution, an untenable practice existed where the A-G in each of the provinces was an agent independent of the executive branch of government. In a number of judgments delivered by the Constitutional Court,

we see the anomaly where the case is listed as the state, whereas the reality was the views represented by 'the state' were not necessarily that of the executive (which is the branch of government responsible for executing the law).[92] The A-G had in effect become a fourth branch of government that could interpret and enforce the law with nominal accountability to the legislature and executive. The function of the A-G is a quintessential executive function.[93] Therefore, the A-G must fall under the control of the executive branch of government and not operate as a free-floating fourth branch of government, minimally accountable to the executive and legislature. The final Constitution restores the position of making the final responsibility for prosecutions an executive decision. The National Director of Public Prosecutions (NDPP) is appointed by the president and is responsible for all prosecutions.

In the *First Certification* decision, the Constitutional Court addressed challenges to the new text, which now made prosecution policy subject to executive control.

In re: Certification of the Constitution of the Republic of South Africa
CCT 23/96 (6 September 1996), now cited as 1996 (4) SA 744 (CC);
1996 (10) BCLR 1253 (CC)
(*First Certification* decision)
(notes omitted)
Unanimous Decision

The Prosecuting Authority
[140] Objection was taken to NT 179 which makes provision for a single national prosecuting authority consisting of a National Director of Public Prosecutions, Directors of Public Prosecutions and prosecutors. In terms of NT 179(2),

the prosecuting authority has the power to institute criminal proceedings on behalf of the state. NT 179(5) provides that the National Director of Public Prosecutions is vested with powers which include the determination of prosecution policy, the issuing of policy directives which have to be observed in the prosecution process, the power to intervene in the prosecution process when policy directives are not complied with and the ability to review a decision to prosecute or not to prosecute.

[141] It was contended that the provisions of NT 179 do not comply with CP VI, which requires a separation of powers between the legislature, executive and judiciary, with appro-

---

[90] In the US, impoundment by the executive is governed by the Impoundment Control Act of 1974, 2 USC, ss 682–688. The statute gives the president authority to delay spending of appropriated funds. However, the ultimate recission will only take place, if congress adopts a recission bill.

[91] Section 4 of the Act limits the removal of the A-G only for misconduct, ill-health, or incapacity.

[92] eg we saw this anomaly in the first judgment delivered by the Constitutional Court where the case was listed as *Zuma and Two Others v The State* CCT/5/94.

[93] *See Heckler v Chaney* 470 US 821 (1985). Here the Court ruled, eg that the failure of the executive branch of government to regulate drugs used in executions is not subject to judicial review. In other words, the power to execute the law lies with the executive branch of government.

priate checks and balances to ensure account-ability, responsiveness and openness. The objection was based primarily on the fact that, in terms of NT 179(1), the National Director of Public Prosecutions is appointed by the President as head of the national executive. There is no substance in this contention. The prosecuting authority is not part of the judiciary and CP VI has no application to it. In any event, even if it were part of the judiciary, the mere fact that the appointment of the head of the national prosecuting authority is made by the President does not in itself contravene the doctrine of separation of powers.

[142] The decision in *Ex parte Attorney-General, Namibia: In 're: The Constitutional Relationship between the Attorney-General and the Prosecutor-General* was relied upon in support of the objection. This case stressed the importance of the prosecuting authority in a constitutional state being independent and pointed to the potential danger of empowering political appointees to decide whether or not prosecutions should be instituted.

[143] The dispute in *Ex parte Attorney-General* arose out of the terms of the Namibian Constitution which provide that there should be an Attorney-General and a Prosecutor-General. The Attorney-General is a political appointment and holds office at the discretion of the President without any security of tenure. The Prosecutor-General is appointed by the President on the recommendation of the Judicial Service Commission and under the Constitution is vested with the power to prosecute in the name of the Republic of Namibia. The Court had to construe the Constitution and determine whether the Prosecutor-General was subject to the instructions of the Attorney-General. It concluded that he was not.

[144] In the course of the judgment reference was made to the lack of uniformity in Commonwealth countries in regard to the status of the prosecuting authority. It was said that '. . . there is no single policy to be discerned in these countries as their constitutions have adopted different models and, in some cases, a hybrid mixture. Moreover in none of them has the same language been used as in the Constitution of Namibia'.

[145] *Ex parte Attorney-General* was concerned with the application of the particular prosecuting model selected by the Namibian Constitution. The decision as to the model to be adopted for the prosecuting authority in the NT is not prescribed by the CPs and was a decision to be taken by the CA. If that decision complies with the requirements of the CPs we have no power to set it aside. The choice that was made is not inconsistent with CP VII nor with any other of the CPs.

[146] NT 179(4) provides that the national legislation must ensure that the prosecuting authority exercises its functions without fear, favour or prejudice. There is accordingly a constitutional guarantee of independence, and any legislation or executive action inconsistent therewith would be subject to constitutional control by the courts. In the circumstances, the objection to NT 179 must be rejected.

In the *First Certification* decision, the Court acknowledges that the constitution-makers selected a certain model of separation of powers making prosecution decisions subject to executive control. The Court draws attention to s 179(4), which provides that '[N]ational Legislation must ensure that the prosecuting authority exercises its functions without fear, favour or prejudice'. This, the Court states, is a constitutional guarantee of independence.[94] Any legislation, or executive action inconsistent with this independence would be subject to the Court's control. There are various examples of theoretical situations where prosecutions may be carried out with favour and prejudice.[95] For example, let us say that it can be established that there is a pattern of prosecuting black but not white youths. Affected parties who can surmount technical barriers such as standing,

---

[94] *Certification I* para 146.
[95] *Yick Wo v Hopkins* 118 US 356 (1886) (where the SC invalidated action which targeted people of Chinese ancestry).

can under s 38 of the Constitution challenge the way the executive enforces the law, including the way prosecutions are conducted, based on grounds of equality, or other violations in the Bill of Rights. In *City Council of Pretoria v Walker*,[96] the applicants successfully challenged the City Council of Pretoria's actions of prosecuting only residents in predominantly white areas for non-payment for water and electricity, while not taking any legal action against residents in predominantly black areas. The Court, *per* Langa DP, held that the conduct of the council officials constituted a violation of the equality clause.[97]

Similarly, any legislation that detracts from the prosecuting authority exercising its functions in an impartial manner can also be subject to scrutiny. Suppose legislation is drawn up in a way that gives the prosecuting authority discretion to target a particular racial group. Such legislation offends the Constitution and the Court would be required to strike it down.

However, as the Court acknowledges in the *First Certification* decision, the Constitution also proclaims in s 179(6): '[T]he Cabinet member responsible for the administration of justice must exercise final responsibility over the prosecuting authority.' What controls are there on the executive's failure to enforce the law? Suppose the legislature passes a law forbidding donations from corporations to political parties. Responsibility for enforcing the law lies with the executive branch, more specifically the NDPP, and ultimately the cabinet member responsible for the administration of justice.[98] Assume, for example, that the NDPP receives information that certain large corporations have made donations to various

political parties. The NDPP does not take action against the corporations, nor the political parties. The executive do not believe that there was any violation of the law. Can another organ of government, or a private party, bring an action requiring the NDPP to take action against the corporations and the political parties?

Under the Irish Constitution, individuals even though they are not directly harmed by the executive's conduct, are allowed to challenge the executive's enforcement of the law.[99] The Irish Supreme Court's position is premised largely on the fear that the A-G himself may be the defendant, and it would be inappropriate to have a situation that any legal action can only be brought with the consent of the wrongdoer.[100] Under the Irish Constitution, the A-G is not a member of the government.[101]

The Criminal Procedure Act also permits private enforcement actions.[102] While the Constitution requires that the prosecutorial function be carried out without fear, favour, or prejudice, it also states that the cabinet member responsible for the administration of justice is ultimately responsible for the prosecuting authority.[103] Resolution of disputes pertaining to enforcement powers depends on how one interprets executive power. Where the law gives the executive the power to interpret certain facts and apply those facts to various situations (unlike the appropriation example where the law imposed a duty on the executive to act in a certain way), courts should accord the executive discretion in interpreting the facts. Decisions to prosecute would come under this discretionary power.[104] Under this interpretation, there should be no right to compel the executive

---

[96] *City Council of Pretoria v Walker* CCT 8/97 (17 February 1998) now cited as 1998 (2) SA 363 (CC); 1998 (3) BCLR 257 (CC).

[97] *Supra* paras 87, 91.

[98] Section 179(6) of the Constitution.

[99] LM Kelly, et al *The Irish Constitution* Dublin: Butterworths 1994, 318–19.

[100] Kelly 319.

[101] Article 30(4) of the Irish Constitution.

[102] Sections 5758 of the Criminal Procedure Act 51 of 1977.

[103] Section 179(6) of the Constitution.

[104] See *Heckler v Chaney* 470 US 821 (1985). Here the Court ruled, eg that the failure of the executive branch of government to regulate drugs used in executions is not subject to judicial review. In other words, the power to execute the law lies with the executive branch of government.

to execute a particular interpretation of the law.[105] Unfortunately, some judges have seen it fit to question the judgement of the A-G regarding how he exercises his powers and interprets facts in particular cases, based on the fact that the appointment of the A-G is a political act.[106] The separation of power model under the Constitution is a political choice made by the political leaders. This is not to say that executive wrongdoing is immune to judicial or other controls. As we have stated, where there is a violation of individual rights, the aggrieved person has the ability to seek redress before the courts. In addition, there are political checks ensuring executive wrongdoing does not go unpunished. There are other independent constitutional organs that can intervene politically such as the Public Protector, the Human Rights and Gender Commissions. In addition, there are direct political checks such as parliamentary censure of the executive. The political checks and the contribution of the other independent constitutional organs should not be underestimated.[107] For example, in the United States, although the enforcement of the law is an executive function, this did not prevent the prosecution of President Nixon and other high-ranking executive officials during the Watergate crisis.[108] The political spotlight on the president made it difficult for President Nixon to dismiss the Special Prosecutor whom he himself had appointed. Separation of powers means checks and balances that include political checks. It could be that mechanisms might be needed to ensure that when wrongdoing on the part of high-ranking executive officers is alleged, these allegations are investigated and prosecuted by an independent prosecutor outside the executive.[109] These are special situations that will need to be dealt with as South African democracy matures. Outside these special situations, the enforcement power should not be taken out of the hand of the executive branch.

The civil service and separation of powers: different approaches

Different public service models

The role of the civil service (public service) does not always fall under the doctrine of separation of powers. Some countries, such as Germany and France, attempt to separate public servants from the other two branches of government. In others, such as Britain, most public servants serve at the will of the executive.[110]

Germany and France represent what are referred to as the 'classic' system of bureaucracy. For example, the German Basic Law gives a permanent status to the civil servant.[111] According to this model, the civil servants must perform their tasks in the interest of the public without political concerns. Members of the bureaucracy are recruited to take up a career in the public service after passing a public service examination.[112] These countries define the circumstances under which civil servants can lose their jobs. If the civil servant is made redundant, compensation must be

---

[105] In the US under the Ethics in Government Act of 1978, executive officers could be investigated by an independent council appointed by a federal judge. However, even then, an independent council investigation was only triggered, if the A-G believed that there was a specific and credible evidence of wrongdoing. The Act lapsed as from 2000.

[106] See criticisms of Van der Walt J in refusing to accede to the A-Gs request that bail is to be granted to the accused. (1998) 11–17 December *Mail and Guardian* 3.

[107] In *Nixon v Fitzgerald* 457 US 731 (1982) (the USSC emphasized that apart from the legal process, there are a number of additional safeguards against executive misconduct including impeachment and constant scrutiny by the media. *Nixon*, at 732.

[108] See *United States v Nixon* 418 US 683 (1974).

[109] eg in the US, the Ethics in Government Act of 1978 allowed for the appointment of an independent council by a special division of the Court of Appeals (District of Columbia Circuit), to investigate and prosecute violations of federal criminal laws by high-ranking officials of the executive branch.

[110] As a result of recent legislation, Britain falls into this category. See Patricia Greer *Transforming Central Government: The Next Steps Initiative* Buckingham: Open University Press 1994, 102.

[111] Article 33 of the German Basic Law.

[112] Ferrell Heady 'Bureaucracies' in *Encyclopedia of Government and Politics*, edited by Mary Hawkesworth and Maurice Kogan. London: Routledge 1992, 306–7.

paid.[113] If the civil servant is dismissed for disciplinary reasons, an elaborate administrative procedure has to be followed.[114]

The idea of a professional and secure civil service is to provide continuity, in an impartial non-political way, in the administration of the state. In mature constitutional systems, where there is a change in government, there are sometimes criticisms that civil servants who become accustomed to the habits and ways in which the old government did things are 'defeatist', and work to obstruct the policies of the new government.[115] By the 1980s, there was a perception by some, in Britain that it was difficult to efficiently implement the policies of a new government with a cadre of civil servants appointed by the old government. Britain finally moved towards the abolition of the permanent civil service. Under current British practice, the executive has the right to change its employees' conditions of service, and employees hold their appointments at the pleasure of the Crown.[116]

Historically in South Africa, the government could alter or terminate the terms of employment of public servants at the government's discretion, subject only to any statutory regulation.[117] Unlike, for example, the Constitution of Germany, which explicitly provides that the status of civil servants shall be protected,[118] the South African Constitution does not expressly guarantee the jobs of the present civil servants. However, unlike the position in Britain, s 195 of the Constitution contains certain basic values and principles which should govern public administration. These include a high standard of professional ethics, efficiency, impartiality, accountability, transparency, and representativeness.

The Constitution in s 197(1), requires the public service to be structured in terms of national legislation. Section 197(2) states that the terms and conditions of public service be regulated by national legislation. The values in s 195 have to underlie legislation that governs the public service. It is possible for the legislature, in furtherance of the values and principles contained in s 195, to provide tenure for certain civil servants. However, there is no requirement to provide tenure. In adopting legislation protecting civil servants, once again the legislature and the courts have to be mindful of two important principles. First, the courts have to consider the context within which South Africa operates, namely a civil service inherited from an old order, against the backdrop of the urgent need to effectively implement socio-economic restructuring.[119] Secondly, executive power should not be encroached upon in violation of the principle of separation of powers.

Basic values and principles: the context

Section 195 of the Constitution spells out the basic values and principles governing public administration: values and principles that have to be interpreted in the context and reality of the South African order. The context and reality is that the overwhelming number of civil servants having been appointed to their positions by the old order, now have to fulfil the mandates of what is essentially a new order. It should be appropriate for the government to take special measures to make the public service more representative, and to instil confidence in the public service. This may require the retiring of and differing treatment of civil

---

[113] F Ridley and J Blondel *Public Administration in France* London: Routledge, 2nd edition, 1969, 46.

[114] Ridley & Blondel 46.

[115] Cabinet members in Prime Minister James Callaghan's Labour Party criticized the civil servants for obstructing the government policies and members of Margaret Thatcher's Conservative Party did likewise when the Conservative Party assumed the government in 1979. See Dennis Kavanagh 'Politics of Great Britain' in *Modern Political Systems: Europe*, edited by Roy C Macridis Englewood Cliffs: Prentice Hall, 7th edition, 1990, 52–3.

[116] *R v Kent County Council ex parte Ashford Borough Council and Others*, 1992 QB LEXIS co/1116/92, at 30 (QB 20 July 1992).

[117] *Sachs v Donges* 1950 (2) SA 265 (A) paras 283–284.

[118] Article 33 of the German Basic Law.

[119] See Ziyad Motala 'Socio-economic Rights, Federalism and the Courts: Comparative Lessons For South Africa' (1995) 112 *South African Law Journal* 61, 63– 9. The author also offers the contextual and systemic method as an approach which the Constitutional Court should adopt in interpreting the socioeconomic provisions of the Constitution.

servants from the old order. There is an instructive lesson to be learned from the approach by the German Constitutional Court in the *Civil Servant* case, which has interesting parallels with the South African situation.[120] After the Second World War, the German government elected to cut the pensions and other benefits of some former civil servants who had served under the Nazi order. One of the issues involved in the *Civil Servant* case, and the *Gestapo* case, was whether the German state was responsible for the claims of public employees who were employed by the Nazi regime and had subsequently lost their tenure, pension, and other privileges accorded to civil servants in Germany. In the *Gestapo* case, the German Constitutional Court observed that the transformation from the Third Reich to the Federal Republic of Germany amounted to more than a change in government, but in effect amounted to a new order. In both the *Civil Servant* case and the *Gestapo* case, the German Constitutional Court ruled that it would be wrong to force the new order to respect the entitlements that civil servants had obtained under the Nazi regime.[121] It is no secret that the majority of civil servants in the South African situation are conservative whites appointed under the apartheid regime.

In South Africa, the problem is more dramatic in that the change is not just a civil service appointed by the old government, but involves a civil service appointed by an old order, which is now entrusted with the responsibility of implementing the policies of the new order. The current civil service is in the position to exercise an anesthetizing influence on major reforms.[122] To reduce this influence, there is a need for new blood in the civil service so as to make the service proactive and less obstructionist. With less civil service obstructionism, the new order will more easily be able to implement policies adopted by the democratically elected legislature.[123] For example, the achievement of recon-

struction and development is important for the success and legitimacy of the new order; the new order cannot afford to have a recalcitrant civil service distort its policies. At this stage in South African history, a very important goal is efficient governance in the transformation of South African society, requiring an accountable and energetic executive. The executive branch of government should have a large degree of discretion with respect to the composition of the public service in the execution of the much-needed social and economic transformation. The nature of change in South Africa is not just in the sphere of government, but a revolutionary change in the entire *Grundnorm* of the legal system from an unrepresentative racist system to a non-racial democratic order. Clearly, South Africa cannot afford to retain forms of 'order' that fail to promote democracy. The Constitution has enough flexibility to allow the issue of job security for civil servants to be dealt with in stages. It is only after the public service has been overhauled and made representative that there should be job protection for certain categories of the public service. Parliament can adopt the model of giving civil servants job tenure. Parliament can also define the criteria for job tenure and removal. However, whatever criteria parliament adopts, such criteria should not encroach on executive power.

Towards an appropriate understanding of separation of powers and the position of the public servant

Section 195(4) of the Constitution provides that the appointment 'of a number of persons on policy considerations is not precluded, but national legislation must regulate these appointments in the public service'. The question is how far can parliament go in regulating these appointments and

---

[120] *See* the *Civil Servant Loyalty* case (1975) 39 BVerfGE 334 and the *Gestapo* case (1957) 6 BVerfGE 132. For a discussion of these cases, see Donald P Kommers *The Constitutional Jurisprudence of the Federal Republic of Germany* Durham: Duke University Press 1989, 233, 263.

[121] Kommers 233, 263.

[122] For an overview of this phenomena in Britain, see Greer. 104. Similar concerns with respect to the civil servants role in SA were expressed by delegates at the last ANC Conference in Bloemfontein in December 1994.

[123] Greer 104.

dismissals. It is arguable that parliament can regulate the rank at which people are employed, as well as the salaries of individuals at different ranks. However, the ultimate responsibility for executive appointments and dismissals of executive appointments must lie with the executive branch. Presumably, policy appointments include individuals that are performing purely executive functions, such as a special adviser to a cabinet member. The president or cabinet member must be free to select close advisers based on individual requirements. Similarly, they must be able to dismiss executive officials in whom they have no confidence. Seeing that the executive is accountable to the legislature, the appropriate approach with respect to executive officers is to allow the executive discretion in the hiring of the civil service, which is responsible for executing the law. Under this concept of separation of powers, it is the executive branch of government that is responsible for executing the law. Therefore, the executive branch should be able to choose the personnel responsible for that execution. If the programmes of the legislature are not adequately executed, it is the executive under this scheme of separation of powers that should be called to task for this failure.

On the other hand, s 195(1) could be interpreted to require a professional and secure civil service, to provide continuity, in an impartial non-political way, in the administration of the state. If so, job security for public servants should be approached in terms of whether the official is engaged in activities of either an executive or an administrative nature. In terms of separation of powers, parliament could have the final say on the appointment and termination of that part of the civil service involved in administrative functions. In other words, the question of whether a particular appointee is ultimately subject to executive control, or can be subject to parliamentary control, should be approached in terms of a functional test whether the job in question is executive or administrative in function.

Insofar as s 197(1) of the Constitution provides that the terms and conditions of service of employees in public administration shall be regulated by national legislation, and that s 195(4) allows for policy appointees, this allows the legislature latitude to adopt appropriate legislation to approach job security in terms of the functional test. However, parliament in exercising its powers in s 195(4) should be consistent with separation of powers principles. The president's ability to carry out his or her executive duties will be materially affected if he or she is fettered in appointing and dismissing executive officials. For example, it would be inappropriate for parliament to require parliamentary approval for the hiring and firing of the president's chief of staff. The tenure provisions in the Public Service Act of 1994 removed the power of executive control over civil servants, even where the civil servant in question is exercising powers in the executive realm. For example, the previous section of the Public Service Act of 1994, providing that the provisions of the Act shall not apply to executive officers without the recommendation of the commission, was untenable.[124] A free-floating agency such as the Public Service Commission should not act as a fetter on the executive when the executive needs to make executive appointments. Similarly, to the extent that the Public Service Act attempted to define 'executing authority' and restricted the definition to a few persons, this ignored the wide number of individuals that could be involved in executive functions, and amounted to a limitation of executive control over individuals engaged in executive functions.[125]

The issue of job security for public service employees should be approached in terms of separation of powers principles, and more specifically in terms of whether the acts performed by the individual public servant pertain to an executive or administrative function. If the activity in question is classified as executive in nature, then the executive branch of government should have discretion about the hiring and termination of

---

[124] Section 2(4) of the Public Service Act of 103 of 1994, now amended under Public Service Laws Amendment Act 47 of 1997 and the Public Service Commission Act 46 of 1997.

[125] Section 2(4) of the Public Service Act 103 of 1994. Chapter 1 of the Act defined 'executing authority' as referring to the office of the president, deputy president, ministers, premiers of provinces and members of the executive council of the provinces.

the employee.[126] If the activity in question is of an administrative nature, than there could be limitations on the ability of the executive branch of government to terminate those individuals.[127] The functional approach draws inspiration from the early United States Supreme Court's approach in *Myers v United States*, where the Supreme Court declared legislation providing for a restriction on the president's removal power in the executive realm as unconstitutional.[128] Myers stands for the proposition that the head of the executive branch of government shall have the power to appoint and remove state officers because this power is integrally related to the president's ability to ensure that laws are faithfully executed. The president, in order to effectively execute the laws, must be able to discipline subordinate officials.

On the other hand, an administrative act involves a ministerial act in a mechanical fashion.[129] The Constitution does not contain a list of executive and administrative functions. Instead, it allows for the legislature to define the different functions through legislation. It is not practical to define the different functions in the Constitution, because there might be a need for a job-by-job determination of whether the particular function involves either an executive or an administrative act. The appropriate categorization will have to be worked out through experience, and through a process of consultation between the legislature, executive, and the constitutionally created Public Service Commission. In addition to s 195(4), which allows for the appointment of persons based on policy considerations, s 195(5) allows for different laws for the various sectors, administrations or institutions in public administration.

The legislature can, through appropriate legislation, insulate administrative officers from executive control. This provides continuity (in an impartial non-political way), in the administrative functions of the state, and the ability to realize the many values spelt out in s 195(1) including professionalism, efficiency, and impartiality. Again, the appropriate legislation should only pertain to administrative functions, and not to executive functions. To take a rudimentary example, someone working in the post office should not be removed from service simply because there is a change in the executive branch of government. Similarly, someone involved in clerical work in some ministry, or a school teacher, should not be removed when there is a change in the executive. However, if there is an official who is entrusted with supervising the way that the post office fulfils its mandate on, for example, a regional basis, it might be appropriate for the executive branch of government to make an executive appointment in terms of s 195(4). Similarly, the director-general in a ministry should also be considered as an executive official. Such an individual should serve as an executive appointee and not as part of an 'impartial' public service.

Independent constitutional organs and state institutions supporting constitutional democracy under the Constitution

Section 181(1) of Chapter 9 of the Constitution creates various independent state institutions separate from the executive and legislature.[130] Section 181 provides:

---

[126] *Myers v United States* 272 US 52, 134 (1926).

[127] See USSC approach in *Bowsher v Synar* 478 US 714, 106 SCt 3181 (1986).

[128] *Myers v United States* 272 US 52 (1926). In this case the statute in question placed a restriction on the president's ability to remove the Postmaster-General without the advice and consent of the US Senate. President Wilson removed Myers on his own arguing that the act of removal was an executive act. The SC sided with the president in declaring that the power of removal of executive officers is part of the power of appointment, and therefore the president has exclusive power of removing officers of the US. *Myers v United States* 272 US at 119.

[129] *Bowsher v Synar* 478 US 714, 732 (1986).

[130] Some of which are defined in Schedule 6, s 520(1) as a 'constitutional institution'.

State Institutions Supporting Constitutional Democracy

Establishment and governing principles

181 (1) The following state institutions strengthen constitutional democracy in the Republic:

(a) The Public Protector.

(b) The Human Rights Commission.

(c) The Commission for the Promotion and Protection of the Rights of Cultural, Religious and Linguistic Communities

(d) The Commission for Gender Equality.

(e) The Auditor-General.

(f) The Electoral Commission.

(2) These institutions are independent, and subject only to the Constitution and the law, and they must be impartial and must exercise their powers and perform their functions without fear, favour or prejudice.

(3) Other organs of state, through legislative and other measures, must assist and protect these institutions to ensure the independence, impartiality, dignity and effectiveness of these institutions.

(4) No person or organ of state may interfere with the functioning of these institutions.

(5) These institutions are accountable to the National Assembly, and must report on their activities and the performance of their functions to the Assembly at least once a year.

In addition, there are various provisions calling for independent bodies to regulate various activities. For example, s 192 requires the creation of an independent broadcasting authority (IBA) to regulate broadcasting in the public interest. Section 196(1) requires the creation of a Public Service Commission (PSC) to advise and oversee the public service. Section 220 requires the establishment of a Financial and Fiscal Commission, which has to be consulted on various matters including government guarantees,[131] and salaries for the members of the executive, the legislature, other organs of government.[132] Section 223 requires the establishment of the South African Reserve Bank, to protect the value of the currency. All these bodies are all required to perform their functions in an independent fashion,[133] and will be referred to as 'independent constitutional organs'.

The state institutions, created under s 181, have investigative and promotional power designed to strengthen democracy. Under s 181(2), the institutions created under s 181 are required to be independent, impartial, and to perform their activities free from political controls. The organs under s 181 are also independent constitutional organs. Given their independence, they constitute a fourth branch of government nominally accountable to the legislature and do not fit easily into the traditional framework of separation of powers. Some of them fulfil executive and others legislative functions, some both legislative and executive functions, some advisory functions, and yet others adjudicative functions. For example, the IBA is required to regulate broadcasting, entailing both lawmaking and administrative functions. The Financial and Fiscal Commission and the PSC primarily have consultative and investigative powers but no lawmaking or enforcement powers. These independent constitutional organs created under s 181 have largely investigative, promotional, and monitoring power. The Electoral Commission has enforcement powers under s 190(1)(b) powers serving to ensure that elections are free and fair. They also have adjudicative functions under s 190(1)(c), because they have to adjudicate the results of elections. The Constitu-

---

[131] Section 218 of the Constitution.

[132] Sections 219(1)(a) and 219(1)(b).

[133] Sections 192, 196(2), 220(3), and 224(2) of the Constitution, for example. Section 192 requires the independent authority to regulate broadcasting in a fair manner; s 196(2) states the PSC must be independent and impartial, and s 220(3) requires the Financial and Fiscal Commission to be independent and impartial. Similarly, s 224(2) states that the SA Reserve Bank must perform its functions independently without fear, favour, or prejudice.

tion permits assigning additional powers to the institutions created under s 181(1).[134]

The independence of the independent constitutional organs is guaranteed in the Constitution which limits the circumstances for removal of members serving on these bodies. Under s 194(1)(a), members serving on bodies created under s 181 can only be removed on grounds of misconduct, incapacity, or incompetence. Such a finding must, under s 194(1)(b), be supported by a committee of the NA. In addition, under s 194(2)(a), the removal of the Public Protector or the Auditor-General, entails the NA passing a resolution supported by at least two thirds of the NA. Under s 194(2)(b), the removal of a member of a commission, entails the NA passing a resolution supported by at least a majority of the NA. Similarly, under s 196(10), members of the PSC may only be removed on grounds of misconduct, incapacity, or incompetence. Under s 196(10)(b), a finding by a committee of the NA, or a committee of the province is required for the removal of a commissioner by the premier of a province. This finding under s 196(11)(c) has to be affirmed by the adoption of a resolution by the NA, or the relevant legislature of the province before the president can remove a commissioner. Although the Constitution does not contain any express job protections for members of the Reserve Bank, the Constitutional Court in the *First Certification* decision stated that if parliament attempted to act in a way which compromised the independence and impartiality of the Reserve Bank, its actions would violate the Constitution.[135]

In the *First Certification* decision, the Court described the function of the Public Protector by stating that:

[161] The purpose of the office of Public Protector is to ensure that there is an effective public service which

maintains a high standard of professional ethics. NT 182(1) provides that the Public Protector has the power 'to investigate any conduct in state affairs, or in the public administration in any sphere of government, that is alleged or suspected to be improper or to result in any impropriety or prejudice'. NT 182(4) provides that the Public Protector must be 'accessible to all persons and communities'. The Public Protector is an office modelled on the institution of the ombudsman, whose function is to ensure that government officials carry out their tasks effectively, fairly and without corruption or prejudice. The NT clearly envisages that members of the public aggrieved by the conduct of government officials should be able to lodge their complaints with the Public Protector, who will investigate them and take appropriate remedial action.

The Court described the role and position of the Auditor-General in the following way:

[164] Like the Public Protector, the Auditor-General is to be a watch-dog over the government. However, the focus of the office is not inefficient or improper bureaucratic conduct, but the proper management and use of public money. To that end, NT 188 provides that the Auditor-General must audit and report on the accounts, financial statements and financial management of all national and provincial state departments and administrations as well as municipalities. The reports of the Auditor-General must be made public and they must also be submitted to any legislature that has a direct interest in the audit. NT 181(2) provides that the office of Auditor-General should be independent and that the powers and functions of the office should be exercised without fear, favour or prejudice. NT 189 provides that the tenure of the Auditor-General must be for a fixed, non-renewable term of between five and ten years. Appointment and removal provisions are the same as those that apply to the Public Protector.

The Court described the role and position of the Reserve Bank in the following way:

---

[134] Section 182(2) allows additional powers and functions to be assigned to the Public Protector; s 184(4) allows additional powers and functions to be assigned to the Human Rights Commission; s 185(4) allows additional powers and functions to be assigned to the Commission for Promotion and Protection of the Rights of Cultural, Religious and Linguistic Communities; s 187(3) allows additional powers and functions to be assigned to the Commission for Gender Equality, and s 188(4) allows additional powers and functions to be assigned to the Auditor-General. Similarly, s 190(2) allows additional powers and functions to be assigned to the Electoral Commission.

[135] *First Certification* decision para 168.

[166] The Reserve Bank is institutionally and functionally very different from both the Public Protector and the Auditor-General. Unlike those two institutions, its primary purpose is not to monitor government. The NT states that its primary object is to protect the value of the currency in the interest of economic growth. The independence and impartiality of the Bank therefore do not require the same type of protection provided to the other two institutions NT 224 provides that in pursuit of its primary object, the Bank must perform its functions independently and without fear, favour or prejudice.

[168] A second objection raised was that the NT contains no provisions relating to the appointment, tenure and removal of the Governor of the Reserve Bank or of its Board of Directors. These matters are currently dealt with in legislation. It was argued that this was a failure to meet the terms of CP XXIX. Given the purpose and nature of the institution, however, it is in our view unnecessary to place such provisions in the Constitution. If the national legislation were to include provisions concerning appointment, tenure and removal which compromised the independence and impartiality of the institution, then such provisions could well be challenged in terms of the Constitution.

[169] The third objection is that NT 224(2), which provides that there shall be regular consultation between the Bank and the member of the executive responsible for financial matters, compromises its independence and impartiality. We cannot adopt the interpretation of the provision offered by the objectors. If the executive interferes with the independence and impartiality of the Bank, that conduct can be challenged. The requirement for consultation in no way undermines the independence of the Bank. Accordingly, the provisions relating to the Reserve Bank comply with the CPs.

The Court described the role and position of the PSC in the following way:

Public Service Commission

[170] The last institution mentioned in CP XXIX is the Public Service Commission (the 'PSC'). Two CPs are relevant to this institution, CP XXIX, which is quoted above, and CP XXX.1, which provides:

'There shall be an efficient, nonpartisan, career orientated public service broadly representative of the South African community, functioning on a basis of fairness and which shall serve all members or [sic] the public in an unbiased and impartial manner, and shall, in the exercise of its powers and in compliance with its duties, loyally execute the lawful policies of the government of the day in the performance of its administrative functions. The structures and functioning of the public service, as well as the terms and conditions of service of its members, shall be regulated by law.'

The CPs require appointments to the public service to meet the criteria set out in CP XXX, but do not require any particular procedures to be followed in making such appointments. As far as CP XXX.1 is concerned, its requirements are met by NT 197 read with NT 195. It is implicit in CP XXIX that an independent PSC should have some role in the process of appointing, promoting, transferring and dismissing members of the public service, but what that role should be is not defined. The institution of an independent public service commission to check executive power in respect of employment in the civil service comes to us from England and is a feature of the constitutions of many Commonwealth countries. The role of a public service commission is to promote fairness and maintain efficiency and standards in the public service. To this end it is usually required to report on its activities to Parliament. The purpose is to ensure that prescribed procedures for making appointments, promotions, transfers and dismissals are adhered to, and that any deficiencies in the organisation and administration of the public service, or the application of fair employment practices, are made public. There is, however, no uniformity in regard to the powers vested in a public service commission for the purposes of carrying out its duties.

Are the terms 'misconduct, incapacity or incompetence' subject to judicial standards? As in the case of the removal of judges, it is arguable that these are more political than legal standards.[136] As the Court noted in passing, in the *Second Certification* decision, that the political conse-

---

[136] All exercise of political power is subject to the legality principle. See *SARFU 2* para 121; *Pharmaceutical Manufacturers Association* para 83 and 85. As in the case of discretionary power of the executive, it is only in the most extreme cases such as bad faith, bribery, or fraud that the Court should intervene.

quences from an abuse of this power are likely to be considerable.[137]

Where power is conferred on an independent constitutional organ through the Constitution or by legislation, the executive branch can neither usurp the power of the independent constitutional organ, nor can it exercise a veto power over how an independent constitutional organ carries out its functions. In *Executive Council of the Western Cape*, the Constitutional Court invalidated ss 2 and 4 of the Local Government: Municipal Structures Act,[138] because under these provisions, the minister was empowered to fix the boundaries for various wards over the Independent Demarcation Board. Section 155(3)*(b)* of the Constitution sought to create a process whereby new municipalities would be created without political interference. The function of determining political boundaries is entrusted to an independent authority, namely the Demarcation Board.[139] The exercise of power by the minister to fix the points of municipal boundaries was invalid and amounted to a usurpation of the power of an independent constitutional organ.[140] Similarly, when an independent constitutional organ exercises its power, it cannot be constrained by the national government. In *Executive Council of the Western Cape*, the Court invalidated s (6)(2) of the Structures Act, which attempted to give the minister discretion as to whether to accept the recommendation of the Demarcation Board as to the demarcation of municipal boundaries.[141]

Although their budget is set by parliament, independent constitutional organs have financial independence from executive control.[142] The executive branch of government cannot exercise control over the budget of an independent constitutional organ.[143] Similarly, an independent constitutional organ has administrative independence over matters pertaining to their functions under the Constitution or in terms of legislation.[144] This independence includes the power to employ whom it wishes.[145]

Executive Council of the Province of the Western Cape v The Minister for Provincial Affairs and Constitutional Development and Another; The Executive Council of KwaZulu-Natal v The President of the Republic of South Africa and Another **CCT 15/99; (2) CCT 18/99 (15 October 1999), now cited as 2000 (1) SA 661 (CC); 1999 (12) BCLR 1360 (CC)** (notes omitted)

[1] These two cases raise important questions relating to the authority to establish municipalities and their internal structures. They arise out of a dispute between the governments of the Western Cape and KwaZulu-Natal, on the one hand, and the national government on the other. The dispute concerns the constitutionality of certain provisions of the Local Government: Municipal Structures Act, No 117 of 1998 ('the Structures Act'). The Structures Act became law on 11 December 1998, but only came into operation on 1 February 1999 ...

[2] The Western Cape government instituted proceedings in this Court on 26 April 1999, on an urgent basis. In its notice of motion it challenged the constitutional validity of sections 5(1) and (2), 6(2), 13(2), 40 to 80, 82 and 91(1) ...

[13] Section 155 deals with the establish-

---

[137] *Certification of Amended Text* para 143.

[138] Act 117 of 1998 (Structures Act).

[139] *Executive Council of the Western Cape* CCT 15/99 paras 50, 54–55.

[140] *Supra* para 58.

[141] *Supra* para 68.

[142] *Supra* para 98.

[143] *The New National Party of South Africa v The Government of the Republic of South Africa and Others* CCT 9/99 (13 April 1999) paras 89 and 96, now cited as 1999 (5) BCLR 489 (CC); 1999 (3) SA 191 (CC).

[144] *Supra* para 99.

[145] *Supra*.

ment of municipalities. It makes provision for three different categories of municipality, namely, category A, self-standing municipalities, category B, municipalities that form part of a comprehensive co-ordinating structure, and category C, municipalities that perform co-ordinating functions. In addition, it also makes provision for national legislation to define different types of municipality that may be established within each such category. It sets out a scheme for the allocation of powers and functions between the national government, provincial government and the Demarcation Board in relation to the establishment of municipalities. In terms of this scheme: (a) national legislation must establish criteria for determining which category of municipality should be established in a particular area, must define the types of municipality that may be established within each such category, must establish criteria and procedures for the determination of municipal boundaries by an independent authority (which is the Demarcation Board), and must make provision for the division of powers and functions between municipalities with shared powers; (b) the Demarcation Board must determine the municipal boundaries in accordance with the criteria and procedures established by such national legislation;19 and (c) provincial legislation must determine which types of municipality should be established in its province. In addition, provincial governments 'must establish municipalities' in their provinces 'in a manner consistent with the legislation enacted in terms of subsections (2) and (3)' of section 155.

[34] Sections 4 and 5 of the Structures Act provide:

Application of criteria

4 (1) The Minister must apply the criteria set out in section 2 and determine whether an area in terms of the criteria must have a single category A municipality or whether it must have municipalities of both category C and category B.

  (2) The Minister may determine that an area must have a category A municipality only after consultation with the MEC for local government in the province concerned, the Demarcation Board, SALGA and organised local government in the province.

Declaration of metropolitan areas

5 (1) If the Minister determines that an area must have a single category A municipality, the Minister, by notice in the *Government Gazette*, must declare that area as a metropolitan area.

  (2) When declaring an area as a metropolitan area the Minister designates the area by identifying the nodal points of the area but must leave the determination of the outer boundaries to the Demarcation Board.'

[35] The principal issue for determination in this regard is the location of the power to apply the criteria for determining the categories of municipality. The relevant provision of the Constitution is section 155, which deals with the establishment of municipalities.

[50] The purpose of section 155(3)(*b*) may well have been to guard against political interference in the process of creating new municipalities, and to this extent the function of determining municipal boundaries is entrusted to an independent authority.

[54]...The independent authority has to determine the boundaries of the different categories of municipality in accordance with criteria and procedures determined by national legislation. That is also how the independent authority must determine the boundaries of the wards. There seems to be no difference. In my view, the Minister could not be empowered to fix nodal points for each of the wards as this would have adverse implications for democracy. The criteria must be applied by the independent authority in accordance with the prescribed procedures. Once this is accepted, there is no reason why the same should not apply to the application of the criteria to decide where different categories of municipality must be.

[57] National legislation is confined to setting criteria for determining categories and criteria and procedures for the determining of

boundaries. It is not specifically authorized to do more than this. If it was contemplated that national legislation could, in addition to setting criteria for categories, also determine who should apply the criteria, one would have expected this to have been said explicitly. Having regard to the careful allocation of powers in section 155, the omission is not without significance.

[58]...What is important for the purposes of the present case is the fact that the Minister is empowered to fix more than one point, and that the fixing of the points determines whether there will be category A municipalities or not. In addition, this has a material impact on where the boundaries of category A municipalities will be. This, in my view, interferes with the function of the Demarcation Board to determine municipal boundaries.

[59] It follows that, in purporting to authorise the Minister to apply the criteria set out in section 2 of the Structures Act, sections 4 and 5 have fallen foul of the provisions of the Constitution. For that reason they are invalid.

[68] In my view, the problem with section 6(2) lies elsewhere. Upon a proper construction, it gives the Minister a discretion to decide whether to accept the recommendation of the Demarcation Board in relation to where the boundaries should be. In the exercise of this discretion the Minister may, therefore, reject a boundary determined by the Demarcation Board. Yet the scheme for the allocation of powers relating to the structure, functioning and establishment of municipalities contemplates that the Demarcation Board should determine boundaries in accordance with the criteria and procedures prescribed by the legislation contemplated in sections 155(2) and (3), and that it should be able to do this without being constrained in any way by the national or provincial governments. If section 6(2) is to have any meaning, it subjects the decision of the Demarcation Board in relation to the municipal boundaries to the discretion of the Minister. This, in my view, is impermissible. To the extent that section 6(2) of the Structures Act gives the Minister a discretion whether to accept the boundaries determined by the Demarcation Board in respect of categories of municipality, it is inconsistent with sections 155(2) and (3) of the Constitution.

National delegation to other legislative bodies

Introduction

Section 44(1)(iii) of the Constitution allows parliament to delegate legislative powers, with the exception of the power to amend the Constitution, to any legislative body in another sphere of government. This power in terms of the express provisions of the Constitution is directed at other legislative organs such as provincial legislatures, or legislatures at the local government level. Delegation of power to the provinces is a feature that was attempted in Canada and struck down as unconstitutional by the Supreme Court of Canada.[146] Section 44(1)(iii) appears very open-ended and allows parliament to assign 'any of its legislative powers' except constitutional amendments. Arguably, there are additional legislative powers that parliament cannot assign to another legislature. For example, it would be absurd to allow a delegation of power that would allow the provincial legislature to enact legislation directing the national executive on how to develop and implement foreign policy.[147] Similarly, it would also be absurd to allow delegated legislation which authorizes a provincial legislature to pass legislation on the structure of the defence force. The powers delegated under s 44(1)(iii) have to be

---

[146] See Peter W Hogg Constitutional Law of Canada Scarborough: Carswell, 3rd edition, 1992, 353–5. For an overview of the Canadian approach to federal–provincial delegation, see Paul C Weiler 'The Supreme Court and the Law of Canadian Federalism' (1973) 23 University of Toronto Law Journal 307, 311–18.

[147] In re: Constitutionality of the Liquor Bill para 46.

consistent with the structure and purpose of the Constitution. This notion is discussed in further detail below.

Delegation to the executive and independent agencies[148]

The Constitution, in s 85(2)(b), allows an Act of Parliament to remove the power to implement national legislation from the executive and lodge it with another body. In terms of the functional test, it is also possible for the legislature to provide security of tenure for officials in other areas where there is a perceived need to leave decision-making to a non-partisan body of experts. For example, it might be that the legislature wants the approval of drugs to be made by a body of experts, as opposed to the executive. It accordingly creates an agency to perform this task free from executive control. Similarly, it might be that decisions pertaining to environmental standards are better made by an independent body of environmental experts. The Constitution (as mentioned above) also permits assigning additional powers to the independent constitutional organs created under s 181(1).[149] The question is what are the limits on the legislature's ability to take away the power to implement national legislation and lodge it in other agencies separate from the executive. In *Premier of KwaZulu-Natal* case,[150] Mahomed DP alluded to a constitutional amendment that has the 'effect of destroying or abrogating the very essentials upon which the Constitutional Principles are premised' a situation which he said did not arise in that case.[151] Parliament should not through ordinary legislation undermine the core premises of the Constitution.[152] The constitutional validity of taking enforcement powers from the executive, or creating agencies free of executive control, or giving additional enforcement powers to the independent constitutional organs, again has to be evaluated in terms of whether the function which is being transferred involves an executive act, or activity that needs to be performed in an impartial manner, free of executive or other political control. For example, when we looked at the approach of the United States Supreme Court in *Myers*, it ruled that the United States Congress could not limit the ability of the president to remove the Post-Master General because the official in question was fulfilling executive functions.[153] However, in *Humphrey's Executor v United States*,[154] the Court ruled that the legislature could limit the power of the president to remove members of the Federal Trade Commission (FTC), because the legislative history indicated that the goal of congress in all instances, was to leave the decision-making in this area to a non-partisan body of experts.[155] The Court said the FTC was not performing executive functions, but administrative functions in an impartial way in accordance

---

[148] This is an adaption (with permission) from Ziyad Motala 'Towards an Appropriate Understanding of the Separation of Powers, and Accountability of the Executive and Public Service under the New South African Order' (1995) 112 *South African Law Journal* 111.

[149] Section 182(2) allows additional powers and functions to be assigned to the Public Protector; s 184(4) allows additional powers and functions to be assigned to the Human Rights Commission; s 185(4) allows additional powers and functions to be assigned to the Commission for Promotion and Protection of the Rights of Cultural, Religious, and Linguistic Communities, and s 187(3) allows additional powers and functions to be assigned to the Commission for Gender Equality. Section 188(4) allows additional powers and functions to be assigned to the Auditor-General; similarly, s 190(2) allows additional powers and functions to be assigned to the Electoral Commission.

[150] *Premier of Kwazulu-Natal and Others v President of the Republic of South Africa and Others* CCT 36/95.

[151] *Premier of Kwazulu-Natal* para 12.

[152] Mahomed DP characterizes such changes as radically and fundamentally restructuring and reorganizing the fundamental premises of the Constitution. *Premier of KwaZulu-Natal* para 64. Another example of a reorganization of the fundamental premise of the Constitution would arise if the legislature attempted to abdicate its lawmaking power (discussed below), and delegate the lawmaking power to another agency. *See* PH Lane *A Manual of Australian Constitutional Law* Sydney: Law Book Co 1995, 180 (who argues that such a broad delegation is unconstitutional).

[153] *Myers*, 272 US at 185.

[154] *Humphrey's Executor v United States* 295 US 602 (1935).

[155] *Supra* at 623.

with legislative standards created by the legislature.[156]

The corollary is that such an agency should not be an agent of parliament. In other words, parliament should not be able to create these agencies and direct the way they perform their functions. While parliament provides the important standards that agencies should administer, it should not be in a position to hire and fire those involved in administering these policies. For example, in *Metropolitan Washington Airports Authority v Citizens for the Abatement of Aircraft Noise*,[157] the United States Supreme Court ruled that where there is a transfer of power from the executive, the legislature cannot invest itself with the enforcement powers.[158] To rule otherwise would give the legislature enforcement powers, which is a departure from its role of lawmaking.[159] Moreover, any matter involving the execution of law, taken out of executive control, must pertain to activities for which there is a strong need for decisions to be made in an impartial way, free of political control.

The creation of these agencies amounts to a fourth branch of government which upsets traditional separation of powers, and accountability of the executive and the legislature. In many developing countries (including independent African countries), over a period of years the role of the legislature in government has declined, and the role of the bureaucracy has increased. Political decision-making should not be transferred willy-nilly to agencies outside the executive and legislature. The fused model of separation of powers allows parliamentary oversight and accountability of the executive, which is a very important feature. The history of many African countries has shown that where the legislature is weak and not involved in the formulation of laws and policies or in the oversight of the executive, power swings in the first instance to the president and ultimately to the bureaucracy. As a result of the decline in the role of the legislature, many people have looked in the direction of the civil service and bureaucracy, which in the circumstances has come to assume greater influence.[160] The decline in the role of the legislature invariably results in the *de facto* administration being done by bureaucrats.[161] The population has no input into the decisions of the bureaucrats[162] and inevitably bureaucratic actions are taken impulsively or even capriciously.[163] The state now becomes an administrative state as opposed to a representative state. Being part of the administrative machinery of the state confers a status, as well as the power to distribute resources and patronage.[164] Being dismissed from one's job in the state machinery carries the consequences of losing not only power to dispense favours, but also results in the loss of vehicle, housing, and medical benefits, and various other allowances not usually found in other areas of employment.[165] The bureaucracy becomes a self-perpetuating institution. In many instances the obtaining of rewards and jobs occurs along tribal lines or in terms of a system of patronage.[166] The ministries or bureau-

---

[156] *Supra* at 628.

[157] *Metropolitan Washington Airports Authority v Citizens for the Abatement of Aircraft Noise* 501 US 252 (1991).

[158] *Supra* at 282.

[159] *Buckley v Valeo* 478 US 714, 756 (1976).

[160] Michael F Lofchie 'Representative Government, Bureaucracy, and Political Development: The African Case' (1976) 16 *African Administrative Studies* 133.

[161] Lofchie 133.

[162] Christian P Potholm *The Theory and Practice of African Politics* Englewood Cliffs: Prentice-Hall 1979, 89.

[163] RF Hopkins 'The Influence of the Legislature on Development Strategy: The Case of Kenya and Tanzania' in *Legislatures in Development: Dynamics of Change in New and Old States*, edited by Joel Smith and Lloyd D Musolf. Durham: Duke University Press 1979, 168. Section 33 of the Constitution requires just administrative action. Pursuant to the mandate in s 33(3), parliament has passed the Promotion of Administrative Justice Act 3 of 2000. However, as the discussion below illustrates, there are numerous problems with an 'administrative state', particularly in developing countries.

[164] Susanne D Mueller *Government and Opposition in Kenya, 1966–1969* Boston: African Studies Centre 1983, 16.

[165] Mueller 16.

[166] Dirk Berg-Schlosser *Tradition and Change in Kenya: A Comparative Analysis of Seven Major Ethnic Groups* Paderborn: F Schoningh 1984, 655.

cracies in many African countries have collectively presided over great corruption. Vast amounts of money are spent on prestige projects such as monuments, hotels, and mansions for leaders.[167] Being part of the elite, that is a senior member of one of the ministries or bureaucracies, presents the opportunity for self-enrichment, including luxury vehicles, apparel, and other forms of ostentation.[168] At times the corruption is so rife that necessary services such as medical care or access to jobs can be obtained only by bribery or by connections to someone in high office.[169] Those jobs that are available reward workers disproportionately to the services they render, with the bureaucrats taking the lion's share of the rewards.[170] These practices confirm the importance of strengthening democratically elected legislatures, and preserving the prerogative of the legislature to pass laws as well as holding the executive accountable, if the laws are not implemented.

Delegation of power: formalism versus functionalism

Delegation of power raises questions as to whether the separation of powers is to be approached in a rigid fashion,[171] or whether the Constitution envisages a functionalist approach to allow some reallocation of power between the legislative and executive branch of government and within an agency beyond the circumstances mentioned in the Constitution.[172] The answer will depend on whether the Constitution represents a formal, or functional approach, in the allocation of power.[173]

Delegation of power within an agency

The Constitutional Court used a functional approach in *Transvaal Agricultural Union*,[174] where the Court upheld legislation that allowed other persons apart from the Commission on Restitution of Land, to mediate land-claim disputes. At issue here was whether s 122(1)(b) of the interim Constitution required the commission itself to deal with all mediation of land disputes. Parliament adopted a statute that authorized the Chief Land Claims Commissioner to appoint mediators or other persons to assist in settling land disputes. The applicants contended that under s 122(1)(b) of the interim Constitution, the commission was required to conduct all mediation on land disputes in person.[175] The argument that the Constitution in setting up the commission, and giving it certain powers, required this body to carry out only designated functions, represents a formalist approach. The unanimous Court, *per* Chaskalson P, declared that the Constitution should not be interpreted with 'the austerity of tabulated legal-

---

[167] Arnold Rivkin *Nation-building in Africa: Problems and Perspectives* New Brunswick: Rutgers University Press 1969, 58.

[168] Ronald E Wraith *Corruption in Developing Countries* New York: Norton 1964, 15.

[169] Wraith 17.

[170] eg the top 5% of the population in the Ivory Coast obtained 29% of the national income; 64% of the national income went to 20% of the population in Sierra Leone; the bottom 40% of the population in Gabon received only 8% of the national income, while the bottom 40% of the population received only 14% of the income in Nigeria.

See studies reported in Irving L Markowitz *Power and Class in Africa: An Introduction to Change and Conflict in African Countries* Englewood Cliffs: Prentice-Hall 1977, 206–9. See also, Basil Davidson *Which Way Africa? The Search for a New Society* Harmondsworth: Penquin, 3rd edition, 1971, 135.

[171] eg where the USSC approached distribution of power in a rigid and formalistic way, see *Buckley v Valeo* 424 US 1, 135–137 140 (1976). See also *Metropolitan Washington Airports Authority v Citizens for the Abatement of Aircraft Noise* 501 US 252 (1991). In both these cases, the Court refused to allow delegation of power to agents outside the executive branch of government, basing its interpretation on a strict notion of separation of powers.

[172] The following two cases represent examples where the USSC deals with the issue in terms of a functional approach: *Morrison v Olson* (1988) 487 US 654; *Mistretta v United States* (1989) 488 US 361 (1989).

[173] Brian C Murchison 'Interpretation and Independence: How Judges use the Avoidance Canon in Separation of Powers Cases' (1995) 30 *Georgia Law Review* 85, 103.

[174] *Transvaal Agricultural Union v The Minister of Land Affairs and Others* CCT 21/96 (18 November 1996), now cited as 1997 (2) SA 621 (CC); 1996 (2) BCLR 1573 (CC).

[175] *Supra* para 43.

ism'.[176] The Court noted that to accept the applicants arguments would result in inordinate delays since the commission would be required to deal in person with all two million potential claims lodged.[177] While the Court permitted delegation of power from one organ to another in *Transvaal*

Agricultural Union, however, in *SARFU 2* the Court held that the decision to appoint a Commission of Enquiry must, under the Constitution, be made by the president.[178] The exercise of this power cannot be delegated to another executive official.[179]

Transvaal Agricultural Union v The Minister of Land Affairs
CCT/ 21/96 (18 November 1996), now cited as 1997 (2) SA 621 (CC); 1996 (2) BCLR 1573 (CC)
(note omitted)
CHASKALSON P

[1] The Transvaal Agricultural Union is a body established to represent the interests of its members who are farmers. It has applied directly to this Court for an order declaring that sections 6(1)*(c)*, 9(1)*(b)*, 11(1), 11(6)*(b)*, 11(7), 11(8), and 13(2)*(b)* of the Restitution of Land Rights Act 22 of 1994, and rules 13 and 14 of the rules regarding the procedure of the Commission on Restitution of Land Rights, promulgated in terms of section 16(1) of that Act, are inconsistent with the Constitution, and accordingly invalid. The provisions are material to the interests of members of the applicant, and it was not disputed that it has standing in terms of section 7(4)*(b)* of the Constitution to bring this application.

[14] Sections 9(1)*(b)* and 13(2)*(b)* of the Act empower the Chief Land Claims Commissioner to direct that attempts be made to settle a disputed claim for restitution of land rights through mediation. The Commissioner may appoint a mediator for such purposes, or the parties may do so themselves. The applicant contends that this procedure is inconsistent with section 122(1)*(b)* of the Constitution, which, so the contention goes, requires the Commission to undertake the mediation itself.

[42] The Constitution contemplates that the Commission will deal with claims for restitution of land rights in respect of dispossessions effected during a period which could be from 19 June 1913 until 27 April 1994. There is one Commission for the whole country. The first respondent in his answering affidavit says that more than 2 million people may be affected by the provisions of the Act. Over 10 000 claims (some from communities) have already been lodged, and the first respondent anticipates that more than double this number of claims are likely to be lodged in the future. The applicant is not in a position to dispute these statistics, but does not suggest that they are incorrect, or surprising.

[43] The Constitution contemplates that the Commission will play a crucial role in sifting claims for restitution and in the process of mediation and negotiation. This is apparent from the provisions of section 121(6) which provides that a claim for restitution:

shall not be justiciable by a court of law unless the claim has been dealt with in terms of section 122 by the Commission established by that section.

The applicant contends that the competences referred to in section 122 have to be performed by all the members of the Commission jointly. If this is so, there would be inordinate delays in processing claims. All members of the Commission would have to deal with each of the thousands of claims that are anticipated, and the functioning of the Commission would be cumbersome and impractical. Even if the Commission were to discharge its functions

---

[176] *Supra* para 44.
[177] *Supra* paras 42–43.
[178] *SARFU 2* para 40.
[179] *Supra*.

through its own employees, in order to perform all the tasks referred to in section 122 itself, namely, to investigate the merits of the claims, mediate and settle disputes arising from such claims, draw up reports on unsettled claims for submission as evidence to the Land Claims Court, and carry out any other functions which may be assigned to it by the contemplated legislation, without having the power to assign or delegate such functions to other functionaries, a large bureaucracy would have to be established to enable the Commission to function effectively and fulfil its mandate, and proceedings would be protracted to the potential prejudice of both the claimants, and the owners and other persons interested in the land.

[44] Parliament has full plenary power to enact legislation within the competences vested in it by the Constitution. It is not to be equated with a subordinate functionary whose powers of delegation must be restricted, nor is the Constitution to be construed with 'the austerity of tabulated legalism'. Section 122(1) of the Constitution does not specifically require the Commission to carry out the functions referred to in that section itself. It vests in the Commission a competence to do so. There is, *prima facie*, nothing in the Constitution which deprives Parliament of the power to enact legislation which authorises the Chief Land Claims Commissioner, who is the senior functionary of the Commission, to appoint mediators to assist in the settlement of disputed claims, or to delegate that power to some other person.

[45] In these circumstances the Supreme Court may well hold that there is not sufficient substance in the contentions raised by the applicant in this regard to warrant the issue being referred to this Court for its consideration.

The Constitution now expressly permits the type of delegation that occurred in *Transvaal Agricultural Union*. Section 238(a) allows an executive organ of state in any sphere of government, to delegate power to any other executive organ of state, providing the delegation is not inconsistent with the legislation in terms of which the power is exercised. The executive, under s 238(b), can delegate authority to another executive organ on an agency or on a delegation basis. The word 'executive' in s 236 is used loosely to depict an organ (at any level of government) having the power to execute the law.

Transvaal Agricultural Union represented delegation of authority within an agency. The next and more contentious form of delegation is the transfer of lawmaking authority from the legislature to the executive, or to independent agencies.

Delegation of power from the legislative to the executive branch

Assuming we say the power distribution should not be approached in a formal way, what are the limits to parliament transferring authority to make law, to the executive or independent constitutional organs? There can be no delegation of power where the Constitution prescribes that a decision has to be exercised by a particular organ.[180] In determining whether the power can be delegated or not, the Court looks at the language of the Constitution and the context in which it is being construed.[181] Where the power is open to delegation, the lawmaker must provide clear standards for the exercise of the delegated power.

There can be no delegation of power in a way which fundamentally alters the balance created under separation of powers. In *Executive Council*

---

[180] *Executive Council of the Western Cape Legislature and Others v President of the Republic of South Africa and Others* CCT 27/95 (22 September 1995) para 51, now cited as 1995 (4) SA 877 (CC); 1995 (10) BCLR 1289 (CC) (*Executive Council of the Province of Western Cape I*); *Executive Council of the Province of the Western Cape v The Minister for Provincial Affairs and Constitutional Development and Another* CCT 15/99 (15 October 1999) para 124; *The Executive Council of KwaZulu-Natal v The President of the republic of South Africa and Another* CCT 18/99, now cited as 2000 (1) SA 661 (CC); 1999 (12) BCLR 1360 (CC) (*Executive Council of the Province of the Western Cape III*).

[181] *Executive Council of the Province of the Western Cape III* para 124; *In re: Constitutionality of the Liquor Bill* para 46.

of the Western Cape I,[182] the Court was faced with the question whether parliament could delegate to the executive the power to make laws, including the power to amend a statute through executive decree. Chaskalson P highlighted the importance of delegating power to other bodies in a modern state.[183] The majority of the Court concurred with Chaskalson P that under the South African concept of separation of powers, which is akin to the United States approach, and unlike the Constitutions of other Commonwealth countries,[184] parliament could not abdicate its legislative authority.[185] Delegated power has to be exercised in terms of the intent laid out by the legislature. This intent cannot include actions that go against the form prescribed in the Constitution. The majority ruled that to allow the executive to amend a statute by executive decree would undermine the Constitution, which lays out the procedure for making law.[186]

Similarly, if the matter is of particular importance to the democratic political process, the Court is less likely to sanction delegation of power. In *Executive Council of Western Cape III,* the Court held that the delegation of power to the national minister to determine the term of office of the municipal council as provided for under s 24(1) of the Structures Act was unconstitutional.[187] Section 159(1) of the Constitution prescribes that the term of a municipal council may be no more than five years, as determined by national legislation. The Constitutional Court held that the term of office of the municipal council was important to the democratic political process. In construing the language of s 159(1), this was a power which parliament could not delegate.[188] There is an inherent subjectivity to the Court's approach. There is a sense that the extent to which they will permit the delegation depends on the Court's perception of how important the power is.

Executive Council of the Western Cape Legislature and Others v President of the Republic of South Africa
CCT 27/95 (22 September 1995), now cited as 1995 (4) SA 877 (CC); 1995 (10) BCLR 1289 (CC)
(Executive Council of the Western Cape I)
(notes omitted)
CHASKALSON P

[2] The case arises from a dispute between the Executive Council of the Western Cape and the national government relating to the validity of amendments to the Local Government Transition Act (the 'Transition Act'). These amendments were effected by the President by proclamation purporting to act in terms of powers vested in him under the Transition Act. The validity of the proclamations embodying the

amendments was challenged on constitutional and non-constitutional grounds.

[51] The legislative authority vested in Parliament under section 37 of the Constitution is expressed in wide terms 'to make laws for the Republic in accordance with this Constitution'. In a modern state detailed provisions are often required for the purpose of implementing and regulating laws, and Parliament cannot be expected to deal with all such matters itself. There is nothing in the Constitution which prohibits Parliament from delegating subordinate regulatory authority to other bodies. The power to do so is necessary for effective lawmaking. It is implicit in the power to make laws for the country and I have no doubt that under our Constitution Parliament can pass legislation delegating such legislative functions to other bodies. There is, however, a difference between delegating authority to make subordi-

---

[182] *Executive Council of The Western Cape I.*

[183] *Supra* para 5.

[184] eg in Canada the delegation of power to the executive cannot be attacked on the basis that legislative power is conferred on the executive. *See* Hogg 343.

[185] *Executive Council of the Western Cape I* para 62.

[186] *Supra.*

nate legislation within the framework of a statute under which the delegation is made, and assigning plenary legislative power to another body, including, as section 16A does, the power to amend the Act under which the assignment is made.

[52] In the past our courts have given effect to Acts of Parliament which vested wide plenary power in the executive. *Binga v Cabinet for South West Africa and Others* 1988 (3) SA 155(A) and *R v Maharaj* 1950 (3) SA 187 (A) are examples of such decisions. They are in conformity with English law under which it is accepted that Parliament can delegate power to the executive to amend or repeal acts of Parliament. Wade and Forsyth *Administrative Law*, pp 863–4 (Clarendon Press, Oxford (7 ed) 1994). These decisions were, however, given at a time when the Constitution was not entrenched and the doctrine of parliamentary sovereignty prevailed. What has to be decided in the present case is whether such legislation is competent under the new constitutional order in which the Constitution is both entrenched and supreme.

[61] … But our Constitution of 1993 shows a clear intention to break away from that history. The preamble to the Constitution begins by stating the 'need to create a new order'. That order is established in section 4 of the Constitution which lays down that:

(1) This Constitution shall be the supreme law of the Republic and any law or Act inconsistent with its provisions shall, unless otherwise provided expressly or by necessary implication in this Constitution, be of no force and effect to the extent of the inconsistency.

(2) This Constitution shall bind all legislative executive and judicial organs of the State at all levels of government.'

Sub-section (2) is of particular importance in the present case.

[62] The new Constitution establishes a fundamentally different order to that which previously existed. Parliament can no longer claim supreme power subject to limitations imposed by the Constitution; it is subject in all respects to the provisions of the Constitution and has only the powers vested in it by the Constitution expressly or by necessary implication. Section 37 of the Constitution spells out what those powers are. It provides that:

The legislative authority of the Republic shall, subject to this Constitution, vest in Parliament, which shall have the power to make laws for the Republic in accordance with this Constitution.

The supremacy of the Constitution is reaffirmed in section 37 in two respects. First, the legislative power is declared to be 'subject to' the Constitution, which emphasises the dominance of the provisions of the Constitution over Parliament's legislative power, *S v Marwane* 1982 (3) SA 717 (A) at 747 H748 A, and secondly laws have to be made 'in accordance with this Constitution'. In paragraph [51] of this judgment we I [sic] pointed out why it is a necessary implication of the Constitution that Parliament should have the power to delegate subordinate legislative powers to the executive. To do so is not inconsistent with the Constitution; on the contrary it is necessary to give efficacy to the primary legislative power that Parliament enjoys. But to delegate to the executive the power to amend or repeal Acts of Parliament is quite different. To hold that such power exists by necessary implication from the terms of the Constitution could be subversive of the 'manner and form' provisions of sections 59, 60 and 61. Those provisions are not merely directory. They prescribe how laws are to be made and changed and are part of a scheme which guarantees the participation of both houses in the exercise of the legislative authority vested in Parliament under the Constitution, and also establish machinery for breaking deadlocks. There may be exceptional circumstances such as war and emergencies in which there will be a necessary implication that laws can be made without following the forms and procedures prescribed by sections 59, 60 and 61. It is possible that circumstances short of war or states of emergency will exist from which a necessary implication can arise that Parliament may authorise urgent action to be taken out of necessity. A national disaster as a result of floods or other forces of nature may call for urgent action to be taken inconsistent with existing laws such as environmental laws. And there may well be other situations of urgency in which this type of action will be necessary. But even if this is so (and there is no need to decide this issue in the present case) the conditions in which section 16A were enacted fall short of such an emergency. There was, of course, urgency associated with the implementation of the Transition Act, but the Minister has regulatory powers under the Act, and legislation could have been passed to authorise the President to issue proclamations not inconsistent with the Act. Whether this could have included a power to amend other Acts of Parliament need not now be decided. An unrestricted power to amend the Transition Act itself cannot be justified on the grounds of necessity, nor can it be said to be a power which by necessary implication is granted by the Constitution to the President.

Standards for delegation of power

Where power is delegated, the standards for exercising that delegated power must be determined by the legislature. In the absence of standards, the Court will strike down the delegated power.[189] In *Dawood*, the Constitutional Court, *per* O'Regan J, struck down s 25(9)(b) read with ss 26(3) and (6) of the Aliens Control Act[190] as unconstitutional. Section 25(9)(b) provided authority for the relevant immigration official to grant permission to, among others, a foreign spouse of a person who is lawfully and permanently resident in South Africa to temporarily stay in the country. Sections 26(3) and (6) governed the grant of temporary residence permits. The Court held that no guidelines were provided under ss 26(3) and (6) as to the circumstances in which it would be appropriate or inappropriate to extend a temporary residence permit.[191] A potential applicant would not know what factors the immigration official would consider when deciding whether to grant or extend a temporary permit.[192] The legislature, when delegating power, must take care that delegated power is exercised in a constitutional manner.[193] This requires that the legislature identify the considerations which need to be taken into account by the relevant agency.[194] South Africa has to be vigilant in preserving its new-found democracy and cannot afford to become a state subject to bureaucratic lawmaking.

In *Ynuico Limited v Minister of Trade and Industry*,[195] the applicants challenged the constitutionality of s 2(1)(b) of the Import Export Control Act.[196] The section gave the Minister of Trade and Industry the power to prevent the import of certain goods into South Africa, if he deemed it necessary or expedient in the public interest. The minister, acting in terms of this power, prevented the importation of certain commodities, including tea.[197] The applicant, a supplier of tea, argued that such a broad delegation of power to the minister violated the interim Constitution, which granted legislative power to parliament. Section 2(1)(b) gave the minister plenary power to legislate. There were no objective guidelines or criteria for the exercise of this power.[198] The Court sustained the statute

---

[187] *Executive Council of Western Cape III* para 126.

[188] *Supra.*

[189] *Dawood and Another v Minister of Home Affairs and Others; Shalabi and Another v Minister of Home Affairs and Others; Thomas and Another v Minister of Home Affairs and Others* CCT 35/99 (7 June 2000) para 40, now cited as 2000 (8) BCLR 837 (CC). See also *Executive Council of the Western Cape I* para 62.

[190] Act 96 of 1991 (Aliens Act).

[191] *Dawood* para 26.

[192] *Supra* para 47.

[193] *Supra* para 48.

[194] *Supra* para 49.

[195] *Ynuico Limited v Minister of Trade and Industry* CCT 47/95 (21 May 1996), now cited as 1996 (3) SA 989 (CC); 1996 (6) BCLR 798 (CC).

[196] Import and Export Control Act 45 of 1963.

[197] *Ynuico* para 2.

[198] *Supra* para 4.

based on the fact that it was passed before the coming into effect of the new Constitution. Legislative authority under the new Constitution had no effect on statutes that were passed under the parliament of the previous order.[199] Section 229 of the interim Constitution required the continuation of all laws passed by the old order until they were replaced or repealed.[200] However, no law would be immune from nullification if it violated a fundamental right entrenched in the Bill of Rights.[201] In *Dawood*, the Court struck down the delegation of power even though it arose from a pre-1994 statute because the absence of standards had consequences which affected rights enshrined in the Bill of Rights.[202]

Similarly, *Executive Council of the Western Cape 1* stands for the propositions that parliament cannot delegate its plenary lawmaking power.[203] Where there is a delegation of power, this delegation has to be traced to legislation adopted by parliament. The legislation must provide clear limits for the way this power is exercised.[204] For example, it is questionable whether parliament could validly delegate power to the Minister of Environment to legislate whatever environmental standards he or she sees fit. In *JW Hampton Jr & Co v United States*, the United States Supreme Court laid out a test to approve the delegation of power to the legislature; namely whether the legislature, has enacted 'an intelligible principle to which the person or body authorized to take action is directed to conform'.[205] Similarly, the German approach is to require the legislature to spell out a guide for the content of any regulation.[206] In other words delegated power must be exercised in terms of an enabling statute, which sets clear parameters for the exercise of the delegated power.[207] If the enabling legislation reflects a policy that is called into question because of new unanticipated developments, the legislature should be required to re-examine the original policy in the light of the changed circumstances.[208] The clear import of the majority approach in *Executive Council of the Western Cape* is to repudiate the idea of a broad delegation of power. This does not mean that the rules should always be defined with precision. For example, the legislature may want to accomplish certain energy goals in the most efficient and safe way. It might be sufficient for parliament to spell out the goals of efficiency and safety in the enabling legislation. The determination as to what is efficient and safe could be left to experts in the environment ministry.[209] It seems appropriate that experts should have delegated power to use their scientific expertise to come up with regulations defining what is most efficient and safe.[210] However, the exercise of the delegated power must be connected to the task the legislature gave, which in our example would be the promotion of the efficient and safe use of energy.[211] In the absence of clear standards, the Constitutional Court would intervene and set aside the delegation of authority, which lacks sufficient guidelines for the exercise of the delegated power.

---

[199] *Supra* paras 5 and 7.

[200] *Supra* para 7.

[201] *Supra* para 8.

[202] *Dawood* para 58.

[203] *Executive Council of the Western Cape I* para 62.

[204] *Supra.*

[205] *JW Hampton Jnr & Co v United States* 276 US 394, 409 (1928).

[206] *Judicial Qualifications* case 34 BVerfGe 52, quoted in Kommers 159.

[207] eg cases where the USSC has struck down legislation based on the non-delegation doctrine, where the legislature has not provided clear standards to the agency exercising delegated power, see the early US cases of *NIRA, Panama Refining Co v Ryan* 293 US 388 (1935). See also, *ALA Schechter Poultry Corp v United States* 295 US 495 (1935).

[208] This is the approach of the German Constitutional Court. See the *Kalkar* case (1978) 49 BVerfGe 89, translated and quoted in Kommers 152.

[209] *Dawood* para 53.

[210] *Supra.*

[211] Tribe 363.

Dawood and Another v Minister of Home Affairs and Others; Shalabi and Another v Minister of Home Affairs and Others; Thomas and Another v Minister of Home Affairs and Others
CCT 35/99 (7 June 2000), now cited as 2000 (8) BCLR 837 (CC)
(notes omitted)

[25] In my view there is a three-fold conclusion. First, section 25(9), read in the context of section 23, establishes a general rule that a regional committee of the Immigrants Selection Board (the agency empowered to grant immigration permits) may grant such permits only when the applicant is not in South Africa. Secondly, section 25(9)(a) creates an exception to this rule in terms of which an applicant for an immigration permit who possesses a valid work permit need not be outside of South Africa when the immigration permit is granted. Thirdly, section 25(9)(b) creates a further exception in terms of which spouses, dependent children and aged, infirm or destitute family members who are in possession of a valid temporary residence permit issued in terms of section 26 also need not be outside South Africa at the time their immigration permit is granted.

[26] The grant of temporary residence permits is governed by section 26(3) of the Act, which provides:

(a) An immigration officer, in the case of an application for a visitor's permit, business permit or a medical permit referred to in subsection (1), or the Director-General, in the case of an application for any of the permits referred to in that subsection, may, on the application of an alien who has complied with all the relevant requirements of this Act, issue to him or her the appropriate permit in terms of subsection (1) to enter the Republic or any particular portion of the Republic and to sojourn therein, during such period and on such conditions as may be set forth in the permit ....

The extension of a temporary permit is governed by section 26(6):

The Director-General may from time to time extend the period for which, or alter the conditions subject to which, a permit was issued under subsection (3), and a permit so altered shall be deemed to have been issued under the said subsection.

It can be seen from these provisions that no guidance is provided as to the circumstances in which it would be appropriate to refuse to issue or extend a temporary residence permit.31 I return to this later. I now turn to the question whether section 25(9)(b) is unconstitutional or not.

[44] ... However, section 25(5) of the Act states that a regional committee, *notwithstanding the provisions of section 25(4)*, may issue an immigration permit to a spouse of a permanent and lawful resident of South Africa. Section 25(5) does not substitute any other criteria for those provided by section 25(4)(a). There is therefore no guidance to be found in either of these provisions as to the circumstances in which immigration officials or the DG may refuse to issue or extend a temporary residence permit.

[45] Can it nevertheless be said that the statute is reasonably capable of bearing a meaning that identifies factors relevant to the refusal to grant or extend permits that should be taken into consideration in addition to the marital or family status of the parties? In determining whether a legislative provision is reasonably capable of a particular meaning, the Court must, as the Constitution requires, 'promote the spirit, purport and objects of the Bill of Rights'.

[46] The Constitution also makes it plain that all government officials when exercising their powers are bound by the provisions of the Constitution. So section 8(1) of the Constitution provides that

[t]he Bill of Rights applies to all law, and binds the legislature, the executive, the judiciary and all organs of state.

There is, however, a difference between requiring a court or tribunal in exercising a discretion to interpret legislation in a manner that is consistent with the Constitution and conferring a broad discretion upon an official, who may be quite untrained in law and constitutional interpretation, and expecting that official, in the absence of direct guidance, to exercise the discretion in a manner consistent with the provisions of the Bill of Rights. Officials are often extremely busy and have to respond quickly and efficiently to many requests or applications. The nature of their work does not permit considered reflection on the scope of constitutional rights or the circumstances in which a limitation of such rights is justifiable. It is true that as employees of the state they bear a constitutional obligation to seek to promote the Bill of Rights as well. But it is important to interpret that obligation within the context of the role that administrative officials play in the framework of government which is different from that played by judicial officers.

[47] It is an important principle of the rule of law that rules be stated in a clear and accessible manner. It is because of this principle that section 36 requires that limitations of rights may be justifiable only if they are authorised by a law of general application. Moreover, if broad discretionary powers contain no express constraints, those who are affected by the exercise of the broad discretionary powers will not know what is relevant to the exercise of those powers or in what circumstances they are entitled to seek relief from an adverse decision. In the absence of any clear statement to that effect in the legislation, it would not be obvious to a potential applicant that the exercise of the discretion conferred upon the immigration officials and the DG by sections 26(3) and (6) is constrained by the provisions of the Bill of Rights, and in particular, what factors are relevant to the decision to refuse to grant or extend a temporary permit. If rights are to be infringed without redress, the very purposes of the Constitution are defeated.

[48]. . .The fact, however, that the exercise of a discretionary power may subsequently be successfully challenged on administrative grounds, for example, that it was not reason-able, does not relieve the legislature of its constitutional obligation to promote, protect and fulfil the rights entrenched in the Bill of Rights. In a constitutional democracy such as ours the responsibility to protect constitutional rights in practice is imposed both on the legislature and on the executive and its officials. The legislature must take care when legislation is drafted to limit the risk of an unconstitutional exercise of the discretionary powers it confers.

[49]. . . It is for the legislature, in the first place, to identify the policy considerations that would render a refusal of a temporary permit justifiable. However, as the legislation is currently drafted, the grant or extension of a temporary residence permit may be refused where no such grounds exist.

[50] The foregoing discussion assists in determining the interpretation of the relevant provisions that would best 'promote the spirit, purport and objects of the Bill of Rights'. In the case of the statutory discretion at hand, there is no provision in the text providing guidance as to the circumstances relevant to a refusal to grant or extend a temporary permit. I am satisfied that in the absence of such provisions, it would not promote the spirit, purport and objects of the Bill of Rights for this Court to try to identify the circumstances in which the refusal of a temporary permit to a foreign spouse would be justifiable. Nor can we hold in the present case that it is enough to leave it to an official to determine when it will be justifiable to limit the right in the democratic society contemplated by section 36. Such an interpretation, of which there is no suggestion in the Act, would place an improperly onerous burden on officials, which in the constitutional scheme should properly be borne by a competent legislative authority. Its effect is almost inevitably that constitutional rights (as in the case of two of the respondents before this Court) will be unjustifiably limited in some cases. Of even greater concern is the fact that those infringements may often go unchallenged and unremedied. The effect, therefore, of section 25(9)(b) read with sections 26(3) and (6) is that foreign spouses may be refused temporary permits in circumstances that con-

stitute an infringement of their constitutional rights.

[53] Discretion plays a crucial role in any legal system. It permits abstract and general rules to be applied to specific and particular circumstances in a fair manner. The scope of discretionary powers may vary. At times, they will be broad, particularly where the factors relevant to a decision are so numerous and varied that it is inappropriate or impossible for the legislature to identify them in advance. Discretionary powers may also be broadly formulated where the factors relevant to the exercise of the discretionary power are indisputably clear. A further situation may arise where the decision-maker is possessed of expertise relevant to the decisions to be made. There is nothing to suggest that any of these circumstances is present here.

[58] In this case, the legislature has sought to give a limited privilege to spouses and certain other family members through enacting section 25(9)(b). However, when that subsection is read with sections 26(3) and (6), it is plain that the privilege afforded by section 25(9)(b) may not in fact be of assistance to the groups section 25(9)(b) seeks to assist (as indeed it was not for Mr Shalabi or Mr Thomas). The privilege is dependent upon the grant of a valid temporary permit. However, the statutory provisions contemplate the refusal of such a permit, but contain no indication of the considerations that would be relevant to such refusal. Whatever the language and purpose of section 25(9)(b), its effect is uncertain in any specific case because of the discretionary powers contained in sections 26(3) and (6). The failure to identify the criteria relevant to the exercise of these powers in this case introduces an element of arbitrariness to their exercise that is inconsistent with the constitutional protection of the right to marry and establish a family. In my view, the effect of section 25(9)(b) read with sections 26(3) and (6) results in an unjustifiable infringement of the constitutional right of dignity of applicant spouses who are married to people lawfully and permanently resident in South Africa. There is no government purpose that I can discern that is achieved by the complete absence of guidance as to the countervailing factors relevant to the refusal of a temporary permit. In my view, therefore, section 25(9)(b) as read with sections 26(3) and (6) of the Act is unconstitutional.

Necessary or implied executive powers

The president has additional powers, which, although not explicitly spelled out in the Constitution, are still constitutionally based. For instance, s 84 of the Constitution proclaims that the president has the powers entrusted by the Constitution and through legislation 'including those necessary to perform the functions of Head of State and head of the national executive'. The latter part of s 84 envisages additional unspecified executive powers. There is no need for legislation to confer additional power on the president. These powers can be term-implied powers. Under s 84, one can argue that executive privilege is part of the Constitution.

It is necessary that the president and the executive enjoy some degree of executive privilege in order to effectively perform their functions. Executive privilege could include the power of the president to refuse to provide certain information, which the other branches of government or the public may have requested. The president has to depend on advisers in fulfilling executive duties. Even though the Constitution does not mention executive privilege, it is necessary for the president and his or her advisers to feel assured that there is confidentiality in their communications and that they do not have to constantly look over their shoulders.[212] If the president is unable to ensure

---

[212] Interestingly, the Promotion of Access to Information Act 2 of 2000 does not apply to a record of the cabinet and its committees in terms of s 12(a).

the confidentiality of these exchanges, the advisers might be hesitant to provide him or her with candid assessments needed by the president and cabinet for making wise decisions. The claim of executive privilege was recognized by the United States Supreme Court in *United States v Nixon*.[213] The Court stated that the claim of executive privilege is constitutionally based and 'fundamental to the operation of Government. Executive privilege although not explicitly mentioned in the Constitution is inextricably rooted in the separation of powers under the Constitution ...'.[214]

In *Nixon*, the United States Supreme Court ruled that the privilege was not absolute but had to be weighed against other interests including the needs of the criminal justice system.[215] For example, assume that there is an allegation of criminal wrongdoing on the part of a cabinet member. It is believed that the president is privy to information pertaining to the wrongdoing, although the president is not directly implicated in the wrongdoing. Can the president refuse to supply the information? Where there is a conflict between the interests of the justice system and the executive invocation of privilege, it is the duty of the court to weigh the competing claims.[216] Where the Court finds the information is privileged, the Court should excise it from the evidence.[217] Where the communication is not privileged and is relevant in a case before the court, the evidence should be allowed.

What if the information is sought by the legislature, or another constitutional organ not in the context of a matter before the courts? For example, parliament or an independent constitutional organ requests information from the president pertaining to exchanges between the president and his or her advisers. In *Attorney General v Hamilton*,[218] the chairman of a Tribunal of Enquiry sought information as to whether a decision taken by a cabinet member at a cabinet meeting, was an instrumentality of the Irish legislature. The Attorney-General argued such a line of questioning was unconstitutional. The majority of the Irish Supreme Court held that questions pertaining to what occurred at cabinet meetings violated the constitutional provisions of collective responsibility of the cabinet.[219] The Court held that although the executive under the parliamentary system is responsible to the legislature, this responsibility only applies in respect to decisions already taken. It does not apply to the process leading up to such decisions.[220] Therefore, the tribunal had no right to demand information pertaining to the content and details of the executive discussions. The Court also based its conclusions of confidentiality on the doctrine of separation of powers.[221] The Court makes a distinction between a plaintiff seeking information in the context of legal proceedings,[222] versus the situation in this case.[223]

The legislature has a legitimate oversight function, and power to investigate and to aid it in its legislative functions. As part of its lawmaking power, parliament or any of its committees could require individuals to testify and to cooperate with its investigations.[224] However, parliament's powers to investigate must be linked to its

---

[213] *United States v Nixon* 418 US 683 (1974).

[214] *Supra* at 708.

[215] *Supra* at 709.

[216] *Nixon* 418 US at 705. This is also the approach of the Irish SC. See Kelly 378–9.

[217] *Nixon* 418 US at 716.

[218] *Attorney-General v Hamilton* [1993] 3 IR 227.

[219] *Supra* at 250.

[220] *Supra* at 257.

[221] *Supra* at 244.

[222] Which privilege the court did not sustain in *Ambiorix Ltd v Minister for the Environment* [1992] 1 IR 277. Here plaintiff sought disclosure of certain cabinet memoranda and cabinet documents. The information was sought during a legal challenge to a decision made by a cabinet minister to set aside certain land for urban renewal. The executive sought to deny delivery of the documents on the ground of privilege. The Court stated that to sustain a general privilege would make it difficult for individual litigants to challenge decisions by the government.

[223] *Attorney-General v Hamilton.*

[224] Section 56 of the Constitution.

lawmaking and oversight functions.[225] The legislature should not be able to investigate or publicize executive or private activity merely for sole exposure.[226] Moreover, parliament should not be able to freely investigate executive communications unless the investigation is connected to some legitimate parliamentary objective such as lawmaking to rule otherwise would encroach on executive power. For example, in the United States, despite the advice of Freeh, the Director of the Federal Bureau of Investigation (FBI), to the Attorney-General to have an independent counsel investigate and deal with allegations concerning discrepancies with President Clinton's 1995–1996 campaign fund-raising, Attorney-General Janet Reno refused to act upon the advice. The House Government Reform and Oversight Committee which investigated the allegation of improper fund-raising, requested a copy of the FBI director's memorandum to the Attorney-General. The Attorney-General refused to supply the memorandum stating that it involved inter-agency communications which she constitutionally does not have to divulge to the legislature.[227] Even in Germany, the Constitutional Court has held that investigations by the legislature, of the executive, must be limited to activities related to the legislature fulfilling its role.[228]

Even in the context of a criminal proceeding before a court, it is not always that the court is best suited to make the determination as to what is privilege. In *Nixon*, the Court recognized that there are certain claims for executive privilege where they would defer to the executive, specifically where the information pertained to military or diplomatic secrets, or national security interests.[229] The Constitution, in s 202(1), makes the president the Commander-in-Chief of the Defence Force. In order to fulfil the military and national security responsibilities, there may be times when the president must withhold sensitive information from the other organs and from public scrutiny. The commander-in-chief has the power to confer certain privileges on the president and to withhold certain information in order to effectively carry out his or her defence functions.

It is arguable that the president also has certain inherent or prerogative powers that can be traced to s 84. The English philosopher John Locke described prerogative power as a discretionary power to act for the public good, without legal authorization and sometimes even against it.[230] In *Executive Council of Western Cape I*, Chaskalson P in dicta entertained the idea of allowing a departure from express constitutional provisions (beyond express executive powers, and emergency powers provided for in the Constitution), in exceptional circumstances such as war and emergencies.[231] The issue was whether parliament could delegate to the president the power to amend a statute by executive decree. The majority concluded that to allow the president the power to amend or repeal legislation goes against the clear provisions in the Constitution. Chaskalson P stated

---

[225] Laurence Tribe *American Constitutional Law* Mineola: Foundation Press, 2nd edition, 1988, 377.

[226] Ibid.

[227] Roberto Suro and Susan Schmidt 'Subpoena Seeks Freeh Memo to Reno; FBI Chief Wanted Independent Counsel' (1997) 6 December *The Washington Post*, A01, 1997 WL 16222483.

[228] Steinberger *152*.

[229] *Nixon*, 418 US at 683. The approach of the Irish SC even in cases of defence of national security is to insist that the court weigh the competing interest. See Kelly 378.

[230] John Locke *Two Treatises on Government*, edited by Peter Laslett. New York: Cambridge University Press 1988, chapter XIV, s 160. For an overview of cases in the US which upheld the idea of prerogative power see *In re: Nagle* 135 US 1, 10 SCt 658, 34 LEd 55 (1890). The SC ruled that the president did not need legislative authorization to assign a marshal to protect a judge. The Court ruled that the president's responsibility to execute the laws extends beyond legislative authorization to include 'the rights, duties, and obligations growing out of the Constitution itself, our international relations, and all the protection implied by the nature of the government under the Constitution'. *Nagle* at 64. However, in *Youngstown*, the Court did not speak with one voice. The majority disapproved of President Truman's innovation of inherent power, as a justification for seizing the nations steel mills during the Korean War. *Youngstown Sheet & Tube Company v Sawyer* 343 US 579 (1952).

[231] Chaskalson P in *Executive Council of Western Cape I* para 62. Ackermann and O'Regan JJ, paras 149–150, preferred to avoid the issue of emergency powers, since the argument was not presented to the Court.

that a national disaster such as a flood may require urgent action inconsistent with the law.[232] One can think of situations where the express provisions of the Constitution cannot be adhered to. For instance, a major disaster, such as a catastrophic nuclear accident might occur, precluding parliament from meeting and declaring a state of emergency, under the procedures provided under s 37 of the Constitution. It is unpalatable to say that an action which goes against the Constitution is acceptable. Rather, the better view is that the Constitution allows, in very extreme situations, extraordinary executive powers which under normal circumstances would be impermissible. Such powers can be implied from s 84 and other sections. For example, in times of war, there may be additional implied powers that the president might legitimately exercise pursuant to his or her power as commander-in-chief.

Foreign Affairs

The executive has sole power for the negotiation and signing of all treaties under s 231(1). This means parliament cannot instigate treaty negotiations. Arguably, the treaty power can neither be delegated to another organ of government, nor can any other organ dictate to the executive the substance of treaty negotiations.[233] All parliament can do is approve or reject a treaty. A Court can invalidate a treaty if it is incompatible with the Constitution.[234] However, even when fundamental rights are implicated, courts are very reluctant to invoke other constitutional values to second-guess the executive and legislature on foreign policy. For example, in the German case of *Pershing 2*, the complainants argued that the stationing of nuclear weapons on German soil

violated various provisions of the German Basic Law, including the right to life.[235] They asserted that the stationing of nuclear weapons posed a greater risk of attack by the Soviet Union. The German Constitutional Court adopted a political question approach in stating that there were no manageable criteria to determine whether the action by the German government posed a greater threat to life.[236] This is an evaluation that the national government has to make. The Court further stated that it must defer to the political branch with respect to how the state must fulfil its affirmative legal duty, to protect basic rights in the sphere of foreign policy and defence matters.[237] Deference to the political organs in foreign policy is important because a country has to speak with one voice in the realm of foreign policy. For the Court to second-guess the political organs would cause great embarrassment to the government abroad.[238]

An international agreement becomes binding on the Republic of South Africa only after it has been approved by parliament. There are some treaties that allow amendments of an administrative or a technical nature to be made by an international organ.[239] For example, technical conventions on matters such as air navigation or postal relations may sometimes require frequent modifications.[240] The conduct of international relations would be very cumbersome if these amendments required ratification of all signatory states. The Constitution recognizes this reality in s 231(3) and provides an exception to parliamentary approval for agreements of a technical, administrative or executive nature. Once entered into by the executive, treaty agreements are binding on the republic.

An executive agreement is an agreement entered into between the executive and a foreign

---

[232] *Executive Council of Western Cape I* para 62.

[233] This is also the approach of the Irish SC. *See Hutchinson v Minister for Justice* [1993] 3 IR 567, 571.

[234] See *Sonderup v Tondelli and Another* CCT 53/00 (4 December 2000), para 27, now cited as 2001 (2) BCLR 152 (CC); 2001 (1) SA 1171 (CC); *Reid v Covert* 354 US 1 (1957).

[235] *Pershing 2* and *Cruise Missile I* case (1983) 66 BVerfGe 39 in Kommers 165–8.

[236] Kommers 167.

[237] Ibid.

[238] *Luther v Borden* 48 US 1, 7 How 1 (1849).

[239] JG Starke *Introduction to International Law* London: Butterworths, 10th edition, 1989, 469.

[240] Louis Richard Henkin, et al *Cases on International Law* St Paul: West Publishing Co, 3rd edition, 1993, 485.

state. The difficulty lies in distinquishing between an executive and other types of agreement. In the United States, the two are treated synonymously.[241] An agreement concluded by the executive, which purports to impose legal obligations in the domestic context, would not be binding without its adoption by national legislation.[242] However, there is nothing to preclude political treaties such as treaties of friendship and alliance through an executive agreement. The Constitution does not spell out how an executive agreement, which is opposed by parliament, should be dealt with. If the treaty requires appropriation of funds for its implementation, parliament can effectively veto the implementation of the treaty by not appropriating funds. There are instances where there might be no need for appropriation of funds. For example, if the president by executive agreement confers recognition on an unpopular government, which decision parliament disapproves off, can parliament override the president's decision? Arguably, parliament cannot override the executive because the Constitution says that the negotiation and signing of all treaties is the responsibility of the executive. Parliament can withhold approval of a treaty presented to them under s 231(2). However, they can neither 'negotiate' unilaterally and pass a treaty, nor can they veto an executive agreement entered into under s 231(3).[243]

A treaty is an agreement between two or more states, or between a state and an international organization. Parliament can legislate over a subject that may be covered in a treaty. For example, an environmental treaty, approved by parliament through legislation, may require a reduction in the emission of certain gases, and concrete collective action and cooperation between states in ensuring pollution control. Parliament through subsequent legislation can, without executive negotiation, change the domestic law on pollution, even if the legislation alters the effects of the treaty. This action is constitutional in terms of parliament's ordinary legislative power. However, parliament cannot on its own initiative, change the terms of the treaty as it pertains to collective action and cooperation between the republic and other states. Foreign policy is an area where a country has to be decisive.[244] The Constitution recognizes the need for expediency and decisiveness in foreign affairs by lodging the power to initiate international agreements with the executive.

Defence

The president under s 201(2) has exclusive power to authorize the use of the defence force. Section 202(1) of the Constitution casts the president as the Commander-in-Chief of the Defence Force. The command of the defence force under s 202(2) is exercised through a cabinet member responsible for defence. Section 201(2) provides three circumstances under which the president may authorize the deployment of the defence force: first, in cooperation with the police force;[245] secondly, in defence of the republic;[246] or thirdly, in fulfilment of an international obligation.[247] The section does not state these are the only conditions under which the defence force may be deployed. Even, assuming s 202(2) is interpreted as the only circumstances where the defence force may be employed, it is unlikely that the validity of the president's decision to employ the defence force could be successfully challenged before the courts. Section 201(2)(b) 'in defence of the Republic' grants the president a wide degree of discretion that is not easily amenable to judicial review.

There is a category of cases, which, despite clear jurisdictional authority, the courts consider nonjusticiable. In chapter 4, the political question

---

[241] Erwin Chemerinsky *Constitutional Law: Principles and Policies* New York: Aspen Law & Business 1997, 271.

[242] Under s 231(4), a treaty only assumes self-executing character after parliament adopts it as national legislation.

[243] This is also the approach of the USSC with respect to executive agreements. See *United States v Belmont* 301 US 324 (1937). See also *Dames & Moore v Reagan* 453 US 654 (1981).

[244] See the USSC pronouncements in this regard in *United States v Curtis-Wright Export Corporation* 299 US 304, 319–20 (1936).

[245] Section 201(2)(a) of the Constitution.

[246] Section 201(2)(b).

[247] Section 201(2)(c).

doctrine was mentioned. Instead of repeating the analysis, several points will be highlighted here. The political question doctrine is invoked by courts in various jurisdictions where the courts consider the matter to be particularly sensitive and better amenable to resolution via the political process.[248] In *Baker v Carr*, the United States Supreme Court made the following observation:

Baker v Carr
369 US 1866 (1962)
(notes omitted)

We have said that 'in determining whether a question falls within [the political question] category, the appropriateness under our system of government of attributing finality to the action of the political departments and also the lack of satisfactory criteria for a judicial determination are dominant considerations'. The nonjusticiability of a political question is primarily a function of the separation of powers. Much confusion results from the capacity of the 'political question' label to obscure the need for case-by-case inquiry. Deciding whether a matter has in any measure been committed by the Constitution to another branch of Government, or whether the action of that branch exceeds whatever authority has been committed, is itself a delicate exercise in constitutional interpretation, and is a responsibility of this Court as ultimate interpreter of the Constitution.

Foreign relations: There are sweeping statements to the effect that all questions touching foreign relations are political questions. Not only does resolution of such issues frequently turn on standard that defy judicial application, or involve the exercise of a discretion demonstrably committed to the executive or legislature; but many such questions uniquely demand single-voiced statement of the Government's views. Yet it is error to suppose that every case or controversy which touches foreign relations lies beyond judicial cognizance. Our cases in this field seem invariably to show a discriminating analysis of the particular question posed, in terms of the history of its management by the political branches, of its susceptibility to judicial handling in the light of its nature and posture in the specific case, and of the possible consequence of judicial action.

Dates of duration of hostilities: Though it has been stated broadly that 'the power which declared the necessity is the power to declare its cessation, and what the cessation requires', here too analysis reveals isolable reasons for the presence of political questions, underlying this Court's refusal to review the political departments' determination of when or whether a war has ended. Dominant is the need for finality in the political determination, for emergency's nature demands. 'A prompt and unhesitating obedience'.... Further, clearly definable criteria for decision may be available. In such cases the political question barrier falls away ....

Validity of enactments: In *Coleman v Miller* [307 US 433 (1939)], this Court held that the questions of how long a proposed amendment to the Federal Constitution remained open to ratification, and what effect a prior rejection had on a subsequent ratification, were committed to congressional resolution and involved criteria of decision that necessarily escaped this judicial grasp. Similar considerations apply to the enacting process: 'The respect due to coequal and independent departments', and the need for finality and certainty about the status of a statute contribute to judicial reluctance to inquire whether, as passed, it complied with all requisite formalities ....

It is apparent that several formulations which vary sightly according to the settings in which the questions arise may describe a political

---

[248] See our earlier discussion of *Pershing 2 and Cruise Missile 1* cases, where the complainants argued that the stationing of nuclear weapons on German soil violated various provisions of the German Basic Law, including the right to life. The German Constitutional Court adopted a political question approach in stating that there was no manageable criteria for them to determine whether the action by the German government posed a greater threat to life. (1983) 66 BVerfGe 39 in Kommers 165–8. For US cases, *see Baker v Carr* 369 US 186 (1962) and *Luther v Borden* 48 US 1, 7 How 1 (1849).

question, although each has one or more elements which identify it as essentially a function of the separation of powers. Prominent on the surface of any case held to involve a political question is found a textually demonstrable constitutional commitment of the issue to a coordinate political department; or a lack of judicially discoverable and manageable standards for resolving it; or the impossibility of deciding without an initial policy determination of a kind clearly for nonjudicial discretion; or the impossibility of a court's undertaking independent resolution or an unusual need for unquestioning adherence to a political decision already made; or the potentiality of embarrassment from multifarious pronouncements by various departments on one question.

The conduct of foreign policy and defence matters is committed to the political branches. On the use of the defence force, pre-eminence is given to the executive. In general, decisions on war and foreign affairs entail policy considerations. There are no manageable judicial standards for making decisions of this nature. The judiciary is not appropriately placed to make these policy decisions nor to second-guess the political branches on, for example, whether the president's action to employ the troops was in defence of the republic. It would also be a grave embarrassment for the country abroad if the president makes a policy decision to commit the defence force into combat only to be overruled by the Court. The ultimate check on the abuse of presidential power in foreign affairs and defence matters is removal by the legislature.

Additional legality requirements

The Constitution, in various provisions, imposes additional legality requirements such as written notification, or consultation between executive officials, before an executive action has legal force.

Under s 101(1), a decision by the president, taken in terms of legislation, or where it has legal consequences, must be in writing. Under s 101(2), a written decision by the president must be countersigned by another cabinet member, if the decision pertains to a function assigned to that cabinet member. Like the German Constitution, the South African Constitution imposes a high degree of rationality and accountability in the way delegated power is exercised.[249] This is designed to ensure that official actions are comprehensible and predictable.[250]

Before appointing certain judicial officers, the president is required to consult with the JSC, political parties represented in the NA, and the President of the Constitutional Court.[251] The president is the Commander-in-Chief of the Defence Force and has the sole authority to authorize the deployment of the defence force.[252] However, when the president decides to deploy the defence force, the president under s 201(3) must inform parliament, or if parliament is not in session, under s 201(4), the appropriate oversight committee of the decision. Similarly, if the president declares a state of national defence, under s 203, he or she is required to notify parliament.

---

[249] Kommers 147.
[250] *Emergency Price Control* case (1958) 8 BVerfGe 274 in Kommers 148.
[251] Sections 174(3) and 174(4) of the Constitution.
[252] Sections 202(1) and 201(2).

7

Fundamental rights

Introduction

Section 7 of the Constitution states:

> (1) This Bill of Rights is a cornerstone of democracy in South Africa. It enshrines the rights of all people in our country and affirms the democratic values of human dignity, equality and freedom.
> (2) The state must respect, protect, promote, and fulfil the rights in the Bill of Rights.
> (3) The rights in the Bill of Rights are subject to the limitations contained or referred to in section 36, or elsewhere in the Bill.

From power to rights

The Constitution serves two primary functions: to grant power, and to limit power.[1] Provisions that serve to grant power are called 'empowerment' or 'power' provisions.[2] Provisions that limit the exercise of government power are called 'rights' or 'limitation clauses'. Some examples of power provisions are s 43 *(a)*, which vests the legislative authority in parliament, and s 85(1), which vests the executive authority in the president. The power provisions provide the constitutional authority to different branches and organs of government to do certain things, describing when which branch of government, parliament, executive, judiciary, or independent government agency, has the authority to act. Similarly, the distribution of competencies between national, provincial, and local government are power provisions, describing which level of government has authority to exercise power. However, by describing the organ or branch of government having authority to act means that there are also limitations arising from the power provision. If the Constitution grants the national parliament certain powers, this might limit the provincial legislature or the executive. Similarly, if the Constitution gives certain power to an independent constitutional organ such as the Independent Broadcasting Authority (IBA), this power limits the executive and the legislature in the regulation of broadcasting. Power limitations seek to avoid governmental tyranny through structural and institutional strategies such as the distribution of power among the three branches of government, the national government, and the provinces. Most of these provisions examined are power provisions.

Next, we look at a different form of constitutional limitation, namely rights limitations. The strategy here contrasts with the previous approach

---

[1] William A Kaplan *The Concepts and Methods of Constitutional Law* Durham: Carolina Academic Press 1992, 18.
[2] Ibid.

in that the emphasis is on individual and human rights. The limitation on government power arises from the Bill of Rights. So while a government agency might have the power to regulate a particular activity, the regulation would be unconstitutional, if it violates a right protected in the Bill of Rights. For example, the executive has the power to negotiate treaties. Parliament has the power to adopt a treaty as binding on individuals. If parliament adopts an anti-terrorism treaty which targets certain individuals based on religion, the legislation would be unconstitutional, if it is found to violate freedom of religion,[3] the equality provision,[4] or freedom and security of the person.[5] The Court will allow the legislation only if it can be established that the legislation satisfies the limitations clause[6] of the Constitution.[7]

In the following chapters we move away from the structural and institutional strategies for preventing government tyranny and focus on the Bill of Rights and interpretation of the fundamental rights protections contained in the Bill of Rights. In interpreting the power provisions, we alluded in previous chapters to jurisprudential differences in defining the scope of executive and legislative power. However, despite these difficulties, the texts for many of the power provisions are easier easy to interpret, and to some extent resemble the methodology of statutory interpretation.[8] For example, the composition of parliament or the method of election of the president is clear from the text of the Constitution. In contrast, almost all of the rights contained in the Bill of Rights are phrased at a level of abstraction. For example, the Constitution provides that '[E]veryone has inherent dignity and the right to have their dignity respected and protected'.[9]

Inherent dignity cannot be interpreted from the text itself. This and other provisions in the Bill of Rights need concrete meanings that can be derived from different sources including methods of philosophy, common law, customary law, natural law, consensus, conventional morality, and discourse in international human rights.

In *Makwanyane*, the Constitutional Court was faced with the question of whether the death penalty constituted cruel, inhuman, or degrading treatment under the Constitution. Didcott J, correctly noted that '[W]hether execution ranks also as a cruel, inhuman or degrading punishment that lends itself to no precise measurement. It calls for a value judgment in an area where personal opinions are prone to differ, a value judgment that can easily become entangled with or be influenced by one's own moral attitude and feelings'.[10] As with other parts of the Constitution, there is the recurring question of whether the judiciary is best placed to discover these values. In *Makwanyane*, Didcott J stated that it is the role of the courts to make decisions of this order, because the training and experience of judges prevents them from making decisions in an unduly subjective way.[11] Whether judges are able to discover the right values in a neutral and detached way is a recurring question in the following chapters.

In human rights discourse, jurists commonly speak about first, second, and third generation human rights.[12] 'First generation rights' is a reference to civil and political rights; 'second generation rights' refer to economic, social, and cultural rights, and 'third generation rights' refer to collective rights such as the right to self-determination, development, and the right to a safe and secure environment.[13] The Constitution

---

[3] Section 15 of the Constitution.

[4] Section 9.

[5] Section 12(1).

[6] Section 36.

[7] The limitations clause is discussed in chapter 14.

[8] This is also the case in the US. Paul Brest and Sanford Levinson *Processes of Constitutional Decision-making: Cases and Materials* Boston: Little Brown, 3rd edition, 1992, 943.

[9] Section 10 of the Constitution.

[10] *S v Makwanyane and Another* CCT 3/94 (6 June 1995) para 177, now cited as 1995 (3) SA 391 (CC); 1995 (6) BCLR 665 (CC).

[11] *Supra.*

[12] DJ Harris *Cases and Materials on International Law* London: Sweet & Maxwell, 3rd edition, 1983, 601.

[13] Op cit 601–2.

contains protections for first, second, and third generation human rights and proclaims that the Bill of Rights is a cornerstone of democracy. It imposes obligations on the state to 'respect, protect, promote and fulfil the rights in the Bill of Rights'.[14] This chapter will focus on core civil and political rights contained in the Bill of Rights. In later chapters we look in greater detail at certain substantive rights, such as equal protection, including affirmative action,[15] right to property,[16] the Constitution and private action,[17] right to fair trial and due process procedures,[18] freedom of speech and association,[19] and freedom of religion.[20] In addition, we look at second generation economic, social and cultural rights, and third generation collective rights such as the right to a safe and secure environment.[21] Finally, we look at the permissible circumstances for derogation or limitation of fundamental rights.[22]

Many of the civil and political rights are contained in the Universal Declaration of Human Rights,[23] and the International Covenant on Civil, and Political Rights,[24] as well as the various regional instruments on human rights, such as the African Charter on Human and Peoples Rights,[25] the European Convention for the Protection of Human Rights and Fundamental Freedoms,[26] and the American Convention on Human Rights.[27] Today many of these rights are considered customary international law, and some even rise to the level of *jus cogens*, which creates binding obligations for all states and from which there can be no derogation.[28]

Human dignity

The Constitution in s 10 proclaims:

> Everyone has inherent dignity and the right to have their dignity respected and protected.

The protection of human dignity means that human beings stand at the centre of the system of government. Human dignity has been defined as a founding value of the new Constitution.[29] The centrality of human dignity is particularly important given the legacy of the apartheid era, which denied the humanity of the majority of South African citizens. The emphasis on human dignity is also found in the Basic Law of Germany.[30] The human dignity clause in the Basic Law marks an endeavour to bring in a new constitution that rejects the previous authoritarian order that showed contempt for human beings. The new South African Constitution, as O'Regan J emphasized in *Makwanyane* 'rejects this past and affirms the equal worth of all South Africans'.[31]

---

[14] Section 57(2) of the Constitution.

[15] See chapter 8.

[16] See chapter 9.

[17] See chapter 10.

[18] See chapter 11.

[19] See chapter 12.

[20] Ibid.

[21] See chapter 13.

[22] See chapter 14.

[23] (1948) III UNGAR 217, adopted by the UNGA on 10 December 1948.

[24] 999 UNTS 171, (1967) 6 ILM 368 (Civil Covenant).

[25] OAU Doc CAB/LEG/67/3/Rev 5 Adopted by the Organization of African Unity on 27 June 1981 and entered into force on 21 October 1986 (African Charter).

[26] European Convention for the Protection of Human Rights and Fundamental Freedoms 213 UNTS 221 ETS. Signed at Rome on 4 November 1950 and entered into force on 3 September 1953 (European Convention).

[27] OAS Official Records OEA/SER K/XVI/ 1.1, Doc 65, Rev 1 Cor 1, 7 January 1970, (1970) 9 ILM 101 and entered into force on 18 July 1978 (American Convention).

[28] John P Humphrey 'The International Bill of Rights: Scope and Implementation' (1976) 17 *William & Mary Law Review* 529. The concept of *jus cogens* has been discussed in greater detail in chapters 2 and 4.

[29] *Makwanyane* para 328.

[30] Article 1 of the German Basic Law, para 3.

[31] *Makwanyane* para 329.

This right is the foundation of many other rights contained in the Bill of Rights.[32] Respect for human dignity means that the exercise of power, particularly governmental power, must be based on the respect of human beings.[33] The legality of government conduct is consistently evaluated in terms of whether human dignity is violated.[34] Even though a particular right might not be expressly contained in the Constitution, the Constitutional Court will give expression to the right if it is related to human dignity.[35]

How do we begin to define human dignity? For Ackerman J, the starting point to human dignity is the individual, and the need to respect the 'uniqueness' of each individual.[36] The uniqueness of each individual requires that each individual be permitted to develop his or her individual talents in an optimal fashion.[37] For Ackermann J, human dignity is the equivalent of personal freedom and individual autonomy.[38]

For other members of the Court human dignity, although concerned with the individual, need not commence from the vantage point of an individual as an isolated entity.[39] For example, Mokgoro J conceptualizes human dignity as part of *ubuntu*, a concept mentioned in the post-amble to the Constitution. Like Ackermann J, Mokgoro J couples human dignity with humaneness.[40] However, it is not the human being as isolated

sovereign, but instead the human being as part of a larger group.[41] Ackermann J's concept of human dignity derives largely from the common-law and the Anglo-American idea of self-reliance. Mokgoro J's concept associates dignity with caring and help for the vulnerable. The concept of *ubuntu* is described as social justice, and showing care and compassion for others.[42] *Ubuntu* draws from traditional African societies that were largely communal in nature.

If we say human dignity is the foundation for other guaranteed rights, then there is potential tension between some individual rights and collective rights which need to be reconciled. Ackermann J's datum for measurement of human dignity proceeds from the classical liberal paradigm. For Ackermann J, any derogation from individual liberty for the collective good must be justified by the limitations clause.[43] For Mokgoro J, the Constitution seeks a balance between the interests of the individual and society. Mokgoro J, therefore, requires reconciliation between individualism and the needs of the community. The balance that Mokgoro J seeks to achieve is more consistent with the overall spirit and purpose of the Constitution, which seeks to promote not only individual rights but also social, economic, and group rights. This balance was recognized by the majority in *Ferreira*, *per* Chaskalson P, where the

---

[32] *Supra.*

[33] *The Government of the Republic of South Africa and Others v Grootboom and Others* CCT 11/00 (4 October 2000) para 83, now cited as 2000 (11) BCLR 1169 (CC); 2001 (1) SA 46 (CC). Kurt Sontheimer 'Principles of Human Dignity in the Federal Republic' in *Germany and its Basic Law, Past, Present and Future: A German–American Symposium*, edited by Paul Kirchoff and Donald P Kommers Baden-Baden: Nomos 1993, 214.

[34] The protection of human dignity looms large in the court's approach to protection of fundamental human rights, eg when we look at the Equality Jurisprudence (see chapter 8), the Constitutional Court has consistently proclaimed whether a classification constitutes unfair discrimination will largely hinge on whether human dignity is violated.

[35] eg recognition of the right to marry and found a family as expressed in *Dawood and Another v Minister of Home Affairs and Others; Shalabi and Another v Minister of Home Affairs and Others; Thomas and Another v Minister of Home Affairs and Others* CCT 35/99 (7 June 2000) para 37, now cited as 2000 (8) BCLR 837 (CC); *Certification I* para 100; the prohibition of the migrant-labourer system as pronounced in *Certification I* para 100; the prohibition of corporeal punishment as pronounced in *S v Williams* para 39.

[36] *Ferreira* para 49.

[37] *Supra.*

[38] *Supra.*

[39] See eg *Makwanyane*, *per* Langa J, para 225, where the right to life is approached in terms of the way the community collectively put value in life and dignity.

[40] *Makwanyane* para 308.

[41] *Supra.*

[42] See the opinion of Madala J in *Makwanyane* para 237. See also Njongonkulu Ndungane 'A new faith for new South Africans' (1998) 20–26 February *Weekly Mail* 34.

[43] *Ferreira* para 52.

president stated that if they accepted Ackermann J's view of individual freedom, the lawmaker would be constrained from effecting vital social and economic reforms required by the Constitution.[44] The approach of Chaskalson P and Mokgoro J is akin to the approach adopted by the German Constitutional Court, which seeks to balance human dignity[45] with the concept of a social state.[46] The German Constitutional Court has resolved the tension as requiring a balance between the individual and the community.[47] Arguably, like the German Basic Law,[48] the Constitution requires the state to respect the dignity of individuals and also, as Sontheimer states in the German context, create equitable social conditions 'in which the individual can develop that dignity and exercise those rights'.[49]

Cole Durham describes the approach in German law as follows:

The German approach is fundamentally more sympathetic to a conception in which the state plays a role in facilitating the actualization of freedom. Rather than being the key power that needs to be constrained if liberty is to be preserved, the state is seen as the vehicle for achieving freedom. This tradition, which I shall refer to as 'facilitative freedom,' has deep roots in the German past, and is manifested in a wide variety of current constitutional doctrines It is a tradition in which freedom tends to be seen not as the polar opposite of community, but as a value that must be achieved in synthesis with community. In this setting, it is natural for the state to assume a more affirmative role in actualizing specific constitutional rights. The claims of *Sozialstaatlichkeit* and economic and social rights dovetail more easily with this view of freedom than with the American counterpart. The 'New Property' of Charles Reich and minimum welfare notions of Frank Michelman, trendy suggestions of the sixties that never took hold in the United States, might well have found a home in the German system. In a deep sense, the German system of facilitative freedom has strong affinities with Kant. The notion of dignity embodied in Article 1 of the Basic Law has roots in Kantian ethics. Similarly, the tendency to think of constitutional law as embodying an objective ordering of fundamental values is consistent with the deontological cast of Kant's thought about the nature of republican institutions. Anti-utilitarian instincts in German adjudication also harmonize with the Kantian heritage. In contrast to Locke, Kant's derivation of private property and other institutions of freedom starts with a world of community, and asks how private holdings are individuated out of the common pool. More generally, Kant thought of justice as 'the aggregate of those conditions under which the will of one person can be conjoined with the will of another in accordance with a universal law of freedom'. This approach, while making freedom and dignity central, connects them to concerns about a community of free persons. The effect of the social compact is for man to abandon the 'wild, lawless freedom' of the Hobbesian state of nature 'in order to find his whole freedom again undiminished in a lawful dependency, that is, in a juridical state of society'. Genuine autonomy in this system will harmonize with reason and universalizable values; arbitrary private choice is mere heteronomy of the will.[50]

Thus far, the Constitutional Court has made several pronouncements on what is human dignity. In *Makwanyane*, the Constitutional Court, *per* Chaskalson P, held that the death penalty violated human dignity,[51] and that the death row phenomena of lengthy incarceration prior to execution also amounts to a violation of human dignity.[52] Imprisonment, while it impairs human dignity, does not violate human dignity.[53] When imposing punishment, the state must

---

[44] *Supra* para 180.
[45] Article 1 of the German Basic Law.
[46] Article 20.
[47] Sontheimer 215.
[48] Ibid.
[49] Ibid.
[50] Cole W Durham 'General Assessment of the Basic Law – An American View' in *Germany and Its Basic Law: Past, Present and Future: A German-American Symposium,* edited by Paul Kirchoff and Donald P Kommers, 45–6 (reprinted with permission).
[51] *Makwanyane* para 84.
[52] Didcott J in *Makwanyane* para 178.
[53] Chaskalson P in *Makwanyane* para 142.

observe standards which respect human dignity. For example, judicial sanctioning of corporeal punishment constitutes a violation of human dignity.[54] Respect for human dignity precludes the pass laws and the institutionalized migrant-labour system, which was a hallmark of the previous order.[55] Human dignity encompasses the right to marry freely and found a family.[56] In *Dawood*, the Court was faced with a challenge to the constitutionality of s 29(9)(b) read with s 26(3) and (6) of the Aliens Control Act,[57] which gave the immigration officials discretion whether to grant a foreign spouse, married to a permanent or lawful resident in South Africa, permission to reside in South Africa. The Constitutional Court held that the sections were invalid because they did not provide standards for the exercise of the discretion.[58] The arbitrary nature of the provisions results in an infringement of the right of dignity of applicant spouses.[59] The legislation restricts the establishment of a marriage relationship constituting a violation of the right to dignity.[60]

Life

Section 11 of the Constitution provides:

> Everyone has the right to life.

International the concept of the right to life is contained in art 3 of the Universal Declaration, art 4 of the African Charter; art 6(1) of the Civil Covenant; art 2(1) of the European Convention, and art 7(2) of the American Convention. The right to life is undoubtably part *jus cogens*. It is made a non-derogable right under s 37(5)(c) of the South African Constitution. It is also a non-derogable

right under art 4(2) of the Civil Covenant. The Constitution, as do international law instruments, states the right to life at the level of abstraction. For example, does the right to life preclude suicide, abortion, and capital punishment?

The Constitution in s 12(2) dealing with freedom and security of person provides in part:

> Everyone has the right to bodily and psychological integrity which includes the right–
> (a) to make decisions concerning reproduction;
> (b) to security in and control over their body ....

Do the above provisions cover both contraception and abortions or only contraception? If it covers both, what limitations may the state place in preventing a woman from obtaining an abortion? For example, can the legislature say life begins at conception, or a few weeks after conception, and therefore mandate that after such period there can be no abortions? In *Makwanyane*, Mahomed J raised the question of what the right to life means.[61] He also raised the question as to whether there can be a conflict between the right to privacy, which includes the right of the mother to control her body, versus the right to life?[62] He further raised the question whether:

[268] the 'right to life', ... preclude[s] the practitioner of scientific medicine from withdrawing the modern mechanisms which mechanically and artificially enable physical breathing in a terminal patient to continue, long beyond the point, when the 'brain is dead' and beyond the point when a human being ceases to be 'human' although some unfocused claim to qualify as a 'being' is still retained? If not, can such a practitioner go beyond the point of passive, withdrawal into the area of active intervention? When? Under what circumstances?

---

54 *S v Williams* CCT 20/94 (9 June 1995) para 39, now cited as 1995 (3) SA 632 (CC); 1995 (7) BCLR 861 (CC).
55 *Certification I* para 100.
56 *Supra.*
57 Act 96 of 1991 (Aliens Control Act).
58 *Dawood* para 58.
59 *Supra.*
60 *Supra* para 37.
61 *Makwanyane* para 268.
62 Mahomed J raised these questions but did not, however, answer them, as these questions were not before the Court.

Abortion

A study of international human rights does not reveal a single approach to the question whether the right to life includes or precludes the right to have an abortion.[63] The issue is one of 'legitimate diversity', meaning there is no consensus in the international community that advocates for the universal adoption of 'a single substantive standard'.[64] The first important question is that of when does life begin? The answer has implications in the approach to abortion in different jurisdictions. There are two primary approaches to the abortion debate – reflected in those of the United States and Germany. The first approach eschews taking a stand on when life begins. The second approach proceeds from the premise that life begins at conception.

The United States courts have expressly declined to espouse any one perspective on when life begins. Similarly, at the regional level, although the American Convention expressly states that the right to life shall be protected 'in general, from the moment of conception', neither the Inter-American Court, nor the Human Rights Commission has embraced this provision literally.[65] For example, in 1981 the Inter-American Commission on Human Rights refused to impute this language to the Universal Declaration to find that abortion laws violated the right-to-life provision of the declaration.[66]

In *Roe v Wade*, the plaintiff, an unmarried and pregnant woman, claimed that Texas statutes which criminalize abortions unless the woman's life was endangered by the pregnancy, were unconstitutional because they precluded her from procuring an abortion by a 'competent, licenced physician, under safe, clinical conditions'.[67] The United States Supreme Court found that the privacy rights guaranteed by the Ninth and Fourteenth Amendments to the United States Constitution, include a woman's right to terminate her pregnancy prior to foetal viability.[68] In the United States, the decision to have an abortion is included in the Right to Privacy. However, this right is 'qualified' and must be balanced against the interests of states including, but not limited to, the states' responsibility to protect life and health.[69] In balancing the competing interests, the Court ultimately established a 'trimester system', which permitted states to constitutionally prohibit abortions during the third trimester. At this stage, the state's interest in protecting 'life' is deemed to outweigh the mother's privacy rights, because of the viability of the foetus.[70]

The decision in *Roe v Wade*, which held that a woman's right to obtain an abortion is part of her privacy rights, has been affirmed in a litany of cases in the United States.[71] However, in its recent decision in *Planned Parenthood v Casey*, the Supreme Court abandoned the trimester approach in favour of the 'undue burden test'.[72] Under the current approach, an abortion statute will be unconstitutional where the state's regulation places an unreasonable obstacle in the path of a woman seeking to terminate her pregnancy prior to foetal viability.[73] Once the woman's right to make the ultimate decision is protected, any state regulation which seeks to discourage a decision to

---

[63] Theodor Meron (ed) *Human Rights in International Law: Legal and Policy Issues* Oxford: Clarendon 1984, 123. See the decision of the Constitutional Court of Austria, Decision of 11 October 974, quoted in Mauro Cappelletti and William Cohen *Comparative Constitutional Law: Cases and Materials* Indianapolis: Bobbs-Merrill 1979, 615–22.

[64] Meron 123.

[65] Francisco Forrest Martin, et al *International Human Rights Law and Practice: Cases, Treaties and Materials* Cambridge: Kluwer Law International 1997, 338.

[66] Ibid.

[67] *Roe v Wade* 410 US 113, 120.

[68] *Supra* at 153.

[69] *Supra*.

[70] *Supra* at 163.

[71] See generally *Maher v Roe* 432 US 464 (1977); *Webster v Reprod Health Servs* 492 US 490 (1989); *City of Akron v Akron Ctr for Reprod Health, Inc* 462 US 416 (1983); *Planned Parenthood v Casey* 505 US 833, 873 (1992).

[72] *Casey*, 505 US at 873 (1992).

[73] *Supra*.

abort will be upheld, provided the means chosen is reasonably related to the state's objective to protect life.[74]

The German courts on the other hand place the abortion dialogue within the context of their hierarchical constitutional value system: the right to life comes before the right to privacy.[75] They proceed from the basis that life begins at conception; therefore, the foetus' right to life supercedes the woman's right to privacy, if there are no extenuating circumstances such as risk to the mother, which would justify changing this order.[76] The right to life provision of the German Constitution imposes an affirmative duty upon the state to protect all life from harm, not only by the government, but by third parties as well.[77] Foetal life is not considered an exception to this rule because it has an independent legal value.[78] Thus, from the moment of implantation (fourteen days after conception), and continuing throughout the pregnancy, the life of the foetus is a life entitled to constitutional protection.[79] Although the right to life is examined within the context of the right to privacy, that is, the woman's right to choose whether she wants to terminate her pregnancy, the right to life is viewed as the preeminent right under art I(I).[80] It is within this context that the intentional destruction of a foetus, being 'an act of killing', constitutes a deprivation of the right to life, which may legitimately be criminally punished by the state.[81] The Polish Constitutional Tribunal has followed the German example in restricting abortion.[82]

Euthanasia

Similarly, the international community has not articulated a bright-line rule either proscribing or permitting voluntary euthanasia.[83] The pivotal question is whether the right to life necessarily mandates that an individual must continue to live, regardless of circumstances that may surround a decision to terminate one's life.[84] In *Cruzan v Missouri*, the petitioner, Cruzan, was severely injured in an automobile accident that left her in a vegetative state. Her parents sought to have her removed from life-support systems arguing that, while competent, she engaged in conversations which indicated her intent to have her life terminated if she could not live 'at least half way normally'.[85] The Mississippi Supreme Court held that in the absence of 'clear and convincing evidence' showing that Cruzan wanted to have her life terminated under circumstances such as these, her parents did not have the authority to effectuate such a request.[86] The Supreme Court affirmed this decision holding that although a competent person has a protected liberty interest which would permit the refusal of medical treatment, it does not follow that this right extends to incompetent persons.[87] In addition, although a

---

[74] *Supra* at 876.

[75] The German approach is reflected in the Court's decision in the opinion (1975) 39 BverfGE 1, the relevant parts of which are translated in Cappelletti & Cohen 586–605. The second seminal decision is the 1993 decision, the relevant parts of which are translated in Vicki C Jackson and Mark V Tushnet *Comparative Constitutional Law* New York: Foundation Press 1999, 134–9. The 1975 opinion is fully canvassed in Donald P Kommers *The Constitutional Jurisprudence of the Federal Republic of Germany* Durham: Duke University Press 1989, 351.

[76] Kommers 351.

[77] David P Carrie 'Positive and Negative Constitutional Rights' (1986) 53:3 *University of Chicago Law Review* 868.

[78] Donald P Kommers 'German Constitutionalism: A Prolegomenon' (1991) 40:3 *Emory Law Journal* 870.

[79] Kommers 351.

[80] Ibid.

[81] Op cit 352–3.

[82] Jackson & Tushnet 143.

[83] See Meron, 123; Richard B Bilder and Mark A Weisburd 'Book Review and Note: Legal and Moral Constraints on Low-Intensity Conflict' (1997) *American Journal of International Law* 375; see also Ellis S Magner 'Therapeutic Jurisprudence Forum: Therapeutic Jurisprudence: Its Potential For Australia' (1998) 67 *Revista Juridica de la Universidad de Puerto Rico* 121, 131 (stating that The Rights of the Terminally Ill Act, 1995 was the first example of euthanasia legislation to be enacted in the world).

[84] Ibid.

[85] *Cruzan* v Missouri 497 US 261, 265–266 (1990).

[86] *Supra* at 268.

[87] *Supra* at 263.

surrogate may sometimes legitimately act on behalf of an incompetent person, the procedural safeguard which requires clear and convincing evidence is constitutionally permissible.[88]

Death penalty

The Universal Declaration and the Civil Covenant did not envisage foreclosing capital punishment. At the time the Universal Declaration was adopted, the majority of states permitted capital punishment. Article 6 of the Civil Covenant provides conditions for the imposition of the death penalty. The American Convention provides limitations on the death penalty, and

precludes the reintroduction of the death penalty in states that have abolished it.[89] In the last three decades, more and more states, as recognized in international conventions, have moved towards the abolition of the death penalty.[90] In *Makwanyane*, all eleven of the justices in separate opinions, ruled that the death penalty as contained in s 277(1)(a) of the Criminal Procedure Act of 1977 constituted a violation of the right to life under the interim Constitution. Chaskalson P, who wrote the order of the Court, referred to the Hungarian Constitutional Court's decision, which found the death penalty to be a violation of the right to life and the right to human dignity.[91]

S v Makwanyane and Another
CCT/3/94 (6 June 1995), now cited as 1995 (6) BCLR 665 (CC); 1995 (3) SA 391 (CC)
(notes omitted)

[83][CHASKALSON P]: An individual's right to life has been described as '[t]he most fundamental of all human rights', and was dealt with in that way in the judgments of the Hungarian Constitutional Court declaring capital punishment to be unconstitutional. The challenge to the death sentence in Hungary was based on section 54 of its Constitution which provides:

(1) In the Republic of Hungary everyone has the inherent right to life and to human dignity, and no one shall be arbitrarily deprived of these rights.
(2) No one shall be subjected to torture or to cruel or inhuman or degrading punishment.

[84] Section 8, the counterpart of section 33 of our Constitution, provides that laws shall not impose any limitations on the essential content of fundamental rights. According to the finding of the Court, capital punishment imposed a

limitation on the essential content of the fundamental rights to life and human dignity, eliminating them irretrievably. As such it was unconstitutional. Two factors are stressed in the judgment of the Court. First, the relationship between the rights of life and dignity, and the importance of these rights taken together. Secondly, the absolute nature of these two rights taken together. Together they are the source of all other rights. Other rights may be limited, and may even be withdrawn and then granted again, but their ultimate limit is to be found in the preservation of the twin rights of life and dignity. These twin rights are the essential content of all rights under the Constitution. Take them away, and all other rights cease. I will deal later with the requirement of our Constitution that a right shall not be limited in ways which negate its essential content. For the present purposes it is sufficient to point to the fact that the Hungarian Court held capital punishment to be unconstitutional on the grounds that it is inconsistent with the right to life and the right to dignity.

[95] The carrying out of the death penalty destroys life, which is protected without reserva-

---

88 *Supra* at 281.
89 Articles 4(2) and 4(3) of the American Convention.
90 Ibid. In 1983, The European Convention was amended to abolish the death penalty. Protocol 6 to The Convention for the Protection of Human Rights and Fundamental Freedoms Concerning the Abolition of the Death Penalty (1983) 22 ILM 538. The Protocol entered into force on 1 March 1985. In *Soering v United Kingdom* (1989) 11 EHRR 439, the European Court of Human Rights held that no state party to the European Convention can extradite any person if that person would face the risk of being put to death in the requesting state.
91 *Makwanyane* paras 39 and 83–84 referring to Decision 23/1990 (X31) AB of the Hungarian Constitutional Court.

tion under ... our Constitution, it annihilates human dignity which is protected ....

[144] The rights to life and dignity are the most important of all human rights, and the source of all other personal rights .... By committing ourselves to a society founded on the recognition of human rights we are required to value these two rights above all others. And this must be demonstrated by the State in everything that it does, including the way it punishes criminals. This is not achieved by objectifying murderers and putting them to death to serve as an example to others in the expectation that they might possibly be deterred thereby.

Torture, cruel, inhuman, or degrading treatment

Section 12 of the Constitution provides for freedom and security of the person which includes freedom from: arbitrary arrest; detention without trial; public or private violence; torture; cruel, inhuman, or degrading punishment, and not to be subjected to medical or scientific experiments without consent. The concept of freedom and security of the person is largely understood as freedom from physical restraint,[92] and is therefore dealt with under the right to fair-trial procedures.[93]

Article 5 of the Universal Declaration prohibits torture, or cruel, inhuman, or degrading treatment. Similar prohibitions are contained in art 5 of the African Charter; art 7 of the Civil Covenant; art 3 of the American Convention, and art 5(2) of the European Convention. The Civil Covenant also prohibits medical or scientific experimentation without the free consent of the individual concerned. It is widely accepted that the prohibition against torture rises to the level of *jus cogens*.[94]

In order to constitute torture, actual physical brutality such as assault or rape is required.[95] This is reflected in the General Assembly Resolution of 1975,[96] which defines torture as an act 'by which severe pain or suffering, whether physical or mental, is intentionally inflicted ...'.[97] The difference between torture, and cruel inhuman or degrading treatment is one of the degree of the suffering inflicted. This is reflected in the above declaration which provides '[t]orture constitutes an aggravated and deliberate form of cruel, inhuman or degrading treatment or punishment'.[98] Degrading treatment is less in intensity then inhuman treatment.[99]

Ireland v United Kingdom
2 EHRR 25 (1979–80)
18 January 1978

The Emergency Situation and its Background

[11] JUDGE: The tragic and lasting crisis in Northern Ireland lies at the root of the present case. In order to combat what the respondent Government describe as 'the longest and most violent terrorist campaign witnessed in either part of the island of Ireland', the authorities in Northern Ireland exercised from August 1971 until December 1975 a series of extra-judicial powers of arrest, detention and internment. The proceedings in this case concern the scope and

---

92 See Chaskalson P in *Ferreira v Levin NO and Others; Vryenhoek and Others v Powell NO and Others* CCT 5/95 (6 December 1995) para 170, now cited as 1996 (1) SA 984 (CC); 1996 (1) BCLR 1 (CC).

93 See chapter 11.

94 American Law Institute *Restatement of the Law Third, Restatement of the Foreign Relations Law of the United States* St Paul: American Law Institute Publishers 1987, 161, 170. See also *Filartiga v Pena-Irala* 630 F2d 876 (2nd Cir 1980).

95 *Yagiz v Turkey* 22 EHRR 573 (1966). In *Yagiz*, the European Commission of Human Rights ruled that beating on the soles of the victims feet and rape both constituted torture.

96 UNGAR 3452 (XXX), The Declaration on the Protection of All Persons from being Subjected to Torture and other Cruel, Inhuman or Degrading Treatment or Punishment.

97 Article 1 of UNGAR 3452 (XXX).

98 Article 2.

99 *Tyrer v United Kingdom*, European Court of Human Rights 26 ECHR (ser A) (1978) 2 EHRR 1 (1979–1980): para 29–30.

the operation in practice of those measures as well as the alleged ill-treatment of persons thereby deprived of their liberty ....

[96] ... [Fourteen suspects in Northern Ireland] were submitted to a form of 'interrogation in depth' which involved the combined application of five particular techniques. These methods, sometimes termed 'disorientation' or 'sensory deprivation' techniques ... consisted of the following:

(a) wall-standing: forcing the detainees to remain for periods of some hours in a 'stress position', described by those who underwent it as being 'spreadeagled against the wall, with their fingers put high above the head against the wall, the legs spread apart and the feet back, causing them to stand on their toes with the weight of the body mainly on the fingers';

(b) hooding: putting a black or navy coloured bag over the detainees' heads and, at least initially, keeping it there all the time except during interrogation;

(c) subjection to noise: pending their interrogations, holding the detainees in a room where there was a continuous loud and hissing noise;

(d) deprivation of sleep: pending their interrogations, depriving the detainees of sleep;

(e) deprivation of food and drink: subjecting the detainees to a reduced diet during their stay at the centre and pending interrogations.

A Torture

Admittedly the word 'torture' included in Article 3 of the Convention is not capable of an exact and comprehensive definition. It is undoubtedly an aggravated form of inhuman treatment causing intense physical and/or mental suffering. Although the degree of intensity and the length of such suffering constitute the basic elements of torture, a lot of other relevant factors had to be taken into account. Such as: the nature of ill-treatment inflicted, the means and methods employed, the repetition and duration of such treatment, the age, sex and health condition of the person exposed to it, the likelihood that such treatment might injure the physical, mental and psycho-logical condition of the person exposed. Whether the injuries inflicted caused serious consequences for short or long duration are all relevant matters to be considered together and arrive at a conclusion whether torture has been committed.

It seems to me permissible, in ascertaining whether torture or inhuman treatment has been committed or not, to apply not only the objective test but also the subjective test.

As an example I can refer to the case of an elderly sick man who is exposed to a harsh treatment – after given several blows and beaten to the floor, is dragged and kicked on the floor for several hours I would say without hesitation that the poor man has been tortured. If such treatment is applied on a wrestler or even a young athlete, I would hesitate a lot to describe it as an inhuman treatment and I might regard it as a mere rough handling. Another example: if a mother, for interrogation, is separated from her suckling baby by keeping them apart in an adjoining room and the baby starts yelling of hunger for hours within the hearing of the mother and she is not allowed to attend her baby, again I should say both the mother and the baby have been subjected to inhuman treatment. The mother by being agonized and the baby by being deprived of the urgent attention of the mother. Neither the mother nor the child has been assaulted.

...

I do not share the view that extreme intensity of physical or mental suffering is a requisite for a case of ill-treatment to amount to 'torture' within the purport and object of Article 3 of the Convention. The nature of torture admits gradation in its intensity, in its severity and methods adopted. It is, therefore, primarily the duty and responsibility of the authority conducting the enquiries from close quarters, after taking into account all the surrounding circumstances, evidence and material available, to say whether in a particular case inhuman ill-treatment reached the degree of torture. In other words, this is a finding of fact for the competent authority dealing with the case in the first instance and, for reasons we give hereunder, we should not interfere with.

In *Makwanyane*, the Constitutional Court, *per* Chaskalson P, ruled that the death penalty consti-tuted cruel, inhuman, and degrading punishment:[100]

S v Makwanyane
CCT/3/94, now cited as 1995 (6)
BCLR 665 (CC) 1995 (3) SA 391 (CC)
(notes omitted)

[26] [CHASKALSON P]: Death is the most extreme form of punishment to which a convicted criminal can be subjected. Its execution is final and irrevocable. It puts an end not only to the right to life itself, but to all other personal rights which had vested in the deceased under Chapter Three of the Constitution. It leaves nothing except the memory in others of what has been and the property that passes to the deceased's heirs. In the ordinary meaning of the words, the death sentence is undoubtedly a cruel punishment. Once sentenced, the prisoner waits on death row in the company of other prisoners under sentence of death, for the processes of their appeals and the procedures for clemency to be carried out. Throughout this period, those who remain on death row are uncertain of their fate, not knowing whether they will ultimately be reprieved or taken to the gallows. Death is a cruel penalty and the legal processes which necessarily involve waiting in uncertainty for the sentence to be set aside or carried out, add to the cruelty. It is also an inhuman punishment for it '... involves, by its very nature, a denial of the executed person's humanity', and it is degrading because it strips the convicted person of all dignity and treats him or her as an object to be eliminated by the state. The question is not, however, whether the death sentence is a cruel, inhuman or degrading punishment in the ordinary meaning of these words but whether it is a cruel, inhuman or degrading punishment within the meaning of section 11(2) of our Constitution. The accused, who rely on section 11(2) of the Constitution, carry the initial onus of establishing this proposition.

[27] The principal arguments advanced by counsel for the accused in support of their contention that the imposition of the death penalty for murder is a 'cruel, inhuman or degrading punishment', were that the death sentence is an affront to human dignity, is inconsistent with the unqualified right to life entrenched in the Constitution, cannot be corrected in case of error or enforced in a manner that is not arbitrary, and that it negates the essential content of the right to life and the other rights that flow from it. The Attorney General argued that the death penalty is recognised as a legitimate form of punishment in many parts of the world, it is a deterrent to violent crime, it meets society's need for adequate retribution for heinous offences, and it is regarded by South African society as an acceptable form of punishment. He asserted that it is, therefore, not cruel, inhuman or degrading within the meaning of section 11(2) of the Constitution. These arguments for and against the death sentence are well known and have been considered in many of the foreign authorities and cases to which we were referred. We must deal with them now in the light of the provisions of our own Constitution.

[90] The United Nations Committee on Human Rights has held that the death sentence by definition is cruel and degrading punishment. So has the Hungarian Constitutional Court, and three judges of the Canadian Supreme Court. The death sentence has also been held to be cruel or unusual punishment and thus uncon-stitutional under the state constitutions of Massachusetts and California.

[91] The California decision is *People v Anderson*. Capital punishment was held by six of the seven judges of the Californian Supreme Court to be 'impermissibly cruel' under the California Constitution which prohibited cruel or unusual punishment. Also, it degrades and dehumanizes all who participate in its processes It is unnecessary to any legitimate goal of the state and is incompatible with the dignity of man and the judicial process.

---

[100] *Makwanyane* paras 90–92.

[92] In the Massachusetts decision in *District Attorney for the Suffolk District v Watson*, where the Constitution of the State of Massachusetts prohibited cruel or unusual punishment, the death sentence was also held, by six of the seven judges, to be impermissibly cruel.

In the *Williams* case,[101] six juveniles convicted for different offences were sentenced to receive a number of strokes with a light cane. Langa J, speaking for a unanimous court, ruled that state sanctioned corporeal punishment, provided for under s 294 of the Criminal Procedure Act of 1977, amounts to cruel, inhuman, and degrading treatment and an affront to human dignity, all of which are prohibited under the interim Constitution. The prohibitions against torture, cruel, inhuman and degrading treatment under s 11(2) of the interim Constitution, are identical in substance to what is contained in s 12 *(d)* and *(e)* of the final Constitution. In his opinion, Langa J alluded to the difference between torture, cruel, inhuman, and degrading treatment as being a difference in degree.

S v Williams and Others
CCT 20/94 (9 June 1995), now
cited as 1995 (3) SA 632 (CC); 1995 (7)
BCLR 861 (CC)
(notes omitted)

[19] LANGA J: Much of applicants' argument was, understandably enough, devoted to the alleged violation of section 11(2) of the Constitution. As the heading indicates, this section deals with '[f]reedom and security of the person' and the subsection provides that '[n]o person shall be subject to torture of any kind, whether physical, mental or emotional, nor shall any person be subject to cruel, inhuman or degrading treatment or punishment'. This is the only provision, among those relied upon by the applicants, that expressly refers to punishment. I propose to deal with the impact, if any, of sections 10 and 11(2) of the Constitution on the conduct which is prescribed by section 294 of the Act.

[20] It is clear that when the words of section 11(2) of the Constitution are read disjunctively, as they should be, the provision refers to seven distinct modes of conduct, namely: torture; cruel treatment; inhuman treatment; degrading treatment; cruel punishment; inhuman punishment and degrading punishment.

[21] In common with many of the rights entrenched in the Constitution, the wording of this section conforms to a large extent with most international human rights instruments. Generally, the right is guaranteed in absolute, non-derogable and unqualified terms; justification in those instances is not possible.

[22] The interpretation of the concepts contained in section 11(2) of the Constitution involves the making of a value judgment which 'requires objectively to be articulated and identified, regard being had to the contemporary norms, aspirations, expectations and sensitivities of the ... people as expressed in its national institutions and its Constitution, and further having regard to the emerging consensus of values in the civilised international community ...'.

[23] While our ultimate definition of these concepts must necessarily reflect our own experience and contemporary circumstances as the South African community, there is no disputing that valuable insights may be gained from the manner in which the concepts are dealt with in public international law as well as in foreign case law.

[24] The *Oxford English Dictionary* defines 'cruel' as 'causing or inflicting pain without pity', 'inhuman' as 'destitute of natural kindness or pity, brutal, unfeeling, savage, barbarous' and 'degrading' as 'lowering in character or quality, moral or intellectual debasement'. In South African case law, definitions of 'cruel,' with regard to treatment or punishment are rare. The

---

101 *S v Williams and Others* CCT 20/94 (9 June 1995), now cited as 1995 (7) BCLR 864 (CC); 1995 (3) SA 632 (CC).

phrase 'cruel treatment' has been used in the context of abuse of animals and has been described variously as 'wilfully caus[ing] pain without justification ... intention of causing it unnecessary suffering'; 'deliberate act causing substantial pain and not reasonably necessary in all the circumstances'.

[25] Whether it is necessary to split the words of the phrase and interpret the concepts individually is a matter which would largely depend on the nature of the conduct sought to be impugned. It may well be that in a given case, conduct that is degrading may not be inhuman or cruel. On the other hand, other conduct may be all three. It was suggested to us that a useful approach might be to grade the concepts on a sliding scale of suffering inflicted, torture occupying the extreme position, followed by cruel, inhuman and degrading, in that order.

[26] International forums offer very little guidance with regard to the meaning to be given to each word, individually. The tendency has been to deal with them as phrases or a combination of words. Thus when the United Nations Human Rights Committee (UNHRC) was called upon to interpret the corresponding section in the International Covenant on Civil and Political Rights (ICCPR), it did not consider 'it necessary to draw up a list of prohibited acts or to establish sharp distinctions between the different kinds of punishment or treatment; the distinctions depend on the nature, purpose and severity of the treatment applied'. According to the UNHRC, the assessment of what constitutes inhuman or degrading treatment depends on all the circumstances of the case, such as the duration and manner of the treatment, its physical or mental effects as well as the sex, age and state of health of the victim.

[27] Article 3 of the European Convention for the Protection of Human Rights and Fundamental Freedoms (European Convention), has been interpreted by distinguishing the concepts primarily by the degree of suffering inflicted. The European Commission of Human Rights (European Commission) described inhuman treatment as that which 'causes severe suffering, mental or physical, which in the particular situation is unjustifiable' and torture

as 'an aggravated form of inhuman treatment'. The European Court of Human Rights (European Court) found the difference between torture and inhuman treatment in the fact that the former attaches 'a special stigma to deliberate inhuman treatment causing very serious and cruel suffering'. The Court also categorised degrading conduct as that which aroused in its victims feelings of fear, anguish and inferiority leading to humiliation and debasement and possible breaking of their physical or moral resistance. The same Court distinguished between inhuman and degrading punishment in *Tyrer v United Kingdom*, and held that suffering had to reach a certain level before punishment could be characterised as inhuman. In a case where a juvenile had been sentenced to three strokes of the birch, the Court found that although that level had not been reached, the birching of the minor nevertheless amounted to degrading punishment.

[31] The decisions of the Supreme Courts of Namibia and of Zimbabwe are of special significance. Not only are these countries geographic neighbours, but South Africa shares with them the same English colonial experience which has had a deep influence on our law; we of course also share the Roman-Dutch legal tradition. Unlike our Constitution, the Namibian Constitution does not have a general limitation clause. Article 22 however specifies how limitations, whether they are built-in or are imposed by other laws, are to be employed. In *Ex parte Attorney-General, Namibia*, Mahomed AJA had no difficulty in arriving at the conclusion that the infliction of corporal punishment, whether on adults or juveniles, was inconsistent with article 8 of the Namibian Constitution and constituted 'inhuman or degrading' punishment.

[32] In *S v Ncube; S v Tshuma* and *S v Ndhlovu*, the Zimbabwe Supreme Court, dealing with the issue of corporal punishment for adults, held that the practice was inhuman and degrading in violation of section 15(1) of the Declaration of Rights of the Zimbabwe Constitution which prohibits 'torture or inhuman or degrading punishment'. The same conclusion

was reached with respect to juvenile whipping by the Zimbabwe High Court in *S v F*. Juvenile whipping was held to constitute inhuman and degrading punishment by the Zimbabwe Supreme Court in *S v Juvenile*. Gubbay JA characterised juvenile whipping as:

> ... inherently brutal and cruel; for its infliction is attended by acute physical pain. After all, that is precisely what it is designed to achieve. In short, whipping, which invades the integrity of the human body, is an antiquated and inhuman punishment which blocks the way to understanding the pathology of crime.

[39] There is unmistakably a growing consensus in the international community that judicial whipping, involving as it does the deliberate infliction of physical pain on the person of the accused, offends society's notions of decency and is a direct invasion of the right which every person has to human dignity. This consensus has found expression through the courts and legislatures of various countries and through international instruments. It is a clear trend which has been established.

Although only the prohibition against torture is considered *jus cogens* under international law, the Constitution makes torture, cruel and unusual punishment, and medical or scientific experimentation without consent, non-derogable under s 37(5). This is analogous to art 4(2) of the Civil Covenant which in addition to torture also makes the prohibition against cruel, inhuman, or degrading treatment or punishment non-derogable.

Slavery, servitude, and forced labour

Section 13 of the Constitution provides:

> No one may be subject to slavery, servitude or forced labour.

The prohibition against slavery is contained in art 4 of the Universal Declaration; art 5 of the African Charter; arts 8(1) and 8(2) of the Civil Covenant; art 4 of the European Convention, and art 6 of the American Convention. Under the Civil Covenant, art 4(2), there can be no derogation from the prohibition against slavery. The prohibition against slavery is also a non-derogable right under the Constitution, s 37(5). The prohibition against

slavery under art 4(2) of the Civil Covenant is also a non-derogable right. The prohibition against slavery is absolutely prohibited and is, therefore, a peremptory norm of international law.[102]

The prohibition against forced labour is not *jus cogens* and is also not listed as a non-derogable right under the Constitution. The Civil Covenant specifies that in addition to hard labour as punishment for a crime,[103] 'forced or compulsory labour' does not include military service,[104] service exacted in cases of emergency,[105] or any service as part of normal civil obligations.[106] Similar exemptions are contained in the regional instruments namely art 6(3) of the American Convention, and art 4(3) of the European Convention. The African Charter in Chapter II contains a list of duties owed to society. Article 29(2) of the African Charter requires an individual to serve the national community by placing his or her physical and intellectual abilities at its service. Therefore, forced community service required of medical graduates, or requirements that other professionals, such as lawyers, perform *pro bono* legal services does not constitute forced or compulsory labour.

Although the prohibition against slavery and servitude has risen to the level of *jus cogens* in the international community, the prohibition against

---

[102] American Law Institute 69. Frank C Newman and Karel Vasek 'Civil and Political Rights' in *The International Dimensions of Human Rights*, edited by Karel Vasak and Philip Alston. Westport: Greenwood Press 1982, 146.

[103] Article 8(3)*(b)* of the Civil Covenant.

[104] Article 8(3)*(c)*(ii).

[105] Article 8(3)*(c)*(iii).

[106] Article 8(3)*(c)*(iv).

forced labour is not absolute. For example, in both the American and European Conventions, labour may be compelled to fulfil 'normal civil obligations' or in 'emergency' situations.[107] An extreme case of economic and social underdevelopment might be enough of an emergency to justify the derogation from this principle.[108] However, some scholars argue that a purely economic purpose, cannot be the driving force behind the compulsion to work.[109] For example, anti-parasite laws that compel all able-bodied citizens to work, are condemned as violating the prohibition against forced labour.[110]

Privacy

Section 14 of the Constitution provides:

> 14 Everyone has the right to privacy, which includes the right not to have –
> (a) their persons or home searched;
> (b) their property searched;
> (c) their possessions seized; or
> (d) the privacy of their communications infringed.

The right to privacy is contained in art 12 of the Universal Declaration; arts 17, and 18 of the Civil Covenant; arts 8(1) and 9(1) of the European Convention, and arts 11 and 12 of the American Convention. The right to privacy is also protected in other parts of the Constitution, such as the sections on freedom of religion,[111] and freedom of association.[112] Although the Constitution does not explicitly spell out the right to worship, to practice belief or religion either privately or in community, freedom of religion and association means the right to worship, congregate and associate on a voluntary basis, which has deep implications for privacy. This is also recognized in the international instruments. For example, the Universal Declaration provides in art 18 that everyone has the freedom of thought, conscience, and religion which can be practised alone or in community with others, in public or in private. The right to practise religion, belief or worship either alone or in community with others is also affirmed in the Civil Covenant art 18(1); the European Convention art 9(1), and the American Convention art 12(1).

Different dimensions to privacy

What precisely does the right to privacy encompass? Does the right to privacy inhere in places, relationships, or people?[113] Privacy also raises difficult questions as to who should define its scope – the lawmaker, or the courts?

The right to privacy is implicated in two primary contexts. First, in the criminal procedure context which is addressed more fully under right to fair trial procedures.[114] In the criminal procedure context, it seeks to ensure that persons, their homes, property, possessions, and communications are not subject to unreasonable searches, seizures or invasion. The first context encompasses privacy mostly in a place-oriented context, such as an individual's home. The object of the protections against unwarranted interference is both the person and his or her home. Any interference by the government has to be subject to certain legal standards. The second context encompasses a liberty interest,[115] to include 'the

---

[107] Meron 125.

[108] R St J Macdonald 'Derogations under Article 15 of the European Convention on Human Rights' (1997) 36 *Columbia Journal of Transnational Law* 236.

[109] Richard B Lillich 'Civil Rights' in *Human Rights in International Law: Legal and Policy Issues*, edited by Theodor Meron. Oxford: Clarendon Press 1984, 126.

[110] Ibid.

[111] Section 15 of the Constitution.

[112] Section 18.

[113] Ralph A Rossum and Alan G Tarr *American Constitutional Law: Cases and Interpretation* New York: St Martin's Press, 3rd edition, 1991, 686.

[114] See chapter 11.

[115] This is most cogently reflected in the decisions of the USSC in cases such as *Griswold v Connecticut* 381 US 479 (1965) and *Roe v Wade* 410 US 113 (1973).

right to be let alone'.[116] The latter context includes a conception of privacy interests which includes a right to 'be left alone', to do 'as one pleases', and to enter into relationships without government interference.[117] While the first idea of privacy seeks to regulate the way the government invades or interferes with a person or his or her property, the idea of privacy under the second context means that there are certain substantive aspects to privacy, which preclude the government from regulating individuals and relationships. For example, in the first context, if the government wants to enter a property, and confiscate private possessions, it has to adhere to certain procedures, more aptly referred to as due process or criminal procedure safeguards.[118] Under the second situation, the process more than the right is the issue. For example, the government cannot prescribe to a man or a woman whom they may or may not marry. This is a fundamental privacy right that belongs to the individual. If the government wants to deprive a person of this right, it needs a justification that can surmount the limitations clause. The right to privacy in the second context involves matters of a personal nature and how one defines one's self.[119]

The right to be left alone

The right to privacy 'as the right to be left alone' is a more difficult concept – particularly considering individual autonomy balanced against the rights of society as a whole.[120] As an extreme example, an individual may want to walk nude in public. The individual's right to define himself or herself in this way may offend the sensibilities of others. In *Bernstein*, Ackermann J alluded to this difficulty and mentioned that '[t]he concept of privacy is an amorphous and elusive one which has been the subject of much scholarly debate'.[121] Ackermann J proceeds with the idea that privacy is linked to the idea of autonomous identity.[122] What is acceptable is often defined in terms of what is acceptable under prevalent community standards.[123] An individual may have a right to walk nude, or exhibit nude pictures in his or her home, but may not have the right to walk nude in public, or exhibit nude pictures in public. There is, however, an inner sanctum of each person that cannot be invaded, for example what they do in the privacy of their own homes, their family life, and their sexual preferences.[124]

Bernstein and Others v Bester NO and Others 1996 CCT 23/95 (27 March 1996), now cited as 1996 (4) BCLR 449 (CC); 1996 (2) SA 751 (CC)
(notes omitted)

[65] ACKERMANN, J: The concept of privacy is an amorphous and elusive one which has been the subject of much scholarly debate. The scope of privacy has been closely related to the concept of identity and it has been stated that 'rights, like the right to privacy, are not based on a notion of the unencumbered self, but on the notion of what is necessary to have one's own autonomous identity'.

[66] In expanding upon this notion Forst acknowledges that communal bonds are not to be substituted with abstract relations, but argues beyond this for a multi-levelled recognition of identity. Besides the concrete and abstract

[116] Samuel D Warren and Louis D Brandeis 'The Right to Privacy' (1980) 4 *Harvard Law Review* 193.
[117] *National Coalition for Gay and Lesbian Equality and Another v The Minister of Justice and Others* CCT 11/98 (9 October 1998) para 30, now cited as 1998 (12) BCLR 1517 (CC); 1999 (1) SA 6 (CC).
[118] See chapter 11.
[119] *Bernstein and Others v Bester and Others NNO* CCT 23/95 (27 March 1996) para 65, now cited as 1996 (2) SA 751 (CC); 1996 (4) BCLR 449 (CC).
[120] Basil S Markesinis *Foreign Law and Comparative Methodology: A Subject and A Thesis* Oxford: Hart 1997, 382.
[121] *Bernstein* para 65.
[122] *Supra* para 65.
[123] *Supra* para 68.
[124] *Supra* para 67; *National Coalition for Gay and Lesbian Equality* para 32.

realms, this thirdly also pertains to societal membership and fourthly to the community of humanity itself.

[67] The relevance of such an integrated approach to the interpretation of the right to privacy is that this process of creating context cannot be confined to any one sphere, and specifically not to an abstract individualistic approach. The truism that no right is to be considered absolute, implies that from the outset of interpretation each right is always already limited by every other right accruing to another citizen. In the context of privacy this would mean that it is only the inner sanctum of a person, such as his/her family life, sexual preference and home environment, which is shielded from erosion by conflicting rights of the community. This implies that community rights and the rights of fellow members place a corresponding obligation on a citizen, thereby shaping the abstract notion of individualism towards identifying a concrete member of civil society. Privacy is acknowledged in the truly personal realm, but as a person moves into communal relations and activities such as business and social interaction, the scope of personal space shrinks accordingly.

[68] ... The unlawfulness of a (factual) infringement of privacy is adjudged 'in the light of contemporary *boni mores* and the general sense of justice of the community as perceived by the Court'.

[69] Examples of wrongful intrusion and disclosure which have been acknowledged at common law are entry into a private residence, the reading of private documents, listening in to private conversations, the shadowing of a person, the disclosure of private facts which have been acquired by a wrongful act of intrusion, and the disclosure of private facts contrary to the existence of a confidential relationship. These examples are all clearly related to either the private sphere, or relations of legal privilege and confidentiality. There is no indication that it may be extended to include the carrying on of business activities.

[73] Use of this term has not been unproblematic, since in terms of a resolution of the consultative Assembly of the Council of Europe this right has been defined as follows:

The right to privacy consists essentially in the right to live one's own life with a minimum of interference. It concerns private, family and home life, physical and moral integrity, honour and reputation, avoidance of being placed in a false light, non-revelation of irrelevant and embarrassing facts, unauthorised publication of private photographs, protection from disclosure of information given or received by the individual confidentially.

And in the final conclusions of the Nordic Conference on the Right to Respect for Privacy of 1967 the following additional elements of the right to privacy are listed: the prohibition to use a person's name, identity or photograph without his/her consent, the prohibition to spy on a person, respect for correspondence and the prohibition to disclose official information. The Commission has connected the right to privacy of Article 8 also with the right to freedom of expression of Article 10 by stating that 'the concept of privacy' in Article 8 also includes, to a certain extent, the right to establish and maintain relations with other human beings for the fulfilment of one's personality. This expansion of the concept by the European Commission is strongly reminiscent of Forst's explanation, *supra*, as to his use of the concept of 'identity', namely that it refers to the ability of a person to relate to him or herself and to be able to relate to others in a meaningful way.

Invasion of privacy can also come about through the reading of private documents, listening to private conversations, and disclosing private facts through a wrongful act or intrusion.[125] The Civil Covenant provides that no one may be subjected to arbitrary or unlawful interference with his or her

---

[125] *Bernstein* para 69.

privacy, family, or home correspondence, or to unlawful attacks on his or her honour and reputation.[126]

In *Griswold v Connecticut*,[127] the United States Supreme Court invalidated the State of Connecticut's law prohibiting the use and distribution of contraceptives. Justice Douglas held that the law violated the right to privacy by prohibiting married couples from using contraceptives.[128] Justice Douglas said '[W]ould we allow the police to search the sacred precincts of the marital bedrooms for telltale signs of the use of contraceptives?[129] The very idea is repulsive to the notions of privacy surrounding the marriage relationships'.[130] Justice Douglas' conclusion was based on the need to protect the privacy of the bedroom from invasion by the state.

Special protection is accorded to individual autonomy exercised within the confines of an individual's home.[131] In *Case*, the applicants were charged with contravention of s 2 of the Indecent or Obscene Photographic Matter Act,[132] which prohibited the possession of sexually explicit material. The sexually explicit video cassettes were seized by the police from the applicants' home. The applicants argued that the provisions of the Act violated their right to privacy under the interim Constitution. The judges unanimously (and in five separate opinions), ruled that the statute violated the right to privacy.[133] What sexually explicit material individuals view in the privacy of their home, for their personal use is the business of neither the state nor society.[134] Similarly in *National Coalition for Gay and Lesbian Equality*, the Court, *per* Ackermann J, held that privacy includes 'a right to a sphere of private intimacy and autonomy' to establish human relationships without interference from others.[135] The way an individual expresses his or her sexuality 'is at the core of this area of private intimacy'.[136] The majority of the justices in *Case* held that the right to view sexually explicit material in the home is not exempt from any limitation.[137] For example, children should not be exposed to pornographic material.[138]

Case and Another v Minister of Safety and Security; Curtis and Others v Minister of Safety and Security CCT 20/95, CCT 21/95 (9 May 1996), now cited as *Case and Another v Minister of Safety and Security and Others; Curtis v Minister of Safety and Security and Others* **1996 (5) BCLR 609 (CC); 1996 (3) SA 617 (CC)** (notes omitted).

[90] DIDCOTT J: These cases concern the possession of material that is hit by the Indecent or Obscene Photographic Matter Act (No 37 of 1967). I underline the word 'possession', then underline it again. Neither case has anything to do with the production of such material, with its importation, publication, exhibition, distribution or dissemination.

[91] What erotic material I may choose to keep within the privacy of my home, and only

---

[126] Article 17.1 of the Civil Covenant.

[127] 381 US 479, 486 (1965).

[128] *Supra* at 485.

[129] *Supra*.

[130] *Supra* at 486.

[131] *Case and Another v Minister of Safety and Security; Curtis v Minister of Safety and Security* CCT 20/95; CCT 21/95 (9 May 1996), now cited as 1996 (3) SA 617 (CC); 1996 (5) BCLR 609 (CC).

[132] Act 37 of 1967.

[133] Mokgoro J, para 65. Didcott J, (concurred by Chaskalson P, Mahomed DP, Ackermann, Kriegler, and O' Regan JJ and Ngoepe AJ) at para 91; Langa J, (concurred by Chaskalson P, Mahomed DP, Ackermann, Kriegler, and O'Regan JJ) para 97; Madala J, para 102; Sachs J, para 108.

[134] Didcott J, para 91.

[135] *National Coalition for Gay and Lesbian Equality* para 32.

[136] *Supra*.

[137] *Case*, Didcott J, para 93; Langa J, para 99. Madala J, para 105.

[138] *Supra*.

for my personal use there, is nobody's business but mine. It is certainly not the business of society or the state. Any ban imposed on my possession of such material for that solitary purpose invades the personal privacy which section 13 of the interim Constitution (Act 200 of 1993) guarantees that I shall enjoy. Here the invasion is aggravated by the preposterous definition of 'indecent or obscene photographic matter' which section 1 of the statute contains. So widely has it been framed that it covers, for instance, reproductions of not a few famous works of art, ancient and modern, that are publicly displayed and can readily be viewed in major galleries of the world. That section 2(1) clashes with section 13 seems to be indisputable.

[93] ... The production of pictures like those, and of further types equally depraved, is certainly an evil and may well deserve to be suppressed.

Perhaps, as a means to that end, the same even goes for their possession, making it both reasonable and justifiable for society to mind the private business of its members. Such questions do not arise at present and are best left unanswered until some future case confronts us with them. But the trouble one now has with section 2(1) is that it hits the possession of other material too, material less obnoxious and sometimes quite innocuous which we cannot remove from its range while it lasts because the parts of section 1 giving it that effect are not satisfactorily severable from the rest. A better target at which to aim in the battle with unbearably vile pictures as matters stand for the time being, a target under fire already from separate legislation as I mentioned earlier, is surely their production whenever that occurs here, the importation of one's produced elsewhere, and the dissemination of all.

Reproductive choices

There is a rich progeny of cases in other jurisdictions which recognize the right to make reproductive choices as flowing from the right to privacy and security of person.[139] In *Morgentaler*, the majority of the justices of the Canadian Supreme Court, *per* Dickson CJ, held that to force a woman, by threat of criminal sanction, to carry a foetus to term constituted a profound interference with a woman's body and a violation of security of the person.[140] The majority concluded that security of the person meant that an individual had the right to control over his or her body and to make decisions about his or her life.[141] In *Eisenstadt*, the Court was faced with the constitutionality of a Massachusetts statute prohibiting the distribution of contraceptives to unmarried individuals, and only allowed physicians to distribute contraceptives to married

persons.[142] Justice Brennan writing for the majority held: '[I]f the right to privacy means anything, it is the right of the individual married or single, to be free from unwarranted governmental intrusion into matters so fundamentally affecting a person as the decision whether to bear or beget a child'.[143] In *Roe v Wade*, the United States Supreme Court held that the Constitution protects the right of a woman to procure an abortion prior to viability of the foetus.[144] The United States Constitution does not expressly mention the right to privacy. The recent decisions on the right to contraception and abortion have been located in the Fourteenth Amendment's concept of liberty.[145] The Canadian Supreme Court has also located the right to seek an abortion as flowing from the right to security of the person. It is unclear that the Constitutional Court will follow the same approach in tying these

---

[139] See the Canadian SC case of *Morgentaler, Smoling and Scott v The Queen* [1988] 1 SCR 30. *Eisenstadt v Baird* 405 US 438 (1972); *Carey v Population Services International* 431 US 678 (1977); *Roe v Wade* 410 US 113 (1973).

[140] *Morgentaler* para 27.

[141] *Supra.*

[142] *Eisenstadt*, 405 US at 440.

[143] *Supra* at 453.

[144] *Roe* 410 US at 153.

[145] *Eisenstadt* 405 US at 446-455; *Roe* 410 US at 153; *Casey* 505 US at 846.

rights to liberty. The South African Constitution has express provisions on privacy,[146] and the right to make decisions over reproduction and control over one's body.[147] In *Ferreira v Levin*, Ackermann and Sachs J interpreted the interim Constitution's freedom and security protections,[148] as also encompassing a residual liberty protection.[149] The majority of the justices felt that freedom and security related primarily to physical integrity,[150] and cautioned that the Court should be careful from straying from this primary sense of what freedom and security represents. However, on a proper construction, they would be prepared to accept that freedom and security need not only protect physical integrity and could include protection of a fundamental freedom not adequately protected in the Bill of Rights.[151]

Control over personal information

Privacy interests include the right to control information about oneself.[152] However, the government can order disclosure of certain information to achieve important state objectives. In *Whalen v Roe*,[153] the United States Supreme Court declared: '[W]e are not unaware of the threat to privacy implicit in the accumulation of vast amounts of personal information in computerized data banks or other massive government files. The collection of taxes, the distribution of welfare and social security benefits, the supervision of public health, the direction of our Armed Forces, and the enforcement of the criminal laws all require the orderly preservation of great quantities of information, much of which is personal in character and potentially embarrassing or harmful if disclosed'.[154] Whether, or not the state can compel disclosure of the information depends on the nature of the information and the context within which it is sought. In *Bernstein*,[155] the applicants challenged the validity of ss 417 and 418 of the Companies Act,[156] these sections required them to appear before an enquiry pertaining to the liquidation of a company, and to produce certain documents relating to the affairs of the company (which was now in liquidation proceedings). The applicants were members of an auditing firm that audited the company in liquidation and argued that the demand that they appear before the enquiry, and the demand that they turn over documents violated their right to privacy. The Constitutional Court, *per* Ackermann J, held that the compulsion to respond to a subpoena does not constitute an invasion of privacy.[157] Under certain circumstances, disclosure of a person's identity might constitute a breach of privacy.[158] The Court also held that disclosure of private information including books and documents could constitute an invasion of privacy.[159] The Court concluded that to properly pronounce on the claim of privacy, the content of the document or information in respect to which the applicant claims a privacy interest, must be

---

[146] Section 14 of the Constitution.

[147] Section 12(2).

[148] Found in s 11(1) of the interim Constitution and now contained in s 12(1) of the final Constitution.

[149] See *Ferreira v Levin* CCT 5/95 (6 December 1995) now cited as 1996 (1) SA 984 (CC); 1996 (1) BCLR 1 (CC)(Ackermann J, at para 69; Sachs J, at para 249).

[150] *Supra, per* Chakalson P, para 170.

[151] *Supra* para 185.

[152] Section 32(1)(a) of the Constitution grants everyone the right to access to information held by the state. Section 32(1)(b) grants a right to access to information held by a private person where the information is required for the exercise or protection of any right. The right to information is regulated in terms of the Promotion of Access to Information Act 2 of 2000. The implications of the Act on private persons and their right to access to information are discussed more fully in chapters 10 and 11.

[153] *Whalen v Roe* 429 US 589 (1977).

[154] *Supra* at 605.

[155] *Bernstein*.

[156] Act 61 of 1973, as amended.

[157] *Bernstein* para 58.

[158] *Suptra* para 64.

[159] *Supra*.

disclosed. Without having that information, the Court cannot make a determination as to whether privacy interests are implicated.[160]

Similarly, in *SARFU 2*, the Court held that a witness before a commission of enquiry could be asked to produce documents or answer questions which might intrude on their privacy.[161] If the document sought and the questions posed are relevant to an investigation of public concern, the invasion of privacy will be sustained.[162]

The German Constitutional Court, in the *Microcensus* case held that a government questionnaire or census that asks questions which intrude into the intimate realm of personal life, could violate the right to privacy and self-determination.[163] Privacy interests are at their greatest when they relate to personal aspects of a person's existence,[164] and are much narrower outside personal matters.[165] This means that privacy protection for an individual is greater than it would be for a corporation or a juristic person.[166] Similarly, if an individual enters into a social relationship such as becoming a director of a public company, a social dimension comes into play, which restricts the scope of an individual's privacy.[167] The state could require the individual

that enters into the public realm to disclose information pertaining to that individual's conduct. In *Bernstein*, the Court held that the knowledge of a director, or an auditor of a company concerning the affairs of the company, does not come within the purview of privacy interests.[168] For example, court proceedings pertaining to marriage and divorce, even though they may concern intimate details about personal relationships are public record.[169]

Even within the private sphere, the state can require individuals to disclose certain information about themselves if the information is needed for legitimate state goals. In the *Microcensus* case, the German Constitutional Court held that a government census (which is aimed at providing information for long-term state planning), so long as it does not require individuals to disclose intimate details about personal life, does not violate the right to privacy.[170] In the *Census Act* case, the German Constitutional Court similarly upheld a government census about personal data such as name, address, sex, marital status, religious affiliation, sources of income, education background, hours of work, and modes of transportation.[171]

---

[160] *Supra.*

[161] *The President of the Republic of South Africa and Others v South African Rugby Football Union and Others* CCT 16/98 (10 September 1999) para 186, now cited as 1999 (10) BCLR 1059 (CC); 2000 (1) SA 1 (CC) (*SARFU 2*).

[162] *Supra.*

[163] (1969) 27 BVerfGE 1 in Kommers 307.

[164] *The Investigating Directorate: Serious Economic Offences and Others v Hyundai Motor Distributors (Pty) Ltd: In re Hyundai Motor Distributors (Pty) Ltd and Others v Smit NO and Others* CCT 1/100 (25 August 2000) para 18, now cited as 2000 (10) BCLR 1079 (CC); 2001 (1) SA 545 (CC).

[165] *Supra. Microcensus* case in Kommers 307.

[166] *Hyundai Motors* para 18.

[167] *Bernstein* para 77.

[168] *Supra* para 83.

[169] See *Carlisle v Fawcett Publications, Inc* 201 CalApp2d 733 (1962)(marriage an event 'of public record' and disclosure does not violate right to privacy); see also *Aquino v Bulletin Co* 190 Pa Super 528; 154 A2d 422(1959) (applying the same rule for divorce); *Green v Uccelli* 207 Cal App 3d 1112, 1120 (1997).

[170] *Microcensus* case in Kommers 307–8.

[171] *Census Act* case (1983) 65 BVerfGE 1 in Kommers 332–5.

Bernstein and Others v Bester and Others NNO
CCT 23/95 (27 March 1996), now
cited as 1996 (4) BCLR 449 (CC); 1996 (2)
SA 751 (CC)
(notes omitted)

[83][ACKERMANN, J]: Although the phrase 'information concerning the ... affairs ... of the company' appears to be quite broad facially, it must be construed in conformity with the aforementioned purpose of the inquiry. It is difficult to see how any information which an individual possesses which is relevant to the purpose of the enquiry can truly be said to be private. One is after all concerned here with the affairs of an artificial person with no mind or other senses of its own; it depends entirely on the knowledge, senses and mental powers of humans for all its activities. In the words of Rogers CJ in *Spedly Securities v Bond Corporation Holdings Ltd Directors and Others* concerned with the management and affairs of a failed company (in which category of persons I would certainly include the auditors) 'owe a duty to creditors and shareholders to provide a candid, full and truthful account of their stewardship'. This duty arises from the very fact that the company has no mental or sensory capacities of its own.

[84] In this regard I find the following observation of Bryson J in *Lombard Nash International Pty Ltd v Berentsen*, when made in relation to precisely this corporate deficiency, acute, sound and relevant: the company in a fair sense ought to be thought of as the owner of the knowledge in their [the officers' of the company] minds. If that is so, and I agree that it is for purposes of present analysis, then it can hardly be said that the knowledge of the director, official or auditor bearing relevantly on the affairs of the company that has failed can be said to fall within such person's domain of personal privacy. I would hold the same in relation to a mere debtor or creditor of the company. If such knowledge is relevant, it is relevant because of some legal relationship between such person and the company, which can hardly be said to be private.

[85] The establishment of a company as a vehicle for conducting business on the basis of limited liability is not a private matter. It draws on a legal framework endorsed by the community and operates through the mobilization of funds belonging to members of that community. Any person engaging in these activities should expect that the benefits inherent in this creature of statute, will have concomitant responsibilities. These include, amongst others, the statutory obligations of proper disclosure and accountability to shareholders It is clear that any information pertaining to participation in such a public sphere, cannot rightly be held to be inhering in the person, and it cannot consequently be said that in relation to such information a reasonable expectation of privacy exists. Nor would such an expectation be recognised by society as objectively reasonable. This applies also to the auditors and the debtors of the company. On the facts of this case the conclusion seems to be unavoidable that no threat to or infringement of any of the applicants' right to privacy as protected by section 13 of the Constitution has been established. The application of the Constitution to the issue of 'sufficient cause' in the present context would operate as follows. The first part of the enquiry is whether answering the particular question would infringe the applicant's right to privacy. If it would, this would constitute 'sufficient cause' for declining to answer the question unless the section 418(5)(*b*)(iii)(*aa*) compulsion to answer the question would, in all the circumstances, constitute a limitation on the right to privacy which is justified under section 33(1) of the Constitution.

Emergency powers

Section 37 of the Constitution provides:

37 (1) A state of emergency may be declared only in terms of an Act of Parliament and only when—
(a) the life of the nation is threatened by war, invasion, general insurrection, disorder, natural disaster, or other public emergency; and
(b) the declaration is necessary to restore peace and order.
(2) A declaration of a state of emergency, and any legislation enacted or other action taken in consequence of that declaration, may be effective only—
(a) prospectively from the date of the declaration; and
(b) for no more than 21 days from the date of the declaration, unless the National Assembly resolves to extend the declaration. The National Assembly may extend a declaration of a state of emergency for no more than three months at a time. The first extension of the state of emergency must be by a resolution supported by a majority of the members of the National Assembly. Any subsequent extension must be by a resolution supported by at least 60 per cent of the members of the Assembly. A resolution in terms of this paragraph may be adopted only following a public debate in the Assembly.
(3) Any competent court may decide on the validity of—
(a) a declaration of a state of emergency;
(b) any extension of a declaration of a state of emergency; or
(c) any legislation enacted, or other action taken, in consequence of a declaration of a state of emergency.
(4) Any legislation enacted in consequence of a declared state of emergency may derogate from the Bill of Rights only to the extent that—
(a) the derogation is strictly required by the emergency; and
(b) the legislation—
(i) is consistent with the Republic's obligations under international law applicable to states of emergency;
(ii) conforms to subsection (5); and
(iii) is published in the national *Government Gazette* as soon as reasonably possible after being enacted.
(5) No Act of Parliament that authorises a declaration of a state of emergency, and no legislation enacted or other action taken in consequence of a declaration, may permit or authorise—
(a) indemnifying the state, or any person, in respect of any unlawful act;
(b) any derogation from this section; or
(c) any derogation from a section mentioned in column 1 of the Table of Non-Derogable Rights, to the extent indicated opposite that section in column 3 of that table.

An emergency is an unexpected event that poses a grave danger to the state. A dictionary definition of an emergency is 'a crisis', or 'a decisive turning point' in a condition or state of affairs – everything depending on the outcome.[172] The definition suggests a pressing situation usually necessitating a difficult choice.[173] The essential idea that emerges from the definition is that the situation confronting the country is not normal and therefore extraordinary measures are required to deal with the crisis.

Section 37 of the Constitution is consistent with international human rights instruments in allowing for human rights derogations in a public emergency. The Civil Covenant and the two regional instruments permit derogation from international obligations under certain circumstances. Article 4(1) of the Civil Covenant allows state parties to derogate from their obligations in times of public emergencies. Similar provisions are contained in art 15 of the European Convention, and art 27 of the American Convention.

With the hindsight of the apartheid order, the Constitution borrows from international law

---

[172] *Webster's Encyclopedic Unabridged Dictionary of the English Language* (1989) 467.
[173] Ibid.

instruments by regulating the imposition of emergency powers. The regulations contain a number of safeguards to prevent the abuse of emergency powers, such as occurred under the apartheid order. The statutory state of emergency powers under the apartheid order conferred on the executive wide discretionary powers in situations other than war. In terms of the Public Safety Act, the state president could proclaim a state of emergency, if he or she believed that events in the country were of such a nature as to pose a threat to public safety. It was a wholly discretionary measure which the state president could exercise in terms of his or her discretion. Since 1960, the statutory state of emergency has been declared three times.[174]

The proclamation conferred on the security forces wide powers. The police had the power to search and seize materials from any place or premises without a warrant. They were empowered not only to impose curfews in any area, but also to remove a person from a particular place. The freedom of press was severely restricted. For example, the press was limited in reporting the activities of the security forces and matters relating to unrest to only what the government had approved for reporting. No person was permitted to incite any civil disobedience or boycott activities. Any person who contravened the state of emergency faced a prison sentence of up to ten years or a fine of up to R20 000, or both. In terms of the state of emergency, thousands of people, including many children, were detained. There were numerous complaints of police brutality and torture of detainees. No civil or criminal proceedings could be brought against the state president, police, or other government official acting pursuant to the state of emergency, even if it lead to injury or death.

The Constitution recognizes the need for strong government action in times of emergency. An emergency can arise in two contexts. First, in a war situation, whether of an international or internal nature. This is also recognized in international law instruments, which speak about war or public emergency threatening the life of the nation.[175] The Constitution speaks about the possible declaration of a state of emergency in war, insurrection, natural disorder, or other public emergency.[176] The term 'other public emergency' was defined by the European Court of Human Rights in the case of *Lawless* as referring 'to an exceptional situation of crisis or emergency which affects the whole population and constitutes a threat to the organized life of the community of which the State is composed.'[177] Disasters such as earthquakes, fires, droughts, floods, and famines could be classified under the categories of natural disaster or other public emergency.[178]

While the Constitution allows for the declaration of a state of emergency, it seeks to balance the need for strong government action in times of emergency against the need for not compromising fundamental liberties. History has shown many examples where in a state of war, there is a tendency for national fervour to reach a heightened pitch, resulting in serious human rights violations, particularly against 'unpopular' groups.[179] This occurs, for instance, in internal or civil wars as shown by the atrocities in Rwanda and Bosnia. An argument can be made that there needs to be greater vigilance during times of war – as required by the Constitution. The Constitution contains detailed provisions as to the conditions that have to be fulfilled, and the procedure that needs to be followed for a declaration of a state of emergency. A state of emergency may be declared

---

[174] The most recent state of emergency was proclaimed in June 1986. Proc 108 of 1986 in *GG* 10279 of 12 June 1986. The restrictions in terms of the state of emergency were from time to time amended and tightened.

[175] Article 15 of the European Convention; art 27(1) of the American Convention.

[176] Section 37(1)*(a)* of the Constitution.

[177] *Lawless v Ireland*, European Court of Human Rights (1961) 3 ECHR (ser A) para 28.

[178] Stephen Marks 'Principles and Norms of Human Rights Applicable in Emergency Situations: Underdevelopment, Catastrophes and Armed Conflicts' in *The International Dimensions of Human Rights*, edited by Karel Vasak and Philip Alston. Westport: Greenwood Press 1982, 176.

[179] At the time of the Second World War, the US government rounded up US citizens of Japanese ancestry, none of whom committed any crime, and kept them under conditions resembling a concentration camp. The action was validated by the USSC as necessary for the war effort in *Korematsu v United States* 323 US 214 (1944).

only in terms of an Act of Parliament, and only when the life of the nation is threatened,[180] and the declaration must be necessary to restore peace and order.[181] The maintenance of a state of emergency needs periodic approval from the National Assembly (NA).[182] After three months, any extension of the declaration of a state of emergency must be approved by at least sixty per cent of the members of the NA.[183] The Court, at all times, is competent to rule on the validity, extension or conditions of the state of emergency.[184] The procedural requirements under the Constitution, with respect to the role of the legislature and the Court reflects emerging consensus on standards for declaration of a state of emergency. For example, the 1991 Conference of Security and Co-operation in Europe (CSCE), consisting of Western and former East European states, promulgated standards for a state of emergency.[185] The standards require that states of emergency can only be declared by a constitutionally lawful body empowered to do so,[186] and require that the legislature must remain functioning – if at all possible.[187] The standards further require that legal guarantees necessary to uphold the rule of law must remain in force.[188]

In addition to the procedural guarantees, there are also substantive rights which under international law need to be respected – even under a state of emergency. Section 37(5)(c) of the Constitution provides that even under a state of emergency, there can be no derogation from the rights characterized as 'non-derogable', under the Bill of Rights. The rights protected from derogation under Table 3 include equality; human dignity; life; freedom from medical or scientific experimentation without consent; slavery and servitude; certain rights of children, and certain rights of arrested, detained, and accused persons. In addition, neither the state, nor any person can be indemnified for an unlawful act.[189]

The international human rights instruments also provide that there are certain rights which cannot be derogated from even in public emergencies. Under the international instruments, there can be no derogation from the right to life;[190] freedom from torture;[191] freedom from slavery,[192] and freedom from retrospective laws.[193] The Civil Covenant and the American Convention also preclude derogation from the right to legal personality[194] and freedom of conscience.[195] The Civil Covenant precludes derogation from imprisonment for civil debt.[196] The American Convention has additional rights[197] from which there can be no derogation. The rights include the rights of the family;[198] right to a name;[199] rights of the

---

[180] Section 37(1)(a) of the Constitution.

[181] Section 37(1)(b).

[182] Section 37(2)(b).

[183] Section 37(2)(b).

[184] Section 37(3).

[185] Document for the Moscow Meeting of the Conference on the Human Dimension of the CSCE 3 October 1991 (Published in (1991) 30 *International Legal Materials* 1670).

[186] Op cit 28.2.

[187] Op cit 28.5.

[188] Op cit 28.9.

[189] Section 37(5)(a) of the Constitution.

[190] Article 6 of the Civil Covenant; art 2 of the European Convention; art 4 of the American Convention.

[191] Article 3 of the Civil Covenant; art 7 of the European Convention; art 5 of the American Convention.

[192] Articles 8(1) and 8(2) of the Civil Covenant; art 4(1) of the European Convention; art 6 of the American Convention.

[193] Article 15 of the Civil Covenant; art 7 of the European Convention; art 9 of the American Convention.

[194] Article 16 of the Civil Covenant; art 13 of the American Convention.

[195] Article 18 of the Civil Covenant; art 12 of the American Convention.

[196] Article 11 of the Civil Covenant.

[197] Which are listed in art 27(2) of the American Convention.

[198] Article 17.

[199] Article 18.

child;[200] right to nationality;[201] the right to participate in government,[202] and judicial guarantees for the protection of fundamental rights.[203] In an advisory opinion, the Inter-American Court of Human Rights has affirmed that independence of the judiciary cannot be ousted in times of emergency.[204] Such independence is particularly important to ensure that *habeas corpus* and a person's physical integrity is preserved.[205] The International Law Association asserts that a right to a fair trial is a non-derogable right.[206] The Constitution recognizes the importance of *habeas corpus* and physical integrity and entrenches judicial review on the declaration of the state of emergency. It further entrenches the right to judicial review with respect to detention without trial.[207] Section 35(6) lists detailed steps to be followed whenever someone is detained without trial.

The Constitution also requires that a declaration of a state of emergency not conflict with international law obligations.[208] For example, under the Geneva Convention[209] there are required humanitarian norms and practices with respect to combatants and civilian populations.[210] Article 27 of the Geneva Convention,[211] requires that religious freedoms in all circumstances be protected. Religious freedom is not a non-derogable right under the Table of Non-derogable Rights in the Constitution.

The Constitution requires that any legislation enacted under the state of emergency may derogate from the Bill of Rights only to the extent that the derogation is strictly required by the emergency.[212] This section might prove difficult to adjudicate in some circumstances. Given the seriousness of an emergency threatening the state of the nation, intervention by the Court, to second-guess the other branches of government can sometimes pose problems. For example, what standards is the Court going to use if the national government has to justify every emergency action, such as rationing of scarce resources, curfews, or limitations on free speech, challenged by individuals while the country is in the midst of a serious war, or natural catastrophe? Having to justify each action before the courts, in terms of rigorous requirements, may hamper the war effort. Whenever non-derogable fundamental rights are not implicated, the national government could in some situations be accorded greater deference under the emergency powers, simply because the Court may not have the necessary fact-finding powers. It is very difficult for the Court to second-guess the national government on what is necessary to prosecute a war. Commenting on the war and emergency powers in the United States, Laurence Tribe notes that while the Supreme Court's deference to the legislative branch of government in *Korematsu v United States*[213] and other cases was wrong, these powers are exercised by the legislative branch in times of emergency. The Supreme Court does not have the fact finding ability that the other branches of government have and 'prudent awareness of the limits of judicial power, and out of simple unfamiliarity with the

---

[200] Article 19.

[201] Article 20.

[202] Article 23.

[203] Article 27(2).

[204] Inter-American Court of Human Rights Advisory Opinion OC-9/87 of 6 October 1987 at paras 20, 29.

[205] *Supra* paras 30–31.

[206] International Law Association, Paris Minimum Standards of Human Rights Norms in a State of Emergency, art 7 (1984).

[207] The right to challenge the lawfulness of the detention, together with a host of other right to fair-trial procedures, is made a non-derogable right.

[208] Section 37(4)*(b)*(i) of the Constitution.

[209] (1950) 75 UNTS done at Geneva on 12 August 1949, entered into force on 21 October 1950.

[210] eg common art 3 of the Geneva Convention prohibits the taking of hostages.

[211] Geneva Convention Relative to the Protection of Civilian Prisoners in Times of War 6 UST 3516, TIAS 3365, 75 UNTS 287.

[212] Section 37(4)*(a)* of the Constitution.

[213] 323 US 214 (1944).

issues raised', means the Court should defer to the other branches of government.[214] This deference applies both to the declaration of the state of emergency as well as the steps taken to deal with the state of emergency. For example, let us assume that the country faces terrible flooding resulting in food and raw-material shortages. Parliament subsequently declares a state of emergency to deal with the crisis. It would be difficult for a Court to second-guess legislative findings as to the scope of the crisis, assuming that parliament takes certain measures, including rationing and price controls, as extraordinary measures to respond to food and raw material shortages. Again, it would be very difficult for the Court to intervene and second-guess the legislature on what is appropriate action to deal with the crisis.

Political rights

Section 19 of the South African Constitution provides:

> 19 (1) Every citizen is free to make political choices, which includes the right –
> (a) to form a political party;
> (b) to participate in the activities of, or recruit members of, a political party; and
> (c) to campaign for a political party or cause.
> (2) Every citizen has the right to free, fair and regular elections for any legislative body established in terms of the Constitution.
> (3) Every adult citizen has the right–
> (a) to vote in elections for any legislative body established in terms of the Constitution, and to do so in secret; and
> (b) to stand for public office and, if elected, to hold office.

The rights contained in s 19 are integrally linked to the achievement of democracy. It is aimed at ensuring that government is based on the will of the people. To ensure that the will of the people is carried out, the Constitution requires free and fair elections for all legislative bodies created under the Constitution. Section 19 begins by recognizing the role of political parties in modern democracies. Therefore, it guarantees every individual the right to form, participate, recruit, and campaign for political parties. Moreover, it guarantees the right to vote and stand as a candidate for public office. Similar protections are contained in art 21 of the Universal Declaration; art 25 of the Civil Covenant; art 13 of the African Charter; art 23 of the American Convention, and art 3 of Protocol 1 to the European Convention.[215]

As regards the type of electoral system adopted, there is a wide degree of discretion available to each country. The European Court of Human Rights has held that the obligation to hold free elections at reasonable intervals under secret ballot, does not create an obligation to introduce a specific system of ballot.[216] In *Certification I*, a challenge was brought to the 'anti-defection clause' in the Constitution which requires any parliamentarian who defects to another political party to vacate his or her seat.[217] The objectors argued that the anti-defection clause undermined accountable, responsive, and democratic government.[218] The Court held that the anti-defection clause is wholly consistent with a democratic system of government. The clause requires members of a political party, who were elected based on their names being on the party's list, to be loyal to the party. The loyalty to the party fulfils the expectations of the electorate who voted for the party.[219]

In all modern democracies, political parties are indispensable agencies through which political organization occurs. Parties serve as the vehicle

---

[214] Laurence Tribe *American Constitutional Law* Mineola: Foundation Press, 2nd edition, 1988, 355.
[215] Protocol 1 to the European Convention For the Protection of Human Rights and Freedoms ETS 9, 213 UNTS 262 (Entered into force in 1954).
[216] *Mathieu-Mohin and Clerfayt v Belgium* European Court of Human Rights 113 ECHR. (ser A) (1987) 10 EHRR 1 (1988) at para 54.
[217] *Certification I* para 180.
[218] *Supra* para 182.
[219] *Supra* para 183.

though which leaders are elected, mobilization is conducted, and common interests are pursued.[220] As Kommers notes, political parties 'recruit leaders, crystallize issues, aggregate interests, organize governments, and make policies'.[221] In *Certification I*, the Court recognized that under the system of proportional representation provided for in the Constitution, a parliamentarian who does not adhere to the party line can lose his or her seat and party affiliation. The Court stated that it is parties 'that the electorate vote for, and parties which must be accountable to the electorate'.[222] While the legislature is democratically elected and conducts itself (in relation to all political parties) in a democratic way, in a political system based purely on party affiliation with proportional representation, major policy decisions are made within the political parties. In light of the reality that political parties are the indispensable and real tool though which democracy and political organization is expressed under our Constitution, it is arguable that there should be an obligation for political parties to conduct their affairs in a democratic manner. Otherwise, democracy in the legislature could be the legislature rubber stamping decisions taken behind closed doors by the party elite. Mindful of this possibility, the German Constitution, therefore, requires that 'political parties shall participate in the forming of the political will of the people. Their internal organization must conform to democratic principles'.[223] As Eckart Klein observes, in the German system, 'the decision-making process within the parties must be organized according to democratic principles; otherwise the line of democratic feedback between the rulers and the people would be interrupted'.[224] This mandate is in a constitutional system that does not have an anti-defection clause.[225]

Self-determination and political rights

The Constitution in s 235 speaks about self-determination and the possibility (by national legislation), of recognition of communities sharing a common cultural and language heritage.[226] The right to self-determination is a legal right recognized in a number of United Nations human rights documents. Article 55 of the United Nations Charter mentions 'the principles of equal rights and self-determination of peoples'.[227] The two International Covenants on Human Rights in article 1 state: 'all peoples and all nations shall have the right to self-determination'.[228] The right to self-determination is reaffirmed in art 20 of the African Charter on Human and People's Rights.[229]

As a concept, self-determination has not been free of problems. Two questions arise: first, whether the right to self-determination arises in a colonial context alone, or secondly, whether the right of groups within a state to secede from that state is accommodated.[230] For a long time, the right to self-determination was seen as only the

---

[220] George Ross 'The Constitution and the Requirements of Democracy' in *New Challenges to the German Basic Law*, edited by Christian Starck. Baden-Baden: Nomos 1991, 123.

[221] Kommers *Constitutional Jurisprudence of the Federal Republic of Germany* 201.

[222] *Certification I* para 186.

[223] Article 21(1) of the German Basic Law.

[224] Eckart Klein 'The Parliamentary Democracy' on *The Constitution of the Federal Republic of Germany: essays on the Basic Rights and Principles of the Basic Law with a translation of the Basic law*, edited by Ulrich Karpen. Baden-Baden: Nomos 1988, 161.

[225] Klein 155.

[226] See also discussion of self-determination in chapter 5.

[227] UN Charter 26 June 1945, 59 Stat 1031, TS 993, 3 Bevans 1153, entered into force on 24 October 1945.

[228] International Covenant On Economic, Social And Cultural Rights 993 UNTS 3, (1967) 6 ILM 360, adopted by the UNGA 16 December 1966 and entered into force on 3 January 1976. International Covenant on Civil And Political Rights 999 UNTS 171, (1967) 6 ILM 368, adopted by the UNGA 16 December 1966 and entered into force on 23 March 1976.

[229] African Charter on Human and Peoples' Rights (Banjul Charter) OAU Doc CAB/LEG/67/3Rev 5; adopted by the Organization of African Unity on 27 June 1981 and entered into force on 21 October 1986.

[230] For the different understandings of the right to self-determination, see chapter 5.

right to be free from colonial or foreign domination.[231] According to this interpretation, there was no further claim to self-determination once a country achieved its independence or freedom from foreign domination.[232] More recently, self-determination has come to mean – under certain circumstances – secession from an existing state, and the formation of a new state.[233]

Self-determination in the South African Constitution is not meant to apply in either of the international law contexts. In the *First Certification* decision, the Constitutional Court stated emphatically that self-determination, as used in the Constitution, does not embody any notion of separation or political independence. Instead, self-determination protects associational rights and institutions providing for democratic governance.[234] Self-determination stands for the right of citizens to choose their own form of government, institutions, and economic and political structure.[235]

Citizenship

Section 20 of the Constitution provides:

No citizen may be deprived of citizenship.

Article 15 of the Universal Declaration proclaims that everyone 'has the right to a nationality', and continues that no one 'shall be arbitrarily deprived of his nationality'. This article was designed to underscore the requirement that individuals should not be arbitrarily stripped of their nationality – as under the Nazi regime.[236] With respect to the regional instruments, only art 20 of the American Convention contains reference to a right to a nationality.

The right to citizenship in the Constitution is important in light of the denationalization of millions of South Africans under the apartheid order – as under the Nazi regime in Germany. The Population Registration Act classified the South African population under different groups,[237] or four primarily racial groups. The African population was further sub-divided into eight additional sub-groups (or tribal divisions), and confined to designated areas where they were considered to be that area's nationals. Simultaneously these groups were stripped of their rights to South African citizenship.

Freedom of movement and residence

Section 21 provides for freedom of movement;[238] the right to leave the republic;[239] right to enter; to remain and live anywhere in South Africa,[240] and the right to a passport.[241] Freedom of movement is contained in art 13 of the Universal Declaration; art 12 of the Civil Covenant; art 12 of the African Charter; art 22 of the American Convention, and art 2 of Protocol 4 to the European Convention.[242] Freedom of moment includes both

---

[231] This view was supported by the UN in its actions in various secessionist conflicts such as in the Congo and Nigeria. In both of these instances, the UN decided against the secessionist movements In the case of Congo, the UN sent troops to crush the irredentist forces. See Christopher O Quaye *Liberation Struggles In International Law* Philadelphia: Temple University Press 1991, 232.

[232] See Ziyad Motala 'Under International Law, does the New Order in South Africa assume the Obligations and Responsibilities of the Apartheid Order: An Argument for Realism over Formalism' (1997) 30 *South African Yearbook of International Law* 294–5.

[233] For a discussion of the historical evolution of the right to self-determination starting from the restrictive view of self-determination meaning only right to be free from colonial rule, to an expanded meaning allowing for fragmentation of existing states, see Richard F Iglar 'The Constitutional Crisis in Yugoslavia and the International Law of Self-determination: Slovenia and Croatia's Right to Secede' (1992) 15 *Boston College International and Comparative Law Review* 213.

[234] *Certification I* para 24. This is discussed in greater detail in chapter 5.

[235] For the understanding that self-determination means internal democratic governance see Hector Gross Espiell *The Right to Self-determination: Implementation of United Nations Resolutions* New York: United Nations 1980, 10.

[236] 3 UNGAR, (1948) C (123 mtg) 352.

[237] Act 30 of 1950.

[238] Section 21(1) of the Constitution.

[239] Section 21(2).

[240] Section 21(3).

[241] Section 21(4).

[242] ETS 46, (1986) 7 ILM 978.

internal freedom – the right to move freely within the country, as well as external freedom – the right to leave and enter the country. The state could impose limitations on the right to leave the country if the state requires an individual to fulfil certain obligations before he or she leaves the country.[243] Assume recent medical graduates want to leave the country before serving the required community probation period. It might be reasonable for the state to require them to fulfil their obligations before leaving the country – even, if only, for travel purposes. In *Peltonen*, the Government of Finland refused to grant Peltonen a passport until he completed his military service. Peltonen argued that this restriction violated his right to travel under art 12 of the Civil Covenant. The Human Rights Commission held that the right to travel could not be invoked to avoid compulsory military service.[244] The commission further held that the restriction that the Finnish government imposed was reasonable, and there was no violation of the right to travel.[245]

---

[243] *Peltonen v Finland* UNHR Committee Communication 492/1992. Views adopted on 21 July 1994 UN Doc CCPR/C/51/D/492/1992 (1994).

[244] Op cit 8.3.

[245] Op cit 8.4.

8

The right to equality

Introduction

Section 9(1) of the South African Constitution proclaims:

> 9 (1) Everyone is equal before the law and has the right to equal protection and benefit of the law.
>
> (2) Equality includes the full and equal enjoyment of all rights and freedoms. To promote the achievement of equality, legislative and other measures designed to protect or advance persons, or categories of persons, disadvantaged by unfair discrimination may be taken.
>
> (3) The state may not unfairly discriminate directly or indirectly against anyone on one or more grounds, including race, gender, sex, pregnancy, marital status, ethnic or social origin, colour, sexual orientation, age, disability, religion, conscience, belief, culture, language and birth.
>
> (4) No person may unfairly discriminate directly or indirectly against anyone on one or more grounds in terms of subsection (3). National legislation must be enacted to prevent or prohibit unfair discrimination.
>
> (5) Discrimination on one or more of the grounds listed in subsection (3) is unfair unless it is established that the discrimination is fair.

The preamble to the United Nations Charter asserts the equal rights of men and women. It further affirms that one of the purposes of the United Nations (UN) is to achieve equal rights and self-determination of peoples.[1] The Charter also proclaims that the purpose of the UN is to promote and encourage respect for human rights and fundamental freedoms for everyone without regard to race, sex, language, or religion.[2] The Universal Declaration, in its preamble, also asserts 'the equal and inalienable rights of all members of the human family'. Article 1 of the Universal Declaration speaks about equality and proclaims that '[e]veryone is entitled to all rights and freedoms set forth in this Declaration without distinction of any kind, such as race, colour, sex, language, religion, political or other opinion, national or social origin, property, birth or other status'. Article 7 further provides that '[A]ll are equal before the law and are entitled without discrimination to equal protection of the law. All

---

[1] Article 1(2) of the Charter.
[2] Article 1(3).

are entitled to equal protection against any discrimination in violation of this Declaration and against any incitement to such discrimination'. Equality is required under art 26 of the Civil Covenant; art 3(1) of the African Charter, and art 24 of the American Convention. In the *South West Africa* case,[3] the International Court of Justice held that to enforce distinctions based on race, colour, descent, national, or ethnic origin is a flagrant violation of the purposes and principles of the UN Charter.[4] The right to equality is part of customary international law, if not *jus cogens*. The prohibition against discrimination is part of the non-derogable rights contained in the 'Table of Non-derogable Rights' in s 37(5)(c) of the Constitution.[5]

Like the interim Constitution,[6] the Constitution expresses equality in two main ways. Section 9(1) states the right positively as a right to be treated equally before the law. Section 9(3) is phrased negatively to preclude discrimination by the state, while s 9(4) precludes discrimination by other parties. The Constitutional Court has resisted interpreting the various equality provisions into watertight compartments.[7] Instead, it prefers to look at the equality provisions in their entirety, as a guarantee to equal treatment under the law.[8] However, s 9(1) also speaks about the right to the equal 'benefit of the law'. Section 9(2) recognizes the need for affirmative action to redress imbalances which historically disadvantaged groups suffer. Sections 9(1) and 9(2) could be interpreted as a mandate for substantive equality, which under certain circumstances requires equality in results and not just in opportu-

nity.[9] Apart from sanctioning affirmative action, the Constitution in s 9(4) requires that national legislation must be enacted to prevent or prohibit unfair discrimination.[10] The Court's treatment of equality is one of the more complex areas of the law. This chapter will attempt to provide an in-depth analysis of the methodology the Court employs in the field of equality. The chapter will consider: the definition of equality; the steps involved in the Court's equality analysis; the difficulties and problems involved in questions of equality; the different types of discrimination, namely facial discrimination, discrimination in application and discrimination in effects; discrimination in relation to corrective/affirmative action; the role of the Court in the context of affirmative action, and the use of immutable characteristics in non-affirmative action contexts.

Definition of equality

How does one define equality? Few laws exist that which do not make distinctions between groups of people. If one wants a driver's licence, there are age requirements that need to be adhered to. The law imposes distinctions between legal and illegal acts. People engaging in illegal acts are subject to punishments not imposed on others. In seeking university admission certain criteria must first be met. Qualifying for government benefits requires following specific rules and criteria. In every classification, some are favoured and others not. A law stating only those of eighteen years or older may receive a driver's licence, naturally excludes a

---

3 'Opinion on the Presence of South Africa in Namibia' (1971) *International Court of Justice Reports.*
4 Op cit para 131.
5 Hereinafter referred to as s 37(5)(c) non-derogable rights
6 Section 9 of the interim Constitution.
7 *Per* Ackermnann, J in *Prinsloo v Van der Linde and Another* CCT 4/96 (18 April 1997) para 20, now cited as 1997 (3) SA 1012 (CC); 1997 (6) BCLR 759 (CC).
8 *Supra* para 22.
9 *National Coalition for Gay and Lesbian Equality and Another v The Minister of Justice and Others* CCT 11/98 (9 October 1998) para 60–61, now cited as 1998 (12) BCLR 1517 (CC); 1999 (1) SA 6 (CC)(Ackerman, J)(*National Coalition for Gay and Lesbian Equality I*). In terms of this concept, the state is entitled and sometimes required to take affirmative steps, to equalize opportunities for differently situated people. The implications of this argument are explored later under affirmative action, and in chapter 13 dealing with social and economic rights. For a discussion of formal versus substantive equality, see John de Waal, et al *The Bill of Rights Handbook* Cape Town: Juta & Co, 2nd edition, 1999, 190–1.
10 Pursuant to this mandate, parliament adopted the Promotion of Equality and Prevention of Unfair Discrimination Act 4 of 2000.

seventeen-year-old. This, even supposing that the under-age driver may be able to demonstrate better driving skills than the eighteen-year-old. What does unequal treatment of people mean? Should we insist that equality requires that anyone, including a minor who can demonstrate that they can drive competently, is entitled to a drivers licence? In *Hoffmann v South African Airways*,[11] the Constitutional Court was faced with a challenge to the practice of South African Airways (SAA) who refused to employ HIV-positive persons as cabin attendants. People suffering from advanced AIDS complications may well be medically unfit to perform their tasks.[12] The question before the Court was whether SAA could adopt a blanket policy of excluding all persons who were HIV positive?

One approach is to assert that all legal distinctions should be treated as discrimination.[13] Any categorization, in order to pass constitutional muster, will have to satisfy the limitations clause of the Constitution. This approach would impact on efficient government and impose high administrative costs on the lawmaker, who will have to satisfy the limitations clause in each and every categorization it adopts. For example, the lawmaker will have to show that a law, precluding a seventeen-year-old from driving a motor vehicle, will impose a heavy burden on the lawmaker – if the legislature has to satisfy the limitations clause.

Unlike the first approach, based on the assumption that all distinctions are *prima facie* invalid, under the second approach the Court is required to investigate whether the differences are valid or invalid. The origin of equality jurisprudence usually lies in the definition of Aristotle that 'things which are equal should be treated equally'. Those that are unequal can be treated unequally in proportion to that inequality.[14] This principle is expressed as requiring equal protection and equal benefit to persons who are similarly situated, and conversely, that persons who are differently situated be treated differently.[15] The problem with the definition is that it is stated at a level of abstraction. What criteria make people similar or dissimilar? How do we determine criteria for similarity or dissimilarity? Human beings are infinitely similar and dissimilar. The definition of Aristotle is further refined to require that differences in treatment can withstand constitutional scrutiny only if the differences between individuals are relevant or unfair.[16] Returning to the example of the driving licence: excluding a seventeen-year-old from receiving a driver's licence is unlikely to be found discriminatory or unfair. However, to exclude a person who has HIV-positive status from seeking employment where that person is fully competent to perform the task required, constitutes an impairment of that person's dignity and unfair discrimination based on prejudice.[17] The following discussion illustrates the overall test the Court employs, and the factors the Court considers in determining whether there is discrimination and whether the discrimination is unfair.

Test for discrimination

In *Harksen v Lane*,[18] the Court summarized the stages of inquiry which need to be conducted to determine whether there is discrimination under s 8 of the interim Constitution, now incorporated in s 9 of the final Constitution.[19] The Court has adopted the equality jurisprudence and the analysis it developed under the interim Constitution as applicable to 'section 9 of the 1996 Constitution,

---

[11] *Hoffmann v South African Airways* CCT 17/00 (28 September 2000) para 32 and 37, now cited as 2000 (10) BCLR 1211 (CC); 2001 (1) SA 1 (CC).

[12] *Supra* para 32.

[13] This is the view advocated by Peter W Hogg *Constitutional Law of Canada* Scarborough: Carswell, 3rd edition, 1992, 1164. See also Patrick Macklem, et al *Constitutional Law of Canada* Toronto: Emond Montgomery Publishers 1994, 616.

[14] Hogg 1159; JM Kelly, et al *The Irish Constitution* Dublin: Butterworths, 3rd edition, 1994, 724–5.

[15] Macklem 612.

[16] Geoffrey R Stone, et al *Constitutional Law* Boston: Little Brown, 3rd edition, 1996, 565.

[17] *Hoffman v South African Airways* paras 32 and 37.

[18] *Harksen v Lane and Others* CCT 9/97 (7 October 1997), now cited as 1998 (1) SA 300 (CC); 1997 (11) BCLR 1489 (CC).

[19] *Supra* para 53.

notwithstanding certain differences in the word-ings of these provisions'.[20]

Harksen v Lane and Others
CCT 9/97 (7 October 1997), now
cited as 1997 (11) BCLR (CC);
1998 (1) SA 349 (CC)
(notes omitted)
GOLDSTONE J (concurred by CHASKALSON P,
LANGA DP, ACKERMANN J, and KRIEGLER J):

The Equality Clause

[53] ... it may be as well to tabulate the stages of enquiry which become necessary where an attack is made on a provision in reliance on section 8 of the interim Constitution. They are:

(a) Does the provision differentiate between people or categories of people? If so, does the differentiation bear a rational connec-tion to a legitimate government purpose? If it does not then there is a violation of section 8(1). Even if it does bear a rational connection, it might nevertheless amount to discrimination.

(b) Does the differentiation amount to unfair discrimination? This requires a two-stage analysis:
    (i) Firstly, does the differentiation amount to 'discrimination'? If it is on a specified ground, then discrimination will have been established. If it is not on a specified ground, then whether or not there is discrimination will depend upon whether, objectively, the ground is based on attributes and characteris-tics which have the potential to impair the fundamental human dignity of persons as human beings or to affect them adversely in a comparably serious manner.
    (ii) If the differentiation amounts to 'discrimination', does it amount to 'unfair discrimination'? If it has been found to have been on a specified ground, then unfairness will be pre-sumed. If on an unspecified ground, unfairness will have to be established by the complainant. The test of unfairness focuses primarily on the impact of the discrimination on the complainant and others in his or her situation.

    If, at the end of this stage of the enquiry, the differentiation is found not to be unfair, then there will be no violation of section 8(2).

(c) If the discrimination is found to be unfair then a determination will have to be made as to whether the provision can be justified under the limitations clause ....

[40] It was further submitted on behalf of Mrs Harksen that the provisions of section 21 of the Act were in violation of the equality clause of the interim Constitution. More particularly it was contended that the vesting provision constitutes unequal treatment of solvent spouses and discriminates unfairly against them; and that its effect is to impose severe burdens, obligations and disadvantages on them beyond those applicable to other persons with whom the insolvent had dealings or close relationships or whose property is found in the possession of the insolvent. Moreover, to the extent that section 21(10) favours solvent spouses who are 'traders', it discriminates against solvent spouses who are not 'traders'. It was submitted further that section 21(2), which entitles a solvent spouse to claim the return of what in fact belongs to him or her, does not save the provision. There may be a number of innocent reasons why the solvent spouse is not able to establish that the property belongs to him or her. Counsel for Mrs Harksen suggested that the provisions of section 21 constituted a violation of both sections 8(1) (a denial of equality before the law and equal protection of the law) and 8(2) (unfair discrimination).

---

[20] *National Coalition for Gay and Lesbian Equality I* para 15.

[42] Where section 8 is invoked to attack a legislative provision or executive conduct on the ground that it differentiates between people or categories of people in a manner that amounts to unequal treatment or unfair discrimination, the first enquiry must be directed to the question as to whether the impugned provision does differentiate between people or categories of people. If it does so differentiate, then in order not to fall foul of section 8(1) of the interim Constitution there must be a rational connection between the differentiation in question and the legitimate governmental purpose it is designed to further or achieve. If it is justified in that way, then it does not amount to a breach of section 8(1).

[43] Differentiation that does not constitute a violation of section 8(1) may nonetheless constitute unfair discrimination for the purposes of section 8(2). The foregoing is my understanding of the judgment in *Prinsloo*. It was there stated in the majority judgment that:

If each and every differentiation made in terms of the law amounted to unequal treatment that had to be justified by means of resort to s 33, or else constituted discrimination which had to be shown not to be unfair, the Courts could be called upon to review the justifiability or fairness of just about the whole legislative programme and almost all executive conduct. The Courts would be compelled to review the reasonableness or the fairness of every classification of rights, duties, privileges, immunities, benefits or disadvantages flowing from any law. Accordingly, it is necessary to identify the criteria that separate legitimate differentiation from differentiation that has crossed the border of constitutional impermissibility and is unequal or discriminatory 'in the constitutional sense'.

Taking as comprehensive a view as possible of the way equality is treated in s 8, we would suggest that it deals with differentiation in basically two ways: differentiation which does not involve unfair discrimination and differentiation which does involve unfair discrimination.

In dealing with differentiation which does not involve unfair discrimination the Court stated:

It must be accepted that, in order to govern a modern country efficiently and to harmonise the interests of all its people for the common good, it is essential to regulate the affairs of its inhabitants extensively. It is impossible to do so without differentiation and without classifications which treat people differently and which impact on people differently. It is unnecessary to give examples which abound in everyday life in all democracies based on equality and freedom. Differentiation which falls into this category very rarely constitutes unfair discrimination in respect of persons subject to such regulation, without the addition of a further element . . . .

It is convenient, for descriptive purposes, to refer to the differentiation presently under discussion as 'mere differentiation'. In regard to mere differentiation the constitutional State is expected to act in a rational manner. It should not regulate in an arbitrary manner or manifest 'naked preferences' that serve no legitimate governmental purpose, for that would be inconsistent with the rule of law and the fundamental premises of the constitutional State. The purpose of this aspect of equality is, therefore, to ensure that the State is bound to function in a rational manner. This has been said to promote the need for governmental action to relate to a defensible vision of the public good, as well as to enhance the coherence and integrity of legislation . . . .

Accordingly, before it can be said that mere differentiation infringes s 8 it must be established that there is no rational relationship between the differentiation in question and the governmental purpose which is proffered to validate it. In the absence of such rational relationship the differentiation would infringe s 8. But while the existence of such a rational relationship is a necessary condition for the differentiation not to infringe s 8, it is not a sufficient condition; for the differentiation might still constitute unfair discrimination if that further element . . . is present.

[44] If the differentiation complained of bears no rational connection to a legitimate governmental purpose which is proffered to validate it, then the provision in question

violates the provisions of section 8(1) of the interim Constitution. If there is such a rational connection, then it becomes necessary to proceed to the provisions of section 8(2) to determine whether, despite such rationality, the differentiation none the less amounts to unfair discrimination.

[45] The determination as to whether differentiation amounts to unfair discrimination under section 8(2) requires a two stage analysis. Firstly, the question arises whether the differentiation amounts to 'discrimination' and, if it does, whether, secondly, it amounts to 'unfair discrimination'. It is as well to keep these two stages of the enquiry separate. That there can be instances of discrimination which do not amount to unfair discrimination is evident from the fact that even in cases of discrimination on the grounds specified in section 8(2), which by virtue of section 8(4) are presumed to constitute unfair discrimination, it is possible to rebut the presumption and establish that the discrimination is not unfair.

What Constitutes Discrimination

[46] Section 8(2) contemplates two categories of discrimination. The first is differentiation on one (or more) of the fourteen grounds specified in the subsection (a 'specified ground'). The second is differentiation on a ground not specified in subsection (2) but analogous to such ground (for convenience hereinafter called an 'unspecified' ground) which we formulated as follows in *Prinsloo*:

The second form is constituted by unfair discrimination on grounds which are not specified in the subsection. In regard to this second form there is no presumption in favour of unfairness . . . .

Given the history of this country we are of the view that 'discrimination' has acquired a particular pejorative meaning relating to the unequal treatment of people based on attributes and characteristics attaching to them. [U]nfair discrimination, when used in this second form in section 8(2), in the context of section 8 as a whole, principally means treating persons differently in a way which impairs their fundamental dignity as human beings, who are inherently equal in dignity.'

Where discrimination results in treating persons differently in a way which impairs their fundamental dignity as human beings, it will clearly be a breach of section 8(2). Other forms of differentiation, which in some other way affect persons adversely in a comparably serious manner, may well constitute a breach of section 8(2) as well.

There will be discrimination on an unspecified ground if it is based on attributes or characteristics which have the potential to impair the fundamental dignity of persons as human beings, or to affect them adversely in a comparably serious manner.

[47] The question whether there has been differentiation on a specified or an unspecified ground must be answered objectively. In the former case the enquiry is directed at determining whether the statutory provision amounts to differentiation on one of the grounds specified in section 8(2). Similarly, in the latter case the enquiry is whether the differentiation in the provision is on an unspecified ground (as explained in para 46 above). If in either case the enquiry leads to a negative conclusion then section 8(2) has not been breached and the question falls away. If the answer is in the affirmative, however, then it is necessary to proceed to the second stage of the analysis and determine whether the discrimination is 'unfair'. In the case of discrimination on a specified ground, the unfairness of the discrimination is presumed, but the contrary may still be established. In the case of discrimination on an unspecified ground, the unfairness must still be established before it can be found that a breach of section 8(2) has occurred.

[48] Before proceeding to the second stage of the enquiry, it is necessary to comment briefly on one aspect of the specified and unspecified grounds of differentiation which constitute discrimination. In the above quoted passage from *Prinsloo* it was pointed out that the pejorative meaning of 'discrimination' related to the unequal treatment of people 'based on attributes and characteristics attaching to them'. For purposes of that case it was unnecessary to

attempt any comprehensive description of what 'attributes and characteristics' would comprise.

What Constitutes Unfair Discrimination

[50] The nature of the unfairness contemplated by the provisions of section 8 was considered in paras 41 and 43 of the majority judgment in the *Hugo* case. The following was stated:

[41] The prohibition on unfair discrimination in the interim Constitution seeks not only to avoid discrimination against people who are members of disadvantaged groups. It seeks more than that. At the heart of the prohibition of unfair discrimination lies a recognition that the purpose of our new constitutional and democratic order is the establishment of a society in which all human beings will be accorded equal dignity and respect regardless of their membership of particular groups. The achievement of such a society in the context of our deeply inegalitarian past will not be easy, but that is the goal of the Constitution should not be forgotten or overlooked.

[43] To determine whether that impact was unfair it is necessary to look not only at the group who has been disadvantaged but at the nature of the power in terms of which the discrimination was effected and, also at the nature of the interests which have been affected by the discrimination.

In para 41 dignity was referred to as an underlying consideration in the determination of unfairness. The prohibition of unfair discrimination in the Constitution provides a bulwark against invasions which impair human dignity or which affect people adversely in a comparably serious manner. However, as L'Heureux-Dubé J acknowledged in *Egan v Canada*, 'Dignity [is] a notoriously elusive concept. It needs precision and elaboration.' It is made clear in para 43 of *Hugo* that this stage of the enquiry focuses primarily on the experience of the 'victim' of discrimination. In the final analysis it is the impact of the discrimination on the complainant that is the determining factor regarding the unfairness of the discrimination.

[51] In order to determine whether the discriminatory provision has impacted on complainants unfairly, various factors must be considered. These would include:

(a) the position of the complainants in society and whether they have suffered in the past from patterns of disadvantage, whether the discrimination in the case under consideration is on a specified ground or not;

(b) the nature of the provision or power and the purpose sought to be achieved by it. If its purpose is manifestly not directed, in the first instance, at impairing the complainants in the manner indicated above, but is aimed at achieving a worthy and important societal goal, such as, for example, the furthering of equality for all, this purpose may, depending on the facts of the particular case, have a significant bearing on the question whether complainants have in fact suffered the impairment in question. In *Hugo*, for example, the purpose of the Presidential Act was to benefit three groups of prisoners, namely, disabled prisoners, young people and mothers of young children, as an act of mercy. The fact that all these groups were regarded as being particularly vulnerable in our society, and that in the case of the disabled and the young mothers, they belonged to groups who had been victims of discrimination in the past, weighed with the Court in concluding that the discrimination was not unfair'.

The discussion that follows looks at how the Court approaches each of the questions when faced with a challenge to a classification on grounds of lack of equality.

Differentiation

In dealing with equality, the Constitutional Court prefers to avoid sweeping interpretations and instead to allow the equality doctrine to develop incrementally 'on a case-by-case basis with special emphasis on the actual context in which each problem arises'.[21] As a general rule, the Court does not want to engage in an enquiry as to the justifiability or fairness of every piece of legislation.[22] It is necessary to identify legitimate and illegitimate classifications.[23] Legislation which differentiates unfairly between groups of people is discriminatory.[24] An essential criterion in many discrimination challenges is whether the fundamental dignity of a human being is affected by the classification.[25] The mere fact that a law treats different people in dissimilar ways is not necessarily discriminatory. Legislation that differentiates between people in a way which impairs their fundamental dignity as human beings *is* discrimination.[26]

In *Prinsloo*, the applicant argued that s 84 of the Forest Act 122 of 1984, which imposed a presumption of negligence on him for veld fires, violated the interim Constitution's equality provisions because it discriminated against defendants in veld-fire cases while dealing differently with defendants in other delictual matters. The defendant further argued that the statute made an irrational distinction by creating a presumption in a non-controlled area but not in controlled areas.[27] The majority, *per* Ackerman J, upheld the constitutionality of the section and stated that it is not possible for the Court to review every legislative programme, and every instance of executive conduct.[28] All laws differentiate between people. The question for the Court is whether the law makes impermissible classifications which rises to the level of discrimination.

Prinsloo v Van de Linde and Another
CCT 4/96, now cited as 1997 (6)
BCLR 759 (CC); 1997 (3) SA 1012 (CC)
(notes omitted)

ACKERMANN J:

[16] In his written argument, counsel pointed to the differentiation between defendants in veld fire cases and those in other delictual matters. According to him, this differentiation had no rational basis, because the apparent object that the legislature sought to achieve by reversing the general rule regarding the incidence of onus that whoever avers must prove, could have been, and, indeed, already was, accomplished by means of common-law aids to proof. He referred in particular to the concept of *res ipsa loquitur* and the practice of triers of fact to require less evidence to establish a *prima facie* case if the facts in issue are peculiarly within the knowledge of the opposing party. A second differentiation which was raised by first respon-dent, relates to the fact that the presumption of negligence applies only in respect of fires in non-controlled areas, and not to those spreading in controlled areas, which at first blush appears to be incongruous. The challenge to constitutionality in both cases would be based either on a breach of the right to equality as guaranteed in section 8(1) or on a violation of the prohibition of discrimination contained in section 8(2). To determine whether either challenge in terms of section 8 is correct, it is necessary to consider first the proper approach to be taken to sections 8(1) and (2).

[17] If each and every differentiation made in terms of the law amounted to unequal treatment that had to be justified by means of resort to section 33, or else constituted discrimination which had to be shown not to be unfair, the courts could be called upon to review the justifiability or fairness of just about the whole legislative programme and almost all executive conduct. As Hogg puts it:

---

[21] *Prinsloo* para 20.
[22] *Supra, per* Ackerman J, para 18.
[23] *Supra* para 17.
[24] *Per* Goldstone J in *Harksen* para 43.
[25] *Per* Ackermann J in *Prinsloo* para 31.
[26] *Per* Goldstone J in *Harksen* para 46. Ngcobo J in *Hoffmann* para 40.
[27] *Per* Ackerman J in *Prinsloo* para 16.
[28] *Supra* para 17.

What is meant by a guarantee of equality? It cannot mean that the law must treat everyone equally. The Criminal Code imposes punishments on persons convicted of criminal offences; no similar burdens are imposed on the innocent. Education Acts require children to attend school; no similar obligation is imposed on adults. Manufacturers of food and drugs are subject to more stringent regulations than the manufacturers of automobile parts. The legal profession is regulated differently from the accounting profession. The Wills Act prescribes a different distribution of the property of a person who dies leaving a will from that of a person who dies leaving no will. The Income Tax Act imposes a higher rate of tax on those with high incomes than on those with low incomes. Indeed, every statute or regulation employs classifications of one kind or another for the imposition of burdens or the grant of benefits. Laws never provide the same treatment for everyone.

The courts would be compelled to review the reasonableness or the fairness of every classification of rights, duties, privileges, immunities, benefits or disadvantages flowing from any law. Accordingly, it is necessary to identify the criteria that separate legitimate differentiation from differentiation that has crossed the border of constitutional impermissibility and is unequal or discriminatory 'in the constitutional sense'.

[18] Even a cursory summary of international experience indicates that there are no universally accepted bright lines for determining whether or not an equality or non-discrimination right has been breached. The varying emphases given in different countries depend on a combination of the texts to be interpreted, modes of doctrinal articulation, historical backgrounds and evolving standards. Questions of institutional function and competence might play a role when reviewing, for example, legislation of a social and economic character.

[23] The idea of differentiation (to employ a neutral descriptive term) seems to lie at the heart of equality jurisprudence in general and of the section 8 right or rights in particular. Taking as comprehensive a view as possible of the way equality is treated in section 8, we would suggest that it deals with differentiation in basically two ways: diffiation which does not involve unfair discrimination and differentiation which does involve unfair discrimination. This needs some elaboration. We deal with the former first.

[24] It must be accepted that, in order to govern a modern country efficiently and to harmonise the interests of all its people for the common good, it is essential to regulate the affairs of its inhabitants extensively. It is impossible to do so without differentiation and without classifications which treat people differently and which impact on people differently. It is unnecessary to give examples which abound in everyday life in all democracies based on equality and freedom. Differentiation which falls into this category very rarely constitutes unfair discrimination in respect of persons subject to such regulation, without the addition of a further element. What this further element is will be considered later.

[25] It is convenient, for descriptive purposes, to refer to the differentiation presently under discussion as 'mere differentiation'. In regard to mere differentiation the constitutional state is expected to act in a rational manner. It should not regulate in an arbitrary manner or manifest 'naked preferences' that serve no legitimate governmental purpose, for that would be inconsistent with the rule of law and the fundamental premises of the constitutional state. The purpose of this aspect of equality is, therefore, to ensure that the state is bound to function in a rational manner. This has been said to promote the need for governmental action to relate to a defensible vision of the public good, as well as to enhance the coherence and integrity of legislation. In Mureinik's celebrated formulation, the new constitutional order constitutes 'a bridge away from a culture of authority ... to a culture of justification'.

[26] Accordingly, before it can be said that mere differentiation infringes section 8 it must be established that there is no rational relationship between the differentiation in question and the governmental purpose which is proffered to validate it. In the absence of such rational relationship the differentiation would infringe section 8. But while the existence of such a

rational relationship is a necessary condition for the differentiation not to infringe section 8, it is not a sufficient condition; for the differentiation might still constitute unfair discrimination if that further element, referred to above, is present.

[27] It is to section 8(2) that one must look in order to determine what this further element is. For reasons which will subsequently emerge it is unnecessary to consider the precise ambit or limits of this subsection. It is, however, clearly a section which deals not with all differentiation or even all discrimination but only with unfair discrimination. It does so by distinguishing between two forms of unfair discrimination and dealing with them differently.

[28] The first form relates to certain specifically enumerated grounds ('specified grounds') on the basis whereof no person may unfairly be discriminated against. The specified grounds are race, gender, sex, ethnic or social origin, colour, sexual orientation, age, disability, religion, conscience, belief, culture or language. When there is *prima facie* proof of discrimination on these grounds it is presumed, in terms of subsection (4), that unfair discrimination has been sufficiently proved, until the contrary is established. These are not the only grounds which would constitute unfair discrimination. The words 'without derogating from the generality of this provision', which introduce the specified grounds, make it clear that the specified grounds are not exhaustive. The second form is constituted by unfair discrimination on grounds which are not specified in the subsection. In regard to this second form there is no presumption in favour of unfairness.

[29] The question arises as to what grounds of discrimination this second form includes. A purely literal reading and application of the phrase 'without derogating from the generality of this provision' would lead to the conclusion that discrimination on any ground whatsoever is proscribed, provided it is unfair. Such a reading would provide no guidance as to what unfair meant in regard to this second form of discrimination. It would provide very little, if any, guidance in deciding when a differentiation which passed the rational relationship threshold

constituted unfair discrimination. It also seems unlikely that the content of the concept unfair discrimination would be left to unguided judicial judgment. We are of the view, however, that when read in its full historical and evolutionary context and in the light of the purpose of section 8 as a whole, and section 8(2) in particular, the second form of unfair discrimination cannot be given such an extremely wide and unstructured meaning.

[31] The proscribed activity is not stated to be 'unfair differentiation' but is stated to be 'unfair discrimination'. Given the history of this country we are of the view that 'discrimination' has acquired a particular pejorative meaning relating to the unequal treatment of people based on attributes and characteristics attaching to them. We are emerging from a period of our history during which the humanity of the majority of the inhabitants of this country was denied. They were treated as not having inherent worth; as objects whose identities could be arbitrarily defined by those in power rather than as persons of infinite worth. In short, they were denied recognition of their inherent dignity. Although one thinks in the first instance of discrimination on the grounds of race and ethnic origin one should never lose sight in any historical evaluation of other forms of discrimination such as that which has taken place on the grounds of sex and gender. In our view unfair discrimination, when used in this second form in section 8(2), in the context of section 8 as a whole, principally means treating persons differently in a way which impairs their fundamental dignity as human beings, who are inherently equal in dignity.

[33] Where discrimination results in treating persons differently in a way which impairs their fundamental dignity as human beings, it will clearly be a breach of section 8(2). Other forms of differentiation, which in some other way affect persons adversely in a comparably serious manner, may well constitute a breach of section 8(2) as well. It is not necessary to say more than this in the present case, for reasons which emerge later in this judgment.

[41] This does not end the matter, because

despite the existence of the aforementioned rational relationship between means and purpose, the particular differentiation might still constitute unfair discrimination under the second form of unfair discrimination mentioned in section 8(2). The regulation effected by section 84 in the present case differentiates between owners and occupiers of land in fire control areas and those who own or occupy land outside such areas. Such differentiation cannot, by any stretch of the imagination, be seen as impairing the dignity of the owner or occupier of land outside the fire control area. There is likewise no basis for concluding that the differentiation in some other invidious way adversely affects such owner or occupier in a comparably serious manner. It is clearly a regulatory matter to be adjudged according to whether or not there is a rational relationship between the differentiation enacted by section 84 and the purpose sought to be achieved by the Act. We have decided that such a relationship exists. Accordingly, no breach of section 8(1) or (2) has been established.

Is there a *nexus* between means and ends?

In mere differentiation the classification must be legitimate, which leads to the question, what is a legitimate classification? Where there is mere differentiation which is not unfair, the categorization will pass constitutional muster if it passes a rationality test. The rationality test requires that the regulation must not be arbitrary so as to serve no legitimate governmental purpose[29] – the test requires a rational reason for the regulation, and a connection between the regulation and the ends pursued.[30]

Statutes that differentiate often present problems of over inclusiveness or under inclusiveness.[31] As in the example of the age limitation on driving licences, the legislature may have decided to draw the line at eighteen years as the minimum age of eligibility for a driver's licence. The line-drawing is related to the state's objective of keeping the roads safe. Similarly, the statute may not prevent people over eighty years old from driving, even though it could be established that their driving ability is not as skilled as the majority of seventeen-year-olds. The statute does not cover a potentially dangerous class of drivers more dangerous than seventeen-year-olds. The line in the above example may have been over inclusive, in that the majority of seventeen-year-olds may be able to drive as competently as eighteen-year-olds. The line is also under inclusive, in that the majority of seventeen-year-olds may be able to drive more competently than the over eighty-year-olds. To require the legislature to establish that every seventeen-year-old is not able to drive as competently as an eighteen-year-old would make line-drawing impossible.[32] Requiring the legislature to draw up a distinction with mathematical certainty that covers older drivers is also an extremely difficult task. To some extent line-drawing includes generalizations that need not be absolutely true.[33] However, where the line-drawing is arbitrary and impairs human dignity, the Court will not defer to the classification scheme.[34]

Under the rationality test, the courts in most jurisdictions apply a low level of scrutiny under

[29] *Per* Goldstone J in *Harksen* para 43.

[30] The rationality requirement is present in the constitutional jurisprudence of many countries including the US, Germany, Ireland, and Canada. See Stone, 567; Volkmar Gotz 'Legislative and Executive Power under the Constitutional Requirements entailed in the Principle of the Rule of Law' in *New Challenges to the German Basic Law*, edited by Christian Starck. Baden-Baden: Nomos 1991, 155–156; Kelly 737; Hogg 1160–1.

[31] See John E Nowak and Roland E Rotunda *Constitutional Law* St Paul: West, 5th edition, 1995, 598–600, for a discussion of the problems which accompany over and under inclusive statutes.

[32] Kelly 734.

[33] Stone 568–9.

[34] Here, the Court will find unfair discrimination which is discussed below. See *National Coalition for Gay and Lesbian Equality and Others v Minister of Home Affairs and Others* CCT 10/99 (2 December 1999) para 32, now cited as 2000 (1) BCLR 39 (CC)(*National Coalition for Gay and Lesbian Equality 2*). *Hoffmann* para 40.

which the following principles can be assumed: the legislature has a wide degree of discretion in deciding what is a reasonable classification;[35] where there is a legal category created, a court is generally going to defer to the legislature unless the classification is arbitrary;[36] the burden of proving that the classification is improper lies with the party challenging the statute; the fact that the government objective could be achieved in a less restrictive way is not sufficient to impugn the classification;[37] and the classification need not be made with mathematical certainty.

In considering statutes which differentiate, the court does not require a close fit between the classification and the objective. As we observed in *Prinsloo*, the statute imposed a presumption of negligence for veld fires on certain property owners in non-controlled areas and not on certain owners in controlled areas.[38] The Court held that the classification bore a rational relationship to a government objective of preventing veld fires. Where there is differentiation, equality doctrine eschews questions as to the desirability of the method chosen, focusing instead on the rationality of the chosen method.[39] The fact that, in *Prinsloo*, the objectives of controlling veld fires could be

pursued without imposing the burdens on the applicant under the presumptions in the Act was not sufficient to attack the constitutionality of the Act.[40] The test for rationality focuses on whether there is a relationship between the categorization and the purpose, and not whether the objective could be obtained in a less intrusive manner.[41]

In *Jooste v Score Supermarket Trading (Pty) Limited and Another*,[42] the Constitutional Court was called upon to review the rationality of s 35(1) of the Compensation for Occupational Injuries and Diseases Act.[43] Section 35(1) precluded the recovery of common-law damages against employers. The applicants contended that the Act discriminated against employers whilst non-employers retained the common-law right to recover damages from the wrongdoer.[44] The Court, *per* Yacoob J, held that the relevant enquiry was whether the impugned section was rationally related to a legitimate governmental objective.[45] It is not open to the Court to say there were better policy choices available. Whether an employer should be able to recover damages both under the Act and the common law is a complex policy determination question which the legislature must make.[46]

---

[35] See Thomas Wurtenberger 'Equality' in *The Constitution of the Federal Republic of Germany: Essays on Basic Rights and Principles of the Basic Law with a Translation of the Basic Law*, edited by Ulrich Karpen. Baden-Baden: Nomos 1988, 72; Stone 568.

[36] *Prinsloo* at para 41.

[37] *Per* Ackermann J in *Prinsloo* para 36.

[38] *Prinsloo* para 16.

[39] Jeewan BP Reddy 'The Jurisprudence of Human Rights' in *Human Rights and Judicial Review: A Comparative Perspective*, edited by David M Beatty. Dordrecht: M Nijhoff 1994, 212.

[40] *Prinsloo* para 36.

[41] *East Zulu Motors (Pty) Ltd v Empangeni/Ngwelezane Transitional Local Council and Others* CCT 44/96 (4 December 1997) para 23, now cited as 1998 (2) SA 61 (CC); 1998 (1) BCLR 1 (CC), *per* O'Regan J.

[42] *Jooste v Score Supermarket Trading (Pty) Limited and Another* CCT 15/98 (27 November 1998), now cited as 1999 (2) SA 1 (CC); 1999 (2) BCLR 139 (CC).

[43] Act 130 of 1993.

[44] *Jooste* para 10.

[45] *Supra* para 12.

[46] *Supra* para 17.

*Jooste v Score Supermarket
Trading (Pty) Ltd and Another*
CCT 15/98 (27 November 1998), now
cited as 1999 (2) SA 1 (CC); 1999 (2)
BCLR 139 (CC)
(notes omitted)

[1] On 27 December 1995 the applicant fell and was injured in the respondent's supermarket where she worked as a cashier. On 29 April 1997 she began an action in the Eastern Cape High Court claiming, *inter alia*, general damages resulting from her injuries, which she alleged were a direct result of the negligence of one or more employees of the respondent during the course and scope of their employment.

[2] In its special plea the respondent took the point that the applicant's claim was barred by section 35(1) of the Compensation for Occupational Injuries and Diseases Act 130 of 1993 ('the Compensation Act'). This special plea elicited a replication which advanced the proposition that section 35(1) was inconsistent with the interim Constitution in that its provisions violated the right to equality before the law and to equal protection of the law and the right not to be unfairly discriminated against, the right of access to courts and the right to fair labour practices, enshrined in sections 8(1) and (2), 22 and 27(1) of that Constitution respectively. The applicant accordingly sought to have the special plea dismissed with costs, alternatively to have the issue of the constitutionality of section 35(1) referred to this Court, presumably pursuant to section 102(1) of the interim Constitution

[10] It was contended in the High Court that section 35(1) infringed both sections 9(1) and 9(3) of the 1996 Constitution. The applicant's equality challenge was based on a contention that employees, by being deprived of the common-law right to claim damages against their employers, are placed at a disadvantage in relation to people who are not employees and who retain that right. The challenge was not based on any of the grounds specified either in section 8(2) of the interim Constitution or section 9(3) of the 1996 Constitution. In dealing with these contentions Zietsman JP said:

The question . . . is whether section 35 of the Act, which denies to employees the right to claim compensation from their employers, has a rational connection to the purpose of the Act. If not it constitutes unfair discrimination against employees.

[12] In oral argument before this Court counsel for the applicant rightly accepted that there was no evidence in support of the proposition that the differentiation in issue amounted to unfair discrimination and advanced no contention in this regard. The submission on behalf of the applicant was accordingly that the only issue of relevance to the equality challenge was whether the impugned section was rationally connected to a legitimate government purpose. If there was a rational connection, the applicant should fail because unfair discrimination had not been established . . . .

[15] The Compensation Act supplants the essentially individualistic common law position, typically represented by civil claims of a plaintiff employee against a negligent defendant employer, by a system which is intended to and does enable employees to obtain limited compensation from a fund to which employers are obliged to contribute. Compensation is payable even if the employer was not negligent. Though the institution of the regime contemplates a differentiation between employees and others, it is very much an open question whether the scheme is to the disadvantage of employees.

[16] Counsel for the applicant did not base his contention on a comparison of the position of the worker under the scheme contemplated by the Compensation Act with the position at common law. He submitted instead that section 35(1) had to be viewed independently of the rest of the Compensation Act because it did not have to be an integral part of the scheme, that there was no reason why a negligent employer should not be obliged to pay both the assessed contributions to the fund and common-law damages, and that there was accordingly no rational basis for the inclusion of section 35(1) as part of the scheme. He said that the assumption that it was unduly onerous for the employer to be obliged to pay both contribu-

tions to the fund and common law damages if negligent was ill founded. Indeed, counsel confessed that his contention concerning the absence of a rational connection amounted to the employee having 'the best of both worlds'. In essence, the contention amounted to this: the nature of the balance achieved by the legislature through the Compensation Act tilts somewhat in favour of the employer while requirements of policy and the nature of the relationship between the employee and the employer indicate that a different balance is appropriate. It was contended that the object of the Act is to provide compensation for workers, not to benefit employers. Section 35(1) benefits only employers. It is therefore not rationally related to the purpose of the legislation.

[17] But that argument fundamentally misconceives the nature and purpose of rationality review and artificially and somewhat forcibly attempts an analysis of the import of the impugned section without reference to the Compensation Act as a whole. It is clear that the only purpose of rationality review is an inquiry into whether the differentiation is arbitrary or irrational, or manifests naked preference and it is irrelevant to this inquiry whether the scheme chosen by the legislature could be improved in one respect or another. Whether an employee ought to have retained the common law right to claim damages, either over and above or as an alternative to the advantages conferred by the Compensation Act, represents a highly debatable, controversial and complex matter of policy. It involves a policy choice which the legislature and not a court must make. The contention represents an invitation to this Court to make a policy choice under the guise of rationality review; an invitation which is firmly declined. The legislature clearly considered that it was appropriate to grant to employees certain benefits not available at common law. The scheme is financed through contributions from employers. No doubt for these reasons the employee's common-law right against an employer is excluded. Section 35(1) of the Compensation Act is therefore logically and rationally connected to the legitimate purpose of the Compensation Act, namely, a comprehensive regulation of compensation for disablement caused by occupational injuries or diseases sustained or contracted by employees in the course of their employment.

Where there is mere differentiation, the Court may not conduct the second and third stages of the enquiry: namely, whether there was discrimination and, if so, was the discrimination unfair, unless there was an impairment of human dignity, or categorization based on immutable or analogous characteristics.[47] If the Court feels strongly that the discrimination is outrageous, it could dispense with the first stage of the enquiry whether there was differentiation. In *Hoffmann*, the Court was faced with a challenge to the policy of SAA not to hire HIV-positive persons as cabin stewards. The Court dispensed with the first stage of the enquiry and proceeded directly to examine whether there was unfair discrimination.[48]

Is the differentiation discrimination?

Even where differentiation passes the rationality test, it may still not pass constitutional muster if it constitutes unfair discrimination. The Court considers the next enquiry in terms of two separate questions: first, was there discrimination, and secondly, if there was discrimination, was the discrimination unfair? Discrimination is determined based on the nature of the categorization

---

[47] Accordingly in *Prinsloo*, the Court did not proceed to the next stages of the enquiry whether there was unfair discrimination, because the classification did not impair the dignity of an owner of land outside a controlled fire area. *Prinsloo* para 41. However, in *National Coalition for Gay and Lesbian Equality 2*, the Court did not proceed to the first stage because the discrimination based on sexual orientation was deemed to impair human dignity. See para 57.

[48] *Hoffmann* para 26.

or impact of the categorization. Suspect categorizations which would be considered discrimination include: categorizations based on a listed ground, and categorizations that impair human dignity.

Categorization based on listed grounds

In conducting the investigation whether the categorization is, or is not valid, one need not presume at the outset that the categorization is unconstitutional. Whether one starts off with the presumption that the categorization is invalid would depend on the nature of the categorization. The Constitution addresses two kinds of categorizations. First, categorizations based on listed immutable characteristics, against certain types of relationships, associations, or groups are presumptively invalid.[49] Secondly, other categorizations although not listed, may be found to be unfairly discriminatory.[50]

Categorization based on listed or inferred immutable characteristics would be assumed to be discriminatory.[51] The Constitution proceeds from a presumption that certain bases for distinguishing between individuals such as race, gender, sex, pregnancy, marital status, ethnic or social origin, colour, sexual orientation, age, disability, religion, conscience, belief, culture, language, and birth, are almost always irrelevant and unconstitutional.[52] The categories listed are based on what the United States Supreme Court has characterized as either immutable characteristics determined solely by the accident of birth, or a class saddled with disabilities, or subjected to a history of unequal treatment, or relegated to political powerlessness, which all require extraordinary protection from the majoritarian political process.[53] Race, gender, sex, ethnic or social

origin, age, and disability are involuntary conditions. The other listed grounds such as religion, culture, belief, marital status, or sexual preference, relate to lifestyle and how individuals seek to define themselves. To use a phrase from United States jurisprudence, categorizations on all these grounds are based on a 'suspect' category.[54] In *Harksen v Lane*,[55] Goldstone J stated:

[49] ... What the specified grounds have in common is that they have been used (or misused) in the past (both in South Africa and elsewhere) to categorize, marginalise, and often oppress persons who have had, or who have been associated with, these attributes or characteristics. These grounds have the potential, when manipulated to demean persons in their inherent humanity and dignity. There is often a complex relationship between these grounds. In some cases, they relate to immutable biological attributes or characteristics, in some to the associational life of humans, in some to the intellectual, expressive and religious dimensions of humanity and in some cases to a combination of one or more of these features.[56]

In terms of s 9(4) of the Constitution, the legislature may add to the list of what constitutes unfair discrimination. In terms of the Employment Equity Act, HIV status has been listed as prohibited grounds of unfair discrimination.[57] Even without such legislation, when the Court finds that the categorization will dehumanize a group or perpetuate and reinforce negative stereotypes, it will rule that the categorization constitutes unfair discrimination.[58] In *National Coalition for Gay and Lesbian Equality 2*, the Constitutional Court held that discrimination against same-sex partners with respect to immigration into South Africa under s 25(5) of the Aliens

---

[49] The characteristics or types of discrimination are listed in s 9(3).
[50] *Prinsloo* para 31.
[51] *National Coalition for Gay and Lesbian Equality 2* paras 26–27.
[52] Section 9(3) of the Constitution.
[53] *Johnson v Robinson* 415 US 361, 375 (1974).
[54] *United States v Carolene Products Company* 304 US 144, 153 (1938).
[55] *Harksen* para 49.
[56] *Supra.*
[57] Section 6(1) of the Employment Equity Act.
[58] *Hoffmann* paras 32 and 40.

Control Act[59] constituted unfair discrimination and a serious invasion of their dignity.[60] Similarly, in *Hoffmann*, the Court held that the policy of SAA not to hire HIV-positive persons as cabin attendants was based on prejudice and constituted an impairment of human dignity.[61]

In addition to the Universal Declaration, the two Covenants and the various regional instruments, there are a number of specific international law instruments which forbid discrimination based on immutable characteristics including race, religion, belief, and gender. The seminal treaties include: the International Convention on the Elimination of All Forms of Racial Discrimination;[62] the International Convention on the Suppression and Punishment of Apartheid;[63] the Declaration on the Elimination of All Forms of Intolerance and of Discrimination Based on Religion or Belief;[64] the Convention on the Elimination of All Forms of Discrimination Against Women (CEDAW),[65] and the Convention on the Rights of the Child.[66]

Categorization based on analogous grounds

Section 8(3) of the Constitution is sufficiently flexible to preclude discrimination not only on the listed grounds, but also on analogous grounds. The listed grounds in s 8(3) reflect the more pervasive basis for discrimination. The Constitutional Court has emphasized that it should not give a narrow definition to these attributes and characteristics. The definition includes other grounds based on immutable characteristics by analogy.[67] For example, in *Larbi-Odam*, the Court invalidated an employment statute which discriminated against non-citizens. The Court held that although citizenship was not a listed ground, non-citizens were politically powerless and vulnerable. Moreover, citizenship was typically an immutable characteristic.[68] The definition of immutable characteristics is therefore subject to expansion beyond the categories listed in s 8(3). In *Harksen*, the Court found the vesting provisions of the Insolvency Act constituted discrimination because they targeted innocent spouses based on their attributes or characteristics: namely, their intimate association with the insolvent spouse, even though under the interim Constitution marriage was not a listed ground.[69]

Where there is an allegation of discrimination based on analogous grounds, the burden of proof lies with the complainant.[70] In interpreting what is an analogous ground, the Court will also consider whether the discrimination impairs human dignity.[71] This contrasts with the position of Hogg, that all distinctions are *prima facie* invalid. In the United States, the Supreme Court approaches the issue in terms of tiers of scrutiny. If a distinction is based on what the Court characterizes a 'suspect category' such as race, or when the legislation touches on a fundamental right, the Court would subject the legislation to strict scrutiny.[72]

In *City Council of Pretoria*, the municipal

---

[59] Act 96 of 1991.

[60] *National Coalition for Gay and Lesbian Equality 2* paras 54 and 57.

[61] *Hoffmann* paras 37 and 40.

[62] 660 UNTS 195, (1966) 5 ILM 352 (Convention on Racial Discrimination).

[63] 1015 UNTS 243, (1974) 13 ILM 50.

[64] (1981) 55 UNGAR XXXVI, (1982) 21 ILM 205.

[65] (1979) 180 UNGAR XXXIV, (1980) 19 ILM 33.

[66] UNGAR 44/25, (20 November 1989).

[67] *Per* Goldstone J, in *Harksen* para 41. *Per* Mokgoro J, in *Larbi-Odam and Others v MEC for Education (North West Province) and Another* CCT 2/97 (26 November 1997) para 16, now cited as 1998 (1) SA 745 (CC); 1997 (12) BCLR 1655 (CC).

[68] *Per* Mokgoro J in *Larbi-Odam* para 19.

[69] *Harksen* para 61.

[70] *Supra* para 53.

[71] *Per* Ackermann J in *Prinsloo* para 31.

[72] See *Carolene Products* 304 US at 153, where Stone J first enunciated the idea that more exacting scrutiny should be employed where a statute affects fundamental rights, or targets discrete or insular groups. For statutes of an economic or social nature, the Court would adopt a more deferential approach, see *Williamson v Lee Optical Company* 348 US 483 (1955). More recently some of the justices have adopted an intermediate level of scrutiny for what they characterize as quasi-suspect classifications such as

authorities adopted different rates for assessing electricity use in historically white and black areas. The different assessment methods were of a temporary nature until the authorities could introduce equal facilities to the different areas. The Court, *per* Langa DP, held that the differentiation was rationally connected to a legitimate government objective of providing services during a period of transition.[73] Although it used the mere rationality test in subjecting the differentiation to scrutiny, the Court in this instance does proceed to the next stage of the enquiry because the statute was discriminatory in that it impacted on people on the basis of race. In other words, even though a statute may differentiate, and the differentiation may be rationally related to a government objective, the differentiation may still constitute discrimination if the statute distinguishes between people based on immutable characteristics,[74] or if the statute impairs the fundamental dignity of a human being.[75]

Categorization based other than on immutable characteristics: impairment of human dignity

As long as discrimination is understood as a prohibition on classifications based on listed or analogous categories, interpretation of s 9 would be more manageable. The Court needs to only look at the legislation in question to see whether it discriminates on one of the listed or analogous grounds, and make their appropriate findings. It is easier to conclude that a law which targets a group based on personal characteristics impairs human dignity and is unconstitutional. Outside these listed categories, the task of determining whether there is discrimination is more difficult. Regardless of whether there is discrimination based on a listed or analogous ground, if the discrimination results in the impairment of fundamental dignity, it will be in breach of the Constitution's equality provisions.[76] As we have stated, there is hardly a law which does not create distinctions or classifications. Returning to the example on driving abilities, it would be manifestly absurd to proceed on the presumption that a law which deprives a seventeen-year-old the opportunity of obtaining a driver's licence is *per se* unconstitutional, unless the legislature can justify the distinctions under the limitations clause. The Court has been called upon to evaluate the constitutionality of a variety of forms of categorizations based neither on immutable characteristics nor on the basis of association. These categorizations, among others, include differences in the appeal procedure between litigants in the magistrates' court and the Supreme Court,[77] differences in the treatment between the solvent spouse of an insolvent and other persons who might have dealings with an insolvent,[78] and different burdens of proof imposed on litigants in civil and criminal cases.[79] The Court has correctly concluded that not all categorizations which differentiate between people are illegal. There is a need to make a distinction between regulations that differentiate between people, and those that discriminate. Mere differentiation between groups of people is rarely found to be discriminatory.[80] The modern state of

---

affirmative action or gender discrimination. See the majority approach in *Metro Broadcasting Inc v Federal Communications Commission* 497 US 547 (1990), where the majority upheld the constitutionality of an affirmative action programme designed to ensure diversity in broadcasting based on the use of an intermediate level of scrutiny.

[73] *Per* Langa DP in *City Council of Pretoria v Walker* CCT 8/97 (17 February 1998) para 27, now cited as 1998 (2) SA 363 (CC); 1998 (3) BCLR 257 (CC).

[74] Goldstone J in *Harksen* para 43.

[75] *Harksen* para 46.

[76] Ackerman J in *Prinsloo* para 33. Goldstone J in *Harksen* para 46.

[77] *Besserglik v the Minister of Trade, Industry and Tourism and Others* CCT 34/95 (14 May 1996), now cited as 1996 (4) SA 331 (CC); 1996 (6) BCLR 745 (CC).

[78] *Harksen.*

[79] *Prinsloo.*

[80] Langa DP in *City Council of Pretoria* para 26. Ackerman J, in *Prinsloo* para 26. O'Regan J in *Besserglik* para 11.

necessity regulates the affairs of its citizens. Regulation is not possible without differentiation which classifies, treats, and impacts on people differently.[81] It is, therefore, not discriminatory if the legislature provides for different procedures for appeals from the Supreme Court and magistrates' court.[82] It is also not discriminatory if the legislature provides different procedures for civil and criminal appeals.[83] The myriad laws that impose differentiation criteria, such as licencing laws; qualifications for receiving benefits, and minimum requirements for admission to universities would not be discriminatory. For purposes of discrimination, treating persons differently principally means 'treating persons differently in a way which impairs their fundamental dignity as human beings, who are inherently equal in dignity'.[84] For example, in *Harksen*, the applicant who was the wife of an insolvent argued that s 21 of the Insolvency Act of 1936 violated the equality provisions of the Constitution by discriminating against solvent spouses and not against other persons having had a close relationship with the insolvent person.[85] Under s 21 of the Act, property of the solvent spouse is divested and vested in the Master of the Supreme Court. The differentiation was not based on any specified ground under the Constitution. However, the majority concluded that there was discrimination because the statute demeans innocent spouses in respect of their inherent humanity and dignity.[86] With discrimination, the statute will not pass

muster unless it can be proved that the discrimination is not unfair. This leads us to the next enquiry what is unfair discrimination?

Is the discrimination unfair?

Central to the finding of unfair discrimination is the question whether the dignity of a human being has been affected.[87] Where discrimination is based on the listed grounds or immutable characteristics, the Court will assume that the discrimination is unfair.[88] The burden of proof is on the lawmaker or on the party wishing to uphold the classification to establish that the classification is not unfair. Under s 13 of the Promotion of Equality and Prevention of Unfair Discrimination Act, the burden of proof is also on the lawmaker, or any person who wants to uphold the classification, if the activity falls within the prohibitions mentioned under ss 7–12 of the Act. Where discrimination is based on analogous grounds such as certain relationships,[89] or where you have discrimination which impairs the fundamental dignity of a human being – not in the context of immutable characteristics[90] – then there is no presumption of unfairness.[91] In the latter instances, the burden of proof is on the complainant to establish that the discrimination is unfair.[92]

Discrimination based on listed grounds

Discrimination based on gender, or race would constitute an example of unfair discrimination.[93]

---

[81] Ackerman J in *Prinsloo* para 24.

[82] *Besserglik* para 11.

[83] *Supra*.

[84] *Per* Ackermann J in *Prinsloo* para 31.

[85] *Harksen* para 40.

[86] *Supra* para 61. The Court also found that the differentiation although not based on a listed ground was based on an unspecified ground in that it targeted spouses based on their close relationship with a solvent spouse.

[87] *Hoffmann* para 27.

[88] Goldstone J in *Harksen* para 43. Sections 7–12 of the Promotion of Equality and Prevention of Unfair Discrimination Act list a range of activities pertaining to race, gender, disability, hate speech, harassment, and dissemination of information in certain contexts, which constitutes unfair discrimination. The Act was passed pursuant to s 9(4) of the Constitution.

[89] *Fraser v The Children's Court, Pretoria North and Others* CCT 31/96 (5 February 1997), now cited as 1997 (2) SA 261 (CC); 1997 (2) BCLR 153 (CC).

[90] *Per* Goldstone J in *Harksen* para 46.

[91] *Prinsloo* para 28.

[92] *Per* Goldstone J in *Harksen* para 62.

[93] *Brink v Kitshoff* CCT 15/95 (15 May 1996), now cited as 1996 (4) SA 197 (CC); 1996 (6) BCLR 752 (CC); see also *Fraser* paras 23 and 25.

In *Brink*, the Court was faced with a challenge to s 44 of the Insurance Act,[94] which required married women – under certain circumstances, when their husbands' estate is sequestrated – to forfeit benefits of life insurance policies. The applicant argued that the forfeiture provisions constitute a violation of the equality provisions of the interim Constitution by discriminating on the basis of gender.[95] The Court held that the statute discriminated on the basis of a listed ground which makes the discrimination unfair.[96]

Brink v Kitshoff
NO CCT 15/95 (15 May 1996),
now cited as 1996 (6) BCLR 752 (CC);
(4) SA 562 751 (CC)
(notes omitted)
O REGAN J (unanimous decision):

[19] The question referred to the court in this matter was whether section 44 of the Insurance Act, 27 of 1943 ('the Act'), is in conflict with the provisions of chapter 3 of the Constitution of the Republic of South Africa Act, 200 of 1993 ('the Constitution'), in so far as it discriminates against married women by depriving them, in certain circumstances, of all or some of the benefits of life insurance policies ceded to them or made in their favour by their husbands.

[22] One effect of these provisions is that, where a life insurance policy has been ceded to a woman, or effected in her favour, by her husband more than two years before the sequestration of her husband's estate, she will receive a maximum of R30 000 from the policy. If it was ceded or taken out less than two years from the date of sequestration, she will receive no benefit from the policy at all. Similarly, once two years has elapsed since the policy was ceded to a wife, or effected in her favour, the policy or any money due thereunder, to the extent that it exceeds R30 000, will be deemed, as against the creditors of the husband, to form part of the husband's estate. Such proceeds may therefore be attached by judgment creditors of the husband in execution of a judgment against him. If less than two years has elapsed since the date of the cession or taking out of the policy and the date of attachment by a creditor of her husband, all the proceeds of the policy will be deemed to be part of the husband's estate. The Act contains no similar limitation upon the effect of a life insurance policy ceded or effected in favour of a husband by a wife.

[24] The facts in the case referred to this court are as follows: a life insurance policy valued at approximately R2 million in respect of Mr P Brink was taken out during 1989. The policy reflected Mr Brink as the owner of the policy and in 1990 he ceded, or purported to cede, it to his wife, Mrs A Brink, who is the applicant before this court. On 9 April 1994 Mr Brink died. Mr A Kitshoff, the Respondent before this court, was appointed as executor of the estate and on 23 May 1994, in terms of section 34(1) of the Administration of Estates Act, 66 of 1965, ('the Estates Act'), he sent a notice to creditors informing them that the estate was insolvent. In terms of section 44 of the Act, the executor demanded that the assurer (Liberty Life Association of Africa) pay into the estate all but R30 000 of the proceeds of the life insurance policy. When the assurer refused to do so, the executor launched an application in the Transvaal Provincial Division of the Supreme Court for an order compelling the assurer to pay over the proceeds. Mrs Brink, the assurer and the Master of the Supreme Court were cited as respondents in that application.

[33] Equality has a very special place in the South African Constitution. The preamble states that

... there is a need to create a new order in which all South Africans will be entitled to a common South African citizenship in a sovereign and democratic

---

[94] Act 27 of 1943.
[95] *Brink* para 31.
[96] *Per* O'Regan J in *Brink* para 43.

constitutional state in which there is equality between men and women and people of all races . . . .

Furthermore, section 33(1) of the Constitution states that rights entrenched in Chapter 3 may be limited to the extent only that it is 'justifiable in an open and democratic society based on freedom and equality'. It is not surprising that equality is a recurrent theme in the Constitution. As this court has said in other judgments, the Constitution is an emphatic renunciation of our past in which inequality was systematically entrenched. (*S v Makwanyane* 1995 (3) SA 391 (CC); 1995 (6) BCLR 665 (CC) at paragraphs 218, 262, 322; *Shabalala and Others v Attorney-General, Transvaal and Another* 1996 (1) SA 725 (CC); 1995 (12) BCLR 1593, at paragraph 26.)

[34] Section 35(1) of the Constitution requires us to have regard to international law to interpret the rights it entrenches. The concepts of 'equality before the law' and 'discrimination' are widely used in international instruments. Article 7 of the Universal Declaration of Human Rights 1948 provides that:

All are equal before the law and are entitled without any discrimination to equal protection of the law. All are entitled to equal protection against any discrimination in violation of this Declaration and against any incitement to such discrimination.

Article 26 of the International Covenant on Civil and Political Rights 1966 provides that:

All persons are equal before the law and are entitled without any discrimination to the equal protection of the law. In this respect, law shall prohibit any discrimination and guarantee to all persons equal and effective protection against discrimination on any ground such as race, colour, sex, language, religion, political or other opinion, national or social origin, property, birth or other status.

In addition, there are other international conventions dealing with specific aspects of discrimination such as the International Convention on the Elimination of all Forms of Racial Discrimination 1966, the Convention on the Elimination of all Forms of Discrimination against Women 1980, the Convention against Discrimination in Education 1960 and the International Labour Organisation (ILO) Discrimination (Employment and Occupation) Convention 1958.

[40] As in other national constitutions, section 8 is the product of our own particular history. Perhaps more than any of the other provisions in chapter 3, its interpretation must be based on the specific language of section 8, as well as our own constitutional context. Our history is of particular relevance to the concept of equality. The policy of apartheid, in law and in fact, systematically discriminated against black people in all aspects of social life. Black people were prevented from becoming owners of property or even residing in areas classified as 'white', which constituted nearly 90% of the landmass of South Africa; senior jobs and access to established schools and universities were denied to them; civic amenities, including transport systems, public parks, libraries and many shops were also closed to black people. Instead, separate and inferior facilities were provided. The deep scars of this appalling programme are still visible in our society. It is in the light of that history and the enduring legacy that it bequeathed that the equality clause needs to be interpreted.

[41] Although our history is one in which the most visible and most vicious pattern of discrimination has been racial, other systematic motifs of discrimination were and are inscribed on our social fabric. In drafting section 8, the drafters recognised that systematic patterns of discrimination on grounds other than race have caused, and may continue to cause, considerable harm. For this reason, section 8(2) lists a wide, and not exhaustive, list of prohibited grounds of discrimination.

[42] Section 8 was adopted then in the recognition that discrimination against people who are members of disfavoured groups can lead to patterns of group disadvantage and harm. Such discrimination is unfair: it builds and entrenches inequality amongst different groups in our society. The drafters realised that it was necessary both to proscribe such forms of

271

discrimination and to permit positive steps to redress the effects of such discrimination. The need to prohibit such patterns of discrimination and to remedy their results are the primary purposes of section 8 and, in particular, subsections (2), (3) and (4).

[43] Sections 44 (1) and (2) of the Act treat married women and married men differently. This difference in treatment disadvantages married women and not married men. The discrimination in sections 44(1) and (2) is therefore based on two grounds: sex and marital status. Section 8(2) does not require that the discrimination be based on one ground only; it specifically states that it may be based on 'one or more' grounds. Nor is it a difficulty for the applicant that section 8(2) mentions only one of the grounds, sex. The list provided in section 8(2) is not exhaustive. The subsection states expressly that the list provided should not be used to derogate from the generality of the prohibition on discrimination. It is not necessary to consider whether the other ground of discrimination, marital status, would be a ground which would constitute unfair discrimination for the purposes of section 8. It is sufficient that the disadvantageous treatment is substantially based on one of the listed prohibited grounds, namely, sex.

Discrimination based on associations or relationships

Unfair discrimination will also be found if the statute discriminates based on the type of association or relationship. In *Fraser v Children's Court, Pretoria North*, the Court was faced with the constitutionality of s 18(4)*(d)* of the Child Care Act,[97] which dispensed with the consent of a father in adoption proceedings where the child was 'illegitimate'. Section 18(4)*(d)* of the Act required that the consent of both parents was needed for the adoption of a child. Where the child was 'illegitimate', only the consent of the mother of the child was needed. The applicant, a father of an illegitimate child that was being put up for adoption, argued that dispensing with his consent violated the equality provisions of the interim Constitution.[98] The Court unanimously invalidated the provisions on the grounds that the statute discriminated based on the type of marriage relationship. The rights of fathers in customary unions, even where the marriage may have been polygamous, was protected under the Black Administration Act 38 of 1927. The effect was to discriminate against fathers of children born from marriages contracted according to other rites.[99] Although not expressly mentioned, it can be inferred from the Court's decision that the Child Care Act also discriminated on the basis of race and culture, by recognizing the rights of fathers married under 'Black Law and Custom', while discriminating against say a 'brown' person married under another religious system. According to Mahomed DP, 'fathers of children from Black customary unions have greater rights than similarly placed fathers from children born from marriages contracted according to the rites of religions such as Islam. This appears to be a clear breach of the equality right in ... the Constitution'.[100]

The Court found two additional grounds for invalidating the statute. The statute deprived a father of consent to adoption simply on the basis of gender.[101] Finally, the Court also found that the statute discriminated between married and unmarried fathers.[102] The interim Constitution did not list discrimination based on marriage status as a listed category. The Court did not develop whether the discrimination between

---

[97] Act 74 of 1983.

[98] *Fraser* para 4.

[99] Per Mahomed DP in *Fraser* para 22.

[100] *Fraser* para 23.

[101] *Supra* para 25.

[102] *Supra* para 26.

married and unmarried fathers in this instance was unfair. Where there is discrimination which impairs the fundamental dignity of a human being, the Court will assume that the discrimination is unfair.[103]

Fraser v Children's Court, Pretoria, North and Others
CCT 31/96 (5 February 1997), now cited as 1997 (2) BCLR 153 (CC); 1997 (2) SA 261 (CC)
(notes omitted)

[1] The applicant is a system developer employed in the computer industry. The second respondent is a violinist employed by the South African Broadcasting Corporation. For some months during the period 1994 to 1995 the applicant and the second respondent became involved in an intimate relationship and lived together as man and wife in a commune in Johannesburg, initially in Melville and subsequently in Malvern. It is common cause that the second respondent gave birth to a boy named Timothy on 12 December 1995 and that the applicant is the father of that child. No marriage was solemnized between the parties.

[2] During April 1995, shortly after the second respondent discovered that she was pregnant with this child she decided that it would be in the best interests of the unborn child that he be put up for adoption. When this became known to the applicant he resisted the proposed adoption and that resistance has given rise to extensive litigation between the parties commencing early in December 1995.

[4] The litigation also included a number of separate hearings before the Commissioner of the Children's Court, Pretoria North, which is the first respondent in the present proceedings. On these occasions the applicant sought to intervene in the adoption proceedings on the grounds that he was an interested party and also on the grounds that he wished to be considered as a prospective adoptive parent. He also sought a stay of the adoption proceedings pending an application to the Constitutional Court to challenge the constitutionality of section 18(4)(d) of the Child Care Act 74 of 1983 ('the Act'), insofar as it dispenses with the father's consent for the adoption of an illegitimate child. This subsection reads as follows:

A children's court to which application for an order of adoption is made ... shall not grant the application unless it is satisfied–

(d) that consent to the adoption has been given by both parents of the child, or, if the child is illegitimate, by the mother of the child, whether or not such mother is a minor or married woman and whether or not she is assisted by her parent, guardian or husband, as the case may be.

[19] The main attack on section 18(4)(d) of the Act made on behalf of the applicant was that, in its existing form it violates the right to equality and the right of every person not to be unfairly discriminated against .

[20] There can be no doubt that the guarantee of equality lies at the very heart of the Constitution. It permeates and defines the very ethos upon which the Constitution is premised. In the very first paragraph of the preamble it is declared that there is a '... need to create a new order ... in which there is equality between men and women and people of all races so that all citizens shall be able to enjoy and exercise their fundamental rights and freedoms'. Section 8(1) guarantees to every person the right to equality before the law and to equal protection of the law. Section 8(2) protects every person from unfair discrimination on the grounds of race, gender, sex, ethnic or social origin, colour, sexual orientation, age, disability, religion, conscience, belief, culture or language. These specified grounds are stated to be without derogation from the generality of the provision. Section 8(3)(a) makes it clear that nothing in sections 8(1) or (2) precludes measures designed to achieve the adequate protection or advance-

---

[103] *Per* Goldstone J in *Harksen* para 46.

ment of persons or groups or categories of persons disadvantaged by unfair discrimination, in order to enable their full and equal enjoyment of all rights and freedoms. Consistent with this repeated commitment to equality are the conditions upon which there can be any justifiable limitation of fundamental rights in terms of section 33 of the Constitution. In order for such a limitation to be constitutionally legitimate it must be 'justifiable in an open and democratic society based on freedom and equality'.

[21] In my view the impugned section does in fact offend section 8 of the Constitution. It impermissibly discriminates between the rights of a father in certain unions and those in other unions. Unions which have been solemnised in terms of the tenets of the Islamic faith for example are not recognised in our law because such a system permits polygamy in marriage. It matters not that the actual union is in fact monogamous. As long as the religion permits polygamy, the union is 'potentially polygamous' and for that reason, said to be against public policy. The result must therefore be that the father of a child born pursuant to such a religious union would not have the same rights as the mother in adoption proceedings pursuant to section 18 of the Act. The child would not have the status of 'legitimacy' and the consent of the father to the adoption would therefore not be necessary, notwithstanding the fact that such a union, for example under Islamic law, might have required a very public ceremony, special formalities and onerous obligations for both parents in terms of the relevant rules of Islamic law applicable.

[22] Whatever justification there might have been for discrimination against the fathers of such unions is destroyed by section 27 of the Act which provides that a 'customary union' as defined in section 35 of the Black Administration Act 38 of 1927 ('the Black Administration Act') is deemed to be a marriage between the parties thereto for the purposes of Chapter 4 of the Act (which includes section 18(4)). That definition in the Black Administration Act defines 'customary union' to mean 'the associa-

tion of a man and a woman in a conjugal relationship according to Black law and custom, where neither the man nor the woman is party to a subsisting marriage'. The effect of section 27 of the Act is therefore to deem a customary union in terms of Black law and custom to be a marriage for the purposes of the Act. The consequence which follows is that, in terms of section 18(4)(d) of the Act, the consent of both the father and the mother would, subject to the provisions of section 19, be necessary for an adoption order to be made in respect of a child born from such a union.

[23] In respect of adoption proceedings under the Act, fathers of children born from Black customary unions have greater rights than similarly placed fathers of children born from marriages contracted according to the rites of religions such as Islam. This appears to be a clear breach of the equality right in section 8 of the Constitution. The question which arises is whether there can be any justification for this discrimination in terms of section 33 of the Constitution. In my view there is none. Such a distinction might or might not have been justified if the 'Black law and custom' referred to in the definition of 'customary union' precluded polygamy. But, in any event, it does not. There appears to me to be no reason why exactly the same recognition should not be afforded to marriages in accordance with the rights of systems which potentially allow polygamy. This invasion of section 8 of the Constitution is, in my view, clearly not reasonable and not 'justifiable in an open and democratic society based on freedom and equality'. The objection to section 18(4)(d) of the Act must, on this ground, therefore be upheld. It is true that what was directly attacked by the applicant is section 18(4)(d) of the Act and not section 27, but the two have to be read together. Section 27 is effectively a definitional section which includes a 'customary union' (as defined in the Black Administration Act) in the definition of marriage.

[24] Apart from the fact that the impugned section unfairly discriminates between some matrimonial unions and others, it might also

be vulnerable to attack on other grounds. A strong argument may be advanced in support of other attacks on the section made in terms of section 8 of the Constitution on the grounds that its effect is to discriminate unfairly against the fathers of certain children on the basis of their gender or their marital status.

[25] Sometimes the basic assumption of the attack on the impugned section based on gender discrimination is that the only difference between the mother and the father of a child born in consequence of a relationship not formalised through marriage is the difference in their genders and on that basis it is suggested that this is expressly made an impermissible basis for discrimination in terms of section 8(2) of the Constitution. In my view, this proposition is too widely stated. The mother of a child has a biological relationship with the child whom she nurtures during the pregnancy and often breast-feeds after birth. She gives succour and support to the new life which is very direct and not comparable to that of a father. For this reason the kind of discrimination which section 18(4)(d) of the Act authorises against a natural father may be justifiable in the initial period after the child is born. My difficulty, however, is that the section goes beyond this. Every mother is given an automatic right, subject to section 19, to withhold her consent to the adoption of the child and that is denied to every unmarried father, regardless of the age of the child or the circumstances. This could lead to strangely anomalous and unfair results. The consent of the father to the adoption of such a child would be unnecessary even if the child is eighteen years old, has the strongest bonds with the father and the mother has not shown the slightest interest in the nurturing and development of the child after the first few months. On those facts the mother's consent would, subject to section 19 of the Act, always be necessary, but not that of the father. It may be difficult to find justification in terms of section 33 of the Constitution for this kind of discrimination. There is a strong argument that the discrimination authorised by

the impugned section is unreasonable in these circumstances and without justification in an open and democratic society based on freedom and equality.

[26] It was also contended before us on behalf of the applicant that section 18(4)(d) of the Act impermissibly discriminates between married fathers and unmarried fathers. There is also some substance in that objection. The effect of section 18(4)(d) of the Act is that the consent of the father would, subject to section 19, be necessary in every case where he is or has been married to the mother of the child and never necessary in the case of fathers who have not been so married. In the context of certain laws there would often be some historical and logical justification for discriminating between married and unmarried persons and the protection of the institution of marriage is a legitimate area for the law to concern itself with. But in the context of an adoption statute where the real concern of the law is whether an order for the adoption of the child is justified, a right to veto the adoption based on the marital status of the parent could lead to very unfair anomalies. The consent of a father, who after his formal marriage to the mother of the child concerned, has shown not the slightest interest in the development and support of the child would, subject to section 19, always be necessary. Conversely a father who has not concluded a formal ceremony of marriage with the mother of the child but who has been involved in a stable relationship with the mother over a decade and has shown a real interest in the nurturing and development of the child, would not be entitled to insist that his consent to the adoption of the child is necessary. The consent of the mother only would, subject to section 19, be necessary even if the only reason why the relationship between the couple has not been solemnised through a marriage is that the mother refuses to go through such a ceremony, either on the ground that she has some principled objection to formal marriages or on some other ground.

Other criteria in evaluating whether the discrimination was unfair

In evaluating what is unfair, particularly with respect to discrimination on a non-listed ground, the Constitutional Court looks at three primary factors: first, the group that has been disadvantaged; secondly, the nature of the power in terms of which the discrimination was effected, and thirdly, the interests which are affected by the discrimination.[104]

The group that has been disadvantaged

An important consideration under the first factor is whether the complainant belongs to a group that is in need of special protection.[105] In *Larbi-Odam*, the North West Province passed a regulation that prevented the employment of non-South African citizens as teachers in a permanent capacity. The applicants included a number of permanent residents and other non-citizens who challenged the constitutionality of the provisions based on violation of the equality clause of the interim Constitution. The Court, *per* Mokgoro J, held that non-citizens were politically powerless and in need of special protection.[106] They were a vulnerable group and the regulations which imposed burdens on them constituted unfair discrimination.[107]

There is no need for the group to be a victim of past discrimination. Accordingly, in *City Council of Pretoria*, the majority of the Court considered the applicants, who were members of the white minority, and who challenged the different electricity rates applied in white and black areas, as a vulnerable group.[108] Their vulnerability was based on their minority racial status. Sachs J, in his dissenting opinion, disagreed with this approach

and argued that unfairness should only be presumed if the statute explicitly uses categorizations based on immutable characteristics.[109] According to Sachs J, if the statute does not explicitly use categories based on immutable characteristics, such as race, then unfair prejudice could only justifiably be invoked if the group from which the complainant comes from was stigmatized by discrimination.[110]

In *Harksen*, the Court found that the statute in question, namely the Insolvency Act, had a discriminatory effect on a solvent spouse in that it required the solvent spouse to vest his or her assets with the Master of the Supreme Court, which was not required of other persons closely related to an insolvent person. However, the majority held that the group which suffered – solvent spouses – were neither a vulnerable group, nor did they suffer past discrimination.[111] Four of the justices, in dissenting opinions by O'Regan J[112] and Sachs J, found the discrimination unfair. O'Regan J did not find that solvent spouses were a historically disadvantaged group. She also did not expressly state that human dignity was infringed upon by the legislation. Instead, she found the section discriminated based on marital status.[113] The overall effect of the legislation, which required the solvent spouse to surrender their property to the Master of the Supreme Court, was too severe, and invasive of the rights of a solvent spouse.[114] The effects of these drastic provisions constituted unfair discrimination.[115] Sachs J in his separate dissenting opinion was of the view that the vesting provisions were unfair discrimination because they intruded on human dignity and privacy.[116] It is debatable whether the majority would adhere to

---

[104] Goldstone J in *Hugo* para 42; *per* Mokgoro J in *Larbi-Odam* para 17. Ngcobo J in *Hoffman* para 28.
[105] In *Larbi-Odam*, Mokgoro J expressed the view that the first factor was the primary consideration: para 23.
[106] *Supra* para 23.
[107] *Supra* para 25.
[108] *Per* Langa DP in *City of Pretoria* para 48.
[109] Sachs J in *City of Pretoria* para 107.
[110] *Supra.*
[111] *Per* Goldstone J in *Harksen* para 64.
[112] Concurred by Madala and Mokgoro JJ in *Harksen*.
[113] O'Regan J in *Harksen* para 92.
[114] *Harksen* paras 97–98.
[115] *Supra* para 101.
[116] Sachs J in *Harksen* para 122.

the approach in *Harksen* if the constitutionality of the vesting provision came before the Court today since the final Constitution now includes marital status as a listed category which forbids discrimination.

The constitutional provision implicated

Under the second factor, the Court will look at what constitutional provision is implicated and how the power is exercised.[117] The primary concern here is who is making the decision and in terms of what power the decision is being rendered.[118] Underlying the Court's methodology is the idea that for certain decisions, deference must be given to one or other organs of government. For example, in *Hugo*, the Court was faced with the question of whether the president had exercised his power to pardon prisoners in a discriminatory manner. The president had issued a decree under which special remission of sentences was granted to a category of female prisoners who had minor children under the age of twelve years. The respondent had a child under the age of twelve, but did not qualify for the remission because of his gender.[119] The majority, *per* Goldstone J, concluded that the discrimination was not unfair because the pardon power here was exercised by the president in a 'blunt-axe' method.[120] The power of pardon under the Constitution was given to the president to determine, in his view, whether the public welfare will be better served by granting a pardon, or a remission of sentence. However, if the decision was made by another branch of government in the legislative or administrative context, the majority felt the classification would in all likelihood be held

to be unfair.[121] Similarly in *Harksen*, the majority considered the role of the legislature to protect the public interest, as one factor in upholding the Insolvency Act, which discriminated against insolvent spouses.[122]

Has human dignity been impaired?

Under the third consideration, the Court considers whether the complainant's human dignity is impaired.[123] The more invasive the nature of the discrimination, the more likely the discrimination will be held to be unfair.[124] For example, in *Harksen*, Sachs J would have invalidated the vesting provisions of the Insolvency Act which required a solvent spouse to surrender his or her property to the Master of the Supreme Court because the vesting provisions constituted too radical an intrusion on human dignity and privacy.[125] In *National Coalition for Gay and Lesbian Equality*, the Court, *per* Ackermann J, held that the law which prohibited sexual relations between consenting male adults impacted on gay men in a way which impacted at a deep level, the dignity, personhood, and identity of gay men.[126] Hence the discrimination was unfair and a breach of s 9(5) of the Constitution.[127]

Unfair discrimination can only be sustained of it satisfies the requirements of the limitations clause

Where discrimination is found to be unfair, a violation of the Bill of Rights exists which, like all fundamental rights' violations, will be sustained

---

[117] Langa DP in *City Council of Pretoria* para 37 (referring to the Court's approach in *Hugo*).

[118] The question in terms of what power the decision is rendered is particularly important in the affirmative action and promotion of diversity contexts, which is discussed later in this chapter.

[119] *Hugo* para 2.

[120] *Supra* para 47.

[121] See *Hugo*.

[122] Goldstone J in *Harksen* para 64.

[123] Langa DP in *City Council of Pretoria* para 38.

[124] O'Regan J in *Hugo* para 112.

[125] Sachs J in *Harksen* para 122.

[126] *National Coalition for Gay and Lesbian Equality 2* para 25.

[127] *Supra*.

only if the discrimination can overcome the requirements in the limitations clause.[128] These requirements – particularly the requirements that the limitation be reasonable and justifiable[129] and that there are no less restrictive means available to achieve the purpose – impose burdens which are not easy to satisfy.[130]

Summary of the test for discrimination

The test for discrimination which the Court follows, as laid out in *Harksen v Lane*,[131] is paraphrased as follows: first, does the provision differentiate between people or categories of people? If there is differentiation, does the differentiation bear a rational connection to a legitimate government purpose? If it does not have a rational connection, then there is a violation of s 9(1). Even if it does bear a rational connection, it might nevertheless amount to discrimination. Secondly, does the differentiation amount to unfair discrimination? This requires a two-stage analysis. The first stage investigates whether the differentiation amounts to 'discrimination'? If it is on a specified ground as contained in s 9(3), then discrimination will have been established. If it is not on a specified ground, then whether or not there is discrimination will depend upon whether, objectively, the ground is based on attributes and characteristics which have the potential to impair the fundamental human dignity of persons as human beings or to affect them adversely in a comparably serious manner.

The second stage asks if the differentiation amounts to 'discrimination' and does it amount to 'unfair discrimination'? If it has been found to have been on a specified ground, then unfairness will be presumed. If on an unspecified ground, unfairness will have to be established by the complainant. The test of unfairness focuses primarily on the impact of the discrimination on the complainant and others in their situations.

If, at the end of this stage of the enquiry, the differentiation is found not to be unfair, then there will be no violation of s 9(3). Alternatively, if the discrimination is found to be unfair then a determination will have to be made as to whether the provision can be justified under the limitations clause.

Inherent subjectivity in determining discrimination: the counter-majoritarian problem

When analyzing the case law, it is apparent that there is difficulty, and an inherent value judgement in many enquiries in determining whether there is discrimination. First, the line-drawing between legitimate differentiation and discrimination is a subjective choice. The line-drawing depends, to some extent, on the way the judges' see prevailing moral and cultural values, and the judges ideas of justice.[132] In *Prinsloo*, Ackermann J alluded to the difficulty and stated that the determination as to whether discrimination exists depends 'on a combination of the texts to be interpreted, modes of doctrinal articulation, historical backgrounds and evolving standards'.[133] In *Brink*, O'Regan J stated that the equality clause must be interpreted in the context of South Africa's history of systematic racial discrimination,[134] and other modes of systematic discrimination inscribed on the country's social fabric.[135] In *Prinsloo*, Ackermann J also alluded to the question of the

---

[128] *Per* O'Regan J in *Brink* para 46–50.
[129] Section 36(1) of the Constitution.
[130] Discussed in chapter 14 below.
[131] *Harksen* para 53.
[132] Wurtenberger 73.
[133] *Prinsloo* para 7.
[134] *Brink* para 40.
[135] *Supra* para 41.

institutional function in reviewing certain types of legislation.[136] Ackermann J's observation on institutional function is central to the entire enquiry. The extent to which the Constitutional Court is prepared to defer to the findings of the other branches of government, or the extent to which they will intervene and substitute their own judgments, ultimately determines the validity of the line-drawing.[137]

The general proposition is that laws which restrict fundamental dignity or freedoms, or discriminate based on personal characteristics, lifestyle, or association, should be subject to the most intense scrutiny. However, defining the terms 'personal characteristics', or 'lifestyle', or 'human dignity' often involves a subjective judgement. Assume the legislature believes that small businesses are more socially and economically desirable than large businesses. It therefore passes a law which provides subsidies to small businesses. Is such a choice that rewards a particular lifestyle constitutional? Assume also that the legislature believes that it is preferable that couples living together should be married. The government accordingly passes a statute that provides a tax break to married couples alone. In the two examples, is the legislature making a lifestyle choice, and if so, is it constitutional for the legislature to determine what is a desirable lifestyle? Ultimately, it is a normative judgement as to whether the classification distinguishes between people based on personal characteristics or human dignity.

Arguably the most subjective part is the determination of unfairness. The Constitution requires the legislature to enact corrective legislation to prevent or prohibit unfair discrimination.[138] As is this case in the United States Congress, parliament has a specific constitutional mandate to enforce the dictates of equality. As Justice O' Connor noted in *Croson*, '[t]he power to "enforce" may at times also include the power to define situations which congress determines threatens principles of equality to adopt prophylactic rules to deal with those situations'.[139] Where to draw the line concerning unfairness, and who is better suited to make that judgment is difficult to establish.[140]

The Court considers three primary factors to determine whether the discrimination is unfair: first, the group which has been disadvantaged; secondly, the nature of the power in terms of which the discrimination was effected, and thirdly, the interests which are effected by the discrimination.[141] Apart from possibly bringing the judgment of the legislature and the Court into conflict, when the Court intervenes, it is not always clear which of the three factors the Court is going to give greater weight to in any specific challenge. It is also difficult to evaluate the prejudices that influence the individual justices in giving these factors expression. The three factors are elastic. In the words of United States Supreme Court Justice William Rehnquist, commenting on the flexibility of the intermediate standard of review, the factors 'invite subjective judicial preferences or prejudices relating to particular types of legislation masquerading as judgments'.[142] We see these different preferences in the way the justices are divided as to whether there was unfair discrimination in cases such as *Harksen*, *Hugo*, and *City of Pretoria*. For example, in *Harksen*, five of the justices (namely Chaskalson P, Langa DP, Goldstone, Ackermann and Kriegler JJ) concluded that the discrimination against solvent spouses was not unfair, based on their conclusion that neither did the solvent

---

[136] *Prinsloo* para 7.

[137] This is demonstrated most clearly in *Hugo*, where the majority upheld the validity of the president's decision to grant recission of sentences only to female prisoners, based on the majority's preference that they should defer to the executive on decisions of this nature.

[138] Section 9(4) of the Constitution. Pursuant to this mandate, parliament has adopted several pieces of legislation, namely the Employment Equity Act 55 of 1998 and the Promotion of Equality and Prevention of Unfair Discrimination Act 4 of 2000.

[139] *City of Richmond v JA Croson Co* 488 US 469, 490 (1989).

[140] Wurtenberger 74.

[141] Goldstone J in *Hugo* para 42; Mokgoro J in *Larbi-Odam* para 17.

[142] *Craig v Boren* 429 US 190, 221 (1976).

spouses as a group, suffer past discrimination, nor was their dignity affected by the statute. [143] Four of the justices (O' Regan, Madala, Mokgoro and Sachs JJ), felt that the discrimination was too invasive an intrusion and therefore unfair. [144] In finding the discrimination unfair, the dissent expressed a competing value judgement against what they considered as an unacceptable concept of marriage. [145] Ackermann J's concern in *Prinsloo* about institutional balance is central to many of the debates. In the choice over competing values, a recurring question arises regarding whether the judges' concept of values is superior to that of the legislature.

Whether human dignity is impaired, resulting in a violation of equality also involves a normative judgement. The case-by-case analysis, though inevitable, presents great challenges to a litigant who is trying to establish that his or her dignity is affected by the classification. Even assuming that a statute differentiates in a way that is rational, and the differentiation does not pertain to a listed ground, one cannot be sure whether the judges will merely employ the first part of the test, or move directly to a detailed enquiry into the second part of the test, to ascertain whether there was in fact discrimination, and whether the discrimination was unfair. Sometimes this depends on the Court's intuitive sense as to whether the classification impairs the fundamental dignity of human beings. [146] For example, in *Besserglik*, [147] the applicants argued that the different procedures for appeals from the Supreme Court and magistrates' court, and the different procedures for civil and criminal appeals were discriminatory. [148] The

Court, *per* O' Regan J, held that equality does not require identical treatment. [149] However, the Court did not ask whether the different procedures were rational. Neither did the Court conduct an enquiry as to whether there was discrimination, and if so was the discrimination unfair. The Court merely assumed that there was no suggestion of unfair discrimination. [150] In *Harksen* on the other hand, even though the legislation was found to differentiate between people, and the differentiation was found to be rational, the Court still proceeded to the second stage of the enquiry, whether the discrimination was unfair. The Court proceeded to examine the question of whether there was discrimination because it found that solvent spouses were dealt with differently because of their attributes of being closely related to the solvent spouse. The disadvantages that a solvent spouse suffered, demeaned their inherent humanity and dignity. [151] There is a clear sense that the Court in *Besserglik* felt that there was not even the faintest demeaning of dignity, if a person is treated differently in civil and criminal appeals. It is also possible for the Court to find unfair discrimination without explicitly considering the three factors. [152] It is also possible for the Court to assume the discrimination is unfair without considering the differentiation part of the test. [153]

Even if there is no classification based on immutable characteristics, or violation of human dignity, the rationality of the legislation is also subject to approval based on the value judgement of the Court. Even under the mere rationality test, ultimately, the justices decide whether there is a

---

[143] *Per* Goldstone J in *Harksen* para 67.

[144] *Per* O'Regan J in *Harksen* para 101; *per* Sachs J in *Harksen* para 120.

[145] Sachs J in *Harksen* para 120 found that the statute promoted a patriarchal notion of marriage.

[146] Ackermann J in *Prinsloo* para 31.

[147] *Besserglik v Minister of Trade, Industry and Tourism and Others; Minister of Justice* CCT 34/95 (14 May 1996), now cited as 1996 (4) SA 331 (CC); 1996 (6) BCLR 745 (CC).

[148] *Supra* para 11.

[149] *Supra*.

[150] *Supra*.

[151] *Harksen* para 61.

[152] In *Fraser*, the Court, *per* Mahomed DP, found that the statute in question unfairly discriminated against fathers based on the form of marriage. Under the interim Constitution, marriage was not a listed factor. In arriving at the conclusion that the discrimination was unfair, he did not explicitly mention the three factors. See generally *Fraser*.

[153] As was done in *Hoffmann*, see para 26.

sufficient relationship between the goals and the means chosen to achieve those goals. The tendency under the mere rationality test is be deferential to the legislature. Commenting on the United States experience, Nowak and Rotunda conclude that whether the classification meets the equal protection guarantee depends to a large degree on whether the judiciary exercises independent review of the legislation.[154] When the Court defers to the legislature's determination of goals, or the appropriate classification to meet those goals, the Court is taking the position that the other branches of government are in a better position to assess these issues.[155] When the Court does not defer to the legislature, it is indeed saying that it should determine these issues separately from the legislature.[156] To some extent, the constitutionality of the categorization will depend on whether the justices choose to independently review the legislation. Independent review is assured when the justices find that the legislation makes distinctions based on immutable or analogous characteristics, or infringes on human dignity. The converse is that independent review is most unlikely when the legislation touches on social and economic aspects.

Deference to legislature on socioeconomic legislation

There is a strong tendency for the Constitutional Court to defer to the legislature where the legislature makes distinctions based on social and economic considerations.[157] This tendency derives from a recognition of the institutional role of the legislature which is viewed as the best institution to adopt appropriate legislation on social and economic questions. The Court's embrace of deference to the legislature on social and economic policies is consistent with other democracies such as the United States,[158] Japan,[159] and Germany.[160] Countries with past histories of authoritarianism, such as Japan, and Germany, like South Africa, have introduced a constitution that elevates human rights. However, the Courts in these countries defer to the legislature on social and economic policies.[161]

In *Ferreira v Levin*,[162] Ackermann J adopted the position that the section on freedom and security in the interim Constitution protects liberty interests. Under this interpretation, an individual has a right not to have obstacles placed before him or her with respect to possible choices and activities.[163] Interpreted in this way, all legislative policy judgments would be subject to the strictest scrutiny not only based on equality, but on violations of liberty. The majority of the Court, *per* Chaskalson P, rejected this interpretation, which would require all regulatory laws as being necessary in order to survive constitutional muster.[164] The majority held that such an interpretation would require the 'courts to sit in judgment on what are essentially political decisions, and in doing so to require the legislature to justify such decisions as being *necessary*'.[165] The

---

[154] Nowak & Rotunda 600.

[155] Thus underlies the majority approach in *Hugo*, where the majority, *per* Goldstone J, defer to the generalization of the president on recission of sentences of certain female, and not male, prisoners. See generally *Hugo* para 38.

[156] Nowak & Rotunda 600.

[157] Chaskalson P in *Fraser* para 30. Ackermann J in *Prinsloo* para 18.

[158] *United States v Carolene Products Company* 304 US 144 (1938); *Williamson v Lee Optical Company* 348 US 483 (1955).

[159] Itsuo Sonobe 'The System of Constitutional Review in Japan' in *Human Rights and Judicial Review: A Comparative Perspective*, edited by David M Beatty. Dordrecht: M Nijhoff 1994, 159–63.

[160] Wurtenberger 75.

[161] Like the US, the Japanese Courts adopt the approach that basic policy must be determined by the legislature. For a survey of Japanese case law, see Sonobe 159–63. For Germany, see Dieter Grimm 'Human Rights and Judicial Review in Germany' in *Human Rights and Judicial review: A Comparative Perspective*, edited by David M Beatty. Dordrecht: M Nijhoff 1994, 294.

[162] See generally *Ferriera and Levin and Others; Vryenhoek and Others v Powell NO and Others* CCT 12/95.

[163] *Supra* para 54.

[164] Chaskalson P in *Ferreira* para 174.

[165] *Supra*.

majority approach recognized that a welfare state calls for regulation and redistribution in the public interest. Such a determination is better made by the legislature. The judges should therefore avoid an interpretation of individual freedom that impedes social policies.[166]

When interpreting social and economic regulations, not only does the Court adopt a mere rationality test to determine whether the legislation is discriminatory, it is also circumspect in applying the override provisions when the legislation is impugned based on *a violation of economic rights*.[167] In *Lawrence*, the applicants argued that the Liquor Act,[168] which prohibited the sale of certain types of alcoholic beverages and regulated the hours and days on which sales could be effected, was unconstitutional because it affected their right to economic activity as contained in s 26 of the interim Constitution.[169] Under the interim Constitution, express authority was given to the state to employ measures to promote economic activity on a number of grounds, including improving the quality of life, economic growth, human development, and social justice.[170] Similarly, under the final Constitution, the practice of a trade, occupation, or profession may also be regulated.[171] The applicants argued that since the right to economic activity was listed as a fundamental right, any encroachment on this right had to be justified by stringent requirements.[172] The majority, *per* Chaskalson P, rejected this interpretation and held that the state has a right to regulate economic activity, be it in the form of town planning, zoning, licensing, and other regulations.[173] Any limitation on this power was contained in s 26(2) itself, which stated the measures will be constitutional – provided these were justified in an open and democratic society based on freedom and equality. The Court, *per* Chaskalson P, held that the power to define the scope of economic activity under the interim Constitution is evaluated under the terms of authority given to the legislature under s 26(2) and not under the proportionality test contained in the limitations clause.[174]

When subjecting the lawmakers' economic classification to scrutiny, the Court gives utmost deference to the lawmakers findings. The applicants in *Lawrence* argued that the measures adopted neither promoted safety, nor led to a decrease in alcohol consumption. Therefore, the restriction on business hours was irrational.[175] The Court held that there was a dispute about facts and when these disputes arise the Court should only ask whether there is a rational basis for the legislature's decision. Providing there is a rational basis for the regulation, the validity of the regulation would be upheld.[176] In other words, the legislative purpose would not be viewed in terms of whether there is an 'objective probability' of achieving its purpose.[177] As a matter of fact, courts are neither equipped to investigate the connection between purpose and end, nor are they supposed to perform such a function.[178] When the Court employs the rational basis test, the Court does not require that the legislation be

---

[166] *Supra* para 180.

[167] *Lawrence* para 36.

[168] Act 27 of 1989.

[169] *Lawrence* para 2.

[170] Section 26(2) of the interim Constitution.

[171] Section 22 of the final Constitution. Unlike s 26(2) of the interim Constitution, the final Constitution does not spell out the matters pursuant to which regulation may be adopted. In a sense, the final Constitution gives the lawmaker a broader discretion on what are appropriate reasons to regulate economic activity.

[172] *Lawrence* paras 27–28.

[173] *Supra* para 34.

[174] Chaskalson P in *Lawrence* paras 29–30.

[175] *Lawrence* para 65.

[176] *Supra* para 36.

[177] *Supra* para 41.

[178] *Supra* para 42.

reasonable as is called for under the limitations clause.[179] The Court would also not set aside legislation merely because it feels that the legislation is ineffective, or because it feels that the goals could be achieved in a more desirable way.[180]

S v Lawrence; S v Negal; S v Solberg
CCT 38/96, 39/36, 40/36
(6 October 1997), now cited as 1997 (1)
BCLR 1348 (CC); 1997 (4) SA 1176 (CC)
(notes omitted)

[42] In the passage relied upon by the appellants Professor Mureinik argued for a more stringent test of legislative purpose – that there be an 'objective probability' that the purpose will be achieved. He was not, however, dealing there with 'economic freedom'. To apply that test to economic regulation would require courts to sit in judgment on legislative policies on economic issues. Courts are ill equipped to do this and in a democratic society it is not their role to do so. In discussing legislative purpose Professor Hogg says:

While a court must reach a definite conclusion on the adjudicative facts which are relevant to the disposition of litigation, the court need not be so definite in respect of legislative facts in constitutional cases. The most that the court can ask in respect of legislative facts is whether there is a rational basis for the legislative judgment that the facts exist.

The rational-basis test involves restraint on the part of the court in finding legislative facts. Restraint is often compelled by the nature of the issue: for example, an issue of economics which is disputed by professional economists can hardly be definitively resolved by a court staffed by lawyers. The most that can realistically be expected of a court is a finding that there is, or is not, a rational basis for a particular position on the disputed issue.

The more important reason for restraint, however, is related to the respective roles of court and legislature. A legislature acts not merely on the basis of findings of fact, but upon its judgment as to the public perceptions of a situation and its judgments as to the appropriate policy to meet the situation. These judgments are political, and they often do not coincide with the views of social scientists or other experts. It is not for the court to disturb political judgments, much less to substitute the opinions of experts. In a democracy it would be a serious distortion of the political process if appointed officials (the judges) could veto the policies of elected officials.'

[43] This accords with the approach of the United States Supreme Court to rational basis review. It has consistently held:

This restriction upon the judicial function, in passing on the constitutionality of statutes, is not artificial or irrational. A state legislature, in the enactment of laws, has the widest possible latitude within the limits of the Constitution. In the nature of the case it cannot record a complete catalogue of the considerations which move its members to enact laws. In the absence of such a record courts cannot assume that its action is capricious, or that, with its informed acquaintance with local conditions to which the legislation is to be applied, it was not aware of facts which afford reasonable basis for its action. Only by faithful adherence to this guiding principle of judicial review of legislation is it possible to preserve to the legislative branch its rightful independence and its ability to function.

[44] Section 26 should not be construed as empowering a court to set aside legislation expressing social or economic policy as infringing 'economic freedom' simply because it may consider the legislation to be ineffective or is of the opinion that there are other and better ways of dealing with the problems. If section 26(1) is given the broad meaning for which the appellants contend, of encompassing all forms of economic activity and all methods of pursuing

---

[179] *Supra* para 45.
[180] *Supra* para 44.

a livelihood, then, if regard is had to the role of the courts in a democratic society, section 26(2) should also be given a broad meaning. To maintain the proper balance between the roles of the legislature and the courts section 26(2) should be construed as requiring only that there be a rational connection between the legislation and the legislative purpose sanctioned by the section. I deal later with how, if it be disputed, the legislative purpose is to be established.

[45] The rational basis test fits the language of the section which, unlike section 33, sets as the criterion that the measures must be justifiable in an open and democratic society based on freedom and equality, but does not require in addition to this that the measure be reasonable. The proportionality analysis which is required to give effect to the criterion of 'reasonableness' in section 33 forms no part of a section 26 analysis.

The propriety of deference to the legislature on social and economic legislation, based on the idea of the Court's institutional role under the doctrine of separation of powers, can be best appreciated from the New Deal crisis in the United States. For almost the first forty years of the twentieth century, the majority of the justices in the United States Supreme Court had their own strong views on appropriate social and economic policy. The justices used their philosophy to consistently strike down elementary economic regulations of every sort, including the prohibitions on monopoly practices,[181] and the right to form trade unions.[182] Minimum-wage laws,[183] and stipulated maximum working hours were also set aside.[184]

Since the New Deal crisis, the approach of the United States Supreme Court has been to defer to the legislature, to adopt whatever economic policy the legislature feels is reasonable to promote public welfare.[185] The Court considers itself as not having the authority to second-guess, or override the legislature's choice on policy issues.[186] In *Williamson*,[187] the Court was faced with a statute that prevented any person except an ophthalmologist or an optometrist from fitting any lens or duplicating any lenses onto frames, except on prescription from an ophthalmologist or optome-

trist. The effect of the legislation was to deny opticians the opportunity to fit prescription lenses. The statute did not prevent a person from buying prescription glasses from a pharmacy without a prescription. The Court rejected a challenge to the statute and stated that the times have passed when it would strike down 'state laws regulatory of business and industrial conditions because they may be unwise, improvident, or out of harmony with a particular school of thought'.[188] At the same time, the United States Supreme Court curtailed its intervention in the realm of social and economic legislation, it extended its role in protecting vulnerable groups and in the protection of fundamental rights.[189] In the latter instances, the Court employs a more exacting scrutiny. The South African Constitutional Court's approach of exercising more exacting scrutiny where the legislation impairs fundamental dignity or affects an insular group, so as to constitute unfair discrimination, mirrors the United States approach.

The more difficult cases arise where the Court has to make economic and social choices, where some provision of the Bill of Rights may be violated, and the violation is not based on immutable characteristics or on group affiliation. For example

---

[181] See *United States v EC Knight Co* 156 US 1 (1895) where the SC invalidated government actions, which attempted to terminate monopoly practices in sugar manufacturing.

[182] *NLRB v Jones & Laughlin Steel Corp* 301 US 1 (1937).

[183] *ALA Schechter Poultry Corp v United States* 295 US 495 (1935).

[184] *Lochner v New York* 198 US 45 (1905).

[185] *Day Brite Lighting v Missouri* 342 US 421,423 (1952); *Ferguson v Skrupa* 372 US 726, 730 (1963).

[186] *Nebbia v New York* 291 US 502, 537 (1976).

[187] *Williamson v Lee Optical Company* 348 US 483 (1955).

[188] *Supra* at 488.

[189] See the celebrated note by Stone J in *United States v Carolene Products Company* 304 US at 153, note 4.

in *Tsoetetsi*,[190] the Court was faced with a statute that limited the amount of damages a victim of a motor vehicle accident could recover under the Multilateral Motor Vehicle Accidents Fund Act.[191] The Constitution confers a right to have disputes settled in a court.[192] As a general rule, a person who is harmed can sue the wrongdoer for compensation based on the actual injury or loss sustained. Can the lawmaker regulate the amount of damages that certain victims can obtain based on social and economic policy factors? For example, let us assume that the government has only a certain amount of money for health care. It wishes to avoid situations where large amounts of money are spent on malpractice damages, resulting in the denial of medical care to needy patients. On the other hand, it also does not want to deny a victim of malpractice a remedy against the wrongdoer. It accordingly adopts legislation that caps all malpractice damages against the state to R50 000. How does one balance the need of a victim to get redress, versus the right of the state to adopt appropriate social and economic policies within the constraints of scarce resources? Is it discrimination to allow full damages to be recovered against the state for most delictual actions, but restrict the amount of recovery for some categories of harm? In *Tsoetetsi*, the applicants did not raise the question of a right to a remedy. Instead, the Court was faced with a more general equality claim based on an injury that took place before the Constitution came into effect. The Court was able to avoid the equality question since the accident occurred before the Constitution came into effect. The Court held that this was not an appropriate case to apply the equality provisions with retroactive effect. However, the Court in dicta, *per* O' Regan J, stated that even if it applied the

Constitution's equality provisions with retroactive effect, it did not consider the breach of equality to be a gross breach.[193] Even if the accident occurred after the Constitution became effective, the Court would in all likelihood have upheld the validity of the legislation.[194] The financial implications of ruling the statute invalid would impose considerable costs and burdens on the state.[195] O'Regan, J stated that the Court should be very circumspect to make an order which would distort the financial affairs of a welfare programme.[196] The approach in *Tsoetsi* was followed in *Jooste v Score Supermarket Trading (Pty) Ltd and Another*,[197] where the Constitutional Court, *per* Yacoob J, upheld s 35(1) of the Compensation Act,[198] which limited the amount of damages an employee could recover from an employer. Even though the Act related to the conduct of a private employer, the Court held that such policy choices are best made by the legislature.[199]

On the other hand, where social and economic choices are made, and such choices affect a group based on immutable characteristics, the Court would exercise more exacting scrutiny, as exemplified in the majority approach in *City Council of Pretoria*.[200] The difference in this case is the finding by the majority that the different bases of assessment for the two areas had a racial impact. In the absence of a finding that the classification scheme is suspect, the Court's role under separation of powers requires it to accord deference to the legislature on social and economic legislation. Once again, there is a subjective element to the enquiry. To return to the malpractice example, can a victim who is unable to work argue that to deny him or her adequate compensation from the wrongdoer, which deprives him or her of the

---

[190] *Tsotetsi v Mutual and Federal Insurance Co* CCT 16/95 (12 September 1996), now cited as 1997 (1) SA 585 (CC); 1996 (11) BCLR 1439 (CC).

[191] Act 93 of 1989.

[192] Section 34 of the Constitution.

[193] *Tsotetsi* para 8.

[194] *Supra* para 10.

[195] *Supra.*

[196] *Supra* para 9.

[197] *Jooste v Score Supermarket Trading (Pty) Ltd and Another* CCT 15/98 (27 November 1998), now cited as 1999 (2) BCLR 139 (CC).

[198] Act 130 of 1993.

[199] *Jooste* para 17.

[200] *Per* Langa DP in *City Council of Pretoria* paras 32–33.

ability to live the rest of his or her 'impaired' life without adequate food or the ability to pay his or her rent, amounts to a violation of one's dignity?

Different forms of discrimination

Article 1 of the Racial Discrimination Convention provides a definition of racial discrimination which includes discrimination based on purpose or effect. This definition recognizes that discrimination can appear in different forms. Equality jurisprudence recognizes that discrimination can appear in three different forms: facial discrimination; discrimination in application; and discrimination in effect.[201] The first is a direct form of discrimination whereas the last two are indirect forms. The last two are concerned with the consequences of law rather than the form of the conduct.[202] Where the Constitutional Court looks at the consequences of the law, proof of intention to discriminate is not necessary.[203]

Facial discrimination

A law may be discriminatory on its face, for example, a law providing that only a particular racial group will be employed in the civil service is discriminatory on its face. The proof of discrimination is apparent from the face of the statute. *Hugo* was a case of facial discrimination because the proclamation provided for remission of sentences for female, and not male, prisoners.

Discrimination in application

A law may be discriminatory in its application,[204] for example, a law may preclude loitering on the streets. Such a law may be neutral on its face but it could be proved discriminatory in its application if it is shown that the law leads to greater arrests of certain racial groups. In *City Council of Pretoria*, the Court was challenged by white residents of Pretoria that the City Council was selectively enforcing the law – for non-payment of water and electricity use – primarily against white residents, and not against black residents. The majority held that the selective enforcement of the law was discriminatory.[205] Similarly, in *Makwanyane*, Ackermann J found the death penalty unconstitutional primarily because the imposition of the death penalty in different situations was arbitrary and hence unequal.[206]

City Council of Pretoria
CCT 8/97 (17 February 1998), now cited as 1998 (3) BCLR 257 (CC); 1998 (2) SA 363 (CC)
(notes omitted)
LANGA DP (concurred by CHASKALSON P, ACKERMANN, KRIEGLER, MADALA, MOKGORO and O'REGAN JJ)

[69] At the time of the trial in the Magistrates' Court in May 1996 approximately 3 000 summonses had been served on defaulting residents in old Pretoria. Although figures do not always tell the whole story, statistics referred to in the evidence reveal that in old Pretoria about 25% of the rate-paying residents were in default and the arrears in that part amounted to R229 million. In old Pretoria steps were taken to enforce payment by suspending services and by the issuing of summons. For reasons of hygiene though, there was no interruption of water supplies. In Atteridgeville, less than one third of the 13 442 ratepayers were in default and in Mamelodi the figure was just under 50 percent of the 25 307 ratepayers. Atteridgeville and Mamelodi owed R12 million and R57,5

---

[201] See Hogg 1179.
[202] See Langa DP in *City Council of Pretoria* para 31.
[203] *City Council of Pretoria* para 43.
[204] See Ackermann J in *S v Makwanyane and Another* CCT 3/94 (6 June 1995) para 156, now cited as 1995 (3) SA 391 (CC); 1995 (6) BCLR 665 (CC). See also *Yick Wo v Hopkins* 118 US 356 (1886).
[205] *City Council of Pretoria* para 81.
[206] *Makwanyane* para 166.

million respectively. Electricity services to individual stands could not be suspended in these townships because there were no means for doing so. Despite the number of residents in arrears no legal action was instituted against them, though summonses were issued against defaulting businesses in those townships.

[72] According to Mr Eicker the policy that was adopted by council officials to address this problem was to enforce payment of arrear charges in old Pretoria, if necessary by means of suspension of services or legal action, and to encourage payment of arrears by residents in Atteridgeville and Mamelodi, but not to take legal action against them while the installation of meters was still in progress. Questions about this appear to have been raised by the attorneys for the BBG and are dealt with in a letter written to them by Mr Eicker on 26 October 1995. He asked them to be patient, saying that the action against the residents who failed to pay their accounts was in a strategic phase of implementation and that to disclose the strategy would undermine what was being planned. This may be the reason why the matter was raised with the council prior to 7 May 1996 when Mr Eicker reported somewhat equivocally to the executive Committee that no credit control measures (in Atteridgeville and Mamelodi) were possible for different reasons, of which the upgrading of services and administration were the most important. That was only a few days before the hearing in the Magistrates' Court commenced. There can be no doubt, however, that the Council must have been aware of the delays and the policy adopted by its officials. There were articles in the press and there were public meetings at which these matters were raised and the build-up of arrear charges in old Pretoria and the townships could not have gone unnoticed.

[73] Section 8 of the Constitution is a guarantee that at least at the level of law-making and executive action, hurtful discrimination such as that which forms part of our painful history, will no longer be a feature of South African life. Equality is one of the core values of the Constitution. Whilst the section clearly calls for more than 'formal equality' and recognises the need to address past disadvantages, the guarantee that it gives extends to all sections of the community, not only those who have been disadvantaged in the past. Whilst there can be no objection to a council taking into account the financial position of debtors in deciding whether to allow them extended credit, or whether to sue them or not, such differention must be based on a policy that is rational and coherent. It goes without saying that a local authority is not obliged to sue every debtor. The Constitution requires only that its debt-collection policy be rational and not constitute unfair discrimination.

[74] Section 8(3) permits the adoption of special measures which may be required to address past discrimination. In the present case, however, although there was mention of it in argument, it was not part of the council's case that the policy of selective enforcement of arrear charges was a measure adopted for the purpose of addressing the disadvantage experienced in the past by the residents of Atteridgeville and Mamelodi. The reasons given for the policy were pragmatic. Apparently the town engineer had indicated that he was anxious to avoid anything that might provoke a hostile reaction from the residents of Mamelodi and Atteridgeville at a time when the contractors were engaged in the installation of meters in the two townships. It was to accommodate this concern that the council officials adopted a policy of enforcing claims against (white) residents of old Pretoria and of not enforcing claims against (black) residents of Atteridgeville and Mamelodi. This was in fact contrary to a council decision that arrear charges should be collected and if necessary enforced by way of legal action against all consumers.

[75] The case advanced by the council was that in the circumstances that existed at that time the selective enforcement, though discriminatory, was not unfair. It was argued on behalf of the council that the policy had the legitimate purpose of facilitating the transition from a system under which municipal services were provided on a separate and unequal basis to one in which equal services would be provided

on an equal basis. Counsel stressed that the arrear charges were not written off, and that the policy was for the short term only, and was to come to an end when all the meters had been installed.

[76] This argument, however, failed to take into account that the policy of selective enforcement of debts owed to the council was not one which was initiated by the council itself. It was one adopted and implemented by its officials apparently without its authority and in conflict with its own express resolution which required action to be taken against all defaulters. Furthermore, as already mentioned, the policy was implemented not only without public notice but secrecy and after untrue and misleading public statements had been made by such officials with regard to that policy. The mere fact that council officials acted without authority and in contravention of council policy does not have as a necessary consequence that the policy implemented by them constituted unfair discrimination. That question must be answered objectively with regard only to what they did or omitted to do. In other words, if the policy would not have been unfair if implemented in terms of council policy, the fact that it was implemented without the council's authority would not make it unfair. At the same time where a policy is deemed by section 8(4) to constitute unfair discrimination on a ground specified under section 8(2), the fact that the

policy is contrary to a fair and rational council resolution and is implemented in secrecy and in contradiction of public statements issued by the council officials, makes the burden of proving the policy not to be unfair more difficult to discharge than it might otherwise have been.

[81] No members of a racial group should be made to feel that they are not deserving of equal 'concern, respect, and consideration' and that the law is likely to be used against them more harshly than others who belong to other race groups. That is the grievance that the respondent has and it is a grievance that the council officials foresaw when they adopted their policy. The conduct of the council officials seen as a whole over the period from June 1995 to the time of the trial in May 1996 was on the face of it discriminatory. The impact of such a policy on the respondent and other persons similarly placed, viewed objectively in the light of the evidence on record, would in my view have affected them in a manner which is at least comparably serious to an invasion of their dignity. This was exacerbated by the fact that they had been misled and misinformed by the council. In the circumstances it must be held that the presumption has not been rebutted and that the course of conduct of which the respondent complains in this respect, amounted to unfair discrimination within the meaning of section 8(2) of the interim Constitution.

Discrimination in effect

A law may also be discriminatory in its effect. For example, a law which imposes an Afrikaans language requirement for employment in the public service, though neutral on its face, may be discriminatory against other groups if the effect of the law is to exclude large numbers of non-Afrikaans speaking people from working in the public service. Such a law is unlikely to be rationally related to any legitimate objective. Moreover, such a law imposes different and

unnecessary burdens on different classes of people.[207] The Employment Equity Act prohibits psychometric testing and other kinds of assessments of an employee unless the test has been scientifically shown to be valid and reliable, can be fairly applied to all, and is not biased against any employee or group.[208] The difficulty arises with respect to determining whether a measure is biased against a group. Is there discriminatory effect if a disproportionately large percentage of one group is adversely affected by a specific measure? In *City*

---

[207] Nowak & Rotunda 621.
[208] Section 8 of the Employment Equity Act.

Council of Pretoria, the Court held that the different methods for assessment of electricity in different parts of Pretoria, although based on neutral criteria, were discriminatory in their effect, on white residents since the measure effected almost only white residents.[209] In effects cases, proof of discrimination is not required.[210] However, the Court would consider the intention of the lawmaker when it determines whether the discrimination was unfair.[211]

The majority approach in *City Council of Pretoria* could result in challenges based on indirect discrimination, to every regulation that impacts disproportionately on a particular group.[212] This could conceivably bring many pieces of legislation before the courts. Sachs J, in a dissenting opinion, advocated that certain restraints should be put into the concept of effects. For example, where there is a claim for indirect discrimination, Sachs J would be more circumspect in finding indirect discrimination where a claim is made by a privileged group, such as the affluent white applicants in *City Council of Pretoria*.[213]

Sachs J raises a legitimate concern: that almost any statute which affects one group one way affects another differently, be it in the realm of taxes, licensing, town-planning regulation or, job qualifications.[214] The United States courts usually reject allegations of racial discrimination based purely on disproportionate racial impact.[215] Instead, in claims based on the law having a discriminatory effect, the United States Supreme Court requires proof of a discriminatory pur-

pose.[216] In *Davis*, the Washington DC police had a qualifying test that applicants needed to pass before they could be considered for the police force. The test was supposed to measure verbal skills, vocabulary and reading skills. A number of unsuccessful black applicants contended that the test unconstitutionally discriminated against them because more blacks than whites failed the test. Plaintiffs also argued that the test was not a reliable predictor of subsequent job performance. The Supreme Court held that disproportionate impact was not sufficient to establish discrimination.[217] Plaintiffs had to show some state contrivance to segregate on the basis of race. State contrivance need not be shown on the face of the statute but it could be shown by the existence of an invidious discriminatory purpose.[218] The Court would consider the totality of facts including the impact of the statute to ascertain whether there was an invidious discriminatory purpose. Mere disparate impact is usually on its own not sufficient for a finding of invidious discrimination.[219] In *Davis*, the majority held that there was no invidious discriminatory purpose because the law served a legitimate and neutral purpose: namely, to test communication skills of applicants.[220]

In *Arlington Heights*,[221] the Court further clarified the factors it takes into account when considering whether an invidious discriminatory purpose exists. Invidious discrimination can be proved by showing the impact of the decision and historical background to the decision. In this regard, was the normal procedure followed; was there a departure from the usual procedure; and

---

[209] *City Council of Pretoria* para 33.
[210] *Supra* para 18.
[211] *Supra* para 44.
[212] Per Sachs J in *City Council of Pretoria* para 117.
[213] *Supra* paras 115–116.
[214] *Supra* para 117.
[215] *Washington v Davis* 462 US 229, 240 (1976).
[216] *Davis* 462 US at 240; see also *Jefferson v Hackney* 406 US 535, 548 (1972) where the Court rejected claims that the Social Security Act was discriminatory based on statistically disproportionate racial impact.
[217] *Davis* 462 US at 239.
[218] *Supra* at 242.
[219] *Supra*; see also *Hackney* 406 US at 548 where the Court rejected claims that the Social Security Act was discriminatory based on statistically disproportionate racial impact.
[220] *Davis*, 462 US at 246.
[221] *Village of Arlington Heights v Metropolitan Housing Development Corporation* 429 US 252 (1977).

what was the legislative or administrative history behind the decision (such as statements by members responsible for taking the decision)?[222] There could be exceptional situations where discriminatory purpose might be inferred from a statute's effect alone. For example, in *Gomillion*, the Court was faced with a statute which mandated that the City of Tuskegee alter its city boundary in such a way so as to remove almost all of the black residents from the city lines.[223] No white voter was removed from the city boundary. The new city boundary, the Court said, was an 'uncouth twenty-eight-sided figure'.[224] Arguably in *Gomillion*, the effect of disenfranchising almost the entire black population was so dramatic that it was not difficult to infer a discriminatory purpose from effect.[225]

Without this kind of dramatic finding, Sachs J is correct when he observed in *City Council of Pretoria* that the Court should proceed carefully in finding discrimination based on the effects of the statute.[226] Similarly, underlying the majority approach in *Davis*, and *Arlington Heights*, is the idea that almost any statute affects one group more than another. If the Court was to intervene to rule that a statute designed to achieve neutral ends is invalid because it impacts on one race more than another, this would invalidate 'a whole range of tax, welfare, public service, regulatory, and licensing statutes that may be more burdensome to the poor and to the average black than to the more affluent white . . .' and that this impact on its own is sufficient to establish discrimination.[227] The approach of the majority in *City Council of Pretoria*, does not accept this reality. Instead, the majority proceeded from the basis that discrimination on a listed ground can be inferred from impact alone, and from this impact you proceed to the next stage: namely, to determine whether the discrimination was unfair.

City Council of Pretoria
CCT 8/97 CCT 8/97 (17 February 1998),
now cited as 1998 (3) BCLR 257 (CC);
1998 (2) SA 363 (CC)
(notes omitted)
LANGA DP (concurred by CHASKALSON P,
ACKERMANN, KRIEGLER, MADALA, MOKGORO
and O'REGAN JJ)

[32] The emphasis which this Court has placed on the impact of discrimination in deciding whether or not section 8(2) has been infringed is consistent with this concern. It is not necessary in the present case to formulate a precise definition of indirect discrimination. The conduct of which the respondent complains is summarised in paragraph 6 of this judgment. It is sufficient for the purposes of this judgment to say that this conduct which differentiated between the treatment of residents of town-ships which were historically black areas and whose residents are still overwhelmingly black, and residents in municipalities which were historically white areas and whose residents are still overwhelmingly white constituted indirect discrimination on the grounds of race. The fact that the differential treatment was made applicable to geographical areas rather than to persons of a particular race may mean that the discrimination was not direct, but it does not in my view alter the fact that in the circumstances of the present case it constituted discrimination, albeit indirect, on the grounds of race. It would be artificial to make a comparison between an area known to be overwhelmingly a 'black area' and another known to be overwhelmingly a 'white area', on the grounds of geography alone. The effect of apartheid laws was that race and geography were inextricably linked and the application of a

---

[222] *Supra* at 268.
[223] *Gomillion v Lightfoot* 364 US 339 (1960).
[224] *Supra* at 340.
[225] *Supra* at 341.
[226] *City Council of Pretoria* para 116.
[227] See *Davis*, 462 US at 248.

geographical standard, although seemingly neutral, may in fact be racially discriminatory. In this case, its impact was clearly one which differentiated in substance between black residents and white residents. The fact that there may have been a few black residents in old Pretoria does not detract from this.

[33] I have had the opportunity of reading the judgment of Sachs J in which the view is expressed that the differentiation in the present case was based on 'objectively determinable characteristics of different geographical areas, and not on race'. I cannot subscribe to this view or to the proposition that this is a case in which, because of our history, a non- discriminatory policy has impacted fortuitously on one section of our community rather than another. There may be such cases, but in my view this is not one of them. The impact of the policy that was adopted by the council officials was to require the (white) residents of old Pretoria to comply with the legal tariff and to pay the charges made in terms of that tariff on pain of having their services suspended or legal action taken against them, whilst the (black) residents of Atteridgeville and Mamelodi were not held to the tariff, were called upon to pay only a flat rate which was lower than the tariff, and were not subjected to having their services suspended or legal action taken against them. To ignore the racial impact of the differentiation is to place form above substance.

[43] In interpreting section 8 of the interim Constitution it seems to me to be of importance to have regard to the fact that it contains both an equal protection clause and an anti- discrimination clause. The purpose of the anti-discrimination clause, section 8(2), is to protect persons against treatment which amounts to unfair discrimination; it is not to punish those responsible for such treatment. In many cases, particularly those in which indirect discrimination is alleged, the protective purpose would be defeated if the persons complaining of discrimination had to prove not only that they were unfairly discriminated against but also that the unfair discrimination was intentional. This problem would be particularly acute in cases of indirect discrimination where there is almost always some purpose other than a discriminatory purpose involved in the conduct or action to which objection is taken. There is nothing in the language of section 8(2) which necessarily calls for the section to be interpreted as requiring proof of intention to discriminate as a threshold requirement for either direct or indirect discrimination. Consistent with the purposive approach that this Court has adopted to the interpretation of provisions of the Bill of Rights, I would hold that proof of such intention is not required in order to establish that the conduct complained of infringes section 8(2). Both elements, discrimination and unfairness, must be determined objectively in the light of the facts of each particular case. This seems to me to be consistent not only with the language of the section, but also with the equality jurisprudence as it has been developed by this Court. It is also consistent with the presumption in section 8(4) which would be deprived of much of its force if proof of intention was required as a threshold requirement for the proof of discrimination.

[44] This does not mean that absence of an intention to discriminate is irrelevant to the enquiry. The section prohibits 'unfair' discrimination. The requirement of unfairness limits the application of the section and permits consideration to be given to the purpose of the conduct or action at the level of the enquiry into unfairness. This is made clear in the passage cited above from the judgment of Goldstone J in *Harksen's* case. It is also made clear in that case that an objective test has to be applied in deciding whether or not discrimination has been unfair.

Sachs J (dissenting):

[115] The concept of indirect discrimination, as I understand it, was developed precisely to deal with situations where discrimination lay disguised behind apparently neutral criteria or where persons already adversely hit by patterns of historic subordination had their disadvantage entrenched or intensified by the impact of measures not overtly intended to prejudice them. I am unaware of the concept being expanded so as to favour the beneficiaries of overt and systematic advantage.

[116] In our still fragmented and divided country, with its legacy of racial discrimination and its deeply entrenched culture of patriarchy, and with it practices and institutions based on homophobia or on a lack of attention to the most elementary rights of disabled people, almost every piece of legislation, and virtually every kind of governmental action, will impact differentially on the groups specified in section 8(2) of the Constitution. There are strong policy and practical reasons for holding that something more than differential impact is required before indirect discrimination under section 8 can be inferred.

[117] An undue enlargement of the concept of indirect discrimination would mean that every tax burden, every licensing or town planning regulation, every statutory qualification for the exercise of a profession, would be challengeable simply because it impacted disproportionately on blacks or whites or men or women or gays or straights or able-bodied or disabled people. If the state in each such case were to be put to the burden of showing that differentiation was not unfair, the courts would be tied up interminably with issues that had nothing to do with the real achievement of equality and protection of fundamental rights as contemplated by section 8. Judicial review would lose its sharp cutting edge and become a blunt instrument invocable by all and sundry in a manner that would frustrate rather than promote the achievement of real equality.'

Corrective or affirmative action

Corrective or affirmative action is authorized under s 9(2) of the Constitution which provides:

> To promote the achievement of equality, legislative and other measures designed to protect or advance persons, or categories of persons, disadvantaged by unfair discrimination may be taken.

Parliament has since passed several pieces of legislation on affirmative action, namely the Promotion of Equality and Prevention of Unfair Discrimination Act;[228] the Employment Equity Act,[229] and the Preferential Procurement Policy Framework Act.[230]

Under equality jurisprudence, there is a tension between prohibitions on discrimination between groups and the view that it is necessary to adopt distinctions that favour groups which have been disadvantaged by past discrimination. The Convention on Racial Discrimination, while prohibiting discrimination, states that measures taken for the purpose of securing the advancement of certain racial or ethnic groups shall not be deemed racial discrimination.[231] Similarly, the Convention on the Elimination of all Forms of Discrimination Against Women (CEDAW) states that affirmative action measures aimed at achieving equality between men and women shall not, for purposes of the Convention, be considered as discrimination.[232] The Convention on Racial Discrimination and CEDAW require that the special measures should be maintained only until the objectives for which they have been taken have been achieved.[233] Under the Convention on Racial Discrimination, state parties are obligated to take concrete measures to ensure the adequate development and protection of certain racial groups or individuals belonging to them.[234]

A positive obligation, which requires corrective steps to be taken to compensate historically disadvantaged groups, moves discrimination dis-

---

[228] Act 4 of 2000.

[229] Act 55 of 1998.

[230] Act 5 of 2000.

[231] Article 1 of the Convention on Racial Discrimination.

[232] Article 4(1) of CEDAW.

[233] Article 1 of the Convention on Racial Discrimination; art 4(1) of CEDAW.

[234] Article 2(2) of the Convention on Racial Discrimination.

course away from a formal concept to a substantive concept of equality. According to this notion identical treatment of unequals results in inequality.[235] Through no fault of their own, certain individuals and groups may find themselves in a position of disadvantage, which deprives them of the benefit of the law. The disadvantage need not be associated with the numerical strength of the group. For example, in most countries, women are the majority of the population, yet it is difficult to deny that they are pervasively discriminated against. In South Africa, the black majority population has been discriminated against and denied access to education and other resources, which puts them at a disadvantage in terms of competing for jobs, housing, and entrance to educational institutions. Under this substantive concept of equality, the law must be adjusted and formulated in a way which allows the historically disadvantaged – still saddled with disadvantages – to also benefit from the protections of the law.[236] In this sense, equality jurisprudence has moved beyond a pure process-oriented (or what one can term a formal legality) approach, to a substantive or results oriented approach.[237] The formal approach – the focus of much or our discussion so far – precludes the use of contradictory measures, be it in the legislative or administrative field. The substantive approach is that it is not sufficient to say the rules apply to all equally, but that under certain circumstances, one needs to ensure that the results achieved are more equal.[238] The lawmaking bodies are obliged take into account factual peculiarities and differences in people.[239] In other words, the law is not there merely to act as a neutral umpire to ensure that rules are applied in a single fashion to all. Instead, under certain circumstances, the law is adjusted to equalize the disadvantages by treating the less fortunate more favourably – this is corrective or affirmative action.[240]

The corrective action can come in a number of forms including subsidies, job preferences, and preferences for positions in educational institutions.[241] Collectively, these actions are designed to direct resources and opportunities to correct the imbalances in economic and human capital which certain groups lack, in order for the deprived groups to participate effectively in the social and economic fabric of society.[242] In *City Council of Pretoria*, Langa DP stated that 'the ideal of equality will not be achieved if the consequences of those inequalities and disparities caused by discriminatory laws in the past are not recognized and dealt with'.[243] The deputy president goes on to quote Goldstone J who remarked in *Hugo*:

We need, therefore to develop a concept of unfair discrimination which recognizes that although a society which affords each human being equal treatment on the basis of equal worth and freedom is our goal, we cannot achieve that goal by insisting upon identical treatment in all circumstances before that goal is achieved. Each case, therefore, will require a careful and thorough understanding of the impact of the discriminatory action upon the particular people concerned to determine whether its overall impact is one which furthers the constitutional goal of equality or not. A classification which is unfair in one

---

[235] See Macklem 611–12.

[236] Like the SA Constitution, the Constitution of India in art 15(4) and 16(4) also authorizes special programmes for historically disadvantaged groups called 'Scheduled Castes', 'Scheduled Tribes' and 'Backward Classes'.

[237] Reddy 212–13.

[238] Karl Joseph Partsch 'Fundamental Principles of Human Rights' in *The International Dimensions of Human Rights*, edited by Karel Vasak and Philip Alston. Westport: Greenwood Press 1982, 69.

[239] Partsch 69.

[240] M Hidayatullah *Constitutional Law of India* New Delhi: Bar Council of India Trust 1984, 258, 263.

[241] Although no affirmative action claim was raised, the Constitutional Court, *per* Langa DP, held in *City Council of Pretoria* para 85, that it was legitimate for a local government to charge different tariffs for electricity and water use, depending on the type of user and the circumstances of the user. Both the Employment Equity Act and the Preferential Procurement Policy Framework Act seek to provide preferences for historically disadvantaged groups in employment and business. See s 2 of the Employment Equity Act. See also s 2 of the Preferential Procurement Policy Framework Act.

[242] See Christopher A Ford 'Challenges and Dilemmas of Racial and Ethnic Identity in American and Post-Apartheid South African Affirmative Action' (1996) 43 *University of California Los Angeles Law Review* 1953, 1981.

[243] *City Council of Pretoria* para 46.

context may not necessarily be unfair in a different context. [244]

Similarly, Ackermann J noted in *National Coalition for Gay and Lesbian Equality*:

[60] ... it is necessary to comment on the nature of substantive equality, a contested expression which is not found in either of our Constitutions. Particularly in a country such as South Africa, persons belonging to certain categories have suffered considerable unfair discrimination in the past. It is insufficient for the Constitution merely to ensure, through its Bill of Rights, that statutory provisions which have caused such unfair discrimination in the past are eliminated. Past unfair discrimination frequently has ongoing negative consequences, the continuation of which is not halted immediately when the initial causes thereof are eliminated, and unless remedied, may continue for a substantial time and even indefinitely. Like justice, equality delayed is equality denied.

[61] The need for such remedial or restitutionary measures has therefore been recognised in sections 8(2) and 9(3) of the interim and 1996 Constitutions respectively. One could refer to such equality as remedial or restitutionary equality.

Two critical questions arise from the observation of Langa DP and Ackermann J. First, whether corrective action which favours historically disadvantaged groups and which imposes burdens on others constitutes discrimination? Secondly, should affirmative action remedies be subjected to scrutiny using the limitations clause? The manner in which the Constitutional Court approaches these questions will have important consequences for attitudes to affirmative action.

Afirmative action should not be viewed as discrimination

For a long time the United States courts were divided as to the appropriate level of scrutiny to employ when subjecting race conscious and affirmative action remedies to scrutiny. The United States approach to equality is very different from that of the South African Constitution – the United States uses a one-step analysis, unlike the South African two-step analysis. However, the dilemmas which United States courts have faced is instructive in terms of whether racial classifications in an affirmative action context should be viewed as suspect, and what level of scrutiny should the courts should employ in subjecting race conscious affirmative action classifications to scrutiny. One school of thought in the United States advocates the position that where a group suffers some disadvantage, corrective action which favours that group is not discriminatory. In other words, a group that does not have the 'traditional indicia of suspectness', that is to say, as a class they have not been subjected to historical discrimination and deprivations, has no claim of discrimination. [245] There is a recognition that racism continues to impose hardships on underprivileged groups while not imposing similar hardships on advantaged groups. Therefore, even though particular individuals from the privileged group were not responsible for the past discrimination, such a sharing of the burden by innocent parties is not unacceptable. [246]

In *City Council of Pretoria*, Sachs J adopted this approach in stating that there is no presumption of unfairness when invoked by a historically privileged group 'to shield continuing advantage gained as a result of past discrimination from the side-winds of remedial social programmes designed to reduce the effect of such structured advantage'. [247] This approach considers race conscious remedies in a remedial context benign and subject to a lenient standard of review. In the United States, Justices Brennan and Marshall argued that the test to evaluate the legislation should not be mere rationality, which as we saw almost always upholds the validity of the statute. It should also not be the stringent test that accompanies other suspect categorizations where the state has to show

---

[244] Goldstone J in *Hugo* para 41.

[245] *Richmond*, 488 US at 553 (Marshall and Brennan JJ dissenting); *Regents of University of California v Bakke* 438 US at 357 (1978); *Metro Broadcasting*, 497 US at 550 (1990)(Brennan J).

[246] Burger J, in *Fullilove v Klutznick* 411 US 448, 484 (1990).

[247] *City Council of Pretoria* para 109.

a compelling need for the classification and that there is no less restrictive alternative available. Since the statute may distinguish based on immutable characteristics, Justices Brennan and Marshall would subject the legislation to an intermediate level of scrutiny, under which they ask the following questions: first, whether there is an important and articulated government purpose behind the remedy,[248] and secondly, whether the classification is substantially related to the achievement of that objective.[249] The statute would be struck down if it stigmatized any group.[250]

The approach followed by the other justices in the United States asserts that all distinctions based on race are suspect in whatever context, and should be subjected to the same stringent scrutiny.[251] Under this approach equal protection standards are not adjusted in different contexts.[252] In order to pass constitutional muster, racial classifications even in an affirmative action context must show a compelling government interest that cannot be achieved by any less restrictive means.[253]

The first approach recognizes that affirmative action is taken as a corrective measure to counter-act the legacy of unfair discrimination. Therefore, it should not be subject to the pejorative label of discrimination. The discrimination is constituted in the effects of the discriminatory laws of the past, and the lingering attitudes that prevent certain groups from fully participating and benefitting as equals. When measures are taken to ensure equality, such measures should not be stigmatized with the derogatory label of discrimination. The Convention on Racial Discrimination correctly states that measures taken for the purpose of securing the advancement of certain disadvantaged racial or ethnic groups shall not be deemed racial discrimination.[254] Similarly, the Indian Supreme Court does not consider affirmative action as discrimination *per se*. On the contrary, affirmative action is viewed as the promotion of equality to compensate for accumulated inequalities as a result of a legacy of past discrimination.[255] In other words, affirmative action in India is not viewed as an exception to equality. Instead, it is a means to accomplish equality and to give equality real meaning. Using the approach that affirmative action is not discrimination, when a court is faced with affirmative action measures, it should not subject the measure to scrutiny in terms of the standards it uses in ordinary equal protection challenges. In other words, if the Constitutional Court finds that the measure is a proper corrective measure, it should not embark into an enquiry of whether there was differentiation which amounts to discrimination, and whether the discrimination was unfair.

Affirmative action in relation to the limitations clause

The Court should also not subject legitimate affirmative action measures to the limitations clause. Instead, it should approach the legality of government action in terms of an enquiry into whether the measures adopted are appropriate corrective measures to remedy against past discrimination. Where the Court is faced with a legitimate affirmative action measure, the Court is to balance the requirement for affirmative action against other rights in the Constitution. The

---

[248] Brennan J in *Bakke*, 438 US at 359.

[249] Brennan J in *Craig v Boren* 429 US 190, 197 (1976).

[250] Brennan J in *Bakke*, at 361.

[251] Powell J in *Bakke*, at 267; O'Connor J in *Adarand Constructors v Pena* 515 US 200, 218 (1995); Stevens J, and Kennedy J, in *Croson*, 488 US at 493.

[252] Powell J in *Bakke*, at 289–290.

[253] O'Connor J in *Adarand*, 515 US at 220 (quoting Powell J in *Wygant v Jackson Board of Ed* 476 US 267 'the level of scrutiny does not change merely because the challenged classification operates against a group that historically has not been subject to governmental discrimination', and stated the two-part inquiry as 'whether the provision is supported by a compelling state purpose and whether the means chosen to accomplish the purpose are narrowly tailored'. In other words, racial classifications of any sort must be subjected to 'strict scrutiny'; O'Connor J, White J, and Kennedy J in *Croson*, 488 US at 472.

[254] Article 1 of the Convention on Racial Discrimination.

[255] Vicki C Jackson and Mark V Tushnet *Comparative Constitutional Law* New York: Foundation Press 1999, 1079.

Constitution gives the lawmaker the power to differentiate in order to implement corrective action. It further recognizes that such corrective action is not discrimination. Since affirmative action is not discrimination, affirmative action measures should not be stigmatized by the tests that are employed for measures which discriminate. It is also unacceptable to find affirmative action to be discrimination.

The Promotion of Equality and Prevention of Unfair Discrimination Act operates under the notion that affirmative action is discrimination which is not unfair.[256] Instead, it should be found that if properly employed, affirmative action is necessary corrective action.[257] In other words affirmative action should not be approached as discrimination in order to to balance against past discrimination. Instead, it should be understood as necessary corrective action to promote equality and to remedy the discrimination of the past.

To say that corrective action should not be judged as discrimination does not mean that every time a measure is labelled as affirmative action, the measure is proper. While appropriate deference has to be accorded to the parliament which is given the power to adopt legislative and other measures to protect or advance certain groups,[258] the approach we advocate is that some level of independent scrutiny should be conducted as to the rationality of the statute.[259] Section 14(2) of the Promotion of Equality and Prevention of Unfair Discrimination Act provides cogent and detailed criteria for evaluating affirmative action and provides that the following must be taken into account:

> (2) In determining whether the respondent has proved that the discrimination is fair, the following must be taken into account:
> (a) The context;

> (b) the factors referred to in subsection (3);
> (c) whether the discrimination reasonably and justifiably differentiates between persons according to objectively determinable criteria, intrinsic to the activity concerned.
> (3) The factors referred to in subsection (2)*(b)* include the following:
> (a) Whether the discrimination impairs or is likely to impair human dignity;
> (b) the impact or likely impact of the discrimination on the complainant;
> (c) the position of the complainant in society and whether he or she suffers from patterns of disadvantage or belongs to a group that suffers from such patterns of disadvantage;
> (d) the nature and extent of the discrimination;
> (e) whether the discrimination is systemic in nature;
> (f) whether the discrimination has a legitimate purpose;
> (g) whether and to what extent the discrimination achieves its purpose;
> (h) whether there are less restrictive and less disadvantageous means to achieve the purpose;
> (i) whether and to what extent the respondent has taken such steps as being reasonable in the circumstances to–
>   (i) address the disadvantage which arises from or is related to one or more of the prohibited grounds; or
>   (ii) accommodate diversity.

In applying the criteria in the Act and in attempting to balance all the considerations, the recurring question is what level of deference should be given to the party claiming the need to apply affirmative action? The degree of deference may be different depending on whether the measure was adopted by parliament, as

---

[256] Section 14(1) of Act 4 of 2000.

[257] It seems the majority would employ the same test of discrimination and unfair discrimination to affirmative action cases as well. See Langa DP in *City Council of Pretoria* para 35.

[258] Section 9(2) of the Constitution.

[259] Etienne Mureneik 'A Bridge to Where? Introducing the Interim Bill of Rights' (1994) 10 *South African Journal of Human Rights* 31.

opposed to a measure adopted by another body or a private party.[260] However, it is conceivable that under the guise of corrective action, the lawmaker, or other parties, could impose further harm on disadvantaged people. For example, let us say that parliament finds that labour costs are too high, resulting in loss of investments and loss of jobs, which has in turn led to massive unemployment. In order to decrease labour costs and as a way of assisting, mostly black, unemployed workers, parliament passes a law exempting employers in some regions of the country from wage laws and from providing certain benefits to employees. How does one evaluate whether a measure is a proper corrective action? Similarly, should we accept a claim by a private employer that Afrikaner males were historically discriminated against and require affirmative action? The ultimate constitutionality of a categorization will depend on the context.[261] Ultimately, the Constitutional Court will provide its interpretation of affirmative action under the Constitution and the various tests and the level of scrutiny to evaluate differentiation in an affirmative context.

If the Court uses the mere rationality test which it employs for most laws that merely differentiate, the Court would in most cases uphold the constitutionality of affirmative action. Where the statute differentiates and confers different privileges or benefits on racial groups, in a non-affirmative action context the measure would be considered suspect, and would constitute discrimination based on immutable traits. The question is when the measure effects different groups based on immutable characteristics, but is employed in an affirmative action context, should it also be subjected to a rigorous analysis in terms of means and *nexus*? There is much merit to the approach of Justices Brennan and Marshall from the United States Supreme Court who advocate that the Court conduct an independent scrutiny of affirmative action classifications. The Court should look at the rationality of the categorization, evaluate its importance, as well as the relationship between the purpose and the means adopted.[262] In an affirmative action context, the Court should avoid presumptions of unconstitutionality. Instead, it should approach such measures with a presumption of constitutionality.[263] Even under the lenient test, it is easy to weed out spurious claims for corrective action. If the Court finds that the measure is not an appropriate affirmative action measure, only then should it avail itself of the test it employs in the discrimination context.

Criteria for affirmative action

Few people would question using economic factors as criteria for disadvantage. What other criteria can be used to identify historically disadvantaged groups? Can these groups be identified on immutable characteristics such as race or gender?

The fact that racial classifications had pernicious consequences under the previous order, should not blind us to the differences between the racial classifications of the past, and the race conscious remedies directed towards the upliftment of the disadvantaged. The reality in South Africa is that race, to a large extent, is a class determinant. There is no reason why race, if properly employed, cannot serve as a surrogate for class. The approach we advocate does not require that each individual show that he or she was a victim of past discrimination before he or she can benefit from corrective action. It is sufficient for the lawmaker to recognize that members of a particular group, such as women or blacks, are victims of past discrimination, or continue to experience the effects of previous discrimination, and accordingly

---

[260] Given the powers given to parliament under ss 9(2) and 9(4), it is arguable that parliament deserves greater deference than other bodies or private persons. In *Fullilove*, 411 US at 472, the USSC, *per* Powell J, adopted the view that it would give greater deference to a finding of congress than it would to another body. Powell J, goes on to observe that congress does not need to provide the same record-keeping as other agencies.

[261] Goldstone J in *Hugo* para 41.

[262] The role of the Court in this regard is explored more fully at the end of this chapter.

[263] See dicta of Sachs J in *City Council of Pretoria* para 112.

tailor a remedy for the victimized group.[264] It is also appropriate for private employers and other groups to recognize the previous discrimination and the legacy of past discrimination and provide preferential remedies for historically disadvantaged groups.[265] The Indian Supreme Court has accepted categorizations based on immutable characteristics. In *Vasanth Kumar*, the majority of the Court accepted caste as a basis to identify a disadvantaged group.[266] Some of the justices also recognized an economic test as a basis for determining disadvantage.[267] In *Adarand* on the other hand, the United States Supreme Court rejected a government plan which gave preference to 'socially and economically disadvantaged individuals' which included 'Black Americans, Hispanic Americans, Native Americans,[and] Asian Pacific Americans'.[268]

As Sachs J pointed out in *City Council of Pretoria*, if the criterion of poverty is used and not race, 'and it so happens that the great majority if not all the beneficiaries happen to be black, then it would be counter to the whole tenor of "the equality provision" to say that this was a case of indirect discrimination against white children who would be left out of the programme, and therefore presumptively unfair to the latter'.[269] Sachs J correctly notes that for a long time poverty relief programmes such as housing, health care and education will inevitably benefit blacks more than whites.[270] Sachs J also correctly notes that it would be a perverse reading of the equality clause, if such programmes were treated as presumptively unfair.[271] Sachs J limits his analysis to effects cases only. However, there is no reason why distinctions based on immutable traits in an affirmative action context should not be treated as presumptively fair. As Justice Brennan correctly noted in *Bakke*, there is nothing wrong with the government taking race into account when it acts not to demean or insult any racial group, but to remedy disadvantage imposed on other groups.[272] Commenting on the reality of the United States racial experience Brennan J correctly noted that 'claims that law must be "color-blind" or that the datum of race is no longer relevant to public policy must be seen as aspiration rather than a description of reality'.[273] The Indian Supreme Court goes even further and states that there can be neither stability nor real progress if large groups of people cannot transcend primitive living conditions because of past discrimination.[274] The use of race in a corrective situation at times is a class remedy which recognizes that a group of people have been discriminated against, not as individuals, but as a group.[275] These individuals continue to experience the legacy of racism not because of what they are as individuals, but because of who they are: individuals perceived to belong to a particular group. In other words, it is not only the discrimination of the past that accounts for black disadvantage. The legacy of the past continues in the present resulting in whites not willing to employ blacks, or allow them access to opportunities. Therefore, in order to get beyond racism, it is necessary to first take account of race, which might require treating people differently.[276] It is hoped that the Constitutional Court would not, as Brennan J warned against in *Bakke*, let 'color blindness become myopia which masks the

---

[264] *Croson*, 488 US at 487–488 (Marshall J dissenting)

[265] See *Johnson v Transportation Agency*, 480 US 616 (1997), where the USSC upheld a voluntary affirmative action programme in favour of women.

[266] *Vasanth Kumar v The State of Karnataka* 72 AIR (SC) 1495 (1985).

[267] *State of Karnataka*, at 1509, *per* Reddy J; see also Desai J in *State of Karnataka*, at 1506–1507.

[268] O'Connor J in *Adarand*, 515 US at 205–206.

[269] Sachs J in *City Council of Pretoria* para 111.

[270] *City Council of Pretoria* para 111.

[271] *Supra.*

[272] *Bakke*, 438 US at 325 (Brennan J, dissenting)

[273] *Bakke*, at 327.

[274] See the opinion of Hegde J in *Viswanath v State of Mysore* quoted in Jackson & Tushnet 1080.

[275] *Bakke*, at 306 (Blackmun J, concurring).

[276] *Supra* at 407 (Brennan J, dissenting).

reality'.[277] In other words, the use of race, or for that matter gender, in an affirmative action context is qualitatively different from its use in other contexts, and hence should not be viewed as suspect.

Types of benefits under affirmative action

The lawmaker can embark on a host of corrective measures including reservation of a certain percentage of jobs,[278] contracts,[279] and educational slots,[280] for historically disadvantaged groups.[281] For example, different qualification tests could pass constitutional muster.[282] In *Kerala v Thomas*,[283] the Supreme Court of India was faced with a challenge to a law which allowed members of certain historically disadvantaged groups a two-year relief from passing a test in order to receive promotions. The Court held that the two-year exemption was a reasonable classification, which was related to the state's objective of increasing the employment of the historically disadvantaged group.[284] Similarly, a certain percentage of educational slots, and government contracts can be reserved for disadvantaged groups, even though their bids may be higher than non-disadvantaged applicants.[285]

Apart from the appearance of treating groups differently, corrective action may be in conflict with other choices such as local autonomy, autonomy for language, or cultural or religious groups. For example, let us assume that the lawmaker wants to integrate schools into a unitary system. It further wants government schools and teachers to reflect the diversity of the population. It is within the competence of the lawmaker to rezone school areas cutting across local autonomy, and bus students from different areas as part of its programme to achieve diversity, even though this may conflict with local autonomy.[286] Similarly, the lawmaker has the ability to assign teachers and change school boundaries, even though this might encroach on local autonomy, in pursuit of its goal of removing vestiges of discrimination.[287]

The courts and affirmative action

The Court has a continual oversight role in affirmative action programmes. Affirmative action to correct past discrimination should only be maintained until the objectives for which they have been taken have been achieved.[288] Even under relaxed scrutiny, the Court must investigate

[277] *Supra* at 327 (Brennan, J dissenting).

[278] See Employment Equity Act 55 of 1998 generally. See also the Indian case of *Balajee v The State of Mysore* AIR (SC) 649 (1963), where the Court approved a reservation of up to 50% of slots for 'backward' classes.

[279] See Preferential Procurement Policy Framework Act. See also *Fullilove*, 411 US 448 where the SC upheld the constitutionality of measures which required a certain percentage of building contracts be awarded to disadvantaged groups.

[280] *Motala v University of Natal* 1995 (3) BCLR (D), where the SC validated an affirmative action programme designed to increase admissions of historically disadvantaged students into the University of Natal Medical School.

[281] Many of these measures are provided for in terms of the Employment Equity Act, Promotion of Equality and Unfair Discrimination Act, and the Preferential Procurement Policy Act. Section 15(3) of the Employment Equity Act, provides for preferential treatment and numerical goals for historically disadvantaged groups.

[282] With a view to achieving employment equity, ss 20(3) and (4) of the Employment Equity Act list different ways in which qualifications may be assessed beyond experience, formal qualifications or learning. Section 20(3)*(d)* read with s 20(4) requires employers to consider the candidate's 'capacity to acquire, within a reasonable time, the ability to do the job'. See the Indian case of *Damodaran v Secretary to Government Hyderabad Educational Department* 78 AIR (AP) 194, 196 (1991). For a rejection of quotas as a remedy, see the majority opinion of O'Connor J, in *Croson*, 488 US at 499.

[283] *State of Kerala v NM Thomas* 63 AIR (SC) 490 (1976).

[284] *Supra* at 500.

[285] Burger J in *Fullilove*, 411 US at 450 ('Congress's use here of racial ethnic criteria as a condition attached to a federal grant is a valid means to accomplish its constitutional objectives, and the MBE provision on its face does not violate the equal protection component of the Fifth Amendment'); O'Connor J in *Croson*, 488 US at 470. For a rejection of quotas as an appropriate remedy see the majority opinion of O'Connor J in *Croson*, at 499.

[286] See *Swann v Charlotte-Mecklenburg Board of Education* 402 US 1, 15 (1971)

[287] *Keys v School District No 1, Denver* 413 US 189, 240 (1973).

[288] See eg the provisions in art 1 of the Convention on Racial Discrimination; see also art 4(1) of CEDAW.

the government purpose, as well as the means used to achieve that purpose.[289] Just as a mere claim of affirmative action is not sufficient, there must also be some reasonable nexus between the means and the end. We made the observation that even though particular individuals from the privileged group were not responsible for past discrimination, such a 'sharing of the burden' by innocent parties is not unacceptable.[290] The Court has an important role in ensuring that there is some proportionality in the corrective action and the burden imposed on innocent persons. As Gajendragadkar J observed in the Indian case of *Balajee v State of Mysore*, 'the interests of weaker sections of society which are a first charge on the states and the Centre have to be adjusted with the interests of the community as a whole'.[291] Ultimately, the question becomes one of balancing the advancement of historically disadvantaged groups against the interests of others in society. For example, in *Wygant*,[292] the United States Supreme Court held that while affirmative action to correct past discrimination was constitutional, in this instance where the government wanted to lay off white workers and replace them with black workers, the measure was too heavy a burden on innocent individuals.[293]

Affirmative action remedies based only on immutable traits sometimes result in benefits to the relatively well-off members from that group who might not be in need of upliftment.[294] The Court should require, insofar as is practicable, that immutable traits should not be the only criteria. To the extent that it is possible, other factors such as the socio-economic condition of the family,[295] occupation, and place of residence, should also be taken into account.[296] The Indian Supreme Court has ordered the government to adopt a means test in order to prevent those members of a historically disadvantaged group, who have adequate resources from benefitting from reservation schemes.[297] A case-by-case evaluation is not always possible. As in all classifications, we again run into the problem of over and under inclusiveness. As Brennan J observed in *Bakke*, '[w]hen individual measurement is impossible or extremely impractical, there is nothing to prevent ... using categorical means to achieve its ends, at least where the category is closely related to that goal ...'.[298]

In the previous discussion, we focused on the role of the Court in validating affirmative action programmes adopted by the lawmaker. The Court has important oversight functions beyond testing the constitutionality of the affirmative action programme. Where there is a history of past discrimination against groups, and the lawmaker has not taken action to redress the wrong, or the wrongdoer is recalcitrant in effecting changes, individuals and groups can petition the Court for corrective action. Beyond an injunction to stop discriminatory practices, or the imposition of fines, the Court can order the body that discriminates to redress the discrimination through affirmative action.[299] The measures the Court can order include an order to hire a minimum number of employees from the discriminated group. In *Sheet Metal Workers*,[300] the United States Supreme

---

[289] This is an exercise constantly engaging the Indian SC. See Jackson & Tushnet 1080.

[290] Burger J in *Fullilove*, 411 US at 484.

[291] Quoted in Jackson & Tushnet 1080.

[292] *Wygant*, 476 US at 267.

[293] *Supra* at 283–284.

[294] Hidayatullah 262–3.

[295] Ibid.

[296] EJ Prior 'Constitutional Fairness or Fraud on the Constitution? Compensatory Discrimination in India' (1996) 28 *Case Western Reserve Journal of International Law* 87.

[297] The seminal case is *Indra Sawhney v Union of India* 80 AIR (SC) 477, 558. The Indian approach is to require criteria that excludes the 'creamy layer' which is a reference to those persons from the targeted group who have achieved independent success. See Reddy 213. For a discussion of *Indra Sawhney*, see Prior 93.

[298] Brennan J in *Bakke*, 438 US at 377–378.

[299] For an overview of the approach of the Indian SC, see Reddy 212–13.

[300] *Sheet Metal Workers Local 28, Sheet Metal Workers International Association v EEOC* 478 US 421 (1986).

Court ordered the union to hire a certain minimum of workers from groups that were discriminated against in the past.[301] Similarly, in *Paradise*,[302] the United States Supreme Court approved a lower court order which required Alabama to ensure a minimum of fifty per cent of all promotions in the police force be awarded to black troopers.[303] The lower court made this finding after over a decade of litigation during which period the relevant authorities failed to redress the racially discriminatory practices.[304] Where there are discriminatory practices in access to facilities, the Court can order an overhaul of the way the services are rendered. For example, in *Swann*, the United States Supreme Court ordered the Education Department to dismantle the system of dual schools.[305] Following many years of litigation, more than half of the black students in the school district, continued to attend schools with ninty-nine per cent black population. Among the measures imposed by the Court were rezoning of school lines and bussing.[306]

Constitutionally permissible use of immutable characteristics in non-affirmative action contexts

The Constitution itself allows distinctions, or permits distinctions, based on immutable characteristics in a number of provisions. For example, only citizens are allowed to vote or be members of the NA,[307] and only citizens can be appointed as judges.[308] In addition, there are various provisions which require diversity, that employers in various state agencies must be reflective of the South African population. Looking at various provisions in the Constitution, it is fair to say that diversity is a legitimate goal. For example, the Commission for the Promotion and Protection of the Rights of Cultural, Religious and Linguistic Communities must be broadly representative of the cultural, religious, linguistic, and gender composition of South African society.[309] The South African Broadcasting Commission is required to ensure diversity of views broadly representative of South African society.[310] Public administration must also be broadly representative of the South African population to redress the imbalances of the past.[311]

Some of the above provisions are not necessarily tied to affirmative action. For example, diversity in broadcasting is aimed at achieving a broad spectrum of views over the airwaves. Similarly, diversity in the Cultural Commission is meant to achieve protection of the cultural interests of different groups in South African society. To achieve the objectives of diversity and representation in the public service, or in broadcasting, parliament needs to suitable adopt legislation. Similarly, it is appropriate that other institutions, both public and private, broadly reflect the composition of South Africa society. We will refer to these classifications as 'diversity classifications'. It is appropriate for the legislature to make distinctions based on immutable characteristics such as race, language, gender, and religion in diversity classifications. For example, s 2 *(b)* of the Employment Equity Act, apart from seeking to accomplish affirmative action, also seeks to ensure 'equitable representation in all occupational categories and levels in the workforce'. Such legislation taken pursuant to the constitutional mandates should also not be subject to the test

[301] *Supra* at 431–432.
[302] *United States v Paradise* 480 US 149 (1987).
[303] *Supra* at 153.
[304] *Supra*.
[305] *Swann v Charlotte-Mecklenburg Board of Education* 402 US 1, 22 (1971).
[306] *Supra* at 8.
[307] Section 47(1) of the Constitution.
[308] Section 174(1).
[309] Sections 186(2)*(a)* and 186(2)*(b)*.
[310] Section 192.
[311] Section 195(1)(i).

used under the discrimination analysis.[312] Instead, legislation adopted in terms of diversity classifications should be subjected to separate scrutiny in terms of the requirements of the various sections, using a more deferential approach. For example, say a law is passed which allocates airtime to various language groups. The constitutionality of such a measure should not be allowed to be impugned under the equality clause simply because the distinctions are based on immutable characteristics. Similarly, a law that says a specific percentage of public service jobs must be given to certain categories of people, in order to make the public service more representative of the population, should not be impugned under the equality clause, on account of the lawmaking distinctions based on immutable traits. The same intermediate level of scrutiny that should be employed in affirmative action cases to remedy past discrimination should be employed in diversity classifications. In other words, affirmative action under certain provisions of the Constitution is directed at achieving diversity, and not always to compensate victims for past discrimination.[313]

---

[312] Under the Employment Equity Act, certain employers are required to take affirmative steps to achieve diversity in the workplace. See s 15 of the Act. Similarly, in terms of s 53, where a business wants to enter into a business contract with the state, preference will be given to businesses who are able to show that they comply with the provisions of the Act. This is further affirmed in s 2 of the Preferential Procurement Policy Framework Act, in terms of which special preference is given to contracting with persons who come from historically disadvantaged groups.

[313] This view of affirmative action was accepted by the majority in *Metro Broadcasting*, 497 US at 548, *per* Brennan J, where the Court upheld a congressional statute which gave preferences to minorities for broadcasting licences. The majority held that the programme was related to an important government purpose of promoting diversity in broadcasting.

9

The right to own property

Introduction

Private law in South Africa has detailed rules on property law. The discussion in this chapter considers the right to property under the Constitution. In attempting to give meaning to the property provisions of the Constitution, the discussion will draw from comparative experiences and international law, both of which might influence the way the Constitutional Court interprets the property provisions of the Constitution. This chapter does not consider the substantive law of property, which exists largely under private law and properly belongs under the purview of property law.

International human rights and the right to property

Article 17(1) of the Universal Declaration states that everyone 'has the right to own property alone as well as in association with others'. Article 17(2) provides that no-one 'shall be arbitrarily deprived of his property'. The right to own property historically was a fundamental principle of international law. With the emergence of new states in Africa, Asia and the growth of communism after the Second World War, the international consensus on the individual right to own property has considerably weakened. The Civil Covenant does not mention a right to own property. The right to property is guaranteed in art 14 of the African Charter; art 1 of Protocol 1 of the European Convention, and art 21(1) of the American Convention. In the last few decades, the right to individual property as an international human right has been called into question by many jurists and countries.[1] For example, the African Charter guarantees the right to property, but with a major departure from other human rights documents in that property is not specifically guaranteed in individual terms.[2] The flexibility in this provision allows the traditional concept of property being communally owned to take root. The failure to mention the right to own property in the Civil Covenant, as well as many differences of opinions on the nature of the right, leads many jurists to

---

[1] Stephen P Marks 'Principles and Norms of Human Rights Applicable in Emergency Situations: Underdevelopment, Catastrophes and Armed Conflicts' in *The International Dimensions of Human Rights*, edited by Karel Vasak and Philip Alston. Westport: Greenwood Press 1982, 183.

[2] Article 17 of the Universal Declaration calls for the right to own property individually and in association with others

conclude that the right to property is not part of customary international law.[3] In *Golak Nath*, Hidayatullah J of the Indian Supreme Court remarked: '[O]ur Constitution accepted the theory that the Right to Property is a fundamental right. In my opinion, it was an error to place it in that category. Of all fundamental rights, it is the weakest'.[4] The right to property has also been limited in the overall interests of society in several European constitutions such as Greece, the Netherlands, Spain, Switzerland and Portugal.[5] In *the First Certification* decision, the Constitutional Court rejected a challenge by petitioners that the right to property is not protected in terms of universally accepted standards. The Court held that there is no uniform formulation or consensus on the status of the right to property.

In re: Certification of The Constitution of the Republic of South Africa, 1996 CCT 23/96 (6 September 1996), now cited as Ex parte Chairperson of the Constitutional Assembly: In re Certification of the Constitution of the Republic of South Africa 1996 (10) BCLR 1653 (CC); 1996 (4) SA 1098 (CC)
(notes omitted)

[71] The first objection raises the question whether the formulation of the right to property adopted by the CA complies with the test of 'universally accepted fundamental rights' set by CP II. If one looks to international conventions and foreign constitutions, one is immediately struck by the wide variety of formulations adopted to protect the right to property, as well as by the fact that significant conventions and constitutions contain no protection of property at all. Although article 17 of the UDHR provides that '[e]veryone has the right to own property' and that '[n]o-one shall be arbitrarily deprived' of property, neither the ICESCR nor the ICCPR contains any general protection for property.

[72] Several recognised democracies provide no express protection of property in their constitutions or bills of rights. For the remainder, a wide variety of formulations of the right to property exists. Some constitutions formulate the right to property simply in a negative way, restraining state interference with property rights .....

The property provisions under the Constitution

The Constitution in s 25 provides:

25 (1) No one may be deprived of property except in terms of law of general application, and no law may permit arbitrary deprivation of property.

(2) Property may be expropriated only in terms of law of general application –

(a) for a public purpose or in the public interest; and

(b) subject to compensation, the amount of which and the time and manner of payment of which have either been agreed to by those affected or decided or approved by a court.

(3) The amount of the compensation and the time and manner of payment must be just and equitable, reflecting an equitable balance between the public interest and the interests

---

[3] The USSC has also referred to the uncertain nature of the international right to property in *Banco Nacional de Cuba v Sabbatino* 376 US 398 (1964).

[4] Justice Hidayatullah in the Indian case of *Golak Nath v State of Punjab*, 1967 AIR (SC) 1639 at 1710. The Constitution of India was subsequently amended in 1978 by the Forty-Fourth Amendment, in terms of which the right to property was deleted from the Constitution.

[5] Christian Starck 'Europe's Fundamental Rights in their Newest Garb' (1982) 3 *Human Rights Law Journal* 110.

of those affected, having regard to all relevant circumstances, including –

(a) the current use of the property;

(b) the history of the acquisition and use of the property;

(c) the market value of the property;

(d) the extent of direct state investment and subsidy in the acquisition and beneficial capital improvement of the property; and

(e) the purpose of the expropriation.

(4) For the purposes of this section–

(a) the public interest includes the nation's commitment to land reform, and to reforms to bring about equitable access to all South Africa's natural resources; and

(b) property is not limited to land.

(5) The state must take reasonable legislative and other measures, within its available resources, to foster conditions which enable citizens to gain access to land on an equitable basis.

(6) A person or community whose tenure of land is legally insecure as a result of past racially discriminatory laws or practices is entitled, to the extent provided by an Act of Parliament, either to tenure which is legally secure or to comparable redress.

(7) A person or community dispossessed of property after 19 June 1913 as a result of past racially discriminatory laws or practices is entitled, to the extent provided by an Act of Parliament, either to restitution of that property or to equitable redress.

(8) No provision of this section may impede the state from taking legislative and other measures to achieve land, water and related reform, in order to redress the results of past racial discrimination, provided that any departure from the provisions of this section is in accordance with the provisions of section 36(1).

(9) Parliament must enact the legislation referred to in subsection (6).

Although there is a lack of consensus in international law on the nature of the right to property, many countries, including South Africa, have elevated the right to property as a fundamental right. Therefore, under the Constitution, the problem is not so much the existence of the right but the precise formulation of the contours of the right.[6] What are the possible limitations on this right? The Constitution allows the expropriation of property in terms of a law of general application, which is not arbitrary,[7] for a public purpose or in the public interest,[8] subject to compensation.[9] The requirement for a law of general application means that the lawmaker cannot direct legislation at specific individuals. The requirement that the law is not arbitrary means that it cannot be capricious or unreasonable. This requires an interpretation of what is unreasonable. The reasonableness of the deprivation of property, and the amount of compensation, therefore, will depend on a number of factors: the most important of which is the purpose behind the deprivation. This raises the question what is public purpose? The Constitution also requires that the amount of compensation and the manner and type of payment be just and equitable.[10] What is just and equitable compensation? The Constitution lists a number of factors that have to be taken into regard in calculating the amount and manner of payment for the compensation.[11] Arriving at appropriate compensation, and the manner and place of payment, also requires an interpretation and balancing of the various circumstances listed in s 25(3).

---

6   Francisco Forest Martin, et al *International Human Rights Law and Practice: Cases, Treaties and Materials* Cambridge: Kluwer Law International 1997, 868–9. The authors make the observation that differences over the contours of the right to property, even among countries that agree on the importance of the right to property, proved to be a stumbling block on including the right to property in the two International Covenants.

7   Section 25(1) of the Constitution.

8   Section 25(2)*(a)*.

9   Section 24(2)*(b)*.

10   Section 25(3).

11   Section 25(3).

Public purpose

The state cannot simply take a person's property even though compensation is given to the property owner. The property taken must be for public use, or in the public's interest. The Constitution, in allowing for the taking of property contains a recognized principle of international law under which a state has the right to nationalize, expropriate, or requisition property for public use.[12] Under the Constitution and under other international-law instruments, the public interest overrides individual or private interests.[13]

How does one measure whether something is in the public interest? Broadly speaking, we are talking about measures which are; in the public good, for public necessity, or for public utility.[14] The Constitution states that public purpose would include the 'nation's commitment to land reform, and to reforms to bring about equitable access to all South Africa's natural resources'.[15] Beyond this, what is in the public interest will vary with the times and conditions in the specific context of each country. Obviously, where a large section of the population will benefit from the measure, it is easier to find a public purpose.[16] In determining whether a measure is in the public interest, one does not engage in the exercise of attempting to count heads in terms of how many people benefit, or how many suffer a disadvantage from the taking. In *James*,[17] the European Court of Justice held that the leasehold measure in question, which gave a number of tenants the right to purchase the land from the landlord, but did not benefit the community at large, was in the public interest, because the measure was pursuant to a legitimate, social, and economic policy.[18] The Court held that the public interest does not mean that the property has to be put into use for the general public or the community generally.[19] It also does not mean that a substantial portion of the population has to benefit from the taking of the property.[20] The public interest requirement is satisfied when the taking of property is calculated to enhance social justice within the community.[21] Public interest could also be directed towards the economic, moral, and material upliftment of a community.[22]

In the context of South Africa's racially divided history, it might be that stability and equity at times may require that property be expropriated from private parties in the interest of a particular region or community. The immediate tangible benefits in terms of monetary rewards may only be reaped in a specific community. However, it may be that long-term stability of the country is better served by this measure which in the short term is seen as benefitting a small segment of the population. In making an assessment of public interest, the Constitutional Court must consider the unique social and economic circumstances of South Africa. When parliament adopts legislation to expropriate property to solve a pressing problem, 'the tests of reasonableness have to be viewed in the context of the issues which faced the legislature'.[23] There are no abstract legal rules to approach these issues These measures are designed to improve people's quality of life; their determination often involves a consideration of economic, social, and political elements.[24] Often there is a

---

[12] See General Assembly Resolution on Permanent Sovereignty over Natural Resources, UNGAR 1803 (XVII) 17 UN Doc A/5217 (1963), arts 1 and 4; see also Declaration on the Establishment of a New International Economic Order, UNGAR 3201 (S-V), (Special) (UNGAOR, SUPP (1) 3, UN Doc A/95559 (1974), art 4; Charter of Economic Rights and Duties of States, UNGAR 3281 (XXXIX), 29 UNGAOR Supp (31) 50 UN Doc A/9631 (1975), art 2.

[13] Article 4 of Resolution 1803.

[14] John E Nowak and Roland E Rotunda *Constitutional Law* St Paul: West, 5th edition, 1995, 464.

[15] Section 25(4)*(a)* of the Consitution.

[16] M Hidayatullah *Constitutional Law of India* New Delhi: Bar Council of India Trust 1984, 413.

[17] *James v United Kingdom* 98 ECHR (ser A), (1986) 8 EHRR 123.

[18] *James* para 40.

[19] *Supra* para 123.

[20] *Supra.*

[21] *Supra.*

[22] Hidayatullah 407.

[23] Ibid.

[24] Michael W Gordon *The Cuban Nationalizations: The Demise of Foreign Private Property* Buffalo: William S Hein 1976, 119.

dynamic interplay between these elements, and a calculation of short-term and long-term public interest – not always be evident to a court. It is not easy or appropriate for a court to weigh economic, social, and political elements; this role is better performed by the democratically elected legislature. Therefore, the legislature must have a large degree of discretion in determining public purpose, or public interest. In *Penn Central Transportation Co*,[25] the United States Supreme Court held that when it comes to controlling and regulating property for public use, all the courts can do is conduct minimal and 'essentially ad hoc, factual enquiry'.[26]

Similarly, the European Court of Justice in *James* held that the notion of public interest is necessarily extensive, and commonly involves considerations of political, economic, and social issues: resulting opinions in a democratic society may reasonably differ widely.[27] In *James*, the applicant trustees were forced by legislation to sell certain houses on prescribed terms and conditions. The Court held that eliminating social justice is the aim of the democratically elected legislature. The only time the Court would intervene is where the legislation is 'manifestly without reasonable foundation'.[28] Without that, the legislature must be given a wide 'margin of appreciation' to adopt legislation directed at achieving social justice, even where the law adopted might interfere with existing contractual obligations between private parties 'and confers no direct benefit on the State or the [c]ommunity at large'.[29] When reviewing the legislation, the Court would proceed by asking the question whether the lawmaker's 'assessment of the relevant social and economic conditions came within the State's margin of appreciation'.[30]

Apart from the general expropriating provisions in s 25, the Constitution also permits the expropriating of property through legislative and other measures to achieve land, water, and related reform to redress past racial discrimination.[31] These measures have to conform with the conditions contained in the property clause. If not, the provisions have to comply with the limitation clause set out in s 36.

Compensation

A recurring question under international law is whether a state must compensate persons whose property has been nationalized. Neither the African Charter, nor Protocol I to the European Convention, contains any reference to compensation for the expropriation of property. Article 21(2) of the American Convention specifies that no-one may be 'deprived of his property except upon payment of just compensation . . .'.

In the United States and other liberal democracies, the traditional position was to insist on just compensation, which has been understood to mean prompt, adequate, and effective compensation.[32] Under this interpretation, where there was an expropriation of property, compensation equivalent to the monetary value had to be provided.[33] Moreover, the compensation had to be paid at the time of the expropriation, or within a reasonable time thereafter (with interest from the date of the expropriation), and the payment had to be effected in a convertible currency.[34] The liberal interpretation of just compensation standing for prompt, adequate, and effective compensation has been challenged vigorously since the 1960s, by a competing principle of compensation in terms of the law of the state taking such

---

[25] *Penn Central Transportation Co v New York City* 438 US 104 (1978).

[26] *Supra* at 124.

[27] *James* para 44.

[28] *Supra* para 46.

[29] *Supra* para 47.

[30] *Supra* para 49.

[31] Section 25(8) of the Constitution.

[32] See Dawson and Weston 'Prompt Adequate and Effective Universal Standard of Compensation' (1962) 30 *Fordham Law Review* 727.

[33] American Law Institute *Restatement of the Law Third: The Foreign Relations Law of the United States* St Paul: American Law Institute Publishers 1990, 712, 197.

[34] Ibid.

measures.[35] The United Nations General Assembly has adopted a number of resolutions – some with overwhelming majorities[36] – conferring a right on states to nationalize property. If property is expropriated, appropriate compensation must be given.[37] In arriving at what is appropriate compensation, individual states must take into account its own relevant laws, regulations, and circumstances.[38] Wherever there is controversy, disputes must be settled by the domestic law of that state.[39]

There is still considerable divergence in domestic practice with respect to compensation. Some constitutions, such as the Constitution of Portugal, allow for nationalization of property without compensation, while Switzerland, the Netherlands, and Sweden allow for nationalization at a rate of compensation to be determined by the legislature.[40] One can safely say that under international law, just compensation does not represent 'prompt, adequate and effective compensation'.[41] As Schachter notes, in the *Charzow Factory* case, the Permanent Court held that just compensation had to be determined in view of all the surrounding circumstances.[42] Tribunals in more recent decisions have also rejected the prompt, adequate, and effective standard.[43] This

leads many scholars to conclude that the proper standard is 'appropriate compensation'.[44]

The interim Constitution made provision for restitution of land to any dispossessed community or person, subject to certain conditions. First, a Commission on Restitution of Land Rights was created, to which all land claims had to be addressed.[45] In *Transvaal Agricultural Union v The Minister of Land Affairs and Another*,[46] the Constitutional Court, *per* Chaskalson P, stated that the interim Constitution required parliament to pass legislation to address the claims of persons and communities who had lost their land as a result of past discriminatory laws.[47] Chaskalson P further stated that the 'existing rights of ownership do not have precedence over claims for restitution'.[48] Section 25(7) of the final Constitution provides:

> A person or community dispossessed of property after 19 June 1913 as a result of past racially discriminatory laws or practices is entitled, to the extent provided by an Act of Parliament, either to restitution of that property or to equitable redress.

Under the interim Constitution, if the land is in the hands of a private owner, the Constitutional

---

[35] See Resolution entitled the Charter of Economic Rights and Duties of States, UNGAR 3281 (XXXIX), 29 UNGAOR, Supp 31, at 50, UN Doc A/9631 (1974), art 2.

[36] See American Law Institute 203.

[37] See the following UNGARs: Resolution on Permanent Sovereignty Over Natural Resources, UNGAR 1803 (XVII) 17 UN Doc A/5217 (1963), art 1, art 4; Declaration on the Establishment of a New International Economic Order, UNGAR 3201 (S-V), (Special) (UNGAOR, SUPP (1) 3, UN Doc A/95559 (1974), art 4; Charter of Economic Rights and Duties of States, UNGAR 3281 ('IX), 29 UNGAOR Supp (31) 50 UN Doc A/9631 (1975), art 2.

[38] Article 2(2)*(c)* of the Charter of Economic Rights and Duties of States.

[39] Article 2(2)*(c)*

[40] Starck 110.

[41] Oscar Schachter 'Editorial Comment, Compensation for Expropriation' (1984) 78 *American Journal of International Law* 121, 123.

[42] Ibid.

[43] See *American International Group, Inc v Iran* 4 Iran-US CTR 96 (1983), where the Iran–United States Claims Tribunal rejected the prompt, adequate and effective as the standard for compensation.

[44] Schachter 127; see also *Texas Overseas Petroleum Co v Gov't of the Libyan Arab Republic* (1978) 17 ILM 3, 29, (1979) 53 ILR 389 (English trans); *Banco Nacional de Cuba v Chase Manhattan Bank* 658 F2d 875 (2d Cir 1981); Arbitration between Kuwait and the American Independent Oil Co (AMINOIL), (1982) 21 ILM 976.

[45] Section 121 of the interim Constitution.

[46] *Transvaal Agricultural Union v Minister of Land Affairs and the Commission on Restitution of Land Rights* CCT 21/96 (18 November 1996), now cited as 1997 (2) SA 621 (CC); 1996 (12) BCLR 1573 (CC).

[47] *Supra* para 33.

[48] *Supra.*

Court has the power to adjudicate over the dispute.[49] Compensation is to be given to the owner if the land is taken away and the Court sets the limit of the compensation. The interim Constitution, however, did not say from where the compensation was to come. The final Constitution also does not address the issue of from what source the compensation is to be paid. An indigent who has been forced off the land is unlikely to be able to afford to buy back land which he or she claims originally belonged to the family. The lawmaker will have to legislate on amounts of compensation, and how payment is to be effected. How does one determine what is appropriate compensation? In the *First Certification* decision, the Constitutional Court recognized the divergence of opinions with respect to compensation.[50]

Certification of The Constitution of the Republic of South Africa
CCT 23/96 1996 (10) BCLR 1653 (CC); 1996 (4) SA 1098 (CC)
(notes omitted)

[73] The second objection was that the provisions governing expropriation, and in particular for the payment of compensation, also fall short of what is universally accepted as contemplated by CP II. The argument was that the NT should stipulate that the compensation should be calculated on the basis of market value and that expropriation should take place only where the use to which the expropriated land would be put is in the interests of a broad section of the public. The objectors also argued that expropriation for purposes of land, water or related reform contemplated by NT 25 fell short of the 'universally accepted' understanding of the right to property. Once again, and for the reasons given in the previous paragraph, we cannot accept these arguments. An examination of international conventions and foreign constitutions suggests that a wide range of criteria for expropriation and the payment of compensation exists. Often the criteria for determining the amount of compensation are not mentioned in the constitutions at all. Where the nature of the compensation is mentioned, a variety of adjectives is used including 'fair', 'adequate', 'full', 'equitable and appropriate' and 'just'. Another approach adopted is to provide that the amount of compensation should seek to obtain an equitable balance between the public interest and the interests of those affected. Some constitutions, too, prescribe that the compensation must be prompt or made prior to the expropriation. Similarly there is no consistency with regard to the criteria for expropriation itself. The approach taken in NT 25 cannot be said to flout any universally accepted approach to the question.

Although the Constitutional Court recognized the different approaches to compensation, the Court did not spell out what the Constitution requires with respect to compensation. The Constitution calls for just and equitable compensation. The word 'just' is not used in the traditional sense as employed by the United States, and now refuted in international law. In arriving at what is just and equitable, the Constitution requires a balance between public and individual interests[51] Furthermore, in arriving at this balance, regard must be given to a number of factors contained in s 25(3): first, current use of the property; secondly, history of its acquisition and use; thirdly, market value; fourthly, extent of direct state investment and subsidy in acquisition and beneficial capital improvement, and finally, purpose of the expropriation.

Moreover, in arriving at what is the public interest, regard must be given to other interests such as the country's commitment to land reform, and other reforms to bring about equitable access

---

[49] Section 123(1) of the interim Constitution.
[50] *Certification I* para 73.
[51] Section 25(3) of the final Constitution.

to all of South Africa's natural resources.[52] The Constitution recognizes that the right to property has both individual and social functions, which can at times be antagonistic.[53] The individual component of the right, for example the right to have a house, is important for personhood and liberty under the first part of the test, 'the current use of the property'. As Kommers notes, in the jurisprudence of the German Constitutional Court, it 'provides space for the exercise of autonomy and self-realization'.[54] This approach is consistent with emerging trends in international law that give greater protections to certain types of property. For example, the UN General Assembly in a resolution in 1991 recommended greater protection for personal property including the residence of one's self and family.[55]

While we have argued that there is no fundamental right to property under international law, the guarantee of the right to property under the Constitution is important for the protection of an individual's home, one's individual possessions, and one's tools of trade. A private home and personal possessions have largely individual relevance. Wherever there is taking of such property, the scales with respect to compensation should weigh heavily in favour of protecting the individual interest. The former Indian Prime Minister Jawaharlal Nehru similarly stated that when it came to compensation for expropriation of property, a distinction had to be made between 'petty acquisitions' and large claims of social reform and social engineering which could not be considered only from the point of view of the individual.[56] Sometimes what is involved is a conflict between individual property not of a

'personal nature', versus the eradication of poverty.[57] Non-personal property such as industrial property, and unutilized land have a greater social dimension. For these kinds of property, the scales with respect to compensation should weigh more heavily in favour of the social aspects, such as 'the purpose of the expropriation'. As the German Constitutional Court held in their decision in *Kleingarten*,[58] the purpose of the restrictions will depend on the degree to which the property has a social function, or is of social relevance.[59] The German Constitutional Court further observed, '[t]he more the individual is depending on the use of another person's property, the greater is the freedom of legal measures by the legislature; this legislative freedom becomes less, if that is not or only to a certain extent the case ...'.[60]

Both the Indian and the German approach adopt the consensus in international human rights discourse – that the individual right to compensation at times is subject to the overall welfare of society. In arriving at what is proper compensation, the individual and the social functions have to be brought into balance. The balance between the social and individual aspect was brought out more forcefully in the challenge to the co-determination laws of Germany.[61] In the *Co-determination* case, shareholders brought a challenge to the co-determination laws which mandated worker participation in the decision-making structures of private companies, on the ground that their property rights were violated. The German Constitutional Court held that the greater the social relevance of the property, the more legislature may limit the content and define the restrictions to property.[62]

---

52 Section 25(4)*(a)*.

53 This is akin to the German Basic Law. See Gunnar Folke Schuppert 'The Right to Property' in *The Constitution of the Federal Republic of Germany Essays on the Basic Rights and Principles of the Basic Law with a Translation of the Basic Law*, edited by Ulrich Karpen. Baden-Baden: Nomos 1988, 108.

54 Donald P Kommers *The Constitutional Jurisprudence of the Federal Republic of Germany* Durham: Duke University Press 1989, 260.

55 UN Doc A/Res 45/98 (Adopted on 22 January 1991), art 3*(a)*.

56 Hidayatullah 399.

57 Ralph H Folsom and Michael W Gordon *International Business Transactions* St Paul: West Publishing Co, 3rd edition, 1995, 1020.

58 BVerfGE 52,1 cited by Schuppert 114.

59 Op cit 115.

60 Ibid.

61 *Co-determination* case (1963) 50 BVerfGE 4, quoted in Kommers 278.

62 Kommers 280–1; see also Schuppert 111.

Admittedly, it is not always easy to make an incisive distinction between an individual and the social dimension of property. An appropriate balance has to be struck. More often than not, the needs of the public would take precedence. For example, in the *Hamburg Flood Control* case of 1968, the Constitutional Court in Germany ruled:

The Basic Law establishes that in the recurring tension between the property interest of the individual and the needs of the public, the public interest may, in case of conflict, take precedence over the legally guaranteed position of the individual ....[63]

In these cases, the overall welfare of society is given preference over that of the individual. For example, after German unification, there were a number of challenges brought before the German Constitutional Court on the subject of compensation for individuals who were deprived of property under the former East German regime. The Court ruled that the unity of the German state is more important than the claims of individual property owners, and in determining the amount of compensation the state could take into account the heavy financial burdens connected with unification.[64] The Court put the common good over the individual right to property and ruled that it was permissible for the state to provide less than full restitution.[65] Ernst Benda argues that the Court acknowledges that after a revolutionary change, one has to look at the political situation that the country finds itself in and accordingly support the appropriate government policy.[66]

In South Africa, no one can dispute that the change from apartheid rule to majority rule represents revolutionary change. The enquiry the Constitutional Court in South Africa will be faced with is: what is the appropriate jurisprudence to approach the property clause and questions of compensation? We argue that the core component of individual property should be respected, but like the welfare constitutions in Europe, the right to compensation should be restrained by certain political values, community norms, and ethical principles which, for example, the German Constitutional Court recognizes.[67] The standards in s 25 of the property clause require, or at minimum are flexible, to permit such an approach.

A bill of rights interpreted in terms of the common law, as in the United States polity, places utmost emphasis on the individual. The United States Supreme Court is not prone to express language of 'community', and 'public good because according to the American view the community does not have any claim upon the individual person'.[68] The German view, on the other hand, is that the polity is the highest expression of the community,[69] which is the approach the Constitutional Court in South Africa should also recognize.

The Constitution provides the factors that need to be considered in arriving at compensation. It requires the parties to agree on the amount and method of payment. If the parties fail to do so, a court will decide these matters.[70] The manner in which the Constitutional Court approaches the issue of compensation will be an important test not only of legitimacy itself, but the legitimacy of the new constitutional order. The property provisions cannot be interpreted as requiring full compensation for property taken where the property was acquired under the apartheid order. There is a need for appropriate deference to the legislature on compensation, particularly where the taking of property has greater social relevance. This is the

---

[63] Kommers 260.

[64] E Benda 'The Position and Function of the *Bundesverfassungsgericht* (Federal Constitutional Court) in a United Germany' in *Federalism-in-the-Making: Contemporary Canadian and German Constitutionalism, National and Transnational*, edited by Edward McWhinney, et al. Dordrecht: Kluwer Academic Publishers 1992, 32.

[65] Ibid.

[66] Ibid.

[67] Donald P Kommers 'Jurisprudence of Free Speech' (1980) 53 *Southern California Law Review* 676.

[68] Op cit 694.

[69] Ibid.

[70] Section 25(2)*(b)* of the Constitution.

approach to which international tribunals such as the European Court of Justice have also adhered.[71] For example, the European Court of Justice has concluded that where there is a taking of property, there is no guarantee of full compensation.[72] In its decision in *James*, the European Court of Justice held that legitimate objectives of public interest such as economic and social reform would justify less than full market value.[73] Moreover, the state has a wide margin of appreciation in determining the amount of compensation.[74]

In *Lithgow*,[75] a challenge was brought against the British government's payment of compensation for nationalization of certain aerospace and shipbuilding industries. The compensation represented only a fraction of the property's value at the date of taking.[76] The industries concerned had been recipients of substantial government assistance in the past. The government felt that the industries would better serve the national interest if they were under greater public control.[77] The European Court of Justice held that under art 1 of Protocol I of the European Convention, there was no guarantee of full compensation. Legitimate objectives of public interest such as economic reform may justify less than full compensation.[78] The Court further held that the decision to nationalize commonly involves consideration of issues about which the legislature has more direct

knowledge. It would be artificial for the Court to separate the decision as to the compensation terms from the decision to take the property.[79] As in the determination of what is in the public interest, it seems that what is appropriate compensation has to also be determined in a way that allows the legislature a wide margin of appreciation.[80] The bottom line is, questions of appropriate compensation should be approached by the courts in a way that is deferential to the legislature, unless the compensation is completely arbitrary or illusory.[81]

In Africa, customary law expressed human rights and property rights in societal terms.[82] The African concept of human rights, unlike the common law, is communal in nature – the group being seen as more important than the individual. In traditional African society, the individual is not viewed as alienated from society, but rights are enjoyed through the group and derived from the relation with the group.[83] Similarly, property in African customary law is seen as a communal possession.[84] The traditional African concepts of property rights, which seek to balance the rights of the individual against that of society, have much in common with rights interpretations that come from current concepts of property rights in international law, and from many European constitutions. Collectively, the emerging trend is for a balance in favour of societal interests where the property is of social relevance.

---

[71] See *James* para 54.

[72] *Supra.*

[73] *Supra.*

[74] *Supra.*

[75] *Lithgow et al v United Kingdom* 102 ECHR (ser A), (1986) 8 EHRR 329.

[76] *Supra* at 108.

[77] *Supra* at 11.

[78] *Supra* at 121.

[79] *Supra* at 122.

[80] *Supra.*

[81] *State of Karnataka v Ranganath Reddy* AIR (1978) SC 215, 224. See also James para 54.

[82] African customary law had a remarkable sense of justice and a deep sense of human rights. John Beattie 'Checks on the Abuse of Political Power in Some African States: A Preliminary Framework For Analysis' in *Comparative Political Systems: Studies in the Politics of Pre-industrial Societies,* edited by Ronald Cohen and John Middleton. New York: Natural History Press 1967, 355, 361–73.

[83] Ziyad Motala 'Human Rights in Africa: A Cultural, Ideological and Legal Examination' (1989) 12 *Hastings International and Comparative Law Review* 381.

[84] Op cit 382–3.

Rules regulating the use of property

Expropriation of property is the most severe exercise of control over property by the state. There are other lesser measures that do not include physical acquisition available to the state. For example, regulations which require a property owner to conduct his or her business in a certain way, such as minimum and maximum charges for petroleum, could deprive the property owner of the full benefit of the property. These regulations in prescribing the limits of profits by property owners would not constitute an expropriation of property unless the rate of return was so low as to be confiscatory.[85] These regulations are economic regulations and are considered under a standard which is deferential to the lawmaker.[86] For example, in *Wickard v Filburn*,[87] the United States Supreme Court was faced with a challenge to the Agricultural Adjustment Act of 1938 which imposed limitations on the amount of wheat each farmer could produce. Congress imposed these limits in order to control the volume of wheat moving in the stream of commerce in order to avoid surpluses and shortages, and thereby, to prevent fluctuations in the price of wheat. Filburn, a farmer, exceeded his allotment of wheat production and, when penalized, argued that the statute was unconstitutional. The Court upheld the constitutionality of the statute and held that the legislature under its economic power could pass regulations of this nature, to prevent volatility in the wheat market.[88] Similarly, the German Constitutional Court has upheld laws which set limits on how one uses one's property, including limits on the amount of land which could be brought under cultivation.[89] Most zoning regulations that regulate the way property is utilized would also be judged by a deferential approach.[90] Providing the zoning regulation advances some reasonable interest, the Court will uphold the zoning requirement.[91] Where there is a reasonable basis for the regulation, there is no requirement to compensate the owner who is restricted in the use of his or her property.[92]

The state can temporarily deprive an owner of use of property in order to realize other important goals.[93] Where the state temporarily deprives an owner of use of his or her property pursuant to a legitimate government objective, there is no requirement to compensate the owner. In *Harksen v Lane*, the applicant was the wife of an insolvent. She argued that s 21 of the Insolvency Act of 1936 violated the property provisions of the interim Constitution. Under s 21 of the Act, property of the solvent spouse is divested and vested in the Master of the Supreme Court. The majority, *per* Goldstone J, held that there is a distinction between an acquisition and a deprivation of property. The first situation is a permanent deprivation of rights of the owner, which would require the payment of compensation.[94] The second situation is not expropriation, since it is a temporary deprivation of property in order to realize an important objective.[95]

---

[85] *Duquesne Light Co v Barasch* 488 US 299, 307 (1989).

[86] Nowak & Rotunda 439.

[87] 317 US 111 (1942).

[88] *Wickard,* 317 US 118.

[89] See reference to the *Vineyard* case, in Kommers 261.

[90] *Euclid v Ambler Realty Co* 272 US 365, 368 (1926).

[91] *Goldblatt v Town of Hempstead* 369 US 590, 592−593 (1962).

[92] *Supra.*

[93] *Harksen v Lane NO and Others* CCT 9/97 (7 October 1997), now cited as 1998 (1) SA 300 (CC); 1997 (11) BCLR 1489 (CC).

[94] *Supra* para 34.

[95] *Supra* para 36.

Harksen v Lane and Others
CCT 9/97 (7 October 1997), now
cited as 1997 (11) BCLR 1489 (CC);
1998 (1) SA 300 (CC)
(notes omitted)
GOLDSTONE J:

[31] The word 'expropriate' is generally used in our law to describe the process whereby a public authority takes property (usually immovable) for a public purpose and usually against payment of compensation. Whilst expropriation constitutes a form of deprivation of property, section 28 makes a distinction between deprivation of rights in property, on the one hand (subsection (2)), and expropriation of rights in property, on the other (subsection (3)). Section 28(2) states that no deprivation of rights in property is permitted otherwise than in accordance with a law. Section 28(3) sets out further requirements which need to be met for expropriation, namely, that the expropriation must be for a public purpose and against payment of compensation.

[32] The distinction between expropriation (or compulsory acquisition as it is called in some other foreign jurisdictions) which involves acquisition of rights in property by a public authority for a public purpose and the deprivation of rights in property which fall short of compulsory acquisition has long been recognised in our law. In *Beckenstrater v Sand River Irrigation Board*, Trollip J said:

[T]he ordinary meaning of 'expropriate' is 'to dispossess of ownership, to deprive of property' (see eg *Minister of Defence v Commercial Properties Ltd and Others* 1955 (3) SA 324 (N) at p 327G); but in statutory provisions, like sections 60 and 94 of the Water Act, it is generally used in a wider sense as meaning not only dispossession or deprivation but also appropriation by the expropriator of the particular right, and abatement or extinction, as the case may be, of any other existing right held by another which is inconsistent with the appropriated right. That is the effect of cases like *Stellenbosch Divisional Council v Shapiro* 1953 (3) SA. 418 (C) at pages 422–3, 424; *SAR & H v Registrar of Deeds* 1919 NPD. 66; *Kent NO v*

SAR & H 1946 AD 398 at pages 405–6; and *Minister van Waterwese v Mostert and Others* 1964 (2) SA 656 (AD) at pages 666–7.

[33] The Zimbabwean Constitution also provides that property may not be compulsorily acquired, save under a law which requires the acquiring authority to pay fair compensation. In *Hewlett v Minister of Finance and Another*, Fieldsend CJ considered the meaning of 'acquire' in those sections of the Constitution. He referred to the following dictum of Innes CJ in *Transvaal Investment Co Ltd v Springs Municipality*:

... juristically, the word 'acquire' connotes ownership; the ordinary legal meaning implies the acquisition of *dominium*. To acquire a thing is to become the owner of it. No doubt it may be used in a wider sense so as to include the acquisition of a right to obtain the *dominium*; but the narrower meaning is the accurate and more obvious one.

Fieldsend CJ continued:

It is true, too, that 'compulsory acquisition' is used in both English and Roman-Dutch law to denote the expropriation of property by an authority – whether State, local or public utility – usually for some public purpose, most commonly in relation to land. It is, of course, common cause that property in s 16 is not limited to land.

Cases relied upon by Mr Kentridge clearly establish that it is not every deprivation of a right which amounts to a compulsory acquisition of property, as for example regulation of a landlord's rights which in effect diminished his rights (*Thakur Jagannatha Baksa Singh v United Provinces* 1946 AC 327 (PC)), regulations which limited an owner's right to build above a certain height on his land (*Belfast Corporation v OD Cars Ltd* 1960 AC 490), and legislation allowing licensed pilots to provide pilotage only if they were employed by the port authority (*Government of Malaysia v Selangor Pilot Association*).

It is perhaps of some significance to note that in almost all the post-colonial constitutions granted by Britain in Africa the section reciting the fundamental freedoms protected refer to the right not to be *deprived* of property without compensation whereas the sections giving actual protection provide that no property of any description shall be *compulsorily taken possession of* and no interest in or right [over] property of any description shall be *compulsorily acquired* except on certain conditions including compensation. This is clear recognition that there is a distinction between deprivation and acquisition, and also an indication that not every deprivation of property must carry compensation with it. Indeed government could be made virtually impossible if every deprivation of property required compensation.'

In *Davies and Others v Minister of Lands, Agriculture and Water Development*, Gubbay CJ cited the aforesaid passages with approval and held that section 11 *(c)* of the Zimbabwe Constitution does not afford protection against deprivation of property by the State 'where the act of deprivation falls short of compulsory acquisition or expropriation'.

[34] The Constitution of India originally had a property clause which recognised the distinction between compulsory acquisition and requisition which was held to be a less intrusive form of deprivation of property. In *HD Vora v State of Maharashtra*, it was said by Bhagwati J:

The two concepts [compulsory acquisition and requisition] . . . are totally distinct and independent. Acquisition means the acquiring of the entire title of the expropriated owner whatever the nature and extent of that title may be. The entire bundle of rights which was vested in the original holder passes on acquisition to the acquirer leaving nothing to the former . . . . The concept of acquisition has an air of permanence and finality in that there is transference of the title of the original holder to the acquiring authority. But the concept of requisition involves merely taking of 'domain or control over property without acquiring rights of ownership' and must by its very nature be of temporary duration.

(It is unnecessary to consider whether there is a difference between the concept of *requisition* used in the Indian provision and *deprivation* used in the interim Constitution.)

[35] While the legal effect of section 21(1) may be to 'transfer' ownership of the property of the solvent spouse to the Master or trustee, in order to determine whether or not such a 'transfer' constitutes an expropriation of that property for the purposes of the property clause, regard must be had to the broad context and purpose of section 21 as a whole. Apart from the question as to whether the transfer of the property of the solvent spouse is for a 'public' purpose, to regard the vesting under section 21(1) as an expropriation, in my opinion, is to ignore the substance of the provision. The purpose and effect is clearly not to divest, save temporarily, the solvent spouse of the ownership of property that is in fact his or hers. The purpose is to ensure that the insolvent estate is not deprived of property to which it is entitled. The fact that the onus of establishing his or her ownership of the property is placed upon the solvent spouse should not in any way be confused with the purpose of the provision. In any vindicatory action the claimant has to establish ownership. The onus of proof had to be placed on either the Master or the trustee or on the solvent spouse. Having regard to which of those parties has access to the relevant facts, the onus was understandably and justifiably placed on the solvent spouse.

[36] Again, on the assumption that the effect of section 21 is to 'transfer' ownership of the property of the solvent spouse to the Master or the trustee, the section does not contemplate or intend that such transfer should be permanent or for any purpose other than to enable the Master or the trustee to establish whether any such property is in fact that of the insolvent estate. Again, there is no intention to divest the solvent spouse permanently of what is rightfully hers or his or to prejudice the solvent spouse in relation to her or his property. Hence the provisions enabling the solvent spouse to seek the assistance of the court in order to obtain the

release of that which is his or hers and to seek the protection of the court in the event of the trustee wishing to sell such property prior to its release. So, too, the provision enabling the court to order the exclusion of property of the solvent spouse from the operation of a vesting order in the event that such spouse is a trader or is likely to suffer serious prejudice by reason of an immediate vesting. The whole thrust of section 21 is merely to ensure that property which properly belonged to the insolvent ends up in the estate. The statutory mechanism employed is temporarily to lay the hand of the law upon the property of both the insolvent spouse and the solvent spouse and to create a procedure for the release by the trustee or the court of that which in fact belongs to the solvent spouse.

[37] In all the circumstances which I have described, the provisions of section 21 do not have the purpose or effect of a compulsory acquisition or expropriation of the property of the solvent spouse whether by a public authority or at all. I am of the opinion therefore that there is no basis for regarding the effect of section 21 as an expropriation of the rights in the property of the solvent spouse.

Affirmative action

Section 25(8) of the Constitution allows a departure from the provisions of the property clause, to achieve land, water, and related reforms in order to redress the results of past discrimination, providing such measures are in accordance with the limitation clause. This provision is difficult to understand in that it allows a departure from the requirements of s 25 itself, but then says that in order to pass muster the departure must comply with the more rigorous standards of the limitations clause. It seems that the framers attempted to cater to a situation of taking of property for corrective action, where the taking could not be justified under the criteria spelled out in the property clause. It is difficult to think of corrective action, to redress past discrimination, properly introduced under the guidelines spelled out in chapter 8, as not being in the public purpose, or in violation of the other requirements in the property clause. Such reforms could therefore pass constitutional muster in terms of the standards laid out in the property clause. Similarly, reforms related to land, water and many other areas concerning economic and social reforms would legitimately come under public purpose. To require that all affirmative action remedies that touch on property rights should satisfy the limitations clause of the Constitution would reflect a serious bias in favour of the status quo. This was also discussed in chapter 8.

10

The Bill of Rights and private action

Application

Section 8 of the Constitution provides:

> 8 (1) The Bill of Rights applies to all law, and binds the legislature, the executive, the judiciary and all organs of state.
> (2) A provision of the Bill of Rights binds a natural or a juristic person if, and to the extent that, it is applicable, taking into account the nature of the right and the nature of any duty imposed by the right.
> (3) When applying a provision of the Bill of Rights to a natural or juristic person in terms of subsection (2), a court —
> (a) in order to give effect to a right in the Bill, must apply, or if necessary develop, the common law to the extent that legislation does not give effect to that right; and
> (b) may develop rules of the common law to limit the right, provided that the limitation is in accordance with section 36(1).

There is considerable debate in liberal schools of jurisprudence as to whether a constitution should govern the relationships between private persons, or whether it should apply only to the state and its institutions.[1] The debate is framed in terms of whether the rights apply in only a 'vertical' application, meaning that the Bill of Rights provides protection against the state, versus the 'horizontal' application, which argues for the Bill of Rights to also govern relations and disputes between private persons.[2] Different countries adopt divergent approaches to horizontality.[3] Under some jurisdictions, the fundamental rights generally apply only to governmental conduct.[4] For example, in Canada, individuals would not

---

[1] See Allen C Hutchinson and Peter Andrew 'Private Rights, Public Wrongs: The Liberal Lie of the Charter' (1988) 38 *University of Toronto Law Journal* 278.

[2] *Du Plessis and Others v De Klerk and Another* CCT 8/95 CCT 8/95 (15 May 1996) para 8, now cited as 1996 (3) SA 850 (CC); 1996 (5) BCLR 658 (CC).

[3] *Supra* para 21–41, the Court, *per* Kentridge AJ, conducted a survey of the divergent approaches adopted in different countries Christian Starck 'Europe's Fundamental Rights in their Newest Garb' (1982) 3 *Human Rights Law Journal* 107.

[4] eg Canada. See Peter W Hogg *Constitutional Law of Canada* Scarborough: Carswell, 3rd edition, 1992, 848. With few exceptions this is also the case in the US. See John E Nowak and Roland E Rotunda *Constitutional Law* St Paul: West, 5th edition, 1995, 470.

generally have an action against another individual based on a breach of fundamental rights in the Canadian Charter.[5]

The approach in the United States would be that private conduct would not run foul of the Constitution, unless either there is state action that aids that conduct, or where the legislature passes rules to cover that private activity.[6] In this situation, the private action is looked at in terms of whether the action is related to a government function, or whether it is aided or encouraged by the state, so as to hold the private parties responsible.[7] In *Shelley v Kraemer*, the United States Supreme Court held that the court's enforcement of an agreement by property owners, not to sell or lease their properties to blacks or other racial groups constituted state action in aiding racial discrimination.[8] In other words, the lower court's involvement in validating the restrictive covenant constituted state action.[9] Lawrence Tribe notes that two questions underlie this approach. First, whether the actors who make a particular decision are government actors or private actors.[10] Secondly, can the law validly distribute authority between governmental and private actors as it purports to do.[11]

Under the second situation, the lawmaker passes a statute which brings the activities of the private party under the statute. For example, the United States Constitution empowers Congress to enforce the XIII,[12] XIV,[13] and XV[14] Amendments by appropriate legislation. When the legislature adopts appropriate legislation, for example, to enforce equal citizenship under the XIII Amendment, this legislation is binding on private citizens.[15] In *Jones*, the Supreme Court upheld the power of Congress to bar racial discrimination in the sale of property.[16] The Court held that the XIII Amendment gave Congress the power to pass laws that would outlaw the vestiges of slavery, including private conduct.[17] In the above example, private action is covered only after the lawmaker has legislated to regulate private activity.[18]

The constitutions of some countries, such as Greece and Spain, cover private action for some activities, without the need for legislative initiatives.[19] The German Constitutional Court approaches the issue of horizontality in terms of an 'indirect' application model.[20] Under this model, the Constitution does not directly apply to private disputes. However, the ordinary courts employ the values in the Constitution to 'influence' the rules of private law in terms of a balancing of individual rights, against the values contained in the Constitution.[21]

---

[5] Patrick Macklem, et al *Constitutional Law of Canada* Toronto: Emond Montgomery Publishers 1994, 209.

[6] Nowak & Rotunda 470.

[7] *Shelley v Kraemer* 334 US 1 (1948).

[8] *Supra* at 19.

[9] *Supra*; see also *Burton v Wilmington Parking Authority* 365 US 715 (1961) (holding that judicial enforcement of discrimination by a state supported facility constituted state action by both the state and the judiciary); *I Griffin v Maryland* 378 US 130 (1964) (holding that judicial enforcement of the unconstitutional acts of one who acts on behalf of the state also constitutes state action).

[10] Lawrence Tribe *American Constitutional Law* Mineola: Foundation Press, 2nd edition, 1988, 1699.

[11] Ibid. Many of the cases in this area are controversial in not laying out a coherent theory with respect to the boundary between private and public. In some instances, the finding of state action is strained. Op cit 1698–1706, 1711–15.

[12] Section 2 of Amendment XIII.

[13] Section 4 of Amendment XIV.

[14] Section 2 of Amendment XV.

[15] *Jones v Alfred Mayer Co* 392 US 409 (1968).

[16] *Alfred Mayer Co*, at 413–417.

[17] *Supra* at 443.

[18] This legislation can cover a variety of activities including eg, outlawing of discrimination, freedom of religion or speech in the work place, or privacy in the work place to name a few. See JM Kelly, et al *The Irish Constitution* Dublin: Butterworths, 3rd edition, 1994, 716. For outlawing of discrimination in the workplace pursuant to a statute, see *Runyon v McRary* 427 US 160 (1976).

[19] eg the Greek and Spanish Constitutions, in art 2, bind private individuals to the protection of some human rights. See Starck 114.

[20] *Du Plessis* para 40.

[21] *Supra*.

In *Du Plessis v De Klerk*, the justices adopted divergent approaches to the question of whether the Bill of Rights under the interim Constitution had horizontal application. In *Du Plessis*, the *Pretoria News* published a series of articles alleging that the plaintiffs were responsible for supplying illegal arms to the rebel movement UNITA in Angola. The plaintiffs sued the defendants and the *Pretoria News*, its editor, and others for defamation and for loss of business. The defendants asserted that the speech was protected in terms of s 15(1) of the interim Constitution which guaranteed the freedom of speech and expression. On the facts, the Constitutional Court held the activity took place before the coming into effect of the interim Constitution. Therefore, the Constitution did not afford the defendants the protection they claimed.[22] The Court, however, still proceeded to address the question whether the interim Constitution had horizontal application because the matter was of public importance.[23] The question before the Court was whether the interim Constitution regulated private relationships? The justices adopted divergent approaches to the question.

Five of the justices expressed a preference for the German approach in interpreting the interim Constitution, in terms of which direct horizontality was rejected.[24] In other words, the Bill of Rights did not ordinarily apply to private relationships.[25] This approach, if interpreted rigidly, could mean that private discrimination, or encroachment by an employer on an employee's freedom of speech need not be an actionable constitutional

wrong.[26] The majority of justices, consistent with the German approach, rejected this rigid approach and preferred to allow the ordinary courts to infuse the common law with the values contained in the Bill of Rights. Under the majority approach, egregious conduct such as private discrimination would not necessarily be condoned. However, this depended on the ordinary courts adopting and infusing the common law with a new ethos.[27]

The majority's rejection of horizontal application in *Du Plessis* was based largely on a textual interpretation – the lack of an express provision that required horizontal application of the Bill of Rights.[28] Similarly, Kentridge J, using a textualist approach, interpreted s 7(1) of the interim Constitution which provided '[t]his chapter shall bind all legislative and executive organs of state at all levels of government' to mean that court decisions do not equate with state action.[29] The effect was that the Bill of Rights did not apply to courts.[30] This is now superseded by the final Constitution, which explicitly provides that '[t]he Bill of Rights applies to all law, and binds the legislative, the executive, the judiciary and all organs of state'.[31] The Constitution further provides that 'the Bill of Rights binds a natural or juristic person . . .'.[32]

With regard to the common law, the Courts are required, as was the case under the interim Constitution, to apply or develop the common law, if there is no legislation to give effect to that right.[33] In terms of the approach of Kentridge AJ (concurred in by Chaskalson P, Langa, and O'Regan JJ) in *Du Plessis*, the application or

---

[22] *Supra* paras 14 and 19.

[23] *Supra* para 30.

[24] *Supra* para 60 (Kentridge AJ).

[25] *Supra* para 48.

[26] Hogg 848.

[27] *Du Plessis* para 62. See also Ackerman J's opinion para 110.

[28] *Du Plessis* paras 45–47. Kentridge AJ stated in para 45 that '[i]t would be surprising if as important a matter as direct horizontal application were to be left or implied'.

[29] *Supra* para 47.

[30] Kentridge AJ, at para 56, invoked the Canadian case of *Retail, Wholesale Department Store Union, Local 580 et al v Dolphin Delivery Ltd* (1987) 33 DLR (4th) 174 for the proposition that Court action is not state action. *Dolphin Delivery* holds that the Canadian Charter of Rights applies to the common law. However, it does not apply in litigation between private parties where the relief is based on the common law.

[31] Section 8(1) of the Constitution.

[32] Section 8(2).

[33] Section 8(3)*(a)*.

development of the common law was restricted to governmental acts or omissions.[34] Kentridge AJ preferred that the values which underlie the Bill of Rights must be taken into account by the courts in private disputes. Whilst the Bill of Rights did not have horizontal application, the values in the Bill of Rights must be taken into account in the development of the common law.[35]

Krieggler J rejected the dichotomy of horizontal versus vertical application of the Bill of Rights. For him, the Bill of Rights applies to all organs of government, including the judiciary.[36] Similarly, the Constitution made no distinction between private and public power.[37] Section 35(3) of the interim Constitution, which required that all courts interpret every law and to apply the common law in light of the 'spirit, purpose, and objects' of the Bill of Rights, constituted an obligation to respect the Bill of Rights which was imposed on all institutions and individuals.[38]

The approach of Mahomed DP was to selectively incorporate the Bill of Rights into private relations.[39] Unlike Kentridge A'js approach, it is not sufficient to say judges would be able to infuse the common law with the new ethos as contained in the Bill of Rights. Instead, any private actions inconsistent with the spirit, purpose and objects of the Bill of Rights should not be legally enforced.[40] Where the courts have not given proper consideration to the spirit, purpose, and objects of the Bill of Rights under Mahomed DP's approach (unlike Kentridge AJ), the Constitutional Court should intervene and make the appropriate determination.[41] This intrusion into private conduct was necessitated by the unique circumstances of South Africa's history.[42] Mahomed DP eloquently summarized the dangers in the Constitutional Court not intervening in private relations and stated:

[85] ... I would have remained profoundly uncomfortable ... that the Constitution was impotent to protect those who have so manifestly and brutally been victimised by the private and institutionalized desecration of the values now so eloquently articulated in the Constitution. Black persons were previously denied the right to own land in 87% of the country. An interpretation of the Constitution which continued to protect the right of private persons substantially to perpetuate such unfairness by entering into contracts or making dispositions subject to the condition that such land is not sold to or occupied by Blacks would have been for me a very distressing conclusion. These and scores of other such examples leave me no doubt that those responsible for the enactment of the Constitution never intended to permit the privatisation of Apartheid or to allow the unfair gains of Apartheid or the privileges it bestowed on the few, or the offensive attitudes it generated amongst many to be fossilized and protected by courts rendered impotent by the language of the Constitution.

Now in light of s 8(3), it is envisaged that the lawmaker will have the ability to restrict the common law, to extend the application of the Bill of Rights to private relations.[43] If the legislature does not do so, the courts, in terms of s 8(1), are required to do so in their own right. Any limitation of fundamental rights under the common law has to be justified under the limitations clause. No longer is there any doubt that the Bill of Rights also applies to private relations.[44] However, there is an important qualification in that the section goes on to further provide that the Bill of Rights binds private parties

---

[34] *Du Plessis* para 49.
[35] *Supra* para 62. In his separate concurring opinion, Sachs J largely agreed with the views of Kentridge AJ. *Supra* paras 177 and 190.
[36] *Supra* para 130.
[37] *Supra* para 136.
[38] *Supra* paras 138–139.
[39] *Supra* para 72, which was also the approach of Madala J.
[40] *Supra* paras 79 and 86.
[41] *Supra* para 87. On this issue, Madala J largely agreed with Mahomed DP. See opinion by Madala J, paras 159 and 161. See opinion by Mokgoro J, paras 166 and 171.
[42] *Per* Mahomed DP in *Du Plessis* para 85; Kriegler J, para 135.
[43] For a full discussion of the scope of s 8(3), see chapter 2.

'if, and to the extent that, it is applicable, taking into account the nature of the right and the nature of any duty imposed by the right'.[45] The qualification relates to whether a particular section of the Bill of Rights would apply to specific private relationships; namely, whether the right can be properly applied in private relationships Some rights such as detention without trial, forming of political parties, citizenship, and socioeconomic rights (such as education) are difficult, if not impossible, to apply to private relationships.[46]

Apart from s 8, other sections of the Constitution provide additional horizontal application for specific rights. For example, s 32(1)*(b)* provides for horizontal application of the right or access to information held by another person.[47] Section 9 of the Constitution requires the enactment of national legislation to prevent or prohibit unfair discrimination and to promote the achievement of equality.[48]

The Constitution, despite its provisions stating that the Bill of Rights applies to private persons, places an onerous task on the courts to determine the suitability of applying the Bill of Rights to specific private relationships. For example, could the reach of the equality clause prescribe to the Catholic Church that it cannot discriminate against women by refusing to ordain female priests? If a religious organization restricts the rights of its members to speak to the press, is this a violation of freedom of speech? These two examples pose a potential conflict between freedom of religion and

association on the one hand, and freedom against discrimination and freedom of speech on the other. Similarly, could an organization for battered women be forced to admit battered men or battered children? The answer to applying the Bill of Rights to private relations will vary from section to section, and the context within which it is being applied.[49] In *Christian Education of South Africa v Minister of Education*,[50] the Court had to balance the right of the parents to educate their children in terms of their religious beliefs – including administering corporeal punishment – against the interest of the state in eradicating corporeal punishment from the schools as a vestige of a painful past. The Court upheld the ban on corporeal punishment and held that the state had a legitimate interest in outlawing such conduct.[51]

Often, interpreting the Bill of Rights and the various statutes which provide for horizontal application involves a balancing of individual and community autonomy.[52] In deciding on the proper balance, the extreme individualistic approach finds inspiration from natural rights theory. Natural law provides a barrier beyond which the government should not penetrate. Natural law is posited as being in existence before positive law, and state law is derived from the former. State violations of this natural law are illegitimate and therefore void.[53] The crucial thread of natural-law theory is the focus on individualism and the protection of individual rights.[54] The priority of the individual is derived

---

[44] Johan de Waal, et al *The Bill of Rights Handbook* Cape Town: Juta & Co, 2nd edition, 1999, 34, 39.

[45] Section 8(2) of the Constitution.

[46] Dennis Davis, et al *Fundamental Rights in the Constitution: Commentary and Cases: A Commentary on Chapter 3 on Fundamental Rights of the 1993 Constitution and Chapter 2 of the 1996 Constitution* Cape Town: Juta & Co 1997, 46.

[47] Pursuant to the mandate in s 32, parliament adopted the Promotion of Access to Information Act 2 of 2000 to give effect to this right. Under s 50(1)*(a)* of the Act, a requestor has a right of access to any record of a private body, if that record is required for the exercise or protection of any right.

[48] Parliament has since passed the Promotion of Equality and Prevention of Unfair Discrimination Act 4 of 2000 and the Employment Equity Act 55 of 1998.

[49] See Starck 112.

[50] *Christian Education of South Africa v The Minister of Justice of the Government of the Republic of South Africa* CCT 13/98 (14 October 1998), now cited as 1998 (12) BCLR 1449 (CC); 1999 (2) SA 83 (CC).

[51] *Supra* para 49.

[52] Macklem 218.

[53] Brendan Francis Brown *The Natural Law Reader* New York: Oceana Publications 1960, 2.

[54] See generally John Locke *Two Treatises on Government*, edited by Peter Laslett. New York: Cambridge University Press 1988. Otto von Gierke *Natural Law and the Theory Of Society, 1500–1800* Cambridge: Cambridge University Press 1958, 96–8.

from a previous state of nature in which no prior group existed.[55]

In the original state of nature, man's natural rights were subject to a state of flux and invasion by others. In order to protect these rights, one enters into a society, and the formation of the state is to guarantee these natural rights.[56] The entering into a society is referred to as the social contract, which reflected a concerted effort to protect natural rights.[57] However, the social contract theorists emphasize that the people were the possessors of all political power, and had subsequently surrendered a part of it to the state.[58] The parts that it had surrendered to the state were the power to prevent violent conflicts and the power to protect natural rights. Since the social contract was formed to protect the individual's natural rights, it was deemed necessary to limit the powers of government and prevent it from transgressing beyond the boundaries of natural law. It was unthinkable to imagine that an individual, on entering into a social contract, would wish to be in a worse position by relinquishing his or her natural rights such as liberty and property.[59]

The social perspective proceeds from the basis that individuals are not isolated sovereign entities. Rather, they exist in a social matrix. Therefore, the individual's rights must be reconciled with those rights of the unit to which he or she belongs.[60] The Constitution does not embrace either of these polar approaches.[61] Instead, it seeks to achieve proportion in both approaches In the *First Certification*

decision, the Court held that in applying the Bill of Rights to private conduct, the Court would have to balance competing rights.[62] On the other hand, there are incidents of egregious personal conduct, which Mahomed DP alluded to in *Du Plessis*, such as the privatization of apartheid,[63] which the Constitution seeks to eradicate. Between these extremes there is an entire grey area, the boundaries of which will, in the words of Hogg, expand or contract based on democratic forces[64] and national ethos. The more public the conduct, the more amenable it is to government regulation.[65] The concept of public versus private rights was explained in previous chapters.[66] Generally, where the right is more closely related to personhood and liberty, the law should respect individual autonomy and self-realization.[67] For example, there are very limited reasons (if any at all) why the public should have a claim on someone's religious beliefs, particularly when the person observes these beliefs individually in the confines of his or her home. Similarly, the public has little claim on an individual's privacy in the home or individual possessions or personal information.[68] However, if in an assumed situation, that individual obtains a licence to broadcast his or her religious beliefs, and the individual and his or her organization expressly states that they will not hire female broadcasters. Where a group excludes women from a broadcast which is made to the public on religious beliefs, it is appropriate for the state and the courts to prevent such discrimination.

---

[55] Gierke 96.

[56] John Locke 'An Essay Concerning the True Original Extent and End of Civil Government' in *Social Contract, Essays by Locke, Hume and Rousseau*, edited by Ernest Baker. Oxford: Oxford University Press 1971, 73.

[57] Locke 180.

[58] Gierke 44–5.

[59] Locke 75, 82; and JJ Rousseau 'The Social Contract' in Locke, 197–8.

[60] Macklem 222.

[61] Dennis Davis, et al 'Democracy and Constitutionalization: The Role of Constitutional Interpretation' in *Rights and Constitutionalism: The New South African Legal Order*, edited by David Van Wyk, et al. Cape Town: Juta & Co 1996, 128.

[62] *Certification I* para 56.

[63] *Du Plessis* para 85.

[64] Hogg 850.

[65] M Hidayatullah *Constitutional Law of India* New Delhi: Bar Council of India Trust 1984, 271.

[66] See discussion on privacy in chapter 7. See also under discussion on compensation in chapter 9.

[67] Donald P Kommers *The Constitutional Jurisprudence of the Federal Republic of Germany* Durham: Duke University Press 1989, 260.

[68] eg s 63 of the Promotion of Access to Information Act, which protects certain private information such as medical records from public disclosure.

The individual has carried religious practices into the public realm. The regulation of private conduct is even more compelling where the egregious conduct is performed outside a private setting or under the licence of the state. In *Christian Education of South Africa*, the Court upheld the prohibition against corporeal punishment in private, religious schools. The Court held that the conduct was not taking place in the intimate and spontaneous atmosphere of the home, but in an institutional environment of the school.[69] The state could, therefore, prevent parents from authorising teachers in private schools to administer corporeal punishment.[70] However, the Court did not similarly state that parents cannot administer corporeal punishment to their children in an intimate or private setting. At times, the Court may be called upon to reconcile conflicting rights and interests protected in the Bill of Rights.[71] There may be instances where the Court might feel that this role may be better performed by parliament.[72]

However, s 8(2) marks a recognition that the complete horizontal application of the Bill of Rights to all private situations is not feasible, and would destroy the core of individual freedom.[73] In the examples provided above, such as insisting that the church leader not be prevented from making public statements on church doctrine, or asking the Catholic church to ordain female priests pursuant to the equality clause, would be unworkable and an infringement of important personal liberties.[74] There should be a personal realm in which people cannot be coerced to subscribe to national or universal values. Freedom of religion, belief, and association would largely partake of this personal character. For example, if persons say they hate blacks and will never marry a black, and will teach their children never to socially associate with blacks, there is no way to force them to marry or associate with blacks in a social context. A religious association for Jews cannot be forced to admit non-Jews. Similarly, the state and the courts have to be very circumspect in ruling on religious doctrine, worship, or forms of association.[75] However, where a group has oppressive features within their practices which harm others, the Bill of Rights may apply in a horizontal manner.[76]

---

[69] *Supra* para 49.

[70] *Supra* para 51.

[71] As was the case in *Christian Education of South Africa*.

[72] See the concerns of Ackermann J in *Du Plessis* para 112.

[73] See Starck 112.

[74] Kelly 716.

[75] In *Ryland v Edros* 1997 (2) SA 690 (C) at 703, Farlen J adopted the position that the new constitutional order permitted the Court to get involved in questions of religious doctrine. This is arguably an erroneous and dangerous position. The full implications of this view will be covered in chapter 12.

[76] eg female genital mutilation as practised in some religions can never be condoned. See Sachs J in *Christian Education of South Africa* para 26.

11

Procedural due process: the right to fair trial and fair administrative procedures

Introduction

The Constitution contains various sections – namely ss 12, 13, 32, 33, 34, and 35 – which require fair action in trial and administrative procedures. These sections borrow largely from provisions in international human rights instruments, such as arts 10 and 11 of the Universal Declaration; art 14 of the Civil Covenant; art 7 of the African Charter; art 6 of the European Convention, and arts 7 and 8 of the American Convention. These international instruments require that due process rights be guaranteed: a fair trial, notice of charges, adjudication by an independent tribunal, presumption of innocence, and the right to remain silent.

Arbitrary state action under the previous order

The importance of the right to fair-trial procedures in the Constitution is best understood against the background of arbitrary state action under the apartheid order when the rule of law lacked normative content. The legislature and executive consistently adopted measures to override fundamental fair-trial procedures. In terms of the principle of parliamentary supremacy, no court of law could pass judgment on the validity of an act of the legislature, regardless of how serious an encroachment the law may have been on fundamental fair-trial procedures. For example, a court could not invalidate the power of the executive to detain persons indefinitely, or to banish individuals to certain areas, or to treat citizens differently, if the actions were sanctioned by an Act of Parliament. Similarly, the freedom of movement of individuals deemed to be a danger to the state, could be restricted by virtue of the power given to the executive to restrict the movement of individuals, or ban them, or both. For example, the Minister of Law and Order could restrict the movement of a person whom the minister had reason to suspect was a danger to the security of the state.[1] The minister could confine that person to a particular area or house for a specified period of time and further prevent him or her from meeting with certain other persons. A further encroachment on individual freedom and freedom of movement was the power, under the Internal Security Act, conferred on the minister, as well as on any police officer, to detain a person considered a danger to the security of the state, for prolonged periods, and without furnishing any details of the person's detention.[2]

---

[1]   Section 19 of the Internal Security Act 74 of 1982.
[2]   Sections 28–29.

Government action under the apartheid order was often arbitrary and outside the framework of clear legal standards. A wide array of discretionary powers were available to the executive under the Internal Security Act. In exercising these discretionary powers, the agents responsible did not need to provide details of their actions in many instances. Moreover, many of the sections of the Internal Security Act were so ambiguously phrased that it was impossible to know whether a person had fallen foul of its provisions. For example, in terms of the detention provisions of the Internal Security Act, it was not clear when an individual's activities were considered to endanger the interests of the state. In terms of the requirements of the rule of law, there were no known rules on which an individual could structure his or her behaviour if he or she wished to conform.

Standards for fair trial under the Constitution

Introduction

In its first judgment,[3] the Constitutional Court, *per* Kentridge AJ, made the observation that the right to a fair trial 'embraces a concept of substantive fairness which is not to be equated with what might have passed muster in our criminal courts before the Constitution came into force'.[4] Since April 1994, criminal trials have had to be conducted with notions of basic fairness and justice.[5] Kentridge AJ writing for a unanimous court ruled that s 25 of the interim Constitution

(containing protections in s 35 of the final Constitution), embodies certain important rights which include 'the right to remain silent after arrest, the right not to be compelled to make a confession which can be used in evidence, the right to be presumed innocent and the right not to be a compellable witness against oneself'. In *Parbhoo*,[6] Ackermann J in a unanimous opinion, noted that the fair-trial guarantees contained in the final Constitution do not differ in any material respect from those in the interim Constitution.[7]

The process of developing appropriate standards for a fair trial is likely to undergo considerable change in providing greater protection to the accused, as the Court interprets the various provisions of the Constitution. As the Court has observed, 'fairness is an issue which has to be decided upon the facts of each case, and the trial judge is the person best placed to make that decision'.[8] Already, there have been seminal pronouncements on various aspects, such as the presumption of innocence,[9] appropriate punishment,[10] the right to bail,[11] and the right to counsel.[12] Section 35(5) provides that evidence obtained in any way that violates any right in the Bill of Rights must be excluded if it would render the trial unfair, or would be detrimental to the administration of justice. In *Key*, Kriegler J stated that at times fairness might require the exclusion of evidence obtained illegally.[13] However, there may also be times when evidence, although obtained through unconstitutional means, nevertheless should be admitted.[14] The Constitutional Court still has to interpret, on a case-by-case basis, many of the provisions of the Constitution. The

---

[3] *S v Zuma* CCT 5/94 (5 April 1995), now cited as 1995 (2) SA 642 (CC); 1995 (4) BCLR 401 (SA).

[4] *Zuma* para 16.

[5] *Supra.*

[6] *Parbhoo and Others v Getz and Another* CCT 16/97 (18 September 1997), now cited as 1997 (4) SA 1095 (CC); 1997 (10) BCLR 1337 (CC).

[7] *Supra* para 9.

[8] Kriegler J in *Key v A-G, Cape of Good Hope and Another* CCT 21/94 (15 May 1996) para 13, now cited as 1996 (4) SA 187 (CC); 1996 (6) BCLR 788 (CC).

[9] *S v Coetzee and Others* CCT 50/95 (6 March 1997) para 17, now cited as 1997 (3) SA 527 (CC); 1997 (7) BCLR 437 (CC).

[10] *S v Williams and Others* CCT 20/94 (9 June 1995) para 39, now cited as 1995 (3) SA 632 (CC); 1995 (7) BCLR 861 (CC); *S v Du Plessis* CCT 2/94 (8 June 1995) para 16, *per* Didcott J, now cited as 1995 (3) SA 292 (CC); 1995 (7) BCLR 851 (CC).

[11] *Bongani Dlamini v The State* CCT 21/98 (3 June 1999), now cited as 1999 (7) BCLR 771 (CC); 1999 (4) SA 623 (CC).

[12] *S v Vermaas.*

[13] *Key* para 13.

[14] *Supra.*

interpretations will have to be seen in the light of questionable trial practices which originate from laws under the apartheid order.[15] This chapter will only consider the salient aspects of the right to a fair trial under the Constitution against international human rights standards, and against the South African Criminal Procedure Act of 1977 (CPA).[16] An in depth enquiry on the right to fair-trial procedures is beyond the scope of this study and belongs within the ambit of criminal procedure.

Right to a remedy

The Constitution in s 38 confers a right on anyone listed in the section, whose rights have been infringed or threatened, to approach a court for appropriate relief. The seminal international human rights instruments guarantee victims a right to a remedy. Article 8 of the Universal Declaration provides '[E]veryone is entitled in full equality to a fair and public hearing by an independent and impartial tribunal, in the determination of his rights and obligations and of any criminal charges against him'. A similar provision is found in art 3 of the Covenant which provides that each state party undertakes '[to] ensure that any person whose rights or freedoms as herein recognized are violated shall have an effective remedy, notwithstanding that the violation has been committed by persons acting in an official capacity'. Similar provisions are contained in art 7(1)(a) of the African Charter of Human and People's Rights; art 25 of the American Convention on Human Rights, and art 13 of the European Convention on Human Rights. The observation has been made that 'human rights without effective implementation are shadows

without substance'.[17] In 1984, the UN General Assembly passed a resolution, the Declaration of Principle of Justice for Victims of Crime and Abuse of Power, which reiterates the right of the victim to seek individual redress and compensation.[18] The widespread reference to a right to a remedy arguably elevates the right to a remedy at least to the level of a customary international norm. The remedy should neither be illusory nor symbolic – it should be an effective remedy.[19]

In *Azanian Peoples Organization and Others v The President of the Republic of South Africa and Others*,[20] the applicants argued that the amnesty provisions of the Promotion of National Unity and Reconciliation Act[21] violated s 22 of the interim Constitution that provided 'every person shall have the right to have justiciable disputes settled by a court of law or, where appropriate, another independent or impartial forum'.[22] The protections in s 22 of the interim Constitution are now contained in s 34 of the final Constitution. Section 20(7) of the Amnesty Act precludes any criminal or civil actions against any individual who confesses to any wrongdoing related to political acts of the past. The Court ruled that s 20(7) of the Amnesty Act impacts upon fundamental rights,[23] but does not violate the Constitution because the Constitution itself, in the epilogue, authorized such a violation.[24] The Amnesty Act, by ousting the right of the victim to seek redress before a competent court, transgressed a fundamental right protected in s 22 of the interim Constitution. Although not canvassed in the decision, s 7(4) was also transgressed. Both of these provisions conferred a right on anyone to apply to a competent court for appropriate relief.

---

[15] *S v Dzukuda; S v Tilly; S v Tshilo;* CCT 23/00 (2) *S v Tshilo* (2) CCT 34/00 (27 November 2000 para 10, now cited as 2000 (II) BCLR 1252 (CC); 2000 (4) SA 1078 (CC).

[16] Act 51 of 1977.

[17] John P Humphrey, quoted in Richard B Lillich 'Civil Rights' in *Human Rights in International Law: Legal and Policy Issues*, edited by Theodor Meron. Oxford: Clarendon Press 1988, 134.

[18] Declaration of Principle of Justice For Victims of Crime And Abuse of Power, (1984) UNGAR 40/30.

[19] Article 3 of the International Covenant.

[20] *Azanian Peoples Organization (Azapo) and Others v The President of the Republic of South Africa and Others* CCT 17/96 (25 July 1996), now cited as 1996 (4) SA 671 (CC); 1996 (8) BCLR 1015 (CC).

[21] Act 30 of 1995 (Amnesty Act).

[22] *Azapo* para 8.

[23] *Supra* para 9.

[24] *Supra* paras 10, 14.

The right to approach a competent court is now contained in s 38 (a) of the Constitution. To the extent that the Amnesty Act curtails the rights of victims to seek individual redress before the courts, amounts to a violation of a fundamental norm of international human rights.

The Constitutional Court, *per* Mahomed DP, has previously recognized the importance of not placing the victim at the mercy of the bureaucratic machinery of the state in order to obtain redress.[25] In *Azapo*, the Amnesty Act took away this fundamental right of seeking redress from the courts and asked the victims to place their confidence in the bureaucracy of the state. In *Mhlungu*, Mahomed DP stated that it is no comfort to an accused to have to rely on the legislative, executive, or bureaucratic machinery of the state to afford the accused relief. The learned judge quoted the Constitution as providing equal protection for every person as a right that must be protected by the courts. The Amnesty Act does not guarantee the victim effective relief, but at the end of the day, whether any relief is provided is within the discretion of the legislature and the executive.[26] In upholding the provisions of the Amnesty Act, which deny the victim's right to a remedy, Mahomed DP forced the victim to accept the dangers alluded to in *Mhlungu*: specifically that the victim now has to rely on the bureaucratic machinery of the state to achieve redress.

The right of redress is widely recognized by international tribunals. In a decision in 1992, The Inter-American Commission of Human Rights[27] declared that the granting of amnesty and foreclosing of a victim's right to redress constitutes a grave violation of non-derogable guarantees under the American Convention. The Commission went on to say that '[T]he present Amnesty law, as applied in these cases, by foreclosing the possibility of judicial relief in cases of murder, inhumane treatment and absence of judicial guarantees, denies the fundamental nature of the most basic human rights. It eliminates perhaps the single most effective means of enforcing such rights, the trial and punishment of offenders'.[28]

In *Uruguay*, as part of the transition to a new constitutional order, the political parties expressly provided amnesty to perpetrators of all crimes. The Uruguayan government argued before the Inter-American Commission that the granting of clemency was within its sovereign prerogative and should be viewed in the political context of reconciliation.[29] The argument in the *Uruguay* case is the same conclusion that the Constitutional Court arrived at in the *Azapo* decision, namely that it is within the power of the legislature to override international law, and that widespread amnesty has to be seen in the context of reconciliation. The Inter-American Commission ruled that Uruguay had violated its international law obligations with respect to the right to a fair trial. The Commission ruled that the effect of the amnesty 'was to deny the victim, or his rightful claimant, the opportunity to participate in the criminal proceedings, which is the appropriate means to investigate the commission of the crimes denounced, determine criminal liability and impose punishment on those responsible, their accomplices and accessories after the fact'.[30]

Right of access to an impartial court

The Constitution marks a fundamental departure from the previous order in not only providing judicial review but in also guaranteeing everyone access to the courts Section 34 provides:

> Everyone has the right to have any dispute that can be resolved by the application of law decided in a fair public hearing before a court or, where appropriate, another independent and impartial tribunal or forum.

---

[25] *Supra* paras 10, 14 at note 6.
[26] See s 28(1)–28(3) of the Amnesty Act.
[27] Report 26/92 Case 10.287 *El Salvador*.
[28] *El Salvador* case, 10.287.
[29] Report 29/92 Cases 10.029, 10.036, 10.145, 10,305, 10.372, 10.373, 10.374 and 10.375 *Uruguay* 2 October 1992.
[30] See generally the *Uruguay* case.

The right of access to an 'independent' and 'impartial' court is contained in art 10 of the Universal Declaration;[31] art 14(1) of the International Covenant;[32] art 6(1) of the European Convention,[\\\$h] and art 8(1) of the American Convention.[34] The right to approach a court is further strengthened by s 38 of the Constitution, which guarantees the right to approach a competent court for appropriate relief whenever a right in the Bill of Rights has been infringed.

Where there is a dispute over property, the right to have the dispute settled before a court or another independent forum precludes one party from resorting to self-help.[35] In *Lesapo*, the Constitutional Court invalidated s 38(2) of the North West Agricultural Bank Act,[36] which permitted the North West Agricultural Bank to seize a defaulting debtor's property, without court authorization, and to sell the property in a public auction to recover the debts owed to the bank. The Court held that the section was unconstitutional and constituted a denial of judicial process insofar as it permitted the bank to resort to self-help without a court adjudicating over the process.[37] The right of access to a court also requires that there should be no unnecessary hurdles preventing the individual's access to a court.[38] In *Mohlomi*, the applicants impugned the constitutionality of s 113(1) of the Defence Act.[39] This section precluded any civil action against the state or any person with respect to actions performed in pursuance of the Act, if the action was instituted six months after the date of the cause of action. The defendants argued that the section violated the Constitution, which gave each person the right to have disputes settled by a court. The Court, *per* Didcott J, observed that time limits on bringing an action are common in all legal systems. They are designed to prevent inordinate delays in litigation which may damage the interests of justice.[40] However, the six-month time period here was unreasonable, given the reality that many individuals in South Africa face poverty and illiteracy, both of which make it very difficult for defendants to exercise their rights within the six-month period.[41] Hence there was a breach of the right of access to a court.[42]

The ordinary meaning of 'independent', with reference to access to an independent tribunal or forum, is independent of other organs of government in terms of the doctrine of separation of powers.[43] Such impartiality and independence cannot be achieved through ad hoc or special tribunals. It is required that the tribunal be 'competent' which is understood to mean that the jurisdiction of the court must have been previously established by law.[44] The tribunal must conduct itself in a way which accords full due process rights to individuals.[45] In *Azapo*, the applicants argued that victims of human rights abuses had a right of access to a court, and that the ouster provisions under the Amnesty Act should

---

[31] (1948) III UNGAR 217.

[32] UNGA. International Covenant on Civil and Political Rights 999 UNTS 171, (1967) 6 ILM 368, and entered into force on 23 March 1976.

[33] European Convention For the Protection of Human Rights And Fundamental Freedoms (1950) 213 UNTS 221 ETS, and entered into force on 3 September 1953.

[34] OAS Official Records OEA/Ser K/XVI/1.1, Doc 65 Rev 1, 7 January 1979, entered into force on 18 July 1978.

[35] *Chief Direko Lesapo v North West Agricultural Bank and Another* CCT 23/99 (16 November 1999), now cited as 2000 (1) SA 409 (CC); 1999 (12) BCLR 1420 (CC). See also *Sheard v Land and Agricultural Bank of South Africa and Another; First National Bank of South Africa Ltd v Land and Agricultural Bank of South Africa and others* CCT 07/00 and CCT 15/00 (9 June 2000) para 5, now cited as 2000 (3) SA 626 (CC); 2000 (8) BCLR 876 (CC). See also *Metrocash Trading Limited v The Commissioner for the South African Revenue Services* CCT 3/00 para 46.

[36] Act 14 of 1981.

[37] *Chief Direko Lesapo* para 14.

[38] *Mohlomi v Minister of Defence* CCT 41/95 (26 September 1996), now cited as 1997 (1) SA 124 (CC); 1996 (12) BCLR 1559 (CC).

[39] Act 44 of 1957.

[40] *Mohlomi* para 11.

[41] *Supra.*

[42] *Supra* para 14.

[43] Lillich 141.

[44] Ibid.

be found unconstitutional. Under the Amnesty Act, a person who testified before the Truth and Reconciliation Commission and was granted amnesty by the Amnesty Committee in respect of any act, omission or offence, enjoyed full immunity from all criminal and civil actions.[46] In his concurring opinion in *Azapo*, Didcott J stated that the Committee on Amnesty and the Committee on Reparation and Rehabilitation, both appointed in terms of the Promotion of National Unity and Reconciliation Act, were independent and impartial.[47] This finding is not consistent with international human rights interpretations to the extent that both the Committee on Amnesty, and the Committee on Reparation and Rehabilitation were temporary and ad hoc bodies whose members were appointed by the executive branch of government.[48] On the other hand, if a statute directs a litigant to a particular court in the hierarchical structure, the requirement of access to a competent court is satisfied.[49]

Contrary to its approach in *Azapo*, the Constitutional Court has recognized the importance of an independent judiciary in the context of a criminal trial. In *Bernstein and Others v Bester NO and Others*, the Constitutional Court, *per* Ackermann J, emphasized the importance of the right to access before an impartial and independent court under the interim Constitution and stated:

[105] . . . When section 22 is read with section 96(2), which provides that '[t]he judiciary shall be independent, impartial and subject only to this Constitution and the

law', the purpose of section 22 seems to be clear. It is to emphasise and protect generally, but also specifically for the protection of the individual, the separation of powers, particularly the separation of the judiciary from the other arms of the State. Section 22 achieves this by ensuring that the courts and other *fora* which settle justiciable disputes are independent and impartial. It is a provision fundamental to the upholding of the rule of law, the constitutional state, the '*regstaatidee*', for it prevents legislatures, at whatever level, from turning themselves by acts of legerdemain into 'courts'. One recent notorious example of this was the High Court of Parliament Act. By constitutionalising the requirements of independence and impartiality the section places the *nature* of the courts or other adjudicating fora beyond debate and avoids the dangers alluded to by Van den Heever JA in the *Harris* case.

Similarly, Ackermann J held in *De Lange v Smuts NO and Others*[50] that fair-trial procedures required the hearing to be presided over by a judicial officer in a court structure established by the Constitution. In *De Lange* the majority of the Court invalidated s 66(3) of the Insolvency Act,[51] which permitted officers in the public service to commit a recalcitrant witness to prison.[52] Ackermann J held:

[59] I will assume all that in favour of the respondents. Such officers do not, however, meet one fundamental and indispensable criterion. However admirable they may be in all the respects mentioned, and I do not for a moment question any of these high qualities, they are officers in

---

45 Inter-American Court of Human Rights Advisory Opinion OC-9/87 of 6 October 1987, para 24.

46 See s 21(7) of the Amnesty Act.

47 The *Azapo* decision para 53.

48 See the decision of the German Constitutional Court of 9 November 1955 [1956] 4 BVerfGE 331 quoted in Mauro Cappelletti and William Cohen *Comparative Constitutional Law: Cases and Materials* Indianapolis: Bobbs-Merrill 1979, 335–40. The German Constitutional Court affirmed the position that independence of judges under the German Basic Law required that the personnel adjudicating over the matter be part of an independent established post, as opposed to a temporary body, which is an outgrowth of the executive. Op cit 337–8.

49 See *Dormehl v Minister of Justice and Others* CCT 10/00 (14 April 2000) para 4, where the Court held s 34 does not confer a right on litigants to approach any court in the court hierarchy for relief. All that the section requires is the right to approach a court of competent jurisdiction.

50 CCT 26/97 (28 May 1998), now cited as 1998 (3) SA 785 (CC); 1998 (7) BCLR 779 (CC) (concurred by Chaskalson P, Langa DP, and Madala J, with separate concurring opinions by Mokgoro, O'Regan and Sachs JJ).

51 Act 24 of 1936.

52 *De Lange* para 61.

the public service – in the executive branch of the state – and therefore do not enjoy the judicial independence which is foundational to and indispensable for the discharge of the judicial function in a constitutional democracy based on the rule of law. This independence, of which structural independence is an indispensable part, is expressly proclaimed, protected and promoted by subsections (2), (3) and (4) of section 165 of the Constitution in the following manner:

(2) The courts are independent and subject only to the Constitution and the law, which they must apply impartially and without fear, favour or prejudice.

(3) No person or organ of state may interfere with the functioning of the courts

(4) Organs of state, through legislative and other measures, must assist and protect the courts to ensure the independence, impartiality, dignity, accessibility and effectiveness of the courts.

[63] The principle articulated in *Brimson* and implicit in the jurisprudence of other democracies is clear: only judicial officers may, consistent with the proper separation of government powers, commit recalcitrant witnesses to prison. Judicial officers enjoy complete independence from the prosecutorial arm of the State, and are therefore well-placed to curb possible abuse of prosecutorial power. However, were executive branch officials to be invested with the power to compel, upon pain of imprisonment, cooperation with their investigative demands, this necessary check on the prosecutorial power would vanish, because it would allow the executive to pass judgment on the lawfulness of its own prosecutorial decisions.

[74] ... Accordingly, when considering whether it is 'appropriate' under section 34 for 'another independent and impartial tribunal' to commit a person to prison under section 66(3) it strengthens the conclusion that this would only be appropriate where such tribunal were constituted, or presided over, by a judicial officer of the court structure established by the 1996 Constitution and in which section 165(1) has vested the judicial authority of the republic.

[75] In sum, officers in the public service, who answer to higher officials in the executive branch, do not enjoy the independence of the judiciary and therefore cannot, without danger to liberty, commit to prison witnesses who refuse to cooperate in proceedings, such as the present. I accordingly conclude that the committal provision of section 66(3) infringes section 12(1)(*b*) of the Constitution, at least to the extent that a person who is not a magistrate is authorised by the subsection, read with section 39(2) of the Insolvency Act, to issue a warrant committing to prison an examinee at a creditors' meeting held under section 65 of the Insolvency Act.

Essential aspects of impartiality are that the judge has an open mind and does not have an interest or previous involvement in the case.[53] Having an open mind means that the judge must be open to persuasion by counsel as opposed to adherence to the views of one party or the personal views and preconceptions of the judge.[54] In *The President of the Republic of South Africa and Others v South African Rugby Football Union and Others*,[55] the Constitutional Court observed that where there is an 'apprehension of bias' a judge should recuse him or herself from the proceedings.[56] The test for apprehended bias is an objective one and the onus for establishing bias rests with the applicant.[57] The

---

[53] *The President of the Republic of South Africa and Others v South African Rugby Football Union and others* CCT 16/99 (4 June 1999) para 12, now cited as 1999 (7) BCLR 725 (CC); 1999 (4) SA 147 (CC) (*SARFU 1*). *South African Commercial Catering and Allied Workers Union and Others v Irvin and Johnson Limited Seafoods Processing Division* CCT 2/00 (9 June 2000) paras 12 and 14, now cited as 2000 (3) SA 705 (CC); 2000 (8) BCLR 886 (CC). *Karttunen v Finland*, UN Human Rights Committee Communication 387/1989 views adopted 23 October 1992 UN Doc CCPR/C/46/D/387/1989 (1992) para 7.2

[54] *South African Commercial Catering* para 14.

[55] *SARFU I*.

[56] *Supra* para 38.

[57] *Supra* paras 45 and 48. *South African Commercial Catering* para 13.

Court will scrutinize whether the apprehension of bias is reasonable.[58] Bias cannot be based upon the judge's political associations prior to the judge's appointment to the bench unless the subject matter before the court arose as a result of the past associations.[59] The Court observed that '[A] judge who sits in a case in which she or he is disqualified from sitting because, seen objectively, there exists a reasonable apprehension that such judge might be biased, acts in a manner that is inconsistent with section 34 of the Constitution, and in breach of the requirement of section 165(2) and the prescribed oath of office'.[60] If a judge incorrectly refuses to recuse him or herself, the other members of the court should refuse to sit with that judge –

otherwise the proceedings would be irregular.[61] Where a judge is related to one of the parties, the impartiality of the Court is open to question.[62] If a later trial involves the same central issues or witnesses, and where a judge had in the previous case expressed strong views on the issues or credibility of the witnesses, the judge should recuse him or herself from the later proceedings.[63] Also if a judge was previously involved in the dispute, impartiality requires that the judge be recused from the subsequent judicial proceedings. Otherwise, public trust and confidence can be eroded. For example, where a judge was previously a prosecutor in a case and there was an objective doubt about the judge's impartiality, which required recusal.[64]

Karttunen v Finland
UN Human Rights Committee Communication 387/1989 views adopted 23 October 1992 UN Doc CCPR/C/46/D/387/1989 (1992).

Authors' note: In a civil trial involving the applicant, one of the judges was an uncle of the complainant, and the brother of another judge was a member of the company involved in litigation against the applicant. The applicant argued that he was therefore denied a right to a fair trial in violation of art 14(1) of the Civil Covenant.

7.1 The Committee is called upon to determine whether the disqualification of lay judge VS and his alleged disruption of the testimony of the author's wife influenced the evaluation of evidence by, and the verdict of, the Rääkyla District Court, in a way contrary to article 14, and whether the author was denied a fair trial on account of the Court of Appeal's refusal to grant the author's request for an oral hearing. As the two

questions are closely related, the Committee will address them jointly. The Committee expresses its appreciation for the State party's frank cooperation in the consideration of the author's case.

7.2 The impartiality of the court and the publicity of proceedings are important aspects of the right to a fair trial within the meaning of article 14, paragraph 1. 'Impartiality' of the court implies that judges must not harbour preconceptions about the matter put before them, and that they must not act in ways that promote the interests of one of the parties. Where the grounds for disqualification of a judge are laid down by law, it is incumbent upon the court to consider *ex officio* these grounds and to replace members of the court falling under the disqualification criteria. A trial flawed by the participation of a judge who, under domestic statues, should have been disqualified cannot normally be considered to be fair or impartial within the meaning of article 14.

---

58 *South African Commercial Catering* para 17.
59 *SARFU I* para 76.
60 *Supra* para 30.
61 *Supra* para 32.
62 *Karttunen* para 7.2.
63 *South African Commercial Catering* para 33.
64 *Piersack v Belgium* 53 ECHR (ser A) 1982.

7.3 It is possible for appellate instances to correct the irregularities of proceedings before lower court instances In the present case, the Court of Appeal considered, on the basis of written evidence, that the District Court's verdict had not been influenced by the presence of lay judge VS, while admitting that VS manifestly should have been disqualified. The Committee considers that the author was entitled to oral proceedings before the Court of Appeal. As the State party itself concedes, only this procedure would have enabled the Court to proceed with the reevaluation of all the evidence submitted by the parties, and to determine whether the procedural flaw had indeed affected the verdict of the district Court. In the light of the above, the Committee concludes that there has been a violation of article 14, paragraph 1.

8 The Human Rights Committee, acting under article 5, paragraph 4, of the Optional Protocol to the International Covenant on Civil and Political Rights, is of the view that the facts before it reveal a violation of article 14, paragraph 1, of the Covenant.

Freedom and security

The Constitution, in s 12(1), provides that every person shall have the right to freedom and security of the person, which shall include the right not to be detained without trial.[65] Freedom, liberty, and security of the person are protected in different parts of the international and regional human rights instruments, namely, art 3 of the Universal Declaration; art 9(1) of the Civil Covenant; art 6 of the African Charter; art 5(1) of the European Convention, and art 7(1) of the American Convention. The various provisions specify that an individual cannot be denied freedom and security without proper procedural safeguards.

Whenever a person is subjected to imprisonment, there should be procedural safeguards, such as a prior hearing with proper notice. In *Coetzee v the Government and Others*,[66] and the companion case *Matiso v The Commanding Officer Port Elizabeth and Others*[67] (referred together as *Coetzee*), the Court was faced with the constitutional validity of various sections of the Magistrates' Court Act[68] relating to imprisonment of judgment debtors. The Act, among other things, provided for a magistrate to issue an order which committed the judgment debtor to prison for contempt of court for failure to pay the debt. Under the Act, a debtor could be sent to prison without receiving a notice of a hearing or of a judgment against them. The effect was to undermine the freedom and security of the debtor. The Court held that if a person is going to be denied freedom and security, it is necessary that there be some notice of a judgment or hearing.[69] In his concurring opinion, Didcott J also emphasized that a person cannot be denied freedom and security without hearing.[70] Similarly, Langa J in a separate concurring opinion stressed that imprisonment is a drastic curtailment of 'freedom and security'.[71] When it is resorted to, there must be procedural safeguards Referring to the inadequacies of the previous order, Langa J stated:

[34] ... Despite the existence of common-law provisions protecting personal freedom and security, many people were imprisoned and detained without the application of principles of procedural fairness and in circumstances where they had committed no offence which would warrant the deprivation of liberty. Thousands of South Africans each year were, for instance, imprisoned for

---

[65] Section 12(1)*(b)* of the Constitution.
[66] CCT 19/94 (22 September 1995), now cited as 1995 (4) SA 631 (CC); 1995 (10) BCLR 1382 (CC).
[67] Cited as one case.
[68] Act 32 of 1944, as amended.
[69] *Coetzee* para 14.
[70] *Supra* para 23.
[71] *Supra* para 33.

breaches of influx control legislation after summary trials which carried few, if any, of the characteristics of a fair trial. In addition, imprisonment was also used to curtail other fundamental freedoms unjustly, including those of association, expression and belief, and, as an instrument of coercion, in order to extract information to be used for prosecutions and various other official purposes. It has therefore been a powerful weapon in the hands of officialdom. In terms of the challenged provisions, this weapon is placed at the disposal of creditors for use against defaulting debtors.

[35] The difference between the past and the present is that individual freedom and security no longer fall to be protected solely through the vehicle of common-law maxims and presumptions which may be altered or repealed by statute, but are now protected by entrenched constitutional provisions which neither the legislature nor the executive may abridge. It would accordingly be improper for us to hold constitutional a system which, as Sachs J has noted, confers on creditors the power to consign the person of an impecunious debtor to prison at will and without the interposition at the crucial time of a judicial officer.

When there is a hearing that could result in imprisonment, the person must be made aware of the possible defences against imprisonment.[72] There must be substantive and procedural safeguards, such as the full explanation of rights and duties by the presiding officer, possible legal assistance, and the ability to approach the court for relief.[73]

What is the precise content of 'freedom and security'? Does it apply only to the absence of physical restraint, or does it encompass all the freedoms and rights necessary in a free democratic order? In *Ferreira*, Ackermann J and Sachs J

conceived of freedom as synonymous with individual liberty.[74] Under this interpretation, the right to freedom meant the right of individuals not to have the state place obstacles before them.[75] Any obstacles placed by the state, in order to pass constitutional muster, have to surmount the limitations clause in the Constitution.[76] The majority of the justices, *per* Chaskalson P, did not accept this definition of freedom and security, choosing instead to limit the scope of freedom and security to physical integrity. Chaskalson P, writing for a six-judge majority, stated that the right to freedom and security, although it could have a broader meaning under the Constitution, is designed 'to ensure that the physical integrity of every person is protected'. This is how a guarantee of 'freedom, liberty and security of the person' would ordinarily be understood. It is also the primary sense in which the phrase, 'freedom and security of the person is used in public international law'.[77] Chaskalson P went on to state that there were many other provisions in the interim Constitution which protect individual liberty without having to infer the concept into the 'freedom and security clause'.[78]

The state can make reasonable demands requiring individuals to appear before an enquiry or tribunal to answer questions and to help resolve crimes and civil disputes. A subpoena to appear before a court does not compromise physical integrity and freedom. In *Bernstein*,[79] the Court, *per* Ackermann J, held that the use of subpoenas to require witnesses to appear before courts, to produce documents, or to give evidence 'is essential to the functioning of the court system'.[80] Witnesses who ignore subpoenas, fail to produce documents, or refuse to answer questions may be subject to

---

[72] *Supra* para 14.

[73] *Supra*.

[74] *Ferreira v Levin NO and Others; Vryenhoek and Others v Powell NO and Others* CCT 5/95 (6 December 1995) paras 52, 245, now cited as 1996 (1) SA 984 (CC); 1996 (1) BCLR 1 (CC).

[75] *Supra* para 54.

[76] *Supra* para 52.

[77] *Supra, per* Mokgoro J, paras 170, 210.

[78] *Supra* para 173.

[79] *Bernstein and Others v Bester and Others NNO* CCT 23/95 (27 March 1996) now cited as 1996 (2) SA 751 (CC); 1996 (4) BCLR 449 (CC).

[80] *Supra* para 51.

penalties including imprisonment. Imprisonment compromises physical integrity. However, sanctions in these situations are legitimate and not subject to the limitations clause of the Constitution.[81]

In *De Lange v Smuts*, the Court (in a plurality decision *per* Ackermann J concurred by Chaskalson P, Langa DP and Madala J, with a separate concurring opinion by Sachs J), held that where a person is committed to prison for failure to answer questions pursuant to any insolvency hearing, the committal can only be ordered by a judicial officer, and not by a public servant.[82] The Court invalidated the provisions of the Act which permitted persons, other than a magistrate, to issue a warrant committing a witness, who refuses to testify, to prison.[83]

Presumption of innocence

Every accused person is presumed innocent and has the right to remain silent and not to testify during a trial.[84] The presumption of innocence is required under art 11(1) of the Universal Declaration; art 14(2) of the Civil Covenant; art 7(1)*(b)* of the African Charter; art 6(2) of the European Convention, and art 8(2) of the American Convention.

Confessions obtained without legal counsel, in the past, were governed only by ss 217 and 218 of the Criminal Procedure Act. The courts would allow the confession into evidence, if it was freely and voluntarily made and without undue influence.[85] Under s 217(1) of the Criminal Procedure Act, the test for coercion centres on whether the confession was freely and voluntarily made, which in turn is dependent upon whether it was induced by undue influence. If so, it would be excluded.

However, the onus was on the accused who had the burden of proving that the confession was not made freely and voluntarily.

The presumption of innocence was first addressed by the Constitutional Court in *Zuma* – the first judgment delivered by the Court.[86] The accused were indicted on two counts of murder and one count of robbery. Two of the accused had made confessions before a magistrate, which the prosecution tendered as evidence. The defence counsel asked the court to rule on the constitutionality of s 217(1)*(b)*(ii) of the Criminal Procedure Act. The section created a presumption that when an accused gave a confession to a magistrate and the confession was reduced to writing, the confession would be presumed to have been freely and voluntarily made by that person. The section placed a burden on the accused to prove that the confession was not made freely or voluntarily. If the accused was not able to disprove this on a balance of probabilities, the presumption would prevail. An accused could, in effect, be convicted not because the elements of the crime were established, but because of the presumption. The unanimous Court, *per* Kentridge AJ, ruled that the section was unconstitutional as it violated the presumption of innocence provided for under the common law and now incorporated into the Constitution.[87] The right to be presumed innocent is central to the fundamental liberty and human dignity of an accused.[88] Where the state substitutes the presumption of innocence with the presumption of guilt, the state needs to provide a cogent justification as to why the presumption should be sustained.[89] There may be some instances where reasonable presumptions should be allowed to assist in effective prosecutions.[90]

---

[81] *Supra* para 53.

[82] *De Lange* paras 57, 61.

[83] *Supra* para 109.

[84] Section 35(3)*(h)* of the Constitution. The right to remain silent is further affirmed in s 35(1)*(a)* and s 35(3)*(j)*.

[85] *S v Radebe and Another* 1968 (4) SA 410 (A).

[86] *Zuma.*

[87] *Supra* para 28.

[88] *S v Manamela* CCT 25/99 (14 April 2000) para 40.

[89] *Supra.*

[90] *Zuma* para 41. In *Zuma*, the Court held that presumptions are of different types, and in some cases legal presumptions may reverse the onus of proof as provided, eg in s 237 of the CPA (evidence on the charge of bigamy). *Manamela* para 29.

S v Zuma and Others
CCT 5/94 (5 April 1995), now
cited as 1995 (4) BCLR 401 (SA);
1995 (2) SA 642 (CC)
(notes omitted)
KENTRIDGE AJ (unanimous opinion)

4   ... It is sub-paragraph (ii) of this proviso that is under attack in the present case. It was introduced into the criminal procedure code in 1977. In the circumstances set out in the subparagraph it places on the accused the burden of proving that the confession recorded by the magistrate was *not* free and voluntary. The words 'unless the contrary is proved' place an onus on the accused which must be discharged on a balance of probabilities. He does not discharge the onus merely by raising a doubt. If, at the end of the *voir dire* (or trial-within-a-trial) the probabilities are evenly balanced the presumption prevails.

6   In the case before us the prosecution tendered confessions which had been made by two of the accused before a magistrate and reduced to writing, and invoked the presumption in proviso (b).

7   The accused were indicted on two counts of murder and one of robbery. At their trial before Hugo J and assessors they pleaded not guilty. Two of the accused had made statements before a magistrate, which counsel for the State tendered as admissible confessions. Admissibility was contested by counsel for the accused and a trial-within-a-trial ensued. At the outset defence counsel raised the issue of the constitutionality of section 217(1)(b)(ii) of the Criminal Procedure Act, and counsel for both the defence and the prosecution consented (in terms of section 101(6) of the Constitution) to the trial Judges deciding that issue. The trial-within-a-trial nonetheless proceeded. The accused testified that they had made their statements by reason of assaults on them by the police and the threat of further assaults. The policemen concerned denied this, but two women

called as witnesses by the defence said that they had seen the police assaulting the accused. At the end of the evidence the court concluded unanimously that while they were not satisfied beyond a reasonable doubt that the statements had been freely and voluntarily made, the accused had failed to discharge the onus upon them under proviso (b) on a balance of probabilities In his judgment, given on 10 August 1994, and reported as *S v Zuma* 1995 (1) BCLR 49 (N), Hugo J said –

Had we been convinced that section 217(1)(b) of the Criminal Procedure Act was still valid and constitutional we would therefore have had little hesitation in accepting that the accused had not discharged the *onus* placed upon them by that section. The constitutionality therefore of section 217(1)(b) of the Criminal Procedure Act is therefore crucial to the decision of this case.

33   The conclusion which I reach, as a result of this survey, is that the common law rule in regard to the burden of proving that a confession was voluntary has been not a fortuitous but an integral and essential part of the right to remain silent after arrest, the right not to be compelled to make a confession, and the right not to be a compellable witness against oneself. These rights, in turn, are the necessary reinforcement of Viscount Sankey's 'golden thread' – that it is for the prosecution to prove the guilt of the accused beyond reasonable doubt (*Woolmington's* case). Reverse the burden of proof and all these rights are seriously compromised and undermined. I therefore consider that the common-law rule on the burden of proof is inherent in the rights specifically mentioned in section 25(2) and (3)(c) and (d), and forms part of the right to a fair trial. In so interpreting these provisions of the Constitution I have taken account of the historical background, and comparable foreign case law. I believe too that this interpretation promotes the values which underlie an open and demo-

cratic society and is entirely consistent with the language of section 25. It follows that section 217(1)*(b)*(ii) violates these provisions of the Constitution.

41 It is important, I believe, to emphasise what this judgment does *not* decide. It does not decide that all statutory provisions which create presumptions in criminal cases are invalid. This Court recognises the pressing social need for the effective prosecution of crime, and that in some cases the prosecution may require reasonable presumptions to assist it in this task. Presumptions are of different types. Some are no more than evidential presumptions, which give certain prosecution evidence the status of *prima facie* proof, requiring the accused to do no more than produce credible evidence which casts doubt on the *prima facie* proof. See for example the presumptions in section 212 of the Criminal Procedure Act. This judgment does not relate to such presumptions. Nor does it seek to invalidate every legal presumption reversing the onus of proof. Some may be justifiable as being rational in

themselves, requiring an accused person to prove only facts to which he or she has easy access, and which it would be unreasonable to expect the prosecution to disprove. The provisions in section 237 of the Act (evidence on charge of bigamy) may be of this type. Or there may be presumptions which are necessary if certain offences are to be effectively prosecuted, and the State is able to show that for good reason it cannot be expected to produce the evidence itself. The presumption that a person who habitually consorts with prostitutes is living off the proceeds of prostitution was upheld on that basis in *R v Downey* by the Supreme Court of Canada. A similar presumption in a United Kingdom statute was upheld by the European Court of Human Rights in *X v United Kingdom* (application number 5124/71, *Collection of Decisions,* ECHR 135). This is not such a case. Nor does this judgment deal with statutory provisions which are in form presumptions but which in effect create new offences See *Attorney-General v Odendaal* 1982 Botswana LR 194 at 226–7.

In a litany of cases, the Court has affirmed its holding in *Zuma* that a reverse onus presumption might be justified in 'regulatory offences' but not for pure criminal offences.[91] For example, reverse onus presumptions would likely be sustained for certain activities in the public domain such as the handling of hazardous products or the supervision of dangerous activities.[92] The same would apply for authenticating public documents for licences or for traffic violations.[93] On the other hand, for 'pure criminal offences', the Court will sustain a

reverse onus presumption only in exceptional situations. In *Bhulwana* and the companion case of *Gwadiso*, the Court was faced with the constitutionality of reverse onus presumptions of the Drugs and Drug Trafficking Act,[94] under which any individual found in possession of dagga (cannabis) in excess of 115 grams would be presumed to be dealing in dagga. The effect of the presumption may result in the conviction of an accused despite the existence of a reasonable doubt as to the guilt of the accused.[95] The Court, *per*

---

[91] *S v Bhulwana* and *S v Gwadiso* CCT 12/95 and 11/95 (29 November 1995), now cited as 1996 (1) SA 388 (CC); 1995 (12) BCLR 1579 (CC); *S v Mbatha* CCT 19/95 (9 February 1996), now cited as 1996 (2) SA 464 (CC); 1996 (3) BCLR 293 (CC); *Scargell v Attorney General* CCT 42/95 (12 September 1996), now cited as 1997 (2) SA 368 (CC); 1996 (11) BCLR 1446 (CC). *S v Coetzee and Others* CCT 50/95 (6 March 1997), now cited as 1997 (3) SA 527 (CC); 1997 (4) BCLR 437 (CC); *S v Ntsele* CCT 25/97 (14 October 1997), now cited as 1997 (11) BCLR 1543 (CC); *Mello and Another v The State* CCT 5/98 (28 May 1998), now cited as 1998 (3) SA 712 (CC); 1998 (7) BCLR 908 (CC).

[92] *Manamela* para 29.

[93] *Supra.*

[94] Act 140 of 1992.

[95] *Bhulwana* para 8.

O' Regan J, held that the imposition of the burden on the accused breached the presumption of innocence.[96] It is the duty of the prosecution to prove all the elements of the criminal charge.[97]

The presumption of innocence does not apply in civil proceedings. In *Prinsloo*,[98] the Court was faced with a challenge to s 84 of the Forest Act,[99] which created a presumption of negligence when a fire occurred outside a designated area. The plaintiff was sued by his neighbour (the first respondent) for a fire which caused damage to the neighbour's farmland. The neighbour relied on the presumption created under s 84 of the Forest Act. The plaintiff argued that the presumption in the Act violated his right to be presumed innocent. A unanimous court rejected the plaintiff's argument and ruled that the presumption of innocence only applied in the criminal context.[100]

Right to remain silent

The interim Constitution did not mention a right against self-incrimination. The Constitutional Court, however, inferred the right against self-incrimination to flow from the cluster of fair-trial rights guaranteed in various parts of the interim Constitution.[101] The final Constitution expressly guarantees the right in various provisions. For example, s 35(1)(c) proclaims that an arrested person has the right 'not to be compelled to make any confession or admission that could be used in evidence against that person'. Section 35(3)(h) provides that every accused has the right to remain silent and not to testify during the proceedings. Section 35(1)(b)(i) imposes a duty on the state to inform the accused of the right to remain silent. The right to remain silent is contained in the art 14(4) of the Civil Covenant, and art 8(2)(g) of the American Convention. Although not explicitly mentioned in the European Convention, the European Court of Human Rights has affirmed the importance of the right not to incriminate oneself as part of the fair-trial procedures.[102]

The right to remain silent as a constitutional right was first recognized in *Ferreira v Levin*.[103] In *Ferreira*, the Court considered the constitutionality of s 417(2A)(b) of the Companies Act.[104] The section required persons to provide evidence in winding-up proceedings. Any evidence gathered in such proceedings could be used against the examinee. The controversial part of the section was the requirement that persons were compelled to answer questions that were put to them despite the fact that the question might incriminate them. If the examinee refused to answer a question, the examinee faced conviction and sentence of a fine or imprisonment or both. If they answered the question, they also ran the risk of prosecution and conviction.[105] The majority of the court found that the section violated the right against self-incrimination.[106] While the right to self-incrimination was not explicitly mentioned in the interim Constitution, Chaskalson P stated that the right against self-incrimination is inextricably linked to the right of an accused to have a fair trial.[107] If a person has been indemnified against prosecution, that person would not be able to claim the right against self-incrimination. The section as it stood did not provide that kind of indemnity and was, therefore, unconstitutional.[108] However, any

---

[96] *Supra* para 15.

[97] *Supra.*

[98] *Prinsloo v Van der Linde and Another* CCT 4/96 (18 April 1997), now cited as 1997 (3) SA 1012 (CC); 1997 (6) BCLR 759 (CC).

[99] Act 122 of 1984.

[100] *Prinsloo* para 10.

[101] See Langa J, (unanimous opinion) in *S v Mbatha, S v Prinsloo* 19/95 (9 February 1996) para 11, now cited as 1996 (2) SA 464 (CC); 1996 (3) BCLR 293 (CC).

[102] *Funke v France* European Court of Human Rights 256-A (1993) ECHR (ser A), at para 13.

[103] *Ferreira v Levin NO and Others; Vryenhoek and Others v Powell NO and Others* CCT 5/95 (6 December 1995), now cited as 1996 (1) SA 984 (CC); 1996 (1) BCLR 1 (CC).

[104] Act 68 of 1973, as amended.

[105] *Ferreira, per* Ackermann J, para 70.

[106] *Supra*, Ackermann J, para 71. Chaskalson P, para 159 (concurred by Mahomed DP, Didcott, Langa, Madala JJ, and Trengove AJ).

[107] *Supra, per* Chaskalson P, para 159. This also has been affirmed under the final Constitution. See *Manamela* para 35.

[108] *Supra*, Chaskalson P, para 159.

indemnity given by the state does not affect any civil actions that may be brought against the individual. [109]

The right to remain silent does not affect the legitimate interest which the state has in requiring individuals to appear before an enquiry or tribunal to answer questions to help resolve crimes and civil disputes. If, in the course of questioning, it appears that an answer might incriminate the individual being questioned, it would be lawful for the individual to refuse to answer the question. In *Bernstein*, [110] the applicants challenged the validity of ss 417 and 418 of the Companies Act, [111] which required them to appear before an enquiry pertaining to the liquidation of a company. The applicants were members of an auditing firm, which audited the company involved the proceedings. The applicants argued that the demand that they appear before the enquiry violated their right to remain silent. The Court, *per* Ackermann J, held that the obligation to appear before the enquiry did not affect the applicants' rights. The state had a legitimate interest in obtaining full information about the affairs of the company, and it attempts to gather the information from such enquiries. [112] If applicants were asked to answer a question which would infringe their fundamental rights, such as privacy, or the right against self-incrimination, applicants could at that stage refuse to answer the question. [113] The majority held that the sections were constitutional since there was nothing in the legislation, which compelled the examinees to answer a question thereby threatening his or her fundamental rights. [114]

A similar finding was reached in *Nel*. *Nel* involved the constitutionality of s 205 of the Criminal Procedure Act, which required any subpoenaed person to present him or herself before a magistrate to answer questions in relation to an offence. [115] A unanimous Court, *per* Ackermann J, held that the section was constitutional, since it did not compel any person to answer a question which would infringe on his or her fundamental rights. [116] The Court also noted that if given indemnity, examinees could not refuse to answer any question put before them. [117]

The Constitution does not expressly specify that the accused's silence cannot be used against them. In terms of the Criminal Procedure Act, the accused is a competent – but not a compellable witness, and in the past was under strong pressure to testify. The Constitution reiterates that an accused has the right not to be a compellable witness against him or herself. [118] However, where the state adduces evidence and the accused chooses to remain silent despite the evidence presented to the court, in the absence of an explanation by the accused, the court is entitled to draw a conclusion that the accused is guilty. [119] In *Boesak*, the prosecutor presented a letter at the trial, which letter contained a signature of the defendant acknowledging receipt of donated money. On appeal, the defendant argued that the state had not proved that the defendant Boesak was the author of the letter. The Court held that if the accused failed to challenge the evidence during the trial, the trial court was entitled to draw a conclusion that the accused was the author of the letter. [120] Similarly, the European Court of Human Rights permits the drawing of adverse inferences

---

[109] Ackermann J in *Bernstein* para 115. See also *Nel v Le Roux and Others* CCT 30/95 (4 April 1996) para 4, *per* Ackermann J, now cited as 1996 (3) SA 562 (CC); 1996 (4) BCLR 592 (CC).

[110] *Bernstein*.

[111] Act 61 of 1973, as amended.

[112] *Bernstein* para 50.

[113] *Bernstein* para 58; see also, Ackermann J in *Nel* para 6.

[114] *Bernstein* para 60.

[115] *Nel* para 2.

[116] *Supra* para 7.

[117] *Supra* para 4.

[118] Section 35(1)*(c)* of the Constitution. This right was affirmed in *Zuma* para 29.

[119] *Boesak v The State* CCT 25/00 (1 December 2000) para 24, now cited as 2001 (1) BCLR 36 (CC); 2001 (1) SA 912 (CC).

[120] *Supra* para 25.

from an accused's silence under certain circumstances.[121] In *Murray v United Kingdom*, the accused chose to remain silent when he was questioned by police officers following his arrest.[122] In addition, he chose not to testify or put forward any affirmative evidence in his defence at trial.[123] The Court held that where the prosecution had established a *prima facie* case, the silence of the accused was one factor which the judge, as fact finder, could consider to determine the defendant's guilt or innocence.[124] In the United States, a court cannot draw an adverse inference from a defendant's silence.[125]

In *Manamela*, the majority sustained the first part of the provision in s 37(1) of the General Law Amendment Act,[126] which required any person found in possession of stolen goods not obtained at a public sale, to show that they did not know the goods were stolen. Given that in most instances the state has no way of establishing the circumstances under which the person acquired the goods, the majority held that the limitation on the right to silence was justified.[127] However, the Court did not sustain the second part of s 37(1), which entitled a court to convict the person found in possession of stolen goods based on a reverse onus presumption.[128]

Right to bail and *habeas corpus*

Section 35(1)(f) of the Constitution confers a right on the accused to be released from detention, subject to reasonable conditions, unless the interests of justice require otherwise. The factors to be considered in the granting or refusal of bail are covered in Chapter 9 of the Criminal Procedure Act.[129] In determining whether bail should be granted, the primary question that courts in many jurisdictions consider: will the accused appear in court as required or will the accused disappear?[130] It is not inappropriate to also consider the nature of the crime involved and public perceptions on the granting of bail.[131]

Section 35(2)(d) of the Constitution provides the detained person with the right to challenge the lawfulness of his or her detention in person before a court, and to be released if such detention is unlawful. If the accused does not raise the question of bail, the Criminal Procedure Act requires the court to take the initiative and determine whatever bail would be appropriate for the accused.[132] Under s 36, the fundamental rights protected in the Constitution can be derogated from only if it is reasonable and necessary. Section 37 of the Constitution allows for the declaration of a state of emergency pursuant to an Act of Parliament under certain conditions. If any individual is detained under a state of emergency, the validity of the detention is to be reviewed by a court of law within ten days.[133] The detainee has the right to constantly apply (within ten-day intervals), to a court of law to review the validity of his or her detention.[134] The state has the burden of showing why the detention is justified.[135] The state also has

---

[121] *Murray v United Kingdom* (1996) ECHR (ser A).

[122] 22 EHRR 29, 4.

[123] Op cit 5.

[124] Op cit 12.

[125] *Griffin v California* 380 US 609 (1965).

[126] Act 62 of 1955.

[127] *Manamela* para 38.

[128] *Supra* para 51.

[129] Act 51 of 1977, as amended by the Criminal Procedure Second Amendment Act 75 of 1995 and the Criminal Procedure Second Amendment Act 85 of 1997.

[130] *Dlamini* para 54. *De Veau v United States* 454 A2d 1308 (DC 1982); *Harp v Hinckley* 410 SO2d 619 (FlaApp 1982); *Nicholas v Cochran* 673 SO2d 882 (FlaApp 1996).

[131] *Dlamini* paras 54–55.

[132] Section 60(1)(c) of the Criminal Procedure Act.

[133] Section 37(6)(e) of the Constitution.

[134] Section 37(6)(f).

[135] Section 37(6)(h).

the duty to supply the detainee with written reasons to justify the detention.[136] During the period of detention, the detainee has the right to full access to legal representation of his or her choice.

Notice of charge

The accused, under s 35(2) of the Constitution, has a right to be informed of the charges against him or her. Under ss 35(1)(d), and (e), a person subject to detention has the right, as soon as it is reasonably possible, but not later than forty-eight hours after the arrest (allowing for weekends and routine closings), to be brought before an ordinary court of law on the first court day after the expiry of that period, and to be charged or informed of the reason for his or her further detention. If this information is not timeously provided, the accused is entitled to be released. Article 9(2) of the Civil Covenant requires that an arrested person be promptly informed at the time of arrest of the reason for his or her arrest and of any charges against him or her. Article 9(3) of the Civil Covenant requires that the arrested person be brought promptly before a judicial authority. Similar requirements are contained in arts 5(2) and 5(3) of the European Convention, and arts 8(1) and 8 (2)(g) of the American Convention.

Section 35(3)(k) of the Constitution provides that the accused be tried in a language which he or she understands or, failing this, to have the proceedings interpreted. Article 14(3)(a) of the Civil Covenant provides that the accused must be informed of the nature and the cause of the charge against him or her in the language that he or she understands. Under art 14(3)(f) of the Constitution, an accused has a right to an interpreter, without charge, if he or she cannot understand the language used by the court. The right to be charged in a language that the accused understands and the right to an interpreter is also required under art 8(2)(a) of the American Convention, and arts 6(2)(a) and (e) of the European Convention.

In *Brozicek v Italy*,[137] the plaintiff, a native of Czechoslovakia who resided in Germany, was charged by Italian police for resisting arrest and assault during a previous visit to Italy. The charge was sent to him in Germany by registered mail. On receiving the notice, plaintiff returned the document to the prosecutor's office with a note stating that he did not understand the contents of the charge. He further requested that the charge be in his mother language or one of the official languages of the United Nations.[138] The plaintiff subsequently received a letter from the Public Prosecutor in Germany informing him that he had been convicted by a court in Italy, and that the conviction had been entered in the German criminal records. The plaintiff subsequently appealed to the European Commission and later to the European Court of Human Rights. Similarly, the European Court of Human Rights held that the plaintiff's rights under art 6(3)(a) of the European Convention had been violated.[139] The Court held that once the Italian authorities received notice that the plaintiff did not understand the contents of the charge, they should have taken steps to comply with art (3)(a).[140]

Under s 34(4) of the South African Constitution, whenever the state is required to give information to the accused, 'the information must be given in a language that the person understands'. In *Harvard v Norway*,[141] the Human Rights Committee of the United Nations held that art 14 of the Civil Covenant protects the right to a fair trial. This includes access to documentary information. However, the right of access to information does not include the right to be furnished with translations of all relevant documents in a criminal investigation into the language which the accused understands.[142]

---

[136] Section 37(6)(h).
[137] European Court of Human Rights (1989) 167 ECHR (ser A), (1990) 12 EHRR 371.
[138] *Supra* para 16.
[139] *Supra* para 46.
[140] *Supra* para 41.
[141] UN Human Rights Committee Communications 451/1991 views adopted 15 July 1994 UN Doc CCPR/C/51/D/451/1991 (1994).
[142] *Harvard v Norway* para 9.5.

Access to information

Section 32(1) of the Constitution provides that everyone has a right to receive any information held by the state,[143] and by any other person 'that is required for the exercise or protection of any right'.[144] Freedom to access information arises in two contexts. First, in the context of a trial where one party, particularly an accused in a criminal trial, seeks access to information from the other party, usually the state. The second instance arises where information in a non-trial related context is sought from the state or private parties The major international human rights instruments require that an accused be given access to information and to examine witnesses against him or her.[145] Freedom of information in the second context, is not a 'classic' first generation or second generation human right. It is a right which has only recently been recognized in human rights discourse. In the *First Certification* decision, the Court noted that details governing freedom of information are not generally found in a constitution, neither is it a 'universally accepted fundamental human right'.[146] However, freedom of information is recognized in art 9(1) of the African Charter, which states '[E]very individual shall have the right to receive information'.

In the past, there was neither the right of an accused to obtain information on the evidence against him or her, nor was there any law which required the prosecution to disclose evidence that was in favour of the accused. At present, s 32(1) allows an accused the right to receive such information from the state. In the context of a trial, there is no rule which obliges the prosecution to disclose the information without a request from the accused. Where the information is required from a private party, there is a threshold enquiry that needs to be satisfied. The information must be required 'for the exercise or protection of any right'. There is no similar limitation under s 32(1)(a) mandating that information be held by the state.

However, the legislature can adopt measures that prescribe the conditions under which individuals have the right of access to information in both contexts. Section 32(2) provides that national legislation must be enacted to give effect to this right.[147] The Constitution does not envisage unlimited and unrestricted access at any time. Instead, the national legislation 'may provide reasonable measures to alleviate the administrative and financial burden on the state'.[148] The legislation also prescribe the substantive conditions for the exercise of the right with respect to non-state parties. For example, there is no right of access to intimate affairs of natural persons.[149] Similarly, confidential, commercial contractual information is protected.[150] With respect to information held by the state, information which pertains to defence, security, or international relations;[151] information which would jeopardize the economic interests or financial welfare of the country;[152] certain research information carried out by third parties;[153] or certain information pertaining to the operations of public bodies,[154] can be withheld from public disclosure.

---

[143] Section 32(1)*(a)* of the Constitution.

[144] Section 32(1)*(b)*.

[145] Article 2*(e)* of the Civil Covenant; art 6(2)*(d)* of the European Convention; art 2*(e)* of the American Convention. The African Charter does not contain anything on the right to examine witnesses. However, the African Charter unlike the other regional instruments expressly mentions in art 9(1) a right to receive information.

[146] *Certification I* para 85.

[147] Which has been done in terms of the Promotion of Access to Information Act 2 of 2000. The Constitution in Schedule 6, s 23(2)*(a)* required that such national legislation be enacted within three years of the Constitution taking effect. Chapter 3 of the Promotion of Access to Information Act regulates the manner of access.

[148] Section 32(2) of the Constitution.

[149] Sections 34 and 63 of the Promotion of Access to Information Act.

[150] Sections 36 and 65.

[151] Section 41.

[152] Section 42.

[153] Section 43.

[154] Section 44.

The concerns which an individual might have for access to information in a trial-related context (namely, to achieve a fair trial) is different from the right to receive information in a non-trial context. It is likely that additional legislation be passed for access to information to records required for criminal or civil proceedings.[155] In *Shabalala*, the Court was called upon to interpret the right to information under the interim Constitution.[156] Under the interim Constitution, everyone had a right of access to information held by the state if such information was required for the exercise or protection of any of his or her rights.[157] Instead of dealing with the case under freedom of information, the Court approached the issue in terms of access to information in order to ensure fair-trial procedures under s 25 of the interim Constitution. The accused in *Shabalala* were charged with murder. They subsequently sought information from police dockets, including witnesses' statements and lists of exhibits which the state had in its possession. The trial court judge held that the information was not 'required' for the exercise of any of their fair-trail rights. On appeal to the Constitutional Court, Mahomed DP writing for a

unanimous court, held that an accused is entitled to be furnished with any particulars alleged in the charge.[158] There can be no blanket prohibition on disclosure. As a rule, the search for truth is advanced rather than hindered by disclosure of all relevant information.[159] Therefore, the accused is ordinarily entitled to access to parts of the police docket and to identify and consult with police witnesses.[160] However, in routine prosecutions in inferior courts for minor offences, where there is no imprisonment, there would be no justification to make the whole docket available to the accused.[161] Even before the passing of the Promotion of Access to Information Act, the Court recognized that statements revealing state secrets, methods of police investigation, and identity of informers are also protected from disclosure.[162] Often, the disclosure of police information depends on the timing of the request. The accused is not entitled to information during the course of the prosecution and police investigation.[163] Similarly, an accused is not entitled to access to the police docket during a bail application.[164] The rule otherwise would compromise the investigation and ultimately the course of justice.[165]

Shabalala and Five Others v The Attorney-General of the Transvaal and Another CCT 23/94 (29 Nov 1995), now cited as 1995 (12) BCLR 1593 (CC); 1995 (1) SA 608
(notes omitted)
MAHOMED DP.

(1) Mr Shabalala and five others ('the accused') were charged with the crime of murder before

Cloete J in the Transvaal Provincial Division of the Supreme Court. Before any evidence was led, various applications were made to the trial Court on behalf of the accused. These included applications for copies of the relevant police dockets, including witnesses' statements and lists of exhibits in the possession of the State.

(2) These applications were all opposed by both the Attorney-General of the Transvaal and the Commissioner of the South African Police,

---

[155] Section 7 of the Promotion of Access to Information Act provides that the Act does not apply to records required for criminal or civil proceedings where the matter is regulated by another law. See s 7(1)(c).

[156] *Shabalala and Five Others v The Attorney-General of the Transvaal and Another* CCT 23/94 (29 November 1995), now cited as 1996 (1) SA 725 (CC); 1995 (12) BCLR 1593 (CC).

[157] Section 23 of the interim Constitution.

[158] *Shabalala* para 20.

[159] *Supra* para 47.

[160] *Supra* paras 37, 69.

[161] *Supra* para 38.

[162] *Supra* para 40.

[163] *Dlamini* para 82.

[164] *Supra*. See also s 23 of the Promotion of Access to Information Act.

[165] *Dlamini* para 81.

who were cited as respondents. They were refused by Cloete J substantially on the grounds that the accused had not satisfied the Court that the relevant documents in the possession of the State, were 'required' by them (within the meaning of section 23 of the Constitution of the Republic of South Africa, 1993 ('the Constitution')) 'for the exercise of any of their rights to a fair trial'.

(26) What is perfectly clear from these provisions of the Constitution and the tenor and spirit of the Constitution viewed historically and teleologically, is that the Constitution is not simply some kind of statutory codification of an acceptable or legitimate past. It retains from the past only what is defensible and represents a radical and decisive break from that part of the past which is unacceptable. It constitutes a decisive break from a culture of Apartheid and racism to a constitutionally protected culture of openness and democracy and universal human rights for South Africans of all ages, classes and colours. There is a stark and dramatic contrast between the past in which South Africans were trapped and the future on which the Constitution is premised. The past was pervaded by inequality, authoritarianism and repression. The aspiration of the future is based on what is 'justifiable in an open and democratic society based on freedom and equality'. It is premised on a legal culture of accountability and transparency. The relevant provisions of the Constitution must therefore be interpreted so as to give effect to the purposes sought to be advanced by their enactment.

(30) The crucial issue which needs to be determined is whether the 'blanket docket privilege' from the pre-constitutional era can survive the application of Chapter 3 of the Constitution. The determination of that issue requires a consideration of the various factors impacting on the consequences of any departure from the rule in *Steyn's* case.

(37) Ordinarily, an accused person should be entitled to have access at least to the statements of prosecution witnesses but the prosecution may, in a particular case, be able to justify the denial of such access on the grounds that it is not justified for the purposes of a fair trial. What a fair trial might require in a particular case depends on the circumstances. The simplicity of the case, either on the law or on the facts or both; the degree of particularity furnished in the indictment or the summary of substantial facts in terms of section 144 of the Criminal Procedure Act; the particulars furnished pursuant to section 87 of the Criminal Procedure Act; the details of the charge read with such particulars in the Regional and District Courts, might be such as to justify the denial of such access. The accused may, however, be entitled to have access to the relevant parts of the police docket even in cases where the particularity furnished might be sufficient to enable the accused to understand the charge against him or her but, in the special circumstances of a particular case, it might not enable the defence to prepare its own case sufficiently, or to properly exercise its right 'to adduce and challenge evidence'; or to identify witnesses able to contradict the assertions made by the State witnesses; or to obtain evidence which might sufficiently impact upon the credibility and motives of the State witnesses during cross-examination; or to properly instruct expert witnesses to adduce evidence which might similarly detract from the probability and the veracity of the version to be deposed to by the State witnesses; or to focus properly on significant matters omitted by the State witnesses in their depositions; or to properly deal with the significance of matters deposed to by such witnesses in one statement and not in another or deposed to in a statement and not repeated in evidence; or to hesitations, contradictions and uncertainties manifest in a police statement but overtaken by confidence and dogmatism in *viva voce* testimony.

(38) In other cases, which might include a substantial number of routine prosecutions in the inferior Courts, there might be scant justification for allowing such access to police dockets in order to ensure a fair trial for the accused. This would be the case where there is a simple charge in respect of a minor offence involving no complexities of fact or law, in which there is no reasonable prospect of

imprisonment, and in which the accused can easily adduce and challenge the evidence which the State might lead against him or her, through an analysis of the charge-sheet and any particulars furnished in respect thereof. Hundreds of routine prosecutions in respect of such minor offences take place every day in the Magistrates' Court following upon some kind of acrimony or brawl during a weekend, in which an accused might have become involved. There would ordinarily be little sense in requiring copies of the whole docket to be prepared and made available to the accused in order to dispose of such prosecutions. In such cases where access to witnesses' statements is nevertheless justified it does not follow that copies of witnesses' statements have to be furnished. It might be sufficient to give the defence an opportunity of looking at such statements. No rigid rules are desirable. It is for the trial Court to exercise a proper discretion having regard to the circumstances of each case.

[40] The approach to the constitutionality of the rule in *Steyn's* case, insofar as it pertains to witnesses' statements, involves an analysis of what that rule seeks to protect. It seems to me that the following is included in the protection–

1 The statements of witnesses which need no protection on the grounds that they deal with State secrets, methods of police investigation, the identity of informers, and communications between a legal advisor and his or her client;

2 The statements of witnesses in circumstances where there is no reasonable risk that such disclosure might lead to the intimidation of such witnesses or otherwise impede the proper ends of justice;

3 The statements of witnesses made in circumstances where there is a reasonable risk that their disclosure might constitute a breach of the interests sought to be protected in paragraph 1; and

4 The statements of witnesses made in circumstances where their disclosure would constitute a reasonable risk of the nature referred to in paragraph 2.

Order

(72) In the result I would make an order declaring that –

A 1 The 'blanket docket privilege' expressed by the rule in *R v Steyn* 1954 (1) SA 324 (A) is inconsistent with the Constitution to the extent to which it protects from disclosure all the documents in a police docket, in all circumstances, regardless as to whether or not such disclosure is justified for the purposes of enabling the accused properly to exercise his or her right to a fair trial in terms of section 25(3).

2 The claim of the accused for access to documents in the police docket cannot be defeated merely on the grounds that such contents are protected by a blanket privilege in terms of the decision in *Steyn's* case.

3 Ordinarily an accused person should be entitled to have access to documents in the police docket which are exculpatory (or which are *prima facie* likely to be helpful to the defence) unless, in very rare cases, the State is able to justify the refusal of such access on the grounds that it is not justified for the purposes of a fair trial.

4 Ordinarily the right to a fair trial would include access to the statements of witnesses (whether or not the State intends to call such witnesses) and such of the contents of a police docket as are relevant in order to enable an accused person properly to exercise that right, but the prosecution may, in a particular case, be able to justify the denial of such access on the grounds that it is not justified for the purposes of a fair trial. This would depend on the circumstances of each case.

5 The State is entitled to resist a claim by the accused for access to any particular document in the police docket on the grounds that such access is not justified

for the purposes of enabling the accused properly to exercise his or her right to a fair trial or on the ground that it has reason to believe that there is a reasonable risk that access to the relevant document would lead to the disclosure of the identity of an informer or State secrets or on the grounds that there was a reasonable risk that such disclosure might lead to the intimidation of witnesses or otherwise prejudice the proper ends of justice.

6   Even where the State has satisfied the Court that the denial of access to the relevant documents is justified on the grounds set out in paragraph 5 hereof, it does not follow that access to such statements, either then or subsequently must necessarily be denied to the accused. The Court still retains a discretion. It should balance the degree of risk involved in attracting the potential prejudicial consequences for the proper ends of justice referred to in paragraph 5 (if such access is permitted) against the degree of the risk that a fair trial may not enure for the accused (if such access is denied). A ruling by the Court pursuant to this paragraph shall be an interlocutory ruling subject to further amendment, review or recall in the light of circumstances disclosed by the further course of the trial.

B 1   Insofar as and to the extent that the rule of practice pertaining to the right of an accused or his legal representative to consult with witnesses for the State prohibits such consultation without the permission of the prosecuting authority, in all cases and regardless of the circumstances, it is not consistent with the Constitution.

2   An accused person has a right to consult a State witness without prior permission of the prosecuting authority in circumstances where his or her right to a fair trial would be impaired, if, on the special facts of a particular case, the accused cannot properly obtain a fair trial without such consultation.

3   The accused or his or her legal representative should in such circumstances approach the Attorney-General or an official authorised by the Attorney-General for consent to hold such consultation. If such consent is granted the Attorney-General or such official shall be entitled to be present at such consultation and to record what transpires during the consultation. If the consent of the Attorney-General is refused the accused shall be entitled to approach the Court for such permission to consult the relevant witness.

4   The right referred to in paragraph 2 does not entitle an accused person to compel such consultation with a State witness:

   (a) if such State witness declines to be so consulted; or

   (b) if it is established on behalf of the State that it has reasonable grounds to believe such consultation might lead to the intimidation of the witness or a tampering with his or her evidence or that it might lead to the disclosure of State secrets or the identity of informers or that it might otherwise prejudice the proper ends of justice.

5   Even in the circumstances referred to in paragraph 4 (b), the Court may, in the circumstances of a particular case, exercise a discretion to permit such consultation in the interest of justice subject to suitable safeguards.

The final Constitution does not contain the same threshold as the interim Constitution 'in so far as such information is required', but instead provides a general right of access to information. The right of access to information reflects a concern that the affairs of government should be conducted in the open, and the information should be open to the public. However, there are legitimate circumstances such as state secrets, and identity of informers, which the Court recognized in *Shabalala*, where the state may still restrict access to information.

While s 35(4) of the Constitution requires that an accused may have a right of access to information translated into a language that he or she understands in the context of fair trial procedures, it is questionable whether he or she has a right to have documents translated into a language he or she understands in a non-trial context.[166] Section 35 goes further than the Civil Covenant, which does not require that documentary information be furnished in the language which the accused understands – even in the context of a criminal trial.[167]

Since the right to information applies not only against the state but against any person, providing the information is required in furtherance of any right, the section could entitle individuals to receive information from a variety of private parties. For example, it could conceivably include the right of trade unions to receive financial information and business strategies about the company with which it is engaged in collective bargaining. It could also include, for example, the right of an individual to receive information concerning why he or she was refused admission to a university.

Right to counsel

Section 35(2)(b) of the Constitution states that every prisoner shall have a right 'to choose, and to consult with, a legal practitioner, and to be informed of this right promptly'. The right to legal representation is contained in art 14(3)(b) of the Civil Covenant; art 7(c) of the African Charter; art 6(3)(a) of the European Convention, and arts 8(2)(c) and (d) of the American Convention.

For indigent prisoners, s 35(2)(c) of the Constitution further requires the state to assign to every prisoner a legal practitioner at the state's expense, if his or her inability to obtain a legal practitioner would otherwise result in substantial injustice. The prisoner must be informed of these rights. In the United States case of *Gidean v Wainwright*,[168] the United States Supreme Court unanimously held that an indigent defendant's right to counsel at the state's expense is essential to a fair trial under the adversarial model.[169] In *S v Vermaas* and *S v Du Plessis*,[170] the Constitutional Court observed that there can be no undue delay in the promise of a fundamental right including the right to counsel.[171] However, the right to counsel at the state's expense does not mean the right to have the counsel of one's choice.[172]

Treatment without delay

Sections 35(1)(d) and (e) of the Constitution deal with an accused person's right to be brought

---

[166] Section 31(a) of the Promotion of Access to Information Act requires that information must be given in the language the requestor prefers. If the record does not exist in the language preferred, s 31(b) requires the information be given in any language in which the record exists.

[167] In *Harvard v Norway*, the Human Rights Committee of the UN held that art 14 of the Civil Covenant protects the right to a fair trial. This includes access to documentary information. However, the right of access to information does not include the right to be furnished with translations in the language which the accused understands, of all relevant documents in a criminal investigation. UN Human Rights Committee Communications 451/1991 views adopted 15 July 1994 UN Doc CCPR/C/51/D/451/1991 (1994), para 9.5.

[168] 372 US 335, 345 (1963).

[169] *Wainwright*, 372 US at 345.

[170] These cases were decided together and cited as CCT/1/94; CCT 2/94 (8 June 1995) respectively, now cited as 1995 (7) BCLR 851 (CC); 1995 (3) SA 292 (CC).

[171] *Vermaas, per* Didcott J (unanimous opinion), para 16.

[172] *Supra* para 15. See the German Constitutional Court decision of 16 December 1958 [1959] 9 BverfGE 36 translated in Cappelletti & Cohen 424–6, where the Court held the right to counsel did not mean the right to counsel of one's choice at state expense.

before an ordinary court, and to be informed of the charge against him or her within a reasonable time. This to be no later than forty-eight hours after arrest, or the first day after the period when the court is not in session. Section 35(3)(d) confers a right to have a trial begin and conclude without unreasonable delay. The right to be tried without undue delay or within a reasonable time is contained in art 14(2)(c) of the Civil Covenant; art 7(1)(d) of the African Charter; arts 5(3) and 6(1) of the European Convention, and art 8(1) of the American Convention.

The requirement for a speedy trial is meant to protect liberty, security, and trial-related interests.[173] Unreasonable delays may also cause the accused to suffer in other ways, including being subject to social stigma. Moreover, the accused could be subject to conditions curtailing his or her liberty such as jail, onerous bail conditions, and the need to repeatedly attend court for formal remands.[174] Justice Powell in *Barker v Wingo*[175] made the observation that the right to a speedy trial 'is a more vague concept than other procedural rights. It is, for example, impossible to determine with precision when the right has been denied. We cannot definitely say how long is too long in a system where justice is supposed to be swift but deliberate.'[176] The imprecise nature of the right led the court to embrace a balancing test that was cited with approval by the Constitutional Court in *Sanderson*.[177] In determining what is unreasonable delay, the court is required to conduct a balancing test in which both the conduct of the prosecution and the accused are weighed. In the balancing process, the court considers the length of the delay, the reason the state gives for the delay, the accused's reasons for a speedy trial, and prejudice to the accused.[178] Central to the entire balancing process is the amount of time taken.[179]

Similarly, in *Firmenich v Argentina*,[180] the Inter-American Commission noted that a reasonable length of time cannot be determined in the abstract. Instead, it should be defined in the circumstances of each case. In *Sanderson*, the Constitutional Court, *per* Kriegler J, held that it is not appropriate for South African courts to adopt preordained times for the prosecuting authority.[181] An undue delay in the hearing of a criminal appeal does not necessarily constitute an infringement of the right to a fair trial.[182]

Sanderson v Attorney-General, Eastern Cape CCT 10/97 (2 December 1997), now cited as 1997 (12) BCLR 1675 (CC); 1998 (2) SA 38 (notes omitted)

Authors' note: The appellant argued that an almost two-year delay in his trial for sexual offences undermined his right to a speedy trial under the interim Constitution.[183] He, therefore, sought a permanent stay of prosecution. The unanimous Court, per Kriegler J, in applying the standards enunciated, held that this was not an appropriate case for a stay of prosecution for the reasons stated below.

[2] Those facts, briefly stated, are as follows

---

[173] *Sanderson v the Attorney-General Eastern Cape* CCT 10/97 para 20. See the *Weimhoff-Neumeister* cases, European Court of Human Rights, Judgments of 27 June 1968 [1968] 11 *Yb Eur Conv on Human Rights* 796 and 812.

[174] *Sanderson* para 23.

[175] *Barker* v Wingo 407 US 514 (1972).

[176] *Supra* at 521.

[177] *Sanderson* para 25.

[178] *Supra.*

[179] *Supra* para 28.

[180] Inter-American Commission on Human Rights Resolution 17/89, Report Case 10037 (13 April 1989) *Annual Report of the Inter-American Commission on Human Rights* OEA/Ser L/V/VII 76 (10 September 1989).

[181] *Sanderson* para 30.

[182] *Per* Chaskalson P in *Pennington & Summerley v The State* CCT 14/97 (18 September 1997) para 41, now cited as 1997 (4) SA 1076 (CC); 1997 (10) BCLR 1413 (CC).

[183] Section 25(3)(a) of the interim Constitution provided that every accused person shall have a right to a fair trial which shall include a trial 'within a reasonable time after having being charged'. This section is analogous to s 35(3)(d) of the final Constitution.

Towards the end of October 1994 the Child Protection Unit of the SA Police Service in Port Elizabeth received information that the appellant, the deputy head of a primary school in Port Elizabeth and a well known singer in local church and musical entertainment circles, had sexually interfered with two girls who, at the time, had been standard five pupils at his school. Investigations commenced and on 1 December 1994 the appellant, at the invitation of the investigating officer, attended at the latter's office. There he was informed by the detective that he was suspected of having contravened section 14(1)(b) of the Sexual Offences Act 23 of 1957, that is, the commission of an indecent act with a girl under the age of 16 years, at his home during 1991 and 1993. Having been cautioned in accordance with the Judges' Rules the appellant denied the accusation and declined to make a statement.

[7] Once again supervening events prevented the trial from starting. On 12 November 1996, some three months after the latest trial dates had been fixed, the appellant launched an urgent application in the South Eastern Cape Local Division of the Supreme Court (as it was then still called) seeking, in the main, an order permanently 'staying' the proceedings pending against him in the Regional Court and '[p]ermanently prohibiting the respondent ... from reinstituting any prosecution against [him] in respect of the charges set out in the indictment' (sic).

[8] The nub of the case made out by the appellant in his founding affidavit is that 'an unreasonable and inexcusable delay in the prosecution of this matter has resulted in a serious infringement of my rights to a speedy trial as contained in' section 25(3)(a) of the interim Constitution. In amplification he alleges that he 'was first charged on 1 December 1994 in relation to the charges arising out of the complaints made by the two complainants' and that he 'was eventually served with a formal charge sheet on 10 May 1996'. He stresses that from the time he became aware of the allegations against him in December 1994 he had constantly exerted pressure on the respon-

dent to conclude the investigation and made clear that he reserved his constitutional right to a speedy trial.

[20] The next step is to examine the phrase 'within a reasonable time'. In seeking to understand the scope and effect of the phrase in the context of the section, a useful starting point is to establish why the right to a trial within a reasonable time was included as one of the specifically enumerated elements of a fair trial. More specifically, in the context of the present case, what kinds of interests is the right intended to protect? Apart from denoting that the right is a component of a fair trial, the section gives one few clues. These issues have been constitutionally scrutinized in Canada and the United States, both of which have constitutional provisions (section 11(b) of the Canadian Charter and the Sixth Amendment to the US Constitution) affording the right to a speedy trial. There has also been some consideration in Australia and England of the status of the right to a speedy trial at common law. In the main, the rights primarily protected by such speedy trial provisions are perceived to be liberty, security and trial-related interests In *R v Morin*, these various interests are defined as follows:

The right to security of the person is protected in s 11*(b)* by seeking to minimize the anxiety, concern and stigma of exposure to criminal proceedings. The right to liberty is protected by seeking to minimise exposure to the restrictions on liberty which result from pre-trial incarceration and restrictive bail conditions. The right to a fair trial is protected by attempting to ensure that proceedings take place while evidence is available and fresh.

Uncertainty in Canada and the United States has revolved around the inclusion of trial-related interests. Although the position in both jurisdictions is that trial-related interests are included, strong dissenting voices have argued that conceptually, trial-related interests have no place – or only a secondary place – in the relevant speedy trial provisions. Fair trial interests, it is argued, are catered for elsewhere –

either in other constitutional provisions, or in statutes of limitation.

[23] The central reason for my view, however, goes to the nature of the criminal justice system itself. In principle, the system aims to punish only those persons whose guilt has been established in a fair trial. Prior to a finding on liability, and as part of the fair procedure itself, the accused is presumed innocent. He or she is also tried publicly so that the trial can be seen to satisfy the substantive requirements of a fair trial. The profound difficulty with which we are confronted in this case is that an accused person – despite being presumptively innocent – is subject to various forms of prejudice and penalty merely by virtue of being an accused. These forms of prejudice are unavoidable and unintended by-products of the system.

In addition to the social prejudice referred to by Lamer J, the accused is also subject to invasions of liberty that range from incarceration or onerous bail conditions to repeated attendance at a remote court for formal remands. This kind of prejudice resembles even more closely the kind of 'punishment' that ought only (and ideally) to be imposed on convicted persons. These forms of non-trial related prejudice have a particular resonance in South Africa. Our recent history demonstrates how the machinery of the criminal justice system can be used to impose extra-curial punishments. Vague statutory crimes which gave the State sweeping scope to investigate, charge and prosecute opponents of the governing party; provisions allowing the attorney-general to prevent bail being considered; invasive bail conditions – all of these have been deliberately used to invade and criminalise people's lives.

[25] Having determined that the section protects three kinds of interest, we are better situated to determine when the provision has been violated. The critical question is how we determine whether a particular lapse of time is reasonable. The seminal answer in *Barker v Wingo* is that there is a 'balancing test' in which the conduct of both the prosecution and the accused are weighed and the following considerations examined: the length of the delay;

the reason the government assigns to justify the delay; the accused's assertion of his right to a speedy trial; and prejudice to the accused. Other jurisdictions have likewise adopted the flexible 'balancing' test of *Barker*. South African courts, too, have used the *Barker v Wingo* balancing test in interpreting and applying section 25(3)(a), as well as considerations set out by the Canadian Supreme Court.

[27] Be that as it may, adjudication of claims under section 25(3)(a) requires an assessment of whether there has been a trial within a reasonable time. Reasonableness is not a novel standard in South African law. Here, as in the common-law context, one makes an objective and rational assessment of relevant considerations. What these relevant considerations are is treated by the foreign case law – in particular the *Barker* decision. I want to consider some of these factors in turn. I do so cautiously, not only for the reasons already stated, but because the test in *Barker*, and the related test in Canada, are designed for remedial contexts significantly different from our own. Our flexibility in providing remedies may affect our understanding of the right. Later I will make some general observations about how these different factors should be assimilated in determining whether or not a lapse of time is reasonable.

[28] The amount of elapsed time is obviously central to the enquiry. The right, after all, is to a public trial 'within a reasonable *time* after having been charged'. Understanding how this factor should be incorporated into the enquiry is not straightforward. In the United States and Canada, time is considered to be a 'triggering mechanism' which initiates the enquiry and it also functions subsequently as an independent factor in the enquiry. In my respectful view, time has a pervasive significance that bears on all the factors and should not be considered at the threshold or, subsequently, in isolation.

[29] Time does not only condition the relevant considerations, such as prejudice, it is also conditioned by them. The factors generally relied upon by the State – waiver of time periods, the time requirements inherent in the case, and systemic reasons for delay – all seek to

diminish the impact of elapsed time. These are factors I consider in greater detail below

[30] The test for establishing whether the time allowed to lapse was reasonable should not be unduly stratified or preordained. In some jurisdictions prejudice is presumed – sometimes irrebuttably – after the lapse of loosely specified time periods. I do not believe it would be helpful for our courts to impose such semi-formal time constraints on the prosecuting authority. That would be a law-making function which it would be inappropriate for a court to exercise. The courts will apply their experience of how the lapse of time generally affects the liberty, security and trial-related interests that concern us. Of the three forms of prejudice, the trial-related variety is possibly hardest to establish, and here as in the case of other forms of prejudice, trial courts will have to draw sensible inferences from the evidence. By and large, it seems a fair although tentative generalisation that the lapse of time heightens the various kinds of prejudice that section 25(3)(a) seeks to diminish.

[31] Let me turn now to a consideration of the most important factors bearing on the enquiry. The first is the nature of the prejudice suffered by the accused. Ordinarily, the more serious the prejudice (on a continuum from incarceration through restrictive bail conditions and trial prejudice to mild forms of anxiety), the shorter must be the period within which the accused is tried. Awaiting-trial prisoners, in particular, must be the beneficiaries of the right in section 25(3)(a). In principle, the continuing enforcement of section 25(3)(a) rights should tend to compel the State to prioritise cases in a rational way. Those cases involving pre-trial incarceration, or serious occupational disruption or social stigma, or the likelihood of prejudice to the accused's defence, or – in general – cases that are already delayed or involve serious prejudice, should be expedited by the State. If it fails to do this it runs the risk of infringing section 25(3)(a).

[34] The second factor is the nature of the case. Unlike the Canadian authorities, I do not believe it appropriate to specify 'normal delays' for specific kinds of cases. That seems an enterprise better conducted by the legislature. Instead, judges must bring their own experiences to bear in determining whether a delay seems over-lengthy. This is not simply a matter of contrasting intrinsically simple and complex cases. Certainly, a case requiring the testimony of witnesses or experts, or requiring the detailed analysis of documents is likely to take longer than one which does not. But the prosecution should also be aware of these inherent delays and factor them into the decision of when to charge a suspect. If a person has been charged very early in a complex case that has been inadequately prepared, and there is no compelling reason for this, a court should not allow the complexity of the case to justify an over-lengthy delay. Furthermore, even cases which appear simple may involve factors which justify delay. The personal circumstances and nature of the witnesses, for example, should be considered – and they seem particularly important in this case. There should also be some proportionality between the kind of sentences available for a crime, and the prejudice being suffered by the accused. Pre-trial incarceration of five months for a crime the maximum sentence for which is six months, clearly points in the direction of unreasonableness.

[35] The third and final factor I wish to mention is so-called systemic delay. Under this heading I would place resource limitations that hamper the effectiveness of police investigation or the prosecution of a case, and delay caused by court congestion. Systemic factors are probably more excusable than cases of individual dereliction of duty. Nevertheless, there must come a time when systemic causes can no longer be regarded as exculpatory. The bill of rights is not a set of (aspirational) directive principles of State policy – it is intended that the State should make whatever arrangements are necessary to avoid rights violations. One has to accept that we have not yet reached that stage. Even if one does accept that systemic factors justify delay, as one must at the present, they can only do so for a certain period of time. It would be legitimate, for instance, for an accused to bring evidence showing that the average systemic delay for a particular jurisdiction had been exceeded. In the absence of such evidence, courts may find it

difficult to determine how much systemic delay to tolerate. In principle, however, they should not allow claims of systemic delay to render the right nugatory.

[37] ... It is the duty of presiding officers to assume primary responsibility for ensuring that this constitutional right is protected in the day-to-day functioning of their courts.

[40] It remains to apply the principles I have attempted to enunciate to the facts of this particular case. I have accepted that the appellant's appearance in the magistrates' court on 2 December 1994 constituted his being 'charged' and thereby started the section 25(3)(a) clock running. It must also be accepted that in the 23 months from that date to the launch of the application in the High Court the appellant suffered considerable and fairly prolonged social prejudice. Occupationally the case had no major effect; the appellant retained his position as a deputy principal and continued with his duties. But he was forced to cancel some stage engagements and there must have been quite significant interference with his everyday life. Serious social embarrassment was inevitable from the very nature of the charges and the appellant's occupation. He also made the point that the newspaper publicity at the time of his arraignment in May 1996 was extensive and tarnished his reputation considerably. Such factors are certainly not irrelevant in assessing the prejudice suffered by the appellant. But the object of the current exercise is not the general disadvantages suffered by an accused in consequence of serious charges being preferred.

Our focus is on *delay* and the prejudice that *it* causes.

[41] One is therefore not so much concerned with the prejudice flowing from the charges and the publicity they initially generated, but with the aggravation of that prejudice ascribable to the delay. Moreover, when one considers the nature and cause of that prejudice, a permanent stay of prosecution certainly does not present itself as an obvious remedy. Release from custody is appropriate relief for an awaiting-trial prisoner who has been held too long; a refusal of a postponement is appropriate relief for a person who wishes to bring matters to a head to avoid remaining under a cloud; a stay of prosecution is appropriate relief where there is trial prejudice.

[42] Without setting these as fixed rules, and accepting that there may be cases in which a permanent stay is appropriate without there being trial prejudice, the facts of this case do not warrant such an order. The appellant was not in custody; he continued working; the postponements were to agreed dates that suited him and did not require frequent attendances at court; he was legally represented and could have opposed the postponements earlier and with greater vigour had he wished the trial to proceed. And, of course, a stay will not remedy the main prejudice of which he complains – it will not clear his name. Weighing these factors with the institutional problems described in the respondent's affidavits and with the difficulty in handling complaints of sexual abuse of children, this is not an appropriate case for a stay.

Search and seizure and the right to privacy

The Constitution enshrines the right to privacy. Section 14 provides that every person has the right of personal privacy including the right not to be subject to searches of one's person,[184] home,[185] property,[186] possessions,[187] or private communications.[188] The right to privacy is also enshrined in art 12 of the Universal Declaration; art 17 of the Civil Covenant; art 11 of the American Convention, and art 8(1) of the European Convention.

---

[184] Section 14(a) of the Constitution.
[185] Section 14(a).
[186] Section 14(b).
[187] Section 14(c).
[188] Section 14(d).

In the criminal procedure context, the privacy protection seeks to ensure that persons, their homes, property, possessions, and communications are not subject to unreasonable searches, seizures, or invasion. The object of privacy is to protect both the person and his or her home from undue state interference. Any interference by the state has to be subject to certain legal standards. A reasonable search should, as a rule, require that any law enforcement officer obtain a warrant from a judicial officer, before a search is executed.[189] The inviolability of the home is one of the essential guarantees under international human rights. The right protects not only the home, but also very importantly, the guarantee of due process in as much as it establishes what can be seized.[190] The law enforcement officer must demonstrate to the judicial officer that there is some basis to believe that the search will furnish evidence of criminal activity.[191]

With respect to communications, individuals have a right to non-interference with their correspondence, and a right to be free from eavesdropping. Any interference with an individual's correspondence, eavesdropping, or wiretapping must follow strict procedural safeguards.[192] It is questionable whether many of the provisions in the Criminal Procedure Act that confer wide search and seizure powers – even without a warrant – will pass constitutional muster.

Under ss 218 and 225 of the Criminal Procedure Act, evidence, although obtained by illegal means or against the wishes of the accused, may still be admitted against an accused. The scope of these provisions is likely to be narrowed in light of s 35(5) of the Constitution, which provides that evidence obtained in a way that violates any right in the Bill of Rights must be excluded if it would render the trial unfair, or be detrimental to the administration of justice. In *Key*, Kriegler J writing for a unanimous Court, stated that at times fairness might require that evidence obtained illegally be excluded. However, there may also be times when evidence obtained through unconstitutional means may nevertheless be admitted.[193]

Right of appeal

Under s 35(3)(o) of the Constitution there is a right of appeal or review to a higher court – other than the court which originally heard the matter. The right of appeal is guaranteed under art 14(5) of the Civil Covenant; art 7(1)(a) of the African Charter; art 8(h) of the American Convention, and Protocol 7(2) to the European Convention.

The right of appeal does not mean that all convicted persons may automatically have their convictions heard by a higher tribunal. It also does not mean that the entire proceedings have to be argued again at the appeals stage.[194] Persons who wish to appeal a conviction or sentence can be made to apply for leave to appeal. This requirement does not violate the Constitution's guarantee of a right of appeal. The purpose of applying for leave to appeal is to protect the higher courts from

---

[189] *Garcia Perez v Peru*, Inter-American Commission of Human Rights Report 1/95, Case 11.0006 I-ACHR 71, OEA Ser L/V/II.88, Doc 9 rev (1995). (Translated in Francisco Forrest Martin, et al *International Human Rights Law and Practice: Cases Treaties and Materials* Cambridge: Kluwer Law International 1997, 645.)

[190] Ibid.

[191] *The Investigating Directorate: Serious Economic Offences and Others v Hyundai Motor Distributors (Pty) Ltd; In re: Hyundai Motor Distributors (Pty) Ltd and Others v Smit NO and Others* CCT 1/00 (25 August 2000) paras 12 and 48, now cited as 2000 (10) BCLR 1079 (CC); 2001 (1) SA 545 (CC).

[192] See *Silver v United Kingdom*, (1983) 61 ECHR (ser A), where the European Court held even a prisoner has the right of correspondence. See *Klass and Others v Federal Republic of Germany* (1978) 28 ECHR (ser A), where the Court stated emphatically that any eavesdropping and surveillance activities must be subject to strict independent supervision, to ensure against abuse of privacy rights.

[193] Kriegler J in *Key* para 13. It seems that the South African approach is more akin to the approach in Italy and under the European Convention of Human Rights. See the *EGIDI* decision in Italy translated in Cappelletti & Cohen 494–6. See also the approach of the European Commission on Human Rights, 507–09. The US approach under the 'fruit of the poisonous tree' doctrine is more strict. See *Davis v Mississippi* 394 US 721 (1969).

[194] *S v Rens* CCT 1/95 (28 December 1995) para 21, now cited as 1996 (1) SA 1218 (CC); 1996 (2) BCLR 155 (CC).

being swamped by appeals which have no likelihood of success.[195]

In civil matters 'a screening procedure which excludes unmeritorious appeals' is also not a denial of a right to access to the court.[196] The screening procedure must be fair.[197] The validity of the screening process will be determined in terms of whether the process 'enables a higher court to make an informed decision as to the prospects of success upon appeal ...'.[198] Where the process does not allow for a full appraisal of the merits of the appeal, the Court could invalidate it.[199] For example, if the Appellate Tribunal does not review, or have access to the proceedings in the lower court, it is likely that there might be a violation of the right of appeal.[200] In *Ntuli*, the Court invalidated s 309(4)(a) of the Criminal Procedure Act. The section prevented a convicted person in the magistrates' court from proceeding with an appeal, if the convicted person was not represented by a lawyer, unless a judge certified that there were reasonable grounds for review. Didcott J, for a unanimous Court, held that the procedure for determining whether to grant a certificate, sometimes made by judges without reading the full record pursuant to s 309(4)(a), was unsystematic and haphazard.[201] Didcott J stated that the certificate procedure at a minimum requires an opportunity 'for an adequate reappraisal of every case and an informed decision on it'.[202]

S v Ntuli
CCT 17/95 (8 December 1995),
now cited as 1996 (1) BCLR 141 (CC);
1996 (1) SA 1207 (CC)
(notes omitted)

(3) [DIDCOTT J]: The case concerns a man named Nicko Ntuli. A regional magistrate convicted him of rape, attempted murder and assault with intent to do grievous bodily harm. For those crimes he was sentenced by the magistrate to terms of imprisonment which amounted effectively to an aggregate of thirteen years. He went to gaol at once. There he resolved to appeal against the convictions and the sentences. He had not been legally represented at his trial. Nor, it seems, could he get a lawyer to prepare and present his appeal. So he planned to perform the tasks personally. But a hurdle had to be surmounted at first, one erected by the provisions of the Criminal Procedure Act 51 of 1977 which regulated appeals lodged by convicts like him.

(4) Section 309(1)(a) of the statute decrees that:

Any person convicted of any offence by any lower court ... may appeal against such conviction and against any resultant sentence or order to the provincial or local division having jurisdiction.

A magistrate's court is a lower one for that purpose, and the provincial and local divisions of the Supreme Court are those thus mentioned. In Ntuli's circumstances, however, his right to appeal was qualified. Section 309(4)(a) stipulates that:

When an appeal under this section is noted, the provisions of ... section 305 shall *mutatis mutandis* apply in respect of the conviction, sentence or order appealed against.

---

[195] *Supra* para 7.

[196] O'Regan J, in *Besserglik v Minister of Trade, Industry and Tourism and Others* CCT 34/95 (14 May 1996) para 10, now cited as 1996 (4) SA 331 (CC); 1996 (6) BCLR 745 (CC).

[197] *S v Twala* CCT 27/99 (2 December 1999) para 14, now cited as 2000 (1) SA 879 (CC); 2000 (1) BCLR 106 (CC).

[198] *Besserglik* para 10.

[199] *S v Ntuli* CCT 17/95 (8 December 1995), now cited as 1996 (1) SA 1207 (CC); 1996 (1) BCLR 141 (CC).

[200] *Steyn v The State* CCT 19/00 (29 November 2000) paras 25 and 26.

[201] *Supra* paras 15–16.

[202] *Supra* para 17.

And this is how section 305 goes in turn:

Notwithstanding anything to the contrary in any law contained, no person who has been convicted by a lower court of an offence, and is undergoing imprisonment for that or any other offence, shall be entitled to prosecute in person any proceedings for the review of the proceedings relating to such conviction unless a judge of the provincial or local division having jurisdiction has certified that there are reasonable grounds for review.

A condition of the same nature therefore governs every appeal that is noted by a prisoner against his or her conviction or sentence.

(5) Ntuli wrote a letter to the authorities, an informal one protesting at the outcome of his trial. The letter was forwarded to the Witwatersrand Local Division of the Supreme Court since the matter fell within its jurisdiction. There Cloete J considered the complaint in chambers. Taking the course usually followed in such a situation, he treated the letter as both a notice of appeal and an application for a judge's certificate. He then wrote a short judgment, saying that he saw:

... no prospect whatever of an appeal court interfering with either the convictions or the sentences.

(12) ... It does not follow in my opinion that, if leave to appeal is a condition compatible with section 25(3)(h), the same must necessarily go for judges' certificates. For the similarities between the two mechanisms are accompanied by a difference important enough, as I view it, to distinguish the one from the other.

(15) Judges' certificates do not fall within a comparable framework. Nor indeed is any procedure prescribed for use when they are sought. The lack of statutory control fashions a pattern with no clear design. It marks the communication from the prisoner which sets the proceedings in motion. He or she has usually composed that, either alone or with the help of some imprisoned sea lawyer. The typical product of such efforts, a product familiar to all with experience of it and hardly surprising in view of its source, is a rambling and incoherent commentary on the trial which misses points that matter, takes ones that do not, and scarcely enlightens the judge about any. The only impressions of the case which the judge gains at the start are those derived from the reasons given by the magistrate for the conviction and the sentence. And they will remain sole impressions unless the record is procured and read. The pattern is noticed again when we look next at calls for the record or their absence. No uniform practice prevails there. Some judges obtain the record habitually, once the case is not the sort where the information already available satisfies them that a certificate should be granted straight away. Others do so rarely, being content by and large to rely rather on the magistrate's account of the trial. The refusal of a certificate on that footing worries one. Those judges who do not read the record will have no means of knowing whether the evidence substantiated the findings made by the magistrate on the credibility of witnesses and other factual issues. They will not learn of any procedural irregularities that may have marred the trial. Nothing dispels their ignorance on those scores. Nothing alerts them to flaws in the magistrate's findings or conduct of the proceedings which are hidden for the time being but the record may in due course reveal. No petition prepared by counsel is there to guide them in that direction. Nor is the possible presence of such defects likely to have been mentioned either by the prisoner or even by the magistrate, the one oblivious to the true character of the features in question, the other failing to attribute any such character to them

[16] The scheme, one therefore sees, is unsystematic and works in a haphazard way. It exposes the process to the real danger that appeals which deserve to be heard are stifled because their merits never attract judicial attention .

[17] The requirement that a judge's certificate has to be obtained obviously operates, in each case hit by it, as a restriction on the full access to the Supreme Court which is enjoyed by those who are free to prosecute their similar appeals to finality and usable for the determina-

tion of the appeals themselves. That is not, however, the end of the matter. The question which we must answer is this. Does a prisoner seeking a certificate exercise his or her constitutional right 'to have recourse by way of appeal or review to a higher court' in that very application, by means of that very application, and irrespective of its result? Does the requirement itself cater sufficiently, in other words, for such 'recourse by way of appeal or review'? That phrase sounds rather vague. But the minimum that it envisages and implies, I believe, is the opportunity for an adequate reappraisal of every case and an informed decision on it. The statute makes no provision for that opportunity. Nor does it ensure that certificates will never be refused without it. So applications for them do not amount to exercises of the constitutional right. And no other occasion for its exercise can arise once a certificate has been refused. The requirement is therefore incompatible with section 25(3)(h).

A person who applies for leave to appeal against a conviction or sentence has the burden of satisfying the court on a balance of probabilities that there are reasonable prospects of success. The test of reasonable prospects of success is a lower burden than deciding whether or not the appeal would succeed.[203] The application may be made orally at the conclusion of the trial, or it may be made through a written application for leave to appeal within the periods prescribed in the Criminal Procedure Act. There is a no right to have an application for leave to appeal heard in public.[204] There is also no right for an accused to be present at the appeals process.[205] Where leave to appeal is denied, there is no requirement for a judge to furnish reasons.[206]

S v Rens
CCT 1/95, now cited as 1996 (2)
BCLR 155 (CC); 1996 (1)
SALR 1218 (CC)
(notes omitted)

[MADALA J]: (4) The applicant was charged with and convicted of abduction and of attempted murder, and received a suspended sentence and a fine in respect of the first charge and ten years' imprisonment on the second. He then sought to appeal against the conviction on both counts as well as against the sentence imposed on the charge of attempted murder. For purposes of this judgment it is not necessary for me to deal with the grounds on which the application for leave to appeal was based, or with any arguments advanced in favour of or against the application. Suffice it to say that Rose-Innes J came to the conclusion that there was no reasonable prospect of another court reversing the conviction or interfering with the sentence of imprisonment. He accordingly would have refused the application for leave to appeal but for the constitutional issue in respect of which he had no jurisdiction.

(5) Section 25(3)(h) forms part of Chapter Three of the Constitution which sets out the entrenched fundamental rights and freedoms It provides:

25(3) Every accused person shall have the right to a fair trial, which shall include the right –
  (h) to have recourse by way of appeal or review to a higher court than the court of first instance.

It was contended on behalf of the applicant, in the Court *a quo*, that this section afforded him

---

[203] *Rens* para 7.
[204] *Per* Chaskalson P in *Pennington* para 48.
[205] *Supra* para 47.
[206] *Mphahlele v The First National Bank of South Africa Limited* CCT 23/98 (2 December 1999) para 12, now cited as 2000 (1) SA 879 (CC); 2000 (1) BCLR 106 (CC).

an automatic right to appeal, and that, therefore, the provisions of section 316(1)(b) of the Act were unconstitutional in that they were repugnant to and in conflict with section 25(3)(h). If this submission is correct, it means that a person convicted in the superior courts does not require leave in order to appeal to a higher court than the court of first instance.

(7) Applications for leave to appeal are governed by Section 316 of the Act. A person who has been convicted by a superior court may apply for leave to appeal against such conviction and/or sentence, and must satisfy the court, on a balance of probabilities, that there are reasonable prospects of success. Such application may be made orally at the end of the trial by the accused or by the accused's legal representative to the presiding judge. Alternatively, the accused person may submit a written application for leave to appeal within a prescribed period. The procedure allows for condonation of late applications in appropriate circumstances. The test of reasonable prospects of success on appeal is lower than that which is applied in deciding whether the appeal ought to succeed or not. If the trial judge refuses the application for leave to appeal, Section 316(6) provides that the accused may petition the Chief Justice. I shall deal with this procedure later. The underlying purpose of these requirements is to protect the appeal court – either the Appellate Division or the full court of the provincial or local division – against the burden of having to deal with appeals in which there are no prospects of success.

(19) It was contended by Mr *Charters* that any procedure that requires leave to appeal to be obtained from the court *a quo* would be inconsistent with Section 25(3)(h). In this regard it was argued that the procedure prescribed by Section 316 of the Criminal Procedure Act offends against the provisions of Section 25(3)(h), firstly, because it requires the trial judge to pronounce on prospects of success on appeal against his or her own judgment, and secondly because the petition procedure does not involve a full hearing with a comprehensive

traversing of the facts of the case in the court *a quo*.

(20) There is no substance in the first submission. The trial judge is not required to say that the judgment is wrong; the test is simply that another court may reasonably come to a different conclusion. If leave is refused section 316(6) of the Act allows the accused, whose application for leave to appeal has been refused by the trial judge, to make use of the petition procedure. In so doing it allows the accused to approach a higher court. The question that has to be decided is whether this constitutes a resort to a higher court by way of appeal or review within the meaning of section 25(3)(h) of the Constitution, and if so, whether the prescribed procedures are consistent with the requirements of fairness implicit in section 25(3)(h).

(21) It was contended on behalf of the applicant that only a reassessment of the issues based on full oral argument would serve to meet the requirements of the right contemplated by section 25(3)(h). I cannot agree with this submission . . . .

[24] It is true that the re-assessment of the case usually lacks full oral argument or a full re-hearing of the matter, but this does not in itself mean that the procedure is not fair, or that it does not constitute resort to a higher court within the meaning of section 25(3)(h). In *Monnell and Morris v United Kingdom*, the European Court of Human Rights held that an application for leave to appeal did not necessarily call for the hearing of oral argument at a public hearing or the personal appearance of the accused before the higher court, and that an accused who had been denied leave to appeal without such a hearing, could not contend for that reason alone that there had been a denial of the right to a fair and public hearing by an independent tribunal. The trial had been conducted in public and this was sufficient in the circumstances to meet the requirements of the Charter. There are indeed other jurisdictions in which oral argument in connection with appeals or leave to appeal is not allowed, or where it is curtailed to some extent.

Double jeopardy

Section 35(3)*(m)* of the Constitution prohibits a person being tried for a second time (double jeopardy) for an offence of which the accused was previously acquitted. Article 14(7) of the Civil Covenant and Protocol 7 to the European Convention prohibit double jeopardy. This is also provided for in the Criminal Procedure Act. Under the Act, the avoidance of double jeopardy only applies if the accused was tried by a competent court and acquitted on merits.

Conviction under ex-*post facto* laws

Section 35(3)(l) of the Constitution prohibits ex-*post facto* laws – a person cannot be convicted for an offence that was not illegal at the time. Section 35(3)*(n)* provides a right to benefit from the least severe of the prescribed punishments, if the prescribed punishment has been changed between the time of the offence and sentencing.

Administrative fairness

Section 33 of the Constitution provides:

> **Just administrative action**
> 33 (1) Everyone has the right to administrative action that is lawful, reasonable and procedurally fair.
> (2) Everyone whose rights have been adversely affected by administrative action has the right to be given written reasons.
> (3) National legislation must be enacted to give effect to these rights, and must –

> (a) provide for the review of administrative action by a court or, where appropriate, an independent and impartial tribunal;
> (b) impose a duty on the state to give effect to the rights in subsections (1) and (2); and
> (c) promote an efficient administration.

Section 33 of the Constitution imposes a requirement that rights of due process be accorded to all administrative proceedings even beyond the criminal justice system. This discussion will only present an overview of the salient aspects of fair administrative process as a complete overview of this properly belongs within the scope of administrative law.

The section was not self-executing and required national legislation for implementation of administrative fairness to be adopted within three years.[207] The interim Constitution contained a transitional provision,[208] dealing with administrative justice (taken from s 24 of the interim Constitution). The transitional provision was to be used until the envisaged national legislation in s 33(3) was adopted. If the legislation was not adopted within three years, the administrative-law provisions in the Constitution would have stood on their own and s 33(3) would have lapsed.[209]

There are three salient aspects to s 33. First, it requires that every person have the right to lawful administrative action. Secondly, that there should be procedural fairness in administrative action, and thirdly, written reasons be provided where administrative action affects the rights and interests of that person.

In determining whether administrative fairness

---

[207] The legislation, namely, the Promotion of Administrative Justice Act 3 of 2000 has since been adopted.

[208] See Schedule 6, s 23(2)*(b)*. Section 33(1) and (2) must be regarded to read as follows:
'Every person has the right to–
  (a) lawful administrative action where any of their rights or interests is affected or threatened;
  (b) procedurally fair administrative action where any of their rights or legitimate expectations is affected or threatened;
  (c) be furnished with reasons in writing for administrative action which affects any of their rights or interests unless the reasons for that action have been made public; and
  (d) administrative action which is justifiable in relation to the reasons given for it where any of their rights is affected or threatened.'
  (3) Sections 32(2) and 33(3) of the new Constitution lapse if the legislation envisaged in those sections, respectively, is not enacted within three years of the date the new Constitution took effect.

[209] In terms of Schedule 6 of s 23(3) of the Constitution.

is required, the process must be of an administrative nature in which a decision has binding consequences. In *Bernstein*,[210] the applicants argued that ss 417 and 418 of the Companies Act which required the applicants to answer questions concerning the operations of a company in liquidation, violated their right to fair administrative action.[211] The applicants further argued that they should be afforded fair administrative fairness including reasons, in writing, for administrative action affecting their rights or interests.[212] The majority, *per* Ackermann J, stated that they found difficulty in characterizing the enquiry as administrative in nature.[213] The questioning under the two provisions in the Companies Act was aimed at gathering information to aid in the liquidation process, and not directed towards making decisions binding on others.[214] Therefore, the applicants were not owed administrative fairness.

Similarly, in *The President and Others v South African Rugby Football Union*,[215] the Constitutional Court held that the appointment of a commission of enquiry by the president is not an administrative action. Therefore, the respondents were not entitled to the procedural fairness requirements under s 33 of the Constitution.[216] The nature of the power being exercised will determine whether the conduct is 'administrative action'.[217] For example, executive functions such as the development of policy and the initiating of legislation are not administrative action.[218] The

setting up of a commission of enquiry is meant to assist the president in obtaining information and advice so that he or she may better formulate policy. The subject matter and exercise of that power is not administrative in nature.[219]

The transitional provision in the Constitution was phrased very broadly and required procedural fairness in administrative action where a person's rights or interests are affected or threatened.[220] It also required administrative fairness when a person's legitimate expectations are affected or threatened.[221] The Administrative Justice Act provides that '[a]dministrative action which materially and adversely affects the rights or legitimate expectations of any person must be procedurally fair'.[222] It remains to be seen how 'interests' or 'legitimate expectations' will be interpreted. It is hoped that the lawmakers and the courts will proceed cautiously and restrict administrative action to situations where a person has a claim of entitlement and not a want of entitlement. A legitimate expectation should mean a real stake based on a legitimate claim of entitlement.[223] An 'expectation' of a claim is not a unilateral claim.[224]

The entitlement could arise from a statute, contract or an agreement upon which one party relies.[225] In *Premier, Province of Mpumalanga and Another v Executive Committee of the Association of Governing Bodies of State-Aided Schools: Eastern Transvaal*,[226] the Constitutional Court, *per* O'Regan J, held that a situation can

---

[210] *Bernstein.*

[211] *Supra* para 93.

[212] *Supra.*

[213] *Supra* para 96.

[214] *Supra* para 97.

[215] CCT 16/98 (4 June 1999) now cited as 1999 (7) BCLR 725 (CC); 1999 (4) SA 147 (CC) (*SARFU 1*).

[216] *Supra* paras 34 and 127.

[217] *Supra* para 141.

[218] *Supra* para 142.

[219] *Supra* para 147.

[220] Schedule 6 s 23*(b)(a)*. The same limits were contained in s 24*(a)* of the interim Constitution.

[221] Schedule 6, s 23*(b)(b)*.

[222] Section 3(1) of the Promotion of Administrative Justice Act.

[223] *Board of Regents of State Colleges v Roth* 408 US 564, 577 (1972).

[224] *Supra.*

[225] *Supra*, 408 US at 577–578.

[226] *Premier, Province of Mpumalanga and Another v Executive Committee of the Association of Governing Bodies of State-Aided Schools: Eastern Transvaal* CCT 10/98 (2 December 1998), now cited as 1999 (2) SA 91 (CC); 1999 (2) BCLR 151 (CC).

arise where a person has an expectation of some substantive benefit, or an expectation of some procedural safeguard.[227] Once a person has a legitimate expectation, the Constitution requires that person be granted procedural fairness if there is to be any administrative action which may affect or threaten that right.[228] In this case, the provincial government had made a representation that state-aided tuition, boarding, and transport bursaries would be paid to private schools. The respondent had a legitimate expectation that the bursaries would be honoured for the academic year of 1995. Based on this expectation, the respondent had drawn up its budget for 1995. In the middle of 1995, the provincial government decided to terminate bursary payments. The Constitutional Court held that the provincial government had a right to terminate the bursaries if it provided reasonable notice.[229] In this instance, it was not reasonable 'to terminate the payment of the bursaries with effect from a date more than month before the date' of the notice. Moreover, if there was to be a termination of a legitimate expectation, procedural fairness requires that the affected party be allowed an opportunity to make representations to the decision-maker.[230] The right to make representations should also include the right to challenge facts or evidence used in the decision-making.[231]

A person is entitled to an explanation only when they are entitled to a legal benefit. In *Roth*, the respondent was hired at Wisconsin State University for one year as an assistant faculty member without tenure. After one year he was not rehired and no explanation was given. Roth argued that he was owed an explanation. The United States Supreme Court held that whether Roth had an interest in the position is not based on whether he wants the position. Instead, it depends on whether he had a legitimate claim of entitlement to the benefit of the position.[232] Roth did not have a valid claim of entitlement because the contract under which he was employed was specific in mentioning that his employment would terminate after a specific date.[233] If the contract stated that he would be rehired based on satisfactory performance, this would create a legitimate expectation of an entitlement.[234] Under these circumstances, the aggrieved party would be entitled to some procedure to safeguard his or her interest in the position.[235]

As mentioned previously, the kinds of safeguard required to comply with fair administrative procedure are essentially matters which fall within the ambit of administrative law. To a great extent, it would also depend on the circumstances of the case[236] and the rights involved.[237] As a minimum, the following should be adhered to: previously declared rules,[238] and a neutral decision-maker, who is neither biased against the individual, nor has a personal interest in the outcome.[239] As s 33(2) provides, the individual being deprived of

---

[227] *Supra* para 36.

[228] *Supra*.

[229] *Supra* para 38.

[230] *Supra* para 41.

[231] See the decision of the German Constitutional Court of 24 July, 1963 [1965] 17 BVerfGE 86 quoted in Cappelletti & Cohen 264–6.

[232] *Roth* at 577.

[233] *Supra* at 578.

[234] *Perry v Sandermann* 408 US 593, 601–603 (1972).

[235] *Supra*.

[236] Section 3(2) of the Promotion of Administrative Justice Act. *Janse van Rensberg and Another v Minister of Trade and Industry and Another* CCT 13/99 (29 September 2000) para 24.

[237] See *The President of the Republic of South Africa and Others v South African Rugby Football Union and Others* CCT 6/98 (10 September 1999) para 219, now cited as 1999 (10) BCLR 1059 (CC); 2000 (1) SA 1 (CC) (*SARFU 3*); Chaskalson P in *Transvaal Agricultural Union v Minister of Land Affairs and the Commission on Restitution of Land Rights* CCT 21/96 (18 November 1996) para 30, now cited as 1997 (2) SA 621 (CC); 1996 (12) BCLR 1573 (CC). Michael Asimov 'Towards a South African Administrative Justice Act' (1997) 3 *Michigan Journal of Race and Law* 1, 9–10.

[238] *Van Rensberg* para 25. John E Nowak and Roland E Rotunda *Constitutional Law* St Paul: West, 5th edition, 1995, 511.

[239] See Nowak & Rotunda 511; see also *Gibson v Berryhill* 411 US 564, 579 (1973).

some right must be given a written statement of reasons.[240]

When a deprivation arises through a change in a statute or regulation, publication of the statute or regulation should be sufficient. More complex is the issue of a hearing. In *Transvaal Agricultural Union*, Chaskalson P stated that it is well established that when a law empowers a public official or body to act in a way prejudicing the rights of an individual, the affected party has a right to be heard either before the decision is taken, or shortly thereafter.[241] The reality is that the right to a hearing cannot be granted in every instance.[242] In *Eldridge*, the state agency decided to terminate disability benefits to Eldridge and informed him of its decision. Eldridge was given an opportunity to respond to the decision. Despite his response, the benefits were still terminated. Eldridge argued that the procedure used by the government agency did not afford him an oral hearing, and that therefore his due process rights were violated.[243] The United States Supreme Court rejected Eldridge's arguments that he was owed an oral hearing. The Court held that due process is not a technical concept with a fixed content unrelated to time, place, and circumstances.[244] Due process requires consideration of three factors: first, the private interest at stake; secondly, the risk of deprivation of such interest through error because of the procedures used; and thirdly, the state's interest, including the function involved and the fiscal and administrative burdens that the additional procedural requirement would entail.[245] The latter consideration is particularly important for South Africa because if every decision taken at a lower level by bureaucrats could be subject to a hearing, large resources would be necessary.[246] Where power is delegated to a subordinate agency, the exercise of delegated power must be in terms of clear standards.[247]

The following extract discusses this:

'Towards a South African Administrative Justice Act'[248]

The rights to administrative justice entrenched in section 33 are precious and vital to democratic government. Nevertheless, their uncertainty and overbreadth present serious practical problems.

First, the section 33 rights will have little impact until they have been construed in a wide variety of contexts and actually applied in practice ... . The right to administrative justice will make little difference to ordinary people until it is implemented by detailed legislation backed up by detailed procedural regulations that tell every unit of government exactly what must be done to take administrative action.

Second, South Africa must devote enormous resources to overcoming the effects of apartheid and neglect on the vast majority of its population. By any analysis the available resources fall far short of what is needed for such a task. It is neither practical nor sensible to use limited resources to overproceduralize government action.

...

Section 33(1) provides that everyone has the right to administrative action that is procedurally fair. At a minimum, the procedural fairness clause entrenches the preconstitutional rules of natural justice, including a fair hearing (the 'audi principle') and an impartial decision-maker. The right to an administrative hearing is of paramount importance because it compels a deci-

---

[240] See also s 3(2)*(b)*(1) of the Promotion of Administrative Justice Act.

[241] *Transvaal Agricultural Union* para 24.

[242] *Matthews v Eldridge* 424 US 319, 324 (1976).

[243] *Supra* at 325. *Permanent Secretary of the Department of Education Eastern Cape and Another v Ed-U College (PE) (Section 21) Inc* CCT 26/00 (29 November 2000) para 22.

[244] *Supra* para 334.

[245] *Supra* para 335.

[246] Michael Asimov (1997) 3 *Michigan Journal of Race and Law* 19.

[247] This is discussed fully in chapter 6. See *Dawood* paras 52–54.

[248] Asimov, 9–10 (reprinted with permission).

sion-maker to see and hear the affected individual and confront that person's side of the dispute. As a result, a hearing may well forestall an incorrect decision or cause an agency to exercise discretion more favorably to the individual than it otherwise would have done. Beyond these utilitarian benefits, a hearing is important because it safeguards an individual's dignitary interest, treating that person as a human being rather than as a computer file. Nevertheless, section 33(1)'s broadly stated right to procedural fairness will present numerous difficulties.

. . .

The interim Constitution, like the common law, limited the right to procedural fairness to administrative action that affected or threatened a person's 'rights or legitimate expectations'. Since this limiting language does not appear in section 33(1), it seems at least possible that procedural fairness would apply to cases of administrative action affecting a person's 'interests' rather than merely that person's 'rights or legitimate expectations'.

. . .

Certainly, South African law of the future will contain a variety of benefactory programs; such programs will be seen as conferring rights or legitimate expectations. Consequently, any reduction or termination in benefits and probably any denial of admission to the program will trigger a requirement that the agency act with procedural fairness under section 33(1).

Moreover, section 33(1) opens the field of mass justice to the requirement of procedural fairness. All the unpleasant interactions between local officials and ordinary people relating to public housing, provision of utility service, prisons, schools, or public hospitals should trigger rights to procedural fairness. Consider prisons, for example: decisions to transfer a prisoner from a minimum to a maximum security prison or to subject a prisoner to denial of privileges because of misconduct might trigger a right to some kind of appropriate procedure under section 33(1). A good case can be made that such proceduralization would be

good for the prison system which is widely viewed as lawless and capricious. Still, proceduralization would entail a significant diversion of the system's resources.

. . . Realistically, it is not possible to grant hearings or other sorts of compulsory processes in connection with the vast bulk of low-level discretionary decisions that street-level bureaucrats make every day.

Defining which government/private interactions trigger the right to procedural fairness is only the first step in applying section 33(1). The second step is to spell out the content of the right – what process must be provided and when must it be provided. Obviously, the question of what qualifies as an appropriate procedure is wholly contextual. There must be sufficient notice of the proposed government action and an appropriate opportunity to respond to the government's contentions. Depending on the context, this may entail the presentation of witnesses, interpreters, confrontation, and cross examination. There must be an impartial decision-maker and a decision based exclusively on the record, but this generalization conceals numerous complex issues relating to separation of functions, ex parte contact, biases of various sorts, and what qualifies as record exclusivity.

Often, the question of timing is critical. Generally, notice and opportunity to be heard should be provided before the government acts, but the timing issue can be resolved only after a careful balancing of interests. A hearing provided after government has acted often comes too late to repair the damage caused by that action. In welfare cases, for example, a mistaken termination of benefits can leave the beneficiary and her family homeless. Yet in many situations, a right to a prior hearing can be very costly to the particular regulatory or benefactory program. In welfare programs, for example, if government must provide a hearing before it terminates benefits, unqualified recipients have an incentive to demand a hearing to keep the checks coming. The result is that many more hearings will be demanded, often leading to significant backlogs, and substantial amounts will be paid to unqualified beneficiaries before the hearing occurs. Therefore, in some circumstances, a balancing of interests may suggest that government need only provide rudimentary procedure before it acts and then a full hearing later. In American due process law, this has become the typical pattern in connection with termination of government disability benefits or discharge of civil service employees.

There are countless issues wrapped up in the question of procedural fairness. It is all very well to say that the right to natural justice is flexible and that the agency is given substantial deference in deciding appropriate procedures, but a court must still decide whether the omission of one or more trial-type elements rendered the particular procedure unfair.

Section 33(2) guarantees a written statement of reasons when a person's rights have been adversely affected by administrative action. The value of the written reasons provision is clear. A decision-maker who is compelled to give reasons must at least consider the appropriate factors and produce an apparently justified decision. A statement of reasons helps persons disappointed by the decision evaluate whether to seek judicial review, and it facilitates judicial scrutiny of the decision. Since there was no right under preconstitutional law to a written statement of reasons, the courts will have little guidance when they confront disputes under section 33(2). For example, courts must decide which 'rights' arising out of mass justice situations are sufficiently important to merit a written (as opposed to an oral) reasons statement, whether a request for reasons must first be made, and how detailed the statement must be. Would check marks on a form that furnishes a list of possible reasons suffice? Must an agency explain a purely discretionary call such as the decision to suspend a licence for one year rather than issue a warning to the licensee?

Preconstitutional South African administrative law imposed no procedural requirements on agencies engaged in generalized action such as rulemaking. Section 33(1) and (2) may well require procedural fairness and written statements of reasons in the case of generalized agency action, because the term 'administrative action' is used in connection with all four rights spelled out in section 33. The words 'administrative action' were intended to describe as wide a range of administrative behavior as possible. Certainly the requirements of lawfulness and reasonableness in section 33 apply to action of generalized applicability. Unless the words 'administrative action' have a different meaning with respect to the different rights to administrative justice, it should follow that the right to procedural fairness and reason statements apply to generalized as well as particularized administrative action.

And this is as it should be. Regulations create law that agencies and courts must follow. A regulation may reduce a civil servant's compensation, disqualify a welfare beneficiary, or compel a discharger to install pollution control equipment or an employer to install safety devices. In such cases, the regulation seriously affects the economic interests of the person affected, even though it has not yet been applied to that person individually.

If the requirements of procedural fairness and statement of reasons apply to rulemaking, the Constitutional Court must decide exactly what these provisions demand. The Court might decide that the Constitution requires something like the traditional notice and comment rulemaking process under the US Administrative Procedure Act (APA). Procedural fairness under section 33(1) would entail notice to the public of what an agency proposes and the opportunity to furnish written comments on the issues. Section 33(2) would be satisfied by a discussion of the purpose of the rule and why alternatives suggested by the public were rejected.

12

Freedom of expression, assembly, association, and religion

Freedom of expression

Section 16(1) of the Constitution provides for freedom of expression which includes that of the press,[1] to receive or impart information,[2] of artistic creativity,[3] and of academic and research.[4] Article 19 of the Universal Declaration provides everyone has the right of free opinion and expression, also including the right to receive and impart information through any media. Protection for freedom of expression and the right to receive information are contained in art 19(2) of the Civil Covenant; art 9 of the African Charter; art 10 of the European Convention, and art 13 of the American Convention.

Justifications for freedom of expression

There are several important justifications for freedom of speech. Some are of instrumental value whereas others are of intrinsic value.[5] Freedom of speech serves as an important instrument for the functioning of the political process.[6] In *South African National Defence Union*, O'Regan J stated that democracy requires that individuals in society be able to hear, form, and freely express their opinions on a wide range of matters.[7] In *Whitney*,[8] Brandies J provided the essence of this view by stating that 'freedom to think as you will and to speak as you think are means indispensable to the discovery and spread of political truth'.[9] Similarly, in *Keegstra*, McLachlin J alluded to the political process rationale by stating that freedom of expression is 'instrumental in promoting the free flow of ideas essential to political democracy and the functioning of democratic institutions'.[10] Freedom of expression is aslo important in the search for

---

[1] Section 16(1)*(a)* of the Constitution.
[2] Section 16(1)*(b)*.
[3] Section 16(1)*(c)*.
[4] Section 16(1)*(d)*.
[5] *Case and Another v Minister of Safety and Security; Curtis v Minister of Safety and Security* 1995 (5) BCLR 609 (CC); 1996 (3) SA 617 (CC) 622 para 27.
[6] *South African National Defence Union v Minister Defence and Another* CCT 27/98 (26 May 1999) para 7, now cited as 1999 (6) BCLR 615 (CC); 1999 (4) SA 469 (CC).
[7] *Supra.*
[8] *Whitney v California* 274 US 357 (1927).
[9] *Supra* at 375.
[10] *R v Keegstra* 3 SCR 697, 61 CCC (3d) 1, 184 [1990]. See also the decision of Mason CJ of the High Court of Australia in *Australian Capital Television Pty Ltd v Commonwealth of Australia* (1992) 177 CLR 106 High Court of Australia.

truth.[11] There is no guarantee that the information conveyed contains the truth. However, freedom of expression, by permitting a variety of viewpoints, will better contribute in the search for the truth.[12] As McLachlin J points out in *Keegstra*, sometimes there is no one correct answer that can be verified. Freedom of expression allows a marketplace of ideas producing a more vibrant and progressive society,[13] which leads to the third important justification for freedom of expression.

Freedom of expression is intrinsically important in that it allows for the growth of the human personality,[14] a freedom allowing human beings to express and define themselves. The importance of freedom of expression to the development of the human personality was affirmed by the Constitutional Court, *per* Mokgoro J, in *Case*[15] where the Court held:

[26] It is useful to relate that reasoning to the foundational purposes for the existence of the right to freedom of expression. The most commonly cited rationale is that the search for truth is best facilitated in a free 'marketplace of ideas'. That obviously presupposes that both the supply and the demand side of the market will be unfettered. But of more relevance here than this 'marketplace' conception of the role of free speech is the consideration that freedom of speech is a *sine qua non* for every person's right to realise her or his full potential as a human being, free of the imposition of heteronomous power. Viewed in that light, the right to receive others' expressions has more than merely instrumental utility, as a predicate for the addressee's meaningful exercise of her or his own rights

of free expression. It is also foundational to each individual's empowerment to autonomous self-development.

Relationship between freedom of expression and the right to information

Section 16(1)(b) of the Constitution provides for 'freedom to receive or impart information'. Freedom of information, and freedom of expression are interrelated. Freedom of information and the right to convey that information are essential for the exercise of most other freedoms.[16] For example, if one is arbitrarily detained, without the ability to communicate the existence and unlawfulness of the detention, it would not be possible to redress the wrong.[17] The importance of the media as a vehicle in the dissemination of information is recognized in s 16(1)(a) of the Constitution.[18] By educating the public, the media contributes to the respect for human rights. However, the media does not have any special protection over other citizens.[19] For example, its members could be forced to disclose their sources, even if the information is needed in the administration of justice.[20]

In the *Spiegel* case,[21] the German Constitutional Court summarized the importance of a free press in a modern democracy. The Court stressed the importance of the availability of information to citizens, if citizens are to make informed choices.[22]

---

[11] Peter W Hogg *Constitutional Law of Canada* Scarborough: Carswell, 3rd edition, 1992, 962.

[12] *Keegstra* at 186.

[13] *Supra* at 187.

[14] Ulrich Karpen 'Freedom of Expression' in *The Constitution of The Federal Republic of Germany: Essays on the Basic Rights and Principles of the Basic Law with a Translation of the Basic Law*, edited by Ulrich Karpen. Baden-Baden: Nomos 1988, 96.

[15] See *Case* para 26.

[16] *Palko v Connecticut* 304 US 319, 327 (1937).

[17] Francisco Forrest Martin, et al *International Human Rights Law and Practice: Cases, Treaties and Materials* Cambridge: Kluwer Law International 1997, 154.

[18] Cameron J alluded to the importance of the media in *Holomisa v Argus Newspapers*, 1996 (6) BCLR 836 (W), 1996 (2) SA 588 (W) at 609.

[19] This view was adopted by Cameron J in *Holomisa*.

[20] *Branzburg v Hayes* 408 US 665, 691 (1972); *Zurcher v Stanford Daily* 436 US 547, 576 (1978).

[21] *Spiegel* case (1966) 20 BVerfGe 162, translated in Donald P Kommers *The Constitutional Jurisprudence of the Federal Republic of Germany* Durham: Duke University Press 1989, 398.

[22] Ibid.

The press plays a vital role in supplying information and orienting public debate.[23] The importance of being able to receive and impart information was affirmed by the Constitutional Court, *per* Mokgoro J, in *Case*[24] where the Court held:

[25] But my freedom of expression is impoverished indeed if it does not embrace also my right to receive, hold and consume expressions transmitted by others. Firstly, my right to express myself is severely impaired if others' rights to hear my speech are not protected. And secondly, my own right to freedom of expression includes as a necessary corollary the right to be exposed to input from others that will inform, condition and ultimately shape my own expression. Thus, a law which deprives willing persons of the right to be exposed to the expression of others gravely offends constitutionally protected freedoms both of the speaker and of the would-be recipients.

Different forms of expression

Section 16(1) speaks about freedom of the press and other media. The media could include different mediums for communication (including print), broadcasting, television, or the internet. The Constitution also speaks about 'freedom of artistic creativity'[25] and 'academic freedom and freedom of scientific research'.[26] In *Case*, the Constitutional Court, *per* Mokgoro J, stated:

[28] ... One may well ask what effective utility freedom of the press and other media would have if that freedom did not include as a corollary the right of persons to actually obtain and read newspapers, and to be exposed to other media. By the same token, the freedom of artistic creativity would be seriously undermined if it did not encompass the right of individuals to unhampered access to sources of artistic and intellectual inspiration, including (or, one may say, especially), those expressions which convey sentiments that are threatened with suppression by the State or with marginalization in civil society, because they are deemed dangerous, offensive, subversive, or irrelevant.

It is arguable that permissible forms of expression are sufficiently wide to include many forms of symbolic speech. The United States Supreme Court has recognized the wide ambit of expression including flag burning,[27] and the wearing of armbands.[28] In *Johnson*, the respondent was charged with violation of a Texas statute that prohibited the desecration of the flag. Several people testified that they found the action seriously offensive.[29] The Court held that the burning of the flag was a political expression. The Court further held that the government could not 'prohibit the expression of an idea simply because society finds the idea itself offensive or disagreeable ...'.[30] In *Tinker v Des Moines*, the Court upheld the right of school children to wear armbands as a protest against the Vietnam War.[31] In *Village of Skokie v National Socialist Party of America*, the American Nazi Party protested the prohibition against their members marching through the village displaying swastikas.[32] The Illinois Supreme Court held that the use of a swastika was a symbolic form of speech that could not be constitutionally enjoined.[33]

---

[23] Ibid. See also Karpen 96.

[24] See *Case* para 25.

[25] Section 16(1)*(c)* of the Constitution.

[26] Section 16(1)*(d)*.

[27] *Texas v Johnson* 491 US 397 (1989).

[28] See eg *Tinker v Des Moines* 393 US 503 (1969); *Village of Skokie v National Socialist Party of America* 373 NE 2d 21 (1978).

[29] *Johnson*, 491 US at 399.

[30] *Supra* at 414.

[31] *Tinkler*, at 505.

[32] See *Village of Skokie*, 373 NE 2d 21 (1978).

[33] *Johnson*, 491 US at 24. (Under the SA Constitution, such expressions of speech would likely be prohibited under hate speech, which is considered in the discussion below).

Regulating of expression

Expression like most rights in the Bill of Rights can be regulated. For example, broadcasting may be regulated, if there is insufficient space on the airwaves. Here, the regulation is not for content but for technical reasons Similarly, regulations can be passed requiring the media to carry different viewpoints.[34] In *Red Lion*, the United States Supreme Court ruled that the state could require a broadcaster to present different views and voices that are representative of the community.[35] Similarly, the German Constitutional Court held in the *Third Television* case that the legislature can adopt substantive organizational and procedural provisions to ensure the diversity of existing opinions in broadcasting.[36]

Restriction on expression

Generally, courts frown upon any prior restraints on speech.[37] Otherwise, the press and the exercise of speech would be beholden to the government.[38] There are, however, exceptional situations where content may be restricted. For example, national security concerns could prohibit the disclosure of some information. During emergency or times of war, freedom of speech may be limited against disclosures that compromise the war effort.[39]

Under the Constitution, limitations on freedom of expression have to be justified under the limitations clause.[40] It is unclear whether every limitation on expression has to be justified under the limitations clause. For example, should a limitation on speech in a public library be justified by the limitations clause? It is arguable that not every governmental restriction on freedom of

assembly, association, or expression has to satisfy the limitations clause. For example, a restriction on assembling and protesting in a court building or a public library should not have to satisfy the limitations clause. In *Committee for the Commonwealth of Canada v Canada*, the Supreme Court of Canada was faced with a governmental regulation which restricted the distribution of political literature in an airport. The Court split over whether all governmental restrictions of expression on public property had to satisfy the limitations clause.[41] Justice L'Heureux-Dube held that all limitations on assembly in a public place had to satisfy the limitations clause of the Constitution.[42] Lamar CJ would not subject rules that further the principal function of the public place and restrict access to public property to the limitations clause.[43] If the expression is compatible with the public place, then any restriction would have to satisfy the limitations clause.[44] The Chief Justice further stated:

... no one would suggest that an individual could, under the aegis of freedom of expression, shout a political message of some kind in the Library of Parliament or any other library. This form of expression in such a context would be incompatible with the fundamental purpose of the place, which essentially requires silence. When an individual undertakes to communicate in a public place, he or she must consider the function which that place must fulfill and adjust his or her means of communicating so that the expression is not an impediment to that function. To refer again to the example of a library, it is likely that wearing a T-shirt bearing a political message would be a form of expression consistent with the intended purpose of such a place.

---

[34] *Red Lion Broadcasting Co v Federal Communication Commission* 395 US 367, 389 (1969).
[35] *Supra.*
[36] *Third Television* case (1981) 57 BVerfGe 295, translated in Kommers 411.
[37] *New York Times v Sullivan* 376 US 254, 276 (1964). John E Nowak and Roland E Rotunda *Constitutional Law* St Paul: West, 5th edition, 1995, 1024–8.
[38] Prior restraint shuts off speech before it occurs. See Thomas Emerson *The System of Freedom of Expression* New York: Random House 1970, 506.
[39] See eg JM Kelly, et al *The Irish Constitution* Dublin: Butterworths, 3rd edition, 1994, 926; Nowak & Rotunda 1009.
[40] *Per* Mokgoro J in *Case* paras 21, 37.
[41] *Committee for the Commonwealth of Canada v Canada* 1 SCR 139 [1991].
[42] *Supra* at 238–239.
[43] *Supra* at 395.
[44] *Supra.*

Lamar CJ held there was nothing incompatible with the airport's function if political literature was distributed in the airport, and therefore held the limitation invalid.[45] There is much merit to the view of Lamar CJ that the limitations clause only comes into play if there is a restriction on expression where the expression is incompatible with the function of the place.

Time, manner, and place restrictions

There are time, manner, and place restrictions on freedom of speech.[46] For example, one cannot falsely shout 'fire' in a theatre.[47] Similarly, it would not be practical to allow a demonstration in a court building or on a public highway. In the above instances, freedom of speech has to be balanced against other interests such as public security or traffic considerations. Similarly, certain forms of expression deemed to be for mature audiences can be regulated against exposure to children.[48] The time, manner, and place restrictions must, however, be content-neutral and, therefore, may not regulate ideas.[49] In other words, a law that regulates whether posters can be put up in the train station or in public buildings, or which restricts speech and assembly at a busy intersection all have an impact on speech. However, the laws are not directed at curtailing the content of speech, nor the freedom of individuals to express themselves, if the law regulates all speech in an even manner. The regulation is directed at the place and manner of the expression in order to protect other legitimate uses of the property.

Hate and violent speech

Speech may sometimes be employed to incite others to violence. It may also be used to insult racial, religious and other groups. The Constitution permits the restriction of freedom of expression where expression incites harm, for example, war propaganda;[50] incitement of imminent violence;[51] or advocacy of hatred based on race, ethnicity, gender, or religion.[52] While restriction on freedom of expression is subject to the limitations clause, speech performed as propaganda for war, or as incitement of violence or hate speech do not have constitutional protection. Once the conduct comes under the above categories, such speech can arguably be outlawed without recourse under the limitations clause, since the Constitution, in s 16, states that freedom of expression does not extend to such actions.[53]

International human rights law recognizes similar instances for circumscribing freedom of expression. Article 20 of the Civil Covenant, prohibits propaganda of war and requires the prohibition of hate speech by providing 'any advocacy of national, racial or religious hatred that constitutes incitement to discrimination, hostility or violence'. Article 4 of the International Convention on the Elimination of All Forms of Racial Discrimination[54] also requires states to make it an offence to engage in hate speech. The American Convention outlaws hate speech in art 13(5).

Does s 16(2)(b) of the Constitution require the incitement of imminent violence to cause physical harm against another, or does it include conduct such as burning of a group's religious text, thereby evoking a violent reaction from persons in the affected group? Also, does incitement to cause harm under s 16(2)(c) require incitement to cause physical harm against a person or group, or does it include face-to-face insults which cause psycholo-

---

[45] *Supra* at 397.

[46] Nowak & Rotunda 1142.

[47] *Per* Holmes J in *Schenck v United States* 249 US 47, 52 (1919).

[48] *FCC v Pacifica Foundation*, 438 US 726, 751 (1978). (Here the Court upheld the prohibition of broadcasting certain material in the early afternoon, when children were likely to be exposed.)

[49] *United States v Grace* 461 US 171, 177 (1983).

[50] Section 16(2)(a) of the Constitution.

[51] Section 16(2)(b).

[52] Section 16(2)(3).

[53] Hate speech is further proscribed under s 10 of the Promotion of Equality and Prevention of Unfair Discrimination Act 4 of 2000.

[54] 660 UNTS, (1966) 195 ILM 352.

gical harm? If the phrase requires physical harm, must the physical harm be imminent? Ultimately, limitations on hate speech will be determined by the Court's interpretation of the advocacy of these phrases. The United States' approach reflects one perspective that places utmost reliance on the right of individuals to express themselves in a maximum fashion. It is only exceptional situations that will permit the curtailing of violent or hate speech. Other jurisdictions such as Canada and Germany, and the international human rights norms such as the Racial Discrimination Convention, reflect a competing approach that places restrictions on mere utterances of hate speech or where an expression is meant to evoke violence. Under the latter approach, the outlawing of hate speech and speech espousing violence is more important than the right of individuals to express themselves.

Ultimately, the Constitutional Court will have to determine what criteria to employ in determining whether the speech is part of 'propaganda for war' or 'incitement of imminent violence'. In an early case, the United States Supreme Court held that advocacy of harmful results, such as the violent overthrow of the government, may be punished.[55] Over the years, the Court has imposed more exacting criteria before permitting punishment, requiring that the words that are used 'in such circumstances and are of such a nature as to create a clear and present danger that they will bring about the substantive evils …'.[56] If the government cannot prevent the state structure from violent attack, it is unlikely that other freedoms can survive.[57] Under *Schenck*, not only must the speech be harmful, but the government must show that the speech, in the context it was used, created a danger, and that the likelihood of harm was present and substantial.[58] Under earlier

formulations, the presence of a clear harm is not the same as success or probability of success.[59] Under earlier formulations, mere conspiracy to advocate a violent overthrow of the government was sufficient even though the danger was remote.[60] More recently, the Court required more than mere advocacy of violence. In *Brandenberg*, the Court held that advocacy of violence was protected so long as there was no 'incitement to imminent lawless action'.[61] Under *Brandenberg*, the state may not punish advocacy of violent overthrow of the government 'except where such advocacy is directed to inciting or producing imminent lawless action and is likely to incite or produce such action'.[62]

Similarly with hate speech, the early approach of the United States Supreme Court in *Chaplinsky*, upheld the conviction of the defendant where defendant's utterances disparaged certain groups based on the notion of 'fighting words'.[63] In *Chaplinsky*, the defendant was a Jehovah's Witness who was charged with using insulting epithets against other religions. The defendant was charged under a statute that outlawed the use of insulting language. The Court upheld the conviction and held that defendant's statements were 'fighting words', which are words 'which by their very utterance inflict injury or tend to incite an immediate breach of the peace'.[64] The Court went on to state that such words have 'no essential part of any exposition of ideas, and are of such slight social value as a step to truth that any benefit that may be derived from them is clearly outweighed by the social interest in order and morality'.[65] Subsequent Court decisions have limited the scope of *Chaplinsky* to words tending to cause an actual breach of the peace. In *Gooding v Wilson*, the Court overturned the conviction of

---

[55] See eg *Abrams v United States* 205 US 616 (1919); *Gitlow v New York* 268 US 652 (1925); *Whitney v California* 274 US 357 (1927).
[56] Per Holmes J in *Schenck v United States* 249 US 47, 52 (1919).
[57] *Dennis v United States* 341 US 494, 509 (1951).
[58] *Schenck*, 249 US at 52.
[59] *Dennis*, 341 US at 509.
[60] *Supra*.
[61] *Brandenberg v Ohio* 395 US 444, 447 (1969).
[62] *Supra*.
[63] *Chaplinsky v New Hampshire* 315 US 568 (1942).
[64] *Supra* at 571–572.
[65] *Supra* at 571.

an anti-war protester who shouted at a police: '[W]hite son of a bitch, I'll kill you'.[66] The Court held that the utterance did not evoke an immediate response from the target.[67] Similarly, in *Terminiello v Chicago*,[68] the Court overturned a conviction for disturbing the peace by Terminiello, who in a public address denounced Jews and blacks. The Court held that the function of speech was to invite dispute, unrest and dissatisfaction, or stir people to anger.[69] It might be that speech may unsettle people, but the alternative would be standardization of ideas which the Court found unacceptable.[70]

With respect to hate speech, the approach in the United States under recent decisions is to drastically reduce the scope of government intervention. In *Collin v Smith*,[71] and *Village of Skokie v Nationalist Socialist Party*,[72] the Seventh Circuit and the Illinois Supreme Court refused to enjoin a neo-Nazi party from marching through a Jewish suburb in Illinois wearing Nazi uniforms and displaying Nazi emblems and flags. Many of the residents of the suburb were Holocaust survivors. The march by the neo-Nazis, together with their Nazi paraphernalia, was liable to cause anguish to many of the people in the area. Despite the abhorrent nature of their speech, the Seventh Circuit and the Illinois Supreme Court held that the neo-Nazis were entitled to exercise their free speech.[73] This restrictive interpretation to control hate speech was affirmed by the United States Supreme Court in *RAV v City of St Paul*,[74] where the Court invalidated a city ordinance that outlawed hate speech in the form of placing on public, or private property, symbols, objects, characterizations, or graffiti (such as a burning cross or a Nazi swastika), 'which one knows or has reasonable grounds to know arouses anger, alarm, and resentment in others on the basis of race, color, religion, or gender'.[75] The Court ruled that the statute drew impermissible content-based distinctions by outlawing expressions of hate based on just a few categories.[76]

Under international human rights norms, such as art 4 of the Racial Discrimination Convention, parties commit themselves to 'condemn all propaganda and all organizations which are based on ideas or theories of superiority or one race or group of persons of one colour or ethnic origin, or which attempt to justify or promote racial hatred …'. Article 4(a) further provides that state parties shall declare it an offence punishable by law to disseminate 'ideas based on racial superiority'. The article also prohibits acts of violence or incitement to cause such acts against any race or group of persons. Under art 4(4), state parties are under an obligation to declare illegal any organization which promotes and incites racial discrimination. Under the Racial Discrimination Convention, states have an obligation to intervene to eradicate utterances of hate speech. In contrast, hate speech in the United States is permitted to continue except under very exceptional circumstances. The approaches to hate speech adopted by the Supreme Court of Canada, the Constitutional Court of Germany and the European Court of Justice are more consistent with international human rights norms. In *R v Keegstra*, the Supreme Court of Canada upheld the hate speech conviction of the defendant, a schoolteacher who made anti-semitic statements in class.[77] In a number of decisions, the German Constitutional Court has proscribed

---

[66] *Gooding v Wilson* 405 US 518, 519 (1971).
[67] *Supra* at 528.
[68] *Terminiello v Chicago* 337 US 1 (1949).
[69] *Supra* at 4.
[70] *Supra*.
[71] *Collin v Smith* 578 F2d 1197 (7th Cir 1978)(cert denied).
[72] *Village of Skokie v Nationalist Socialist Party* 69 Ill2d 605 (1978).
[73] *Collin*, 578 F2d at 1210; *Skokie*, 605 US at 615.
[74] *RAV v City of Paul* 505 US 377 (1992).
[75] *Supra* at 380–388.
[76] *Supra*.
[77] *R v Keegstra* 3 SCR 697, 755–758 (1990).

parties that espouse hate speech, or the overthrow of the democratic state.[78]

The European Court of Justice has adopted an even more lenient standard in allowing the state to act against speech which offends groups. In *Otto-Preminger Institute v Austria*,[79] the European Court of Human Rights affirmed the right of the Austrian government to seize a film that portrayed Roman-Catholic and other religious beliefs in a disparaging way. The European Court held that the Austrian government had the right to ensure the peaceful enjoyment of beliefs under art 9 of the European Convention on Human Rights. The state can act against methods employed by some which have the effect of inhibiting the freedom of beliefs.[80] The screening of the film was sufficiently public to cause offence to the religious beliefs of others. It was, therefore, appropriate for the state to seize the film.[81] In *Wingrove v United Kingdom*,[82] the European Court of Human Rights affirmed the right of the British government to prevent distribution of a film that portrayed certain religious figures in a sexual setting.[83]

It is arguable that the incitement requirements under s 16 of the Constitution do not adopt the rugged individualistic approach to free speech, where that speech rises to the level of hate speech, or speech which incites violence, or offends the sacred beliefs of others. Under international human rights norms, including the Canadian and German approaches, the probability of violence or lawless action is not a requirement for the suppression of speech. Under apartheid, the media, schools, and other institutions, incessantly impressed on the country the inferiority of people of colour. This undoubtedly has affected and continues to affect large groups of people. International human-rights law recognizes that hate speech causes psychological harm on target groups. Moreover, hate speech allows for the reinforcement of racist notions leading to further racism. Given the legacy of racism, affirmative steps have to be taken to eradicate racist and hate speech.

Obscene speech

Speech may be limited based on its obscenity or harmful effects.[84] Pornography and obscenity are two of the more difficult areas to define. Justice Stewart, although unable to define obscenity, noted 'I know it when I see it'.[85] In *Roth v United States*, Brennan J stated that obscenity is 'utterly without redeeming social importance'.[86] Justice Brennan further held that an expression is obscene if 'to the average person, applying contemporary community standards, the dominant theme of the material taken as a whole appeals to prurient interests'.[87] In *Miller v California*,[88] the United States Supreme Court was faced with a challenge to a California law that prohibited the mailing of unsolicited obscene material. The Supreme Court, *per* Burger CJ, provided a three-part test for identifying obscenity: first, whether the average person, applying contemporary community standards would find that the work, taken as a whole, appeals to the prurient interest; secondly, whether the work depicts or describes, in a patently offensive way, sexual conduct specifically defined by the applicable state law, and thirdly whether the work, taken as a whole, lacks serious literary, artistic, political, or scientific value.[89]

---

[78] See the *Socialist Reich Party* case (1952) 2 BVerfGe 1, translated in Kommers 223–6. See also the *Communist Party* case (1963) 5 BverfGE 4, quoted in Kommers 221.

[79] *Otto-Perminger Institute v Austria* (1994) 295-A ECHR (ser A).

[80] *Supra* para 47.

[81] *Supra* para 56.

[82] (1996) ECHR (ser A).

[83] *Otto-Perminger Institute v Austria* para 58.

[84] *JT Publishing (Pty) Ltd and Another v Minister of Safety and Security and Others* CCT 14/95 (21 November 1996) para 2, now cited as 1997 (3) SA 514 (CC); 1996 (12) BCLR 1599 (CC).

[85] *Roth v United States* 354 US 476, 484 (1957).

[86] *Supra* at 484.

[87] *Supra* at 489.

[88] *Miller v California* 413 US 15 (1973).

[89] *Supra* at 24.

More recently, feminists have opposed pornography because it exploits and degrades women as sexual objects.[90] The Constitutional Court, *per* Mokgoro J, endorsed the harm-based model in *Case*.[91] In *Case*, the Court was faced with a challenge to s 2 of the Indecent or Obscene Photographic Matter Act,[92] which makes it an offence to possess indecent or obscene photographic material. The Court held that the right to possess sexually expressive material is protected under the Constitution.[93] However, the Court also held that harmful, sexually expressive material may be regulated. Mokgoro J held that '[I]t is common cause in this matter that certain categories of pornographic material may constitutionally be subjected to state regulation. Most commonly singled out as legitimately subject to such regulation was pornography involving the exploitation of women and children, in contexts of violence, degradation and victimization'.[94] The Court nevertheless invalidated the statute because of its over breadth, nature which could not be cut down.[95] In order for legislation to pass muster, the Court admonished the legislature to provide precise guidelines to regulate harmful sexually explicit material, as opposed to painting all sexually explicit material as obscene.[96] In their separate concurring opinions, Didcott and Madala JJ reiterated that possession of pornographic material by consenting adults, in the privacy of their homes may not generally be prohibited.[97] However, there is no constitutional protection for obscene material such as child pornography. In *JT Publishing*,[98] the Constitutional Court in a unanimous decision, *per* Didcott J, once again reiterated that censorship of material that is egregious could be restricted in the public interest, where it could be shown to have a pernicious effect.[99]

The Supreme Court of Canada has also endorsed the harm-based approach. In *R v Butler*,[100] the Court was faced with a challenge to a statute that criminalized the selling and possession of obscene material. The Court majority, *per* Sopinka J, divided pornography into three categories: the first depicting explicit sex with violence; the second depicting explicit sex without violence but which subjects people to treatment that is degrading or dehumanizing; and the third depicting explicit sex without violence that is neither degrading nor dehumanizing.[101] The first two categories would constitute the exploitation of sex, whereas the third category will not usually qualify as the exploitation of sex.[102] The majority recognized the difficulty in ascertaining harm. In this case, the majority reasoned that there was considerable evidence that pornography caused harm to women and to society as a whole. This led the Court to uphold the conviction of the defendant.[103]

Speech and libel

The exercise of speech brings up potential lawsuits for common-law libel. Traditionally, courts in South Africa adopted a very restrictive approach to freedom of the press, and held the press strictly liable for defamatory speech.[104] With the Constitution's guarantee of free speech, it is question-

---

90 Catherine A MacKinnon 'Not a Moral Issue' (1984) 2 *Yale Law and Policy Review* 291.
91 *Case* para 52.
92 Act 37 of 1967, as amended.
93 *Case* para 35.
94 *Supra* para 52.
95 *Supra* paras 61–62.
96 *Supra* para 63.
97 *Supra* paras 91, 105 (Didcott and Madala JJ concurring).
98 See *JT Publishing (Pty) Ltd.*
99 *Supra* para 2.
100 *R v Butler* 1 SCR 452, 70 CCC (3d) 129 (1992).
101 *Supra* at 470.
102 *Supra* at 471.
103 *Supra* at 498.
104 *Pakendorf en Andere v De Flamingh* 1982 (3) SA 146 (A).

able whether this restrictive approach would be adhered to by the Constitutional Court.[105] The widest protection for free speech from libel is provided in the approach of the United States Supreme Court in *New York Times Co v Sullivan*.[106] In *New York Times*, the Court was confronted with a challenge to an Alabama statute which made it libelous for a publication to injure a person's reputation. The *New York Times* had published an advertisement which criticized the treatment of black people in Montgomery by the Alabama police. The advertisement contained a number of minor factual errors. Sullivan was a commissioner in Montgomery, Alabama. He claimed that the advertisement libelled him under the Alabama statute. The majority of the justices held that libel actions cannot serve as a deterrent for freedom of speech where the speech relates to a public official.[107] The press should not be held responsible for erroneous statements which were honestly made.[108] In order for the defamation action to succeed, the plaintiff must show that the defendant had made the statement with malice.[109] In order for there to be malice, the statement must be made with reckless disregard, meaning that at the time the statement was made, there were serious doubts as to the accuracy of the publication.[110]

The German Constitutional Court similarly accords protection to speech unless the speech uttered is known to be incorrect.[111] For example, where the media quotes someone inaccurately, and the misquotation impairs a person's reputation, the media could be held liable.[112] A misquotation has to be distinguished from an interpretation communicated to a reader who is able to discern that what is communicated is an opinion.[113] Therefore, where a politician in a campaign speech called another politician a Nazi, the German Constitutional Court held that there was no actionable wrong, since the statement offered was a value judgement.[114] Value judgements even though caustic and exaggerated are meant to convince others, and to protect the speaker's opinion.[115] The protection is greater where the speech relates to public figure.[116]

Underlying the United States Supreme Court's reasoning in *New York Times*, and the German Constitutional Court's decision in the *Campaign Slur* case is the idea that libel laws cannot serve as a deterrent to honest criticism of public figures. The greater protection accorded to speech where it relates to a public figure is also recognized by the European Court of Human Rights.[117] In *Lingens*, an Austrian journalist published two articles in which he accused the Austrian premier of being sympathetic to Nazism. The chancellor brought a defamation action against the reporter. The European Court of Human Rights held that the limits of acceptable criticism and value judgements are wide when it comes to politicians.[118] The action against Lingens constituted a violation of his freedom of speech.[119]

The definition of a 'public figure' poses a problem. In later cases, the United States Supreme Court has expanded the protection of speech to include coverage of non-public officials where their conduct is of public interest. For example,

---

[105] See Cameron J in *Holomisa*.

[106] *New York Times v Sullivan* 376 US 254 (1964).

[107] *Supra* at 264.

[108] *Supra* at 278.

[109] *Supra* at 279.

[110] *Supra* at 280.

[111] *Boll* case (1980) 54 BVerfGE 208 in Kommers 420.

[112] Op cit 420.

[113] Op cit 421–2.

[114] *Campaign Slur* case (1982) 61 BVerfGE 1 in Kommers 389–90.

[115] Op cit 390.

[116] Op cit 391.

[117] *Lingens v Austria* (1986) 103 ECHR (ser A).

[118] *Supra* at 42.

[119] *Supra* at 47.

reporting on a newsworthy item where a private individual is thrust into the public limelight would be protected.[120] The Hill family were held hostage in their home by three escaped convicts This incident was covered by the national media. Some years later, *Life* magazine printed a story on the incident that included some falsehoods. The Court held that the same standard of recklessness was applicable to false reports where the matter is of public interest.[121]

However, these same standards do not apply where the person involved is not a public figure and the reporting involves something which is not of public interest.[122] The South African Constitution provides for protection of everyone's privacy and dignity. There are legitimate privacy interests which the media has to respect, especially where the individual is not a public figure, or where his or her activity is not of public interest. In the *Lebach* case, the German Constitutional Court held that the right 'to the free development of one's personality and human dignity secure for everyone an autonomous sphere in which to shape one's private life by developing and protecting one's individuality. This includes the right to remain alone, to be oneself within this sphere, and to exclude the intrusion of or the inspection by others'.[123] The Court further held that the public interest cannot justify 'an infringement of the personal sphere'.[124]

The contours of speech in relation to libel and other personal intrusions will have to be defined by the lower courts and the Constitutional Court. In arriving at the proper interpretation of libel, there are a variety of approaches to consider, which the Constitutional Court recognized in *Du Plessis and Others v De Klerk and Another*.[125] The majority, *per* Kentridge AJ, held:

[58] Our jurisdiction under section 98 is not suited to the exposition of principles of private law. I have made this

point in relation to the Matrimonial Property Act 1984. The common law of defamation illustrates this point even more clearly. We are asked to find that the law currently applied by the courts is inconsistent with section 15 of the Constitution. Let that be so. What regime is to replace the existing law? In the development of the common law of defamation a multitude of choices is available. The Defendants, it would seem from their written arguments, are attracted by the far-reaching revision of the common law adopted by the United States Supreme Court in *New York Times Co v Sullivan*, in terms of which a "public person", however grossly defamed in relation to his or her public conduct, can only succeed in an action for defamation by proving that the defamatory statement was false and, what is more, by proving with "convincing clarity" that it was made by the defendant with knowledge of its falsity or with reckless disregard whether it was false or not. I would suggest that before adopting this rule as part of our law, a court would have to consider among other things the sharp criticisms of that rule both academic and judicial, within the United States, and its rejection by the Supreme Court of Canada in *Hill v Church of Scientology of Toronto*. Presumably a court would also wish to consider the rule adopted by the High Court of Australia in the interests of freedom of speech, namely that in an action for defamation by a person engaged in politics or government it is a defense for the defendant to prove that he honestly and reasonably believed in the truth of what he published.

The Australian rule introduces the concept of a duty to exercise care into the law of defamation. A South African court would have to consider the appropriateness of introducing such an element into a delict of intent (*injuria*) in which hitherto *culpa* has not been an element. It would also doubtless consider whether the Australian rule was not right in placing the burden of proof on the defendant rather than the plaintiff – in that respect among others refusing to follow *New York Times v Sullivan*. At least equally important would be the

---

[120] *Time Inc v Hill* 385 US 374 (1967).

[121] *Supra* at 387–388.

[122] *Gertz v Robert Welch, Inc* 418 US 323, 348 (1974).

[123] *Lebach* case (1973) 35 BVerfGE 202 in Kommers 414–15.

[124] *Op cit* 415.

[125] *Du Plessis and Others v De Klerk and Others CCT 8/95 (15 May 1996) para 58, now cited as 1996 (5) BCLR 658 (CC); 1996 (3) SA 850 (CC).*

consideration of the development of the South African law of defamation. Unlike some of the other rights embodied in Chapter 3, freedom of speech and of the press is not a newly created right. When not suppressed or restricted by statute it was emphatically endorsed and vindicated in many judgments of South African courts. Any law of defamation is a restriction on freedom of speech in the interest of other rights thought worthy of protection. More particularly, in cases of defamation, courts have tried to strike a balance between the protection of reputation and the right of free expression. Presumably, too, a court would wish to take account of the fact that the Constitution, like that of Germany but unlike that of the United States, expressly recognizes the right to dignity and to personal privacy, and might find guidance in the German cases to which have been referred to, as well as in the American cases. On the other hand, a court might also wish to consider the desirability of cutting down the concept of a defamatory statement in the interests of freer political criticism. It may similarly consider whether the rule that the press and the broadcasting media, unlike other litigants, cannot avail themselves of the defence of absence of *animus injuriandi* ought to be varied in the light of the values embodied in s 15 of the Constitution. Those values might also require the development of a broader concept of the public interest, entailing a reconsideration of the *Neethling* case. For present purposes, the point is that these are not choices which this Court can or ought to make. They are choices which require consideration perhaps on a case-by-case basis by the common-law courts. The common law, it is often said, is developed on incremental lines

Certainly it has not been developed by the process of 'striking down'.

Lower courts have adopted different approaches to the question of libel.[126] In *Holomisa v Argus Newspapers*, and in *Gardener v Whitaker*, the Court recognized that the traditional rules of defamation were impacted by the new Constitution.[127] In *Holomisa*, Cameron J rejected the broad American approach to free speech in *New York Times v Sullivan*,[128] in favour of the Australian High Court approach.[129] Under this approach, the Court accords protection to free speech in the political arena, even though the speech may be false or defamatory.[130] Plaintiff would only have an action if able to prove that the publisher acted unreasonably.[131] In *Bogoshi*, the Supreme Court, *per* Eloff JP, upheld the traditional rules of defamation. Eloff JP concluded that the traditional rule of liability without fault, of newspapers for publication of defamatory matter was unchanged by the new Constitution.[132] On appeal, the Supreme Court of Appeal emphatically rejected Eloff J's approach in *National Media Limited and Others v Bogoshi*.[133] The Court, *per* Hefer J, held that, 'the common good is best served by the free flow of information and the task of the media in the process, it must be clear that strict liability cannot be defended and should have been rejected in *Pakendorf*. Much has been written about the 'chilling' effect of defamation actions but nothing can be more chilling than the prospect of being mulcted in damages for even the slightest error'.[134] The Court further held that publication of false and defamatory material would be protected if found to be reasonable and in the public interest.[135] This protection is not accorded

---

[126] See *Bogoshi v National Media Ltd and Others* 1996 (3) SA 78 (W); *Potgieter en 'n Ander v Kilian* 1995 (11) BCLR 1498 (N); 1996 (2) SA 276 (N); *Holomisa v Argus Newspapers Ltd* 1996 (6) BCLR 836 (W); 1996 (2) SA 588 (W); *Gardener v Whitaker* 1994 (5) BCLR 19 (E); 1995 (2) SA 672 (E).

[127] See Cameron J in *Holomisa* paras 588, 603. Froneman J in *Gardener v Whitaker*

[128] See generally, *Holomisa* para 613.

[129] *Theophanous v Herald & Weekly Times Ltd* (1994) 124 ALR 1 (HC).

[130] See generally *Holomisa* paras 616–617.

[131] *Supra* para 617.

[132] See *Bogoshi v National Media* para 13.

[133] *National Media Ltd and Others v Bogoshi* 1998 (4) SA 1196 (W).

[134] *Supra* para 1210.

[135] See *National Media Ltd and Others v Bogoshi*.

to the press when it publishes information with the knowledge that it was untruthful. [136]

Advertising

Advertising is also a form of speech meant to educate or persuade the audience. [137] Historically, severe limitations have been placed on the advertising by certain sectors such as attorneys and medical practitioners. The validity of these limitations are open to question in light of the guarantee of free speech. [138] There are legitimate governmental interests in preventing misleading and irresponsible advertising. In *Case*, the Constitutional Court, *per* Mokgoro J in dicta, warned against limitations such as a blanket ban on advertising, which is overbroad in its scope, and might violate the freedom of speech. [139] On the other hand, there are legitimate governmental interests in protecting consumers against misleading expressions on matters such as quality, price, and accuracy. [140]

Case and Another v Minister of Safety and Security; Curtis v Minister of Safety and Security
1996 (5) BCLR (CC)
(notes omitted)

[50] Overbreadth analysis is properly conducted in the course of application of the limitations clause. To determine whether a law is overbroad, a court must consider the means used, (that is, the law itself, properly interpreted), in relation to its constitutionally legitimate underlying objectives. If the impact of the law is not proportionate with such objectives, that law may be deemed overbroad. The Canadian case of *Royal College of Dental Surgeons of Ontario v Rocket*, offers an example of this analysis in the free expression setting. The Canadian Supreme Court struck down as over broad a ban on dentists' advertising, using an analysis conducted under the Canadian Charter's limitation clause. The Court held that while there was no doubt a legitimate government interest in preventing irresponsible and misleading advertising by dentists, the blanket ban challenged also struck at legitimate advertising, with the result that the test of proportionality between the effect of the legislative measure and its purpose was not met: The aims of promoting professionalism and preventing irresponsible and misleading advertising ... do not require the exclusion of much of the speech which is prohibited by [the statute].'

Contempt of court

Historically, there was an aura of infallibility created around the South African judiciary. [141] Under apartheid, it was not common to scrutinize the pattern of judicial appointments or to publicly comment on judicial appointments. [142] Criticisms of the members of the South African judiciary and examination of their backgrounds and patterns of judgments was something not looked upon favourably, and could be subject to contempt-of-court proceedings, if it was felt that the dignity of the court was impaired. Also, comments which questioned the integrity of the judiciary and the administration of justice were punishable by contempt-of-court proceedings. [143] The threat of ever looming contempt proceedings constrains

---

[136] *Supra*

[137] See eg *Rocket v Royal College of Dental Surgeons* 1 SCR 232 (1990); *Virginia State Board of Pharmacy v Virginia Citizens Consumer Council* 425 US 748 (1976).

[138] See *Bates v Bar of Arizona* 433 US 350 (1977) striking down the ban on advertising by attorneys.

[139] Mokgoro J in *Case* para 49.

[140] Hogg 970. See also *Zauderer v Office of Disciplinary Counsel* 471 US 626 (1985), where the SC upheld the disciplining of an attorney who provided misleading information.

[141] See Hugh Corder *Judges at Work: The Role and Attitudes of the South African Appellate Judiciary, 1910–1950* Cape Town: Juta & Co 1984, 2.

[142] See Sydney Kentridge 'Telling the Truth about Law' (1982) 99 *South African Law Journal* 652.

[143] See the contempt proceedings against the late Professor Barend Nan Niekerk, *S v Van Niekerk* 1970 (3) SA 654 (T); *S v Van Niekerk* 1972 (3) SA 711 (A).

honest criticism of the judiciary or investigation of the judicial function. The impartiality of the judiciary and their ability to mediate between the interests of different sectors cannot just be assumed and protected. Freedom of speech should permit questions regarding the appointment of the judiciary, the background of the judiciary, they way they arrive at decisions and how a judge is perceived to be fulfilling his or her functions. In the *Prison Privacy* case, the German Constitution Court had to rule on whether the defendant's reference to the judges as 'prodigious clowns' who if they had any conscience, would not be able to sleep peacefully at night, amounted to a gross insult against the judiciary.[144] The German Constitutional Court held that the defendant had a right to express his opinion even though it was inaccurate or intemperate.[145] Similarly, in the Irish case of *Attorney General v O'Ryan*,[146] Maguire P stated that:

judges and others in authority are open to criticism. Fair and free criticism is allowable and should be welcomed. We must safeguard the rights of the citizens and the rights of newspaper editors. The last thing I would wish is that citizens should feel that the courts are too ready to use against legitimate criticism this powerful weapon of attachment for contempt of court, I would rather err on the other side.

In *Executive Council of the Western Cape Legislature and Others v The President of the Republic of South Africa and Others*, the Constitutional Court, *per* Chaskalson P, criticized the third applicant who questioned the impartiality of the Constitutional Court.[147] The president stated that '[a]ll

citizens are free to attend court, to listen to proceedings, to comment on them and on the judgments, even vigorously, where it is appropriate to do so, but it is irresponsible to make unfounded statements which impugn the integrity of the Court'.[148] In the past, it would be contempt of court to comment on apending case in such a way as to influence the court on how to rule. It seems nonsensicl to say that jurists and public opinions, rendered before a case is heard, would likely sway a judge on how to decide the case. In *Bridges v California*, Black J held that there must be a 'clear and present danger 'that a petitioner's statements criticizing a pending court proceeding would bring about an evil which requires curtailment of the freedom of speech.[149]

Freedom of assembly and association

Essence of the right to assemble and associate

Section 18 of the Constitution guarantees freedom of association. Section 17 guarantees freedom of assembly, demonstration, petition and picket. Freedom of assembly is also protected in terms of the right to form trade unions under s 23(2), and the right to form employee organizations under s 23(3).[150] Freedom of assembly and association is also protected under s 15 – the freedom of religion clause.[151]

Freedom of assembly and association are contained in arts 17 and 20 of the Universal Declaration; arts 21 and 22 of the Civil Covenant;

---

[144] Kommers 395.

[145] Ibid.

[146] [1946] IR 70 (1945), quoted in Kelly 933.

[147] *Executive Council of the Western Cape Legislature and Others v The President of the Republic of South Africa and Others* CCT 27/95 (22 September 1995), now cited as 1995 (10) BCLR 1289 (CC); 1995 (4) SA 877 (CC).

[148] *Executive Council of the Western Cape Legislature* para 122

[149] *Bridges v California* 314 US 252, 270 (1941).

[150] The constitutionalization of labour rights, particularly the right to fair labour practices, is a unique feature of the SA Constitution and is likely to have wide-ranging consequences on the development of labour law. Dennis Davis, et al *Fundamental Rights in the Constitution: Commentary and Cases: A Commentary on Chapter 3 on Fundamental Rights of the 1993 Constitution and Chapter 2 of the 1996 Constitution* Cape Town: Juta & Co 1997, 212. For an overview of the right to labour, see Davis 232–6. See also Johan de Waal, et al *The Bill of Rights Handbook* Cape Town: Juta & Co, 2nd edition, 1999, 379–88.

[151] Freedom of religion is dealt with below.

arts 10 and 11 of the African Charter; arts 15 and 16 of the American Convention; art 11 of the European Convention; art 5 of the Racial Discrimination Convention, and art 7 of CEDAW. The right to formation of labour organizations is recognized in art 21(4) of the Universal Declaration; art 22(3) of the Civil and Political Covenant, and art 11(1) of the European Convention. The right to fair labour practices, although unique in a Constitution, is recognized under international law. For example, art 23(1) of the Universal Declaration provides a right to just and favorable conditions of work. Similarly, in art 15, the African Charter provides a right to work under just and equitable conditions.

The right to assemble, demonstrate, and associate derives from the right to influence public opinion through speech and assembly.[152] Assembly and association, although sometimes listed as one right (as in the Universal Declaration), are two distinct rights. For example, one does not have to be a member of an organization to assemble or petition the government.[153] Similarly, one can be a member of an organization without ever attending a meeting.[154] However, there is often an important group element which involves meeting with others, discussing, and organizing to further common objectives. The ability to get together, organize, and take collective action is important in modern democracies where most political action and labour organization is taken through groups, organizations or political parties.[155] Often, the ability to influence

the government and population depends on organization.[156] Without the ability to associate, political, religious and worker organization, to name a few, would not be possible. Consequently, there can be no adverse consequences flowing from exercising the right to associate.[157] In *NAACP v Alabama ex rel Patterson*, the United States Supreme Court invalidated an order by the State of Alabama requiring a civil rights organization to provide a list of all its members. The Court ruled that the order constituted an invasion of the members' right to associate.[158] The Court further held that privacy in group associations may prove indispensable to the preservation of freedom of association especially where the organization espouses dissident beliefs.[159]

Restrictions on freedom of assembly and association

Generally, there is a wide degree of freedom to assemble and associate in public places. The right to assemble and associate is not, however, absolute. As in freedom of expression, the right to assemble and associate is subject to reasonable regulations including time, manner, and place restrictions, along with public safety, and other important interests.[160] It seems reasonable for the government to restrict the circumstances under which people can assemble on a busy road. Important governmental objectives might validly preclude certain officials of the state from being involved in

---

[152] Kommers 395.

[153] John P Humphrey 'Political and Related Rights' in *Human Rights in International Law: Legal and Policy Issues*, edited by Theodor Meron. Oxford: Clarendon Press 1984, 188.

[154] Ibid.

[155] Ivor Jennings *Law and the Constitution* London: University of London Press, 5th edition, 1977, 277.

[156] The right to associate as a fundamental right can be traced back to the French Revolution of 1789. Its importance to democracy was emphasized in a landmark decision by the French Constitutional Court in 1971. For a discussion of the 1971 'Decision on Freedom of Association', see Vicki C Jackson and Mark V Tushnet *Comparative Constitutional Law* New York: Foundation Press 1999, 558–60.

[157] *NAACP v Alabama ex rel Patterson* 357 US 449, 461 (1958).

[158] *Supra*.

[159] *Supra* at 462.

[160] For US cases on time, manner and place restrictions, see eg *Police Department of Chicago v Mosley* 408 US 92 (1972); see also *Madison Joint School District v Wisconsin Employment Relations Commission* 429 US 167 (1976). For an overview of Indian cases on permissible controls on public meetings, see M Hidayatullah *Constitutional Law of India* New Delhi: Bar Council of India Trust 1984, 326–8.

political parties.[161] In India, under Indian doctrine, the restrictions necessary to pass muster, have to be found to be reasonable in pursuit of some other important objective.[162]

Under the South African Constitution, as in the Canadian Constitution, restrictions on freedom of assembly and association have to satisfy the limitations clause. It is debatable whether every governmental restriction on freedom of assembly and association, as with freedom of expression, have to satisfy the limitations clause. For example, should a restriction on assembling and protesting in a court building or a public library have to satisfy the limitations clause? In *Committee for the Commonwealth of Canada v Canada*, the Supreme Court of Canada was divided over this issue. Lamer CJ would not subject rules, which further the principal function of the public place and restrict access to public property, to the limitations clause.[163] If the expression is compatible with the public place, then any restriction would have to satisfy the limitations clause.[164] As in freedom of expression, there is much merit to the view of Lamar CJ that the limitations clause only comes into play if there is a restriction on assembly and association where the expression or association is compatible with the function of the place. For example, the government should not have to justify prohibitions on assembly and picketing on a busy highway using the limitations clause.

The United States Supreme Court, in evaluating the validity of the restriction, considers the nature of the forum in terms of three categories.[165] In the first category, any limitations on speech in places which have, by tradition, been devoted to debate such as parks and streets, would be subject to the highest scrutiny, and will only pass muster if the state is able to establish that the restriction serves a compelling government interest.[166] In the second category are places which the state has dedicated as sites for communication such as auditoriums, meeting places, and theatres. Restrictions on assembly in such places would also be subject to the strictest scrutiny.[167] The third category includes places which are not, by tradition, designed for public communication. Here the state can impose reasonable limitations to maintain the forum for its intended purposes so long as the restriction is not designed to suppress speech.[168]

It is unlikely that the Constitution provides a general right to assemble on private property without the owner's consent. Assembling on private property without the owner's consent would most likely constitute trespass under the common law.

As in hate and violent speech, the state can proscribe organizations that seek to overthrow the government through violent and illegal means, as well as organizations which espouse hate speech. The Racial Convention requires state parties 'to declare illegal and prohibit organizations ... which promote and incite racial discrimination'.[169] The German Basic Law expressly prohibits organizations that seek to impair or abolish the basic democratic order.[170] The outlawing of such organizations is to be determined by the German Constitutional Court.[171] The German Constitutional Court has exercised its powers under the

---

[161] The Constitution has a host of provisions which require the impartiality of certain officials including the Public Protector and the public service. It would be valid for the lawmaker to pass legislation restricting certain categories of civil servants from involvement in political organizations and political campaigns. See *United Public Workers of America v Mitchell* 367 US 1 (1961).

[162] *United Public Workers of America* at 328.

[163] *Committee for the Commonwealth of Canada* 1 SCR 139, 395.

[164] *Supra.*

[165] *Perry Educational Association v Perry Local Educators Association* 460 US 37 (1983).

[166] *Supra* at 45.

[167] *Supra* at 45–46.

[168] *Supra* at 46.

[169] Article 4*(b)* of the Racial Discrimination Convention.

[170] Article 21(2) of the Basic Law.

[171] Article 21(2).

section to prohibit organizations that seek to do away with the democratic state.[172]

In *Scales v United States*, the United States Supreme Court upheld the conviction of the Chairman of the North Carolina and South Carolina Districts of the Communist Party, under an Act which made it an offence to belong to any 'organization which advocates the overthrow of the Government by force or violence'.[173] The Court held that advocacy to commit violence under the direction of a political party is not protected association.[174] The government has the authority to prohibit associations that further such ideas and activities.[175]

Freedom of religion

Section 15 of the South African Constitution guarantees everyone 'freedom of conscience, religion, thought, belief and opinion'. An additional layer of protection under the Constitution is provided in terms of s 31 which provides that persons belonging to a cultural, religious, or linguistic community have the right to enjoy their culture, practise their religion, and use their language with other members of their community.[176] Individuals also have the right 'to form, join and maintain cultural, religious, and linguistic associations, and other organs of civil society'.[177] The Constitution also permits legislation recognizing traditional marriages, or religious, personal, or

family law.[178] Section 15(3)(*b*) requires that recognition of traditional or religious law must be consistent with the Constitution. Therefore, if for example, traditional law allowed the abuse of women or other groups, this would be seen as unconstitutional

Freedom of religion is contained in art 18 of the Universal Declaration; art 18(1) of the Civil Covenant; art 8 of the African Charter; art 9 of the European Convention, and art 12 of the American Convention. In 1982, the UN General Assembly passed the Declaration on the Elimination of all Forms of Intolerance and of Discrimination Based on Religion or Belief.[179] The Religious Declaration affirms the right to freedom of thought, conscience, and religion.[180] There should be no coercion which impairs freedom of religion or belief.[181]

Like freedom of assembly, there is both an individual and group element in freedom of religion. Belief and opinion can be very individual and private. The concept of belief and opinion covers believers, atheists, agnostics, and the right of others to believe what their individual consciences permit.[182] Freedom of religion and belief also has a group dimension in that prayers are often exercised in community with others.[183] Consequently, s 31 guarantees the right to practise this belief in association with others. Like freedom of speech, it is a right which permits the teaching and proselytizing of others.

---

[172] *Socialist Reich Party* case (1952) 2 BVerfGE 1 selectively in Kommers *Constitutional Jurisprudence v the Federal Republic of Germany* 223–6; See also the *Communist Party* case (1963) 5 BverfGE 4 (Kommers 221); Walter F Murphy 'Excluding Political Parties: Problems for Democratic and Constitutional Theory' in *Germany and its Basic Law, Past, Present and Future: A German-American Symposium*, edited by Paul Kirchoff and Donald P Kommers Baden-Baden: Nomos 1993, 180–1.

[173] *Scales v United States* 367 US 203 (1961).

[174] *Supra* at 228–229.

[175] *Supra* at 229.

[176] Section 31(1)*(a)* of the Constitution.

[177] Section 31(1)*(b)*.

[178] Section 15(3)(1)–(ii).

[179] (1981) UNGAR 55 ('VI), (1982) 21 ILM 205 (Religious Declaration).

[180] Article 1(1) of the Religious Declaration.

[181] Article 1(2).

[182] *Kokkinakis v Greece* (1993) 260-A ECHR (ser A), (1994) 17 EHRR 397, para 31.

[183] *Supra* para 31.

Relationship between religion and the state

There are three possible approaches to the relationship between state and religion. The first is the adoption by the state of a single religion, as in the case of the Church of England in Britain, or the position of Judaism under the laws of Israel.[184] This approach elevates one religion as pre-eminent over other beliefs.

The second is a strict separation between religion and state, as exemplified by the majority approach of the United States Supreme Court in recent times, as well as that of the Japanese Supreme Court.[185] Under this approach, religion belongs exclusively within the domain of private activity. The consequence is that the state, to the maximum extent possible, should not be involved in the promotion of any religious matter. The Supreme Court of Japan has noted that 'to eliminate all ties between the State and religion, it has also been necessary to enact rules providing for the separation of religion and the state'.[186] Similarly, the United States Supreme Court perceives the United States Constitution as having 'erected a wall between church and state. That wall must be kept high and impregnable'.[187] This approach operates on the premise that the choosing of one belief results in the exclusion of people who belong to other faiths. Therefore, the state cannot set up a church, nor adopt laws which aid any religion, or prefer one religion over another.[188]

The third approach is a cooperative approach which seeks to accommodate religion in the state subject to certain conditions, namely that the state should not establish a religion, nor should there be any coercion.[189] The South African Constitution in s 15(2) (as in s 14 of the interim Constitution), permits religious observance at state, or state-aided institutions. In *Lawrence and Others v The State and Another*, the Constitutional Court was faced with an interpretation of freedom of religion under s 14 of the interim Constitution. The Court, *per* Chaskalson P, held that the Constitution does not contain an establishment clause which prevents the advancement or inhibition of religion by the state.[190] The approach to religion under the Constitution is similar to the German approach of cooperation between religion and state.[191]

Where the state aids religion, s 15(2)(b) requires that religious observance must be conducted on an equitable basis. This means that there cannot be a preference for one religion over another.[192] This is unlike the United States Constitution establishment clause,[193] which requires a separation between church and state. Where the state sanctions religious observance in state, or state-aided institutions, under s 15(2)(c), attendance at religious functions must be free and voluntary. In other words, non-coercion means that the state cannot decide what a person must believe.[194] Non-coercion provisions are contained in art 18 of the Universal Declaration; art 18(2) of the Civil Covenant, and art 12(2) of the American Convention. A proclamation of belief in God in

---

[184] The 1948 Declaration of the Establishment of Israel proclaims the establishment of a Jewish state. See Ruth Lapidoth 'Freedom of Religion and of Conscience in Israel' (1998) 47 *Catholic University Law Review* 441.

[185] *Everson v Board of Education* 330 US 1, 15 (1947). See *Kakunaga v Sekiguchi* 31 Minshu 4 at 533 (1977) (SC of Japan, Grand Bench) in Jackson & Tushnet 1190–4.

[186] Op cit 1191.

[187] Ibid.

[188] Ibid.

[189] This approach also has its supporters in the US. See eg the interpretation of Justice Rehnquist in his dissenting opinion in *Wallace v Jaffre* 472 US 98, 106 (1985); see also opinion of Kennedy J in *Allegheny County v Greater Pittsburgh ACLU* 492 US 573, 660 (1989).

[190] *S v Lawrence; S v Negal; S v Solberg* CCT 38/96; 39/96; 40/96 (6 October 1997) para 100, now cited as 1997 (10) BCLR 1348 (CC); 1997 (4) SA 1176 (CC).

[191] Cole W Durham 'General Assessment of the Basic Law: An American Overview' in *Germany and its Basic Law, Past, Present and Future: A German–American Symposium*, edited by Paul Kirchoff and Donald P Kommers Baden-Baden: Nomos 1993, 43.

[192] The requirement for equitable treatment was stressed by Chaskalson P in *S v Lawrence* para 103.

[193] As interpreted from the First Amendment to the US Constitution.

[194] The requirement for non-coercion was stressed by Chaskalson P in *Lawrence* para 103.

the Constitution does not amount to coercion. In *Certification of the Constitution of The Western Cape*, the Constitutional Court held that the reference in the preamble to the Western Cape Constitution and the Constitution of South Africa has no operative effect, nor any constitutional significance.[195] The reference to God, the Court held 'is a time honoured means of adding solemnity, used in many cultures and in a variety of contexts'.[196]

Accommodation versus coercion

The critical question is what constitutes coercion? It would be coercion for the state to force someone to behave in a particular way which goes against that individual's religious beliefs. In *Lawrence*, the Constitutional Court was faced with the question of whether a statute which prevented the third appellant from selling wine on Sundays constituted religious coercion. The appellant argued that the purpose behind the prohibition was to induce compliance with Christian beliefs, and Christian ideas of Sunday being the day of the sabbath.[197] The Court, in a plurality decision *per* Chaskalson P, held that a law which 'compels sabbatical observance of the Christian sabbath offends against the religious freedom of those who do not hold such beliefs'.[198]

The President of the Court referred to the Canadian case of *R v Big M Drug Mart*, which affirmed the position that a law which had a purely religious purpose to compel adherence to a particular belief constituted coercion.[199] The Act in question in *Lawrence* was different from the one in *Big M Drug Mart*, because the purpose of the Act in *Lawrence* was to curtail the consumption of alcohol on certain days, as opposed to compelling adherence to a particular religious belief.[200]

Therefore, Chaskalson P found that the law which prohibited the appellant from selling wine on Sunday did not constitute coercion.[201]

The plurality further held that the restriction on economic activity on Sunday, although of a religious character, also had a secular meaning. The majority of people in South Africa take off on Sunday because it is convenient to have a uniform day of rest.[202] The recognition of Sunday as a day of rest is contained in labour agreements and other business practices.[203] Chaskalson P further stated in *Lawrence* that:

[104] There may be circumstances in which endorsement of a religion or a religious belief by the state would contravene the 'freedom of religion' .... This would be the case if such endorsement has the effect of coercing persons to observe the practices of a particular religion, or of placing constraints on them in relation to the observance of their own different religion. The coercion may be direct or indirect, but it must be established to give rise to an infringement of the freedom of religion.

[105] Whatever connection there may be between the Christian religion and the restriction against grocers selling wine on Sundays at a time when their shops are open for other business, it is in my view too tenuous for the restriction to be characterized as an infringement of the freedom of religion.

O'Regan J in her dissenting opinion (concurred by Goldstone and Madala JJ), found that the prohibition of sale on Sundays was coloured by Christian beliefs. Unlike the plurality who focused on the narrow question of whether the prohibition on the selling of wine by grocers on Sundays was unconstitutional, O'Regan J looked at the totality of the provisions of the Act which prohibited the selling of wine on Sundays and on two out of twelve public holidays, all of which are associated

---

[195] *Case* para 28.
[196] *Supra.*
[197] *Lawrence* para 85.
[198] *Supra* para 89.
[199] *Supra* para 90 (*R v Big M Drug Mart Ltd* (1985) 18 DLR (4th) 321).
[200] *Supra.*
[201] *Supra* para 105.
[202] *Supra* paras 95–96.
[203] *Supra* para 96.

with Christian religious beliefs.[204] The effect of these provisions was to accord special recognition to one religion over others.[205] The Constitution requires not only non-coercion, but also equity of treatment, which meant that one religion could not be favoured over another.[206]

No doubt over time, the Constitutional Court will have to give further expression to 'coercion' and 'equitable basis'. For example is it coercion to begin school with prayer of a particular belief?[207] Moreover, is it coercion to conduct religious classes in regular schools? Is it permissible for state institutions to place religious symbols, such as a crucifix, on state property? In the *Classroom Crucifix* case, the German Constitutional Court held that the placing of a crucifix in a classroom violated the requirement for the state to be neutral in matters of religion.[208] Such icons, when displayed in a school, have a psychological impact on other children who have different beliefs.[209] To the extent that other religious groups have to be accommodated in church–state relations, what are the standards for 'equitable basis'? Courts in different jurisdictions have struggled with, and come to different conclusions on, these questions.[210] The German Constitutional Court has ruled that school prayers need not amount to coercion providing that those who wish not to participate could absent themselves.[211] Adopting and enforcing one belief would seem to be coersion.[212] In *Lawrence*, Chaskalson P stated in dicta that mandatory school prayers constitute a violation of freedom of religion.[213] The President

of the Court further stated that sometimes even voluntary prayers could constitute a violation of freedom of religion by putting pressure on children to participate. The president stated:

[103] [i]n the context of a school community and the pervasive peer pressure that is often present in such communities, voluntary school prayer could also amount to the coercion of pupils to participate in the prayers of the favoured religion. To guard against this, and at the same time to permit school prayers, ... there should be no such coercion. It is in this context that it requires the regulation of school prayers to be carried out on an equitable basis. I doubt whether this means that a school must make provision for prayers for as many denominations as there may be within the pupil body; rather it seems to me to require education authorities to allow schools to offer the prayers that may be most appropriate for a particular school, to have that decision taken in an equitable manner applicable to all schools, and to oblige them to do so in a way which does not give rise to indirect coercion of the 'non-believers'.

Unlike art 4 (2) of the Civil Convention which makes freedom of religion a non-derogable right, the Constitution does not make freedom of religion a non-derogable right. Laws directed at suppressing freedom of religion or a particular religious belief are invalid unless they can satisfy the limitations clause. As in any other law which restricts a fundamental right, a restriction on religious freedom cannot target a particular group or belief.[214]

---

[204] *Supra* para 125.

[205] *Supra* para 127.

[206] *Supra* para 128.

[207] The German Constitution Court has upheld a ban on school prayer. See German *School Prayer* case (1979) 52 BVerfGE 223. The USSC has held that school prayer violates the establishment clause. See *Engel v Vitale* 370 US 421 (1962).

[208] Case referred to in Emily Mosely 'Defining Religious Tolerance: German Policy Toward The Church of Scientology' (1997) 30 *Vanderbilt Journal of Transnational Law* 1129, 1164–6.

[209] Op cit 1166.

[210] See Patrick Macklem, et al *Constitutional Law of Canada* Toronto: Emond Montgomery Publishers 1994, 314–17; Kommers 466–77.

[211] Durham 48.

[212] *Per* Chaskalson P in *Lawrence* para 102.

[213] *Supra*.

[214] *Church of Lukumi Babalu Aye, Inc v City of Hialeh*, 508 US 520, 542 (1993). In *Church of Lukumi Babalu Aye*, the USSC invalidated a city ordinance which prohibited slaughter of animals for ritualistic purposes. The SC held that the city law was not a neutral statute directed at all slaughtering, but only directed at a particular religious group.

Defining religion

Assume someone claims an exemption to permit him or her to smoke marijuana because his or her religion requires him or her to do so. This brings up the question: what is religion? At the heart of religion is faith, doctrine, belief, or disbelief which is part of an individual's spiritual well-being.[215] It is extremely difficult to formulate a definition of religion that takes into account all the variety of beliefs and practices. To do so raises a problem of choosing a single definition which could mean choosing one religion over the other religion.[216]

The approach of the United States Supreme Court is that courts and governments should not be in the business of declaring whether a belief constitutes a religion.[217] If religious beliefs entitle someone to certain benefits, then there might be an inducement to profess those beliefs. As opposed to stating whether a belief constitutes a religion, the United States Supreme Court focuses on whether the person's belief is genuine.[218] Whether the Court can prove the sincerity of beliefs is questionable. Under this approach, if a person makes a religious claim that he or she has miraculous powers to cure diseases, the Court would not test whether the person actually had this power. In *United States v Ballard*, Justice Douglas stated that '[M]en may believe what they cannot prove. They may not be put to the proof of their religious doctrines or beliefs. Religious experiences which are as real as life to some may be incomprehensible to others. Yet the fact that they may go beyond the ken of mortals does not mean that they can be made suspect before the law.'[219] The Court will not ask the person to prove the validity of the religious belief. There is merit to the approach that a single definition would exclude beliefs which fall outside the definition. For example, the German Basic Law allows for the exclusion of 'non-traditional' groups, such as the Church of Scientology from the religious freedom protections of the Basic Law.[220] This results in the exclusion of persons based on governmental non-acceptance of the excluded group's preference. As Justice Douglas remarked in *Ballard*, if one could be sent to jail because a court 'found those teachings false, there would be little left of religious freedom'.[221]

The courts and religious law

There are two divergent approaches which the civil courts can adopt when faced with a question of interpretation of religious law. The first is for the court to take it upon itself to provide an interpretation of religious law. Under the second approach, the court would adopt the position that it should not involve itself in decisions pertaining to religious doctrine. The first approach is exemplified in the approach of the Supreme Court of India, which conducts an investigation to ascertain whether the practice is an 'essential' part of that religion.[222] The Indian approach casts the court in the role of a high priest who has the final authority to determine religious practice.[223] In *Ryland v Edros*,[224] the Cape High Court was faced with the questions whether, under Islamic law – specifically under the Shafi school of thought – a divorced wife was entitled to a consolatory gift when a dissolution of marriage is at the behest of a husband, and was the former wife entitled to an equitable share of the husband's estate.[225] Farlam J adopted the position that with the coming into effect of the new Constitution, the courts would

---

[215] MK Bhandara *Basic Structure of the Indian Constitution: A Critical Consideration* New Delhi: Deep & Deep 1993, 240.

[216] Erwin Chemerinsky *Constitutional Law: Principles and Practice* New York: Aspen Law and Business 1997, 972.

[217] See Nowak & Rotunda 1285–6.

[218] *United States v Ballard* 322 US 78 (1944).

[219] *Supra* at 86–87.

[220] See Mosely 1129, 1168.

[221] *Ballard* at 87.

[222] Jeewan BP Reddy 'The Jurisprudence of Human Rights' in *Human Rights and Judicial Review: A Comparative Perspective*, edited by David Beatty. Dordrecht: M Nijhoff 1994, 200.

[223] Reddy 201.

[224] 1997 (2) SA 690 (C).

[225] *Supra* para 700.

now be called upon to adjudicate over doctrinal disputes among a religious group.[226] On the facts, the Court felt that there was no doctrinal entanglement in relation to the issues before it.[227] However, the Court was still faced with two competing views (based on the testimony of expert witnesses) on the question of whether a divorced wife was entitled to an equitable distribution of the husband's estate.[228] The Court finally made a choice as to which interpretation reflected the 'correct' view under Islamic personal law.[229]

The second approach, as exemplified by the United States Supreme Court and the German Constitutional Court, adheres to the idea that religious freedom means that religious disputes are to be resolved by the religious institutions.[230] The merit of this approach is that it does not place the Court in the role of arbiter over religious beliefs. Unlike the approach of the Supreme Court of India and the South African approach in *Ryland v Edros*, the second approach operates from the premise that the courts should refrain from involvement in religious disputes, pronouncing on religious doctrine, and deciding what constitutes 'true' belief.[231]

For example, let us assume that different Jewish denominations are fighting over whether a particular establishment serves 'valid' kosher food. The court should not rule on matters of religious law on whether the food is kosher – this concerns the Jewish religion alone. Arguably, there is nothing to suggest that the Constitution casts the courts as interpreters of religious doctrine. Therefore, it was inappropriate for the Court in *Ryland v Edros* to judge what is proper religious

law. In *Gonzalez v Roman Catholic Archbishop of Manila*, the United States Supreme Court held that a state court had no authority to determine matters of ecclestical law, such as the qualification of a chaplain.[232] In that case, there was a dispute as to whether an individual was entitled to money under an estate which left money for the creation of a chaplaincy. The Court held that it was for the Roman Catholic Church, through its structures, to make the determination as to who was qualified to be a chaplain.[233] The German Constitutional Court has arrived at the same conclusion: that religious freedom precludes the state from governing religious institutions or regulating internal church matters.[234]

Similarly, the courts should not rule on matters of religious doctrine.[235] In *Thomas v Review Board of the Indiana Employment Security Division*, the applicant, a Jehovah's Witness employed by the defendant, was transferred to department that produced military hardware. The applicant left and claimed that his religious beliefs prevented him from working in the production of armaments. The state denied him unemployment benefits on various grounds: in the main that other members of the same faith worked in the same department, and testified that it was not forbidden by their religion. The Court held that it is not the function of the Court 'to inquire whether the petitioner or his fellow worker more correctly perceive the commands of their common faith. Courts are not arbiters of scriptural interpretation'.[236]

The Court can, however, resolve disputes where the decision is dependent entirely on secular principles.[237] Where different religious groups resort to the civil courts to settle their

---

[226] *Supra* para 703.
[227] *Supra.*
[228] *Supra* paras 714–715.
[229] *Supra* para 717.
[230] *Kedroff v St Nicholas Cathedral* 344 US 94, 121 (1952); Kommers 472.
[231] *Gonzales v Roman Catholic Archbishop of Manila* 280 US 1, 26 (1929).
[232] *Supra* at 16.
[233] *Supra.*
[234] Mosely 1129, 1162–3.
[235] *Thomas v Review Board of the Indiana Employment Security Division* 450 US 707 (1981).
[236] *Supra* at 715–716.
[237] *Jones v Wolf* 443 US 595 (1979).

differences, courts should only render a decision based on the secular issues.[238]

The non-interference on matters of religious law further means that the state should not rule on the hiring and removal of religious employees where religious authorities make decisions based on religious doctrine.[239] For example, let us assume that a religious organization decides to terminate an employee for straying from the beliefs of the organization. The state should be restricted from regulating employer–employee relations in this situation. In *National Labor Relations Board v Catholic Bishop of Chicago*, the United States Supreme Court held that the state could not regulate the relations between an employer and employee in a religious school.[240] The majority held that a consideration of the terms and conditions of employment might involve an interpretation of religious doctrine. This was not an appropriate role for a state agency to perform.[241] In the balancing process that has become a hallmark of German constitutional jurisprudence, the German Constitutional Court has given a similar preference to freedom of religion over government regulations in the employer–employee field. For example, the German Constitutional Court has arrived at the conclusion that the right to religious autonomy is so central that it even overrides the basic labour rights of people employed by these institutions.[242]

Freedom of association and discrimination

More controversial is religious law that discrimi-

nates against others: such as women or other distinct groups If religious law precludes the ordaining of females, can secular law intervene to outlaw this practice? Non-discrimination is a basic principle of the Constitution. How does one balance the need for non-discrimination under secular principles with different concepts of equality that flow from religious law? Arguably, this is an example where the state should not touch private action.[243]

There is much merit in the approach of the United States Supreme Court that the courts should not intervene in what appears as a discriminatory practice where the association involved pertains to intimate activity.[244] In *Roberts v United States Jaycees*, the Court was faced with a challenge to the Jaycees club that refused to admit women into the organization. The Court, *per* Brennan J, made a distinction between two kinds of association. The first consisted of associations of a personal or intrinsic kind.[245] The second were associations which have a more public dimension.[246] The first type pertains to intimate activities involving deep attachments and commitments. Brennan J referred primarily to family groups 'who shared a special community of thought, experiences, and beliefs' as an example of an association of an intrinsic kind. State interference in these intimate associations would undermine the intrinsic nature of the right to associate.[247] The Jaycees failed to qualify as an intrinsic association because they engaged in public activities such as lobbying, civic work, and charitable work.[248] Similarly, in *Board of Director of Rotary International, et al v Rotary Club of*

---

[238] The approach of non-interference was adhered to in *Presbyterian Church v Mary Elizabeth Blue Hull Memorial Presbyterian Church* 393 US 440 (1969), where the Court was asked to resolve a property dispute. The SC held that freedom of religion is jeopardized when religious litigation involving religious doctrine has to be resolved by the ordinary courts.

[239] *Roman Catholic Archbishop of Manila* at 26.

[240] *National Labor Relations Board (NLRB) v Catholic Bishop of Chicago* 440 US 490 (1979).

[241] *NLRB v Catholic Bishop of Chicago*, 440 US at 501.

[242] David M Beatty 'The Last Generation: When Rights lose their Meaning' in *Human Rights and Judicial Review: A Comparative Perspective*, edited by David M Beatty. Dordrecht: M Nijhoff 1994, 335, 345.

[243] See Nowak & Rotunda 1331. (The authors make the observation that Title VII of the Civil Rights Act of 1964 exempts religious groups from the statutory prohibitions against discrimination in employment, on the basis of religion.)

[244] *Roberts v United States Jaycees* 468 US 609 (1984).

[245] *Supra* at 620.

[246] *Supra.*

[247] *Supra.*

[248] *Supra.*

Duarte et al, the Court held that the Rotary Club, as a private business, could be compelled to not discriminate against women in its admissions policies.[249]

The Court's holding in *Roberts* was limited to small intimate associations. In *Hurley v Irish-American Gay, Lesbian and Bisexual Group of Boston*,[250] the Court held that gays and lesbians could be excluded from a public parade.[251] The Court held that the parade, although a public event, was meant to deliver a message, and the participation of gays and lesbians could be prevented if it would alter the message presented.[252]

In chapter 10, we argued that the South African Constitution does not envisage complete horizontal application of the Bill of Rights to all private situations. To insist otherwise would destroy the core of individual freedom.[253] In *Christian Education of South Africa v Minister of Education*,[254] Sachs J in dicta, stated that the right to associate 'on the basis of language, culture, and religion cannot be used to shield practices which offend the Bill of Rights'.[255] In the context of religious belief, how far can the court go to force a religious group to desist from certain practices because it does not conform to the court's view of equality? In the examples of labour practices above, or if the state was to order the Roman Catholic Church to ordain female priests, or admit homosexuals pursuant to the equality clause, the state would either be interpreting religious doctrine or forcing members to act against their religious beliefs. Such an order would be unworkable and an infringement on important personal liberties.[256] Religious beliefs are intensely personal and people cannot be coerced to subscribe to

national or universal values on such intimate matters.

Conflict between religion and important state objectives

Having made the observation that the state should not pronounce on religious beliefs, does this mean that every person has the right to protection to carry out practices in accordance with his or her own standards on matters of faith – no matter how unconventional the standards might appear? There are examples of religious practices, such as the Hindu custom of immolation of wives at their husbands' funeral, which would be unacceptable in most societies. The fact that the practice is based on religious custom does not mean that the state must always accommodate the conduct. If the state has an important social interest in regulating the activity, the Court has to balance the freedom of religion with the other important objectives. In the example of smoking marijuana, although the state cannot pronounce on the validity of a religious belief, the state has the power to prohibit conduct such as smoking marijuana or other dangerous substances, on health, safety, or other grounds. In *Christian Education of South Africa*, the Court was faced with a challenged to s 10 of the South African Schools Act,[257] which prohibited the administering of corporeal punishment in schools. The appellants cited to the Bible and argued that the Act violated the rights of parents of children in independent schools, who according to their religious beliefs, had consented to the use of corporeal punishment.[258] The Court, *per* Sachs J, held that the state should as far as possible aim to accommodate believers.[259] However, the state

---

[249] *Board of Director of Rotary International v Rotary Club of Duarte* 481 US 537 (1988).
[250] *Hurley v Irish-American Gay, Lesbian and Bisexual Group of Boston* 515 US 557 (1995).
[251] *Supra* at 580.
[252] *Supra* at 576.
[253] See Christian Starck 'Europe's Fundamental Rights in their Newest Garb' (1982) 3 *Human Rights Journal* 112.
[254] CCT 4/00.
[255] *Supra* para 26.
[256] Kelly 716.
[257] Act 84 of 1996 (Schools Act).
[258] *Christian Education of South Africa* para 4.
[259] *Supra* para 35.

could regulate oppressive features of internal relationships in which the Bill of Rights has horizontal application.[260]

In order to sustain these restrictions, the laws must be neutral and must not single out a specific religion. In *Church of Lukumi Babulu Aye*, the United States Supreme Court invalidated a city ordinance that banned the sacrifice of animals as part of religious rituals because the law was targeted specifically at a particular group.[261] Similarly, in *Employment Division v Smith*, the Supreme Court upheld the prohibition of peyote, a hallucinogenic substance used by native Americans in their rituals, since the law applied to everyone and did not target a particular religion.[262] Justice Scalia, writing for the majority, held that the right to practise one's religion does not mean that an individual has no obligation to comply with a neutral law of general applicability on the grounds that the law conflicts with that persons religious tenets.[263]

Similarly, in *Jacobson v Massachusetts*, the United States Supreme Court upheld the state's interest in public health in requiring individuals to have vaccinations, even though the vaccination might infringe upon an individual's freedom of religion.[264] In the early case of *Reynolds v United States*, the Court upheld the prohibition against polygamous marriages as within the power of Congress to preserve good order, even though the ban infringed on the beliefs of the Mormon religion.[265]

Freedom of religion and the limitations clause

Does every law that interferes with religious practices have to satisfy the limitations clause in order to pass constitutional muster? For example, if a law requires all schools to be accredited by the Department of Education in order to ensure that minimum secular standards are complied with, should the law have to satisfy the limitations clause? A law which requires schools to take minimum fire and health safety precautions may also impose those rules on religious schools. The courts in Canada make a distinction between laws that have a 'trivial or insubstantial' effect on freedom of religion.[266] Arguably, those laws should not have to satisfy the limitations clause.[267]

Where the Court is faced with two competing clauses in the Constitution, the test might well entail a balancing of the two interests as opposed to considering whether the one can sustain the limitations clause.[268] For example, a ban on marijuana, or a law requiring vaccinations, and any other law which is neutral and of general application, should not have to be justified under the limitations clause. Even the United States Supreme Court under its standards of scrutiny, has moved away from strict scrutiny when evaluating laws which burden religious practices, and where the law is neutral and of general applicability.[269] Where the law is neutral and of general applicability, it would pass constitutional muster if it can satisfy the rational basis test.[270] In the United States, it is only where the law is not neutral nor of general applicability that the Court would evaluate it under the strict scrutiny test.[271] For example, in

---

[260] *Supra* para 26.

[261] *Church of Lukumi Babalu Aye*, 508 US at 520.

[262] *Employment Division v Smith*, 494 US 872 (1990).

[263] *Supra* at 879.

[264] *Jacobson v Massachusetts*, 197 US 11 (1905).

[265] *Reynolds v United States*, 98 US (8 Otto) 145, 166–167 (1878).

[266] Hogg 807–8.

[267] In *Lawrence*, Sachs J applied this *de minimis* rule, but still applies the limitations clause to sustain the statute; *Lawrence* para 168–169.

[268] This is explored in greater detail in chapter 14.

[269] *Per* Justice Scalia in *Employment Division v Smith* 494 US at 888.

[270] *Supra*.

[271] *Per* Kennedy J, in *Church of the Lukumi Babulu Aye* 508 US at 531, 532.

the South African case of *Lawrence*, four of the judges in two separate dissenting opinions by O'Regan J,[272] and Sachs J,[273] found that the prohibition on the selling of wine on Sundays and certain public holidays by grocers constituted a violation of freedom of religion. O'Regan J, in a decision concurred by Goldstone and Madala JJ, further found that the statute, in identifying with Christian holidays, could not be justified under the limitations clause.[274]

However, where the law is neutral and meant to advance a competing interest in the Bill of Rights, arguably, the Court should not use the limitations clause. In *Christian Education of South Africa*, Sachs J, writing for a unanimous Court upheld the prohibition of corporeal punishment in terms of the Schools Act under the limitations clause of the Constitution.[275] The Court did not expressly state that the administering of corporeal punishment in an institutional setting violates the dignity of children. However, the Court recognized that there were a number of overlapping and competing constitutional values and interests involved. On the one hand, the parents have the right to live their lives and bring up their children according to their religious beliefs. The right to dignity of the parents was negatively affected in terms of the state prescribing to them how to bring up and discipline their children. The children, on the other hand, are also entitled under the Constitution to the right to dignity, freedom and security, and protection from maltreatment.[276] This was a case involving competing interests and clauses in the Constitution. Ultimately, the validity of the Schools Act should have depended on the balancing of two competing interests, as apposed to whether the Schools Act can sustain the limitations clause.[277] Moreover, the conduct being regulated was in a public setting, as opposed to the privacy of the home.[278]

---

[272] *Lawrence* para 129.

[273] *Supra* para 164.

[274] *Supra* para 132.

[275] *Christian Education of South Africa* para 32.

[276] *Supra* para 15.

[277] See chapter 14.

[278] For a discussion of the importance of whether the conduct was private or public, see chapters 8, 9 and 10.

13

Social welfare rights

Introduction

The Constitution provides:

Housing

26 (1) Everyone has the right to have access to adequate housing.

(2) The state must take reasonable legislative and other measures, within its available resources, to achieve the progressive realisation of this right.

(3) No one may be evicted from their home, or have their home demolished, without an order of court made after considering all the relevant circumstances. No legislation may permit arbitrary evictions.

Health care, food, water and electricity

27 (1) Everyone has the right to have access to—

(a) health care services, including reproductive health care;

(b) sufficient food and water; and

(c) social security, including, if they are unable to support themselves and their dependants, appropriate social assistance.

(2) The state must take reasonable legislative and other measures, within its available resources, to achieve the progressive realisation of each of these rights.

(3) No one may be refused emergency medical treatment.

Children.

28 (1) Everyone has the right to have access to—

(a) health care services, including reproductive health care;

(b) sufficient food and water; and

(c) social security, including, if they are unable to support themselves and their dependants, appropriate social assistance.

(2) The state must take reasonable legislative and other measures, within its available resources, to achieve the progressive realisation of each of these rights.

(3) No one may be refused emergency medical treatment.

Education

29 (1) Everyone has the right—

(a) to a basic education, including adult basic education; and

(b) to further education, which the state must take reasonable measures to make progressively available and accessible.

(2) Everyone has the right to receive education in the official language or languages of their choice in public educational institutions where that education is reasonably practicable. In order to ensure the effective access to, and implementation of, this right, the state must consider all reasonable educational alternatives, including single medium institutions, taking into account—

(a) equity;

(b) practicability; and

(c) the need to redress the results of past racially discriminatory law and practice.

(3) Everyone has the right to establish and maintain, at their own expense, independent educational institutions that–

(a) do not discriminate on the basis of race;

(b) are registered with the state; and

(c) maintain standards that are not inferior to standards at comparable public educational institutions

(4) Subsection (3) does not preclude state subsidies for independent educational institutions.

Positive rights and legitimacy

The majority of South Africans will judge the new constitutional order in terms of whether it addresses their pressing economic and social needs. Since the Second World War, many constitutions have recognized that unrestricted private property, unrestricted individual freedom, and a passive state can result in large concentrations of wealth and power in the hands of a few. As a result, a large majority of the population continues to reside in poverty despite the fiction of legal equality.[1] The response has been the institution of so-called welfare constitutions, which institutionalize welfare rights into the legal order.[2] The Constitution of South Africa moves away

from 'pure' liberalism with its emphasis on completely autonomous individuals and an essentially passive state, in the direction of a welfare state. The Constitution represents a legal, political, social and, moral foundation which, in the words of Herman Schwartz, 'reflects the triumphs and sorrows of a nation's past and its hope for the future'.[3] The Constitution is an instrument that not only sets up the institutions of power, but also directs the institutions to funnel resources from the privileged sector towards the general welfare of the majority.[4] For example, s 26 speaks about the right to housing.[5] Section 27 speaks about the right to health care,[6] food, water and social security. Section 28(1)(c) provides every child with a right to basic nutrition, shelter,[7] basic health care, and social services.[8] Section 29 enshrines the right to education. Section 22 speaks about the right to freedom of trade, occupation and profession. Section 23 provides worker rights to fair labour practices and the right to join a trade union. Section 30 provides a right to language and cultural protection. The exercise of cultural rights touches on the right to expression and association.[9]

In human rights discourse, the above-mentioned social welfare rights, and what are referred to as 'group rights', are commonly referred to as 'second generation' human rights. Underlying the welfare rights is a belief that individual well-being requires a minimum adequacy of economic and social conditions.[10] Implicit in the cultural and language rights is a recognition that there are

---

[1] Jurgen Dalberg-Larsen *The Welfare State and its Law* Berlin: Tesdorph 1987, 50.

[2] For a discussion of how Sweden has approached the institutionalizing of welfare rights, see Deborah Kenn 'One Dream, Another's Reality: Housing Justice in Sweden' (1996) 22 *Brooklyn Journal of International Law* 63.

[3] Herman Schwartz 'Why Economic and Social Rights Belong in the New Post-Communist Constitutions in Europe' (1992) Fall *East European Constitutional Review* 25.

[4] Schwartz 25.

[5] The leading case, which discusses the right to housing is *The Government of the Republic of South Africa and Others v Grootboom and Others* CCT 11/00 (4 October 2000), now cited as 2000 (11) BCLR 1169 (CC); 2000 (1) SA 46 (CC).

[6] The leading case to discuss the scope of this right is *Soobramoney v Minister of Health, KwaZulu-Natal* CCT 32/97 (27 November 1997), now cited as 1998 (1) SA 765 (CC); 1997 (12) BCLR 1696 (CC).

[7] For an understanding of the right to shelter, see *Grootboom* para 73.

[8] For an overview of the positive obligations owed to a child, see *Minister for Welfare and Population Development v Fitzpatrick and Others* CCT 08/00 (31 May 2000) paras 16–17. See also *Grootboom* paras 73–78.

[9] As discussed in chapter 12.

[10] David M Trubek 'Economic, Social, and Cultural Rights in the Third World: Human Rights Law and Human Needs Programs' in *Human Rights in International Law: Legal and Policy Issues*, edited by Theodor Meron. Oxford: Clarendon 1984, 205.

important attributes within society which are essential to the relationships between people, and their right to associate and develop as groups based on common attributes within their society.[11]

More recently international human rights discourse has recognized 'third generation' human rights, such as the right to a safe environment and the right to information.[12] The right to a safe environment is protected by s 24 of the Constitution. This chapter concerns itself primarily with social welfare rights. The realization of social welfare rights, more so than first generation rights, requires the balancing of the interests of the individual against those of the community.

Welfare rights under international law

The obligation to provide social welfare benefits is required under international law. Article 55 of the Charter of the United Nations requires the UN to promote 'higher standards of living, full employment, and conditions of economic and social progress and development'.[13] The Charter further requires the promotion of 'solutions of international economic, social, health, and related problems; and international cultural and educational co-operation'.[14] The Charter also requires member states to achieve these goals both individually and in cooperation with the UN.[15] Social welfare rights are also contained in the

Universal Declaration of Human Rights, which among other rights protects economic social and cultural rights;[16] social security;[17] the right to work and join trade unions;[18] the right to an adequate standard of living including food, health care, clothing, and housing;[19] unemployment security;[20] and the right to education.[21] More detailed protections of welfare rights and cultural rights are contained in the International Covenant on Economic, Social and Cultural Rights,[22] which spells out the duties and responsibilities of states in the furtherance of these rights.

Welfare obligations versus political objectives

The welfare functions required under the South African Constitution are different from the welfare functions provided in both the British system and federal and some local governments in the United States.[23] Under the Constitution, there is an affirmative duty for the state to realize certain educational, housing, and social security objectives.[24] In other words, the state is required to actively intervene to provide high material standards of living for all, as opposed to leaving this function to be fulfilled in the market place.[25]

A right granted under the Constitution does not only mean the state has to provide facilities. In some instances, it also means an obligation on the part of the state to create conditions whereby

---

[11] Vladimir Kartashkin 'Economic, Social and Cultural Rights' in *The International Dimensions of Human Rights*, edited by Karel Vasak and Philip Alston. Westport: Greenwood Press 1982, 127.

[12] Frank Newman and David Weissbrodt *International Human Rights: Law Policy and Process* Cincinnati: Anderson Publishing, 2nd edition, 1996, 81.

[13] Article 55*(a)* of the UN Charter.

[14] Article 55*(b)*.

[15] Article 56.

[16] Article 22 of the Universal Declaration.

[17] Article 22.

[18] Article 23(1).

[19] Article 25(1).

[20] Article 25(1).

[21] Article 26(1).

[22] 993 UNTS 3, (1967) 6 ILM 360 (Economic Covenant).

[23] eg the WIC (Women's, Infant's and Children's) programme providing food stamps to lower-income households.

[24] Sections 26, 27, 28 and 29 of the Constitution. *Grootboom* para 20.

[25] This is also found in European welfare states. David S Marsh *The Welfare State* London: Longman 1970, 1.

individuals could have access to certain rights.[26] Where the obligation is to provide access to a right, the nature of the obligation would differ in different parts of the country. In *Grootboom*, the Court observed:

[37] The state's obligation to provide access to adequate housing depends on context, and may differ from province to province, from city to city, from rural to urban areas and from person to person. Some may need access to land and no more; some may need access to land and building materials; some may need access to finance; some may need access to services such as water, sewage, electricity and roads. What might be appropriate in a rural area where people live together in communities engaging in subsistence farming may not be appropriate in an urban area where people are looking for employment and a place to live.

Several European constitutions expressly include provisions that call on the state to fulfil this role of constructing a just socioeconomic system.[27] The German Basic Law defines the country as a social federal state.[28] The Basic Law calls on the states to adopt provisions that conform with the principles of a democratic and social state.[29] It also proclaims that the community has a duty to protect and maintain every mother.[30] The Constitution of Sweden imposes similar duties on the state.[31] More recent constitutions in Europe, for example

in Greece, Portugal, and Spain, also confirm this evolution towards a social state in the youngest democracies of Europe.[32]

On the other hand, in the United States, the welfare functions are pursued more as a political purpose. The United States Supreme Court does not interpret the Constitution as requiring the federal government to intervene in the economy, or to assist the poor sectors of society. While the United States has a bill of rights, its government only as a negative obligation to refrain from depriving the citizens of protected rights.[33] The common-law tradition does not regard affirmative rights (such as duties which force the government to provide social welfare or take positive steps to help the needy), as enforceable rights There are exceptional situations, (such as when the state places an individual in danger), where the courts would hold the government to an affirmative obligation. For example, under the United States Constitution the state has an affirmative obligation to provide legal assistance to the indigent accused.[34] Outside these limited circumstances, the Court has consistently interpreted the Constitution as imposing no obligation on the state to provide education, health care, or other social welfare activities.[35] The United States Constitution is viewed as a charter of negative rights. The dominant mode of interpretation that many justices have employed in recent times in the

---

[26] *Grootboom* para 35. The Court held that the right to housing under s 26(1) entailed a right of access to housing. In order for a person to have this access, the state had to create certain conditions like making land available and providing certain services such as water and sewage. Similarly, s 28, which confers rights on children, requires the state to adopted measures to ensure that childrens rights are protected. These measures, in the first instance, mean that legal obligations are created compelling parents to fulfil their responsibilities to their children. *Supra* para 75.

[27] The German Basic Law calls on the state to construct a just social order. Donald P Kommers *The Constitutional Jurisprudence of the Federal Republic of Germany* Durham: Duke University Press 1989, 247–8. See also the constitutions of Denmark and Norway, which provide for a right to work. See Jurgen Dalberg-Larsen *The Welfare State and its Law* Berlin: Tesdorph 1987, 14–15.

[28] Article 20 of the German Basic Law.

[29] Article 28(1).

[30] Article 6(5).

[31] The Swedish Constitution provides that the personal economic, and cultural welfare of the individual shall be fundamental aims of the activities of the community. Constitution of Sweden, Chapter 1, art 2. This Chapter also provides a right to housing, education, social care, security, and a favourable living environment.

[32] These countries adopted liberal constitutions more recently (in the 1970s) and all include various social rights. For a catalogue of rights included in these constitutions, see Christian Starck 'Europe's Fundamental Rights in their Newest Garb' (1982) 3 *Human Rights Law Journal* 114–16.

[33] David P Currie 'Positive and Negative Constitutional Rights', (1986) 53 *Chicago Law Review* 864, 871.

[34] The VI Amendment to the US Constitution. See L Bendes 'The Negative Constitution' (1990) 88 *Michigan Law Review* 2277.

[35] See eg *De Shaney v Winnebago County Department of Social Services* 489 US 189, 196–7, 109 SCt 998, 103 L Ed2d 249 (1989).

United States is the 'living constitution' approach.[36] This method implies that the Constitution is not a static document, but has to be interpreted to take account of modern realities. Although many of the justices have embraced the living constitution idea, their interpretations have been influenced by the common law and a particular strain of liberal theory that perceives the role of government in negative terms. If one adheres to the notion of a living constitution, then the negative concept of rights in the constitution is not an interpretation that the justices are compelled to reach. However, the majority of United States Supreme Court justices are most comfortable with this interpretation.

For example, in *De Shaney v Winnebago County Department of Social Services* the Court ruled that the government has no affirmative duty to provide positive rights to individuals.[37] Similarly, in *Webster v Reproductive Health Services*, the Court ruled that the government has no affirmative duty to provide medical care to individuals.[38] Bendes makes the point that the Court's approach in these and other cases is drawn from a particular liberal conception that the best government is the one that leaves its citizens alone; to provide positive freedom would be to limit the content of individual freedom.[39] The philosophical assumptions of negative conceptions of rights have, in turn, influenced the common law and its assumptions that the individual is the focus of government.[40]

Where the federal and local governments in the United States intervene to provide assistance, the intervention is done to assist the most needy sectors of society. Under the constitutional welfare state on the other hand, social welfare is institutionalized as a democratic right to which all citizens are entitled. In the latter instance, where the government provides services, the services are provided 'to integrate and include the entire population rather than target its resources toward particular problem groups'.[41]

Socioeconomic rights as fundamental rights

In the *First Certification* decision, an objection was lodged against the inclusion of socioeconomic rights in the Constitution. The Constitutional Court responded by stating that:

[76] Sections 26, 27 and 29 in the NT provide rights of access to housing, health care, sufficient food and water, social security and basic education. NT 28, among other things, provides such rights specifically to children. These rights were loosely referred to by the objectors as socio-economic rights. The first objection to the inclusion of these provisions was that they are not universally accepted fundamental rights. As stated, such an objection cannot be sustained because CP II permits the CA to supplement the universally accepted fundamental rights with other rights not universally accepted.

[77] The second objection was that the inclusion of these rights in the NT is inconsistent with the separation of powers required by CP VI because the judiciary would have to encroach upon the proper terrain of the legislature and executive. In particular the objectors argued it would result in the courts dictating to the government how the budget should be allocated. It is true that the inclusion of socio-economic rights may result in courts making orders which have direct implications for budgetary matters. However, even when a court enforces civil and political rights such as equality, freedom of speech and the right to a fair trial, the order it makes will often have such implications. A court may require the provision of legal aid, or the extension of state benefits to a class of people who formerly were not beneficiaries of such benefits. In our view it cannot be said that by including socio-economic

---

[36] eg there is nothing expressly providing for the right to privacy or right to abortion in the US Constitution. Yet through the living constitution approach, the Court has found the right to privacy and abortion to be located in various parts of the Constitution.

[37] 489 US 189, 196–7, 109 SCt 998, 103 L Ed2d 249 (1989).

[38] 492 US 490, 109 SCt 3040, 106 L Ed2d 410 (1989).

[39] Bendes 2314–15.

[40] Op cit 2317.

[41] Kenn 76–7.

rights within a bill of rights, a task is conferred upon the courts so different from that ordinarily conferred upon them by a bill of rights that it results in a breach of the separation of powers.

[78] The objectors argued further that socio-economic rights are not justiciable, in particular because of the budgetary issues their enforcement may raise. They based this argument on CP II which provides that all universally accepted fundamental rights shall be protected by 'entrenched and justiciable provisions in the Constitution'. It is clear, as we have stated above, that the socio-economic rights entrenched in NT 26 to 29 are not universally accepted fundamental rights. For that reason, therefore, it cannot be said that their 'justiciability' is required by CP II. Nevertheless, we are of the view that these rights are, at least to some extent, justiciable. As we have stated in the previous paragraph, many of the civil and political rights entrenched in the NT will give rise to similar budgetary implications without compromising their justiciability. The fact that socio-economic rights will almost inevitably give rise to such implications does not seem to us to be a bar to their justiciability. At the very minimum, socio-economic rights can be negatively protected from improper invasion. In the light of these considerations, it is our view that the inclusion of socio-economic rights in the NT does not result in a breach of the CPs.

In our opinion, the Constitutional Court errs by stating that socioeconomic rights are not fundamental human rights. It is true that for a long time, most Western concerns on human rights dealt only with civil and political rights, while ignoring the social and economic conditions of many people.[42] The right to vote was seen as more important than the right to food and shelter for the people. The Court adopted the liberal approach to fundamental human rights by conceptualizing human rights as a liberal system of values,[43] which is the way fundamental human rights were traditionally viewed. When we look at the drafting of the Universal Declaration and its adoption by the UN in 1948, one finds few African or other 'Third World' countries represented there.[44] The recent decades have seen a change in emphasis as African and other 'Third World' representation has expanded.[45] The cultural orientations and priorities of the new nations were different from those of the Western systems. Since the 1960s in line with this changing pattern of UN membership, the definition and scope of human rights has been broadened and is reflected in the subsequent covenants and conventions of the UN.[46] Even before this change in composition of nations, many non-common-law European countries had incorporated socioeconomic rights into their constitutions.[47]

Many writers from common-law jurisdictions continue to be critical of the international covenants which they consider as going beyond universal rights.[48] According to their test, the emphasis on economic rights and cultural rights, which emphasizes the rights of only the individual, are neither essential nor universal. Such views are indicative of the parochial nature of human rights thinking. Human rights are viewed purely from the ideological standpoint of the speaker, and are conceived of as the achievement of civil and political rights.[49] The Teheran Conference on Human Rights organized under

---

[42] The US State Department in reporting on human rights violations only concerns itself with civil and political rights. See M Hamalengwa 'The Political Economy of Human Rights in Africa: Historical and Contemporary Perspectives' (1983) 9 (3) *Philosophy and Social Action* 25.

[43] This is the view adhered to in many Western countries. See Egon Schwelb *Human Rights in the International Community: The Roots and Growth of the Universal Declaration of Human Rights* Chicago: Quadrangle Books 1964, 12.

[44] At the time the Universal Declaration was drawn up there were only three independent black African countries Egypt, Ethiopia, and Liberia.

[45] Howard Tolley Jnr *The UN Commission on Human Rights* Boulder: Westview Press 1987, 83.

[46] International Covenant on Economic, Social, and Cultural Rights, 16 December 1966, 993 UNTS 3.

[47] eg Germany. See George Ross 'The Constitution and the Requirements of Democracy in Germany' in *New Challenges to the German Basic Law*, edited by Christian Starck. Baden-Baden: Nomos 1991, 138.

[48] Maurice Cranston *What are Human Rights?* New York: Taplinger Publishing Co 1973, 68–69.

[49] Ibid.

the auspices of the UN, stressed the importance of economic, social and cultural rights, and affirmed '[i]n our day political rights without social rights, justice under law without social justice, and political democracy without economic democracy no longer have any true meaning'.[50] This holistic approach was endorsed by the South African Constitutional Court in *Grootboom*, where Yacoob J stated:

[23] Our Constitution entrenches both civil and political rights and social and economic rights All the rights in our Bill of Rights are inter-related and mutually supporting. There can be no doubt that human dignity, freedom and equality, the foundational values of our society, are denied those who have no food, clothing or shelter. Affording socioeconomic rights to all people therefore enables them to enjoy the other rights enshrined in Chapter 2. The realisation of these rights is also key to the advancement of race and gender equality and the evolution of a society in which men and women are equally able to achieve their full potential.

[24] The right of access to adequate housing cannot be seen in isolation. There is a close relationship between it and the other socioeconomic rights. Socioeconomic rights must all be read together in the setting of the Constitution as a whole. The state is obliged to take positive action to meet the needs of those living in extreme conditions of poverty, homelessness or intolerable housing. Their interconnectedness needs to be taken into account in interpreting the socioeconomic rights, and, in particular, in determining whether the state has met its obligations in terms of them.

This idea of unity and interdependence of civil, political, and social welfare rights was endorsed by the UN General Assembly in a resolution in 1977.[51] Similarly, the rights and duties embodied in the African Charter reflect a belief in overall human rights (ie economic, social, cultural, moral, political) and the need for development which overall is consistent with the African tradition of humanism in viewing man holistically.[52] The African Charter reflects a belief that political rights and economic, social and cultural rights are inter-linked in achieving development.[53] Human rights should be viewed holistically, and the traditional balancing should be maintained. In the words of Professor Vojin Dimitrijevic:

There can be no either or thinking in this realm. The moment one human right, or group of rights, is sacrificed for the attainment of some other, more 'important' or 'essential' human right, whenever freedom is opposed to equality or material well-being, the structure of universal values is undermined: at the end there is neither bread nor liberty.[54]

This approach has also been accepted by the German Constitutional Court, which has stated that civil and political rights are interconnected with economic and social rights.[55] A minimum of material welfare is vital to the realization of freedom, as much as a welfare state in its purest form would destroy freedom.[56]

In the *First Certification* decision, the South African Constitutional Court unfortunately approached the welfare provisions in the Constitution in terms of the old nineteenth-century notion of the rule of law that is prevalent in the Anglo-American tradition. This tradition conceives of the rule-of-law as encompassing only negative rights. It restrains the government from arbitrary action; instead of looking at the rule-of-law as a dynamic concept. These traditional Anglo-American notions of the rule of law, considers the concept in

---

[50] The Final Act of the International Conference on Human Rights, Teheran 1968. See UN Doc A/Conf 32/41
[51] For a summary and commentary of the pivotal aspects of the resolution, see Theodor C van Boven 'Distinguishing Criteria of Human Rights' in *The International Dimensions of Human Rights*, edited by Karel Vasak and Philip Alston. Westport: Greenwood Press 1982, 51.
[52] This idea was canvassed in chapter 2.
[53] See s 8 of the preamble to the African Charter on Human and People's Rights (African Charter).
[54] Vojin Dimitrijevic 'Development as a Right' unpublished paper presented at the Seminar on Law and Human Rights in Development in Gaberone, Botswana (24–28 May 1982) 86.
[55] Ross 138.
[56] Ibid.

terms of government operating under law in a manner guaranteeing important individual rights derived from the common law. The rule of law is a dynamic concept. The jurisprudence that emerges from many of the non-common-law traditions, and which was recognized by Yacoob J in *Grootboom*, operates in terms of an expansive and dynamic concept of the rule of law that embodies a recognition of the importance of social and economic rights. The constitutional recognition of socio-economic rights is consistent with developments in international human rights, most notably the formulation by the UN of the Covenant of Social Economic and Cultural Rights. Today, this covenant is seen as part of the international Bill of Human Rights.[57] It marks a recognition that a certain economic standard is an important condition for the rule of law.[58] In terms of this dynamic concept of the constitutional welfare state, the classical notion of the passive state is no longer tenable.

The constitutional demand on the government to intervene in social and economic affairs is a major departure from the Anglo-American tradition and the common-law assumption of an essentially passive government. The use of affirmative action provisions to achieve economic and social rights is also a departure from the common-law tradition. The Anglo-American systems, on the one hand, conceive the social contract as a relationship between the state and autonomous individuals where the power of the state is restricted in favour of maximum protection for individual rights. Under the South African Constitution, there is a greater consideration and balancing (like the European constitutions) of the actions of the individuals against those of the society at large, and a balancing between individual and community interests.[59]

Socioeconomic rights and justiciability

There is always difficulty in determining how to enforce socioeconomic rights.[60] The Constitutional Court noted in the *First Certification* decision, that these rights are readily justiciable.[61] But socioeconomic rights cannot always be supervised by the judiciary to the same extent as civil and political rights. When we speak about the right against torture and freedom from arrest, these are rights that can be implemented immediately with appropriate legislation. There are some socioeconomic rights which can also be immediately implemented with appropriate legislation (such as the right to fair labour practices and the right to form trade unions). However, in the implementation of most other social welfare rights such as the right to housing, health, and education, one needs programmes of implementation that are dependent on the availability of resources.[62] States may not have the resources to provide these economic rights. When we talk about rights, generally we mean entitlements which are readily subject to judicial supervision. With socioeconomic rights, the question arises whether the courts should dictate how the budget of the state must be allocated. The answer is to be found in the correct understanding of the language used in most socioeconomic rights provisions.

Let us look at the international documents referring to social welfare rights, such as the

---

[57] International Covenant on Economic, Social, and Cultural Rights, 16 December 1966, 993 UNTS 3.

[58] Ulrich Karpen 'The Constitution in the Face of Economic and Social Progress' in *New Challenges to the German Basic Law*, edited by Christian Starck. Baden-baden: Nomos 1991, 89.

[59] This is also encapsulated in art 28 of the German Basic Law, which states that the constitutional system must conform to the principles of republican, democratic, and social government based on the rule of law.

[60] See Etienne Mureinik 'Beyond a Charter of Luxuries: Economic Rights in the Constitution' (1992) 8 *South African Journal of Human Rights* 464; Nicolas Haysom 'Constitutionalism, Majoritarian Democracy and Socio-economic Rights' (1992) 8 *South African Journal of Human Rights* 451.

[61] *First Certification* decision para 78.

[62] *Grootboom* para 32. In *Grootboom*, the Court refrained from defining a minimum core obligation with respect to housing. The German Constitutional Court has also restrained itself from awarding legal claims because it does not want to take the budget power away from parliament. Ross 139.

Economic Covenant. We find that the convenant speaks about a right which the parties 'recognize', or about rights which the parties 'undertake to ensure', or 'undertake to guarantee'. The way the right is framed suggests that there is an element of discretion. Similarly, the European Social Charter requires state parties to progressively realize the rights contained in the agreement. When we look at civil and political rights in the Civil Covenant, the right is simply stated which suggests that there is an immediate binding obligation that the state should not act in a way that transgresses on the right. This does not mean that all civil and political rights are of a negative nature. The right to a fair trial, which ordains a right to counsel, requires government expenditure in order for the right to become a reality. These and other examples where the government is forced by the judiciary to act in a positive manner, represent exceptional situations and are usually meant to ensure that the process through which rights are exercised is fair. For example, the right to counsel at state expense is required, because the state has acted to place an individual in danger. There is, therefore, a need to balance the scales.[63] In other instances where, for example, courts order the state to increase spending on jails or legal aid, it is usually due to reasons such as lack of equality and fair process.[64]

On the other hand, social welfare rights are more resource driven. Similar to international instruments, the South African Constitution states that the right to housing, health care, food, water, social security, and education must be provided by the state within its available resources.[65] While there is an obligation on the state to provide these welfare rights, these obligations cannot always be judicially policed in the same way as civil and political rights. To demand that a government supply a judicially determined content of health care for all citizens is qualitatively different from the example where a government places a person in custody, and he or she has a right to counsel at state expense, or a right to a speedy trial. In *Grootboom*, the Court was faced with the question of what the state's obligations were in relation to housing. The Court, in interpreting the socioeconomic rights and the right to housing, held that the first obligation was one of progressive realization.[66] The second obligation is one of means the state cannot be forced to do more than its available resources allow.[67] The Court stated that 'both the content of the obligation in relation to the rate at which it is achieved as well as the reasonableness of the measures employed to achieve the result are governed by the availability of resources'.[68] What this means is that individuals cannot claim socioeconomic rights such as housing and shelter on demand. However, the state is obligated to devise and implement a coherent and coordinated programme to meet its obligations.[69] Where the state does not have any programme, the court will not hesitate in holding the state in breach of its obligations.[70]

Similarly, international law recognizes that all states do not have the resources to realize social welfare rights. At the time of the drafting of the Economic Covenant, one of the participants made the observation that the 'covenant would recognize rights whose content would differ greatly from country to country, depending on available resources, and it therefore could not impose absolute obligations on the state parties to it'.[71] The crucial difference is that obligations with respect to most social welfare rights are obligations of progressive realization, over a period of time, taking into account available resources.[72] Recently the European Economic Community has

---

[63] Bendes 2277.
[64] Beatty 351.
[65] Sections 26(2), 27(1), 27(2), and 29(1) of the Constitution.
[66] *Grootboom* para 34.
[67] *Supra* para 46.
[68] *Supra*.
[69] *Supra* para 95.
[70] *Supra*.
[71] Quoted in Newman & Weissbrodt 54.
[72] Trubek 214.

attempted to tighten up enforcement of social rights through the Maastrict Guidelines on the margin of appreciation, which requires states to fulfil certain core social obligations.[73] However, there is as yet no guidance as to how core obligations are determined.[74] Where the allocation of resources is concerned, there is an obligation under international law to take steps to effect the rights given the available resources.[75] Similarly, the Constitution provides that social welfare rights must be achieved in terms of the principle of progressive realization.[76]

The welfare constitutions in European countries face the same dilemma, leading some commentators to argue that the welfare provisions are not directly applicable law, but rather directive principles, and they call on the state to embark on adopting programmes towards the achievement of these goals.[77] The social welfare provisions serve as a stimulator rather than as a norm.[78] In other words, the welfare provisions constitute fundamental aspirations to utilize the resources of the nation for the common good.[79] The degree of implementation will depend on the state of the economy. The German Constitutional Court has said that the social state is a legal norm, which the legislator must keep in mind as an objective that must be achieved. If this is done, the legislature will be accorded broad discretion as to the extent and means to be used to achieve the social protection.[80] Ultimately its implementation is dependent on the political process.[81] To date, the Constitutional Court in Germany has not ruled that any legislation is invalid because of lack of state action under the principles of social justice.[82] In the *Numerus Clausus 1* case, dealing with admission of students to university, the German Constitutional Court ruled that the notion 'that the individual has an unlimited claim [which is enforceable] at the expense of the community as a whole is incompatible with the principle of a social federal state ... '.[83] It is up to the legislature to determine what may be reasonably claimed and what to prioritize given the multitude of welfare concerns.[84]

Similarly, the Supreme Court of Japan, in interpreting art 25 of the Japanese Constitution, which deals with the right to maintain a living, has ruled that it is up to the Diet (parliament) to decide what measures to take to accomplish the purposes.[85] The Court ruled that '[t]he authority to determine what constitutes the minimum standard of wholesome and cultured living ... is in principle, vested within the discretionary power of the Minister ...'.[86] In the *Horiki* case, again dealing with the interpretation of art 25 of the Japanese Constitution, the Supreme Court of Japan similarly ruled that the section must be given expression by the legislature based on the financial conditions in which the state finds itself,

---

[73] See 'Maastrict Guidelines on Violations of Economic, Social and Cultural Rights', reprinted in *African Legal Aid Quarterly*, January-March 1997, 25–30. See Yvonne Donders 'Commentary on the Guidelines' (1997) January–March *African Legal Aid Quarterly* 22–5. Under art 8 of the Guidelines, states cannot use the principle of progressive realization as a pretext for non-compliance. Under art 9, there is a minimum core of obligations, which all states must ensure.

[74] Donders 24.

[75] Kartashkin 114.

[76] Sections 26(2), 27(1), 27(2) and 29(1) of the Constitution.

[77] Karpen 93.

[78] Philip Kunig 'The Principle of Social Justice' in *The Constitution of the Federal Republic of Germany: Essays on the Basic Rights and Principles of the Basic Law with a Translation of the Basic Law*, edited by Ulrich Karpen. Baden-Baden: Nomos 1988, 203.

[79] Jeewan BP Reddy 'The Jurisprudence of Human Rights' in *Human Rights and Judicial Review: A Comparative Perspective*, edited by David Beatty. Dordrecht: M Nijhoff 1994, 177.

[80] Jacques-Yvan Morin 'The Rule of Law and the *Rechtsstaat* Concept' in *Federalism-in-the-Making: Contemporary Canadian and German Constitutionalism, National and Transnational*, edited by Edward McWhinney, et al. Dordrecht: M Nijhoff 1992, 77.

[81] Kunig 203–4.

[82] Morin 77. See also Kunig 201.

[83] 33 BVerfGE 303 quoted in Kommers 300.

[84] Ibid.

[85] Itsuo Sonobe 'The System of Constitutional Review in Japan' in *Human Rights and Judicial Review: A Comparative Perspective*, edited by David M Beatty. Dordrecht: M Nijhoff 1994, 168–9.

[86] Op cit 170.

taking into account technical, professional and policy factors.[87] Under art 26(2) of the Japanese Constitution, free compulsory education is provided. In the *Free Textbook* case, plaintiffs brought a challenge against the law which charges students for textbooks. The Japanese Supreme Court ruled that such determinations as to who bears the costs and other fiscal matters must be made by the legislature.[88] It is only when the exercise of these discretionary powers become extremely unreasonable would the Court intervene.[89]

The same conclusion has been reached by the Supreme Courts of both Ireland and Spain, when asked to look into the validity of social policy in terms of their Constitutions.[90] It is one thing for the state not to act, in which case the Court might rule the inaction unconstitutional. In *Grootboom*, the respondents were a group of people who were rendered homeless as a result of successive evictions and were in a situation where they had nowhere else to go.[91] The Constitutional Court found that there was no programme in place to deal with the respondents' desperate situation.[92] Not having a programme at all was unreasonable and a violation of the state's obligation.[93]

However, the decision as to what resources to allocate for social welfare programmes, in a sense, involves constitutional politics as opposed to constitutional law.[94] The decisions from the various tribunals confirm that courts would neither define the content of what the rights entail, nor the means that should be used to fulfil those rights.[95] Although socioeconomic rights are not readily amenable to supervision in the same way as civil and political rights, the Court can, in the development of its jurisprudence, constantly remind the legislature of its social welfare obligations. For example, the German Constitutional Court has played an active role in reminding the government of its social obligations towards the establishment of a just social order.[96] While the Court has been reluctant to award legal claims for socioeconomic rights, the Court has on several occasions stated that the function of the state is not only to protect individual rights, but that it is also obliged to be active in promoting the social and educational advancement of the community.[97]

'The Last Generation: When Rights lose their Meaning'[98]
(notes omitted).

In terms of the everyday world of politics and policy formulation, it is easy to identify the line from which the courts have consistently recoiled. In functional terms the line is drawn around the power to fix a community's political priorities and to control the fiscal or the purse.

The fact is that no matter how much encouragement the words of a constitution may seem to provide, no court has ever stood up to the other two, elected branches of government and told them that the actual amounts or levels of financial or cultural support they have provided are inadequate as a matter of constitutional law. Except in cases when a finding of discrimination or unequal treatment as been made out, whenever claimants have asked a court to

---

[87] Ibid.

[88] Op cit 169.

[89] Op cit 171.

[90] JM Kelly, et al *The Irish Constitution* Dublin: Butterworths, 3rd edition, 1994, 1119. Starck 103, 116.

[91] *Grootboom* para 9.

[92] *Supra* para 52.

[93] *Supra* paras 68–69.

[94] This is a distinction introduced by Philip Kunig when considering the German reality. See Kunig 198.

[95] *Grootboom* paras 41–42. Donald P Kommers 'German Constitutionalism: A Prolegomenon' (1991) 40 *Emory Law Journal* 837, 862.

[96] Donald P Kommers *The Constitutional Jurisprudence of the Federal Republic of Germany* 248.

[97] Ibid. This is the pervasive message which comes out of the *Grootboom* opinion.

[98] David Beatty in *Human Rights and Judicial Review: A Comparative Perspective*, edited by David M Beatty. Dordrecht: M Nijhoff 1994, 347–53, 355 (published with permission).

second guess the amount of money a Government has decided to spend on particular social or cultural programmes, they have, without exception, gone away empty-handed.

In legal parlance, the courts have consistently and without exception held that claims of this kind which asks them to establish basic levels of economic and cultural well-being beyond those fixed by the elected representatives of the people are 'non-justiciable'. In lay terms, all of the courts recognize that the elected branches of government have the ultimate authority to decide how much of a community's resources will be spent educating, housing and healing its people and how much will be set aside to alleviate the suffering of those facing conditions of poverty and extreme privation. Even when a constitution explicitly guarantees people a sweeping right to a minimum standard of 'wholesome cultural living' or provides very specific entitlements to social assistance, pensions and health care programmes, as in Japan and Italy, the courts have acknowledged that legislators possess the final discretion to settle, as a matter of hard currency, what meaning these constitutional entitlements will have. Even the Supreme Court of India, which has been especially vocal in urging governments to be responsive to the plight of those forced to live at the margins of human existence, has stopped short of ordering the central or one of the regional Governments to provide work or higher levels of social assistance.

The steadfast refusal of the judiciary to assume responsibility for the budget and the fiscal priorities of the state is not difficult to understand. It is based on the idea, central to all liberal democratic theories of government should be kept separate and distinct. Policy formulation and administration are the principal tasks of the legislature and executive. Election to these branches of government is based, in the most general sense, on platforms which showcase preferred packages of social policies and political priorities. The election of Governments carries with it a mandate to raise whatever resources are necessary to implement the programmes which the people preferred.

Judges, on the other hand, are not elected except only in the mot indirect and attenuated sense because of their political or social philosophies. Their task is to enforce, not revise the law, which includes the constitution of course. From the decisions they have made about people's economic and group rights, we have seen that the role of the third branch of government is to guarantee that all laws and official action taken in the name of the state must meet what are, in effect two very basic measure of distributive justice or formal equality. For the most part, the principles of rationality and proportionality impose duties on how those elected to govern must 'act' in translating their political platforms into law; not on what the content of their policies and programmes should be.

To borrow a phrase Ronald Dworkin has popularized, one could say the role of the court is to ensure that those who are entrusted with the powers of the state show equal concern and respect for those whose lives they can affect. The principle of rationality guarantees everyone a measure of equal respect by ruling unconstitutional laws which restrict their freedom unnecessarily or gratuitously. The principle of proportionality ensures Governments will show the same concern for everyone's life by insisting that there is some consistency in how burdens and benefits which are contained in the law are distributed.

So long as the courts restrict their role to the impartial application of these broad precepts of equality and personal autonomy, they can with good reason be called 'the least dangerous branch' of government. Indeed, the duties and obligations which these principles impose on the 'will of the people' and on the powers of the other two, elected branches of government are not only consistent with, they actually promote the same values and ideals which underlie democracy and popular sovereignty as well. By contrast, it would constitute a serious setback for the forces of democracy and the sovereignty of the people if judges ever did assume that, in addition to being guardians of the constitution, they held ultimate power over the purse. The juxtaposition of such sweeping powers in the branch of government least representative of and accountable to the pole would be to signal a regression to the kind of oligarchic institutions which distinguished (and ultimately discredited) colonial ideas of 'responsible' government.

Now at this point, if not before, human rights activists will undoubtedly want to assert a (constitutional?) right of intervention and reply. Many will have had enormous difficulty with an account which accepts indeed endorses the courts' refusal to recognize what they regard to be the essence of the new generations of rights. They will say the protection of human rights will be only partial and incomplete until the courts take up the task of ensuring that Governments guarantee every person a satisfactory level of physical and spiritual well-being. For them, talk of economic and group rights would be a charade if it did not guarantee substantial social and economic entitlements.

To the separation of powers argument advanced by the courts, they will reply that the jurisprudence shows that the line which is supposed to divide the judiciary from the other two branches of government is crossed all the time. Human rights activists are well aware of the jurisprudence we have reviewed and they often make the point that the courts routinely issue judgments which require Governments to take specific legislative initiatives which can involve very substantial costs for the state. To support their claim, reference is often made to those cases in which courts have ordered the state to provide free legal aid or appoint more judges to satisfy the guarantees, common to all constitutions, that everyone has a right to be tried fairly and fairly expeditiously.

As well, they commonly cite those judgments, which we have already noted, in which the courts have extended the benefits of various social assistance programmes to individuals and groups which the Governments who designed them meant to exclude.

Human rights activists argue that judgments such as these undermine the force of the separation of powers argument. They will say that if it is appropriate for the courts to order

Governments to guarantee a basic level of legal and social services in cases such as these, there can be nothing wrong also insisting that politicians respect whatever minimum standards of housing, health care, education, income etc are preconditions for enjoying a 'wholesome and cultured' life. Without guarantees of this kind, they will say, ideas of formal equality and personal freedom can be used to legitimate living conditions of extreme inequality and deprivation.

Both in spirit and as a matter of empirical observation, the case of the human rights activist pulls hard on most people's sympathies. The cause of the dispossess and the disadvantaged is a compelling one and the fact is, as we have seen for ourselves, on many occasions judges have been very strong and direct in their dealings with the elected branches of government and insisted that initiatives be taken and social programmes extended at considerable cost to the state.

But however appealing the claim of the human rights activists may first appear, neither the justice of their cause nor the past jurisprudence of the courts warrants assigning the third branch of government ultimate power over the purse. It is never a sufficient answer to say that the ends justify the means, and on closer examination it turns out that there is nothing in the way the courts have protected economic and group rights so far which can be used as precedent for judges taking over the job of fixing the levels of social welfare and cultural wellbeing which must be guaranteed in any particular community.

In fact, as we have seen, the courts have never challenged the sovereignty of the people to maintain control of the purse. To the contrary, they have consistently recognized and adhered to the principle of separation of powers between themselves and the other two, elected branches of government. They have never disputed the levels at which any programme of social welfare have been set. Instead, there has been a universal recognition that denying the legislative branch the authority to say just how 'wholesome and cultured' life in each community will be would constitute a massive compromise of the principle of democratic rule.

The decisions to which human rights activists point in support of their case do not really involve the judiciary laying claim to the power of the purse. In fact, they are of a quite different kind. For the most part they follow logically from a straightforward application of the principle of formal equality. Rather than take issue with the level of assistance a programme may guarantee, the courts have simply required legislatures and Governments to make whatever services they do provide available to everyone in a non-discriminatory way. There is no attempt to tell the elected representatives of the people how rich such programmes have to be. Rather than question the practical goals and objectives (the levels of assistance) the people and their representatives set for themselves, in these cases the focus of the courts is strictly on the means the criteria of distribution that are chosen to identify who the beneficiaries of these programmes will be.

Even the cases in which the effect of the court's decision has meant that Governments had to spend considerable sums of money on legal aid schemes or in the construction and staffing of more courts, the idea of equality has done much of the work. Essentially, the reasoning of the courts in cases of this kind has been that Governments should set up legal aid schemes in those proceedings when one of the parties (including the state in criminal trials) will have counsel to represent them. Even the decision of the Supreme Court of Canada, ordering one of its regional Governments to provide more facilities and staff for the courts so that people could have their cases decided within a reasonable time, was based on a gross inequality in how those charged with similar offences in different parts of the country were brought to trial.

Those judgments in which courts have ordered a state to pay a person's legal costs are like those in which the judges have insisted that there must be some social, economic, environmental etc programme or policy in place but have stopped short of asking whether in substance and in detail what has been done is good enough. In all of these cases the courts have recognized that Governments may have different options, with different price tags, available to them to ensure that the legal process id equal and fair, and they have respected the sovereignty of the people and their elected representatives to choose the policy that best suits their needs. Indeed, the Constitutional Court of Italy, regarded by some as the most active court in the filed of social and economic rights, upheld the constitutionality of a system of legal aid which provided no compensation for the lawyers involved in part on the ground that questions concerning the adequacy of social programmes like the provision of legal aid do not raise issues within the domain of constitutional law.

So human rights activists have no answer to the judges who insist on respecting a separation of powers between themselves and the other two, elected branches of government. There is, in fact, no precedent for the judiciary fixing the priorities and levels of state support for people's most basic economic and interpersonal needs. The judiciary has been steadfast in refusing all invitations to assume power over the fiscal, and it is difficult to imagine what circumstances could justify changing its view. To recognize a right to go to court to require Governments to improve the levels of economic and cultural well-being in their communities would mean the end of peoples' sovereignty to define their own political priorities and community values.

In the absence of any satisfactory accounting for the principle of separation of powers and democratic rule, human rights activists act blindly, if not irresponsibly, in continuing to agitate for the entrenchment and judicial definition of minimum standards of social and economic well-being. They encourage people to engage in what will only be fruitless and wasteful litigation, and ultimately to lose respect for the constitution as an inspirational charter of what their community's standards of justice should be. Unless and until they can reconcile such constitutional guarantees with the principle of democratic rule, human rights activists must only look to the courts to promote the ends of justice with the two basic principles of equality of rationality and consistency which have guided their work for the past two hundred years.

That human rights activists must lower their sights in what they can legitimately expect of the courts does not mean that they must close their eyes. Disappointment need not lead to despair. Even if their prescription of how people can improve the level of social justice in their communities is wide of the mark, their instinct that courts can do better than they have in the past must surely be right. However highly one rates the performance of the courts in the enforcement of constitutional bills of rights, on this point everyone critics and activists alike should agree.

Consistent with the approach in other jurisdictions, the Constitutional Court has held that '[t]he precise contours and content of the measures to be adopted are primarily a matter for the legislature and the executive'.[99] When the state is challenged as to whether it has met its positive obligations, the Court will ask the question 'whether the legislative and other measures taken by the state are reasonable'.[100] In looking at whether the measure is reasonable, the Court will not enquire whether there are better alternatives available because policy choices are better left to the other two branches of government.[101] In *Soobramoney v Minister of Health (KwaZulu-Natal)*, the Court held that it was very reluctant to interfere with decisions made by the political organs as to how to allocate scarce medical resources.[102] In *Soobramony*, the applicant requested the Court to issue an order directing the health authorities to make renal dialysis treatment available to him. The applicant based his claim on several provisions of the Constitution, particularly the right to emergency treatment contained in s 27(3). The Court held that all of the social welfare provisions, be it the right to housing, health care, food, water, and social security, were resource driven.[103] The state had to manage its limited resources, which might mean that particular individuals might not receive

life saving treatment.[104] Therefore, the Court would not order the state to provide the plaintiff with treatment.

The Constitutional Court in *Tsotetsi v Mutual and Federal Insurance Company Ltd,* held that it would not easily review a social benefit programme established by the state.[105] The applicant asked the Court to declare parts of ss 46 and 47 of the Multilateral Motor Vehicle Accidents Fund Act,[106] limiting damages that could be recovered from an accident, to be unconstitutional. The Constitutional Court held that, were it to declare the limitations on recovery of damages unconstitutional, this would have serious financial implications for the state.[107] The Court would not readily make an order that would distort the financial affairs of a welfare programme.[108]

The fact that a constitutional provision is not readily amenable to judicial enforcement does not lessen the importance of the right. For example, we made the observation that sometimes the exercise of discretionary executive power, like the granting of pardons by the president, is not easily amenable to judicial control, even where it may be exercised in an unequal manner. The difficulty of subjecting executive discretionary powers to justiciability standards (in terms of a right through a lawsuit enforceable by sanctions) does not lessen

---

[99] *Grootboom* para 41.

[100] *Supra.*

[101] *Supra.*

[102] *Soobramony v Minister of Health (KwaZulu-Natal)* CCT 32/97, *per* Chaskalson P, para 29.

[103] *Supra* para 11.

[104] *Supra* para 31.

[105] CCT 16/95 (12 September 1996), now cited as 1997 (1) SA 585 (CC); 1996 (11) BCLR 1439 (CC).

[106] Act 93 of 1989.

[107] *Tsoetsi* para 9.

[108] See the concerns raised by the Court in *Grootbooom* para 81, where Yacoob J noted that the effect of any order that constitutes a special dispensation for the respondents on account of their extraordinary circumstances is to accord that preference.

the importance of equality under the Constitution. In chapters 2 and 8, we demonstrated how courts have adopted different attitudes towards statutes, depending on the nature of the law. With respect to legislation of an economic matter, there is a tendency in most jurisdictions to accord the greatest latitude to the legislature. In *Soobramony*, Sachs J in his concurring opinion, correctly noted that courts are not the proper place to make these kinds of choices.[109]

Soobramony v Minister of Health (KwaZulu-Natal) CCT 32/97 (27 November 1997), now cited as 1997 (12) BCLR 1696 (CC); 1998 (1) SA 430 (D)
(notes omitted)
CHASKALSON P

[1] The appellant, a 41-year-old unemployed man, is a diabetic who suffers from ischaemic heart disease and cerebro-vascular disease which caused him to have a stroke during 1996. In 1996 his kidneys also failed. Sadly his condition is irreversible and he is now in the final stages of chronic renal failure. His life could be prolonged by means of regular renal dialysis. He has sought such treatment from the renal unit of the Addington State Hospital in Durban. The hospital can, however, only provide dialysis treatment to a limited number of patients. The renal unit has 20 dialysis machines available to it, and some of these machines are in poor condition. Each treatment takes four hours and a further two hours have to be allowed for the cleaning of a machine, before it can be used again for other treatment. Because of the limited facilities that are available for kidney dialysis the hospital has been unable to provide the appellant with the treatment he has requested.

[2] The reasons given by the hospital for this are set out in the respondent's answering affidavit deposed to by Doctor Saraladevi Naicker, a specialist physician and nephrologist in the field of renal medicine who has worked at Addington Hospital for 18 years and who is currently the President of the South African Renal Society. In her affidavit Dr Naicker says that Addington Hospital does not have enough resources to provide dialysis treatment for all patients suffering from chronic renal failure.

Additional dialysis machines and more trained nursing staff are required to enable it to do this, but the hospital budget does not make provision for such expenditure. The hospital would like to have its budget increased but it has been told by the provincial health department that funds are not available for this purpose.

[3] Because of the shortage of resources the hospital follows a set policy in regard to the use of the dialysis resources. Only patients who suffer from acute renal failure, which can be treated and remedied by renal dialysis are given automatic access to renal dialysis at the hospital. Those patients who, like the appellant, suffer from chronic renal failure which is irreversible are not admitted automatically to the renal programme. A set of guidelines has been drawn up and adopted to determine which applicants who have chronic renal failure will be given dialysis treatment. According to the guidelines the primary requirement for admission of such persons to the dialysis programme is that the patient must be eligible for a kidney transplant. A patient who is eligible for a transplant will be provided with dialysis treatment until an organ donor is found and a kidney transplant has been completed.

[4] The guidelines provide that an applicant is not eligible for a transplant unless he or she is '[f]ree of significant vascular or cardiac disease'. The medical criteria set out in the guidelines also provide that an applicant must be

Free of significant disease elsewhere eg ischaemic heart disease, cerebro-vascular disease, peripheral vascular disease, chronic liver disease, chronic lung disease.

The appellant suffers from ischaemic heart disease and cerebro-vascular disease and he is therefore not eligible for a kidney transplant.

---

[109] *Soobramony* paras 58–59.

[5] The appellant has made arrangements to receive dialysis treatment from private hospitals and doctors, but his finances have been depleted and he avers that he is no longer able to afford such treatment. In July 1997 he made an urgent application to the Durban and Coast Local Division of the High Court for an order directing the Addington Hospital to provide him with ongoing dialysis treatment and interdicting the respondent from refusing him admission to the renal unit of the hospital. The appellant claimed that in terms of the 1996 Constitution the Addington Hospital is obliged to make dialysis treatment available to him. The respondent opposed the application. The matter came before Combrinck J who dismissed the application.

[7] The appellant based his claim on section 27(3) of the 1996 Constitution which provides:

No one may be refused emergency medical treatment.

and section 11 which stipulates:

Everyone has the right to life.

[8] We live in a society in which there are great disparities in wealth. Millions of people are living in deplorable conditions and in great poverty. There is a high level of unemployment, inadequate social security, and many do not have access to clean water or to adequate health services. These conditions already existed when the Constitution was adopted and a commitment to address them, and to transform our society into one in which there will be human dignity, freedom and equality, lies at the heart of our new constitutional order. For as long as these conditions continue to exist that aspiration will have a hollow ring.

[10] Sections 26 and 27 contain the following provisions:

26 Housing
Everyone has the right to have access to adequate housing.
(2) The State must take reasonable legislative and other measures, within its available resources, to achieve the progressive realisation of this right.

27 Health care, food, water and social security
(1) Everyone has the right to have access to—
   (a) health care services, including reproductive health care;
   (b) sufficient food and water; and
   (c) social security, including, if they are unable to support themselves and their dependants, appropriate social assistance.
(2) The state must take reasonable legislative and other measures, within its available resources, to achieve the progressive realisation of each of these rights
(3) No one may be refused emergency medical treatment.

[11] What is apparent from these provisions is that the obligations imposed on the State by sections 26 and 27 in regard to access to housing, health care, food, water and social security are dependent upon the resources available for such purposes, and that the corresponding rights themselves are limited by reason of the lack of resources. Given this lack of resources and the significant demands on them that have already been referred to, an unqualified obligation to meet these needs would not presently be capable of being fulfilled. This is the context within which section 27(3) must be construed.

[21] The applicant suffers from chronic renal failure. To be kept alive by dialysis he would require such treatment two to three times a week. This is not an emergency which calls for immediate remedial treatment. It is an ongoing state of affairs resulting from a deterioration of the applicant's renal function which is incurable. In my view section 27(3) does not apply to these facts.

[22] The appellant's demand to receive dialysis treatment at a State hospital must be determined in accordance with the provisions of sections 27(1) and (2) and not section 27(3). These sections entitle everyone to have access to health care services provided by the state 'within its available resources'.

[23] In the Court a quo Combrinck J held that '[i]n this case the respondent has conclu-

sively proved that there are no funds available to provide patients such as the applicant with the necessary treatment'. This finding was not disputed by the appellant, but it was argued that the State could make additional funds available to the renal clinic and that it was obliged to do so to enable the clinic to provide life saving treatment to the appellant and others suffering from chronic renal failure.

[24] At present the Department of Health in KwaZulu-Natal does not have sufficient funds to cover the cost of the services which are being provided to the public. In 1996/1997 it overspent its budget by R152 million, and in the current year it is anticipated that the overspending will be R700 million rand unless a serious cutback is made in the services which it provides. The renal unit at the Addington Hospital has to serve the whole of KwaZulu-Natal and also takes patients from parts of the Eastern Cape. There are many more patients suffering from chronic renal failure than there are dialysis machines to treat such patients. This is a nation-wide problem and resources are stretched in all renal clinics throughout the land. Guidelines have therefore been established to assist the persons working in these clinics to make the agonising choices which have to be made in deciding who should receive treatment, and who not. These guidelines were applied in the present case.

[25] By using the available dialysis machines in accordance with the guidelines more patients are benefited than would be the case if they were used to keep alive persons with chronic renal failure, and the outcome of the treatment is also likely to be more beneficial because it is directed to curing patients, and not simply to maintaining them in a chronically ill condition. It has not been suggested that these guidelines are unreasonable or that they were not applied fairly and rationally when the decision was taken by the Addington Hospital that the appellant did not qualify for dialysis.

[27] The appellant avers in his affidavits that better use could be made of the dialysis machines at the Addington Hospital by keeping the clinic open for longer hours. He says that some of the nurses 'moonlight' at other hospitals after their normal working hours in order to earn extra income, and that if they were given overtime opportunities at the Addington Hospital more people could be treated.

[28] The appellant's case must be seen in the context of the needs which the health services have to meet, for if treatment has to be provided to the appellant it would also have to be provided to all other persons similarly placed. Although the renal clinic could be kept open for longer hours, it would involve additional expense in having to pay the clinic personnel at overtime rates, or in having to employ additional personnel working on a shift basis. It would also put a great strain on the existing dialysis machines which are already showing signs of wear. It is estimated that the cost to the State of treating one chronically ill patient by means of renal dialysis provided twice a week at a state hospital is approximately R60 000 per annum. If all the persons in South Africa who suffer from chronic renal failure were to be provided with dialysis treatment and many of them, as the appellant does, would require treatment three times a week the cost of doing so would make substantial inroads into the health budget. And if this principle were to be applied to all patients claiming access to expensive medical treatment or expensive drugs, the health budget would have to be dramatically increased to the prejudice of other needs which the State has to meet.

[29] The provincial administration which is responsible for health services in KwaZulu-Natal has to make decisions about the funding that should be made available for health care and how such funds should be spent. These choices involve difficult decisions to be taken at the political level in fixing the health budget, and at the functional level in deciding upon the priorities to be met. A court will be slow to interfere with rational decisions taken in good faith by the political organs and medical authorities whose responsibility it is to deal with such matters.

[30] Although the problem of scarce resources is particularly acute in South Africa

this is not a peculiarly South African problem. It is a problem which hospital administrators and doctors have had to confront in other parts of the world, and in which they have had to take similar decisions. In his judgment in this case Combrinck J refers to decisions of the English courts in which it has been held to be undesirable for a court to make an order as to how scarce medical resources should be applied, and to the danger of making any order that the resources be used for a particular patient, which might have the effect of denying those resources to other patients to whom they might more advantageously be devoted. The dilemma confronting health authorities faced with such cases was described by Sir Thomas Bingham MR in a passage cited by Combrinck J from the judgment in *R v Cambridge Health Authority, ex parte B*:

I have no doubt that in a perfect world any treatment which a patient, or a patient's family, sought would be provided if doctors were willing to give it, no matter how much it cost, particularly when a life was potentially at stake. It would however, in my view, be shutting one's eyes to the real world if the court were to proceed on the basis that we do live in such a world. It is common knowledge that health authorities of all kinds are constantly pressed to make ends meet. They cannot pay their nurses as much as they would like; they cannot provide all the treatments they would like; they cannot purchase all the extremely expensive medical equipment they would like; they cannot carry out all the research they would like; they cannot build all the hospitals and specialist units they would like. Difficult and agonising judgments have to be made as to how a limited budget is best allocated to the maximum advantage of the maximum number of patients. That is not a judgment which the court can make.

[31] One cannot but have sympathy for the appellant and his family, who face the cruel dilemma of having to impoverish themselves in order to secure the treatment that the appellant seeks in order to prolong his life. The hard and unpalatable fact is that if the appellant were a wealthy man he would be able to procure such treatment from private sources; he is not and has

to look to the State to provide him with the treatment. But the State's resources are limited and the appellant does not meet the criteria for admission to the renal dialysis programme. Unfortunately, this is true not only of the appellant but of many others who need access to renal dialysis units or to other health services. There are also those who need access to housing, food and water, employment opportunities, and social security. These too are aspects of the right to

... human life: the right to live as a human being, to be part of a broader community, to share in the experience of humanity.

The State has to manage its limited resources in order to address all these claims. There will be times when this requires it to adopt a holistic approach to the larger needs of society rather than to focus on the specific needs of particular individuals within society.

SACHS J:

[58] Courts are not the proper place to resolve the agonising personal and medical problems that underlie these choices Important though our review functions are, there are areas where institutional incapacity and appropriate constitutional modesty require us to be especially cautious. Our country's legal system simply 'cannot replace the more intimate struggle that must be borne by the patient, those caring for the patient, and those who care about the patient'. The provisions of the bill of rights should furthermore not be interpreted in a way which results in courts feeling themselves unduly pressurised by the fear of gambling with the lives of claimants into ordering hospitals to furnish the most expensive and improbable procedures, thereby diverting scarce medical resources and prejudicing the claims of others.

[59] The applicant in this case presented his claim in a most dignified manner and showed manifest appreciation for the situation of the many other persons in the same harsh circumstances as himself. If resources were co-extensive with compassion, I have no doubt as to what my

decision would have been. Unfortunately, the resources are limited, and I can find no reason to interfere with the allocation undertaken by those better equipped than I to deal with the agonising choices that had to be made.

Balancing group and individual rights

Often, in the implementation of social and economic legislation, there will be a balancing of group and individual rights. The Constitutional Court should, when faced with socioeconomic legislation, be careful not to render decisions which make it difficult to implement that legislation. Appropriate deference should be accorded to parliament to shape social and welfare policy. In the previous discussion, we made reference to the approach of the German Constitutional Court that the social state is a legal norm that the legislator must keep in mind as an objective which has to be achieved, and the legislature will be accorded broad discretion as to the extent and means to be used to achieve that social protection.[110] The German concept of the rule of law includes social justice; there the rule of law is not viewed as independent from social justice.[111] The social welfare concept has been used by the legislature and accepted by the Court on a number of occasions to justify social welfare legislation over objections that it interferes with individual rights. If we conceive of a situation where the South African government adopted an economic policy resulting in the taking of resources, either directly or indirectly, from the wealthier sector of society and directing the resources towards the construction of housing for the indigent sector of society; in the United States tradition, this could in terms of the South African Constitution represent deprivation of liberty and taking of property.[112] However, the Constitutional Court has it within its powers to interpret the welfare obligations in a way favouring societal interests over those of the individual. For example, in Germany after the Second World War, some sectors of German industry had tremendous financial problems re-establishing themselves. The federal parliament passed a law imposing a special tax on certain manufacturers and traders with the object of funding those industries experiencing problems. Several corporations filed a constitutional complaint claiming the legislation imposed a special tax on them, and that this violated the equality provision of the German Constitution. In the *Investment Aid 1* case of 1954,[113] the German Constitutional Court declared:

The image of man in the Basic Law is not that of an isolated, sovereign individual. On the contrary, the Basic Law has resolved the tension between the individual and society in favor of coordination and interdependence with the community without touching the intrinsic value of the person.[114]

The German Constitutional Court went on to say:

The individual has to accept those limits on his freedom of action which the legislature imposes to cultivate and maintain society. In turn, such acceptance depends upon the limits of what can reasonably be demanded in a particular case, provided the autonomy of the person is preserved.[115]

Similarly, in Sweden after the Second World War, the legislature introduced detailed laws to provide housing for the majority of the population. One of the cornerstones of this government policy was to remove speculation and profit-making on the cost of land.[116] Local government was able to expropriate

---

[110] Morin 77.

[111] Op cit 78.

[112] See eg *Dolan v City of Tigard* 1994 US Lexis 4826 (24 June 1994).

[113] *Investment Aid 1* case (1954) 4 BVerfGe 7 in Kommers 249.

[114] Op cit 250.

[115] Ibid.

[116] Kenn 80.

land, and to control land sales. In addition, the government introduced widespread cost controls. With this combination of measures, the government was able to allocate significant resources to the building of and distribution of housing.[117] Again, it is possible that such legislation might encroach on individual autonomy and property. As the German Constitutional Court remarked, it is not authorized to judge the wisdom of legislation, and that the state does have the power to pass laws in the interest of particular groups. This approach is adhered to by the highest courts in India, Canada, and the United States, which consistently resist invitations to balance competing interests between those of the individual, and society's need for social programmes.[118] The approach of the highest courts in these various jurisdictions confirms that the legislature is the institution which is best placed to make these kinds of determinations.[119]

The South African Constitutional Court should draw on this jurisprudence. Where the pursuit of social welfare programmes touches on individual rights, it need not be justified under the limitations clause. What we have is a balancing between individual rights and group rights. Parliament is required to achieve social welfare rights. Under traditional liberal thought, individuals should not be used to achieve state objectives. In chapter 2 we argued that the Constitution does not embrace this rugged individualism. The Constitution moves beyond the common law and its concept of *atomistic* individuals, towards a consideration of the interests of the majority. Individuals can be required to make sacrifices for the common good. Parliament should be allowed the discretion to adopt appropriate programmes to meet societal needs. In a landmark address to the Transvaal Law Society, Constitutional Court President Arthur Chaskalson remarked that young lawyers should be required to perform community service to aid in the delivery of legal services to the indigent.[120] Arguably, where such programmes are embarked upon, the validity of these programmes should be judged under the mere rationality test. Moreover, since the programmes are undertaken pursuant to a constitutional mandate, the limitations clause should not be used to justify limitations on individual autonomy. In the balancing process, only in the extreme cases, where the intrusion on individual autonomy is particularly severe,[121] should the Court intervene.[122] In *Lawrence and Others v The State and Another*, the Constitutional Court, *per* Chaskalson P, appropriately adopted the mere rationality test in subjecting social and economic regulation to scrutiny.[123] The Canadian Supreme Court similarly distinguishes between cases where the state acts against an individual as opposed to the situation where the state acts to mediate priorities and allocate resources between different groups. In the latter instance, greater deference is accorded to the legislature.[124]

---

[117] Op cit 81.

[118] M Hidayatullah *Constitutional Law of India*, Vol 1. New Delhi: Bar Council of India Trust 1984, 476–7. Patrick Macklem, et al *Constitutional Law of Canada* Toronto: Emond Montgomery Publishers 1994, 138.

[119] David M Beatty 'The Last Generation: When Rights lose their Meaning' in *Human Rights and Judicial Review: A Comparative Perspective*, edited by David M Beatty. Dordrecht: M Nijhoff 1994, 30.

[120] (1997) 12 November *The Star and SA Times International* 10.

[121] eg where there is a violation of human dignity. See discussion on equality in chapter 8.

[122] Macklem 515.

[123] CCT 38/96; 39/96; 40/96 (6 October 1997) para 44–45, now cited as 1997 (10) BCLR 1348 (CC); 1997 (4) SA 1176 (CC).

[124] Macklem 183–4.

S v Lawrence; S v Negal; S v Solberg
CCT 38/96; 39/96; 40/96
(6 October 1997), now cited as
1997 (10) BCLR 1348 (CC);
1997 (4) SA 1176 (CC)
(notes omitted)

Authors' note: The applicants argued that the Liquor Act 27 of 1989, which prohibited the selling of wine after certain hours, violated the interim Constitution which guaranteed the applicants' right to economic activity.

[42] In the passage relied upon by the appellants Professor Mureinik argued for a more stringent test of legislative purpose that there be an 'objective probability' that the purpose will be achieved. He was not, however, dealing there with 'economic freedom'. To apply that test to economic regulation would require courts to sit in judgment on legislative policies on economic issues Courts are ill equipped to do this and in a democratic society it is not their role to do so. In discussing legislative purpose Professor Hogg says:

While a court must reach a definite conclusion on the adjudicative facts which are relevant to the disposition of litigation, the court need not be so definite in respect of legislative facts in constitutional cases. The most that the court can ask in respect of legislative facts is whether there is a rational basis for the legislative judgment that the facts exist.

The rational basis test involves restraint on the part of the court in finding legislative facts. Restraint is often compelled by the nature of the issue: for example, an issue of economics which is disputed by professional economists can hardly be definitively resolved by a court staffed by lawyers. The most that can realistically be expected of a court is a finding that there is, or is not, a rational basis for a particular position on the disputed issue.

The more important reason for restraint, however, is related to the respective roles of court and legislature. A legislature acts not merely on the basis of findings of fact, but upon its judgment as to the public perceptions

of a situation and its judgments as to the appropriate policy to meet the situation. These judgments are political, and they often do not coincide with the views of social scientists or other experts. It is not for the court to disturb political judgments, much less to substitute the opinions of experts. In a democracy it would be a serious distortion of the political process if appointed officials (the judges) could veto the policies of elected officials.'

[43] This accords with the approach of the United States Supreme Court to rational basis review. It has consistently held:

This restriction upon the judicial function, in passing on the constitutionality of statutes, is not artificial or irrational. A state legislature, in the enactment of laws, has the widest possible latitude within the limits of the Constitution. In the nature of the case it cannot record a complete catalogue of the considerations which move its members to enact laws. In the absence of such a record courts cannot assume that its action is capricious, or that, with its informed acquaintance with local conditions to which the legislation is to be applied, it was not aware of facts which afford reasonable basis for its action. Only by faithful adherence to this guiding principle of judicial review of legislation is it possible to preserve to the legislative branch its rightful independence and its ability to function.

[44] Section 26 should not be construed as empowering a court to set aside legislation expressing social or economic policy as infringing 'economic freedom' simply because it may consider the legislation to be ineffective or is of the opinion that there are other and better ways of dealing with the problems. If section 26(1) is given the broad meaning for which the appellants contend, of encompassing all forms of economic activity and all methods of pursuing a livelihood, then, if regard is had to the role of the courts in a democratic society, section 26(2) should also be given a broad meaning. To maintain the proper balance between the roles of the legislature and the courts section 26(2) should be construed as requiring only that there be a rational connection between the legislation

and the legislative purpose sanctioned by the section. I deal later with how, if it be disputed, the legislative purpose is to be established.

[45] The rational basis test fits the language of the section which, unlike section 33, sets as the criterion that the measures must be justifiable in an open and democratic society based on freedom and equality, but does not require in addition to this that the measure be reasonable. The proportionality analysis which is required to give effect to the criterion of 'reasonableness' in section 33 forms no part of a section 26 analysis

[46] In coming to the conclusion that section 26(2) calls for a rational basis review I have given consideration to the decision in *Public Servants'*

Association of South Africa and Another v Minister of Justice and Others. This case deals with the meaning of the words 'designed to achieve' in section 8(3) of the interim Constitution and takes an approach that is different to the approach taken by me in this judgment. I specifically refrain from commenting in any way on the correctness of that decision or on the interpretation to be placed on section 8(3). That section raises difficult issues, the consideration of which must be deferred until the occasion arises for this Court to do so. It is not necessary to express any view as to whether the test for rational review under section 26 is in any way different to the test for rational review under section 8.

Other methods of implementation: the role of the Human Rights Commission

While there is an obligation to give priority to social welfare rights, which is not readily amenable to judicial supervision, there are other non-judicial methods of implementation. The independent constitutional organs, such as the Human Rights Commission; the Cultural, Religious and Linguistic Commission, and the Gender Commission have important constitutional roles in the promotion and achievement of human rights. Of the three, the Human Rights Commission has a particularly vital role in the promotion of social welfare rights.[125] The Cultural, Religious and Linguistic Commission has a critical role in the promotion of cultural rights.

Functions of the Human Rights Commission
184 (1) The Human Rights Commission must—
    (a) promote respect for human rights and a culture of human rights;
    (b) promote the protection, development and attainment of human rights; and
    (c) monitor and assess the observance of human rights in the Republic.

(2) The Human Rights Commission has the powers, as regulated by national legislation, necessary to perform its functions, including the power—
    (a) to investigate and to report on the observance of human rights;
    (b) to take steps to secure appropriate redress where human rights have been violated;
    (c) to carry out research; and
    (d) to educate.
(3) Each year, the Human Rights Commission must require relevant organs of state to provide the Commission with information on the measures that they have taken towards the realisation of the rights in the Bill of Rights concerning housing, health care, food, water, social security, education, and the environment.
(4) The Human Rights Commission has the additional powers and functions prescribed by national legislation.

Commission for the Promotion and Protection of the Rights of Cultural, Religious and Linguistic Communities: Functions of Commission
185 (1) The primary objects of the Commission for the Promotion and Protection of the Rights of Cultural, Religious and Linguistic Communities are—
    (a) to promote respect for the rights of

---

[125] As spelled out in s 184(3) of the Constitution.

cultural, religious and linguistic communities;

(b) to promote and develop peace, friendship, humanity, tolerance and national unity amongst cultural, religious and linguistic communities, on the basis of equality, non-discrimination and free association; and

(c) to recommend the establishment or recognition, in accordance with national legislation, of a cultural or other council or councils for a community or communities in South Africa.

(2) The Commission has the power, as regulated by national legislation, necessary to achieve its primary objects, including the power to monitor, investigate, research, educate, lobby, advise and report on issues concerning the rights of cultural, religious and linguistic communities.

(3) The Commission may report any matter which falls within its powers and functions to the Human Rights Commission for investigation.

(4) The Commission has the additional powers and functions prescribed by national legislation.

The task of the above-mentioned constitutional organs is to promote human rights protection. Their actions are directed towards promotion of protections, as opposed to imposing sanctions. Therefore, their mandate is expressed in terms of promotion, monitoring, and assessing the respect and observance of human rights. The Human Rights Commission is specifically directed towards the monitoring of social welfare rights 'concerning housing, health care, food, water, social security, education, and the environment'.[126] Its promotional task moves beyond the judicial processes (which are not precluded),[127] towards other techniques, including investigating and reporting;[128] research,[129] and education.[130] These other techniques require a dialogue and interaction with other organs of government, particularly the legislature.

The task of the Human Rights Commission is, in many ways, similar to the role of the principal organs of the UN, particularly the role performed by the specialized agencies of the UN, in the implementation of social welfare rights. The UN General Assembly has the power of initiating studies and making recommendations in assisting in the realization of human rights.[131] The Economic and Social Council (ECOSOC) has similar powers to make recommendations for the promotion and respect for human rights.[132] Under the Economic Covenant, state parties undertake to provide periodic reports to ECOSOC, on measures which they have taken to secure the implementation of rights contained in the covenant.[133] The aim of these reports is to evaluate the progress of states in the achievement of the rights contained in the covenant. These reports indicate the factors and difficulties that the state parties encounter in the fulfilment of the obligations.[134] The reports are evaluated by the expert Committee on Economic, Social and Cultural Rights whose task is to assist ECOSOC in monitoring states' compliance with international social welfare obligations.[135] The reports are also sent to the various specialized agencies.[136]

The work of the Human Rights Commission in the field of social welfare rights, under the

---

[126] Section 184(3).

[127] Section 184(4) permits the Human Rights Commission to exercise additional powers as prescribed by parliament. Section 184(2) *(b)* provides for taking steps to secure redress where there are human rights violations. Arguably, the judicial process is more suited to the securing of civil and political rights given the specific mandate to secure information from the relevant organs of state with respect to social welfare rights.

[128] Section 184(2)*(a)*.

[129] Section 184(2)*(c)*.

[130] Section 184(2)*(d)*.

[131] Article 13(1)*(b)* of the UN Charter.

[132] Article 62(2).

[133] Article 16 of the Economic Covenant.

[134] Article 17.

[135] Newman & Weissbrodt 72.

[136] Article 16(2)*(b)* of the Economic Covenant.

Constitution, is even more analogous to the role performed by the UN specialized agencies, which are ultimately responsible under international law for the implementation of social welfare rights. Most of the economic social and cultural rights under the Economic Covenant are supervised by specialized agencies such as the International Labour Organization (ILO), UN Educational and Scientific Organization (UNESCO), World Health Organization (WHO), and the Food and Agriculture Organization (FAO). [137] Each of the specialized agencies has a system of reporting and method of evaluation as to whether the objectives which fall under their purview are being achieved. [138] Under the international system, the specialized agencies play a pivotal role in the designing of effective programmes in the context of specific states. [139] They also provide standards and guidelines for the progressive realization of social welfare rights. [140] Just as in the international setting, the Human Rights Commission need not accept the legislature's determination as to which resources are adequate for meeting social welfare needs. The Human Rights Commission is in a position to gather information about problems and resources, and can subject governmental decisions on allocation of resources to public scrutiny. It can make the legislature account for the amount it spends or fails to spend in the social welfare realm, and expose situations which it considers a dereliction of the states' duties. Through the reports it receives from governmental organs, and its studies and investigations, the Human Rights Commission should, through a process of dialogue with the other organs of government, play a vital role in the design and implementation of social welfare programmes. To the extent that the government is derelict in prioritizing social welfare rights, the Commission has a vital function in the political process through its reporting and educational role. As observed previously, implementation on social welfare rights is ultimately dependent on the political process. [141] There is a political and moral obligation on the government to implement these rights. If the government fails to do so, it will suffer the political consequences for failing to fulfil these obligations. [142]

---

[137] Kamleshwar Das 'United Nations Institutions and Procedures founded on Conventions on Human Rights and Fundamental Freedoms' in *The International Dimensions of Human Rights*, edited by Karel Vasak and Philip Alston. Westport: Greenwood Press 1982, 332.

[138] Ibid.

[139] David M Trubek 'Economic, Social and Cultural Rights in the Third World: Human Rights, Law and Human Needs Programs' in *Human Rights in International Law: Legal and Policy Issues*, edited by Theodor Meran. Oxford: Oxford University Press 1984, 1220.

[140] Op cit 221. In the area of health care, see op cit 242.

[141] Kunig 203–4.

[142] Schwartz 28.

14

The limitations clause

Introduction

Very few rights are absolute.[1] All the international instruments on human rights contain limitations clauses, which lay out circumstances under which derogation from rights may be allowed.[2] In South Africa, in order to sustain a limitation on a fundamental right, the limitation must satisfy the limitations clause found in s 36(1) of the Constitution, which provides:

> The rights in the Bill of Rights may be limited only in terms of law of general application to the extent that the limitation is reasonable and justifiable in an open and democratic society based on human dignity, equality and freedom, taking into account all relevant factors including:
> (a) the nature of the right;
> (b) the importance of the purpose of the limitation;
> (c) the nature and extent of the limitation;
> (d) the relation between the limitation and its purpose; and
> (e) less restrictive means to achieve the purpose.

The test under the limitations clause

Review of legislation by the Court proceeds in two stages under the Constitution:[3] first, the Court is asked whether there is a violation of a right protected in the Constitution. At this stage, the Court is concerned with the definition and interpretation of the right. If it is found that the right has been violated, the Court proceeds to the second stage where it considers whether the limitation is permissible under the limitations clause. Therefore, unlike the United States

---

[1] The table in s 37(5)(c) of the Constitution lists the non-derogable rights under the Constitution.

[2] For examples of few limitations clauses, see art 29(2) of the Universal Declaration; arts 19(3), 20(2) and 21 of the Civil Covenant; arts 9(2) and 11(2) of the European Convention of Human Rights; arts 10(1), 11 and 14 of the African Charter on Human and Peoples Rights, and arts 15, 16(2) and 21(2) of the American Convention on Human Rights.

[3] *Per* Langa J in *S v Henry Williams and Others* CCT 20/94 cited as 1995 (7) BCLR 861 (CC), para 64; 1995 (3) SA 632 (CC), see also Chaskalson P in *Makwanyane* CCT 3/94 cited as 1995 (6) BCLR 665 (CC), para 100; 1995 (3) SA 391 (CC). The two-stage approach was adopted from the Canadian constitutional model. Judge Zakeria Mohammed Yacoob 'Salient Features of the Negotiating Process' (1999) 52 *Southern Methodist University Law Review* 1581–2. Dennis Davis, et al *Fundamental Rights in the Constitution: Commentary and cases: A Commentary on Chapter 3 on Fundamental Rights of the 1993 Constitution and Chapter 2 of the 1996 Constitution* Cape Town: Juta & Co 1997, 6.

approach of strict scrutiny, the limitations clause is applied in a nuanced and contextual mode.[4] Often, the factors which the Court considers in the formulation of the right are also considered during the limitations enquiry.[5]

The first requirement is that any limitation must be in terms of a law, and the law must be of general application.[6] This requirement is also an affirmation of the rule of law, which is meant to prevent the arbitrary exercise of power. Under the principle of the rule of law, a law must be known to all beforehand, so that individuals can structure their behaviour in terms of the legal requirements. It is also meant to curtail the spectre of violations committed at the whim and fancy of state officials. The requirement that the law be of general application is meant to prevent the targeting of specific individuals. It is debatable as to what the precise reach of this requirement is when it comes to, for example, corporations and other artificial entities. Let us assume that the state passes a law against a particular entity which exercises a monopoly, to break that monopoly's stronghold over the economy. Would such singling out of a single firm be a violation of the requirement of a law of general application?[7]

Section 36(1) of the Constitution lists a number of requirements that have to be considered in subjecting a limitation to scrutiny. A number of factors can be distilled from the Court's jurisprudence. A limitation which violates an entrenched right must be cogently established and must be manifestly reasonable.[8] The state bears the burden of proving that the limitation is permissible.[9] For example, in a litany of cases dealing with reverse onus presumptions, the Court has stated that it is up to the lawmaker to justify any limitation on the presumption of innocence.[10] In *Scagell*, the state wanted the Constitutional Court to uphold the reverse onus presumptions contained in the Gambling Act.[11] The applicants argued that the presumption violated various provisions in the interim Constitution Bill of Rights. The Court held that the state bore the burden of proving why a law that violated fundamental rights should be upheld.[12]

In assessing the other factors under the limitations clause, ultimately the evaluation comes down to an assessment of proportionality. In *Makwanyane*, Chaskalson P stated that where there is a limitation of a right, there needs to be a balancing of competing values and ultimately an assessment on proportionality.[13] The president further observed:

In the balancing process, the relevant considerations will include the nature of the right that is limited, and its importance to an open and democratic society based on freedom and equality; the purpose for which the right is limited and the importance of that purpose to such a society; the extent of the limitation, its efficacy, and particularly where the limitation has to be necessary, whether the desired ends could reasonably be achieved through other means less damaging to the right in question.

---

[4] *Christian Education of South Africa v Minister of Education* CCT 4/00 (18 August 2000) para 31, now cited as 2000 (10) BCLR 1051 (CC); 2000 (4) SA 757 (CC).

[5] See the admonition of Sachs J in *Coetzee v The Government of the Republic of South Africa and Others; and Matiso and Others v The Commanding Officer, Port Elizabeth Prison and Others* 19/94 recorded as 1995 (10) BCLR 1382 (); 1995 (4) SA 631 (CC) para 46. Sachs J stated that there is a commonality that runs through the two stages There are values which must suffuse the whole process which are derived from the concept of an open and democratic society based on freedom and equality.

[6] *Hoffmann v South African Airways* CCT 17/00 (28 September 2000) para 41, now cited as 2000 (10) BCLR 1211 (CC); 2001 (1) SA 1 (CC).

[7] The Indian SC has held otherwise in *Chiranjit Lal v UOI* AIR (1951) SC 41 alluded to in Hidayatullah, 263. (The Court treated the enterprise as a class in itself.)

[8] Per Kriegler J in *S v Makwanyane and Another* CCT 3/94 (6 June 1995) para 210, now cited as 1995 (3) SA 391 now cited as 1995 (6) BCLR 665 (CC); 1994 (3) SA 868 (A).

[9] *Supra* para 184.

[10] *Scagell and Others v Attorney-General of the Western Cape and Others, 1996* CCT 42/95 (12 September 1996) para 9, now cited as 1997 (2) SA 368 (CC); 1996 (11) BCLR 1446 (CC).

[11] Act 51 of 1965.

[12] *Scagell* para 2.

[13] Per Chaskalson P in *S v Makwanyane* para 104.

Scagell and Others v Attorney-General of the Western Cape and Others
CCT 42/95 (12 September 1996), now cited as 1997 (2) SA 368 (CC); 1996 (11) BCLR 1446 (CC)
(notes omiited)
O'REGAN J:

[1] I n this case we are concerned with the question of whether sections 6(3), 6(4), 6(5), 6(6) and 6(7) of the Gambling Act, 51 of 1965 (the Act) are inconsistent with the provisions of the Constitution of the Republic of South Africa, Act 200 of 1993 (the Constitution). They are challenged on the ground that they are in breach of section 25(3) of the Constitution which guarantees the right to a fair trial and, more particularly, on the ground that they are in breach of section 25(3)(c) which protects the presumption of innocence and the right to remain silent.

[9] In this case, the State filed written evidence to establish the purpose and effects of the Act. In his affidavit, Mr CL Fismer, then Minister for General Services, pointed to the negative effects on our society of unlicensed gambling and the consequent need to control such gambling. No evidence was produced as to particular difficulties faced by the police or the Attorney-General in investigating and prosecuting people for illegal gambling. No evidence was led concerning the need for a sweeping presumption of the sort contained in section 6(4) or for that matter any of the other presumptions. Nor was any convincing evidence provided to suggest that conventional policing tactics, such as, for example, the use of plain-clothes police officers, could not provide the necessary evidence for the prosecution of such offences. Evidence lodged to meet the requirements of section 33 needs to persuade us that the particular provisions under attack are justifiable in terms of section 33, not merely address the justifiability of the overall legislative purpose sought to be achieved by the statute.

The limitations clause under both the interim and final Constitutions resembles s 1 of the Canadian Charter of Rights and Freedoms. Not surprisingly, the Constitutional Court has relied on Canadian cases in interpreting the limitations clause.[14] In *Makwanyane*, Chaskalson P further elaborated on the extent of any permissible limitation by citing the Canadian case of *R v Oakes*, which described the components of proportionality. They require a rational connection to the objective sought, and should impair the right in question in as minimum a fashion as possible.[15]

Makwanyane involved the interpretation of various rights under the interim Constitution limitations clause. The factors that need to be considered under s 36(1) of the final Constitution reflect the requirements that the Constitutional Court, *per* Chaskalson P, laid out in *Makwa-nyane*.[16] There are some differences in the wording of the limitation clause under the interim Constitution and the final Constitution. For example, under the interim Constitution limitations clause s 33(1)(b), there was a requirement that any limitation must not negate the essential content of the right in question. For some rights that were listed in ss 33(1)(b)(aa) and (bb), the limitation had to be necessary. Both of the above standards are not mentioned in s 36(1) of the interim Constitution. Another difference is that under the final Constitution, any limitation must have regard to human dignity, a requirement that was not contained in the interim Constitution. Even though the wording of the limitations clause under the interim Constitution differs from that of the final Constitution, the enquiry which the Court is required to conduct in subjecting the limitation to scrutiny remains largely the same;

---

[14] Although Kentridge AJ stated in *Zuma*, that the Court would not follow the criteria employed by the Canadian courts, but would instead employ the criteria spelt out in the limitations clause itself, *S v Zuma and others* CCT 5/94 (5 April 1995) para 34, now cited as 1995 (4) BCLR 401 (SA); 1995 (2) SA 642 (CC).

[15] See *S v Makwanyane* paras 105, 107.

[16] Davis 317.

except that now the Court is required to follow its formulation in *Makwanyane*.[17]

Ultimately, the question is one of proportionality.[18] When considering the factors mentioned in s 36(1), there is no absolute standard for determining what is reasonable and justifiable in an open and democratic society.[19] The question can also not be answered in a mechanical fashion.[20] Application of these principles can only be performed on a case-by-case basis, which is inherent in the requirements of proportionality which calls for the balancing of different interests.[21] Therefore, there is no absolute standard for determining reasonableness.[22] There is a high

---

National Coalition for Gay and Lesbian Equality and Another v The Minister of Justice
1998 (6) BCLR 726 (W); 1999 (1) SA 6 (CC).
(notes omitted)

[33] Although section 36(1) of the 1996 Constitution differs in various respects from section 33 of the interim Constitution its application still involves a process, described in *S v Makwanyane and Another* (41) as the ... weighing up of competing values, and ultimately an assessment based on proportionality ... which calls for the balancing of different interests.

[34] In *Makwanyane* the relevant considerations in the balancing process were stated to include ... the nature of the right that is limited, and its importance to an open and democratic society based on freedom and equality; the purpose for which the right is limited and the importance of that purpose to such a society; the extent of the limitation, its efficacy and, particularly where the limitation has to be necessary, whether the desired ends could reasonably be achieved through other means less damaging to the right in question. The relevant considerations in the balancing process are now expressly stated in section 36(1) of the 1996 Constitution to include those itemized in paragraphs *(a)* to *(e)* thereof. In my view this does not in any material respect alter the approach expounded in *Makwanyane*, save that paragraph *(e)* requires that account be taken in each limitation evaluation of less restrictive means to achieve the purpose [of the limitation]. Although section 36(1) does not expressly mention the importance of the right, this is a factor which must of necessity be taken into account in any proportionality evaluation.

[35] The balancing of different interests must still take place. On the one hand there is the right infringed; its nature; its importance in an open and democratic society based on human dignity, equality and freedom; and the nature and extent of the limitation. On the other hand there is the importance of the purpose of the limitation. In the balancing process and in the evaluation of proportionality one is enjoined to consider the relation between the limitation and its purpose as well as the existence of less restrictive means to achieve this purpose.

---

[17] *National Coalition for Gay and Lesbian Equality and Another v The Minister of Justice* CCT 11/98 (9 October 1998) para 33, *per* Sachs J, now cited as 1998 (6) BCLR 1517 (CC); 1999 (1) SA 6 (CC); *De Lange v Smuts NO and Others* CCT 26/97 (28 May 1998) para 163, *per* O'Regan J, now cited as 1998(7) BCLR 779(CC); 1998 (3) SA 785 (CC).

[18] *S v Mbatha; S v Le Roux and Others* CCT 19/95, CCT 35/95 (9 February 1996) para 14, now cited as *S v Mbatha; S v Prinsloo* 1996 (3) BCLR 293 (CC); 1996 (2) SA 464 (CC) (The question whether a limitation is proportional is a question, which courts address in many constitution systems in subjecting fundamental rights limitations to scrutiny); David Beatty *Constitutional Law in Theory and Practice* Toronto: University of Toronto Press 1995, 105. Volkmar Gotz 'Legislative and Executive Power under the Constitutional Requirements entailed in the Principle of the Rule of Law' in *New Challenges to the German Basic Law*, edited by Christian Starck. Baden-Baden: Nomos 1991, 152–4. Patrick Macklem, et al *Constitutional Law of Canada* Toronto: Emond Montgomery Publishers 1994, 182–3.

[19] See *S v Makwanyane* para 105.

[20] *S v Manamela and Others* CCT 25/99 (14 April 2000) para 32, now cited as 2000 (3) BCLR 491 (CC); 2000 (3) SA 1 (CC).

[21] See *Makwanyane*, *per* Chaskalson P, para 104

[22] *Manamela* para 32.

threshold that has to be satisfied where there is a direct violation of an entrenched right, [23] or a violation that is considered to be inconsistent with a free and democratic society. [24] This applies particularly to rights involving privacy and the inner sanctum of the individual. [25] In addition, there are some rights such as the right to life, right against torture and slavery, which are absolutely inviolable. In *Makwanyane*, the Court unanimously found that the imposition of the death penalty was too severe a sanction and therefore could not be upheld. Similarly, in *Williams* the Court found that corporeal punishment despite the possibility of deterring crime was too severe an encroachment on human dignity. [26] Where there is no convincing evidence of a *nexus* between the means chosen and the ends sought, the Court would not sustain the limitations. For example, in *Brink v Kitshoff*, the Court held that the state had not proved that a statute on insurance which discriminated against married women, by requiring them to surrender proceeds from an insurance policy in the event of their husbands death, was rationally related to the protection of the interests of women. [27] In this instance, the law was not related to meeting its aim. Where there are less

intrusive means available to achieve the state's objective, the Court would require the state to follow the less restrictive means. [28] In *Williams*, the Court held that the state could adopt preventive detention instead of corporeal punishment as a deterrent to crime. [29] Also, where an intrusion is over-inclusive, and there are less restrictive means available, the Court would require that the less restrictive means be followed. [30]

The cases that follow are meant to provide an overview of the balancing process that goes into the consideration of proportionality. It is a balancing process which, in the words of Sachs J, focuses on the synergetic relation between the values underlying the guarantees of fundamental rights and the circumstances of the particular case. [31] Sachs J notes that there is no legal yardstick for making this decision. Ultimately, the Court is engaged in value judgements based on its understanding of the values upon which society is based, in relation to the facts of the case presented to the Court. [32] As in the definition of the rights, the social and political outlook of the individual judge will inevitably influence the extent to which he or she intervenes to invalidate governmental restrictions.

S v Williams and Others CCT 20/94 (9 June 1995; 1995 (3) SA 632 (CC), now cited as 1995 (7) BCLR 864 (CC); 1995 (3) SA 632 (CC) (notes omitted)	[1] This matter has been referred to this Court by the Full Bench of the Cape of Good Hope Provincial Division of the Supreme Court (Conradie, Scott and Farlam JJ). It is a consolidation of five different cases in which six juveniles were convicted by different magistrates

---

[23] *Makwanyane, per* Krieggler J, para 210. *Manamela* para 32.

[24] *S v Williams and Others* CCT 20/94 (9 June 1995) para 62, now cited as 1995 (7) BCLR 864 (CC); 1995 (3) SA 632 (CC); *S v Mbatha,* and *S v Prinsloo* para 18–19.

[25] *Bernstein and Others v Bester and Others NNO* CCT 23/95 (27 March 1996) para 67, now cited as 1996 (4) BCLR 449 (CC); 1996 (2) SA 751 (CC).

[26] *Per* Langa J in *S v Williams.*

[27] *Brink v Kitshoff* CCT 15/95 (15 May 1996) para 47–48, now cited as 1996 (6) BCLR 752 770; 1996(4) SA 197 (CC).

[28] *Per* Ackerman J, *Ferreira v Levin and Others; Vryenboek and Others v Powell NO and Others* CCT 5/95 (6 December 1995) (also known as CCT 3/95) para 127, now cited as 1996 (1) BCLR 1 (CC); 1996 (2) SA 621 (CC).

[29] See *S v Williams.*

[30] See eg *S v Mbatha* and *S v Prinsloo; Coetzee v The Government of the Republic of South Africa and Others; Matiso and Others v The Commanding Officer, Port Elizabeth Prison and Others* CCT 19/94, 22/94 (22 September 1995) now cited as 1995 (10) BCLR 1382 (CC); 1995 (4) SA 631 (CC).

[31] *Coetzee v The Government of the RSA and Others* para 46.

[32] *Supra. Manamela* para 32.

and sentenced to receive a moderate correction of a number of strokes with a light cane. The issue is whether the sentence of juvenile whipping, pursuant to the provisions of section 294 of the Criminal Procedure Act, is consistent with the provisions of the Constitution.

[58] The enquiry involves testing the measures adopted against the objective sought to be achieved. The gist of it, put in the context and the language of section 33(1), really amounts initially to three questions, namely: (a) whether the means used are reasonable ; (b) whether they are justifiable in the context of the civilized society we hope we are or which we, through this Constitution, are aspiring to be; and (c) whether they are necessary to attain the objective. The test relies on proportionality, a process of weighing up the individual's right which the State wishes to limit against the objective which the State seeks to achieve by such limitation.

[59] This evaluation must necessarily take place against the backdrop of the values of South African society as articulated in the Constitution and in other legislation, in the decisions of our courts and generally against our own experiences as a people.

[60] In *State v Makwanyane and Mchunu* Chaskalson P deals with the proportionality test which is also implicit in the limitation of rights in Canada and the European Court. As a general conclusion he notes that the limitation of constitutional rights for a purpose that is necessary in a democratic society involves the weighing up of competing values, and ultimately an assessment based on proportionality. He points out how the German Constitutional Court applies the proportionality test in dealing with limitations authorised by the German Constitution: It has regard to the purpose of the limiting legislation, whether the legislation in fact achieves that purpose, whether it is necessary therefor, and whether a proper balance has been achieved between the value enhanced by the limitation, and the fundamental right that has been limited.

[61] The grounds on which the State sought to justify juvenile whipping were, firstly, that it

made good practical sense to have juvenile whipping as a sentencing option. The practice had advantages for both the offender and the State, particularly in view of a shortage of resources and the infrastructure required for the implementation of other sentencing options for juveniles. Secondly, it was suggested that juvenile whipping was a deterrent.

[62] The purpose of section 294 of the Act is to provide a sentencing option for the punishment of juvenile offenders. What must be addressed is whether it is reasonable, justifiable and necessary to resort to juvenile whipping, notwithstanding the fact that it constitutes a severe assault upon not only the person of the recipient, but upon his dignity as a human being. The primary argument advanced in favour of juvenile whipping was that it constitutes a better alternative to imprisonment, particularly in the so-called grey area crimes This was a reference to instances where a court has to deal with an offence which is not so serious as to merit a custodial sentence but is serious enough to render inappropriate the use of softersentences

[63] It was argued that sentencing alternatives for juveniles were limited and that this country did not have a sufficiently well-established physical and human resource base which was capable of supporting the imposition of alternative punishments. This is of course an argument based on pragmatism rather than principle. It is a problem which must be taken seriously nevertheless. It seems to me, however, to be another way of saying that our society has not yet established mechanisms to deal with juveniles who find themselves in conflict with the law; that the price to be paid for this state of unreadiness is to subject juveniles to punishment that is cruel, inhuman or degrading. The proposition is untenable. It is diametrically opposed to the values that fuel our progress towards being a more humane and caring society. It would be a negation of those values precisely where we should be laying a strong foundation for them, in the young; the future custodians of this fledgeling democracy.

[64] We nevertheless need to examine

available resources to determine whether there are indeed appropriate sentencing options. It has to be borne in mind that the presence of various options in a number of legislative provisions may not always reflect practical realities. It is important that resources should be made available and that they should be utilized properly, so that the values expressed in the Constitution may be upheld and maintained. It bears mentioning that although changes in the criminal justice system have been occurring, albeit at a painfully slow pace, there has been a perceptible shift in approach and attitude towards punishment. I mention three aspects of this process:

[67] The introduction of correctional supervision with its prime focus on rehabilitation, through section 276 of the Act, was a milestone in the process of humanizing the criminal justice system. It brought along with it the possibility of several imaginative sentencing measures including, but not limited to, house arrest, monitoring, community service and placement in employment. This assisted in the shift of emphasis from retribution to rehabilitation. This development was recognized and hailed by Kriegler AJA in *S v R* as being the introduction of a new phase in our criminal justice system allowing for the imposition of finely-tuned sentences without resorting to imprisonment with all its known disadvantages for both the prisoner and the broader community.

[74] To the extent that facilities and physical resources may not always be adequate, it seems to me that the new dynamic should be regarded as a timely challenge to the State to ensure the provision and execution of an effective juvenile justice system. The wider range of penalties now provided for in the Act permits a more flexible but effective approach in dealing with juvenile offenders.

[75] There is indeed much room for new creative methods to deal with the problem of juvenile justice. During argument, we were informed that interesting sentencing options were being increasingly applied in the Western Cape and that Conradie J's suggestion to

magistrates was a further encouragement to the process There are, for instance, community service orders which are linked to suspended or postponed sentences These are structured in such a way that they meet the punitive element of sentencing while allowing for the education and rehabilitation of the offender. There is also the victim-offender mediation process in terms of which the victim is enabled to participate in the justice process, receive restitution while the offender is assisted to rehabilitate. There are sentences which are suspended on condition that the offender attends a juvenile offender school for a specific purpose. These orders are structured in such a way that they yield benefits to the victim of the crime, the offender and to the community. Doubtless these processes, still in their infancy, can be developed through involvement by State and non-governmental agencies and institutions which are involved in juvenile justice projects.

[80] The State stressed the deterrent nature of juvenile whipping. Deterrence is, obviously, a legitimate objective which the State may pursue. We live in a crime-ridden society; the courts and other relevant organs of the State have a duty to make crime unattractive to those who are inclined to embark on that course. The concerns which the provision seeks to address are indeed pressing and they are substantial. But, as already stated, the means employed must be reasonable and demonstrably justifiable. No clear evidence has been advanced that juvenile whipping is a more effective deterrent than other available forms of punishment.

[84] What has not been shown is that such deterrent value as might exist is sufficiently significant to enable the State to override a right entrenched in the Constitution. All indications are to the contrary. While juvenile whipping has a brutalizing effect, it has not been shown that it has the capacity to deter more than other punishments would do. Moreover, I agree with the remarks of Fannin J in *S v Kumalo and Others*. Within comparatively recent times corporal punishment of quite horrifying severity were inflicted for a great number of offences, and I, for one do not believe that the general

deterrent effect of such punishments justified the suffering and indignity which were inflicted upon those who were so punished. I am of the opinion that a whipping is a punishment of a particularly severe kind. It is brutal in its nature and constitutes a severe assault upon not only the person of the recipient but upon his dignity as a human being. The severity of the punishment depends, to a very large extent, upon the personality of the officer charged with the duty of inflicting it, and over that the court ordering the punishment can have little, if any, control.

[85] Howie AJA, quite correctly in my view, warned against the idea that the accused should be sacrificed on the altar of deterrence. To this I would add that this is even more so when the court is dealing with a youthful offender.

[86] If, as I have found, the deterrence value is so marginal that it does not justify the imposition of this special punishment, involving as it does the deliberate infliction of physical pain, one has to conclude that the sole reason for retaining it is to satisfy society's need for retribution. While retribution is, in itself, a legitimate element of punishment, it is not the only one; it should not be the overriding one. It cannot, on its own, justify the existence of the punishment.

[91] No compelling interest has been proved which can justify the practice. It has not been shown that there are no other punishments which are adequate to achieve the purposes for which it is imposed. Nor has it been shown to be a significantly effective deterrent. On the other hand, as observed by Page J in *S v Motsoesoana*, its effect is likely to be coarsening and degrading rather than rehabilitative. It is moreover also unnecessary. Many countries in the civilized world abolished it long ago; there are enough sentencing options in our justice system to conclude that whipping does not have to be resorted to. Thus, whether one looks at the adjectives disjunctively or regards the phrase as a compendious expression of a norm, it is my view that at this time, so close to the dawn of the 21st century, juvenile whipping is cruel, it is inhuman and it is degrading. It cannot, moreover, be justified in terms of section 33(1) of the Constitution.

[92] I accordingly find that the provisions of section 294 of the Act violate the provisions of sections 10 and 11(2) of the Constitution and that they cannot be saved by the operation of section 33(1) of the Constitution. Although the provision concerned is a law of general application, the limitation it imposes on the rights in question is, in the light of all the circumstances, not reasonable, not justifiable and it is furthermore not necessary. The provisions are therefore unconstitutional.

***

National Coalition for Gay and Lesbian Equality and Another v The Minister of Justice CCT 11/98 (9 October 1998), now cited as 1998 (6) BCLR 1517 (CC); 1999 (1) SA 6 (CC)
(notes omitted)

Authors' note: The Constitutional Court was faced with the constitutionality of various statutes that made homosexual relations between consenting males a criminal offence. The High Court had declared the outlawing of homosexual relations between consenting males under the common law and under the various statutes unconstitutional and could not be saved by the limitations clause.

ACKERMANN J:

[36] The criminalization of sodomy in private between consenting males is a severe limitation of a gay man's right to equality in relation to sexual orientation, because it hits at one of the ways in which gays give expression to their sexual orientation. It is at the same time a severe limitation of the gay man's rights to privacy, dignity and freedom. The harm caused by the provision can, and often does, affect his ability to achieve self-identification and self-fulfilment. The harm also radiates out into society generally and gives rise to a wide variety of other discriminations, which collectively unfairly prevent a fair distribution of social goods and

services and the award of social opportunities for gays.

[37] Against this must be considered whether the limitation has any purpose and, if so, its importance. No valid purpose has been suggested. The enforcement of the private moral views of a section of the community, which are based to a large extent on nothing more than prejudice, cannot qualify as such a legitimate purpose. There is accordingly nothing, in the proportionality enquiry, to weigh against the extent of the limitation and its harmful impact on gays. It would therefore seem that there is no justification for the limitation.

S v Mello and Another
CCT 5/98 (28May 1998), now cited as S v Mello and Another 1998 (8) BCLR 943 (CC); 1998 (3) SA 712 (CC)
(notes omitted)

MOKOGORO J:

[1] The appellants, with two other persons, stood trial in the Pretoria Magistrate's Court on charges dealing in alternatively possession of dagga in contravention of the Drugs and Drug Trafficking Act (the Act). The evidence established that several packages of dagga were found hidden in various parts of a truck driven by one of the accused and in which the other accused were passengers. The appellants and one other accused were found guilty and convicted on the alternative charge. In convicting them, the magistrate relied on the presumption created by section 20 of the Act which reads as follows:

6] This Court has on previous occasions pronounced on the unconstitutionality of similar legal presumptions which also create a reverse onus. In S v Bhulwana; S v Gwadiso and S v Ntsele such presumptions were held to be in direct conflict with the presumption of innocence. Similarly, I have no difficulty in finding that the presumption created by section 20 offends against the very essence of the right to a fair trial which includes the right to be presumed innocent and is protected by section 25(3)(c) of the interim Constitution.

[7] Accordingly, section 20 of the Act can only be saved by the provisions of section 33(1) of the interim Constitution, if it constitutes a limitation which is reasonable, necessary and justifiable in an open and democratic society based on freedom and equality.

[8] In Mbatha, this Court had found with regard to the presumption created by section 40(1) of the Arms Act that: The presumption is couched in wide terms and no attempt has been made to tune its provisions finely so as to make them consistent with the Constitution and to avoid the real risk of convicting innocent persons who happen to be at the wrong place at the wrong time. It may be invoked in a wide range of circumstances and against any number of categories of persons, as long as they have been in, on or at a particular place at the relevant time. The Court was further of the view that the presumption had a disproportionate impact in relation to the purpose for which the right in question is limited. It was found that if the purpose of the provision is to promote the legitimate law enforcement objective of separating innocent bystanders from genuine suspects, then it should be cast in terms limited to serving that function only. A legislative limitation motivated by strong societal need should not be disproportionate in its impact to the purpose for which that right is limited. If restrictions are warranted by such societal need, they should be properly focused and appropriately balanced.

[9] This Court considered a similar presumption in Ntsele and found that: The fundamental rights bound up with and protected by the presumption of innocence are so important, and the consequences of their infringement potentially so grave, that compelling justification would be required to save them from invalidation. None is apparent here. On the contrary, the importance of the values in issue and the extent and nature of the risk involved in their erosion outweigh any societal interest likely to be advanced by the presumption.

[10] The presumption with which we are now concerned does not seem to differ in any material respect from section 40(1) of the Arms

Act with which we dealt in *Mbatha*. Nor does there appear to be any material distinction to be drawn between the principles set out in *Bhulwana*, *Julies* and *Ntsele* on the one hand and those that are applicable in the present case on the other. Furthermore, no argument springs to mind in favour of risking false convictions by keeping alive a provision which hits at the core of the right to be presumed innocent until proven guilty; a right which protects the basic values of justice in an open and democratic society based on freedom and equality. I find section 20 to be unjustifiable. In the result it is unconstitutional.

Mistry v The Interim National Medical And Dental Council of South Africa v Enslin and Others
CCT 13/97 (29 May 1998), now cited as 1998 (7) BCLR 880 (CC); 1988 (4) SA 1127 (CC)
(notes omitted)

Authors' note: The applicant a medical doctor, argued that s 28(1) of the Medicines Act 101 of 1965, pursuant to which his premises was searched, was unconstitutional in that in encroached on his privacy rights.

[8] The central problem in this case is whether the powers of entry, examination, search and seizure given to inspectors by section 28(1) of the Medicines and Related Substances Control Act are consistent with the provisions of section 13 of the interim Constitution which guarantee personal privacy. The matter comes to this Court both as a referral of a constitutional issue and as an appeal under the interim Constitution. To avoid confusion the parties are referred to as in the court of first instance.

[9] The applicant is a registered medical practitioner in private practice. The chain of events which led to the present proceedings was initiated by a letter of complaint by a patient to the Interim National Medical and Dental Council of South Africa (the Council, which is the first respondent). It alleged that the applicant was fraudulently claiming reimbursement from the patients medical aid fund for services which he had not in fact rendered. In response, the Council ordered an inspection of the premises by a senior legal advisor on its staff, Mr Enslin (who is the second respondent) and a doctor in private practice in Durban, Dr Moodliar (who is the fifth respondent).

[10] Prior to carrying out the order of the Council, Mr Enslin informed the chief medicines control officer of the Department of Health and an inspector of medicines, Mr Coote (who is the fourth respondent), of the impending inspection. The three inspectors went together to the applicants surgery and proceeded to search it in the absence of the applicant, who arrived when the search was almost complete. The inspectors claim they were informed by staff at the surgery that the applicant had not been in full-time attendance for some months. Shortly after his arrival, Mr Coote purchased a container of Persivate cream from the applicants receptionist. In the course of the search he seized numerous items, while Mr Enslin and Dr Moodliar seized various other items which, however, do not form part of the present matter since they were subsequently returned as a result of a court order.

[16] Section 28(1) of the Medicines Act reads as follows:

An inspector may at all reasonable times—
(a) enter upon any premises, place, vehicle, vessel or aircraft at or in which there is or is on reasonable grounds suspected to be any medicine or Scheduled substance;
(b) inspect any medicine or Scheduled substance, or any book, record or document found in or upon such premises, place, vehicle, vessel or aircraft;
(c) seize any such medicine or Scheduled substance, or any books, records or documents found in or upon such premises, place, vehicle, vessel or aircraft and appearing to afford evidence of a contravention of any provision of this Act;
(d) take so many samples of any such medicine or Scheduled substance as he may consider necessary for the purpose of testing, examination

423

or analysis in terms of the provisions of this Act.

[17] To understand the scope and effect of these powers, it is necessary to locate them within the scheme of the Medicines Act as a whole. In *Administrator, Cape v Raats Röntgen and Vermeulen (Pty) Ltd* Kriegler AJA pointed out that the Medicines Act 14 [was] directed at the control of two main categories of substances, namely medicines and so-called related substances. His judgment makes it clear that the purpose of the 15 Medicines Act was not merely to regulate the manner in which scheduled substances were made available to members of the public, but to control the quality and supply of medicines generally: Manifestly the Act was put on the statute book to protect the citizenry at large. Substances for the treatment of human ailments are as old as mankind itself; so are poisons and quacks. The technological explosion of the twentieth century brought in its wake a flood of pharmaceuticals unknown before and incomprehensible to most. The man in the street — and indeed many medical practitioners — could not cope with the cornucopian outpourings of the world-wide network of inventors and manufacturers of medicines. Moreover, the marvels of advertising, marketing and distribution brought such fruits within the grasp of the general public. Hence an Act designed, as the long title emphasizes, to register and control medicines. The enactment created a tightly meshed screening mechanism whereby the public was to be safeguarded: in general any medicine supplied to any person is, first, subject to stringent certification by experts; then it has to be clearly, correctly and comprehensively packaged and labeled and may only be sold by certain classes of persons and with proper explanatory information; to round it out detailed mechanisms for enforcement are created and ancillary measures are authorized.

[23] For the purposes of the present case, it is not necessary to determine precisely when an inspection becomes a search, and I expressly refrain from trying to do so. Neither is it necessary to decide whether an extensive or narrow meaning should be given to the word property, nor exactly what was contemplated by the term private possessions. Such determinations would be of a threshold nature, that is, they would establish whether or not there had been a breach of section 13. What is clear, nevertheless, is that however the terms search and seizure may be interpreted in a particular case, to the extent that a statute authorizes warrantless entry into private homes and rifling through intimate possessions, such activities would intrude on the inner sanctum of the persons in question and the statutory authority would accordingly breach the right to personal privacy as protected by section 13. There can be no doubt that the language of section 28(1) is so sweeping as to permit such entry and inspection. Accordingly it is in breach of section 13 and has to be justified by the state as being reasonable and justifiable in terms of section 33 of the interim Constitution.

[24] In *S v Makwanyane and Another* this Court held that there was no absolute standard which could be laid down for determining reasonableness and justifiability. Principles could be established, but the application of those principles to particular circumstances could only be done on a case-by-case basis.

This is inherent in the requirement of proportionality, which calls for the balancing of different interests. In the balancing process the relevant considerations will include the nature of the right that is limited and its importance to an open and democratic society based on freedom and equality; the purpose for which the right is limited and the importance of that purpose to such a society; the extent of the limitation, its efficacy and, particularly where the limitation has to be necessary, whether the desired ends could reasonably be achieved through other means less damaging to the right in question.

The nature of the right that is limited, and its importance to an open and democratic society based on freedom and equality.

[25] The existence of safeguards to regulate the way in which state officials may enter the private domains of ordinary citizens is one of the

features that distinguish a constitutional democracy from a police state. South African experience has been notoriously mixed in this regard. On the one hand there has been an admirable history of strong statutory controls over the powers of the police to search and seize. On the other, when it came to racially discriminatory laws and security legislation, vast and often unrestricted discretionary powers were conferred on officials and police. Generations of systematized and egregious violations of personal privacy established norms of disrespect for citizens that seeped generally into the public administration and promoted amongst a great many officials habits and practices inconsistent with the standards of conduct now required by the Bill of Rights. Section 13 accordingly requires us to repudiate the past practices that were repugnant to the new constitutional values, while at the same time re-affirming and building on those that were consistent with these values.

The purpose for which the right is limited and its importance for an open and democratic society based on freedom and equality.

[26] There is nothing to suggest that the broad objectives of section 28(1) raise echoes of the racism and authoritarian de-personalization which characterized the earlier era. Indeed, the purpose of the Medicines Act is manifestly beneficent; it was put on the statute book to protect the citizenry at large. Its purpose is to provide for proper inspection and regulation of the multiple health undertakings in modern society which impact on the welfare and general well-being of the community. It furnishes protection both for the public and for honest health professionals, and cannot be enforced without the existence of inspectors who are appropriately empowered.

The extent of the limitation.

[27] For the purpose of the present case it has not been necessary to determine whether or not regulatory inspections should be regarded as searches and seizures as contemplated by section 13. Yet, even if one were to accept in favor of applicant that there were situations where they did so qualify, it would be necessary to decide on a case-by-case basis how invasive any such regulatory inspections would be. The more public the undertaking and the more closely regulated, the more attenuated would the right to privacy be and the less intense any possible invasion. In *Bernstein and Others v Bester and Others NNO* Ackermann J posited a continuum of privacy rights which may be regarded as starting with a wholly inviolable inner self, moving to a relatively impervious sanctum of the home and personal life and ending in a public realm where privacy would only remotely be implicated. In the case of any regulated enterprise, the proprietors expectation of privacy with respect to the premises, equipment, materials and records must be attenuated by the obligation to comply with reasonable regulations and to tolerate the administrative inspections that are an inseparable part of an effective regime of regulation. The greater the potential hazards to the public, the less invasive the inspection. People involved in such undertakings must be taken to know from the outset that their activities will be monitored. If they are licensed to function in a competitive environment, they accept as a condition of their licence that they will adhere to the same reasonable controls as are applicable to their competitors. Members of professional bodies, for example, share an interest in seeing to it that the standards, reputation and integrity of their professions are maintained. In *Almeida-Sanchez v United States*, Stewart J, writing for the majority, highlighted well the expectations of privacy involved in the modern world of closely regulated enterprises: The businessman in a regulated industry in effect consents to the restrictions placed upon him. As the Court stated in *Biswell*: ... When a dealer chooses to engage in this pervasively regulated business and to accept a federal license, he does so with the knowledge that his business records, firearms, and ammunition will be subject to effective inspection ... The dealer is not left to wonder about the purposes of the inspector or the limits of his task.

[28] Had section 28(1) confined itself to authorizing periodic inspections of the business premises of health professionals, such inspec-

tions would accordingly have entailed only the most minimal and easily justifiable invasions of privacy, if they had qualified as invasions of privacy at all. Indeed, all legitimate health professionals can only welcome such regulatory inspections. It is clear however that section 28(1) does not limit itself to authorizing regulatory inspections of the premises of doctors and chemists. It expressly empowers inspectors to enter not only premises, but also any place, vehicle, vessel or aircraft. There can be no doubt that the word place is meant to have a wider meaning than premises, otherwise there would have been no need to put it in. The description is accordingly so broad as to authorize the inspectors to enter private homes, whether they be the dwellings of health professionals or of other persons. Similarly, the vehicles, vessels and aircraft that inspectors may search are not limited to ambulances, hospital ships or the planes of flying doctors, nor could they reasonably be confined to such. Although it has become almost a judicial cliché to say that the object is . . . [to protect] people, not places, that is, to safeguard personal privacy and not to protect private property, there can be no doubt that certain spaces are normally reserved for the most private of activities. The section is so wide and unrestricted in its reach as to authorize any inspector to enter any persons home simply on the basis that aspirins or cough mixture are or are reasonably suspected of being there. What is more, the section does not require a warrant to be issued in any circumstances at all.

[29] It is difficult to see how the achievement of the basic purposes of the Medicines Act requires that inspectors be allowed at will to enter private homes and inspect private documents. If only periodic regulatory inspection of the premises of health professionals was in issue, then a requirement of a prior warrant might be nonsensical in that it would be likely to frustrate the state objectives behind the search. Once the investigation extends to private homes, however, there would seem to be no reason why the time-honoured requirement of prior independent authorization should not be respected. Whether that would require a prior warrant from a judicial

officer in all circumstances where homes were being searched need not be decided now. If, however, the circumstances were in fact such that even trained police officers would be required to get such a warrant, all the more reason for medical inspectors to do so; it would be odd if the law allowed personnel who might be medical experts but forensically untrained to rush in where even experienced police officers must refuse to tread. Furthermore, even a subjective belief of the investigator that some offence or another was being committed might not be enough — here not even that is required. Inspectors, like any other persons exercising power on behalf of the state, are as entitled as the public to know the precise framework within which they can lawfully and effectively carry out their functions. The statute gives hardly any guidance. All is left to the discretion of the inspectors and their superiors. The fact that the Medicines Act is manifestly in the public interest in no way diminishes the need for the powers of inspection to be exercised according to constitutionally valid criteria and procedures. Lord Actons famous statement about all power tending to corrupt and absolute power corrupting absolutely was made in the context of power being exercised by the most worthy people, not the least. It follows that the desired and permissible ends of regulatory inspection could easily be achieved through means less damaging to the section 13 right.

[30] To sum up: irrespective of legitimate expectations of privacy which may be intruded upon in the process, and without any predetermined safeguards to minimise the extent of such intrusions where the nature of the investigations makes some invasion of privacy necessary, section 28(1) gives the inspectors carte blanche to enter any place, including private dwellings, where they reasonably suspect medicines to be, and then to inspect documents which may be of the most intimate kind. The extent of the invasion of the important right to personal privacy authorised by section 28(1) is substantially disproportionate to its public purpose; the section is clearly overbroad in its reach and accordingly fails to pass the proportionality test laid down in *S v Makwanyane and Another*.

S v Mbatha; S v Le Roux and Others
CCT 19/95, CCT 35/95
(9 February 1996), now cited
as *S v Mbatha; S v Prinsloo* 1996 (3)
BCLR 293 (CC); 1996 (2) SA 464 (CC)
(notes omitted)

[1] Two matters come to this Court by way of referrals from the Witwatersrand Local Division of the Supreme Court. The accused in the first case is Wellington Mbatha who was tried and convicted in the Regional Court at Germiston. Nicolaas Marthinus Prinsloo, an accused in the second matter, is standing trial in the Witwatersrand Local Division with 25 others in the case of the *S v Le Roux and Others*. I shall refer to the two accused persons as the applicants.

[2] In the first matter, the applicant appealed against his conviction on two counts under the provisions of the Arms and Ammunition Act 75 of 1969 (the Act). The charge concerned the unlawful possession of two AK47 rifles and twelve rounds of ammunition, in contravention of sections 32(1)(a) and 32(1)(e) of the Act respectively. The sentences imposed, of eight and two years' imprisonment respectively, were ordered to run concurrently. On appeal, the matter was in turn referred to this Court by Leveson J, with MacArthur J agreeing, for a decision on the constitutionality of the presumption contained in section 40(1) of the Act.

[3] The twenty-six (26) accused in the second matter were indicted on various charges, 96 counts in all, arising out of a series of bomb explosions which took place before the national elections in April 1994. After the close of the prosecution case, Flemming DJP refused an application for the discharge of all the accused on all counts. The applicant and six others were acquitted on all but four of the counts, namely, counts 80 to 83, which relate to the unlawful possession of machine guns, firearms and ammunition, in contravention respectively of sections 32(1)(a) and 32(1)(e) of the Act. In refusing to discharge the applicant on those remaining counts, the trial Judge stated that he relied solely on the presumption in section 40(1) of the Act. He then suspended the proceedings and made the referral order in terms of section 102(1) of the Constitution of the Republic of South Africa Act 200 of 1993 (the Constitution) on the basis that it was in the interests of justice that the issue be resolved at this stage of the proceedings. The case has been postponed to 16 February 1996.

[4] The issue in both matters is the validity of the presumption contained in section 40(1) of the Act in the light of the provisions of section 25(3)(c) and (d) of the Constitution. The applicants complain that the presumption offends against the 'fair trial' provisions in the Constitution, in particular, the right to be presumed innocent and the privilege against self-incrimination. Section 40(1) of the Act provides:

Whenever in any prosecution for being in possession of any article contrary to the provisions of this Act, it is proved that such article has at any time been on or in any premises, including any building, dwelling, flat, room, office, shop, structure, vessel, aircraft or vehicle or any part thereof, any person who at that time was on or in or in charge of or present at or occupying such premises, shall be presumed to have been in possession of that article at that time, until the contrary is proved.

[15] The State argued that the inroads which section 40(1) of the Act makes on the presumption of innocence are reasonable, justifiable and necessary and that they do not negate the essential content of the right. Relying on remarks in *S v Zuma*, it was argued that the reverse onus provisions in the present case are justifiable and therefore constitutionally permissible. In the passage referred to, Kentridge AJ pointed out that the effect of the judgment in that case was not to invalidate every legal presumption reversing the onus of proof as some presumptions may be justifiable as being rational in themselves, requiring an accused person to prove only facts to which he or she has easy access, and which it would be unreasonable to expect the prosecution to disprove .... Or there may be presumptions which are necessary if certain offences are to be effectively prosecuted, and the State is able to

show that for good reason it cannot be expected to produce the evidence itself …. The State contended that circumstances existed which rendered section 40(1) of the Act justifiable, regard being had to the context and the manner in which its provisions were implemented.

[16] The State characterized the objective of the presumption in the present case as being to assist in combating the escalating levels of crime as part of the government's duty to protect society generally. The contention was that the provision is intended to ensure effective policing and to facilitate the investigation and prosecution of crime as well as to ease the prosecution's task of securing convictions for contraventions under the Act. Such an objective is truly laudable and its importance, in the current climate of very high levels of violent crime, cannot be overstated. Information in papers submitted to us reveals that during the period 1990 to 1994, there was a distressing increase in crimes of violence. The common denominator in most of them is the involvement of firearms. In a discussion document titled: Recent Crime Trends, Dr Lorraine Glanz of the Human Sciences Research Council observed that the face of crime is becoming increasingly violent and more serious, and that the rampant crime levels must have a profound negative effect on the quality of life in communities. If left unchecked, a protracted increase in violent crime in particular is a threat to social stability. I could not agree more. A further ugly feature allied to the actual deeds of violence is the incidence of illegal smuggling, sale and possession of arms. We were told that trafficking in arms and drugs from neighboring countries into South Africa is taking place on a significant scale. There is a proliferation of illegal firearms throughout the country and this, no doubt, contributes in no small measure to the high incidence of violent crime. This state of affairs is obviously a matter of serious concern, not only for the courts, but for the legislature, the police and the entire population which is affected by it. There is no doubt that, whatever the causes, crimes of violence particularly those involving firearms have reached an intolerably high level

and that urgent corrective measures are warranted.

[17] The problems which the government has to contend with in fulfilling its duty to protect society were given to us in some detail. We were informed that the detection of people in possession of illegal arms and ammunition is often very difficult. Police have to depend on informers or pure chance to trace offenders. The use of informers who infiltrate gun-smuggling networks is a helpful but often time-consuming and dangerous process. Gunrunners make extensive use of couriers to transport arms; some of the couriers, especially women and children, are used without their knowledge. Even vehicles such as ambulances and official government cars are sometimes used, without the people in control of the vehicles knowing it. Sometimes aircraft and motor vehicles equipped with false panels and compartments for storage are used in the illegal transportation of arms. The problem of policing is compounded by geographical factors; the borders of South Africa are extensive and impossible to patrol effectively 24 hours a day, making it easier for cross-border dealers and smugglers of arms to ply their trade and evade detection. The severe shortage of trained personnel has adverse effects on the capacity of the police to conduct raids and searches in places like hostels and informal settlements, to look for places used for concealment of illegal arms and to trap motor vehicles used in illegal conveyance of arms. Ordinary members of the community often withhold information because they are too terrified and intimidated by armed gangsters and traffickers in narcotic drugs and illegal arms.

[18] It is difficult not to have sympathy for representations of this nature, coming as they do from officials of the State whose task it is to deal with what has become a truly serious problem. These are real and pressing social concerns and it is imperative that proper attention should be given to finding urgent and effective solutions. The issue before us, however, is not simply whether there is a pressing social need to combat the crimes of violence – there clearly is – but also whether the instrument to be used in meeting

this need is itself fashioned in accordance with specifications permitted by the Constitution. Although the relevant legislative provision was enacted before the Constitution came into force, the enquiry is whether the limitation it imposes on constitutionally protected rights is consistent with the provisions of the Constitution. This involves a consideration of the other factors referred to in Makwanyane's case, and in particular, the importance of the impugned right in an open and democratic society, and the extent to which that right has been limited. As O'Regan J said in *S v Bhulwana* (at paragraph 18), the more substantial the inroad into fundamental rights, the more persuasive the ground of justification must be.

[19] The presumption of innocence is clearly of vital importance in the establishment and maintenance of an open and democratic society based on freedom and equality. If, in particular cases, what is effectively a presumption of guilt is to be substituted for the presumption of innocence, the justification for doing so must be established clearly and convincingly.

[20] It was argued that without the presumption it would be almost impossible for the prosecution to prove both the mental and physical elements of possession. I do not agree. The circumstances of each case will determine whether or not the elements of possession have been established beyond reasonable doubt. The evidence need not necessarily be direct. It may be, and often is, circumstantial and will often be sufficient to secure a conviction without the assistance of the presumption. There will no doubt be cases in which it will be difficult to prove that a particular person against whom the presumption would have operated, was in fact in possession of the prohibited article. If that person was in fact guilty, the absence of the presumption might enable him or her to escape conviction. But this is inevitably a consequence of the presumption of innocence; this must be weighed against the danger that innocent people may be convicted if the presumption were to apply. In that process the rights of innocent persons must be given precedence. After all, the consequences of a wrong conviction are not trivial. Apart from the social disapprobation attached to it, heavy penalties are attached to contraventions of the Act. In the cases before us, the sentence prescribed by the Act for the illegal possession of a firearm is imprisonment for a period not exceeding 25 years with a minimum of five years. Illegal possession of ammunition attracts a sentence of imprisonment for a period not exceeding 25 years.

[22] The application of the presumption does not depend on there being a logical or rational connection between the presumed fact and the basic facts proved, nor can it be claimed that in all cases covered by the presumption, the presumed fact is something which is more likely than not to arise from the basic facts proved. The mere presence of the accused in, on or at the premises at the same time as the prohibited article does not, as a matter of course, give rise to the inference of possession. There are clearly circumstances where this connection can be reasonably sustained. Circumstances may even arise where such an adverse inference would be warranted without the accused having been present in, on or at the particular premises when the firearm was found. An example is a case where it is proved beyond a reasonable doubt that a firearm was found in the glove compartment of a locked car which had been driven by its owner and in which there had been no passengers. If the accused's exculpatory version is found to be false (also beyond a reasonable doubt), the conviction would be defensible. That would be so, not because of the presumption created by section 40(1) of the Act, but as a matter of logical inference. The problem with the provision is that it contains no inherent mechanism to exclude those who are innocent and who would otherwise be included within its reach. If, for example, a single firearm were to be found on a crowded bus, each passenger on the bus would be liable to be arrested and prosecuted, and would be presumed guilty unless he or she were able to establish innocence.

[24] If the purpose of the provision is to promote the legitimate law enforcement objective of separating innocent bystanders from

genuine suspects, then it should be cast in terms limited to serving that function only. A legislative limitation motivated by strong societal need should not be disproportionate in its impact to the purpose for which that right is limited. If restrictions are warranted by such societal need, they should be properly focused and appropriately balanced. The foundations of effective law enforcement procedures should always be the thorough collection of evidence and the careful presentation of a prosecution case. The sweeping terms of the presumption, however, encourage dragnet searches followed by dragnet prosecutions in which innocent bystanders, occupants and travellers can be required to prove their innocence and the normal checks and balances operating at the pre-trial stage cease to operate. Immense discretionary power is given to the police, in the first instance and to the prosecuting authorities thereafter, as to whether or not to proceed with arrest and indictment. From a practical point of view, the focus of crucial decision-making on guilt or innocence thus shifts from the constitutionally controlled context of a trial to the unrestrained discretion of police and prosecutor. The possibility cannot be excluded that overworked police and prosecuting authorities would understandably be tempted to focus on merely getting sufficient evidence to raise the presumption of possession; they can then rely on a poor showing by the accused in the witness box to secure a conviction. Yet the law gives no guidance to investigators and prosecutors as to when it is appropriate to rely on the presumption to proceed with a case and when not. Innocent persons may be put to the inconvenience, indignity and expense of a trial simply because they were in a bus, on a ship, or in a taxi, restaurant or house where weapons happened to be discovered. At the same time, the objectivity and professionalism of the police and prosecution are undermined by the lack of principled criteria governing their actions. In my view, in order to catch offenders and secure their convictions, it is not reasonable and justifiable either to expose honest citizens to such open-ended jeopardy or to impose such ill-defined responsibility upon those charged with law enforcement.

[26] Based on the assessment of the potential effect of the provision on innocent people, I am not persuaded that the presumption, as it stands, satisfies the requirements of reasonableness and justifiability. I am fortified in this conclusion by the fact that it has also not been demonstrated that its objective, that is, facilitating the conviction of offenders, could not reasonably have been achieved by other means less damaging to constitutionally entrenched rights. Although the choice of the appropriate measures to address the need is that of the legislature, it has not been shown that an evidentiary burden, for example, would not be as effective. I should not be understood as suggesting that any provision imposing an evidentiary burden, particularly if it is framed as broadly as the presumption in the present case, would be immune from constitutional attack. But by requiring the accused to provide evidence sufficient to raise a reasonable doubt, such a provision would be of assistance to the prosecution whilst at the same time being less invasive of section 25(3) rights. That it might impact on the right of an accused person to remain silent is true; but on the assumption that the rampant criminal abuse of lethal weapons in many parts of our country would justify some measured re-thinking about time-honoured rules and procedures, some limitation on the right to silence might be more defensible than the present one on the presumption of innocence. The accused could of course be exposed to the risk of being convicted if he or she fails to offer an explanation which could reasonably possibly be true, regarding physical association with the weapons; there would however be no legal presumption overriding any doubts that the court might have. At the end of the day and taking into account all the evidence, the court would still have to be convinced beyond a reasonable doubt that the accused was indeed guilty.

[27] I accordingly find that although the provision in question is a law of general

application, it has not been shown to be reasonable as required by section 33(1) of the Constitution. It is furthermore so inconsistent with the values which underlie an open and democratic society based on freedom and equality that it cannot be said to be justifiable. In view of this finding, it is not necessary to canvass the question whether the essential content of the right is negated, nor whether the limiting provision is necessary within the meaning of section 33(1) of the Constitution. Section 40(1) of the Act is unconstitutional inasmuch as it is an unreasonable and unjustifiable violation of the presumption of innocence.

Bongani Dlamini v The State CCT 21/98;
Vusi Dladla and Others v The State
CCT 22/98; *S v Mark David Joubert*
CCT 2/99; *S v Jan Johannnes*
Schietekat CCT 4/99 (3 June 1999), now
cited as 1999 (7) BCLR 771 (CC);
1999 (4) SA 623 (CC)
(notes omitted)

[1] Each of the four cases considered in this judgment is concerned with the constitutional validity of one or more provisions of the South African law relating to bail. These provisions relate to the admissibility of the record of bail proceedings at trial, the test in the grant of bail particularly where serious offences are concerned, and access to the police docket for purposes of a bail application. Some provisions are challenged in more than one of the cases; several of the challenges rely on more than one constitutional ground and many of the provisions being challenged are interrelated. It is therefore sensible to examine the various constitutional challenges together rather than on a case-by-case approach.

[54] It would be appropriate next to focus on sub-ss 60(4)(e) and (8A), which were struck down in *Schietekat* and *Joubert* not only because they were held to constitute an unconstitutional deeming provision, but also because, as it was termed, they constituted lynch law. Counsel for the accused in *Dladla* and *Schietekat* urged the Court to uphold the invalidation of sub-ss (4)(e) and (8A) on substantially the same ground, albeit more prosaically couched. The two subsections, so the argument ran, deviate from the established principle that in considering bail the court focuses on the accused and on the charge against him or her, his or her record, his

or her likely behaviour if released, etc., whereas these two provisions turn the attention away from the accused. Looking at public opinion and taking into account the likely behaviour of persons other than the detainee, so counsel suggested, smack of preventive detention and infringe a detainees liberty interest protected by s 35(1)(f) of the Constitution. Elevating the sentiments of the community above the interests of the detainee is constitutionally impermissible.

[55] There is force in the argument. Ordinarily, the factors identified in s 60(4)(e) and (8A) would not be relevant in establishing whether the interests of justice permit the release of the accused. It would be disturbing that an individuals legitimate interests should so invasively be subjected to societal interests. It is indeed even more disturbing where the two provisions do not postulate that the likelihood of public disorder should in any way be laid at the door of the accused. The mere likelihood of such disorder independently of any influence on the part of the accused, would suffice. Nevertheless, albeit reluctantly and subject to express qualifications to be mentioned shortly, I believe the provisions pass constitutional muster. I do so on the basis that although they do infringe the s 35(1)(f) right to be released on reasonable conditions, they are saved by s 36 of the Constitution. It would be irresponsible to ignore the harsh reality of the society in which the Constitution is to operate. Crime is a serious national concern, and a worrying feature for some time has been public eruptions of violence related to court proceedings. In the present context we are not so much concerned with violent public reaction to unpopular verdicts or sentences, but with such reactions to unpopular grants of bail. There is widespread misunder-

standing regarding the purpose and effect of bail.

Manifestly, much must still be done to instil in the community a proper understanding of the presumption of innocence and the qualified right to freedom pending trial under s 35(1)(f). The ugly fact remains, however, that public peace and security are at times endangered by the release of persons charged with offences that incite public outrage.

Schietekat is a good example. *Dladla* again exemplifies a different type of situation where continued detention is in the interests of the public peace. Experience has shown that organised community violence, be it instigated by quasi-political motives or by territorial battles for control of communities for commercial purposes, does subside while ringleaders are in custody. Their arrest and detention on serious charges does instil confidence in the criminal justice system and does tend to settle disquiet, whether the arrestees are war-lords or drug-lords. In my view, open and democratic societies based on human dignity equality and freedom, after weighing the factors enumerated in paragraphs *(a)* to *(e)* of s 36(1) of the Constitution, would find sub-ss 60(4)(e) and (8A) reasonable and justifiable in the prevailing climate in our country.

[56] That conclusion is based, first, on the inherently temporary nature of awaiting trial detention when weighed against the compelling interest in maintaining public peace. In the second place, there is a close relationship and appropriate fit between the temporary withholding of liberty and the disruption that release would unleash. I do not wish to be understood as saying anything in favour of detention without trial. We are concerned here with detention or release in anticipation of a proper trial. We are moreover and more importantly concerned with possible detention following upon a proper and public hearing before a judicial officer. And in that judicial process we know that the scheme introduced by the 1995 amendment was not to prescribe but to guide, substantially ameliorating its bite. If a court, or certain courts, elevate this particular factor to a pre-eminence it should not have, that is not a constitutional issue to be resolved in this Court.

Courts will no doubt be alive to the danger of public sentiment being orchestrated by pressure groups to serve their own ends. The constitutional principle is clear: a court may, not *must*, take the factors enumerated in sub-s (8A) into account, and must do so judicially; and the ordinary appeal and review mechanisms can remedy any undue deference that may be afforded to public sentiment.

Limitation of a right under another provision of the Constitution

Section 36(2) of the Constitution provides that the only other occasion there can be a limitation of a right contained in the Bill of Rights is if there is another provision in the Constitution that authorizes the limitation. The issue first appeared in *Azapo*,[33] where the plaintiffs challenged the constitutionality of the Promotion of National Unity And Reconciliation Act. The epilogue contained in the last clause of the interim Constitution as a post-end bill,[34] stated that the adoption of that Constitution provided a foundation for South Africans to transcend the divisions and strife of the past. It further proclaimed that there was a need for reconciliation, understanding, and reparation, but not for vengeance and retaliation. The applicants challenged the constitutionality of s 20(7) of the Amnesty Act by arguing that it is unconstitutional for the Amnesty Committee to grant amnesty for gross human rights violations, such as murder and torture. The applicants further argued that the amnesty provi-

---

[33] *Azanian Peoples Organization (Azapo) and Others v President of the Republic of South Africa and Others* CCT 117/96 (25 July 1996), now cited as 1996 (8) BCLR 1015 (CC); 1996 (4) SA 562 (C).

[34] Constitution of the Republic of South Africa Act 200 of 1993 (interim Constitution).

sions violated s 22 of the interim Constitution, which provided that 'every person shall have the right to have justiciable disputes settled by a court of law or, where appropriate, another independent or impartial forum'.[35] The applicants, in oral argument, also asserted that section 20(7) of the Amnesty Act was unconstitutional in all respects because the Constitution did not authorize the granting of such civil or criminal amnesty.[36] The Constitutional Court ruled that s 20(7) of the Amnesty Act impacts upon fundamental rights,[37] but did not violate the Constitution because the Constitution itself in the epilogue authorized such a violation.[38]

Similarly, in *Lawrence and Others v The State and Another*,[39] the Court held that where a provision in the Bill of Rights provides the lawmaker with additional powers to take measures to regulate an activity or right in the Bill of Rights, the Court would not subject the design of that measure to scrutiny under the limitations clause.[40] In *Fraser*, the applicants argued that a prohibition on the selling of liquor on Sunday and other public holidays constituted a violation of the right to engage in economic activity, as guaranteed in s 26(1) of the interim Constitution. Section 26(2) of the interim Constitution gave the legislature the power to provide measures to promote certain values and goals providing the measures are justifiable in an open and democratic society based on freedom and equality. The Court, *per* Chaskalson P, held that the power to define the scope of economic activity under s 26(2) is evaluated under the terms provided in that section and not under the proportionality test contained in the limitations clause.[41]

A third situation where the limitations clause should not be used is where two fundamental rights come into conflict. In this instance, the task of the Court is to balance the two rights. For example, where the state legislates pursuant to a constitutional mandate, and where the state actions encroach on another fundamental right, the Court should not subject the legislation to scrutiny under the limitations clause.[42] Let us imagine the lawmaker, in advancing the right to housing under s 26, taking action which limits the conditions under which landlords may use their property, for example, regulating rentals. The state has an obligation to respect, protect, promote, and fulfil the rights in the Bill of Rights.[43] In the above example, it might be that in the promotion of one right the state may encroach upon another right in the Bill of Rights. Arguably, when faced with two provisions in the Bill of Rights, the task of the Court is to harmonize the provisions Commenting on the German Constitutional Court's approach, Donald Kommers makes the observation that when the Court is faced with two constitutional values it seeks to preserve and protect both in a harmonious fashion.[44] The German Constitutional Court seeks to resolve the tension in a way that avoids minimizing the importance of each right.[45] This harmonization should not be performed by using the limitations clause.

In *Gardener v Whitaker*, the Constitutional Court, *per* Kentridge AJ, referred to the situation of reconciling conflicting rights in the Bill of Rights.[46] The Court, *per* Kentridge AJ in dicta, refrained from endorsing the view of the lower court that when faced with this situation, the rights

---

[35] *Azapo* decision para 8.

[36] *Supra* para 15.

[37] *Supra* para 9.

[38] *Supra* paras 10 and 14. See the discussion in chapter 4 where this view is criticized.

[39] *Lawrence and Others v The State and Another* CCT 38/96; 39/96; 40/96 (6 October 1997), now cited as 1997 (10) BCLR 1348 (CC); 1997 (4) SA 1176 (CC).

[40] *Supra* para 30.

[41] *Supra.*

[42] This is the approach followed by Froneman J in *Gardener v Whitaker* CCT 26/94 (15 May 1996) para 691, now cited as 1996 (6) BCLR 775 (E); 1995 (2) SA 672 (E) and alluded to in the Constitutional Court by Kentridge AJ in *Gardener v Whitaker*.

[43] Section 7(2) of the Constitution.

[44] Donald P Kommers 'German Constitutionalism: A Prolegomenon' (1991) 40 *Emory Law Journal* 837, 851.

[45] See generally Kommers.

[46] See *Gardener v Whitaker*.

have to be looked at as inherently of equal value.[47] In the balancing of the rights, the Court, however, stated that it does not matter whether one is a plaintiff or a defendant.[48] The observation of Kentridge AJ is critical, because it stands for the proposition that what is important are different rights, which have to be balanced and accommodated, as opposed to the usual burdens which accompany whether one is a plaintiff or a defendant. However, in *Christian Education of South Africa v Minister of Education*,[49] the Court, *per* Sachs J, used the limitations clause to uphold a limitation on religious freedom, prohibiting corporeal punishment.[50] This was an instance of balancing competing interests in the Bill of Rights, including the rights of the child. The Court should not have resorted to the limitations clause, but should have balanced the two rights.

The Constitutional Court does not insist that every law which makes it more difficult to exercise a fundamental right should be subject to the limitations clause.[51]

In *National Party of South Africa*, the Court was faced with a challenge to aspects of the Electoral Act, which regulated the way voters registered before they could exercise the right to vote. The applicants argued that the requirement that only certain types of identity documents would be accepted as suitable identification for purposes of voting amounted to an infringement of the right to vote.[52] The majority, *per* Yacoob J, held that it was reasonable for the legislature to create a process of registration for managing the election process.[53] Yacoob J went on to state that it was for parliament, and not the courts, to decide the means by which voters must identify themselves. So long as the scheme adopted by the legislature was rational, the Court should not intervene to substitute its choices for that of parliament.[54] In her dissenting opinion, O'Regan J argued that where the legislation in question touches on a fundamental right such as the right to vote, the Court should insist that the legislation be reasonable under the limitations clause.[55] The majority adopted the view that the question of reasonableness only arises, if the legislation in question results in the infringement of the right to vote.[56] In this case, even though the requirements made it more difficult to vote, the registration and identity documents had a rational purpose and applied equally to all citizens.[57]

---

[47] *Supra* para 10.

[48] *Supra.*

[49] CCT 4/00, now cited as 2000 (10) BCLR 1051 (CC); 2000 (4) SA 757 (CC).

[50] *Supra* para 31.

[51] *The New National Party of South Africa v The Government of the Republic of South Africa and Others* CCT 9/99 (13 April 1999) para 24, now cited as 1999 (5) BCLR 489 (CC); 1999 (3) SA 191 (CC).

[52] *Supra* para 9 (Referring to the Electoral Act 73 of 1998).

[53] *Supra* para 16.

[54] *Supra* para 19.

[55] *Supra* para 122.

[56] *Supra* para 24.

[57] *Supra* para 48.

Subject index